# www.wadsworth.com

*wadsworth.com* is the World Wide Web site for Wadsworth and is your direct source to dozens of online resources.

At *wadsworth.com* you can find out about supplements, demonstration software, and student resources. You can also send email to many of our authors and preview new publications and exciting new technologies.

**wadsworth.com**
Changing the way the world learns®

# Psychopharmacology for Helping Professionals

## *An Integral Exploration*

### R. Elliott Ingersoll
*Cleveland State University*

### Carl F. Rak
*Cleveland State University*

**THOMSON**

**BROOKS/COLE**

Australia • Canada • Mexico • Singapore • Spain
United Kingdom • United States

Executive Editor: *Lisa Gebo*
Counseling Editor: *Marquita Flemming*
Assistant Editor: *Shelley Gesicki*
Editorial Assistant: *Christine Northup*
Technology Project Manager: *Barry Connolly*
Marketing Manager: *Caroline Concilla*
Marketing Communications Manager: *Tami Strang*
Project Manager, Editorial Production: *Rita Jaramillo*
Art Director: *Vernon Boes*

Print/Media Buyers: *Lisa Claudeanos, Becky Cross*
Permissions Editor: *Stephanie Lee*
Production Service: *Scratchgravel Publishing Services*
Copy Editor: *Linda Purrington*
Cover Designer: *Chris Hample Design*
Cover Printer: *Transcontinental Printing/Louiseville*
Compositor: *Scratchgravel Publishing Services*
Printer: *Transcontinental Printing/Louiseville*

Printed in Canada

1  2  3  4  5  6  7  09  08  07  06  05

For more information about our products,
contact us at:
**Thomson Learning Academic Resource Center**
**1-800-423-0563**

For permission to use material from this text or product, submit a request online at
http://www.thomsonrights.com.
Any additional questions about permissions can be submitted by email to thomsonrights@thomson.com.

Library of Congress Control Number: 2004117047

ISBN 0-534-61182-6

**Thomson Brooks/Cole**
**10 Davis Drive**
**Belmont, CA 94002**
**USA**

**Asia**
Thomson Learning
5 Shenton Way #01-01
UIC Building
Singapore 068808

**Australia/New Zealand**
Thomson Learning
102 Dodds Street
Southbank, Victoria 3006
Australia

**Canada**
Nelson
1120 Birchmount Road
Toronto, Ontario M1K 5G4
Canada

**Europe/Middle East/Africa**
Thomson Learning
High Holborn House
50/51 Bedford Row
London WC1R 4LR
United Kingdom

**Latin America**
Thomson Learning
Seneca, 53
Colonia Polanco
11560 Mexico D.F.
Mexico

**Spain/Portugal**
Paraninfo
Calle Magallanes, 25
28015 Madrid, Spain

# Contents

**2   An Overview of Physiology Relevant to Psychopharmacology     16**

**3   Intrapsychic Issues in Psychopharmacology     38**

## PART THREE

## Newer Issues    193

## 9    Medicating Children: Perspectives, Dilemmas, and Future Paradigms    194

# Acknowledgments

Writing a book is an experience that illustrates the vast interconnectedness that typifies our lives, whether or not we are aware of it. We would both like to thank Cleveland State University and Dean Jay McLoughlin. We were both serving in administrative roles while writing this book, and Jay always offered his support when we needed to quietly slip away while the phones were ringing and the emails were pouring in. We also have been supported in mind and spirit by several of our graduate students, including Laura Burns, Carla Gilenko, Alia Lawlor, Elizabeth O'Donnell, Dr. Lalitha Prakash, and Karen Wallis. They have provided copyediting, research services, and manuscript reading at different points, offering helpful suggestions. We also want to thank Marquita Flemming for her belief in this project, as it is a departure from the typical psychopharmacology book. Our individual acknowledgments are below.

—R.E.I. and C.F.R.

I want to thank Ken Wilber for his truly Kosmic framework, which serves as the template for this book. His openness and encouragement to apply his model are deeply appreciated. My gratitude also goes to Jeff Salzman, Bert Parlee, and Willow Pearson, who have welcomed my questions and supported my efforts to apply Integral Theory. My thanks to Fred Kofman, who turned me on to Rumi and tuned me into my Self when I most needed it. Although this book utilizes the Integral Model in only a general way, it is the Integral framework that opens the door to really explore the whole truth about psychopharmacology. I want to emphasize that our use of the Integral Model as a template for the book does not reflect the full richness of the model, and we assume full responsibility for any mistakes related to the model. I have been consistently supported by my friendship with Dr. Ann Bauer, who has spent many hours working with me on applications of Integral Theory as well as reminding me not to take myself too seriously. As always, my wife, Jennifer, and my son, Brady, provide me the stability to work on projects like this. They also made it possible for me to meet Ken Wilber in March 2004. Finally, I thank Carl for joining me in this project. Without his support, clinical wisdom, and detailed cases, this book could never have been written.

—R.E.I.

I want to thank Christine Zeh and Christie Palumbo for their diligent and tenacious efforts to uncover almost all the articles and books written on child and adolescent psychopharmacology. I am equally grateful to Wanda Pruett-Butler for all her copy support and friendship. I deeply appreciate the questions and profound concerns raised by Nancy Waina, Director of School Guidance at Beaumont High School–Cleveland, about the impact of psychotropic medications on adolescent girls suffering from trauma, eating disorders, or major depression.

I am very thankful for the array of assistance and support from my friend and colleague, Dr. Elizabeth Welfel, who had more confidence in my efforts than I did at times. Thanks to my oldest daughter, Jennifer, who always offered her word-processing skills, nuggets of support, and technology skills to this endeavor. Finally to my wife, Georgine, I owe a debt of gratitude for her tireless support, editing, and word-processing skills. Her helpfulness and patience were greatly appreciated.

Thank you, Elliott, for inviting me on this very important adventure and for your incredible, detailed knowledge of this important subject.

—*C.F.R.*

# Psychopharmacology for Helping Professionals

# PART ONE

# An Integral Overview of Psychopharmacology

In this part of the text we introduce you to four important perspectives on psychopharmacology. Chapter One provides an overview of the several issues that are rarely discussed in psychopharmacology books and how we use Ken Wilber's Integral Model as the framework for this material. Psychopharmacology used to be considered a branch of science that studied and created psychotropic medication. Although this much is still true, there is far more to psychopharmacology than that. In Part One we introduce issues of how consciousness, culture, and social institutions relate to psychopharmacology. We include these topics because, even though they are not addressed in most psychopharmacology books, they have a profound impact on clients and mental health clinicians. For example, clients and clinicians may not be aware that many psychotropic medications are prescribed "off label." This means the medications are not specifically approved by the Food and Drug Administration (FDA). Off-label prescribing may benefit a client, but it is important for the client and the mental health professional to know that the drug is being used off label and what the risks are.

We also cover the important physiological aspects of psychopharmacology in Part One, including an outline of important central nervous system structures, the general story of neurotransmission, and common mechanisms of drug action. Another important topic covered in Part One is the subjective experience of the client who is taking the medication. We need to understand the subjective effects clients report, because this helps us understand when their symptoms are improving and when the side effects may be worse than the symptoms. The client's subjective experience of symptoms and the effects of the medication are also related to compliance.

Finally, in Chapter Four we introduce important cultural and social issues related to psychopharmacology. These include cultural differences in attitudes toward psychotropic medications; ethnic, racial, and gender differences in physiologic response to psychotropic medications; and how large social institutions such as the Food and Drug Administration and the pharmaceutical companies affect the manner in which drugs are researched and marketed.

# CHAPTER ONE

# Introduction

## Encouragement to the Reader

Many of you reading this book may begin with some anxiety because this is a totally new area for you. You may imagine that psychopharmacology is exclusively a "hard science," and perhaps you don't think of yourself as a "hard science" kind of person. You may even feel uncertain about your ability to master basic psychopharmacological concepts. First, let us assure you that our goal is to make this topic accessible to readers who are practicing as or studying to be mental health professionals, many of whom may not have a background in the physical or organic sciences. Second, let us recommend to those teaching a course in psychopharmacology that, because of the rapid nature of change in the field, teaching styles that rely on memorization are of limited use in this area. We recommend helping students master basic concepts and then applying these concepts to cases. To facilitate that process we supply cases and Study Questions and Exercises in this book. Finally, we invite you students to join us in an incredible journey centering on the most complex organ known to humanity—the human brain. We hope you can revel in the complexity of the brain and the sheer magnitude of its power. We hope you can resist the temptation to want simple and concrete answers to many of the questions this journey will raise. As authors and researchers who have traveled this path before us will attest, there are no simple or even known answers to many of

the questions that arise (Grilly, 1994; Schatzberg & Nemeroff, 1998). We encourage a mixture of trying to comprehend the information while dwelling in the mystery that is the context for the information. Before moving on, we offer a mantra to help you implement this recommendation.

## A Mantra

Even though psychopharmacology is in its embryonic stage, it is a vast and complex area. Several years ago I (Ingersoll) engaged in some multicultural counseling training with Paul Pederson. In that training, Dr. Pederson commented, "Culture is complex, and complexity is our friend." We offer a paraphrase as a mantra for psychopharmacology students: "Reality is complex, and complexity is our friend." We remind the reader of this mantra throughout the book. You might try saying it aloud right now: "Reality is complex, and complexity is our friend." If you reach a passage in this book that is challenging for you or that arouses anxiety, stop, take a deep breath, and practice the mantra.

The primary audience for this book is mental health clinicians who may not have had much training in biology, neurology, and psychopharmacology. This includes counselors, psychologists, clinical social workers, and substance abuse counselors. We will refer specifically to these different mental health professionals throughout the book as well as including all of them in the phrase "mental health professionals." Although there are significant differences in the training models of these different professionals, they all draw on the same knowledge base when treating clients in school or clinical settings. We also want to add that there are several labels used to describe the therapeutic relationships clients have with mental health professionals. These labels include counseling, therapy, and psychotherapy. There is great debate across the mental health professions about whether and how these labels differ, but in this book we use them synonymously for the sake of simplicity. At the same time, because we take an **Integral** approach to psychopharmacology, we expect this book to be useful to all professionals who treat clients suffering from the symptoms of mental or emotional disorders. While reading this book, you will notice technical terms highlighted with bold print the first time they appear. These terms are defined in the Glossary at the end of the book. Although not all key terms are highlighted, those that nonmedical mental health professionals are less likely to have been exposed to are defined in the Glossary. We encourage you to keep a dictionary handy for other terms that may be new to you. If you meet a word you do not understand, stop reading and check the definition in the glossary or a dictionary. Many readers skip over unfamiliar words assuming the meaning will become clear in a later sentence. Clarifying unfamiliar words when they occur adds to the enjoyment of reading the book and facilitates a better understanding of the topic.

## Scientific Truth and the Acceleration of Knowledge

It is no secret that knowledge accumulation is accelerating. In the early 1970s the French economist Georges Anderla (1973, 1974) prepared a statistical estimate of how quickly knowledge has been growing, based on a variety of indicators. According to Anderla, if you begin in the year 1 C.E. (which stands for Current, or Common, Era) it took 1500 years for knowledge to double. The second doubling took only 250 years (1750). The third doubling took only 150 years (1900), the fourth 50

years (1950), and the fifth doubling only 10 years (1960). If there is any accuracy in Anderla's model, knowledge is estimated to be doubling almost monthly at present (Wilson, 1992). This increase in knowledge about the human brain is particularly pronounced.

The final decades of the 20th century unearthed more knowledge about the human brain than all prior centuries combined. One of the most exciting fields benefiting from these developments is psychopharmacology. Pharmacology is the science of the preparation, uses, and effects of drugs. Psychopharmacology is the branch of pharmacology related to the psychological effects of drugs and the use of drugs to treat symptoms of mental and emotional disorders. These drugs are called *psychotropic medications* ("psyche" colloquially refers to "mind," and "tropic" means "acting on" or "moving toward").

Developing neuroscience technologies have helped accelerate brain research and change in the field of psychopharmacology by letting scientists peer more deeply into the brain and nervous system. The latest technological advances include positron emission tomography (PET) scans, magnetic resonance imaging (MRI), and magneto-encephalography. PET scans for brain functions work thus: The technician injects a radioactive form of oxygen into a person and then asks the person to perform a particular task under a PET scanner. Because the brain area most active during the task requires more oxygen, the PET scanner can trace the radioactive oxygen to those sites in the brain used in the task. The computer scanner then generates a picture that maps the brain activity. MRI scans generate images by magnetizing hemoglobin (the iron-containing colored matter in red blood corpuscles that carry oxygen to tissues) and by tracing changes in blood oxygen levels in the brain. Like the PET scan, MRI images of the brain can be used for diagnostic or research purposes. Magnetoencephalography measures the magnetic field associated with electrical currents in the brain to trace activity levels across brain structures when subjects are engaged in a particular task (Bloom, Nelson, & Lazerson, 2001).

Computer technology has also enabled pharmaceutical researchers to generate three-dimensional models of brain cell receptors and the drug molecules that bind to them. Brain-scanning technologies have allowed us to see how the nervous system reacts neurologically to the presence of drug molecules (**pharmacodynamics**) and how those molecules are moved through the body and eventually eliminated (**pharmacokinetics**). These are only some of the advances that have contributed to the exponential increase in the number of drugs developed annually.

Despite the explosion of advances in psychopharmacology in the last 30 years, the field is still in an embryonic stage (Julien, 2001). Although scientists know a lot about the physiological mechanisms of many psychotropic medications, we know little about how they actually change mood. Researchers are just now beginning to explore how the effects of psychotropic medication differ depending on the age, sex, and race of the person taking them (Heinrich & Gibbons, 2001). Although this society is emerging from a postmodern era where multiculturalism was heavily emphasized, little research has been done on differing cultural worldviews regarding psychotropic agents, let alone how such agents differentially affect people of various racial and ethnic backgrounds. In addition, people are now rethinking whether current diagnostic categories for mental and emotional disorders apply to younger children (McClure, Kubiszyn, & Kaslow, 2002a) and how medications affect the dozens of developmental lines that are so variable in this age group. Although the Human Genome Project has initiated efforts to understand human DNA, scientists are still unclear about the role of over 90% of human DNA (Suurkula, 1996). Efforts to describe the human genetic code and mechanisms of gene expression hold great promise for drug development, but there is still a great deal to be learned.

As recently as 30 years ago, psychopharmacology was a medical subspecialty for psychiatrists in particular. At that time, nonmedical mental health providers could ethically practice with little knowledge of psychotropic medications. As long as they had a medical professional to whom they could refer clients, their knowledge of psychotropic medications could be minimal. This is no longer the case. Most (if not all) mental health professionals work with clients taking psychotropic medications and

need to be knowledgeable about the drugs their clients are taking. The Integral perspective we emphasize in this book provides a template that, when applied properly, suggests that understanding the physiological properties of psychotropic medications is merely the beginning of the journey. We use the Integral Model to address many pressing issues rarely discussed in books on psychopharmacology. For example, most psychopharmacology books simply discuss what medications are used for particular symptoms but do not address how to deal with cultural issues that may influence a client's resistance to taking a prescribed medication. This important perspective becomes included when we take an Integral view of psychopharmacology. Another example is the place of direct-to-consumer advertising. Although mental health professionals may know that changes in federal law in the 1980s allowed pharmaceutical companies to advertise directly to consumers via television ads and other media, they may not know that there is a fierce debate over whether such advertising for psychotropic medications is ethical.

Pharmacologists working in controlled conditions in laboratories may have the luxury of limiting their focus to interactions between drug molecules and neurotransmitters. But mental health professionals in the field must understand clients' perceptions and subjective experiences of taking medications, cultural views of psychotropic medications, group differences in response to the medications (according to sex, age, race, and so on), developmental considerations, socioeconomic institutions that mediate access to medications, and competing worldviews and theories on what causes mental health symptoms. The Integral framework, which requires consideration of these topics, sets this book apart from other books on psychopharmacology. Although this consideration requires more effort, it contributes to a well-rounded knowledge of psychopharmacology that translates into better clinical practice.

### Everybody Is Right (About Something): The Many Faces of Truth

History shows that extremists, despite the strength of their convictions, are rarely correct. (Radin, 1997, p. 205)

In this book we consider multiple dimensions of and perspectives on psychopharmacology. Although it would be convenient to state that all mental and emotional symptoms derive from some malfunction of brain chemistry, there is no evidence to support this statement. Many people are surprised to hear this, so it is important to restate: There is no evidence that all mental and emotional symptoms derive from some malfunction of brain chemistry. Today pharmaceutical companies advertise directly to consumers and often give the impression that psychological disorders are really "medical disorders" that can be alleviated with a particular medication, much as antibiotics can alleviate a bacterial infection. If psychological disorders were like medical disorders, then studying the brain, brain chemistry, and scientific method would suffice. This is not the case, though, so we also need to study the mind, the sociocultural contexts in which mind and brain function, and the consciousness underlying both mind and brain.

The whole truth of psychopharmacology cannot be explored solely through scientific method. Like a diamond, truth has many facets, which are complementary (but not necessarily competing). As philosopher Ken Wilber (2003) notes, no mind is capable of 100% error, so everyone is right about something but not everyone is equally right about everything. Given that insight, exploring the different faces or perspectives of psychopharmacology need not produce warring factions championing mutually exclusive theories of etiology and treatment. Taking different perspectives in exploring psychopharmacology reveals different truths about it.

Lest you think we are lapsing into some type of **radical constructivism** or **relativism** (we are not), consider these questions: What sort of blood test would you use to determine your political philosophy? How might exploring your feelings about your mother help diagnose a streptococcus infection? How can a firsthand understanding of a person's religion be used to tell you how much money he or she earns? How could data about your yearly income be used as an indicator of your sexual orientation? These questions are meaningless, because each proposes an incorrect tool for finding the answer. Because different perspectives reveal different faces of truth, they require tools matched to the task. There are different types of truth, and different types of knowledge and different tools are employed in seeking these different types of knowledge. We emphasize this point because many people believe that medical science (or science in general) is the only tool and that it can solve any problem.

**The Medical Model Perspective**

The perspective of medical science (and science in general) clearly reflects one type of truth, and we draw amply from it in this book. Whereas a relativist would say that one perspective or type of truth is just as good as another for any job, we maintain that some perspectives and tools are better than others for particular tasks. Everyone knows that no blood test can determine a person's political philosophy. Does this mean one's preference for a political philosophy does not exist? No. It simply means a blood test is not a good tool to use to explore the issue. In this case, dialogue is far better than a blood test. To find out a person's political philosophy, you talk with the person to learn what his or her political philosophy is. Regarding the diagnosis of streptococcus infection, a throat culture is a far better test than discussing feelings about one's mother.

Scientific truth is objective truth that can be verified by some observable measurement. This is the type of truth emphasized by the tools of scientific method, the medical model, and most psychopharmacology books. The perspective of scientific truth is an important cornerstone of psychopharmacology. In this book we call this viewpoint the **medical model perspective.** It is characterized by its focus on objective, measurable data related to individuals. Although labeled "medical model" for the purposes of this book, this perspective also includes schools of psychology that rely heavily on objective measurement (such as behaviorism). In psychopharmacology, the medical model perspective helps us understand parts of the brain that seem correlated with symptoms of mental or emotional disorders and things such as the molecular structure of drugs. But mental health professionals are concerned with more than the correlations of symptoms and brain functions or the molecular structures of drugs. As professionals, we are also concerned with how clients feel about taking medications, how and whether psychotropic medications alter their consciousness, relevant cultural issues that may affect their attitudes or increase their preference for alternatives to psychotropic medications, aspects of group membership (race, sex) that may predict differential responses to psychotropic medications, as well as how our clients' place in society affects their ability to get the drugs they may need.

### The Intrapsychic Perspective

Other perspectives complement the medical model and help mental health professionals build a well-rounded understanding of psychopharmacology. These other perspectives reveal other faces of truth that the medical model is not equipped to explore but that are equally important for mental health professionals. As Wilber (1997) noted, the techniques of the medical model perspective can trace the electrical currents in a subject's brain but can only give scientific verification about the electrical activity in that brain—they cannot tell whether the person is thinking about opening a homeless shelter or robbing a liquor store. Further, there is no evidence that the experience of consciousness is caused solely by electrical activity in our brains (Chalmers, 1995).

Information about what other people (including our clients) are thinking can only be obtained through truthful dialogue with them. This introduces the second perspective we use in this book, the **intrapsychic perspective.** Although the name is awkward, it is more exact than "the psychological perspective." Although psychology is derived from the goal of studying the mind or soul, it has evolved into the scientific study of mind and behavior and has come to greatly resemble the medical model. Schwartz and Begley (2002) assert that psychologists have become overly attached to a version of the medical model that dismisses conscious experience and focuses only on what is observable or measurable. They conclude, "Surely there is something deeply wrong, both morally and scientifically, with a school of psychology whose central tenet is that people's conscious life experience . . . is irrelevant" (p. 6). They describe the intrapsychic perspective as "what consciousness feels like from the inside" (p. 256). We include the intrapsychic per-

spective because clients' **phenomenological** experiences of the world cannot be dismissed as irrelevant and are often a key ingredient in their growth.

The intrapsychic perspective deals with consciousness. Although one of the most ambitious pursuits of scientific knowledge is the Human Genome Project there exists an equally ambitious (even if less well known) human consciousness project. The intrapsychic perspective as revealed by the consciousness project is summarizing millennia of knowledge about the human mind, the subjective human experience, consciousness, the domain of the unconscious, and the farther reaches of human nature. This knowledge is different from knowledge generated by the medical model perspective but is no less important for mental health professionals who deal with the whole person. The subjective knowledge about oneself that counseling, psychotherapy, and meditation explore is different from the type of knowledge that science produces to tell us about how nerve cells fire in our brain. It is truly odd that although psychotropic medications are actually supposed to modify experienced consciousness, very few books on the topic actually address that and instead prefer just to discuss how drug molecules bind to neuronal receptors.

Suppose for example that you experience an insight about yourself that leads to more effective ways of living. For the sake of the example, assume the insight is that you fear emotionally depending on others, so you tend to push them away and isolate yourself. When you experience this insight, certainly nerve cells will fire in your brain, but no one can prove the cells are "causing" the insight—they simply accompany it. Further, others cannot learn about the insight by reading a PET scan of your brain taken when you had the insight. You must truthfully share the insight in order for others to learn about it—no physical measurement of any type (brain cells firing, heart rate, blood pressure, and so forth) will reveal the insight—you must share it. This is an important type of knowledge of the sort commonly shared and explored in counseling sessions.

The intrapsychic perspective also includes people's unconscious life experience. The many tools we use to explore the intrapsychic perspective include introspection, dialogue about that introspection, interpreting dialogue, and sharing our interpretation to assess its accuracy. Although we can only be aware of those things that are conscious, by definition, the tools of the intrapsychic perspective can help clients bring to awareness things that were previously unconscious. As Wilber (2003) noted, psychotherapy is always about increasing awareness and this increase in awareness is experienced through the intrapsychic perspective. These tools are familiar to anyone trained in the mental health professions, but it is amazing how easily we forget their importance.

### The Cultural Perspective

A third perspective or type of truth concerns how people should treat one another as well as the beliefs and worldviews people may share. These shared beliefs constitute aspects of culture. Culture, ways of living that groups of humans transmit from one generation to another, includes the shared beliefs and worldviews that different groups develop to understand the world and their place in it. Because shared worldviews are so important to culture, we refer to this third perspective as the **cultural perspective**. The word *culture* may refer to a subgroup of people who share similar genetic and social histories, as in "African-American culture" or a subgroup that comes about for other reasons, such as a business or industry, as in the culture of a pharmaceutical company. Again, no number of PET or MRI scans of brains can show what worldview a person holds, which ways of relating or worldviews are better than others, or whether a person prefers to be "in time" or "on time." As Wilber (1995) puts it, scientific knowledge can never tell us why compassion is better than murder, why social service is better than genocide. Michael Polanyi (1958) also articulated this insight. Polanyi was a Nobel Prize–winning chemist who realized during the communist revolutions in Europe that the revolutionaries were trying to build a culture and a society on scientific principles (the Lenin-Trotsky five-year plan) and that those principles were the wrong tools for the task. Polanyi understood that the tools of science could never help these revolutionaries build a culture or a society worth living in. History has validated his

judgment. Although the design of the Soviet Union tried to account for and control all the measurable aspects of society, it severely underestimated the cultural/ethnic differences that, since its dissolution, have erupted between former member nations. Scientific truth can tell us which psychotropic medication has the greatest probability of easing a client's suffering. But the scientific truth and the medication cannot erase nonbiological sources of suffering nor address what this suffering means to the client. For example, if the client shares a worldview that is highly suspicious of taking psychotropic medication, the client is unlikely to comply with the prescription.

### The Social Perspective

A fourth type of truth, which concerns the structure and impact of social institutions, we call the **social perspective**. Social institutions are based in shared beliefs, policies, and laws that affect people in observable, measurable ways. Whereas the medical model perspective deals with measurable, observable data about individuals, the social perspective deals with measurable, observable data about groups and particularly institutions. One good example in psychopharmacology is the ongoing debate about whether a person can and should be medicated against his or her will (Gelman, 1999). Although the legal system is ideally based on the public's shared understanding of how we need to be regulated with laws, laws prohibiting or permitting forced pharmacological treatment have profound impact on individuals. Besides the legal institutions of our society, other institutions relevant to psychopharmacology include the government (for example, the Food and Drug Administration, the Drug Enforcement Agency) and the pharmaceutical industry in general. Issues such as whether people in the United States should be able to import medications from Canada are the domain of the social perspective. (Again, imagine the absurdity of trying to resolve this import question through the medical model perspective.)

Most books on psychopharmacology focus on scientific or medical model perspectives of what medications seem to do, how they correlate with symptom relief, how much of the medication is needed, and so on. Although we cover these issues in detail, we also discuss the other perspectives that are pertinent to mental health professionals. For example, what does it mean to a client to take a psychotropic medication (intrapsychic perspective)? What does it mean that a significant number of children in this society are referred for medication instead of for counseling (social perspective)? How should we interpret and interact with a family that believes psychotropic medication is spiritually damaging (cultural perspective)? It is time for humanity to integrate the various types of knowledge people have access to, and a study of psychopharmacology can benefit by such integration. We believe this so deeply that we decided to model that integration in this book, and thus we needed a framework to organize the book so the reader can experience it in an integrated manner.

One thinker/writer who has created such a framework for integration is Ken Wilber, and we used his system—the Integral Model—to draw together these different types of truth regarding psychopharmacology. We have titled this book *Psychopharmacology for Helping Professionals: An Integral Exploration* because the model was so influential in our design and writing of the book, particularly in the inclusion of the four perspectives we have outlined here. An in-depth presentation of the Integral Model can be found in Wilber's books, but any Integral exploration uses the four perspectives we have outlined. In addition, an Integral exploration must address development, including levels and lines of development. Although very little research has been done on how psychopharmacology affects development, we have summarized the literature that does exist. Finally Wilber's Integral Model also includes exploration of states of consciousness and types. The relationship between states of consciousness and psychotropic medication is just beginning to be researched (Bitner, Hillman, Victor, & Walsh, 2003), and the issue of psychopharmacology and gender (unlike sex) has yet to be studied systematically. The notion of "types" is primarily related to gender and personality style (for example, styles reflected in tests such as the Myers-Briggs Type Indicator or the Enneagram). Research is limited on how different types may seek out or respond

to medication differently, but it is important to be alert to how this aspect of the Integral Model relates to psychopharmacology. For example, research summaries of depression are mixed regarding the degree to which each gender suffers from depression. Some researchers conclude that depression affects women more than men (the key variable being sex). Other researchers state this is more a reflection of gender in that women are more likely to seek out help than men, and men may engage in more self-destructive behaviors when depressed, such as substance abuse or "workaholism." In terms of psychopharmacology this plays out in antidepressants being disproportionately marketed toward women. This summary of the Integral Model should give you an understanding of how it is generally reflected in this book. So for general purposes, when we use the word "Integral" (with capital "I"), we mean the Integral Model.

## Psychopharmacology and Magical Thinking

R. Stivers, in his book *Technology as Magic* (2001) suggests that as different technologies "disenchant" our sense of the world, people may respond with magical thinking by endowing those technologies with magical attributes. "Today our expectations for technology are magical" (p. 7). You can see this change particularly in psychopharmacology. We have had clients who thought that if they took antidepressant medication prescribed for their symptoms it would (almost magically) erase all suffering from their lives. We agree with Stivers that this society has almost magical expectations of pharmaceutical companies, their products, and the medical professionals who prescribe those products. One practice tied to this expectation is what we call "word magic." Although we are borrowing this phrase from Wilber (1999a), we define it differently than he does.

"Word magic" is the use of words in such a way so as to create the illusion of certainty where certainty does not exist. Word magic is used to increase one's control over the world (and other people), to artificially reduce the complexity of reality, and to help one deal with the insecurity experienced in the face of complexity. Particularly in the service of control, word magic can be used to trigger strong emotions in a reader or listener for the purpose of increasing the speaker's own power. Former U.S. Attorney General A. Mitchell Palmer and Senator Joseph McCarthy engaged in word magic, wielding the key term "communist" to increase their political power during "red scares" in the early and mid 20th century. The same type of word magic was used in the witch hunts, in the Inquisition, and is still being used in the current "war on drugs" (which is really a war on drug users) in the United States (revisited in Chapter Ten).

How does this relate to pharmacology? When various professionals, groups, or companies use words to convey pharmacological certainty where little certainty exists, they are engaging in word magic and in some cases trying to increase their own power. This can result in what Charles Tart (1997) refers to as scientism: "a dogmatic, psychological hardening of materialistic belief systems with emotional attachments, rather than authentic science" (p. 22). Frequently this hardening of belief systems with emotional attachments takes the form of proclaiming something to be much simpler than it is in reality. An example is when pharmaceutical companies, in ads for antidepressants, state, "Depression is a serious medical disease." The payoff for pharmaceutical companies in framing depression this way is that if the general public thinks of depression first and foremost as a medical disease, their first response if feeling depressed will be to go to a medical doctor for a prescription rather than to a mental health professional for counseling. As we will show, depression is an overdetermined set of symptoms that may be biological, psychological, or spiritual in etiology. Just because depression is described in the *International Classification of Diseases* (the diagnostic manual for physicians) does not mean it is a medical disease in the same sense that influenza is a disease. Tart goes on to explain that we are conditioned to assume people in lab coats are dealing with certainty and that sometimes people in lab coats perpetuate that misunderstanding.

We propose that people who commit category errors are more vulnerable to using and abusing word magic. A category error is basically assuming one tool can do any job that needs to be done. With regard to the four perspectives just outlined, a category error is trying to account for all four types of truths with only one perspective. When a pharmaceutical company perpetuates the notion that "major depressive disorder" is a "medical disorder" like streptococcus infection, it is committing a category error. Although something like major depressive disorder may be treated in a medical setting and exist as a thus-named disorder in the International Classification of Diseases (ICD), to suggest it is only a medical disorder denies the complexity of the etiology of depression and cultivates the misperception that the first line of treatment is to take a pill. You can imagine the impact on pharmaceutical sales if all the people who felt depressed decided that the first thing they should do is go to the family doctor for a prescription.

## Moving On: What We Know, What We Do Not Know

To avoid committing category errors or engaging in word magic, people must be willing to admit what they do not know. Studying the mind and brain moves us all to the knowledge frontier of the 21st century. Consider this: Despite considerable success in developing medications that ease the symptoms of mental and emotional disorders, scientists have little understanding of how most of these medications work. Researchers are learning more about how psychotropic agents act on the brain and body (pharmacodynamics) and how the body disposes of them (pharmacokinetics), but scientists still know very little about why certain drugs decrease certain symptoms and contribute to emotional and behavioral changes. Even more interesting (although less publicized) is that in a great number of studies, as many participants respond to placebos as respond to the actual medications being investigated (Fisher & Greenberg, 1997). There are many unanswered questions about the brain, the mind, and the relationship between the two. All together now: "Reality is complex, and complexity is our friend."

An example of this complexity is the case of Louise. Throughout the book we provide cases that illustrate good responses to medications, treatment-resistant symptoms, side effects, client intrapsychic issues related to medications, and cultural and social considerations. The cases illustrate the complementary types of truths we have summarized as the medical model, intrapsychic, cultural, and social. Although it would be much simpler only to use cases where clients have symptoms, take medications, then get better, this has seldom been our experience. Louise's case illustrates many of the perspectives we have introduced in this chapter. It does not lend itself to a single interpretation that relies solely on one perspective. Read the case, and consider the questions following it.

### The Case of Louise

Louise is a 34-year-old architect who has suffered for many years with acute anxiety, depression, **lability** of mood, dissociations, and brief psychotic episodes. Between the ages of 20 and 24 she was hospitalized several times and received several diagnoses and was taking, at different times, an array of psychotropic medications that did not help her. Eventually Louise found a therapist at a public mental health center and began a course of twice-weekly psychoanalytically oriented psychotherapy with psychiatric support. The psychiatrist prescribed 5 mg of loxapine (an antipsychotic) once a day and 20 mg of fluoxetine (the brand antidepressant Prozac) to be taken in the morning. In sessions, the client said she was never sure that medications helped her.

Louise is an only child of European parents from a strict religious orthodox background. She was severely traumatized and sexually abused by an uncle who used to look after her when her parents went out. She was often raped and choked by this uncle between the ages of 3 and 6. The abuse stopped when the uncle hung himself. Her parents insisted that she not speak to anyone about these family secrets and ordered her to make up a disease to explain all her hospitalizations in her 20s.

From the intrapsychic perspective, this client presented many dilemmas. Although she often demonstrated an incredible cognitive capacity for understanding, her awareness was blunted by her traumatic past. She could provide a history up to a point, but her sense of self and self-understandings were often limited and chaotic. She brought many states of herself to therapy, and the therapist perceived her as a divided self. She expressed mixed feelings about taking medications, "I desperately need them, but I must be able to survive without them . . . sometimes I feel better off the meds." She maintained many conscious and unconscious secrets about her past life with her parents, such as their internment. Both had been in concentration camps during World War II, which she discovered as a young adult. It took a great deal of therapy time and attention to the transference to bring her complex issues to the foreground. Louise, at different moments in the therapy, treated her therapist like her aloof father, her passive and secretive mother, her abusing uncle, and some other significant people in her life. These varying and unpredictable transferences made the therapy and the use of therapeutic interventions very complicated.

Culturally, this client struggled with her parents' rigid religiosity and with the power of unspoken rules about keeping mental illness private, with the accompanying shame. She further struggled with the attitudes and styles of her parents at different moments in the Christian church year. Her culture was highly suspicious of "shrinks" and often mandated that one must lie to physicians and therapists to protect the family. So not only did she struggle with all her symptoms and her diminished ego capacity, but she also battled the imposed cultural imperatives of her family and religion. Her mother easily invoked great guilt and shame in her, which resulted in Louise denying truths during many therapy hours.

From the medical model perspective, Louise could present herself very well. She was articulate, bright, and in very good health. She had three master's degrees (one in social work), so she could take psychological tests in a way that masked her deep disturbances. She was very healthy but very sensitive to the side effects of many psychotropic medications and only received brief relief from most. Louise often puzzled her doctors and therapists.

From the social perspective, Louise was greatly influenced by the stigma of mental illness in her capacity to find work and the cost of her psychotherapy. She chose not to use her health insurance because she believed she would forever be "labeled" insane. She tried to avoid any mention of her prior hospitalizations. She accepted the added burden of self-payment, which became a serious complication in the transference over the 11-year treatment.

For 7 of the 11 years, Louise did not use any psychotropic medications until a crisis at work triggered a severe anxiety-panic reaction with cognitive impairment and psychotic features. The therapist then referred her to a new psychiatrist, a woman (her former psychiatrist of 9 years had closed his practice) who prescribed paroxetine (an SSRI, or specific serotonin reuptake inhibitor, antidepressant). She felt almost instant relief, but this psychiatrist observed over the next several weeks that Louise's behavior began to become gradually increasingly manic. She was so "hyper" at work that she was sent home, and her female psychiatrist changed her *DSM* diagnosis to Bipolar II Disorder and told her this illness would be with her for life. Her therapist disagreed, considering it a manic reaction to the paroxetine, a possible side effect of SSRIs. After a tumultuous period, Louise stopped the paroxetine, refused lithium, and gradually stabilized as she identified and discussed the forces that contributed to her chaotic episode.

### *Questions on the Case of Louise*

Given this short case synopsis, answer the following questions. It is best to do these in a small group, but you can do them alone if necessary.

1. From what little you know about medical model thinking and the intrapsychic perspective, what sort of debate might ensue between a biologically oriented psychiatrist and a humanistically oriented counselor regarding Louise's case? If you are in small groups, role-play the debate.
2. What sort of therapeutic issues seem most relevant from the medical model, intrapsychic, cultural, and social perspectives? What role do you imagine medication might play for each issue you identify? What role do you imagine counseling or psychotherapy might play for each issue you identify?
3. Experiment with intentionally committing category errors regarding the case. Pretend you are

going to view the case from one perspective only (the medical model, intrapsychic, cultural, or social). Given your knowledge of theories of etiology and treatment, explain the case from each perspective, offering theories of what caused the symptoms and how best to treat them.
4. Finally, summarize any insights you gained by engaging in the last question.

You may have found that in answering the questions about the case of Louise, you began questioning just how much of a role the client's mind played in the symptoms and how much of a role the brain played. Because the mind–brain problem is inherent in viewing psychopharmacology from multiple perspectives, we provide an overview of it next.

## The Mind–Brain Problem

If you were on a game show and the host asked you (for $1000) to clearly define mind, brain, and the difference between the two, how would you answer? How you answer is basically how you conceptualize the mind–brain problem. The mind–brain problem is an old philosophical issue that addresses whether or not the mind and brain are distinct entities and what their relationship is. Scientific knowledge of both the mind and the brain is incomplete. No one knows what the mind is, where it comes from, or how it interacts with the brain (Dossey, 2001). However, numerous scholars have noted that even if there were complete knowledge of the mind and brain, the problem might still be unsolvable (Gabbard, 2001). Consider being asked to define "the mind." At first glance this might seem a simple task for a mental health counselor or a student training in one of the mental health professions. In fact, it is a rather vexing question with a multitude of answers depending on your theoretical orientation. As much as many hate to admit it, to "define" what "mind" means first requires a leap of faith in the theory or theories you believe most accurately reflect the reality of what the mind is. To say you adhere to a particular theory of the mind–brain problem is fine; to claim a particular theory is ultimately true is at this point in history is scientism, not science. Generally, the mind–brain problem has been explored through two hypotheses, the epiphenomenon hypothesis and the dual-substance hypothesis, discussed as follows.

### The Epiphenomenon Hypothesis

The first hypothesis is called the **epiphenomenon** hypothesis. The theory underlying this is what might be called *radical materialism.* The basis of radical materialism is that all things, including the mind, derive from other things that can be objectively observed and measured. This hypothesis states that the mind derives from the brain. In other words, the mind is an epiphenomenon of the brain. In a sense, this theory claims that your mind, including your sense of self, is a "side effect" of having a developed brain. The 19th-century biologist Thomas Huxley (known as "Darwin's Bulldog" for his fervent support of Darwin's theory of evolution) popularized this hypothesis. More recently Damasio (2000), Dennett (1991), and Churchland (1995, 1999) have set forth varieties of the theory. Sometimes the theory is not stated outright but implied, as if this were the only acceptable theory on mind and brain. Richard Thompson (2000) gave one example when he wrote, "What is consciousness and how does it arise from the brain?" (p. 481). His implication that it does arise from the brain is a theoretical assumption, not an indisputable fact even though he presents it as such. This is another example of word magic—using words to create an illusion of certainty where there is none.

Advocates of the epiphenomenon hypothesis support it by first noting a brain structure responsible for a particular function (such as the relationship of Broca's area to speech, for example). Next they point out that, for example, if Broca's area is damaged, speech is impaired. The reasoning is that one's sense of self (one's mind) is a consequence of brain functioning and if those parts of the brain responsible for the sense of self are damaged, the sense of self is either impaired or vanishes, just as speech becomes impaired if Broca's area is damaged.

Perhaps the quintessential example used to support the epiphenomenon hypothesis is the 19th-century case of Phineas Gage. Gage was a railroad construction worker who had a tamping iron driven through his skull as the result of an explosion. Although he miraculously survived the accident, his personality became so altered that those who knew him say Gage was a different person after the accident. Damasio (1995) hypothesized that from a materialist perspective Gage, the person, had changed because the areas of his brain that maintained and expressed personality had changed when damaged in the accident.

The sense of self is somewhat more complicated than other functions that are traced to specific brain areas, so researchers do not yet know exactly which areas, and the relationships between them, result in the sense of self. Damasio (2000) and others have begun to tackle this problem, but science is far from an explanation. Thus to accept the radical materialist position is a statement of faith that neuroscientists will be able to completely map out the brain and its functions (and that they are correct in thinking such knowledge would resolve the mind–brain problem).

As you can imagine, those who adhere to the medical model of mental and emotional disorders often support the epiphenomenon hypothesis. This model is the basis of allopathic medicine. Allopathic medicine (as opposed to homeopathic or osteopathic) is the branch of medicine that adheres to the philosophy that to treat or cure a disease process, you introduce an agent (such as a drug) that acts in a manner opposite to the process you are trying to treat or cure. Although it is often assumed that if scientists know a disease process they also know its etiology (cause), this is far from true. Thus there is no foundation for the allopathic assumption that identifying a disease process (depressive symptoms for example) and decreasing or stopping that process means that the process had a physical origin. Strict adherence to the medical model leads to unfounded assumptions that all mental or emotional disorders derive from faulty functioning in the brain or nervous system. Many follow this strict adherence despite strong evidence that the mind (at least the thought processes and emotions of the mind) influences the body as much as any organ like the brain. There is even evidence that what we call "mind" has connections to every part of our body and particularly the "gut," which accounts for what are colloquially called "gut feelings" (Radin, 1997). We take this up in our discussion of the next hypothesis on the mind–brain problem.

### The Dual-Substance Hypothesis

The dual-substance hypothesis is often dated back to the philosopher René Descartes who lived in the early 17th century, although it certainly predates Descartes, because it exists to some extent in both Hindu and Buddhist philosophy. Descartes proposed both that a divine being exists and that this divine being created thinking things (*res cogitans*) and material things (such as bodies) that extend into the material realm (*res extensa*). He thought thinking things do not actually exist in time and space and cannot be externally observed. The extended beings do exist in time and space and can be externally observed. Although Gabbard (2001) believes that substance dualism has fallen out of favor, there is still ample support for variations on the hypothesis. Most variations equate "mind" with "consciousness."

Those holding a spiritual worldview often accept the dual-substance argument (in various formulations). Such a worldview may endorse a belief in a God or Divinity of some sort and possibly some notion of an eternal soul. This is not necessary, however, because the Buddhist view, for example, refers to different types of consciousness. One such type is a nonmaterial, ever-present "subtle consciousness" that we are thought to be most in touch with in deep sleep, advanced meditation, sneezing, and orgasms (think about that next time you sneeze!). From the Tibetan Buddhist perspective, epiphenomenalism and radical materialism fall into the trap of reifying physical phenomena (Descartes's *res extensa*) and denying the existence of mental phenomena (Descartes's *res cogitans*) (Wallace, 1999). From this perspective, to say that consciousness depends on the brain for existence is akin to saying that food depends on a stomach for existence. Physician Deepak Chopra (1993) has asked why, if the mind is merely a side effect of the body or brain, how is it that our sense of self remains consistent even though every atom in our body is replaced almost yearly? Psychologist Dean Radin (1997) wrote, "The average neuron consists of about 80

percent water and about 100,000 molecules. The brain contains about 10 billion cells, hence about $10^{15}$ molecules. Each nerve cell in the brain receives an average of 10,000 connections from other brain cells, and the molecules within each cell are renewed about 10,000 times in a lifetime" (p. 259). Radin then asked why, despite this continuous change, the patterns of our sense of self remain stable even though the physical material supporting that sense of self is in constant flux. The body you have while reading this (including your brain) is not at all the same body you had three years ago, but your sense of self is.

Transpersonal psychiatrist Stanislav Grof (2000) has likened the relationship of consciousness and the brain to that of television transmission waves to a television. Grof critiqued the epiphenomenon hypothesis, noting that if you break the picture tube of a television, the broadcast waves cannot be totally expressed through the damaged television; however, the waves still exist. Equally, if damage to Broca's area of the brain hinders speech, that does not mean the consciousness seeking to express speech has its origin in the brain it is trying to express speech through.

In addition to these two perspectives on the mind–brain problem, there are also variations such as interactionism (mind and brain are different but mutually causal) and parallelism (mind and brain are totally separate and do not communicate). Wilber (1997) noted that the mind–brain problem cannot be solved through any of these theories, because they rely *either* on psychological understandings *or* physiological understandings, both of which are the very things that need to be united (mind–brain). Instead, Wilber claimed that the practices of the transcendental traditions (meditation and contemplative prayer) are the appropriate tool to resolve the paradox.

Whether you agree with Wilber or not, the mind–brain problem is an important context for the study of psychopharmacology. If this context is ignored, it is far easier to ignore things, such as the placebo effect, that hold important truths, as yet untapped, that may contribute to our knowledge of healing the symptoms of mental/emotional disorders. Ignoring the mind–brain problem also makes it easier to commit category errors and support them with word magic (such as asserting that all depression is caused by a "chemical imbalance").

## The Layout of This Book

### Part One

The first part of this book covers introductory material on the basic principles of psychopharmacology derived from the medical model as well as material representing the different truths or perspectives that complement the medical model. The information in Chapter Two basically tells the story of neurotransmission. The story of neurotransmission is the story of how brain cells (neurons) communicate both electrically and chemically. If you know this story, you have a general understanding of how psychotropic medications are designed and what they are supposed to do. The story of neurotransmission gives you a sense of the complexity of neurotransmission and a sense of how much people have yet to learn about it. By understanding the story of neurotransmission presented in Chapter Two, you will also be able to conceptualize what we currently know about mechanisms of action of psychotropic medications and about strategies pharmaceutical companies use to develop newer drugs.

Chapter Three gives an overview of relevant issues from the intrapsychic perspective—the subjective sense of or experience of life. Intrapsychic issues also include interpersonal issues relevant to mental health practioners working with clients and other professionals. These issues include how to talk with clients about medication and compliance, how to approach collaboration with prescribing professionals, and how to process particular issues in supervision. In Chapter Four, the last chapter in Part One, we cover important social and cultural issues. We give an overview of cultural, racial, and gender differences regarding responses to psychotropic medication and then discuss the relevance of powerful institutions such as the pharmaceutical industry and the Food and Drug Administration.

### Part Two

The second part of the book contains four chapters (Chapters Five through Eight) covering commonly prescribed psychotropic drugs used to treat depression, anxiety, psychosis, mood instability, and a host of other conditions. Each chapter includes some history on the discovery and use of each category of drugs. This history provides the context that informs the four perspectives we comment on in each chapter. In addition to the history, we present medical model theories of how the drugs work and cover common drugs in each category including their side effects. Then, in each chapter, we include relevant material from the intrapsychic, cultural, and social perspectives. Note that a medication approved by the FDA for some use has both a generic name and a brand name (or brand names). For example, Prozac is a brand name for a drug, the generic name for which is *fluoxetine*. Throughout the book when we refer to a drug in an example we try to provide the reader with both generic and brand names. The *PDR*, the *Physicians Desk Reference*, is the standard reference book on drug names, both generic names and brands. It is available both at the reference desk of most public libraries, and also online.

### Part Three

Part Three of the book, titled "Newer Issues," addresses psychotropic medications for children, what we know about stimulant medications, and an update on herbaceuticals. Each separate chapter contains study questions that should help you review and integrate the information in that chapter. The chapters in this part differ from those in Part Two in that these are newer areas and often have been the subject of fewer research studies. Many of the agents discussed in Part Two and used with adults are still being investigated for efficacy with children. Although scientists have done a great deal of research on the medical model of how stimulants affect children, they have only just begun to deal with which children are really good candidates for stimulant therapy and what the medicating of young children means for this society. Note that each chapter contains study questions and exercises for the reader.

## Study Questions and Exercises

1. Describe the four perspectives derived from the Integral Model and introduced in this chapter.
2. Consider a client living in an inner-city environment of chronic stress. The client suffers from

acute attacks of anxiety (although several of his neighbors do not). How might someone describe the client's anxiety from the medical model perspective?

3. Outline some of the differences between a medical disorder that can be treated allopathically, such as a bacterial infection, and a mental/emotional disorder, such as depression.

4. Give an example of word magic used by one of your professors.

5. Discuss with your classmates the mind–brain problem and your beliefs about the role of the mind and brain. In the context of your beliefs, discuss why you chose to enter a mental health profession.

6. As you embark on this journey of discovery in psychopharmacology, what do you feel are the most important things you need to learn?

7. Write down your expectations for medical technology to alleviate mental and emotional disorders. To what extent do you think these expectations are magical? To what extent do you think they are reasonable? Explain.

# CHAPTER TWO

# An Overview of Physiology Relevant to Psychopharmacology

In this chapter we provide an overview of the central nervous system, the brain, and the brain's individual cells, called *neurons.* We cover **pharmacodynamics** (how drugs act on your body) and **pharmacokinetics** (how the body responds to drugs). This material has been the focus of most psychopharmacology texts, but remember, it is only part of the story—an important part that discloses truth—but not the whole truth.

In studying this material some students become anxious, thinking, "I don't really have any background in biology or physiology." Relax. If "hard science" doesn't come naturally to you, think of the brain and the nervous systems as miraculous works of art that you can experience even if you cannot fully understand them. Set aside quiet study time to read this material. If it is new to you, don't expect to grasp it reading in 20-minute intervals or in a distracting environment. Approach this chapter as a "brain appreciation" tour. Remembering our mantra and the fact that the best "hard science" minds in the world are really just starting to understand the brain, sit back with a warm drink and join us for this tour through the most complex organ known to human beings.

## A Few Basics

We start with a sketch of the **central** and **peripheral nervous systems.** Figure 2.1 illustrates key parts in both systems. Although we focus on central nervous

system effects from various medications, it is important to understand some basics of the peripheral nervous system, because many drugs have **side effects** on this system. Much of the information in this section is drawn from Bloom, Nelson, and Lazerson (2001), Carlson (2001), Julien (2001), and Thompson (2000). Readers interested in full expositions of the brain and central nervous system are referred to their work.

The central nervous system includes the brain and spinal cord. The peripheral nervous system (the nervous system outside the brain and spinal cord) is divided into the **somatic** and **autonomic** (or visceral) **nervous systems.** The somatic nervous system connects with sense receptors and skeletal muscles while the autonomic nervous system controls involuntary functions related to the glands, smooth muscles, heart, and viscera. This is important, because the goal for **psychotropic** drug compounds is to get them into the central nervous system. Remember that "psychotropic" means acting on or moving toward the mind, but because we lack a clear understanding of the relationship between mind and brain (as discussed in Chapter One) the medical model perspective assumes most psychotropic medications have to reach the brain. Note that there is also ample evidence that what we call "mind" may have correlates in other parts of the body, such as the gut (as in a "gut feeling"). Although current research focuses on the impact of psychotropic medications on the central nervous

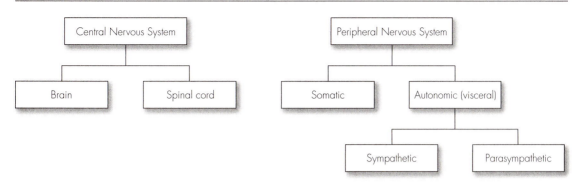

**FIGURE 2.1** Basic Overview of Human Nervous Systems

system, don't be surprised if future research explores how psychotropic medications impact "mind" through other areas of the body (Chopra, 1993; Dossey, 2001).

The nerves in your body and head that send information to and from the central nervous system are peripheral nerves. As you can see in Figure 2.1, the peripheral nervous system consists of the somatic and autonomic nervous systems. The somatic nervous system consists of peripheral nerves (nerves outside the central nervous system) that connect with sense receptors (receptors for vision, taste, and so on) and with skeletal muscles. The somatic nervous system regulates voluntary activity and relays information from the sensory organs to the central nervous system and from the central nervous system to the skeletal muscles. Thus when you see a pint of Haagen-Dazs ice cream, the somatic nervous system relays the visual stimulus to the central nervous system where you decide to reach for the pint (and a spoon). Next the signal for reaching for the ice cream is relayed back to the skeletal muscles, and that signal brings a creamy delight within your reach.

The autonomic (visceral) nervous system regulates activities that are primarily involuntary. For example, once you have enjoyed your ice cream the autonomic nervous system is correlated with activities such as digesting, so you can just bask in the afterglow of a good "sugar high." The autonomic nervous system is further subdivided into the sympathetic nervous system (active during arousal such as fight, flight, or freeze responses) and the parasympa-

thetic nervous system (active during conservation of energy). Activation of the sympathetic nervous system mobilizes your bodily resources and prepares you to expend energy. For example, if you left the Haagen-Dazs on the counter and your dog spied it just before you reached for it, your sympathetic nervous system would help you spring into action, thwarting Fido and capturing your prize. The activation of the parasympathetic nervous system deactivates organs that the sympathetic nervous system activated. Once the ice cream is safe in your grasp, your parasympathetic nervous system returns your body to **homeostasis** so you can settle down.

A ready example of how a drug affects the peripheral nervous system is the popular antidepressant fluoxetine (Prozac). Physicians often recommend that patients take fluoxetine with food. This is because a common side effect of fluoxetine (and most similar antidepressants) is nausea. This nausea occurs because the fluoxetine affects serotonin receptors, and the peripheral nervous system in our digestive tracts is rich in these receptors. Because the drug must pass through these peripheral nervous system structures to get into the bloodstream and eventually the central nervous system, along the way any receptors to which the drug binds are affected. This also returns us to the interesting point about the "mind" being linked with the "gut." Could antidepressants acting on these gut receptors be causing more than just "side effects"? Even if the mind did turn out to be totally generated by the brain (the epiphenomenon hypothesis in Chapter One), what if the "brain" we are referring to includes the entire nervous system? Until researchers can secure funding to think beyond the limits of the current models, such questions remain unexplored.

## Exploring the Central Nervous System

As noted, the central nervous system consists of the brain and the spinal cord. The brain has three general "layers" that developed through evolution, commonly called the **reptilian brain**, the **mammalian brain**, and the **neocortex**. The brain has structures in and across these layers that we have correlated with particular functions. There are several ways to classify brain structures. We have followed the systems used by Julien (2001) and Carlson (2001), because these authors are highly respected in the field. Note that although some names of the brain structures may seem unfamiliar, they are usually Latin or Greek words for rather mundane objects and we will translate them as we go.

### *Exploring the Brain Stem*

The brain stem includes structures that function to keep us alive. Figure 2.2 illustrates the structures of the brain stem and midbrain. When drugs interfere with the function of these structures, the results can be life threatening. For example, when a person drinks so much alcohol that it inhibits the neurons in these structures, the result can be coma and death.

The medulla oblongata is described as "the continuation of the spinal cord in the brain" (Thompson, 2000, p. 14) and controls breathing, heart rate, blood pressure, skeletal muscle tone, and digestion. This small, complex structure forms many connecting links between brain and spinal cord. Shaped like a pyramid, it is about an inch long and less than an inch across at its widest area. Its name comes from the Latin for "long marrow." The structure is so dense in neurons that the tissue looks dark, like bone marrow. Sometimes it is simply called the "medulla."

There is an important cluster of neurons in the brain stem called the **locus coeruleus** (pronounced *sa roo lee us*), from the Latin for "blue disc"; the cluster of neurons has a blue appearance. This structure consists of neurons that release norepinephrine and appear to help the person set priorities on incoming signals and decide where to place attention. Because of this link with attention, the role of the locus coeruleus is being investigated for links to the symptoms of Attention Deficit Hyperactivity Disorder.

The pons (from the Latin for "bridge") connects the medulla oblongata and the midbrain. It also connects the two halves of the cerebellum. The pons extends into the reticular formation (part of the midbrain) and governs alertness, waking, sleeping, muscle tone, and some reflexes. The reticular formation has a netlike appearance (from the Latin *reticular*, "netlike"). The brain stem also includes the raphe nuclei (meaning "nerve cells forming a seam"). The raphe nuclei contain serotonin neurons and are thought to trigger slow-wave sleep. You can imagine the importance of understanding this if a client is going to take a drug that radically increases levels of serotonin in the brain. By increasing serotonin in this area, the drug is also going to

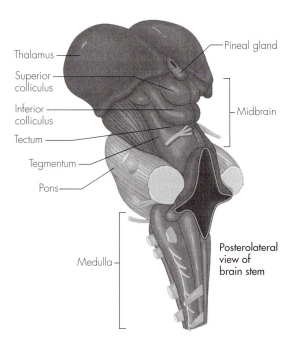

**FIGURE 2.2**   The Brain Stem and Midbrain

*Source:* From *Biological Psychology*, 7th ed., by J. W. Kalat. © 2001. Reprinted by permission of Wadsworth, a division of Thomson Learning, Inc.

cause sleepiness and possibly disrupt the sleep cycle, because serotonin is involved in sleep functions in the brain.

### Exploring the Midbrain

The midbrain is usually labeled **mesencephalon** (Greek for "midbrain") and is a continuation of the brain stem (see Figure 2.2). It merges into the thalamus and hypothalamus and encompasses what Julien (2001) calls the "subthalamus." The subthalamus, combined with the basal ganglia, constitutes one of our motor systems called the **extrapyramidal motor system.** All information that passes between the brain and the spinal cord travels through the midbrain. As mentioned, the reticular formation is an interconnected network of neurons

that extends from the spinal cord into the midbrain. These neurons are implicated in sleep, arousal, and a number of vital functions. The medulla, pons, and midbrain are thought to have developed early in human evolution (thus the common name "reptilian brain").

*The Cerebellum*  The cerebellum (from the Latin, meaning "little brain") looks like a little brain attached onto the larger cerebrum (illustrated in Figure 2.3). The cerebellum lies over the pons and is crucial to things such as balance and smooth, coordinated movement. It has connections with the vestibular system (the balance system located in the inner ear), the auditory, and the visual systems. The cerebellum, the subthalamus, and the basal ganglia

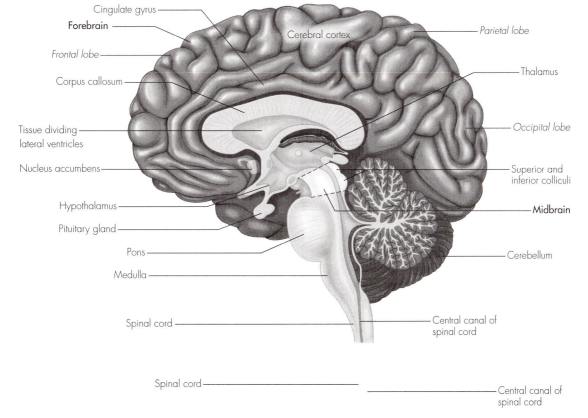

**FIGURE 2.3**  A Sagittal Section Through the Human Brain

*Source:* Adapted from *Biological Psychology*, 7th ed., by J. W. Kalat. © 2001. Reprinted by permission of Wadsworth, a division of Thomson Learning, Inc.

make up the **extrapyramidal system**, which helps coordinate movement, including initiation, smoothness, and termination of movement. If people take a medication that interferes with the functioning of the extrapyramidal system, they will likely suffer from involuntary movements called **extrapyramidal side effects**. We discuss these in detail in our treatment of antipsychotic medications.

### Exploring the Diencephalon

"Encephalon" is a Greek word that simply means "brain." "Di" means "between," so the diencephalon is between the telencephalon and the brain stem. There are several important structures in this brain area. The thalamus, a large group of nerve cells, acts as the final relay area for the major sensory systems that project to the cerebral cortex: the visual, auditory, and somatic sensory systems (Thompson, 2000). Oddly enough, the translation of the Latin word *thalamus* is "bedroom" or "receptacle." Although "receptacle" means basically "final relay area," we have yet to figure out how "bedroom" fit in for the ancient translators, but feel free to use your imagination.

The hypothalamus ("below the thalamus") is a collection of cells that lie above the pituitary gland and immediately in front of the midbrain. The hypothalamus controls the autonomic nervous system and endocrine system and maintains the body's homeostasis (internal state). It also regulates temperature, fluids, metabolism, appetite for specific nutrients, as well as what are called the "four Fs" (Fighting, Feeding, Fleeing, and Mating—again, use your imagination). Hormones secreted by the hypothalamus control the pituitary gland. Part of the wide-ranging influence of the hypothalamus is related to its control over the pituitary gland. Together, they act as a "master control system. The hormones they release act on the other **endocrine glands** such as the thyroid, adrenal, and pituitary glands that secrete certain substances, particularly hormones, directly into the blood. The hormones released by the endocrine glands then act back on the pituitary gland and hypothalamus to regulate their activity, an example of feedback control" (Thompson, 2000, p. 17). The hypothalamus is also located near and has influence over what Olds and Milner (1954) dubbed the brain's **pleasure centers**.

### Exploring the Limbic System

The limbic system is a series of brain structures that help us attach emotional meaning to sensory stimulation. In some systems of classification the limbic system is associated with the diencephalon, and in others it is associated with the telencephalon. The limbic system includes the amygdala (Latin for "almond," which it resembles), the septum (Latin for "dividing wall" or "enclosure"), the hippocampus (Latin for "seahorse" and based on resemblance), and portions of the thalamus. The amygdala integrates and directs emotional behavior, attaches emotional significance to what the senses signal, and mediates defensive aggressive behavior. Damage here produces **Kluver-Bucy syndrome**, which is characterized by decreased fear and aggression. The septum inhibits emotionality, as evidenced by the fact that lesions in the septum produce septal rage syndrome. In this syndrome, damage to the septum leads to uninhibited emotional expression, particularly the expression of anger and aggression. The septum is also part of the pleasure centers of the brain. The hippocampus is a curved ridge in the limbic system, involved in moving signals from short-term memory to long-term memory.

### Exploring the Telencephalon

The **telencephalon** consists of the right and left halves of the cerebrum (*tel* is a variation of the Greek *tele*, meaning "end" or "complete," so the translation is "end of the brain" or "completion of the brain"). The outer portion of the cerebrum is the cerebral cortex. This is the brain's outermost layer, the image you are probably familiar with from pictures of the human brain. This cortex is divided into four lobes (roundish projections) by sulci (deep grooves in the surface). The four lobes are named for the bones of the skull covering them (see Figure 2.3) (Carlson, 2001). This part of the brain is correlated with the functions related to self-awareness or sentience that make humans unique in the animal kingdom. The tissue in the lobes can generally be mapped according to function, although in many cases, if an area is damaged another part of the brain may pick up that function. For most functions their expression is contralateral ("opposite-sided"), meaning that an area on the right side of the brain controls something on the left side of the body. Next we summarize the four main lobes and some of their general functions.

The frontal lobes of the cerebral cortex are generally involved in motor behavior, expressive language, concentration, orientation (time, place, and person) thinking, and reasoning. These lobes contain the pyramidal system that is involved in fine, intricate movements. The left frontal lobe contains **Broca's area**, which is involved in speech production, and damage to this area can produce the experience of *expressive* aphasia (a self-conscious deficit in the ability to articulate or express language). The temporal lobes (located near the areas of your head called the "temples") are related to receptive language, memory, and emotion. These lobes contain **Wernicke's area,** which is involved in comprehending language. Damage to this area can produce *receptive* aphasia. The parietal lobes are located under the skull on the top of your head and contain the primary **somatosensory cortex**. This area receives and identifies sensory information from tactile receptors and processes visual and auditory sensations. Damage to the parietal lobes can produce Gertsmann's syndrome, which includes agraphia (inability to write), acalculia (difficulty with mathematical calculation), and right-left confusion. Finally, the occipital lobes (at the back of your head at the base of the skull) are largely associated with the **visual cortex**. Damage to the occipital lobes produces visual agnosia (the inability to recognize familiar objects on sight).

Under the cortex lie the smaller areas of the telencephalon (Bloom, Nelson, & Lazerson, 2001). The basal ganglia lie at the central regions of the cerebral hemispheres and are systems of cell **nuclei** that effect voluntary movement. They form the primary part of the extrapyramidal motor system (described earlier). Next we focus on the nerve cells in these structures and their function, so that we can begin to explain the mechanisms of action in psychotropic medications.

## An Overview of Neurons

The brain weighs about 3 pounds and has a volume of about 3 pints. It contains a lot of **neurons**. Accounts conflict on to how many neurons the brain

contains: about 100 billion (Churchland, 1995), about 140 billion (Barlow & Durand, 2002)? Others estimate closer to 20 billion (Beulow, Herbert, & Beulow, 2000). Perhaps we are best off estimating "many billions of neurons in every human brain" (Thompson, 2000, p. 29) (or as Carl Sagan might have put it, "billions and billions"). As cells, neurons are unique in that they are created before we are born and have the capacity to live as long as we do. Up until the beginning of the 21st century scientists commonly believed that at birth human beings had all the neurons they were ever going to have. This view is changing, as researchers now confirm that neurogenesis (the growth of new neurons) occurs in adults (Shors et al., 2001; vaan Praag, Christie, Sejnowski, & Gage, 1999) and correlates with the learning of new tasks (Gould, Beylin, Tanapat, Reeves, & Shors, 1999).

Although all human cells renew themselves, not all cells divide regularly. One reason that neurons may not divide as regularly as other types of cells is that they form essential functional units in brains. As Thompson (2000) pointed out, everything people are or do has correlates in the sequencing of neurons and their interconnections. If neurons had to keep dividing to replace themselves, valuable sequences and interconnections might not form.

Although neurogenesis research continues to explore questions about how new neurons may form, most knowledge about the correlation of neuronal function concerns the growth of axons and dendrites from existing neurons. This growth (called **arborization**) is prolific in the first few years of life. Moreover, you may have heard the saying "Size doesn't matter," and this is particularly true of the brain. Whales and dolphins have larger brains than humans, and although these mammals are no slouches intellectually, they do not match the human brain capacity for representational power. Nor do the *number* of neurons matter; it is the number of connections between the neurons that is important.

The neurons of the human brain have an enormous representational capacity. By way of analogy, Churchland (1995) compares this capacity to a standard 17-inch television screen. Such a screen has a representational capacity of about 200,000 pixels (a pixel is the smallest element of an image that can be processed). To get enough pixels to match the representational power of your brain, you would have had to cover all four sides of the Sears Tower in Chicago with such screens—and you have it all between your ears, as the saying goes. Such is the representational power of the brain.

### The Basic Anatomy of a Neuron

Figure 2.4 is a simplistic rendering of a neuron. Neurons come in many different types and shapes, but they all have structures similar to the ones in the figure. The importance of learning the basic parts of the neuron will become clear as we discuss mechanisms of action of psychotropic medications. Using Figure 2.4 as your guide, let us begin by discussing the soma or cell body of the neuron. The dark spot on the figure of the soma is the cell nucleus, which contains the genetic material of the cell. The soma contains the **mitochondria,** which are structures that provide energy for the neuron. Extending from the soma in one direction are **dendrites,** which are structures that receive inputs or messages from other cells through receptors. The receptors are typically pictured as located on the ends of the dendrites but can occur anywhere on the neuron. Receptors are basically chains of proteins that act as communication devices, allowing neurotransmitters (chemical messengers) to bind to them.

Extending in the other direction from the soma is the axon. Many elements made in the soma (such as enzymes and receptors), as well as the "raw materials" for these elements, are transported up and down the axon. The axon also transmits electrical signals that can cause the cell to "fire." When a cell "fires," it releases neurotransmitter molecules from its terminal button. At the far end of the axon are the terminal buttons. The terminal buttons contain sacks (called *synaptic vesicles*) of neurotransmitter molecules. When the electrical signal causes the cell to "fire," these sacks merge with the **permeable** membrane of the terminal button and the neurotransmitters are released into the synaptic cleft (the space between the terminal button and the neighboring receptors to which the neurotransmitter will bind). Although there is a universe of activity in each cell, this glance at the general components will suffice until later in the chapter, when we discuss neurotransmission in more detail.

Now, we say that chemical neurotransmission occurs at the **synapses,** which Stahl (2000) defines as "specialized sites that connect two neurons" (p. 1). Neurons send synaptic information through firing and releasing neurotransmitter molecules. They receive synaptic information through their receptors. The number of synapses (points of connection between a neuron and neighboring neurons) on each neuron varies from around 5000 on a mammalian motor neuron to some 90,000 on a single Purkinje cell in the cerebral cortex. (This type of cell, named after the Czech physiologist

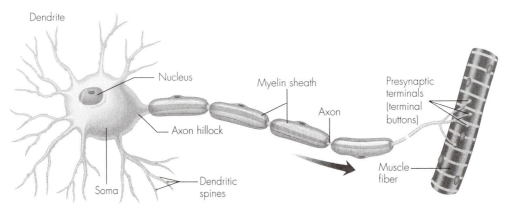

**FIGURE 2.4**   Components of a Motor Neuron

*Source:* From *Biological Psychology,* 7th ed., p. 32, by J. W. Kalat. © 2001. Reprinted by permission of Wadsworth, a division of Thomson Learning, Inc.

who first charted its function, is related to the contraction of the heart).

When the body is resting, the brain, which accounts for only about 2% of the body's mass, consumes about 20% of the body's oxygen. This is a lavish consumption of energy! The brain needs all this energy to maintain ionic gradients essential to receiving and sending information via the synapses. An ionic gradient is merely a charged signal (an electrical charge). You can think of this charge as a rate of change in relation to the distance of the axon. When the electrical charge reaches a certain threshold, the cell fires, or releases its neurotransmitter. To carry an electrical charge down an axon, positive ions must flow in. Once the charge is carried down the axon, these positive ions are pumped back out of the cell. As you will see, these ionic gradients play the key role in determining whether or not neurons fire. Imagine: A single neuron handles a thousand signals in the space of a second, and it may fire several hundred times a second, so its energy consumption must be huge.

One energy-saving device neurons have is myelin (pictured in Figure 2.4). Myelin is peculiar to vertebrates, although not all neurons in vertebrates are myelinated. For example, phylogenetically older fibers such as the C-fibers that innervate the skin and carry information about pain are less myelinated. If you have ever been pounding a nail and the hammer slipped, smashing your finger, you may recall having that split-second knowledge that it is going to hurt in a few milliseconds. With more myelin, you wouldn't have those milliseconds to anticipate the coming pain. Myelin is like the insulation on electrical wiring. The more myelinated an axon is, the better insulated it is and the faster it can conduct a signal. When you see a person with a disease that degrades the myelin (such as multiple sclerosis), you see that he or she has difficulty moving, because the nerves coordinating the signals for the movement cannot send the electrical signals efficiently.

Myelin is made from a type of cell called a "glial cell." "Glial" means "glue," and glial cells form different types of protective barriers (sheaths) around neurons (of which myelin is one). Glial cells usually outnumber neurons by a ratio of 10:1. In different parts of the body, glial cells have different names that reflect the person who discovered them or their function. In the peripheral nervous system, Schwann cells perform the myelinating function; in the central nervous system, oligodendrocytes perform the same function. A third glial cell type, astrocytes, function as fences and filters for the blood–brain barrier, and a fourth type, microglia, function as scavengers cleaning up dead neurons and other disintegrated material. We'll take another look at the blood–brain barrier shortly.

A well-myelinated axon in a human motor neuron can conduct an impulse as fast as 130 meters per second (equivalent to approximately 300 miles per hour), whereas an unmyelinated fiber conducts at about .5 meters per second (a little over 1 mph). Events in the world of silicon chips happen in the nanosecond (a one-billionth of a second), whereas events in the world of neurons happen in the millisecond (a one-thousandth of a second). Brain events are quite slow in comparison to computer events, but in complex tasks such as recognition, brains leave computers "in the dust," because brains accomplish recognition more quickly. Neurons are plastic and dynamic. Their information-relevant parts grow and shrink. The axons and dendrites are constantly changing, establishing new connections and removing old connections. This "arborization" is an important concept in psychopharmacology, because many drugs exert an influence to change the information-relevant parts of the neurons. Neurogenesis research findings are so new that speculations on the implications for pharmacology have just begun.

## The Blood–Brain Barrier

Over 100 years ago, Paul Ehrlich discovered that if blue dye is injected into an animal's bloodstream, all the tissues are tinted blue *except* the brain. You must inject the dye into the brain ventricles to get that tissue to turn blue. Although Ehrlich was working for a dye company on a different project, he thus unwittingly discovered the blood–brain barrier. In most of the body, the cells that form the capillaries are not spaced tightly together, so substances can move from blood plasma to the tissue.

In the central nervous system, the capillary cells do not have the same gaps, because they are filled by the astrocytes that make up the blood–brain barrier. This barrier blocks many substances from entering the central nervous system. In some areas the barrier is weaker than others, to allow specific functions that have developed through evolution. One example of such an area is the *area postrema*, which signals vomiting. The barrier is weak here, so toxins in the blood can be detected. Once it detects toxins, the brain triggers the vomiting response to preserve the organism.

The blood–brain barrier serves an important survival function by keeping foreign elements such as toxins out of the brain. But what about things such as nutrients? Nutrients such as glucose must be transported through the capillary walls by special proteins. This is very important, because to exert their effects all current psychotropic medications must reach the central nervous system. To do so they must pass through the blood–brain barrier. The glial cells that make up the blood–brain barrier have a high fat content. The myelination of the brain in infancy is one reason babies need a lot of fat in their diet. We refer to fatty cells as fat-soluble (the technical term for this is **lipophilicitous**—another great cocktail party word). Thus, to pass through the blood–brain barrier, a molecule also must be highly fat-soluble. Almost all psychotropic medication molecules are fat-soluble, with perhaps the sole exception of lithium, which must be carried across the blood–brain barrier by other means.

## Types of Neurotransmitters

The brain has approximately a dozen known or suspected neurotransmitters. Scientists may discover many more. To be considered a neurotransmitter, a substance must (1) be synthesized in the **presynaptic** neuron, (2) be released from the presynaptic terminal, (3) cause excitatory or inhibitory signals, and (4) have some mechanism for removing it from the site of action (Churchland, 1995). Table 2.1 lists neurotransmitters commonly involved in the actions of psychotropic medications.

Neurotransmitters are made from **precursor compounds** in the neuron. You can think of precursors as the "raw materials" with which neuro-

**TABLE 2.1**    Neurotransmitters Involved in Psychotropic Medications, and Their Abbreviations

| | |
|---|---|
| Glutamate | Glu |
| Gamma-aminobutyric acid | GABA |
| Acetylcholine | Ach |
| Dopamine | DA |
| Norepinephrine | NE |
| Epinephrine | Epi |
| Serotonin | 5-HT |

transmitters are made. These compounds include amino acids, glucose, and certain amines such as choline. You take many of these precursors into your body through the foods you eat. Think of neurotransmitters as chemical messengers in the nervous system. As we explain later, when a cell fires and releases neurotransmitters, these same transmitters bind to receptors on other neurons, conveying information and further exciting or inhibiting neighboring neurons.

Now we provide an overview of the primary neurotransmitters. Become generally acquainted with them, so that when we discuss mechanisms of action in drugs you can recognize the primary neurotransmitters involved. Although scientists generally think that neurons only produce one type of neurotransmitter, each neuron may be outfitted with receptors for multiple neurotransmitters. Thus although a neuron that produces only dopamine releases only dopamine, it can be affected by changes in available serotonin, norepinephrine, acetylcholine, and so on. This multiple sensitivity produces a "ripple effect": Using a drug to affect the levels of only one neurotransmitter may end up affecting the levels of many neurotransmitters.

### Glutamate (Glu)

Glutamate (also called *glutamic acid*) is one of the nonessential amino acids, meaning it is synthesized in the body and not required in the diet. One of the main sources of glutamate in the body is the breakdown of **glucose**. Most neurons have glutamate receptors. Glutamate serves an excitatory function, encouraging neurons to fire, and plays a key role in sensory functions and in some brain structures we have discussed in this chapter, including the pyramidal and extrapyramidal nervous systems, the hippocampus, and the cerebellum. Glutamate may be the dominant excitatory neurotransmitter in our brains. Julien (2001) noted that a newer drug for narcolepsy actually works by augmenting glutamate neurotransmission (as opposed to drugs such as amphetamines that augment dopamine neurotransmission). Researchers hope that a drug augmenting glutamate transmission will not show the dependence-inducing properties that amphetamines have.

### Gamma-Aminobutyric Acid (GABA)

GABA (gamma-aminobutyric acid) is one of the amino acid neurotransmitters and occurs almost exclusively in the brain. GABA reduces the firing of neurons and may be the predominant inhibitory neurotransmitter of the brain. Paradoxically, glutamate is a precursor for GABA, but whereas glutamate is excitatory, GABA is inhibitory. GABA is so common in the central nervous system that neurologists believe a full one third of synapses are receptive to it (Zillman & Spiers, 2001). Although GABA is inhibitory, it is important not to oversimplify this into the erroneous belief that all GABA transmission "mellows you out." For example, some areas of your brain (such as your sleep centers), when stimulated, calm you down. If GABA molecules inhibit these areas, then the end result is the *opposite* of calming you down. GABA-ergic areas of the brain also help people control motor behavior. People with **Huntington's chorea** have difficulty controlling their motor behaviors, and physiologists believe this is caused by losing GABA-ergic neurons (Zillman & Spiers, 2001).

### Acetylcholine (Ach)

Acetylcholine was the first major neurotransmitter to be identified, in the 1920s. (Epinephrine was discovered in 1904 but is less important in psychopharmacology.) Acetylcholine is prominent in the peripheral and central nervous systems. It is present peripherally at the muscle–nerve connection for all voluntary muscles and at many involuntary nervous system synapses. The exact role of acetylcholine neurons is becoming clearer with research. Gener-

ally, they are believed to be involved in alertness, attention, and memory. Acetylcholine is made from choline (an amine and one of the B-complex vitamins) and **acetate**. Choline is supplied by foods such as kidneys, egg yolk, seeds, vegetables, and legumes. Acetylcholine has been linked to cognitive functioning, because Alzheimer's-type dementia is correlated with the degeneration of acetylcholine-rich tissues in the brain. Drugs that temporarily slow the progression of Alzheimer's do so almost exclusively by enhancing the action of acetylcholine in the brain.

### Monoamine Neurotransmitters

Monoamine neurotransmitters are a class of neurotransmitters that share similar **molecular structures**. The monoamines include dopamine, norepinephrine, epinephrine, and serotonin. A subclass of monoamines is the catecholamines. The three catecholamine neurotransmitters are dopamine, norepinephrine (in the central nervous system), and epinephrine in the peripheral nervous system. The first two play important roles in both legal and illegal psychotropic compounds.

### Dopamine (DA)

Dopamine was discovered in 1958. Dopamine is a major transmitter in the **corpus striatum** (cerebrum), regulating motor behavior and playing a large role in the so-called pleasure or reward centers. It is derived from tyrosine, which is an amino acid in our diets. The dopamine pathways in the frontal cortex, nucleus accumbens, and ventral tegmental area (VTA) underlie the pleasure centers. The firing of dopamine neurons in these areas is augmented by certain drugs, which seems to lead some people to use these drugs in ways that are described as "abuse" and that may induce psychological or physical dependence. We look at primary dopamine tracts when we discuss antipsychotic drugs in Chapter Seven.

### Norepinephrine (NE)

In the 1930s the neurotransmitter norepinephrine was found in the both the central and peripheral nervous systems and in the sympathetic nerves of the autonomic nervous system (governing heart rate, blood pressure, bronchial dilation, and so forth). Norepinephrine is derived from tyrosine (an amino acid), and the cell bodies of most norepinephrine neurons are located in the brain stem in the locus coeruleus. From this area, norepinephrine neurons project widely throughout the brain and are involved in many responses, including feelings of reward, pain relief, mood, memory, and hormonal functioning.

### "It's Greek to Me"

A few notes on terms: The word *norepinephrine* is synonymous with *noradrenaline*. Norepinephrine is similar to epinephrine, which is a hormone produced by the adrenal medulla (the core of the adrenal gland). *Epinephrine* is synonymous with *adrenaline*. You may ask (as we did), Why are there two words for both norepinephrine and epinephrine? Good question, and we don't have an answer, but here is a little background.

Basically, one word is derived from the Greek language and the other from Latin. *Epinephrine* is derived from Greek (*epi*, "on"; *nephron*, "kidney"). *Adrenal* is derived from Latin ( *ad*, "toward"; *renal*, "kidney"). The prefix "*nor*" indicates that norepinephrine is a precursor to epinephrine. So to say a drug is "noradrenergic" means it enhances the action of noradrenaline/norepinephrine.

### Serotonin (5-HT)

Serotonin is distributed throughout the body. Researchers in the 1950s initially investigated it as a central nervous system transmitter, because of its similarity in structure to **lysergic acid diethylamide (LSD).** In the central nervous system, serotonin is the primary transmitter of the raphe nuclei, the group of neurons in the medulla and pons. From there these neurons project throughout the cerebral cortex, hippocampus, hypothalamus, and limbic system (Julien, 2001). Serotonin is heavily involved in the sleep–wake cycle as well as in mood and emotion. It is derived from tryptophan, an essential amino acid that people must obtain through diet.

## Reality Is Complex and . . .

It is important to understand that each neurotransmitter may have a number of different receptors to which it can bind. These subfamilies of receptors may play varying roles in mental/emotional disorders. For example, there are numerous serotonin (5-HT) receptors, variously referred to by numeric labels (5-HT1, 5-HT2, 5-HT3, and so on) (Bloom, Nelson, & Lazerson, 2001).

Julien (2001) has noted that researchers think neurotransmitters fit various receptors much like a key fits a particular lock. Thus a drug that mimics the action of serotonin by binding to serotonin receptors may interact differently with different receptor subfamilies. This also has implications for the number of side effects a drug may have. Drugs described as "dirty" affect several receptors and subfamilies of receptors and have more side effects. The "cleaner" the drug is, the more focused its action and the fewer its side effects.

Another complexity is important here. Although researchers once hoped that certain neurochemicals would be specific to certain brain sites, they aren't. Moreover, there is no sharp distinction between chemicals found in the brain and hormones found in rest of the body. Hormones once thought unique to the rest of the body have been found in the brain, and chemicals once thought unique to the brain have been found in the rest of the body. In addition, neurotransmitters may work with other peptides (chain-links of amino acids), forming cotransmitter pairs. For example, dopamine works with enkephalin (a naturally occurring protein with morphine-like properties). Researchers are beginning to see that to influence neurotransmission, pharmacologists may need multiple drug actions. This area in the leading edge of psychopharmacology is also known as **polypharmacy,** which is the use of multiple psychotropic medications to bring about symptom relief. This practice may result in a person being placed on numerous drugs because of the presumed interactions among the drugs. Thus you may hear of a drug such as methylphenidate (Ritalin) "potentiating" fluoxetine (Prozac). In that instance the methylphenidate enhances the action of the fluoxetine. Polypharmacy has also led to the practice of combining two medications in a formulation for a single dose. An example is one of the newest mood-stabilizing medications (Symbyax), which combines an antipsychotic medication (olanzapine) and an antidepressant (fluoxetine).

# The Story of Neurotransmission

Most psychopharmacology is the story of how different medications interfere with neurotransmission. If you become fluent in the language of neurotransmission, you can begin to understand the actions of medications on the brain. Stahl (2000) has offered two similes to help us understand neurotransmission: "wires" and "soup." In some respects the nervous system is like an electrical system (wires) in the sense that connections between neurons are like millions of phone wires within thousands of cables. The big difference is that, unlike a phone or electrical system, neurotransmission is not all electrical. The impulse from the receptor of a cell to the terminal button is electrical. After the cell fires, the neuron sends neurotransmitters out into the extracellular fluid (the chemical "soup"), where the chemical messengers (the neurotransmitters) bind to receptors on other neurons. So neurotransmission is both electrical and chemical. Psychotropic medications can exert effects on both dimensions of neurotransmission. Stahl also discusses the notion of time and neurotransmission. Some neurotransmitter signals are fast (such as GABA or glutamate signals that occur in milliseconds), whereas others are slower (such as norepinephrine, with a signal lasting up to several seconds).

## Neurotransmission: The Team Players

We now introduce some of the key players in neurotransmission. After this we present the entire process of neurotransmission, and then the ways psychotropic drugs interfere with the key players and the process to exert their influence on the nervous system.

### Deoxyribonucleic Acid (DNA)

Deoxyribonucleic acid (DNA)is a **macromolecule,** a very large molecule consisting of hundreds or thousands of atoms, housed in the nucleus of the neuron, that has two interconnected helical strands (the well-known double-helix shape). These strands and associated proteins make up the chromosomes that contain the organism's genetic code. When DNA is active, it makes ribonucleic acid (RNA) and gives RNA the genetic code. The messenger RNA then leaves the cell nucleus and attaches to ribosomes (protein structures that serve as the site of protein production) to create more proteins that serve as the basis for building other structures in the cell. Basically, the DNA acts as a template for messenger RNA synthesis; mRNA is a template for protein synthesis. DNA and RNA govern the production of enzymes, receptors, transporters, and other chemical supplies in and around the neuron's nucleus. DNA is still an uncharted frontier. Although the Human Genome Project has led to advances in understanding DNA, approximately 97% of DNA sequences are noncoding sequences and remain mysterious (Flam, 1994; Suurkula, 1996).

### Transporters

Transporters are just what the name sounds like—they move things around inside the neuron, outside the neuron, and in and out of the neuron. Transporters create a type of recycling program: First the cell fires neurotransmitters into the synaptic cleft. Then the neurotransmitter binds to a receptor. When it eventually unbinds, it is then picked up by this transporter, taken back inside the cell, and stored for future use. Some transporters move enzymes around the neuron so they can carry out their functions.

### Enzymes

Enzymes have multiple functions in the neuron, but typically they put together substances such as neurotransmitters in some areas, whereas they may dismantle neurotransmitters at other areas. Enzymes are also transported (by transporters) outside the cell where they break down neurotransmitters in the synaptic cleft. The enzymes and other elements are then transported down the axon. Enzymes also provide the energy for the transporters to "recycle" the neurotransmitter in the synaptic cleft.

### Receptors

Receptors are also protein molecules (chains of amino acids) created in the soma (cell body) and transported by transporter molecules to different parts of the neuron. They are then inserted through the neuronal membrane by enzymes to perform functions in neurotransmission. Receptors weave in and out of the cell membrane (often in a circular fashion), so part of them is outside the cell (extracellular) and part of them is inside the cell (intracellular). The binding site for the neurotransmitter is typically extracellular (outside the cell).

### Back to Neurotransmitters

As we have already noted, enzymes in the cell make neurotransmitter molecules. The enzymes then package the neurotransmitter into synaptic vesicles that are transported to the terminal button for storage. The synaptic vesicles protect the neurotransmitter from other enzymes that break down the neurotransmitter.

## Ions

Ions are atoms or groups of atoms electrically charged by loss or gain of electrons. Cations are positively charged. Examples of cations are sodium (Na from the Latin *natrium*) and potassium (K, from the Latin *kalium*). Anions are negatively charged ions. Chloride (Cl) is an example of an anion. Ions flow in and out of neurons, increasing or decreasing the electrical charge. If the charge is positive enough, the neuron fires. If the charge is negative enough, the neuron resists firing.

### Ion Channels

Ion channels are channels across the neuron membrane. They can open to allow positively or negatively charged ions into the channels, increasing or decreasing the chance that the neuron will fire depending on what sort of ion was let in. These channels can also remain closed. A cell in its **resting state** has anions intracellularly and cations extracellularly. In this state the cell is *polarized*, with the positively charged ions on the outside and the negatively charged ions on the perimeter of the inside. If cellular events increase this state by resisting opening the ion channels or by letting in only negatively charged ions, the cell is *hyperpolarized*, decreasing the chance it will fire. If ion channels open the cell to positively charged ions, it then becomes *depolarized*, increasing the likelihood of firing.

## A View Within the Cell

You can think of the cell as a little "universe." In this universe, the DNA and mRNA are initiating

protein synthesis in the ribosomes and those proteins are then used to create everything from enzymes to transporter molecules. The transporter molecules are busy transporting elements up and down the neuron axon, to and from the cell body, and moving in and out of the cell with other elements. The enzymes at some points are busy creating neurotransmitters from precursors, at other points dismantling neurotransmitters that have been fired, and at still other points providing energy for various functions of the cell.

Some readers may find a manufacturing metaphor useful. In the metaphor, the DNA and mRNA are the "brains" behind the outfit, planning how each element will function and what the outcomes will be. The enzymes and transporters are like workers with different functions. One of the primary products is the neurotransmitter, and it is packaged in the synaptic vesicles (much like workers producing cell phones may package them in a plastic container for shipping). The transporters are like tractor-trailer rigs that take care of transportation and shipping needs for the business.

## The Process of Neurotransmission

Now we describe a general sequence of events in neurotransmission. Again, remember that if you generally understand this sequence you will be able to understand how particular drugs interfere with the sequence and exert some of their effects. In this process we talk about presynaptic neurons and postsynaptic neurons. These are really relative terms. To understand this, draw an image of three neurons side by side, using the image in Figure 2.4 as a guide. Make sure each neuron you draw has a cell body (soma), dendrites with receptors, and a terminal button. Label the three neurons "A," "B," and "C."

In doing this you can see that the terminal button of neuron A is next to the dendrites for neuron B. The terminal button for neuron B is next to the dendrites of neuron C, and so on. Although this figure is oversimplified, it communicates the basic details. Remember that a synapse is the point where neurons communicate with each other and the synaptic cleft is merely the slight space between these two points. So with regard to the synaptic cleft between neuron A and B, A is the presynaptic neuron and neuron B is the postsynaptic neuron. With regard to the synaptic cleft between neuron B and C, neuron B is the presynaptic neuron and neuron C is the postsynaptic neuron. The labels merely reflect the position of each neuron with respect to a particular synaptic cleft. So in one sense every neuron is a presynaptic neuron to some other neuron and a postsynaptic neuron with respect to still others. Similarly, when you are driving on a crowded freeway, you are in front of some driver and behind some other driver.

### First-Messenger Effects

With the notion of presynaptic and postsynaptic neurons in mind, let's begin with the example. Note that when a cell "fires" (sends neurotransmitters out into the synaptic cleft), we call this *exocytosis* (exo, "outside"; "cytosis" "cell"—outside the cell). So, in

our example, neuron A fires and sends its chemical messengers (the neurotransmitters) out into the synaptic cleft. There some of them bind to receptors on neuron B. This initial binding is called a "**first-messenger effect**." The effect can be an excitatory effect (depolarizing the cell to increase the likelihood of firing) or an inhibitory effect (hyperpolarizing the cell to decrease likelihood of firing). The effect is not tied so much to the neurotransmitter that is binding but to what ion channels the receptors it is binding to control. In some presentations, the excitatory or inhibitory effect is labeled with reference to the synapse. Figure 2.5, from Kalat (2001), shows an example.

Remember that the resting state of the cell is called the *polarized state*. If the receptors open ion channels that allow only negatively charged ions to filter into the cell, then the cell becomes hyperpolarized or less likely to fire. In this scenario, the first-

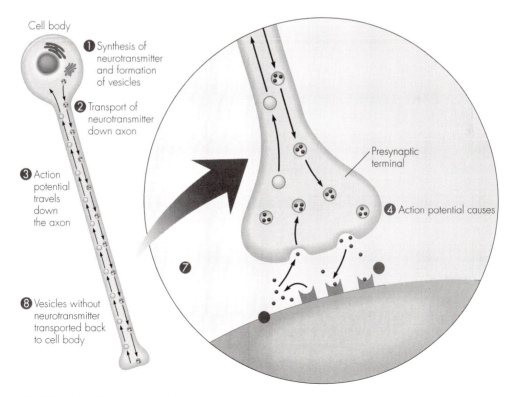

**FIGURE 2.5** The Process of Neural Communication

*Source:* From *Biological Psychology*, 7th ed., p. 59, by J. W. Kalat. © 2001. Reprinted by permission of Wadsworth, a division of Thomson Learning, Inc.

messenger effect is inhibitory. If the receptors to which neurotransmitters are binding open ion channels that let positively charged ions into the cell, then the cell becomes depolarized or more likely to fire. In this scenario, the first-messenger effect is excitatory.

Remember, although part of the receptor is outside of the cell, the receptor also goes through the cell membrane into the cell. The chemical neurotransmitter binding at an excitatory synapse can initiate an electrical impulse that is carried through the receptor into the neuron. That signal may be strong enough to open ion channels to allow positively charged ions to enter the cell. The positively charged ions further facilitate the electrical signal, letting it continue down the axon to the terminal button. When a charge of sufficient intensity reaches the terminal button, the cell "fires" and the synaptic vesicle merges with the terminal button wall, letting neurotransmitter molecules flow out of the neuron.

Once outside the neuron, the neurotransmitters are in the chemical soup (extracellular fluid). There they gravitate toward receptors and, if they fit the receptors in question, bind to them. Once bound, they may exert an agonist or antagonist effect on other cells, and the process continues. Remember that there are billions of neurons, with trillions of synapses where each may communicate with the others.

Once fired from the neuron, neurotransmitters cannot just stay in the synaptic cleft indefinitely. They also do not bind forever to receptors but bind and release or are displaced by other molecules (drug or natural) that then bind to the receptor. The neurotransmitters are then either "recycled" by transporter molecules that carry them back into the cell for future use (reuptake), or they are deactivated by enzymes in the extracellular fluid and their constituent parts are either destroyed or recycled as precursors. Precursors derived from used neurotransmitter or from dietary intake are carried into the cell and then used to create the various elements we have been discussing here.

### Second-Messenger Effects

There are also **second-messenger effects** that take more time than first-messenger effects, are more complicated, but also have a profound impact on neurotransmission. Researchers are just beginning to learn about this chain of events. The difference between second- and first-messenger effects seems to lie in the type of receptor being stimulated. Some receptors, rather than directly opening ion channels, initiate this series of chemical events. A second-messenger effect begins just the same as a first-messenger effect: A neurotransmitter binds to a receptor. This receptor is referred to as "metabotropic" because it requires the neuron to expend metabolic energy. When a neurotransmitter binds to the metabotropic receptor, the receptor activates a **G protein** located nearby within the cell. From there a portion of the G protein breaks away and attaches to a binding site near an ion channel. The channel then opens, allowing the ions to pass through. In a second type of second-messenger system, the G protein attaches to and activates an enzyme inside the cell and the enzyme can prompt the production of chemicals in the cell that can alter the cell's functioning. Compared with first-messenger effects, these second-messenger effects take longer to occur and last longer after they occur. The benefit of second-messenger effects is that they provide the cell with an efficient way to extend and amplify the cell's response to the transmitter (Bloom, Nelson, & Lazerson, 2001).

These first- and second-messenger effects may seem hard to imagine at first, but bear in mind that we are really just reviewing a sequence of events that affect the way the cell functions. Understanding of these events is still in the embryonic stage and will likely change a great deal over the next few years. Just remember that it is important to generally understand the sequence of neuronal events so you can understand (1) how psychotropic medications interfere with those events and (2) what effects are then correlated with specific types of interference. It is interesting to note that researchers hypothesize that second-messenger events can reach all the way back to the cell nucleus, where they may decrease the creation of receptors, reducing the sensitivity of the neuron. This effect, called **downregulation,** is one of the effects correlated with antidepressant-induced improvement in symptoms of depression. We return to this effect in Chapter Five. A second-messenger effect can also increase the synthesis of receptors, increasing the sensitivity of the neuron. This is called **upregulation**. Obviously not all these effects are necessarily good or therapeutic effects. These unwanted effects are called *side effects*, and one example caused by upregulation is **tardive dyskinesia**, an involuntary movement disorder. This is a side effect of older antipsychotic medications to which we return in Chapter Seven. We do want to note here that the further away from a first-messenger effect, the less well understood are the mechanisms of action.

### A Quick Review

Let's review this information: A neuron gets a chemical impulse from a neurotransmitter that (via a first- or second-messenger system) may open ion channels or keep them closed. Depending on which channels are open, this leads the neuron to fire or not fire (exocytosis).

Firing causes the release of stored neurotransmitter and related events (exocytosis). The neurotransmitters shoot across the neuronal synapse to bind to receptors. Neurotransmitter binding to receptor is analogous to a key fitting into a lock. If the neurotransmitter in question (key) does not fit into the receptor structure (lock), binding does not occur there. If the fit is good enough, however, the chemical signal is changed into another electrical signal, and the process goes on.

## What Happens When Neurotransmitters Bind to Receptors?

The neurotransmitter binding to the receptor is the first messenger. It may trigger changes alone or in the cell through second messengers. As a first messenger (quick signal), the neurotransmitter may alter the neuron's ionic gradient to make it fire, releasing more neurotransmitter. Depending on what type of receptor the neurotransmitter is binding to, it may inhibit the cell, preventing exocytosis.

The second messenger (slow signal) is an intracellular chain reaction created by the first-messenger neurotransmitter occupying the receptor. As noted, in second-messenger systems the

neurotransmitter may change the shape of the intracellular part of the receptor. This change then triggers a portion of a G protein to either open ion channels or to bind intracellularly to an enzyme that may then cause subsequent changes inside the cell. The G protein then changes shape so that intracellular enzymes can bind to it.

### And What Happens to the Released Neurotransmitter?

The released neurotransmitter may be recycled and taken back into the cell by transporter molecules to be used later, it may be broken down by enzymes and its precursors reused by the cell at some point, or it may be broken down and metabolized.

This sequence of events can be altered by introducing psychotropic medications into the body, but as Stahl (2000) reminds us, that does not mean researchers have even begun to understand these events or all the effects of psychotropic medications on these events (let alone why any of the latter would decrease the symptoms of mental or emotional disorders). As Stahl wrote, most of these events are still mysteries to neuroscientists. It is important to note there are nonchemical means of altering this sequence of events, such as aerobic exercise and meditation. We say more about such means later in the book.

## Pharmacodynamics: How Psychotropic Medications Affect Neurotransmission

As we noted, we want you to understand the events of neurotransmission so that you can better understand how drugs interfere with those events and how the interference correlates with effects on symptoms. You have perhaps noticed that we keep avoiding the phrase "how drugs decrease symptoms of mental and emotional disorders." We are consciously avoiding it because, in most cases, scientists simply don't know how drugs decrease symptoms. We want you to keep that in mind. This is one of the most compelling reasons for teaching psychopharmacology from multiple perspectives. There are so many variables and so little clear-cut knowledge that even to imply that biochemistry explains it all is purely and simply word magic.

What scientists do know a good deal about is pharmacodynamics, defined as how drugs act (or try to act) in and on the body. Although this is a broad area, for our purposes we focus on 11 general mechanisms of drug action, with an example of each. Bear in mind that psychotropic drugs do not use all these mechanisms of action and may also exert more than one mechanism.

### Agonism and Antagonism

When discussing agonism and antagonism, we refer to the various mechanisms as causing agonist or antagonist effects. The easiest way to think of agonist or antagonist effects is in terms of what the cell would do naturally. Something that assists or facilitates these functions is an agonist. Something that interferes with these functions is an antagonist. Because most cells fire naturally, anything that decreases the probability of this happening can be said to be an antagonist. Anything that increases the probability of this happening is an agonist. As usual, reality is more complex than this. This literature specifies not just agonism and antagonism but partial agonism, inverse agonism, partial inverse agonism, partial antagonism, inverse antagonism, and partial inverse antagonism. Although these concepts are much more exact, for this book the two broad categories of agonism and antagonism are enough.

### Mechanisms of Action With Effects on Production

Drugs can affect the intracellular production of various elements. Earlier we noted that transporters and other proteins carry into the neuron precursors from which things such as neurotransmitter are created. Drugs can interfere with this process by acting like precursors and thus increasing the amount of precursor material available. One such drug is levodopa (brand name Sinemet). This drug basically functions as a precursor to dopamine, allowing more dopamine to be made than normal. This is particularly important in Parkinson's disease, because the disease causes the degeneration of dopamine neurons and thus decreases available dopamine. The drug, at least for a while, corrects the shortage caused by degeneration of dopamine

neurons. Levodopa is an example of a drug exerting an agonist action, because its end result is to help the cells do what they would naturally do.

Drugs can also inactivate enzymes whose job it is to create neurotransmitters. In this case, such a drug artificially decreases the levels of neurotransmitter in a cell by inactivating the enzymes that put the neurotransmitters together in the first place. Such a drug has an antagonist action, because it is stopping a cell from doing what it would do naturally. An example of a drug that acts in this manner is parachlorophenylalanine (PCPA). In addition to being a mouthful to say, this drug inactivates enzymes that create serotonin. Because the release of serotonin is necessary for inducing sleep, such a drug causes insomnia. Interestingly, it may also be one of the few aphrodisiacs in existence. Because serotonin is also related to subduing sexual response, animal studies have correlated hypersexuality with its artificial decrease from taking PCPA.

In our story of neurotransmission, we discussed transporters in and outside the cell that have various functions. One such function is the storage of newly created neurotransmitter molecules in the synaptic vesicles that protect them. The vesicles protect them from other enzymes whose job it is to break down neurotransmitter molecules. Thus a drug that inactivates the transporter that carried the neurotransmitter into the synaptic vesicle leaves the neurotransmitter vulnerable to enzymatic breakdown. Such a drug, by interfering with this crucial storage, ultimately acts as an antagonist. Drugs using this mechanism of action also inactivate the proteins that help with exocytosis. A good example of a drug using these mechanisms of action is reserpine (Serpasil). Reserpine is no longer on the market, because it had unacceptable side effects, but its main mechanism of action affected acetylcholine, dopamine, norepinephrine, and serotonin. It was used to investigate depression because it caused a depressogenic (depression-inducing) response in animals. In the 1950s physicians also used reserpine as an antipsychotic.

Another mechanism of action that affects neurotransmitter production has to do with a special type of receptor called an *autoreceptor*. Autoreceptors seem to monitor levels of neurotransmitter in the synaptic cleft. For example, if there is enough dopamine in the synaptic cleft to bind to an autoreceptor, the autoreceptor sends a signal back into the neuron that basically says, "Slow down the synthesis and release of neurotransmitter." When an autoreceptor is open, production continues as normal. Thus two mechanisms of action here may affect neuronal production of neurotransmitter. The first is a drug that blocks an autoreceptor antagonistically (sending no signal for the cell to slow down production of neurotransmitter). Such a blockage in fact results in more neurotransmitter being produced and released, because the mechanism to signal a decrease has been effectively disabled. Clonidine (Catapres) works in this manner. The other mechanism is to introduce a drug that mimics the endogenous neurotransmitter and increases the signals going into the cell to slow down production and release of neurotransmitter.

### Mechanisms of Action With Effects on Release of Neurotransmitter

As noted, the key element in exocytosis is the release of neurotransmitter into the synaptic cleft. Drugs may have mechanisms of action that can inhibit or facilitate this element. For example, drugs can stimulate the release of neurotransmitter from the terminal button. Such drugs act as agonists. Now here, remember our mantra. Students often assume that an agonist ultimately stimulates the nervous system, but this is clearly not true. We noted that the neurotransmitter GABA has an overall inhibiting influence on the nervous system, so if a drug facilitates the release of GABA that drug is still an agonist, whereas the end result of the GABA release is ultimately inhibitory. Two substances that work by stimulating the release of neurotransmitter from the terminal button are black widow spider venom and sea anemone toxin. Both substances pierce the membranes of the neuron and synaptic vesicles, causing the neurotransmitter to leak out. In the case of the human central nervous system after the human has been bitten by a black widow spider, the venom causes acetylcholine to leak out. Although most bites from a black widow spider are not usually lethal because the spider injects minute amounts of

toxin when biting, the venom itself is 15 times as toxic as the venom from a prairie rattlesnake.

A substance that prevents the release of neurotransmitter from the neuron is botulinum toxin. This toxin has been anxiously discussed in the early 21st century as concerns about chemical warfare grow worldwide. Researchers estimate that one teaspoonful of pure botulinum toxin could kill the entire world's population (Carlson, 2001). This poison works by preventing the release of acetylcholine, which can paralyze muscles (including those used to breathe) and cause death. Oddly enough, diluted botulinum toxin is used dermatologically. Injected locally into wrinkled skin, it paralyzes the area, locally giving the skin a smoother appearance. The drug is available under the brand name Botox.

Another way that a drug can affect the release of neurotransmitter from the neuron is by imitating a first messenger. Nicotine is an excellent example. There are two subtypes of acetylcholine receptors: nicotinic and muscarinic. Acetylcholine binds to both types. Nicotine is structurally similar enough to acetylcholine to bind to the nicotinic receptors. Once there, it causes a release of the neurotransmitters in the neurons it binds to. This release is associated with the reinforcing properties of the drug. The body responds to the presence of nicotine by increasing the number of nicotinic receptors, resulting in the person needing more nicotine to get the desired effect (tolerance to the drug). This is why nicotine is associated with withdrawal symptoms. Although the number of nicotinic receptors eventually returns to the prenicotine state, this can take time. Julien (2001) notes that nicotine withdrawal can last up to several months.

Drugs can also interfere with first-messenger effects by blocking receptors. In this instance, they block the receptor and exert no action; thus such drugs are antagonists. Older antipsychotics act in this fashion by blocking dopamine receptors and not allowing dopamine to bind. Curare also acts in this way by blocking acetylcholine receptors. As you may recall, acetylcholine is the neurotransmitter at most muscle–nerve junctions, so blocking the receptors in this area causes the paralysis for which curare is so well known.

### Mechanisms of Action Targeting Neurotransmitter Deactivation

The two final mechanisms of action we outline are particularly known in antidepressants. They are both agonists in that they facilitate the action and duration of neurotransmitters in the synaptic cleft. The first is enzyme deactivation. As you may recall, once neurotransmitters are released into the synaptic cleft, enzymes that are also in the extracellular fluid can deactivate the neurotransmitters. By deactivating the enzymes that deactivate the neurotransmitters, a drug can artificially lengthen the amount of time the neurotransmitters can exert their influence in the synaptic cleft. Antidepressants called *monoamine oxidase inhibitors (MAO inhibitors)* work in this manner. The second mechanism of action that targets neurotransmitter deactivation is called *reuptake inhibition.* You will also recall that when neurotransmitters are in the synaptic cleft, they can be picked up by proteins called *transporter molecules* and taken back into the cell to be recycled. If a drug disables or slows down these transporter molecules, this drug effectively increases the length of time the neurotransmitters can exert their influence. Almost every antidepressant on the market uses this mechanism in some manner (except for MAO inhibitors).

Remember that a drug can use more than one of these mechanisms of action. It is also important to remember scientists simply do not know all the mechanisms of action for many drugs. It is hoped that future research will help map these mechanisms more effectively.

## Pharmacokinetics: How the Body Responds to and Eliminates Psychotropic Medications

Whereas pharmacodynamics is how drugs act on your body, pharmacokinetics is what your body does with a drug once you ingest it. Pharmacokinetics is "the process by which drugs are absorbed, distributed within the body, metabolized, and excreted" (Carlson, 2001, p. 98). Obviously, to be effective a drug must reach its intended site of action. We noted earlier that for psychotropic drugs this intended site is the central nervous system, so the drug must somehow get across the blood–brain barrier.

Pharmacokinetics involves routes of administration. What is the first thing you must do with a drug for it to have its desired effect? Take it, of course. There are several routes, although not all are commonly used for administering psychotropic medications. The most common route is oral. For a drug to be taken orally, the drug must be capable of being dissolved (soluble) and must retain its integrity in the stomach fluids. This is one reason there are no psychopharmacologically effective nicotine products one swallows. Nicotine cannot withstand stomach fluids and breaks down before it can get to the central nervous system to exert its effects. So if you hear of a new cola advertising nicotine for the "extra jolt," save your money.

Inhalation is a predictable and direct route of administration with many applications. Recreational drug users such as cigarette smokers learn early on how efficient and rewarding this delivery system can be. Although we know of no psychotropic compounds taken by inhaler, cannabis (which has psychotropic properties) is being piloted in the United Kingdom in inhaler form for patients with chronic pain caused by a variety of disorders (Reuters, 2001).

Rectal administration is less efficient than oral or inhaler administrations but can be useful for patients who have digestive tract difficulties. Again, we know of no rectally administered psychotropic medications.

Drugs can be administered via the mucus membranes (mouth or nose), which result in fairly direct absorption into the bloodstream. Also, drugs can be administered through a dermatological "patch" (such as the nicotine "patch" used to help people wean off nicotine).

A common route of administration for psychotropic medications is by injection. Injections may be intravenous, intramuscular, or subcutaneous. The intravenous (IV) is the fastest acting and usually used only in particular situations where a client is either in danger or is endangering someone else. For example, if a client is suffering from debilitating symptoms of mania, an intravenous benzodiazepine may be administered to stabilize the symptoms. Intramuscular (IM) injections have the advantage of being time released because the medicine diffuses slowly from the muscle tissue into the bloodstream, which frees the client from taking pills daily or several times a day. Probably the most common use of IM injections was for older antipsychotic medications. As we discuss in Chapter Seven, these medications are becoming less popular, because they are outdated by the benefits of newer antipsychotic medications.

## Types of Tolerance

It is important to generally understand the types of tolerance clients can develop to drugs. Please note that in this book we avoid using the word "addiction." The emotional hysteria around this word, and the lack of operational definitions, make it too inexact to be helpful. As Julien (2001) reminds us, physical dependence is linked with the term *addiction* and implies that withdrawal signs are "bad" and only linked to drugs of abuse. He concludes that "this is certainly far from the truth: rather severe withdrawal signs can follow cessation of such therapeutic drugs as the SSRI type of clinical antidepressants" (pp. 32–33).

Instead, we discuss types of tolerance and dependence. Julien (2001) defines **tolerance** as the clinical state of reduced responsiveness to a drug that can be produced by a variety of mechanisms, all of which result in the person needing increased doses of the drug to achieve the effects previously provided by lower doses. **Dependence** is defined as a physical tolerance produced by repeated administration of a drug and a concomitant withdrawal syndrome when the drug is discontinued (Stahl, 2000. Julien outlines three primary types of tolerance: metabolic, cellular, and behavioral conditioning processes.

*Metabolic tolerance* is an increase in the enzymes that metabolize a drug, an increase caused by the presence of that or similarly acting drug. The most common enzyme system for metabolizing drugs is the **cytochrome P-450 enzyme** family. These enzymes, produced in the liver, have evolved over 3.5 billion years to accomplish the detoxification (metabolism) of ingested elements such as chemicals and food toxins. There are several families of these enzymes, some more specific to certain substances than others. Thus metabolic tolerance begins when you take a drug that is broken down by any one of these families. If you take the drug consistently, your body responds by elevating the level of enzymes needed to break the substance down. The elevated enzyme level breaks down the drug more efficiently, leading to the need for a larger dosage; thus the cycle begins. The drug, the amount taken, and the individual body's response to it, all determine the pattern of metabolic tolerance. This pattern does not inevitably spiral out of control to the point where the drug cannot be used. For example, many people take benzodiazepines such as Valium or Xanax on an "as needed" (p.r.n., from the Latin *pro re nata*, meaning "as needed") basis. Such a person may only take 0.25 mg of Xanax once or twice a week. Such a low dose is unlikely to produce any problems with metabolic tolerance. This raises another important point, though, namely that similar drugs can produce cross-tolerance. For example, if the same person who took one dose of alprazolam (brand name Xanax) once or twice a week was in the habit of drinking two to three alcoholic beverages each day, probably he or she would not get as much response from the Xanax as someone who only drank two to three alcoholic beverages per week. The person drinking alcohol daily has likely developed some metabolic tolerance to it, and the families of enzymes that break down alcohol are also involved in breaking down Xanax, thus diminishing the effect of the latter. For the record, anyone taking a benzodiazepine such as Xanax or Valium should not drink alcohol.

*Cellular tolerance*, which is more related to pharmacodynamics, occurs when receptors in the brain adapt to the continued presence of a drug (Julien, 2001). A common form of cellular adaptation is downregulation, in which neurons decrease the number and/or sensitivity of receptors because of the presence of a drug. We return to this topic in Chapter Five when discussing antidepressants.

Another type of tolerance involves *behavioral conditioning processes*. The environmental cues associated with taking drugs can become conditioned stimuli that "elicit a conditioned response that is

**TABLE 2.2**   Five Important Pharmacokinetic Terms

| | |
|---|---|
| Half-life | Amount of time required for plasma concentration of a drug to decrease by 50% after a person stops taking it. |
| Steady state | The state when the concentrations of a drug in a person's bloodstream reach a plateau so that the amount being taken in each dose is roughly equivalent to the amount being eliminated. |
| Loading dose | An initial dose of drug that is higher than subsequent doses, given for the purpose of achieving therapeutic levels rapidly. |
| Maintenance dose | The regular dose of the medication that maintains the steady state plasma concentration in the therapeutic range. |
| Titration | The art and science of balancing a drug dose against the patient's symptoms. Upward titration is gradually increasing the dose, and downward titration is gradually decreasing the dose. |

opposite in direction to, or compensation for, the direct effects of the drug" (Julien, 2001, p. 33).

Table 2.2 defines a few more concepts related to pharmacokinetics: half-life, steady state, loading dose, maintenance dose, and titration.

These terms are frequently used in medical practice and may be confusing to the layperson. Clients often ask questions about these terms. One client mistakenly thought he could stop taking medication after the loading dose because he interpreted "loading" in a manner akin to computer software—once loaded, no further loading needed. The half-life is particularly important in understanding how long it takes a drug to clear out of a person's system. This concept is helpful in explaining to clients why they are still experiencing side effects days after discontinuing medication.

## Summary

Although an Integral study of psychopharmacology involves more than physiology, physiology forms the base knowledge in the field. This knowledge base focuses on how psychotropic medications affect the central nervous system, which includes the brain and spinal cord. Medications can also impact the peripheral nervous system, including the sympathetic and parasympathetic nervous systems.

Understanding the story of neurotransmission is also crucial to understanding how psychotropic medication works. This understanding begins with learning about the structure of neurons, neuro-

transmitters, and their functions and interactions. The story of neurotransmission includes how neurotransmitters bind to receptors on neurons and the effects of this binding. Psychotropic medications can mimic or block binding, producing effects on the central nervous system. Once you understand the story of neurotransmission, you will better understand how psychotropic medications interfere with neurotransmission to produce various effects (some desired, some not).

This chapter has covered what we believe to be the most pertinent material on psychopharmacology from the medical model perspective. A basic understanding of the brain structures as well as the events involved in neurotransmission will facilitate mastering the subsequent material in the book on specific types of medications. We cannot overemphasize the importance of this, and we encourage the reader to work (in groups or individually) with the following Study Questions and Exercises.

## Class Exercise:
## The Psychodramatic Neuron

Using placards that students can hang around their necks, label the primary parts in the story of neurotransmission. You will need cards to assign the following parts:

- Three receptors
- Three synaptic vesicles
- One transporter molecule

- One electrical charge
- Two enzymes
- Two ion channels

Mark off an area in your classroom to create a psychodramatic neuron. You can use a table or desk for the synaptic cleft. On one side, line up the synaptic vesicles (in the terminal button) of the presynaptic neuron. On the other side, line up the receptors. One enzyme stands at the end of the row opposite the makeshift cleft. This enzyme is going to put a neurotransmitter together from precursors. The other enzyme and one transporter molecule stand at the side of the table representing the cleft. These will compete for the neurotransmitter once it has bound to and released from the receptors. The person playing the electrical charge stands at the end of the row opposite the makeshift cleft. The people playing the ion channels stand outside the row; one holds a sign indicating a positive electrical charge while the other holds a sign indicating a negative electrical charge. Use Lego-type pieces for the neurotransmitter—about four pieces per neurotransmitter.

The action starts with each synaptic vesicle holding three neurotransmitters (each made of at least four Lego pieces). The electrical charge moves down the axon (the row). If the negative ion channel sign is in the row, the charge must stop and return to the top of the row. If the positive ion channel sign is in the row, the charge can proceed to the end, tapping the synaptic vesicles, which is their cue to "fire" the neurotransmitter into the cleft (set the Lego pieces on the table). The receptors should then pick up the neurotransmitter, one per hand only, count to five, then set them back down on the table. At this point the enzyme and transporter compete for the released neurotransmitter. The transporter hands the neurotransmitter intact back to the synaptic vesicle, or the enzyme takes the neuro-

transmitter apart and carries the parts back to the enzyme near the soma, who puts them back together and carries them down the axon to the synaptic vesicles. The instructor should direct the action, stopping to interview the various parts, asking them what they are doing, what they will do next, and so on. As different drugs are introduced throughout the course, you can write them into the script of the psychodramatic neuron to show how they interfere with the action and exert their influences.

Although this exercise may seem odd, it really helps conceptualize the story of neurotransmission. The first author went to a Halloween party (come as your favorite neuron part) where the game was played well into the night.

## Study Questions and Exercises

1. Define the following terms: *psychopharmacology, pharmacodynamics, pharmacokinetics.*
2. Describe the anatomy of a neuron. Include a definition of synapses and their critical importance in the process.
3. Discuss the importance of the blood–brain barrier and the qualities necessary for a psychotropic medication to cross this barrier.
4. Identify at least five primary neurotransmitters. Describe how each is thought to influence brain activity.
5. Outline the steps in the process of neurotransmission from exocytosis in the presynaptic neuron to reuptake and enzymatic breakdown of the released neurotransmitter.
6. Discuss the difference between an agonist and an antagonist, in the context of neurotransmission.
7. Discuss the various mechanisms of action through which psychotropic medications can interfere with neurotransmission.

# CHAPTER THREE

# Intrapsychic Issues in Psychopharmacology

As we stated in Chapter One, a primary goal of ours is to explore the topic of psychopharmacology in an **Integral** fashion. The Integral approach prepares readers to understand and work with the multiple truths or perspectives relevant to psychopharmacology. If reality is complex and complexity is our friend, then category errors and oversimplification are always temptations. Recall that a **category error** is when you mistake a partial truth for the whole truth or when you assume that one tool works for all jobs.

A common example of a category error in psychopharmacology is extreme advocates of the medical model perspective trying to explain something such as trauma response (an intrapsychic phenomenon) solely through brain chemistry (for example, claiming a client developed Post-Traumatic Stress Disorder (PTSD) because of a chemical/genetic response to a trauma). Ross and Pam (1995) have noted that this category error is rooted in the misguided belief that finding a biological factor in a mental/emotional disorder makes it "more real," because biology is "more real" than psychology (p. 114). This is clearly not true; biology and psychology explore different faces of truth and thus require different tools.

As we noted in Chapter One, there is no conclusive support for the notion that minds are just a "side effect" of signals in brains. However, even if we were to accept that the mind is a "side effect" of the brain, there is still evidence that the mind can affect or act

on the brain (Sperry, 1988) These conclusions, which are very different from radical understandings of the medical model, are giving rise to new subdisciplines in which scientists are examining these issues. One example is positive psychology, which seeks to understand the importance of subjective states of consciousness and how they affect the brain (Seligman & Csikszentmihalyi, 2000).

Even materialist theorists admit that many "disorders" such as PTSD are a result of multiple variables (biological, psychological, cultural, and social), so why do we still find people committing category errors? Most of us struggle with temptations leading to category errors daily. At times, out of sheer exhaustion, we deeply desire simple solutions, and exhaustion and desire for simplicity tempt us toward category errors. Often there is enormous political pressure in organizations or academic departments to hold certain views that reinforce category errors (Schwartz & Begley, 2002). Oversimplification becomes tempting, particularly when the counselor's own self-image is on the line. Sometimes it is far more palatable to view as "resistant" a client who is making no progress, rather than to consider that the counselor has not been able to help the client. Similarly, category errors such as assuming that all mental/emotional symptoms have underlying biological causes relieve the ineffective clinician from difficult self-examination.

Category errors remain ever-present obstacles on the search for truth. The search for truth may be so exhausting that people become willing to settle for the illusion of a partial truth masquerading as the whole truth. It is existentially simpler to believe that the unruly child disrupting so many adult lives simply has a "chemical imbalance" in his or her brain and that all the physicians need to do is concoct the right chemical cocktail for the child. As the philosopher Nietzsche (1985/1974) noted, the unknown confronts people with danger, discomfort, anxiety, and worry, so the first instinct is to abolish these painful sensations. Simply put, any explanation may seem better than no explanation. If clinicians are not willing to look for these weaknesses in their own awareness, the unchallenged gaps will ultimately harm clients.

In Chapter Two we reviewed the perspective of the medical model and discoveries made using the tools of scientific method. In this chapter we explore the intrapsychic perspective, which deals with the phenomenological, subjective aspects of consciousness that the objective tools of science do not easily measure. Learning about a client's intrapsychic perspective entails developmentally tailoring dialogue and interpretation to the client. For example, for young children, whose cognitive tools for dialogue are limited, techniques such as play therapy can help the counselor learn about what is happening in the child's mind.

The intrapsychic perspective also deals with what is happening in the mind of the clinician, particularly with the clinician's vulnerability to category errors and word magic. And it includes interpersonal variables such as ethical dialogue between counselors and clients about psychotropic medication and issues related to collaboration with other health care professionals. Counselors and other mental health therapists often have their own conflicts around psychotropic medication, conflicts that show up in consultation and/or must be handled in supervision (all mental health clinicians have occasion to consult colleagues and to work under supervision at some point in their careers). We also include a section on themes related to medication that often arise in supervision.

Finally, we must remain mindful of the power of intention, attention, and consciousness in general. The power of intention and attention are already

inherent in accepted nonmedical treatments for many mental and emotional disorders. Philosopher David Chalmers (1995) proposed that consciousness cannot be reduced to matter and may qualify as a fundamental building block of reality. If this view of consciousness holds up under scrutiny, then the ability of consciousness to have an impact on material reality (as well as the **nonlocal qualities of consciousness**) also must be considered. This opens up new avenues in understanding and treating mental and emotional disorders. In addition, if consciousness is a fundamental building block of the universe, activities that direct consciousness and expand awareness (such as counseling or meditation) can be examined on their own terms instead of in terms of biological mechanisms hypothesized to underlie them (Dossey, 2001). Such directions for research also help us describe symptoms in ways other than the medical model approved by the American Psychiatric Association. This shift in focus of course could cause huge shifts in power, and those who hold power rarely give it up willingly.

Having cited some of the larger issues related to an intrapsychic perspective of psychopharmacology, we now focus on particular topics: issues of self-worth and stigma, client reactions to the medical model of mental illness, the unconscious, issues about compliance and adherence, talking to clients about medications, and specific supervision issues.

## Issues of Self-Worth and Stigma

Many intrapsychic issues that clients may have related to psychotropic medications are illustrated in discussing **compliance** with medication. Even when a person suffers from terrible **ego-dystonic symptoms** that may be treated with a medication, if taking medication is incongruent with the person's self-image, noncompliance or nonadherence may be an issue. We recall one client (Agnes) who interpreted taking a medication as a sign of weakness that she avoided thinking about. Agnes had lost her husband two years before she consulted a physician for her "nerves." She was experiencing what is called "complicated grief" in the *Diagnostic and Statistical Manual of the American Psychiatric Association* (APA, 2000), was not eating or sleeping, and met the *DSM* criteria for a Major Depressive Episode. Her sense that taking the medication would be a sign of weakness began as a subjective, psychological experience that she did not share with her prescribing physician or with me (Ingersoll), her counselor. She finally told me she was not taking the medication (an antidepressant) her doctor had recommended. She said, "That doctor must think I'm crazy!" Her response was clearly related to her own perceptions of psychotropic medication, which reflected the cultural stigma attached to mental/emotional disorders.

Understanding such stigma is an important variable in understanding clients who may resist or feel conflicted about taking medication (Knudsen, Hansen, Traulsen, & Eskildsen, 2002), but the stigma seems to vary from culture to culture (Britten, 1998; Priest, Vize, Roberts, & Tylee, 1996). Mental health professionals must be willing to commit the time with clients to explore issues such as stigma. For Agnes, cognitive techniques helped her reframe her understanding of weakness and try a medication that could help her through a stressful period. She took it for four months, during which she came to deal directly with her grief. After four months, she had made considerable progress and was sleeping and eating better. At this point her doctor titrated her off the medication, and she continued to do well and was able to get on with her life.

## Client Reactions to the Medical Model of Mental Illness

Certain qualitative studies examine the way clients perceive the medical model description of their symptoms. In one study of women suffering from symptoms of Schizophrenia (Sayre, 2000), most of the sample seemed to have been given a medical model explanation of their symptoms (for example, "Schizophrenia is a brain disorder"). Client responses fell into six general categories. The members of one group more or less accepted the disease explanation and viewed their problems as related to some externally caused illness that could be remedied by medication. The members of another group (labeled the "problem group") saw their symptoms as arising from personal qualities and behaviors that were the root causes. The members of

a third group (the "crisis group") viewed their symptoms as a response to some crisis or other recent stressor. In a fourth group (the "ordination group"), the members saw their symptoms as a sign of special powers or responsibilities (as in the shamanic traditions of many indigenous people). In the fifth group (the "punishment group"), members saw their symptoms as punishment for past actions. In the final group (the "violation group"), members viewed their hospitalization as an attack on them by hospital staff and the idea that they had an illness an excuse for detaining them. In the case of Schizophrenia, although there is support for a theory of biological etiology, the symptom presentation is still heterogeneous and many clients present atypical symptoms that do not respond to antipsychotic medication.

Even if a clinician believes there is no evidence to support etiological theories outside the medical model, it is important for the therapeutic relationship to consider the intrapsychic manner in which the client makes meaning of his or her symptoms. Clearly, some perceptions of illness recorded in the Sayre (2000) study may reflect the illness more than they represent any personal or cultural aspects of the client. For example, **illusions** or **hallucinations** may be perceived as a sign of special powers (as in shamanic initiation) but also may reflect **megalomania,** which manifests in many people suffering from severe disorders such as Schizophrenia or Bipolar I Disorder. Although cases of megalomania are more common than visions related to spiritual initiation (even in indigenous societies), there are ways to differentiate spiritual or transpersonal crises from psychopathology (Grof, 1998).

Although we ourselves, as authors, maintain that mental health professionals need an Integral view of psychotropic medications, it is important to remember that some clients prefer to use the medical model perspective to explain their symptoms. In such cases, the intrapsychic perspective can help counselors understand why some clients have this preference. Although ideally clients will become able to face all the variables related to their symptoms, this may take time. In some cases of depression the medical model may provide the best explanation; however, where the depression is **overdetermined,** the medical model may serve as what Yalom (1995) called an "explanatory fiction." An explanatory fiction is an explanation that is more allegory than fact corresponding to some external truth. One client (let's call him James) had low **self-efficacy** and was actively suicidal. This followed a series of difficult life events, including the loss of a job, being dumped by a long-time girlfriend, and the death of his mother from pancreatic cancer. Clearly, these life experiences were strongly related to his depression but for James, the explanatory fiction of his depression as a medical illness made it easier to accept help in the form of counseling and antidepressant medication. James took the antidepressants for eight months while also engaging in counseling. After eight months his doctor titrated him off the medication. James terminated the counseling relationship after one year, at which time he was functioning much better.

The medical model as explanatory fiction or useful metaphor is illustrated in the notion that alcoholism (or any substance dependence) is a "disease" with a biological etiology. This notion is not supported by science or logic (Ross & Pam, 1995), but the metaphor of alcohol dependence as a disease has helped some clients avoid becoming crippled by guilt and self-recrimination so they can more fruitfully engage in treatment. Certainly the reverse holds true as well—some clients use the metaphor of alcoholism as a disease to avoid taking any responsibility for their drinking ("I can't help it—I have a disease"). Ethically, the clinician needs to know when the medical model perspective seems to be the best explanation for symptoms and when it seems the best metaphor to help the client engage in treatment. When metaphors are mistaken for facts, however, the potential exists for damaging word magic and category errors. One example of this was a case of a fifth-grade student that I (Ingersoll) consulted on. The student was diagnosed with Attention-Deficit-Hyperactivity Disorder (ADHD), Inattentive type. The school counselor and I learned that the diagnosis had been made in a physician's office without an assessment of the child's behavior across several settings. The child appeared to have the inattentive type of ADHD because in school she would unpredictably stare off into space or get up and meander around

the classroom. The physician told the parents that their child had a "chemical imbalance." They took this to mean that the medication (a stimulant in this case) would correct the problem. Although the medication seemed to help the daydreaming, it also seemed to exacerbate the behavior of getting out of her chair and wandering around the room. The school counselor and I referred the child to a specialist who helped children with mild to moderate symptoms of ADHD. The parents agreed, and the counselor worked with the student on learning how to concentrate and helped the parents and teacher at the school cue and reinforce appropriate behavior in the student. After six months the child was able to be titrated off the medication. Had the parents continued under the assumption that their child had "a chemical imbalance," the child might not have received the help she needed or would have received it later than she did.

With regard to the stigma of mental illness, some clients benefit from the medical model perspective of mental/emotional symptoms as constituting an illness and their medication as treatment for this illness. This can especially occur when clients view psychological counseling as having a negative stigma (Ben-Porath, 2002). Such clients may not be ready to realize that variables outside of the medical model perspective, which they control, are contributing to their symptoms. Initially, they may prefer the external locus of control that comes with the disease explanation—the sense that the problem is outside of them, not within them. Ideally, good mental health treatment expands the clients' awareness to include these variables and helps them develop the ego strength to cope better.

Schreiber and Hartrick (2002) described how female clients in their study used the medical model perspective of depression to help deal with the stigma they experienced as a result of others' perceptions. Again, reality is complex, and complexity is our friend. Even though in many cases a client's depression is truly overdetermined, that same client may prefer to exclusively use the medical model to explain his or her symptoms to others. In a way this is a category error on the client's part to which clinicians need to be alert. Unaddressed factors that are contributing to symptoms will manifest in one way or another if the client does not deal with them—whether or not the client is taking medication.

Even though a client may prefer a medical model explanation of symptoms because it is less threatening to his or her sense of self, mental health professionals must resist being caught up in the word magic of the medical model. We recall attending a presentation at a professional conference where the presenter lectured for three hours on the biological bases for mental disorders, without producing one reference or fact to support his thesis. He seemed far too mesmerized by the medical model to bother to provide factual support for his claims. Even though he was trained in psychosocial interventions, he did not mention the ones we know are effective for many of the disorders he covered (such as ADHD). In addition, this psychologist supported the movement to give psychologists the legal power to write prescriptions for psychotropic medications. As such, he was clearly biased. A better approach would have been to set his presentation in the context of his position that psychologists should be allowed to prescribe psychotropic medications. Within this context he then could have addressed the hypotheses concerning the biological etiology of mental and emotional disorders and the how to balance between medical and psychosocial interventions.

A study of adolescents with mental/emotional disorders summarized their perceptions of treatment. These teenagers shared the common negative perception that staff relied too much on the medical model to explain depression. They reported that the staff seemed to just want to give them medication and to not talk to them about what was really bothering them (Buston, 2002). What was "really bothering them" in this case were psychological and cultural variables that they saw as related to their depression. These adolescents wanted to discuss their intrapsychic perspectives with clinicians rather than just have their symptoms described as a disease process treatable with pills.

## The Unconscious

Although many counselors, social workers, and psychotherapists ignore or disregard the unconscious, learning to recognize the power of the unconscious helps clients improve. For the Integral Model, the unconscious plays a prominent role in the intrapsychic perspective. Because, by definition, we cannot learn anything from a client's intrapsychic perspective unless she or he shares it, this model relies on clients being aware of intrapsychic elements they can share. Clients may also be aware of intrapsychic variables and may choose not to share them or may choose to lie about them (for example, a client who enjoys being intoxicated more than anything else in life often lies about the negative impact of drinking until he or she becomes motivated to consciously explore this impact).

We are all aware of the potential unconscious meaning in jokes, momentary slips (**parapraxes**), troubling dreams, or forgetful periods. Freud (1895/1955) discussed how he uncovered memories in patients to which they did not have access. He noted, "These experiences are completely absent from the patient's memory in a normal psychical state, or are only present in a high summary form" (p. 9). Freud asserted that this condition, which he named the unconscious, is universal.

Gabbard (1994) wrote of the unconscious that it exists in the deep recesses of the mind. He also said that the psychoanalytic theory of the unconscious lets the therapist transcend descriptive psychiatry/psychology to enter the complexity of the client's mind. An example of uncovering an unconscious force with a client was my (Rak's) work with a woman who would take her prescribed psychotropic medication only when in emotional crisis. Both I and her psychiatrist encouraged her to take her medication daily as directed, and at each visit she promised to do so, but again failed to do so. One afternoon in a counseling session she spoke of how her adoptive mother always directed her as a child to "take pills only when you feel the worst." This unconscious rule from childhood had arisen to block improvement, so counseling now focused on enhancing her awareness about the previously unconscious rule to only take pills when things were terrible. Overcoming this barrier helped her improve.

## Client Intrapsychic Issues About Compliance and Adherence

**Compliance** is the overall extent to which a client takes medication as prescribed. **Adherence** is more specific, referring to the extent that the client takes the prescribed medication at the exact time and in the correct dose (Demyttenaere, 2001). We discuss adherence in discussing compliance.

Perhaps the best way to begin this section is to ask the reader a simple question. Have you ever (1) not taken a medication as directed, (2) taken more of a medication than prescribed, (3) taken less of a medication than prescribed, (4) stopped taking a medication before your doctor recommended it, (5) resumed taking a medication left over from an earlier prescription without checking with your doctor for the new episode? If you have done any of these, you have not followed—technically, you have been noncompliant with—a medication plan. (When we ask this question in class, 80 to 90% of our students raise their hands; we do, too.) Researchers estimate that only 50% of people on any prescription medication always take it as prescribed (Patterson, 1996).

Although there is no absolute way to predict which clients will be most compliant with medication regimens, some characteristics can be assessed. In general, people who follow medication plans are usually emotionally mature, in stable family situations, employed, and pay for their own or part of their treatment. From an Integral perspective, this profile implies that the further along a client is developmentally, the more likely he or she is to follow a medication plan. Although there are dozens of lines of development, some key lines such as cognitive, emotional, and ego development seem particularly germane here. When you talk to a client about medication, you must consider his or her developmental level as well as lifestyle to get a sense of how compliant that person is likely to be. Predictors of noncompliance include being male, being young, and experiencing severe side effects (Demyttenaere, 2001).

It is also important to examine the clinician's attitude toward compliance. Many interns go into a mental health field with the misconception that part of their job is to make sure the client stays on prescribed psychotropic medications. This is untrue and may reflect anything from unresolved power issues, to poor training, to the unresolved power issues of their supervisors in the field. It is not the job of a mental health professional to make sure

clients stay on their medications. It is the job of a mental health professional to help clients weigh the benefits and risks of taking medications, to help clients process conscious and unconscious resistance to medication, and to work with any number of theories to explore the risks and benefits of medications and how the medications relate to the goals a client has set in counseling. In the end, it is always the client's choice whether or not to take medications, even when not doing so will likely result in incarceration or confinement in a more restrictive treatment setting.

## Reasons That Clients May Not Comply

When the noncompliance issue arises, mental health professionals must explore it with clients. Noncompliance can be caused by many things, including cost of the treatment, forgetfulness, and client values and beliefs (Demyttenaere et al., 2001). Beck, Rush, Shaw, and Emory (1979), who researched irrational beliefs that contributed to noncompliance, concluded that clients on antidepressants were often noncompliant because of irrational thoughts about their medications. These researchers found the following three irrational thoughts among the primary ones associated with medication noncompliance: "The medication won't work," "I should feel good right away," and "My depression is incurable."

### *"The Medication Won't Work"*

Sometimes the client just thinks the drug will not work, without any evidence to support that notion. You may find the client has a pessimistic worldview—part of what Beck and associates (1979) called the *cognitive triad of depression.* Another possibility is that perhaps the client is involved in what is called a negative feedback loop. In a **negative feedback loop,** the client for some reason stopped getting reinforcers that up to a point were satisfying. An example is when a client suffers the breakup of a romantic relationship that he or she experienced as reinforcing. The result of losing these reinforcers was depression, but the depressive symptoms then began prompting reactions in other people, reactions that became reinforcing. In the latter example, assume the client then started getting more calls from friends who were concerned about him or her. Those calls then become reinforcing and, rather than seeking out another relationship, the client may come to rely on those calls. This pattern is colloquially referred to as "getting some secondary gain from the symptoms." In such cases, clients prefer to believe no drug will work for their symptoms, because if they lose the symptoms they lose the secondary gains.

### "I Should Feel Good Right Away"

It would be ideal if all medications worked immediately. But that simply is not the case with most psychotropic medications, particularly antidepressants, that may take anywhere from two to six weeks for the full therapeutic effects to manifest (if they work at all). Counselors and other therapists must help clients deal with the early onset of side effects and later onset of therapeutic effects. It is wise to let the client describe how he or she is feeling before the counselor asks direct questions about non–life-threatening side effects. In some instances (outlined by Greenberg & Fisher, 1997), side effects actually have some placebo value in that the client may interpret them as the medication "working."

### "My Depression Is Incurable"

If a client seems to feel his or her depression is incurable, here again counselors should investigate what possible secondary gains the person may be getting from the symptoms (the negative feedback loop may be operating). This belief may also be a manifestation of one aspect of the **cognitive triad of depression**. Readers may recall that Aaron Beck stated that the cognitive triad of depression was comprised of negative feelings about self, the world, and the future. A third possibility is that the client actually has a subtle death wish and is mentally prepared to decompensate (decline in functioning) to the point where he or she may have the nerve to attempt suicide. A final possibility is that the client has engaged in several unsuccessful treatments and has come to believe there is no treatment for his or her condition. Taking a thorough treatment history is invaluable in identifying this last dynamic.

Patterson (1996) added that clients may not comply with their medication plan because of trouble with routines, or inconvenience; medication as evidence of an undesirable self; misinformation; and other issues.

### Trouble With Routines, or Inconvenience

Trouble with routines, or inconvenience, is often a problem for clients with impaired cognitive functioning. The client may forget or become confused about the medication regimen, grow tired of taking the medication, or may not be able to afford the medication (or believes she or he can't afford it). Clients who do shift work, for example, may have changes in routine that hinder remembering when to take medication. This is one reason pharmaceutical companies try to develop medication formulations that allow once-daily doses or even intramuscular injections that let a client get the medications injected once a month.

Problems of inconvenience often relate to side effects. One client we treated felt lethargic and sedated when taking her medication. She worked in a university setting as a recruitment coordinator. Her job required enthusiastic presentations and campus tours throughout the day. This particular client felt the side effects made her job much more difficult. The extra effort to get through the workday was so inconvenient that she responded by stopping her medication.

### Medication as Evidence of an Undesirable Self

The notion that taking medication shows undesirable personal traits is particularly important when considering the client's intrapsychic perspective. Such a client may believe that requiring medication is a sign of weakness or indicates some personal flaw or the perceived stigma related to mental illness. The client may be embarrassed at the prospect of other people finding out about her or his taking medication. Other clients may say they feel they are not their "real selves" while on medication. Although this may in fact be true, it is also possible that the client has been experiencing symptoms for so long (as in **dysthymia**) that he or she has included the symptoms in his or her definition of "real self." Generally speaking, clients who negatively interpret taking medication are concerned about losing control over their lives. They may feel their symptoms have taken control of their lives to some extent and that the medications further decrease their control. This resistance can be complicated by paranoia that is part of the client's symptom profile or that arises when the client (sometimes for good reasons) does not trust the therapist or prescribing physician.

In such cases, one excellent strategy is based on Rogers's (1957) six core conditions of constructive personality change. First, make sure the client is capable of making psychological contact. Clients with psychotic or manic symptoms may not be able or willing to make psychological contact. Second, if the client is able/willing to make psychological contact, Rogers's conditions posit that he or she is in a state of incongruence between ideal self and what he or she currently perceives as the self. In this situation we assume that the lack of congruence is related to mental/emotional symptoms and the prospect of taking medication for those symptoms. Third, Rogers stipulates a therapist who is congruent, meaning that he or she is aware of both the client's ideal and current sense of self, how they overlap and where they may not. Fourth, the counselor experiences unconditional positive regard for the client. In this case unconditional positive regard includes a nonjudgmental acceptance of the client's conflicts about taking the medication, including an acceptance of extreme feelings (for example, some clients say they would rather die than take medication). Fifth, the counselor experiences an empathic understanding of the client's perspective, and sixth, when the counselor experiences this empathic understanding of the client he or she conveys it to the client. When these conditions are met the stage is set, according to Rogers, for constructive personality change—in this case, dealing with medication issues. If you are using another model of counseling, remember that it is most helpful to clients to work with a counselor who is empathic and willing to talk with them about their fears related to psychotropic medications.

### Misinformation

Misinformation can be an easily remedied reason for noncompliance. In some cases fixing **misinformation** simply requires referring the client to a credible source of information or sharing that information in the counseling session. One problem is related to the labels categories of medications have. One client, who was taking olanzapine (Zyprexa) to control his symptoms of Bipolar I Disorder, heard that the medication was an "antipsychotic" and promptly replied, "Well, I'm not psychotic, so that must be the wrong medicine." A good part of an entire session was spent discussing how such medicine categories are labeled and how they really do not relate well to different uses with different clients. To the notion of misinformation we add the idea of disinformation contamination. **Disinformation** is the intentional spreading (usually by a government body) of information that is patently untrue, for political or other purposes. When disinformation concerning drugs (such as "All drugs cause addiction") contaminates a client's consciousness, it is possible that person may then assume any drug, even one that could help, is more dangerous than it actually is. The U.S. government's "war on drugs" has been built on disinformation for political purposes, such as labeling marijuana and heroin "narcotics," which gives the impression that they are similar substances (they are not). Until the government accepts a reasonable policy on drug use, this disinformation will continue to contaminate the thoughts of the public regarding all medications.

### Other Issues

Sometimes, when symptoms are controlled, a client believes she or he is cured (as with an antibiotic) and stops taking the medication. This is another illustration of how different psychiatry is from other branches of medicine. In the **allopathic treatment model,** symptom cessation often means the condition has in fact been cured. This is not necessarily so with the many mental/emotional disorders where "cure" is not necessarily due to medications. Clients suffering from depression that appears psychological in origin may take medications such as antidepressants for six months and engage in counseling at the same time. For many such clients, the medication provides a chemical window of opportunity wherein they get the energy to deal with the psychological issues related to the depression. Once they have resolved some of the psychological issues, their doctors can titrate them off the medicine. Other clients may suffer from psychological symptoms that seem to have a strong biological component (such as symptoms of Bipolar I Disorder). These clients may be facing years or a lifetime of some medication regimen and face different issues from those who need medication for only a short period.

At the other end of the spectrum is the client who stops taking the medication after a short period because she or he does not notice any effect. As we emphasize throughout this book, many of these medications may take weeks before their therapeutic effects begin. In addition, some clients who discontinue their medication do so because they do not like the side effects. Our experience is that such clients would do better to contact their prescribing professional to see if there is a different medication they may be better able to tolerate. Although mental health clinicians cannot make medical recommendations, they can refer clients back to their doctors when the clients seem to be having trouble with medication.

Patterson (1996) also noted that some clients believe their medications are not working because they have unrealistic expectations for the medication. These fall into the category of magical beliefs that we discussed in Chapter One. One client we recall who was taking an antidepressant was astonished at how sad she became at the funeral of a beloved aunt. She had a history of being overwhelmed by powerful depressive episodes and had developed a defense of warding off strong feelings, assuming that if she could do that, she could maintain emotional control. She said she sobbed throughout the funeral as if she hadn't cried for years (and in fact she hadn't). This client had an unrealistic expectation that the medications were akin to a vaccine against sadness. With her counselor, the client came to see her emotional expression at the funeral as a personal victory in that she expressed her true feelings and was able to grieve with loved ones but wasn't overwhelmed by the grief. Whether this victory was the result of the therapy, the antidepressant, or both could not be differentiated, but it was one of the first signs of improvement in quality of life for this client.

Another basis for noncompliance concerns faulty reasoning about the medications. For example, a client may assume that more is better and may increase a dose without consulting the prescribing professional. Another problem (although not as common as supposed) is clients who abuse their prescription medication because they like the effects or get a "high" from the medication. Of greatest concern among the psychotropic medications are the benzodiazepines, which can be abused to induce an altered state of consciousness and can potentially induce dependence. Although this is a concern for a minority of clients, most clients on these medications do not abuse them and once government disinformation is sifted out, the risk is relatively minor.

Perhaps the most problematic situation is when the medication seems to work for the client but it is precisely these therapeutic effects that the client does not want. This may be the case particularly when the symptoms are pleasant or somehow reinforcing for the client. We recall one client (Jacob) who suffered from Bipolar I Disorder and who really missed the manic "highs." When Jacob suffered from mania his "highs" eventually became incapacitating, leading him to high-risk behaviors that twice ended with his incarceration. He said that although the medication seemed to preclude the mania, it made him feel "normal." For Jacob, "normal" was not as good as he felt in a manic phase. The client tried three times to titrate off his medication over a period of five years. Each time he relapsed within eight months. This was truly frustrating for him, because his manic episodes always ended with him incarcerated or in an inpatient treatment facility. In cases such as Jacob's, an existential counseling approach is very helpful. Such approaches help clients develop a sense of meaning in the middle of difficult or even unacceptable existential givens (such as illness, infirmity, and mortality). John Brent's (1998) article on time-sensitive existential treatment is an excellent synopsis of an approach that can be used with clients such as Jacob. In Jacob's case, he had to work through the difficult reality that every time his doctor titrated him off his medication, he relapsed within one year. The existential givens for Jacob included a nervous system that seemed to require medical intervention for Jacob to be able to function in Western society.

## Talking to Clients About Medications: Know and Educate Thyself

The variation on the **Delphic motto** ("Know thyself") in the subheading "Know and Educate Thyself" is another good mantra for any counselor or mental health professional in training. Your own attitudes about and past experiences with psychotropic medication can seriously affect your work with clients. It is of the utmost importance that all mental health counselors be aware of their own intrapsychic issues with medication, to preclude countertransference reactions. Recall that countertransference occurs when a client's issue triggers unresolved issues in the counselor which the counselor may not be aware of. If left unaddressed, these can then render the counselor less effective with the client. One counseling student we worked with had been an excellent student and had done equally well in her internship until she got her first client being treated with mood-stabilizing medication (lithium). She felt the client should stop taking the medication because of the severe side effects and almost went so far as to say that in a session with the client. This intern, who was normally open, interested, and very present in counseling and supervision sessions, became emotionally "closed off." In supervision, it turned out she had had a sister who suffered from Schizophrenia and had committed suicide. The intern had experienced a great deal of anguish in watching the effects of the medication on her older sister and to some extent blamed the low quality of her sister's life—and her eventual suicide—on the medication. Although the counselor's sister had been on a different medication (haloperidol, discussed in Chapter Seven), the issues the counselor's client was dealing with were similar enough to trigger the counselor's own unresolved issues related to psychotropic medication.

If your client is on medication, take a minute to check in each session with the client about therapeutic effects, side effects, and compliance. If there

seem to be problems with compliance, shift the focus of the session to that. Remember, however, that the aim of counseling or psychotherapy is not to make sure your client stays on his or her medication. Your client is another human being who has a right to make choices about her or his life and the treatment of his or her symptoms . Many beginning therapists are so consumed with worry over their client's compliance with a medication regimen that they cannot be present—attentive—for the client in the session.

When mental health therapists are talking to clients about medication, Patterson (1996) strongly advocates client education, and we agree. As indicated by many of the irrational thoughts about psychotropic medication just described, most people are not aware of what such medications can and cannot do for them. Patterson points out that the therapist must emphasize that these medications are treatments, not cures, and that the client ultimately must manage his or her own life. Understanding the main effects, the side effects, and how the medication is supposed to alleviate the symptoms is important knowledge for the client. Patterson also recommends, when talking to clients, using the word *medications* rather than *drugs*, because the latter term may be confused with drugs of abuse—about which very few people actually have good information, as we noted earlier in the chapter.

Ingersoll (2001) noted that the mental health clinician is in the role of "information broker," which requires some real work. To be a good information broker, you must first be able to differentiate good information from bad information. For our purposes, good information draws from clinical case summaries, peer-reviewed literature, and one's own clinical observations. The biggest problem with peer-reviewed literature is that it may be biased toward the medical model, for reasons we discuss later in the book. Because of this bias, peer-reviewed literature should also be complemented with clinical case observations published in medical journals and newsletters on psychopharmacology. In addition, it is always important to read the sections of peer-reviewed articles that describe who funded the research. As we discuss in Chapter Four, research funded by a pharmaceutical company may be biased toward that company's products. Obviously, to be a good information broker, you also need at least an adequate understanding of research design. This enables you to see the difference between a study that truly supports the efficacy of a drug and a study design that merely supports a particular *view* of a drug.

## Specific Supervision Issues

The student intern case discussed in the last section gives one example of how supervision plays an important role in dealing with clients who take psychotropic medication. In all supervision, the key is assuring quality treatment for clients. For clinicians in nonmedical fields such as counseling and psychology, supervisors are there to monitor client welfare by assuring that clinicians comply with legal and ethical standards as well as standards of good practice. An important component of supervising mental health clinicians is discussing medications that clients are taking and how the clinician is talking about these with clients. As Ingersoll (2001) notes, there are no clear prohibitions against nonmedical mental health professionals discussing psychotropic medications with clients, and codes of ethics and standards state that clinicians should be knowledgeable about all treatment options that clients may encounter. As Buelow, Herbert, and Buelow (2000) note, legal problems are currently more likely to arise from mental health clinicians *not* learning about psychotropic medications than from discussing them.

What are some of the important supervision issues relevant to psychopharmacology? Berardinelli and Mostade (2003) have listed the following categories of responsibilities, which include activities for supervisors and supervisees: assessment, monitoring, advocacy, and issues of diversity.

### Assessment

In the assessment phase of a counseling relationship, the mental health clinician needs to learn what current medications clients are taking, including dosage, frequency, and formulation. In addition, clinicians need to assess the client's use of other licit or illicit recreational drugs. Fulfilling this responsibility assumes some knowledge of the categories, effects, and side effects of psychotropic medications on the part of both the supervisor and, ideally, the supervisee. As Ingersoll (2001) notes, this is where training in psychopharmacology becomes important, particularly for supervisors. The American Psychological Association (APA) has created curricula for three levels of training in psychopharmacology, and the first level (or its curricular equivalent) (APA, 1995) should be required for supervisors of mental health professionals.

The assessment phase should include getting a signed release from the client to view copies of the file on the client kept by the prescribing professional. Assessment may also include (with client permission) contacting the prescribing professional for consultation and to let him or her know (again, only with the client's signed release) what you are treating the client for, and ask about the professional's sense of how the medication is working for the client (along with any other questions you may have). This is an opportunity to at least establish a connection with the prescribing professional, learn about his or her prescribing style, and make a good first impression. With that in mind, you should know what condition the prescribing professional has prescribed the psychotropic medications to treat and be familiar with the medications prescribed. Supervisors will want to make sure the supervisee is following these guidelines and adequately understands the topics relevant to his or her clients at each stage of assessment.

Berardinelli and Mostade (2003) also noted that supervisors should monitor exactly how supervisees are discussing medication side effects with clients. Although it is important to make sure the client is aware of potential side effects, it is also important not to ask leading questions that elicit from clients complaints of side effects. There is clearly more art than science to this. The initial topic can be discussed with open-ended questions about how the client is feeling, whether he or she has followed the medication prescription, and how he or she thinks the medication is working. Depending on the client, opening a session with specific questions that list side effects such as "Are you experiencing any sexual side effects, headaches, dizziness, or nausea?"

may not be the best strategy unless there are compelling reasons to take this approach Some clinical judgment is necessary here. Clients who are more prone to obsessively worrying about side effects may respond to such concrete questions as a list of things they then imagine they are experiencing. However, clients who are functioning at a concrete intellectual level may need direct questions to share side effects that are occurring. Unless you feel direct questions are necessary (as in the case of clients who are concrete thinkers), you can begin asking open-ended questions to elicit the client's thoughts about how the medication seems to be working.

## Monitoring

Monitoring is an important component of the therapeutic relationship and supervision. Supervisors should make sure supervisees are checking in with clients at each session about medication, updating medication information as it changes, and keeping records of medication compliance as well as the client's response to medications. The last item is particularly important, especially for clients who do not see the same prescribing professional on a regular basis or for clients who have not given the clinician permission to contact their prescribing professional. The record of client responses to medication is also important in relation to the record of what is happening with the client intrapsychically.

For example, in one case we treated, the client suffered from Bipolar I Disorder and seemed to show subtle signs of improvement just before the onset of manic symptoms. This happened twice, with two different medications the client was on. The first time the therapist took the shift as a signal of improvement in mood, but the second time the therapist saw it as the first sign of approaching manic symptoms. The client learned in this case the difference between mood stabilization and the onset of manic symptoms. Genuine improvement in this client appeared similar but was followed by increasing insight and unimpaired reality testing.

In another case, the client's perceptions of how helpful the medication was correlated with how events were unfolding in her personal life. When her personal life was going the way she wanted, she felt the medication (in this case an antianxiety medication) was helping. When events in her personal life were not going well, she complained that all she got from the medication were side effects. In tracking this relationship, the issue of locus of control emerged as important in counseling. The client came to realize that she had, over a period of years, established the medication as an external locus of control and that the medication now provided a convenient target when things weren't going well. After six months of work on this locus-of-control issue, this particular client asked her doctor to titrate her off the medication. After a year she was still functioning well without it.

## Advocacy

Although we cover many advocacy issues in Chapter Four, some deserve mention here. For mental health professionals, advocacy is actively supporting the client to make sure she or he is getting the best service possible. Where medication is concerned, supervisors must make sure their supervisees' efforts at advocacy do not cross the line between support and actually recommending medication. Although mental health professionals do not recommend medications, they can ask prescribing professionals questions on the client's behalf (for example, "My client is taking an older antipsychotic with severe side effects. Do you think she would benefit from one of the newer antipsychotic medications?") We address this issue in more detail later. According to Berardinelli and Mostade (2003), advocacy issues include recognizing client needs and the particular needs of certain client populations, integrating medication issues into counseling, and knowing when to refer clients for case management and other services. Advocacy in this sense requires that supervisors and supervisees be familiar with community resources, including medication programs and trials, and programs that help clients pay the cost of medications and provide education to significant others and employers when necessary and when desired by the client.

An interesting question is whether mental health professionals should suggest to prescribing professionals that a particular client may benefit from a particular medication. The short answer is no. In the most conservative sense, in this situation the mental health clinician is assuming he or she has the same level of knowledge of psychotropic medications as the prescribing professional. Although this is possible, the most conservative interpretation of such action could be that the mental health professional is practicing medicine without a license. Obviously, cases in which mental health professionals have the proper training and legal mandate to prescribe (as in certain states and territories where psychologists have the right to prescribe psychotropic medications) do not apply here.

The long answer is that because reality is complex we must look at the context of the situation and how the clinician approaches the prescribing professional. Ingersoll (2001) noted that much can be accomplished by assuming the "one down" position and approaching the prescribing professional with the attitude of requesting education. For example, if a client is prescribed risperidone for Bipolar I Disorder, the mental health clinician may wonder why olanzapine was not prescribed (olanzapine has Food and Drug Administration approval for treatment of Bipolar I Disorder, but risperidone does not). In this example the clinician may ask, "I've heard that some clients with this disorder take olanzapine. How do you think risperidone compares to olanzapine in treating Bipolar I symptoms?" If a clinician seriously questions the work of a medical professional, there are several possible approaches. If the work of the clinician appears to constitute malpractice, a report to the prescribing professional's licensing board is in order. If the questions simply revolve around whether the best medication was selected for the client, the clinician can reinforce the client's right to ask the prescribing professional questions or seek a second opinion if that is an option. We emphasize that this advocacy issue is very murky, and clinicians would do best to exercise conservative judgment here.

### Issues of Diversity

Although we cover some issues related to diversity in Chapter Four, here we should note that supervisors need to know that both social and cultural factors are important for the supervision relationship. Group factors that are more objective in nature include differential responses to medication related to race, ethnicity, age, and sex. Group factors that are more subjective include cultural attitudes toward medication, the medical establishment, and counseling/psychotherapy. If clinicians ignore any of these issues, it is up to the supervisor to make sure they are addressed, because they could directly influence the outcome of therapy.

## Some Final Thoughts on Consciousness

Although it is not the primary topic of this book, the issue of consciousness must be addressed in any serious book on mental health, particularly a book on psychopharmacology that is including the intrapsychic perspective. In Chapter One we summarized the mind–brain problem and noted that many professionals adhering to the medical model perspective put their trust in the belief that mind arises from brain. Each individual is free to choose his or her own beliefs whether or not there is evidence to support them. When treating clients, however, a licensed professional is ethically obligated to practice awareness of his or her own biases and to be alert to alternatives to those biases.

The field of consciousness research is rich with potential for complementing the medical model's pharmacologic treatment of mental and emotional disorders. This notion of complementarity is an important one, from an Integral perspective. Integral treatment does not simply entertain alternatives to dominant models of treatment but actively seeks to explore how all possible treatments fit together for the best overall map of how to help people. Consciousness research properly points to a body, mind, and spirit orientation. Here "body" means the clients' physical body. Mind is the client's subjective experience, including thoughts and feeling, that, when problematic, may manifest as symptoms the client seeks to get rid of. Spirit may be defined in many ways, but one simple description is that which is always present and aware of mind and body.

Consider your experience reading right now. You can be aware of this book in your hands and the sense of your body in contact with the furniture and so on. Your mind, in addition to translating the symbols of these words, may also be aware of sounds in your environment, thoughts about what else you have to do today, and feelings about situations in your life. In addition to these things you also possess awareness—you are aware of being aware of all the things just described. This awareness is currently registering your thoughts and feelings. If you can be aware of your thoughts and feelings, you are not these things, not the same as these things. If anything, you are the awareness that registers them. If you think about it, this awareness has always been with you—in some sense, it is you. Becoming alert to this ever-present awareness is one of the most common routes to identifying spirit. A main finding in consciousness research is that getting in touch with this ever-present awareness can itself cure mental and emotional symptoms. The age-old practice of meditation is one of the most common ways to notice this ever-present awareness. The two main forms of meditation are awareness or insight meditation and concentration medication. The goal of awareness meditation is to expand awareness to as many physical and mental events as possible. The basic practice is to allow thoughts and physical/emotional feelings to arise, take note of them but not become focused on them. The goal of concentration meditation is to restrict attention to a single interior or exterior object for long periods (Engler, 1986). We recommend the practice of different forms of meditation for clients, depending on the state of their ego structure. Although Eastern and Western perspectives on psychopathology differ regarding the role of self in suffering, we rely on the Western notion of ego as a stable sense of self. It is this sense of self that is expanded in meditation practice. The more stable the ego structure of a client, the more comfortable we are in recommending a complementary practice of meditation. Although meditation is not always appropriate for all clients at all times, most clients with adequate ego functioning find meditation a useful Integral adjunct to conventional counseling and psychotropic medications.

## Summary

Many intrapsychic issues arise in our clients when either psychotropic medication is recommended or taken. Clients use several strategies to avoid medication, including irrational beliefs about medications, secondary gains from symptoms, and difficulty with routines..

Multiple truths and realities govern the way clients respond to a course of psychotropic medication. Therapists need to recognize how clients accept psychotropic medications into their intrapsychic and unconscious worlds. It is helpful to talk to our clients about the strengths and limitations of both medications and conventional therapy. In addition, mental health clinicians need to know how to collaborate with medical professionals as well as how to review medication issues in supervision sessions.

## Study Questions and Exercises

1. In a small group, compare experiences from the field or your personal life regarding noncompliance with medication regimens. Do your examples fit the ones we have outlined here? Explain.
2. What is your definition of the unconscious? Give an example from your personal or professional life of the unconscious at work.
3. As you reflect on your awareness of intrapsychic issues and psychotropic medication, list three types of workshops that could contribute to your professional development.
4. Discuss some strategies for talking to your clients about their medication each time you see them in counseling.
5. Take a moment to differentiate among body, mind, and spirit as introduced in the section on meditation. Can you be aware of your body *and* your thoughts and feelings *and* the awareness that registers the existence of all these things? Explain.

CHAPTER FOUR

# Group Issues

## *Social and Cultural Perspectives*

As we noted in Chapter One, the cultural and social perspectives in psychopharmacology deal with a variety of topics. These perspectives include information about the differential responses to medications based on race, ethnicity, sex, and gender; shared worldviews and belief systems; laws, policies, and other aspects of the institutions of society; and how all these issues impinge on the client's symptoms and treatment. In the Integral Model, the social and cultural perspectives mirror aspects of the medical model and intrapsychic perspectives. Where the medical model perspective explores objective, measurable aspects of the individual, what we are calling the *social perspective* explores objective, measurable aspects of groups or society in general. And where the intrapsychic perspective explores the subjective experience of the individual, the *cultural perspective* explores the subjective experiences (shared beliefs) of groups. The issues in this chapter are particularly important for mental health professionals, such as counselors, who place a great deal of emphasis on client advocacy within the helping relationship. We begin by discussing the new discipline of ethnopharmacotherapy and some of the key elements in this new subdiscipline.

## Ethnopharmacotherapy: Group Differences in Response to Psychotropic Agents

**Ethnopharmacotherapy,** a relatively new subdiscipline of psychopharmacology, explores ethnic and racial differences in response to medications, differ-

ences that appear to be physiologically based. Scientists have known for years that people of different racial and ethnic backgrounds may have genuine physical differences that make them more or less sensitive to certain drugs or medications. Alcohol has always been a quintessential case in point (Westermeyer, 1989). People of Asian descent and women have less of the enzyme that breaks down alcohol (alcohol dehydrogenase). This makes these groups more susceptible to the effects of alcohol (Gordis, 2000; Julien, 2001). Now, of course, this does not mean they are more likely to develop patterns of abuse or dependence, just that they are more sensitive to the effects. If such differences exist across groups regarding alcohol, many researchers began wondering whether such differences also exist for psychotropic medication, and in fact they do. These physiological differences can also be further accentuated by cultural differences in diet; use of substances such as herbs, alcohol, and caffeine; and the extent of environmental pollutants (Bhugra & Bhui, 2001).

## Sex and Gender Differences

This section of the chapter, in addition to adding to our knowledge of group differences, also contains information on what Integral Theory refers to as "types," particularly male and female. Types likely include elements from both gender and sex, but we will be clear in this section when we are referring to gender differences and when we are referring to sex differences. We identify gender as a cultural category containing socially endorsed an sanctioned attributes for each of the sexes. Sex in contrast refers to biological makeup identified as male or female. We recognize that neither sex nor gender are clear-cut categories and that there are gray areas in both. Note that "types" also refers to psychological types and there is no research we know of addressing the relationship between psychological types and attitudes toward medication or responses to medication. In this sense, it would be interesting to know if people differ in their attitudes or responses to medication based on a type such as those assessed by the Myers Briggs Type Indicator or the Enneagram.

After some stark initial findings, scientists now agree that extensive work is needed to explore sex differences in response to psychotropic medication (Jensvold, Halbreich, & Hamilton, 1996). Strong evidence shows that males and females respond differently to medication, but little research is devoted to understanding this difference. For example, Robinson (2002) has documented that although women are the primary consumers of most types of psychotropic medication, and although sex differences appear in the absorption, metabolism, and excretion of many medications, little attention has been paid to these differences in research. This gap implies an ethical imperative for pharmaceutical companies. If they target women in direct-to-consumer advertising, then they must conduct research supporting the safety and efficacy of these medications for women. Until such a research database is built, clinicians must advocate for clients by keeping up-to-date on the research that exists on psychotropic medications and responses of females.

Differences in absorption exist between premenopausal women and men, with premenopausal women moving material more slowly through the digestive tract. This delays peak levels and lowers blood concentrations of medications. Women also typically weigh less than men, have less total blood volume than men, and carry a higher percentage of body fat than men. For example, women may initially have low blood levels of a compound, but if the compound is stored in fat cells then levels may rise overall, eventually providing women with higher levels of the compound than men would have. The fact that women clear drugs more slowly

than men means that optimal doses for males may be too high for females. Robinson (2002) notes that this may be why women experience side effects from psychotropic compounds about twice as often as men. Along these lines, Hamilton (1986) found that women taking older antipsychotic medications (covered in Chapter Seven) have higher rates of tardive dyskinesia (a disorder of abnormal, involuntary movement) than do men taking the same medications. In addition to these differences, women's physiology changes through the menstrual cycle. Premenstrual changes include a slowed rate of gastric emptying and decreased gastric acid secretion. Both these changes tend to raise blood serum levels of psychotropic medication before menstruation.

It is important to know that many psychotropic medications appear to interfere with fertility. If a client on psychotropic medications is trying to become pregnant, she should discuss this decision with her physician, who can help her weigh the risks. This is an area where female clients may need the support and advocacy of mental health professionals. Many clients still believe they cannot question their doctors and cannot participate in treatment decisions.

Several psychotropic medications have also been linked to **teratogenesis** (the development of birth defects). Obviously if a woman is pregnant, she should, if possible, refrain from taking any psychotropic medications. Although this is not always possible, the risks to the unborn child must be weighed against potential risks to the mother should she stop taking a particular medication. Such decisions are typically difficult. One client whom I (Ingersoll) treated in the late 1980s was taking mood-stabilizing medications that had been shown to put the fetus at risk. She chose to go off the medication during her pregnancy, which resulted in her decompensation and the need for a more restrictive treatment setting (an inpatient facility, in this case). Although we may never know the impact of her emotional suffering (as a result of relapse related to going off medication) on her child, we do know that going off the medication decreased the child's risk of heart malformation associated with the medication the mother was taking.

The Food and Drug Administration (FDA) requires that prescription medications that may

TABLE 4.1    Examples of Antimanic Medications and Teratogenic Risks

| Medication | Risk | Citation |
| --- | --- | --- |
| Lithium | Ebstein's anomaly | Altshuler, Burt, McMullen, & Hendrick, 1995 |
| Carbamazepine | Craniofacial defects<br>Neural tube defects | Jones, Lacro, Johnson, & Adams, 1989<br>Rosa, 1991 |
| Valproic acid | Neural tube defects | Koren & Kennedy, 1995 |
| Antidepressants | Neonate CNS depression and<br>urinary retention | Preston, O'Neal, & Talaga, 2002 |

cause harm to the developing fetus be classified according to one of five categories (A, B, C, D, X). Category A includes medications for which controlled studies in women fail to show risks to the fetus in the first trimester and the risk of harm appears low. Category B includes medications for which animal studies have not shown fetal risk but there are no controlled studies in pregnant women or for which a risk shown in animal studies was confirmed in studies with women. Category C includes medications for which either studies with animals have shown teratogenic effects or there are simply no animal or women's studies. Category D includes medications for which there is positive evidence of human fetal risk. Such medications have warning sections in their labeling. Category D medications may still be used if the risk–benefit analysis shows that more harm may come to the mother if the medication is *not* used. Category X includes medications for which studies in animals or humans clearly link the medication to fetal abnormalities and the use is unacceptable. This information is listed in the **contraindications** section of the label.

Robinson (2002) has summarized some of the literature on teratogenic effects (causing malformations) of particular medications. Most of these effects are due to antimanic drugs and are risks primarily in the first trimester. These are summarized in Table 4.1. Please note that this is not an exhaustive list. Although many medications have teratogenic properties, scientists are not sure about many other medications yet. A good source of information is the Pregnancy Environmental Hotline Teratogen Information Service at 1-800-322-5014.

Many states have set up their own web sites dealing with teratogenic information. For example, the Massachusetts Pregnancy Environmental site is at www.thegenesisfund.org/pehteratogen.htm. Discussing the prospect of psychotropic medication for pregnant women, Preston, O'Neal, and Talaga (2002) comment, "It is important to remember that absolute data in this area is disturbingly incomplete" (p. 229). Therefore the mental health professional concerned with client advocacy must keep up with the literature in the area and be willing to help the client (and/or guardians) weigh the risks of particular medications.

In addition to teratogenesis (malformation of the fetus), psychotropic medications may affect the developing fetus, the newborn, the actual process of birth, and breastfed infants. Psychotropic medications may result in behavioral problems in the child who is exposed to these drugs in utero. Finally, because pregnancy induces so many changes in a woman's body, these changes can radically alter the action of psychotropic medications (Preston, O'Neal, & Talaga, 2002).

## Racial Differences

In addition to cultural differences in attitudes and trust toward psychotropic medication and the doctors who prescribe them, scientists are now learning that psychotropic medications affect people with different racial backgrounds in significantly different objective ways. Here is a summary of a few of the racial differences that researchers have found in physiological responses to psychotropic medications:

- Some studies have found that African-Americans taking older antipsychotic medications are more likely to develop tardive dyskinesia than Caucasians taking the same medications (Glazer, Morgenstern, & Doucette, 1994; Morgenstern & Glazer, 1993). This may also be related to the fact that many studies have consistently found that African-Americans receive higher doses of these medications (Strickland, Lin, Fu, Anderson, & Zheng, 1995) or to reasons that may be related to racism. In a recent study reviewing prescription trends by racial group, Daumit and colleagues (2003) found that African-Americans were still more likely to receive older antipsychotics as opposed to the newer, supposedly more effective, atypical antipsychotics.
- Asians and Asian-Americans report more adverse effects from antipsychotic and tricyclic medications than do Caucasians. They also show higher plasma levels than do Caucasians at the same dosage (Bond, 1990; Bowden, 1995; Pi, Gutierrez, & Gray, 1993). This evidence tends to point toward the need for lower doses for these clients.
- African-Americans appear to be more sensitive to tricyclic medications than are Caucasians in terms of both therapeutic and side effects (Lin & Poland, 1995).
- Also, African-Americans seem to have a host of different influences affecting their rates and expression of depression, compared to other racial groups in the United States (Meyers, 1993).
- Recall in Chapter Two we discussed the cytochrome P-450 enzyme system that governs metabolism of, among other things, psychotropic medication. The differences outlined in the following studies seem to be based on racial differences in this important enzyme system (Lin, Poland, & Anderson, 1995; Lawson, 1999). These differences may vary for genetic and environmental reasons. Various enzymes vary dramatically across different racial groups (Lin, Poland, & Nakasaki, 1993). This same mechanism may also partly cause the increased risk of **hypertension** in African-Americans (Strickland, Lin, Fu, Anderson, & Zheng, 1995).

In comparing data from across different societies, one confounding factor is that average daily dose of medication or minimum effective dose frequently varies from one society to the next. For example, minimum effective dosage of a medication is often higher in the United States than in other countries (Bhugra & Bhui, 2001). Also note that much research on racial group differences in adverse effects focuses on older medications (tricyclic antidepressants, older antipsychotics) that are slowly being phased out with the arrival of newer agents with better side effect profiles. Even though newer medications ostensibly have fewer side effects, the data on older medications point to differences between groups that will likely also have implications for newer compounds. In addition, because many minorities live in lower socioeconomic brackets, they may be prescribed older psychotropic medication that is available in less expensive, generic form because the patent has expired.

What should the nonmedical mental health therapist do with this information? First, we hope this information makes clinicians better information brokers, as we mentioned earlier. For better or worse, prescribing professionals may fail to take racial/ethnic differences into account and mental health clinicians need to raise these relevant points for the well-being of the client. This is particularly true in clinic settings where prescribing professionals (doctors and psychiatrists) are so overwhelmed with work that they may only get 10 or 15 minutes with clients. Clinicians must be willing to advocate for their clients. Later in this chapter we offer one model on how to collaborate with prescribing professionals. In monitoring the therapeutic and side effects of medications on their clients, therapists need to be alert to the differences we have discussed. As a starting point, Bhugra and Bhui (2001) recommend screening the items in Table 4.2 for clients receiving psychotropic medication.

As noted, there has been little research on ethnopharmacotherapy. Although a small number of committed researchers are making important contributions in this area, the nonmedical mental health clinician must regularly review the literature, because these studies are frequently not included in books on psychotropic medications.

**TABLE 4.2**    Important Cultural Dimensions
Related to Psychotropic Medications

The client's diet

Any dietary restrictions

Relevant religious taboos

Alcohol, caffeine, and nicotine intake

## A Focus on the Cultural Perspective

Recall that what we call the *cultural perspective* describes subjective, shared experience and beliefs. It is the dimension that describes phenomenological aspects of groups. In this sense *culture* can refer to shared worldviews and beliefs clustering around race, ethnicity, socioeconomic status, sexual orientation, spiritual tradition, sex, gender, ability/disability, or age. Culture can also refer to shared worldviews and beliefs clustering around one's professional identification. Thus one can speak of the culture of the pharmaceutical industry, the culture of the counseling profession, and the culture of the psychiatric profession.

Because a mental health professional's main tool is the therapeutic encounter, the impact of culture on that encounter must be figured in. The therapeutic encounter is supposed to improve the interpersonal functioning and the subjective comfort of the client. This necessarily implies defining "normal" and "abnormal" behavior, and cultural milieu determines to a large extent whether a person's behavior or emotional state is considered "normal" or "abnormal." Students in the mental health professions have increasingly addressed cultural variables with regard to mental health diagnosis and treatment (Labruzza, 1997), but how does culture relate to psychopharmacology? There are two dimensions to this relationship: the shared beliefs of cultural groups, and group differences in response to medications. We already explored the latter through the social perspective. We now address what scientists know about those factors relating to the shared worldviews and beliefs of groups. As Lin (1996) noted, psychopharmacologists simply do not

know much about how cultural or ethnic factors affect whether or not a particular medication will be helpful for a particular condition.

### Shared Belief Systems Regarding Psychopharmacology: Multicultural Variables

Human beings in the 21st century are still grappling with the challenges presented by diversity in the species. Wilber (1999a, 1999b) has pointed out that all human beings share what he refers to as "deep structures" that are universal. These structures are physical (such as 208 bones, a triune brain, and a particular number of organs), psychological (such as personal developmental processes through universal stages across cultures), and spiritual (for example, mystical literature across cultures details strikingly similar mystical experiences when awareness expands beyond ego). In addition, human beings express surface structures that derive from these deep structures. The surface structures vary from culture to culture; in fact, they are the culture. For example, although the human body generally has a universal structure, it is adorned and altered differently across cultures and even subcultures (witness the current increase in tattooing in U.S. youth culture). Although many personal developmental sequences occur across cultures, cultures label and facilitate them differently (Gardiner & Kosmitzki, 2001). And finally, although mystical awareness of oneness is described across cultures, the manner differs in which this awareness is then translated through the structures of the culture (Wilber, 1999a).

To use a game simile, deep structures are like the rules of the game (for example, checkers) and surface structures are what the various materials the game board and pieces are made of (such as glass, clay, or wood). The point is that the deep structures are universal, but the surface structures may vary from culture to culture (Wilber, 1999a). In human development terms, deep structures include Piaget's stages of cognitive development (sensorimotor, preoperational, concrete operational, and formal operational) (Gardiner & Kosmitzki, 2001), but the surface structures of culture choose the forms through which these deep structures are expressed—especially at the formal operational level.

This is important to note, because many mental health clinicians merely advocate addressing and recognizing surface structures (cultural differences) and neglect deep structures. An example of this error is when something like spirituality that is found in all cultures is reduced to its surface structures and treated merely as an artifact of culture rather than being understood as a human characteristic that manifests through the vehicle of culture.

Many surface structures of culture may make Western forms of mental health work challenging. Consider, for example, an Arabic student who is suffering from symptoms of depression and who comes to a college counseling center at the urging of his roommate. Also consider that for this client, sharing intimate personal information outside the family may be anathema. Further, consider that this client also may view taking psychotropic medication as a sign of weakness. True, this client shares deep structures of a triune brain and the accompanying nervous system and a complement of developmental structures for the various lines of personal development. However, without understanding and attempting to accommodate this client's cultural background, a therapist is unlikely to succeed in accessing these deep structures to effect treatment.

### Discrimination and Oppression

The cultural perspective also provides a vehicle to explore shared worldviews that stem from a history of discrimination and oppression. Many African-American clients with whom we have worked approach counseling and psychotherapy with a great deal of suspicion. Without understanding the shared worldview that underlies this suspicion, mental health professionals may misinterpret it as paranoia or resistance. There is ample justification for African-Americans to mistrust mental health treatment systems. Flaherty and Meagher (1980) documented that in mental health systems, African Americans tend to receive the least desirable treatments. In addition, many researchers have noted that African-Americans have been more likely to be hospitalized (Lawson, Hepler, Holladay, & Cuffel, 1994), involuntarily committed, and placed in restraints than members of other ethnic groups (Lawson, 1999). In addition, as Lawson (1999)

explained, mental health providers are often not African-American and may have views of treatment very different from the views of African-Americans.

Many clients of African-American and Hispanic background may share a suspicion of mental health counseling and psychotropic medication, believing that basically these interventions are tools of oppression and to be avoided. Moreover, until very recently psychotropic medication trials were conducted largely with Caucasian, male samples and then assumed to generalize to other cultural groups. Again, to interpret this as symptomatically significant paranoia only exacerbates the misunderstanding. African-American resistance to participation in the mental health treatment system occurs in light of the Tuskegee study sponsored by the U.S. government in the 1930s. It is now widely known that in this study treatment was withheld from African-American men with syphilis. The study continued for some 40 years before it was ended by a newspaper exposé. The federal government finally acknowledged the study officially in the 1990s, under then-president Bill Clinton. I (Ingersoll) worked with a granddaughter of one man in the Tuskegee experiment, in a sociodramatic recreation of the devastation wrought by the study. This gave me a firsthand understanding of how "paranoia" regarding medical interventions was a healthy defense for members of this family.

A substantial body of literature supports the charge that minority clients with mental and emotional disorders have often been misdiagnosed, which has led to incorrect treatment (Lawson, 1999). Strickland et al. (1995) demonstrated that African-Americans and Hispanics are overdiagnosed with Schizophrenia and more likely to be given antipsychotics when such medications are not needed. Bell and Mehta (1980, 1981) made a strong case that African-Americans suffering from Bipolar I Disorder (and showing excellent lithium response) were often initially diagnosed with Schizophrenia and therefore given antipsychotic medication. Stratkowski, McElroy, Keck, and West (1996) have also demonstrated that African-Americans with mood disorders are more likely to have psychotic symptoms associated with these disorders. Their conclusion was that this required more careful differential diagnosis so that African-American males who were really suffering from Bipolar I Disorder were not mistakenly diagnosed with Schizophrenia. As Lawson (1999) noted, this evidence is especially problematic because there is also evidence that African-Americans are more likely to develop tardive dyskinesia in response to antipsychotic medications.

Ideally, in the first encounter with culturally different clients the counselor or prescribing professional will be aware of these issues and (if psychological contact permits) will explore them with clients who appear highly guarded or suspicious. In many cases, frank discussion of the issues is the best approach. Generally speaking, the professional should also note that stress plays an important role in shaping compliance with a medication regimen and in the patient's response to the medication. Many culturally different people are under enormous amounts of stress including financial stress, stress related to relocation, and stress resulting from isolation when they move to a new country and leave family and community supports. Prescribing professionals need to consider the possibility of these stressors for such clients (Bhugra & Bhui, 2001).

## Case Study: The Case of Rafael

Rafael, a 57-year-old married Mexican man, came to counseling at a mental health center because he complained of hearing many voices. He visited his priest, who was unable to assist him and who referred him to the mental health center. The staff psychiatrist evaluated Rafael and prescribed Loxitane (loxapine), an antipsychotic for his hallucinations and disorganized thinking. He told Rafael to take his medication daily and assigned him to an agency counselor.

Each week Rafael reported to his counselor that he took his medication, but this puzzled her, because he seemed ever more psychotic and disorganized. However, he reported compliance. Rafael became so confused and impaired that he could no longer drive to his appointments, so his wife brought him. After one very perplexing session, the counselor asked his wife if Rafael was taking his medications. She looked away and said quietly, "Only on the days he comes to see you. On all the other days he prays to the Blessed Virgin for his health with his men friends." The counselor learned that Rafael encountered great resistance about medications from his cohort of friends, who urged him not to take his medication but to pray for sanity and health to the Blessed Virgin. So the only times he took Loxitane were on the days he had an appointment with his counselor. Fortunately his counselor was able to seek the assistance of the Latina counselor on staff and Rafael's priest to intervene with Rafael and his wife and prevent further decompensation and possible hospitalization.

Obviously, it is an error to prescribe psychotropic medications with the assumption that all people from all cultures will receive support and understanding of the process in their homes. People from many cultures have various rules, rituals, and ideas about the danger of "pills for the mind," and the levels of resistance are legion.

The astute reader may have a question at this point that goes something like this: "So in reality, all Rafael's prayer did not cure his psychosis, but the Loxitane seemed to help. Doesn't this validate the importance of the medical model intervention (medication) over the prescribed cultural cure (prayer)?" Certainly Rafael's symptoms seemed to benefit from the medication, but that intervention needed to be complemented with the support from his prayer time with friends. Without seeing a way to integrate these two things, Rafael simply stopped taking the medication. In this case, the counselor also consulted with Rafael's priest, who met with Rafael to discuss the difference between praying for healing and praying for a cure. When Rafael was able to engage in this dialogue, he came to understand that although his prayers to the Blessed Virgin did not produce a "cure" per se, he did receive "healing" of sorts in the form of comfort and the strength to eventually go on the medication despite the opinions of his friends. Here the prayer and the medication served as different tools that brought about different types of healing.

# A Meeting of Subcultures: Collaboration With Prescribing Professionals

In Integral Theory, the cultural perspective also addresses elements related to subcultures and the shared beliefs with which an individual may identify. This perspective can also deal with interactions between professional subcultures such as counseling and psychiatry or, more generally, between prescribing professionals and nonmedical mental health therapists.

Western culture shares a belief in a hierarchy among health professionals, with doctors at the top. The mental health hierarchy has psychiatrists at the top. Neal and Calarco (1999) noted that in the past medical training always emphasized that the doctor is in charge in any team approach to treatment and that some doctors, having internalized this belief, can be quite authoritarian even when they have not studied and do not understand psychotherapeutic approaches. Although one can certainly deconstruct this, place it in nested contexts, or argue that it is a "patriarchal hangover," it still exists as a shared belief with which nonmedical mental health clinicians must deal.

Ingersoll (2001) noted that the nonmedical therapist's approach depends on the attitude of the prescribing professional toward psychotherapy. If a psychiatrist does not value psychotherapeutic approaches, the mental health professional may find a "one down" approach helpful. In this approach the nonmedical therapist presents him- or herself as willing to learn about medications from the prescribing professional. This approach can begin the alliance-building process between the medical and nonmedical members of a treatment team and can give the mental health professional an opportunity to practice equanimity.

In collaborating with prescribing professionals, mental health clinicians can benefit from a judicious combination of equanimity and what we would colloquially call "people skills." Centuries ago, Buddhism introduced equanimity as one of the four sublime states (the other three being love, compassion, and sympathetic joy). **Equanimity** is the

practice of approaching an interaction with respect and caring while remaining unattached to how the interaction unfolds and how you are treated (Gunaratana, 2002). Although this approach can be challenging, it is possible. Reflecting on the good that could come to the client you share with the prescribing professional can be enough to foster the equanimity you need. Also, if a particular prescribing professional thinks poorly of mental health professionals in general, you are not likely to change his or her mind in one interaction.

Next, use good interpersonal skills. This is obvious, but worth noting because people can forget these skills in the press of a crisis or busy day. Most prescribing professionals are equally busy and well intentioned. Reminding ourselves of this can serve as a cue to enter the interaction in a courteous manner regardless of how frantic the setting or your mind-set may be. Ideally both professionals approach the relationship with some mutual respect, because this inevitably helps the client, who would likely be disadvantaged by friction between providers. As Balon (1999) points out, good collaboration is important because the team approach is an economic necessity and likely to remain so.

How the collaboration is set up is important. In agency work, therapists do not have much choice about which doctors they are going to work with. In private practice there is more choice, depending on which practitioner can be persuaded to collaborate. Evidence is growing that a good therapist–prescriber relationship is correlated with more positive client outcomes (Neal & Calarco, 1999). Next we discuss some important elements of collaboration.

### Conditions of the Relationship

Each professional should know the credentials of all other collaborating professionals as well as the areas of specialization and populations each party has worked with. As noted, mental health professionals want to know the medical practitioner's attitude toward counseling and psychotherapy, because a negative attitude can diffuse the therapeutic alliance. Also, it is important to define the role (if any) the mental health clinician plays in giving feedback to the medical practitioner (and whether the professional will welcome or resist feedback).

### Confidentiality Issues

Regardless of whom the client met first (doctor or mental health professional), the recommendation for either therapy or medication presupposes that the client's case will be fully disclosed to the prescriber and that appropriate documentation and releases must be obtained. This is even more important since the enactment of the Health Insurance Portability and Accountability Act of 1996 (HIPAA).

### Confrontation Issues

At times clients either decompensate in reaction to a psychotropic medication or quickly develop adverse effects to the medications. The treating medical professional may be either oblivious to the changes or may insist that the medications are correct for this client. To prepare for such conditions, the mental health clinician must develop assertive and appropriate confrontation skills to advocate well for the client.

### Transference and Countertransference Issues

Finally, transference and countertransference issues must be addressed when they arise, and a vehicle must be set in place for addressing them. To avoid triangulation, which will likely undermine the treatment plan, each professional must be aware of his or her transference and countertransference relationships with the client and with each other. Whenever a third party is brought to the relationship, the impact on the client must be assessed.

## Social Institutions and Their Impact on Psychotropic Medications

Although many social institutions could be examined here, we focus on the Food and Drug Administration and on pharmaceutical companies in general, because they have the most profound impact on psychotropic medications. It would be nice if mental health professionals could operate in a vacuum unaware of what the FDA and pharmaceutical companies were doing, but responsible advocacy requires at least a general understanding of these two forces.

### The Food and Drug Administration

The Food and Drug Administration (FDA) is the federal U.S. government agency charged with overseeing drug testing and development, approving new drugs and compounds, and monitoring approved drugs and compounds. Currently the FDA has nine different centers or offices, performing a variety of functions. In the early 20th century, the FDA was part of the U.S. Department of Agriculture. As recently as 1929, consumers got all but 5% of their medications directly from pharmacists, with no prescription from doctors necessary (Temin, 1980). This changed with the passage of the 1938 Food, Drug, and Cosmetic Act, which was amended in 1962. The FDA has historically addressed three distinct (and at times antithetical) risks:

1. The risk of overpaying for a drug (because of diluted form or low quality)
2. The risk of an adverse drug reaction
3. The risk of failing to recover after taking a drug as prescribed

These risks receive different emphasis at different times in history, but the results have largely been of the "good news / bad news" type (Temin, 1980). The good news is that although regulation has not eradicated risk, it has decreased some risks by requiring standards of dosage, potency, and proof of efficacy. The bad news is that the result has been to further remove the power of choice from the consumer and from the prescribing professional. These results take on a surreal quality today, when, as psychologist Robert Anton Wilson (2002) noted, there is no "war on drugs," only a war on *some* drugs. Although tens of thousands of citizens are denied access to medical marijuana because it is allegedly "addictive," millions are prescribed legal antidepressants that are clearly "addictive" and that in many studies perform no better than placebo. We discuss these issues further in Chapters Five and Ten.

## Some FDA History

It is important to have at least a general understanding of the FDA and the process it uses to enforce its regulations, because both play an important role in how drugs get developed and which drugs get developed. Again, reality is complex, and complexity is our friend. The FDA is mandated by Congress to ensure the efficacy and safety of all new medications. The history of FDA legislation is (like reality) complex. Some believe most FDA legislation came about in response to a crisis (Breggin, 1997). Others note that legislation evolved over periods of years before it was enacted and reflected not just reactions to crises or special interests but also bureaucratic concerns and compromises (Temin, 1980).

The FDA was separated from the U.S. Department of Agriculture in 1931 and introduced the first reform legislation in 1933. This bill failed to pass Congress that year (presidential support was also lacking) and only passed, in a much-diluted form, five years later. In 1938 Congress passed the Food, Drug, and Cosmetic Act, which officially recognized the FDA as separate from the Department of Agriculture. This act was passed partly in response to the deaths of 100 people from ingesting a sulfa drug that contained a toxic solvent. Massengill Company, which produced the drug, could not be prosecuted under the criminal laws at that time and was fined $26,000—the largest fine ever up to that point but small in comparison to the loss of 100 human lives (Temin, 1980). This tragedy fueled passage of the Food, Drug, and Cosmetic Act.

In 1962, the Kefauver-Harris amendments added several elements to the act, including the requirement that researchers notify the FDA before testing a compound on human subjects. The initial impetus in this case was Senator Estes Kefauver's hearings on the drug industry, which opened in 1959. The hearings exposed the enormous gap between medication prices and manufacturing costs. Kefauver introduced legislation in 1961 to increase FDA surveillance over drug manufacturing and the introduction of new compounds. Despite some promises, President John Kennedy did not support the bill, which was so altered in subcommittee that Kefauver refused to floor-manage the bill himself. The group responsible for rewriting Kefauver's bill proposed its own version, headed by Congressman Owen Harris. Three days after this bill was rewritten, the public became aware that thalidomide had caused a rash of birth defects in Europe. This seems to have added to the momentum that eventually resulted in the bill being passed.

A U.S. company had submitted a new drug application for thalidomide, which the FDA had rejected several times as providing too little information. Because the FDA did not have the authority to supervise clinical testing under the 1938 law, thalidomide had been distributed in the United States for this purpose (approximately 2.5 million tablets to 1200 doctors). The clinical testing tragically resulted in thalidomide-related birth defects in the United States as well, but not to the same extent as in Europe. According to Temin (1980), Kefauver's staff took news of the birth defects to *The Washington Post*. This rallied public support for the Kefauver and Harris bills. The two were combined as the Kefauver-Harris amendments and signed into law in 1962. Although they did not address Kefauver's concern over the inflated price of medications, the amendments gave considerable power to the FDA to regulate drug development and the production and sales of new drugs.

## The FDA Process

Getting a drug compound through the FDA approval process is an expensive undertaking for pharmaceutical companies. Logan (2003) estimates that each medication approved by the FDA takes a journey from the lab to the drug store that lasts 15 years and can cost hundreds of millions of dollars. The FDA has a process for drug applications that starts with animal experimentation and proceeds through several phases. The preclinical-phase research development includes identifying the drug, laboratory (in vitro) studies, and tests with animal models and human cells. Computer simulations also help researchers isolate the action of the drug. This phase lasts about six years on average. Next, the company investigating the formulation files an Investigational New Drug Application. Only one in five formulations get from this point to actual approval, a journey that may cost $200 to $900 million (Bodenheimer, 2000; Pediatric Pharmacotherapy, 1995).

From this point the FDA has 30 days to decide if clinical trials will be allowed. If they are, typically there are then three more phases of clinical research and another phase of postmarket surveillance. At this point, research on humans is a standard part of the protocol. In the first phase of human research, researchers usually recruit 20 to 100 healthy volunteers. Here researchers are looking at the impact of the drug on a healthy person. This phase lasts approximately one to two years. In Phase 2, clinical trials are larger and involve patients who may benefit from the drug (100 to 300 volunteers). In these trials adverse and side effects are recorded. This phase lasts about two years. In phase-3 clinical trials, larger numbers of patients (1000 to 3000) are used and equivalency with standard therapies is assessed. In Phase 3 the drug is also compared to placebo. As you will see in upcoming chapters, this can be done in several ways, each of which yields different results. Phase 3 clinical trials usually last about 18 months. The FDA guidelines require that at least two pivotal studies show statistically significant results for the efficacy of the compound. One criticism of this process is that companies may conduct many studies that show no significant results, but as long as two do, the process can continue.

After these three phases of clinical trials on humans are completed, the pharmaceutical company files a New Drug Application. This is basically a compilation of all the data on the research. These applications may be up to 100,000 pages in length. From this point, the FDA has 24 months to render a decision. Despite the time and expense involved in the entire process, the actual clinical trials of medications last only four to six weeks on average (Breggin, 1997). If the drug is approved, the FDA creates a label for marketing a drug. Approval of the label is the final step before the drug can go to the market. The label appears in a drug's package insert (PI) and is included in the *Physician's Desk Reference (PDR)*. The label has many functions, including listing all possible side effects and what the drug's "on-label" use is.

Drugs can be prescribed as on-label or off-label. **On-label** means the drug has specific FDA approval for the disorder it is prescribed to treat. **Off-label** means that the prescribing professional believes, based on clinical experience and case studies, that the drug will help the condition she or he is prescribing it for, but using it for that purpose has not been specifically approved by the FDA (Julien, 2001). A final phase in drug development begins when the drug is approved, and involves monitoring the drug for newly discovered problems. The FDA seeks to monitor the safety of medications through MedWatch, the FDA Medical Products Reporting and Safety Information Program. Doctors and patients can report to MedWatch any adverse effect they believe is associated with the drug. This can be done online at http://www.fda.gov/medwatch/.

MedWatch files each adverse effect report in an Adverse Events Reporting System, which staff examine to determine prevalence and significance of the effects. Thereafter, if a significant problem with a medication is found (life-threatening conditions, permanent disability, or birth defect) the FDA can issue recalls and withdrawals or make labeling changes (Logan, 2003). According to Breggin (1997), this phase is given relatively low priority compared to drug development. Table 4.3 summarizes the phases of the FDA drug approval process.

As Logan (2003) noted, just because a drug compound makes it through this arduous process to receive an on-label designation does not mean that the drug is totally safe or that it is safe or effective for everyone.

### Criticisms of the FDA

Critics of the FDA come from two perspectives. The first is the perspective that the FDA regulatory process interferes with the free market. Leber (1996) asserts that this criticism is inaccurate, because medication is not a commodity like steel or pork bellies. Also, as Senator Estes Kefauver noted in the original version of his 1961 bill, the relationships in pharmaceuticals are atypical in that the person who orders the medication (the doctor) is not the person who purchases it (the patient or insurance carrier) (Temin, 1980). Leber also notes, pointing to the highly unregulated medication market in the late 19th and early 20th centuries, the free market does not effectively drive dangerous

**TABLE 4.3**   Phases of the FDA Approval Process

Preclinical research and development using animal models (can last up to 6 years).

Filing and approval of Investigational New Drug Application.

After approval of Investigational New Drug Application, FDA has 30 days to decide if clinical trials will be allowed.

*Phase 1*: If the drug is approved, clinical trials begin with a small number of healthy volunteers (lasts about 18 months).

*Phase 2*: Phase 2 clinical trials include patients who might benefit from the drug (lasts about two years)

*Phase 3*: Phase 3 clinical trials proceed with a large number of patients where the drug is tested against placebo. This phase must yield at least two "pivotal" trials with statistically significant results. Trials typically last 4 to 6 weeks (entire phase requires about 18 months).

When Phase 3 is over, the company files a New Drug Application summarizing data.

The FDA then has 24 months to approve or not.

If the New Drug Application summarizing data is approved, the FDA then must approve the label for the drug.

Finally, after approval of label and after marketing begins, the drug must be monitored in the market for newly discovered problems.

drug products from the market. In addition, the financial scandals of the early 21st century, if anything, indicate the abuses that can occur even in a moderately regulated market.

The second criticism, from the consumer perspective, typically accuses the FDA of not regulating enough or of being unduly influenced by big business. Breggin (1997) has outlined numerous problems with the current FDA approval process. First, the process does not require pharmaceutical companies to demonstrate in animal or human models that the brain recovers from the effects of psychiatric medication, although there is ample reporting about drug effects on the brain's neurons and neurotransmission. Second, the FDA does not require testing to determine if any cognitive impairment or brain dysfunction is associated with the treatments. Third, the FDA does not require pharmaceutical companies to show that any patients actually recover from their mental/emotional disorders as a result of the drug treatment. Fourth, for a drug to be approved, is the FDA does not require that the patients rate themselves improved as a result of the drug. Fifth, even where known risks are associated with a drug (such as the tardive dyskinesia caused by older antipsychotics) the FDA does not require that a pharmaceutical company explore

a new drug's risks for this problem even if the new drug is in the same category as the older one. Finally, Breggin notes, the FDA does not conduct any drug studies on its own. It relies heavily on research generated by and paid for by the pharmaceutical companies themselves. We explore this problem further in the next section.

In response to such criticisms, Leber (1996) makes several points. First, the FDA is given a huge mandate, frequently without the resources to carry it out. He stated that the FDA has been given a mandate so gargantuan in nature that "no institution, even one with infinite resources and time, could accomplish it" (p. 72). This point is validated when one compares the demands on the FDA with its budget. Second, Leber points out that the FDA interprets the 1938 Food, Drug, and Cosmetics Act requirement that a medication be safe for use as justifying its risk–benefit ratio. Leber (1996) writes, "the absurdity of the literal assignment is not always appreciated by the public" (p. 72). Third, Leber responds to the criticism that regulatory bodies fail to enforce laws and regulations the way their critics would like those laws and regulations enforced. To this criticism he points notes that legislation is always a compromise reached among parties with opposing interests and goals. The 1938 law and the

Kefauver-Harris Amendments are a case in point. Given that, it is thus highly unlikely that legislation and its regulations will ever be enforced in a manner that totally satisfies those on one side of the issue. Echoing our mantra in this book, Leber states that regulation is complex, points of law are hardly ever as straightforward as they are portrayed to be, and the evidence is hardly ever one-sided. This complexity requires informed advocates and consumers, because both the FDA and the pharmaceutical companies have enormous power—and power always requires checks and balances.

### The Power of Pharmaceutical Companies

Drug companies have enormous power in all Western economies, and their power is also growing in Eastern economies. They were among the few companies to survive the Great Depression with little negative impact (Healy, 1997). Because they have enormous economic power, they also have important responsibilities once a given drug is released. Companies must inform the FDA of any new adverse reactions, must monitor the literature regarding their medication, and must report adverse reactions found in that literature as well. Pharmaceutical companies are legally obligated to make changes in their drug labels if the changes regard risks and hazards of the drug. Although many companies make earnest efforts to meet these obligations where psychotropic drugs are concerned, the points raised by critics such as Breggin (1997) deserve to be heard because the stakes for the consumer are so high. Breggin writes, "According to a 1990 Government Accounting Office (GAO) report, more than 50% of all drugs approved by the FDA between 1976 and 1985 were found during postmarketing to have previously undetected 'serious' side effects, sometimes requiring removal from the market" (p. 222). Some of the serious side effects not detected in premarket phases include neuroleptic malignant syndrome and tardive dyskinesia in antipsychotics. We described **tardive dyskinesia** earlier. **Neuroleptic malignant syndrome** is a potentially life-threatening reaction to certain antipsychotic medications and affects approximately 1% of people admitted to inpatient settings for psychiatric problems. Other examples of serious side effects

not noted in initial research are the agitation and depression sometimes seen in patients taking fluoxetine (Prozac).

As we discuss further in Chapters Five and Seven, there are many problems related to the FDA process and the manner in which pharmaceutical companies conduct research. One of the largest revolves around companies hiring their own researchers to conduct studies that have literally millions of dollars riding on the outcome. Whereas in the past drug companies contracted with teaching hospitals and other clinical facilities to test compounds, they have found it much faster to hire their own firms to conduct the research. Bodenheimer (2000) has noted that this research practice has sprung up in the last 10 years. Critics raise questions about the ethical aspects of a company paying researchers to test products that may potentially bring the company large profits. In addition, Bodenheimer (2000) has documented numerous cases where companies prevented important research findings from being published because results of the compound being tested were not favorable. The ethical dilemmas surrounding such research need to be resolved.

### *Pharmaceutical Company–Sponsored Research*

A problem recently explored in medical journals concerns pharmaceutical companies contracting with medical colleges to conduct research on company compounds. Researchers have raised the problems of conflict of interest (Boyd & Bero, 2000) and publication bias (Rivara & Cummings, 2002). Although these specific areas are indeed problematic, recently the focus has shifted to overall bias in industry-sponsored research. The bias includes the sponsor's role in the study design, investigators' access to data, and control over publication (Schulman et al., 2002). The conflict-of-interest biases were addressed by the Association of American Medical Colleges guidelines on the management of financial interests related to biomedical research (Task Force on Financial Conflicts of Interest in Clinical Research, 2001). The International Committee of Medical Journal Editors (ICMJE) also revised guidelines requiring full disclosure of the sponsor's role in the research as well as requiring that investigators be independent of the sponsor, be fully accountable for the study design, have access to all study data, and have control of all editorial and publication decisions (International Committee of Medical Journal Editors, 2001). Recently, the International Committee of Medical Journal Editors (which includes editors from the *New England Journal of Medicine* and JAMA, the *Journal of the American Medical Association*) adopted a policy that requires studies on medications be listed on a public registry before enrollment of human subjects. The committee felt this would give the public access to many of the studies with negative findings that pharmaceutical companies frequently keep private. This policy was adopted in the wake of unpublished data linking some antidepressants with suicidal behavior in children (Tanner, 2004).

Although these seem reasonable guidelines to safeguard the research process, the question remains, Are the guidelines adhered to? In a national study of U.S. medical school agreements to conduct research for pharmaceutical companies, Schulman et al. (2002) found that the ICMJE guidelines were rarely followed. The authors gathered results from 108 of 122 medical colleges. The median number of site agreements per college per year was 103. The researchers found that agreements between pharmaceutical companies and medical colleges rarely required an independent committee or monitoring board as a condition of the agreement. Agreements rarely addressed collection or monitoring of data, or analysis and interpretation of results. Only in 17 cases of 108 did institutional review boards routinely review agreements. In addition, most colleges got low compliance scores for access to data and power over publishing results. The authors conclude, "A reevaluation of the process of contracting for clinical research is urgently needed" (p. 1340).

Nonmedical mental health clinicians may wonder what this has to do with them. The short answer is that an overview of the influence of pharmaceutical companies seems to call into question how much clinicians can rely on published research to give a sense of the efficacy and safety of psychotropic medications. It is also important for client advocates to think critically about prescription medications. Although pharmaceutical companies certainly have improved the quality of life for many, they are among the wealthiest companies in the United States and, as such, have enormous political influence. This requires oversight and monitoring by the government, consumer groups, and those who advocate for consumers—including mental health clinicians. Those who have power rarely give it up willingly, so it must be monitored by those under its influence. However, having too much government regulation may also block a person who wants/needs a particular compound from getting it.

### Pharmaceutical Companies and Direct-to-Consumer Advertising

The economic power of the pharmaceutical industry is enhanced by its direct link to the consumer through advertising. Pharmaceutical companies are now allowed to advertise directly to consumers via print and media campaigns for medications. This is called direct-to-consumer (DTC) advertising. Before the ban on such advertising was lifted in the late 1980s, pharmaceutical companies spent approximately $12 million a year on drug advertisements, mostly aimed at prescribing professionals. Since DTC advertising has been allowed, companies spent $600 million on such advertising in 1996 and $900 million in 1998 (Hollon, 1999). Companies are currently including psychotropic compounds for children in their marketing strategies for those few drugs (such as stimulants) that do carry FDA on-label approval.

Supporters of the DTC movement note that it can be an excellent way of providing educational information to the consumer (Hollon, 1999). Critics note the considerable profit margins correlated with advertising and suggest that, without medical oversight, whatever quality information is available will get lost in the race for profits (Hollon, 1999). Many advertisements for psychotropic medication make a point of stating that the psychological disorder (whichever is being targeted in the ad) is a "medical illness," thus seeking to capitalize on the association with allopathic models for treating disease processes such as bacterial infections. Taken literally, this could severely affect mental health professionals. Imagine if the relevant regulatory bodies agreed that mental/emotional disorders were strictly "medical illnesses." If this stricture were taken to the logical extreme, we could all be accused of practicing medicine without a license. DTC advertising is correlated with significantly larger profits. In the year 2000, the most advertised drugs saw increases in sales of 32% (Express Scripts, 2001). This trend, for better or worse, will certainly drive pharmaceutical companies to get FDA on-label approval for as-yet-untapped markets such as children and adolescents.

### The Subculture of the Pharmaceutical Industry

A culture is a group of people with a shared belief system or worldview, and each pharmaceutical company, as well as the industry as a whole, develops its own subculture. With the repeal of laws banning direct-to-consumer advertising, pharmaceutical companies have more opportunities than ever to portray themselves to the public. In many commercials, pharmaceutical companies portray themselves in almost heroic fashion as being on the front lines of battle against some disease or on the brink of some discovery that will revolutionize medicine. At the same time, critics have had more opportunities than ever to point to the tactics underlying DTC advertising and to what they feel are misrepresentations of facts about medicine and medical science. As MacDonald (2001) pointed out, such ads are more designed to sell the medications in question than to inform the public. Although both perspectives may have merits, the truth probably lies somewhere in the middle. The culture of pharmaceutical companies exists in the semi–free-market economy (one dynamic that prevents a purely free-market system is the granting of huge government subsidies to large corporations), and the bottom line is that the companies must make profits. How much profit they should make has been a point of contention since Estes Kefauver opened his hearings on the drug industry in the late 1950s.

The culture of pharmaceutical companies cannot be divorced from the fact that they are among the wealthiest and most powerful industries in the world. Critics such as Ariana Huffington (2000) note that the prescription drug industry cloaks its "self-interest in language about pharmaceutical re-search and the public good" (p. 169). Huffington chronicled the efforts of several pharmaceutical companies to stop production of inexpensive AIDS drugs in South Africa. The companies wanted South Africans to pay U.S. prices for the drugs, but the U.S. price of $500 a week equaled the annual per capita income of sub-Saharan Africa. Three companies sued South Africa to keep the South African law allowing access to these medications from taking effect. The companies also lobbied for severe trade sanctions against South Africa. Huffington raises serious questions about the ethics of an industry that makes among the largest profits in the world, neglecting research on lethal diseases in favor of developing yet more antidepressant medications or pharmaceuticals for pets (pet pharmaceuticals gross about $1 billion annually in the United States).

On the other side of the argument, commentator Thomas Sowell (2002) notes that the costs of medications reflect years of research and development, as we have seen in reviewing the FDA process. He also notes that although other countries have scientists and facilities capable of developing new medicines, economic and political situations in those countries discourage companies from investing as hugely as U.S. pharmaceutical companies do in developing new products. Sowell makes the case that the U.S. patent laws allow the company to recoup its investment and make a profit. Other countries often ignore or evade U.S. patent laws to get medications more cheaply. He also adds that the United States produces a disproportionate share of the life-saving drugs in the world.

When we ask doctors what they feel the main impact of DTC advertising is, they say it increases the numbers of patients who come in asking for some medication they saw advertised. These doctors also add that rarely do the clients fully understand what the medication can actually do for them and what the possible adverse effects are. Mental health clinicians therefore need to be aware of the connection between the way pharmaceutical companies portray themselves and those companies' economic interests, because clinicians must bridge the information gap for their clients. Students in mental health areas may feel it is hard enough keeping track of all the new medications, let alone understanding other Integrally related things such as the FDA and the culture of the pharmaceutical companies. But education that is only utilitarian in nature is incomplete and potentially dangerous. The clients whom mental health professionals are pledged to serve deserve clinicians who can help them navigate complex reality by weighing the claims made for any medication in the given social and cultural environment.

### The Drug Enforcement Agency

The federal Drug Enforcement Agency (DEA) is another agency that has enormous power in the United States. Reports conflict regarding the extent to which the DEA uses this power wisely, the extent to which it abuses this power (see, for example, Szasz, 1992), and the extent to which it actually violates civil rights (Wilson, 2002). The DEA is in charge of defining and enforcing the federal drug schedules, Schedule I through Schedule V. We discuss these categories because it is important to understand that these drug categories are set up for law enforcement purposes rather than pharmacological clarity. The closer to Schedule I, the more closely monitored the drug. In many instances the DEA guidelines refer to substances by names that are pharmacologically incorrect (for example, calling marijuana or LSD "narcotics"). In addition, Schedule I drugs supposedly have no medical benefit, but this is often debated, as in the case of medical marijuana.

Table 4.4 summarizes the five drug schedules. Although very few psychotropic medications de-scribed here are in the first two schedules, a few, such as methylphenidate (Ritalin), are on Schedule II. Readers can review the relevant laws and drug schedules on the DEA web site at www.usdoj.gov/dea/.

## Conclusions

We have covered a broad spectrum of issues in this chapter that are not normally addressed in books on psychopharmacology, yet all can have profound effects on clients. The primary activity that unites the diverse elements covered here is advocacy. Different professionals approach advocacy differently. Some mental health professionals such as counselors and social workers give a great deal of attention to client advocacy in their training and enter the field expecting to advocate for their clients in a variety of ways. Others, such as psychiatrists, may not really reflect on advocacy much while training but may develop a passionate commitment to it in the field. Moreover, different treatment settings deal with advocacy in different ways. We authors have both worked in agencies that used a treatment team approach, where the division of labor included advocacy in the job descriptions of some team members but not all. However advocacy issues are approached, it is important that the material introduced in this chapter be considered, because, as noted earlier in this chapter, the stakes for the client are very high.

Many readers who previewed this material told us it was easy to feel overwhelmed by the enormity

**TABLE 4.4**   Summary of Drug Enforcement Agency Drug Schedules

| Schedule | Drugs Defined as Having . . . | Examples |
|----------|-------------------------------|----------|
| I | A high potential for abuse and no accepted medical use | Marijuana, heroin, mescaline |
| II | High abuse potential and liability for dependence. Prescriptions cannot be phoned in or renewed | Morphine, amphetamine |
| III | Some potential for abuse but less than drugs in the first two categories | Some stimulants and CNS depressants; lower-dose opioids |
| IV | Lower potential for abuse than those in Schedules I to III | Valium, antidepressants |
| V | The lowest potential for abuse | Drugs that contain small amounts of narcotics for antidiarrheal purposes |

and number of issues to consider. Here are some suggestions on ways that counselors and other mental health therapists can begin to integrate the issues in their practice:

- Consider practicing Integral diagnosis of the type suggested by Ingersoll (2002). This source gives a framework for evaluating clients with respect to social and cultural variables in addition to the standard five-axis *DSM* diagnosis. This complementary model to standard *DSM* diagnosis requires that clinicians review physical, behavioral, psychological, cultural, and social factors relevant to the client. In addition, before a diagnosis is made, the model requires that clinicians consider relevant lines of development in the client's case.

- Talk to your clients about the issues raised in this chapter and get their perspectives. Often clients know much more about their conflicts and cultural mores than you do and can teach you about their perspectives. Asking your clients to teach you about their culture can be rewarding and also contribute to the therapeutic process.

- Address cultural and social issues in your supervision, or form a special supervision group around cultural and social issues.

- Whether you work in private practice or at an agency, consider developing a web site of peer-reviewed journal articles on topics such as ethnopharmacotherapy. If you have a supervision group, perhaps everyone could commit to reviewing one article per month and posting the review or abstract with the full reference on the web site.

- As an exercise in professional development, have staff consider a case with and without the cultural/social variables and then discuss how adding these variables to the case summary may enrich treatment possibilities.

- Keep an anonymous file in Excel or some other database program for your clients on medication. List diagnosis, medication, dosage, race, gender, age, and ethnicity if known. If you work in an agency where you may see hundreds of clients per year, such records can reveal interesting patterns.

## Summary

Perhaps more than any other, this chapter illustrates how an Integral view of psychopharmacology expands the things we consider. Although generations of psychotropic medications were tested on Caucasian adult males, only recently has the sub-discipline of ethnopharmacotherapy questioned the legitimacy of generalizing from such studies to people of different sexes, races, and ethnic backgrounds. Further, mental health clinicians need to understand the cultures that their clients identify with so that they can better understand how culture may impact the way a client reacts to the idea of taking a psychotropic medication.

Although culture, sex, race, and ethnicity are important factors to consider in psychopharmacology, the impact and power of social institutions must also be considered. Institutions such as the Food and Drug Administration, the Drug Enforcement Agency, and the pharmaceutical industry hold enormous power that must be held accountable to checks and balances. Along the lines of culture and the impact of social institutions on clients, mental health clinicians must be prepared to advocate for clients when necessary.

## Study Questions and Exercises

1. When recommending to female clients that they be evaluated for psychotropic medication, several unique issues and concerns arise. Discuss in detail these problems, and develop a strategy of how you will address them.
2. How do you perceive the FDA and the pharmaceutical industry to be relating to clients who take psychotropic medications? Give examples.
3. How might you try to influence outcomes relevant to the FDA or pharmaceutical companies that concern you?
4. Do you support direct-to-consumer advertising? Why or why not?
5. Generally discuss your perspective on free-market economies and whether or not indigent clients should have access to expensive medications. How do you support your views? If you support both free-market economic theory and

access to medical treatment for the poor, how do you reconcile these two positions?

6. Are there any psychotropic prescription medications that you think should be over-the-counter? Explain your rationale.

7. From your personal or professional experience and the examples cited in this chapter, develop a strategy for talking with a client from a culture other than your own about taking psychotropic medication.

8. How would you deal with a Mexican man who refused medication because he believes his symptoms are a message from God telling him that he is one of the chosen few?

### PART TWO

# An Integral View of Drug Discovery

This second part of the book contains four chapters covering commonly prescribed psychotropic medications used to treat depression, anxiety, psychosis, and mood instability. Each chapter includes some history on the discovery and use of each category of drugs. This history provides the context that informs the four Integral perspectives (medical model, intrapsychic, cultural, and social) we comment on in each chapter. After the history, we present medical model theories of how the drugs are thought to work, and we describe common drugs in each category as well as their side effects. Then in each chapter we include relevant material from the intrapsychic, cultural, and social perspectives. Please note that material regarding the use of each category of medications with children has been placed in Chapter Nine in Part Three of this book. Because the research, political, and developmental aspects of prescribing psychotropic medications to children are so unique, they warrant separate treatment.

## Some History on the Discovery of Psychotropic Medications

We include the following historical information in the introduction to Part Two of the book because it is relevant to all categories of medication discussed.

Throughout recorded history (and probably even before), human beings have medicated themselves and one another for various mental or emotional symptoms. Although each category of psychotropic medications has its own history of discovery and development, the development of antidepressants and antipsychotics has particular significance for all psychotropic medications. How these compounds were developed illustrates many concepts that are important in a well-rounded view of psychopharmacology.

Many drugs have been tried throughout history to alleviate symptoms of what we now call *depression*. Opioids have a long history as antidepressants (Snyder, 1996), and although they are no longer widely used for that purpose, Kramer (1993) has noted that a few treatment-resistant depressed patients still respond to opioids. Some depressed clients even respond to antipsychotics.

Like reality, the history of any psychotropic medication is complex. One way to delve into the complexity is to explore the discovery of the different medications. This exploration is so complex that it has never been determined who actually discovered antidepressants and antipsychotics. The history of discovery in pharmaceuticals is a history of serendipity, coincidence, and good, old-fashioned "mammalian politics." Exploring the question of discovering any psychotropic drug helps us understand drug development and marketing as well as their impact on clients. In the Integral approach to psychopharmacology taken in this book, the impact of such influences as marketing and development is important for clinicians to understand.

## The Discovery of Antipsychotics and Antidepressants

The story of the discovery of modern antipsychotics and antidepressants begins with the coal tar industry. As Healy (1997) remarked, modern culture rests on three industries: atomic physics, evolutionary biology, and organic chemistry. Organic chemistry was developed in the late 19th century and gave birth to the coal tar industry, which laid the foundation for the rapid development of pharmaceuticals, dyes, photographic chemicals, and explosives (Findlay, 1938). When coal is heated in the absence of oxygen, a variety of compounds result, which can then be refined to create other compounds. The coal tar industry initially focused on dyes, and almost all pharmaceutical companies began as dye companies (for example, Ciba, Sandoz, and Bayer). From those beginnings, the story increases in complexity. Some highlights drawn from Healy's (1997) history of the pharmaceutical industry may convey the story. For a complete history, read Healy's excellent account.

In 1868 Carl Graebe and Carl Liebermann synthesized a dye called "alizarin" from coal tar. An arrangement was made with Badische Anilin und Soda Fabrik (BASF [Bath Aniline and Soda Factory]) to produce the dye commercially. BASF then went on to create a dye product line from alizarin, including one dye called *methylene blue.*

In 1883 August Bernthsen was working to produce different compounds from methylene blue. One of these was the first phenothiazine compound. Phenothiazines later became the basis for all early antipsychotics medications and for tricyclic antidepressant compounds.

From this point several years passed before numerous paths converged toward the arrival of the first antidepressant. Before World War II, surgeons and physicians had begun to suspect that a state of shock that caused cardiac collapse was related to a

release of histamine in the body. This shock state occurred after a severe loss of blood or as the result of infection. These observations led the medical community to the coal tar industry, where, researchers hoped, some of the volatile compounds discovered could be developed into powerful antihistamines. From here, the trail leading to the discovery of antidepressants continues.

In the 1930s, Daniel Bovet of the Pasteur Institute was searching for antihistamines to preclude the condition of patient shock just described. His compounds proved too toxic for human beings, but research was continued at Rhone-Poulenc Pharmaceuticals (which had a relationship with the Pasteur Institute). Rhone-Poulenc succeeded in developing and marketing useful antihistamines, several of which are still used today (for example, diphenhydramine—familiar under the brand name Benadryl).

Rhone-Poulenc chemist Paul Charpentier was also working with phenothiazines in the hope of developing antimalarial compounds. Although the compounds he was investigating were not antimalarial, they did seem to be antihistamines. In 1949, a French Surgeon named Henri Laborit noted that phenothiazine compounds had central effects, including sedative and analgesic properties.

Laborit's observation led Rhone-Poulenc to charge Pierre Koetschet to work with these compounds to heighten their central nervous system effects. Koetschet delegated Paul Charpentier to synthesize a further series of phenothiazines. Among this series was chlorpromazine (known better under the brand name Thorazine).

Physicians all over France, including Laborit, were given Thorazine to try on various patients. Because Thorazine seemed to have powerful central nervous system effects of sedation, Laborit convinced a psychiatrist, Cornelia Quarti, to try some herself. She did and reported that it induced a feeling of detachment. Based on Quarti's self-experiment, they concluded it might help psychiatric patients.

In 1950 Jean Delay and Pierre Deniker gave Thorazine to 38 patients suffering from psychotic symptoms. They found it significantly calmed these patients, published their findings, and in 1955 organized a Paris conference around the breakthrough. Deniker and others visited the United States and Canada, speaking and giving demonstrations about Thorazine. After reading one of Delay and Deniker's papers, Heinz Lehmann, a psychiatrist working in Canada, tried Thorazine on 70 patients, with what Healy calls dramatic results. From this point the use of Thorazine spread quickly through American hospitals. Healy estimates that in 1955, almost all patients in mental asylums were given Thorazine, and Smith Kline and French, producers of the drug, made $75 million from its sale in that year alone.

From this point, the notion of a profitable psychiatric drug was clearly established and, as Healy noted, "Other companies, not surprisingly, decided they wanted a piece of the action" (p. 46). Before continuing with how these developments related to the discovery of antidepressants, notice, reviewing the history just traced, how difficult it would be to decide who discovered antipsychotics. Should the credit go to the various chemists and pharmacologists who synthesized the various compounds? Should credit go to the doctors who forwarded the drugs to psychiatric colleagues? Should the credit go to the psychiatrists who actually used the drugs on clients? How about the first clients and Cornelia Quarti (the first human subject)? Should they receive some credit too? These questions have been so difficult to answer that no Nobel Prize has ever been awarded for the discovery.

At this point, remember that the time frame was still the 1950s, when mental health and illness were viewed predominantly through a Freudian lens. Depression was thought to result from **object loss**. So although there was great enthusiasm for Thorazine, many people doubted that a drug could ever be developed to counteract depression. Heinz Lehmann and Jean Delay, mentioned earlier, believed otherwise. They experimented with different compounds and even had some success with one (isoniazid). They published their findings in 1952. Although these findings were significant, Lehmann and Delay lacked the other necessary elements that fuel continued research. At the same time in the

United States, Nathan Kline was having success with iproniazid (a chemical cousin of isoniazid) as well as with fueling the research.

## "Discovering" Antidepressants in the United States and Europe

The development of compounds that came to be known as *antidepressants* occurred simultaneously in Europe and the United States.

### *Developments in the States*

In the United States, there is an apocryphal story about an Associated Press photo that showed patients dancing and clapping outside the Seaview Sanitarium for tuberculosis on Staten Island. The caption under the photo supposedly references their recovery from TB as the reason for their levity, but others felt their elevated mood was more related to one of the drugs they had been given—iproniazid. Originally developed as an antituberculosis drug, iproniazid turned out to be the first monoamine oxidase inhibitor (MAO inhibitor). Although iproniazid did reduce the number of **tubercule bacilli** in patients' systems, other antituberculosis drugs later surpassed it. The job of examining effects of iproniazid on the mind and mood fell to psychiatrist Nathan Kline.

Kline noticed iproniazid seemed to have an energizing effect on depressed patients. Using the Freudian terminology dominant at the time, he proposed that there were drugs, iproniazid among them, that actually functioned as "**psychic energizers**." These drugs increased the id energy available to the ego, and this resulted in a sense of joy and optimism (Kramer, 1993). (Healy [1997] believes the success of fluoxetine [brand name Prozac] has resurrected the psychic energizer theory.) At the time, Kline worked at the Rockland State Research Facility in Maryland and had conducted and published several studies supporting the hypothesis that iproniazid was useful to treat depression.

Interestingly, from an Integral perspective, although a researcher such as Kline may demonstrate that a particular compound such as iproniazid has mood-elevating properties, it still takes a pharmaceutical company with money and motivation to develop and market the compound. At the time, the developers of iproniazid (Roche) were not at all interested in a "psychic energizer" (Healy, 1997; Kramer, 1993). Here the public relations genius of Kline appears. Although he knew Roche was not interested in developing and marketing the drug to treat depression, Kline made clear to Roche's president that he was going to present the findings as publicly as possible (Healy, 1997, p. 68). Kline thus persuaded Roche to continue research. He presented his findings in 1957 at a congressional hearing and in a *New York Times* story.

Within one year the drug's use to treat depression had spread. It was pulled from the market shortly afterward because of side effects, but the line of research had been started, largely by Kline. He was very influential in not just the clinical advances with antidepressants but in lobbying the government to make more funding available for mental health research. In 1955 Kline testified before Congress and influenced the passage of the Mental Health Studies Act of 1955. He then used his Washington, DC, connections to write research grants for studying antidepressant medications.

### Developments in Europe

Other companies also saw a chance to profit from psychotropic drug development and began looking at **phenothiazine compounds** and **antihistamines**. The chief of pharmacology at Geigy, Robert Domenjoz, had encouraged the company to explore compounds with structures similar to phenothiazines. Geigy had a storehouse of compounds developed over the years, and those with phenothiazine-like structures were re-examined. One such compound, iminodibenzyl, had been synthesized in 1898, but no use had been found for it. This compound was to become the prototypical tricyclic antidepressant. A series of 42 other compounds were put together from iminodibenzyl by Geigy chemists and were tested on animals and company employees—including many scientists. Given these tests, Geigy researchers thought one compound in particular could be useful in anesthesia or as a **hypnotic**. Among several scientists who tested the drug was Roland Kuhn of Munsterlingen Hospital near Konstanz, Germany.

Although Kuhn noticed few effects from the compound, the success of the chemically similar chlorpromazine fueled continued research.

Kuhn then tested a similar compound labeled G22335. The results were dramatic, and Kuhn proposed that the compound was an effective treatment for depression. The compound, named *imipramine*, was the first marketed antidepressant. Kuhn claimed imipramine was an antidepressant, not a **"euphorant,"** because it helped lift depressed mood but did not induce euphoria, or an elevated, blissful state. He also noted that it might take up to 4 weeks to work, but he didn't know why. In 1957 it was launched as Tofranil in Switzerland and other European countries. In 1958 clinical trials of imipramine began in North America, but it was four years before another tricyclic antidepressant was added to the market.

Geigy was not sure how much credence to give the enthusiastic observations of Kuhn and couldn't understand how something could be so chemically similar to Thorazine and have such a totally different effect. Kuhn's interest was in psychopathology; Geigy's was in estimating market share. Geigy insisted that a drug that lifted mood was a stimulant, but Kuhn maintained it was different. Part of the difficulty in understanding antidepressant action was no one really knew exactly how imipramine or iproniazid worked. Finally in 1965, the main mechanisms of action were summarized into a working chemical hypothesis of depression, and the antidepressant era was on its way. The discoveries that led to biochemical theories of depression are covered later. First, however, it is important from an Integral perspective to understand how you cannot have a theory of a disease until you have a consistent category of a disease about which to theorize. That is where the "selling of depression" plays a role in psychopharmacology and clinical practice.

## Relationships Among Categorical Psychiatry, Economics, and Developments in Psychopharmacology

Psychotropic drug development depends to a large extent on the categories in the *Diagnostic and Statistical Manual* of the American Psychiatric Association. The concepts of mental and emotional disorders play a key role in how psychotropic medications are released in the United States. The relationship of a disorder called Major Depressive Disorder to the development of antidepressant medications is a particularly stark example of this principle.

Prior to 1900 the concept of depression did not exist. There were analytic references to melancholia, but this state was considered a variation on a neurotic disturbance. Until the publication of *DSM-III* in 1980, categories of psychiatric problems were more dimensional than descriptive. The dimensional approach presented symptoms on a continuum or several continua, whereas the descriptive approach tries to establish key symptom lists for each disorder through statistical analysis (Dilts, 2001).

The descriptive approach seems more beneficial in medicine proper than in psychiatry. As professionals, we talk about the weaknesses in descriptive psychiatry (as opposed to dimensional psychiatry). For example, we may have a client who suffers from symptoms on a continuum from anxiety to depression. Sometimes the depression is dominant; sometimes the anxiety is dominant. To diagnose the client, descriptive psychiatric **nosology** (see the *DSM*) would likely result in the client receiving two axis one diagnoses (perhaps Major Depressive Disorder and Anxiety Disorder not otherwise specified, or NOS); however, in treating the client these exclusive diagnoses are merely artifacts of the *DSM* nosology and the symptoms seem to blend together.

## Descriptive Psychiatry and Magic Bullets

The advent of descriptive psychiatry can be tied to Emil Kraepelin in 1896 after **diphtheria** antitoxin was created. The diphtheria antitoxin allowed the medical profession to confirm the hypothesis that there were discrete biological illnesses that would respond to discrete medications. Kraepelin quickly hypothesized there may be discrete psychiatric diseases too that would also respond to specific agents, nicknamed "magic bullets" because they enter the body of the patient and fight disease symptoms without extensively damaging the rest of the organism.

Following Kraepelin's lead, Paul Ehrlich set forth the "magic bullet theory" in the early 20th century. Ehrlich (who used dyes to discover the blood–brain barrier) was impressed with how antibodies produced by vaccines could zero in on and destroy target cells without destroying surrounding tissue. He began searching for such a compound to treat syphilis. This led to the discovery of the first "magic bullet" by Gerald Domagk, who was working with dyes with a sulfur-nitrogen chain. He developed a series of compounds called *sulfonamides* that in mice acted like antibiotics. These are now called *sulfa drugs*. It is important to note that Kraeplin and Ehrlich were generalizing from allopathic treatments of diseases to psychiatric treatments for diseases and assuming the diseases were similar in etiology. Allopathic medicine is the dominant branch of medicine today (as opposed to homeopathic or osteopathic). The term *allopathic* refers to the practice of introducing an agent into the patient that works in a fashion different from or opposite to the disease the patient is suffering from. For example, if a person is suffering from diabetes and not producing enough insulin, one allopathic treatment is to introduce insulin into the patient's system. Although many proponents of the medical model in psychiatry today make the same allopathic assumptions about treatments for psychiatric disorders, they are the first to admit that they do not have physiological markers for mental and emotional disorders as physicians do for the disorders they treat allopathically (Andreasen, 2001; Colbert, 2002).

As noted, the dye companies working with coal tar extracts were really the laboratories that birthed organic chemistry and psychopharmacology. Growth on a large scale erupted quickly as new coal tar compounds were discovered that led to new psychotropic medications. The first successful medications (antipsychotics) reinforced clinicians who wanted a descriptive psychiatry that departed from the dimensional, psychodynamic models that dominated through the mid 20th century. The development of antidepressants further increased the dominance of descriptive psychiatry. The momentum was provided by the thrust toward descriptive psychiatry and by the merging of psychiatric and allopathic approaches in such models as the magic bullet theory.

One psychiatrist involved was Frank Ayd, who published in 1961 the first book on the syndrome of depression, *Recognizing the Depressed Patient*, based on his clinical work. At the same time, Merck, Geigy, and Roche were filing for a patent on amitriptyline (brand name Elavil—the second tricyclic antidepressant to go to market). Merck won because of greater market sophistication. Merck promptly bought 50,000 copies of Ayd's book and distributed them around the world, because the book strengthened the case for the existence of the disorder the new drug was to treat. As Healy (1997) wrote, Merck not only sold a drug, it sold the idea of an illness called depression and in the process strengthened the descriptive approach to mental disorders. As we show in later chapters, pharmaceutical companies learned a great deal from Merck's example in marketing.

## The Relationship Between *DSM* Categories and FDA Approval of Drugs

One temptation of the human condition, is to use word magic to oversimplify complex things, thus committing category errors. Although the descriptive categories in the *DSM* offer a common language and general symptom markers, they do not explain the **etiology** of the disorders described— meaning how the disorders come about (American Psychiatric Association, 2000b). Although it is tempting to believe that most mental/emotional symptoms have exclusively biological causes that can be treated with the right medication, this belief is unrealistic and oversimplifies something as complex as depression. If you succumb to that type of word magic, you may be vulnerable to the images pharmaceutical companies encourage that mental and emotional disorders such as depression are exclusively biologically driven. As we noted in Chapter One, if this were the case, then mental health professionals treating depression would be practicing medicine without a license. As we stated in Chapter One, it is not that the medical model perspective is incorrect—it is simply incomplete.

Category errors such as believing that the medical model provides a full account of mental illness

reinforce categorical psychiatry. Such thinking is further reinforced by the FDA requirement that drugs must undergo **double-blind randomized placebo-controlled trials**. These elements evolved separately and came together in the 1950s. In 1955 Linford Rees reported one of the first double-blind studies at an international symposium. The results supported Nathan Kline's contention that imipramine worked but also demonstrated that the effect was nowhere near as strong as Kline had concluded. As noted, Kline was working under the American model of psychoanalysis. He proposed that psychic conflicts bound up ego energy, leading to inhibited states (less energy, less active psychological states). He thought that perhaps imipramine somehow took energy away from the id and released it for use by the ego; that imipramine was a psychic energizer. Up to this point, medications were tested in trials, of various sizes, using close observation of client responses by clinicians. Much of Kline's work began with this method and Roland Kuhn in Europe basically developed the notion of an "antidepressant" by observing the effects on his clients of taking tricyclic compounds.

The idea of randomized, placebo-controlled trials (RCTs) seemed more appealing after the Contergan disaster in Europe. In 1957 an over-the-counter compound named Contergan was launched in Germany. Generically known as *thalidomide*, it soon became apparent that it caused birth defects. This influenced (but not solely) the passage in 1962 of the Kefauver-Harris drug amendments, which placed more rigorous requirements on drug manufacturers to show that a drug was safe and effective for the disease it was designed to treat. The amendments specify a drug must be effective for a particular disease, and categorical psychiatry provides a lexicon of such diseases in the *DSM*. Without categories of illnesses, how does one persuasively describe ailments? This was the final boost needed to thrust the categorical model of *DSM* into prominence.

The 1962 amendments also institutionalized the view that RCTs are the only scientific means to establish the efficacy of a treatment. The amendments concluded that the FDA "was in the business of licensing compounds for indications that medical experts agreed were the indications for which the compound was needed—diseases" (Healy, 2002, p. 27). Again, if all drug development is for treating different diseases, no field can use the drugs without a nosology of diseases. In 1980, Paul Leber of the FDA pushed through a formula that all compound submissions must contain evidence of at least two pivotal studies. Here, "pivotal" means randomized, placebo-controlled trials. Note, there are no restrictions on how many trials a company may commission before it gets the two "pivotal" trials. One result, as reported by Khan, Leventhal, Khan, and Brown (2002), is that when all studies for depression in the FDA database were examined, a majority (52% in this case) showed no more significant results than placebo. And as Olson and colleagues (2002) noted, studies that do not show positive results are far less likely to be published and to be in the public arena.

Healy (1997) also notes how *DSM* and the development of rating scales such as the Hamilton Depression Scale boosted the standardization of psychiatry. Such scales play a large role as dependent variables in RCTs. This leads to a curious phenomenon regarding psychiatric categories. Some RCTs support that Prozac is effective for Major Depressive Disorder of moderate severity. Clinicians assume it is effective for dysthymia (mild, chronic depression) but in fact have little evidence (at least no RCTs) to support that. This is where dimensional versus categorical psychiatry is important. Also, we know that Prozac and drugs chemically similar are used to treat Obsessive-Compulsive Disorder (OCD), Social Phobia, Generalized Anxiety Disorder (GAD), and Post-Traumatic Stress Disorder (PTSD) to name a few. If one compound can treat all these, are they all really distinct categories of illness? This question has yet to be answered. As far as the definition of disease is concerned, Healy notes, "Disease is coming to be defined, neither as a pathological process nor in terms of unwelcome experiences, but rather as what third-party payors will reimburse" (p. 109). When we limit the notion of mental or emotional disease to the descriptive categories in the *DSM* or other nosologies, we reduce the complexity and artificially narrow the field of treatment.

If we need a category of disease to test a drug's efficacy, can we do so with a proposed category that has not been approved as a mental or emotional

disorder? Apparently the answer is yes. Consider the category of Pre-Menstrual Dysphoric Disorder (PMDD—formerly Late Luteal Phase Dysphoric Disorder). Technically this is not a disorder but a criteria set that did not have sufficient evidence to be labeled a "disorder" in *DSM-IV* and *DSM-IV-TR*. Even though it is technically not a disorder, Eli Lilly Pharmaceuticals marketed a drug for it. The drug is fluoxetine hydrochloride (brand name Prozac), given a new brand name for this indication (Sarafem).

## The Problem of Placebo Response

In this introduction we also want to alert readers to the problem of **placebo response**. These responses vary across the different types of medications discussed in Part Two, but for some medications the rates of placebo response are quite high. For example, evidence indicates that a majority of depressive symptoms in primary care settings respond to placebo. The placebo response rate in studies looking at antidepressants and children reaches 40% in some studies, meaning, 40% of patients taking the placebo show statistically significant improvement. In addition, most of the effectiveness levels in these same studies are around 40 to 50%, meaning that only 40-50% of patients taking the medication show statistically significant improvement (Kutcher, 1998). As noted, the more recent analysis by Khan and colleagues (2002) points to the fact that in most of the trials pharmaceutical companies did on antidepressants, the placebo did as well as the antidepressant. Greenberg and Fisher (1997) have outlined how the effectiveness of a compound is directly related to design of the study to test the compound. Building on the work of Wechsler, Grosser, and Greenblatt (1965), they assert that drug treatments appear more effective in studies that do not use a placebo. They use studies on imipramine as an example, noting that only one in nine placebo-controlled trials show the drug to be more effective than placebo for at least 65% of the study participants. By contrast, the studies that did not use placebo showed drug effectiveness for at least 65% of the participants in seven of nine studies.

Ross (1995) has noted that "30 percent of every treatment response obtained by biological psychiatry is due to the placebo effect. Yet the placebo effect receives virtually no research funding in and of itself within psychiatry. This does not make scientific sense" (p. 113). Ross also notes that many participants in research trials get better on placebo within the first two weeks or drop out of studies because of side effects they are getting from placebos.

In addition, the type of placebo used affects the significance of responses to the compound. A placebo can be active or inert. An active placebo is only active to the extent that it gives the client some sensation, which is not linked to treating the hypothesized disorder. Such a response may be a slight tingling sensation of the skin. An inert placebo by contrast exerts no effects, and the person taking it simply feels no effect from it. The interesting thing is that many clients taking active placebos feel something and make the attribution that the "drug" is "working" and subsequently may "experience" symptom reduction. Whether this response is due to the power of autosuggestion or of experimenter expectation is unresolved, but the point is that something interesting and potentially healing is happening when there is a placebo response. These responses merit further study in and of themselves.

What is most disturbing from an Integral perspective is that many pharmaceutical companies are trying to find ways to screen out placebo responders from their trials. Abboud (2004) reported that Eli Lilly and Pfizer were attempting to develop ways to identify and exclude placebo responders because these participants weaken the effect size for the medication. This is disturbing on several levels. First, as Kay Dickersin from Brown University was quoted in the Abboud article as saying this is a subtle manipulation of what is supposed to be an "objective" process. By taking placebo responders out of trials, companies would, in our opinion, be artificially inflating the effect size. Even if placebo responders could be identified prior to a study, it would advance our knowledge far more to compare these people to those who respond to pharmacological treatment to see if variables can be isolated that correlate with placebo response (Jeff Soulen, personal communication, June 23, 2004).

## Conclusion

We hope these points help readers think critically as they review the medications we cover in Part Two. Here are some questions readers should always ask regarding a psychotropic compound:

1. In studies on the drug what type of placebo is used?
2. In studies on the drug, to what extent do therapeutic responses occur in the placebo group, and how do researchers address these responses?
3. When a drug is marketed for numerous, apparently different, mental disorders, how do theorists address the discrepancy?
4. When a new drug is released and approved by the FDA, how many trials were conducted before the two pivotal trials occurred?
5. Do clinicians "sell" the concept of mental and emotional disorders to clients? If so, how do they do this?
6. What is the general structure of randomized, placebo-controlled, double-blind trials? Describe for a layperson.

Being able to reflect on these questions can also make you a better advocate and educator for your clients.

# CHAPTER FIVE

# The Antidepressant Era

The title of this chapter derives from a book of the same title by David Healy (1997). Healy points out (as we noted in the introduction to Part Two) the important but overlooked fact that depression proper (what the *DSM-IV-TR* calls Major Depressive Disorder) (American Psychiatric Association, 2000b) was basically unheard of as recently as 40 years ago. For Healy, the antidepressant era has unfolded against a backdrop of battles within the psychiatric profession (people endorsing the medical model perspective battling those endorsing models emphasizing an intrapsychic perspective), regulatory agencies such as the Food and Drug Administration (FDA), and the pharmaceutical industry. In addition to guiding readers through various theories of depression and antidepressant action, we also take you on an Integral Model tour of antidepressant medication.

## The Current Impact of Antidepressants

A television commercial features a grimacing young man with his face against a wall. The commercial's narrator lists several symptoms of fear and anxiety related to Social Phobia (colloquially called Social Anxiety Disorder). The last scene in the commercial shows the same young man smiling, rising from a table in a crowded room apparently to receive acclaim for some accomplishment. The ad ends by repeating the name of the medication and informing the viewer, "Your life is waiting." A cur-

rent debate in the American Medical Association concerns whether such ads are a valuable source of information (for example, "A drug exists to treat your symptoms") or prey on the misconceptions many people have about such drugs being "magic potions" to change their lives (for example, "Even if you don't have symptoms, this drug will make you happier") (Kramer, 1993). In the early 21st century such commercials are commonplace, the result of laws passed in the 1980s and 1990s deregulating "direct-to-consumer" advertising for pharmaceutical companies (Hollon, 1999; Holmer, 1999). At this writing, antidepressants are one of the most advertised psychotropic medications. Antidepressants for adults constitute a multibillion-dollar market globally, and in the last five years prescriptions for children have increased at an exponential rate (Bostic, Wilens, Spencer, & Biederman, 1997) despite a lack of evidence to support their use for children and growing evidence that these drugs may exacerbate symptoms such as suicidal ideation in child and adolescents.

Antidepressants are used both on and off label for numerous disorders. When antidepressant medications were introduced about four decades ago, physicians primarily used them to treat depression. Currently, antidepressants are used to treat a variety of disorders, including a number of anxiety disorders, impulsive aggression, and even chronic pain. Although antidepressants may help people with a variety of depressive symptoms, most studies on antidepressants examine their use in treating Major Depressive Disorder as defined by *DSM-IV*. Thus, before discussing the history of antidepressants, let's review Major Depressive Disorder proper.

## Major Depressive Disorder (MDD)

In this text when we discuss the prevalence of *DSM* disorders, we may speak of lifetime prevalence or point prevalence. **Lifetime prevalence** is an estimate at a given time of all the individuals who have ever suffered from the disorder, and **point prevalence** is the estimate of the percentage of the population thought to suffer from the disorder at a given point in time (Ingersoll & Burns, 2001). Prevalence for most disorders is not well established for children and adolescents. Researchers think prepubertal boys are more likely than prepubertal girls to be affected by MDD but believe this changes after puberty (Cyranowski, Frank, Young, & Shear, 2000).

We encourage you to take prevalence estimates with the proverbial "grain of salt" because of the myriad problems with epidemiological data in general and self-report in particular. That said, the lifetime prevalence of MDD varies between 10 and 25% for females and 5 and 12% for males. The point prevalence varies from 5 to 9% for females and 2 to 3% for males. Recurrence estimates range from between 50 and 85% (American Psychiatric Association, 2000a). From 20 to 35% people with MDD have persistent residual symptoms and impaired social or occupational functioning. Researchers consider adolescent and adult females twice as likely to suffer from MDD (single or recurrent) than adolescent and adult males. Although this may be true, it may also be true that females are more likely to self-report symptoms, whereas males may be more likely to self-medicate with things such as alcohol.

## Comorbidity of Depression and Anxiety

As we pointed out in Chapter One, reality is complex, and complexity is our friend. Depression and anxiety, two of the most common symptom types seen by mental health professionals, are often comorbid (occur together) in adults as well as children. This highlights the importance of an accurate diagnosis, because a client may suffer from depression with some secondary anxiety, anxiety with some secondary depression, or from both an anxiety disorder as well as a mood disorder. Even when a client's symptoms fall into one diagnostic cluster at the time of intake, such a client may later show symptoms outside that cluster. Diagnosis is a process that continues throughout the therapeutic relationship and goes well beyond the limited medical categories of the *DSM*. Although we focus mainly on depression in this chapter and on anxiety in Chapter Six, these are rather artificial distinctions we use for instructive purposes. Just as students must learn the "laws" of Newtonian physics before they can understand the exceptions to those laws that occur in particle physics, students must also learn how classes of medications evolved around diagnostic categories and how market and clinical forces exploit the permeable nature of these classes. In the next section we discuss theories of antidepressant action from the medical model perspective.

## Theories of Antidepressant Action From the Medical Model Perspective

Researchers have sought to delineate profiles of clients with depression, to gauge the degree to which a particular client's depression is biological in nature. They have assumed that clients with depression that was more biological in nature would be better candidates for antidepressant medications, whereas clients whose depression was more psychological in nature would be better candidates for counseling or psychotherapy. As Stahl (2000) concluded, however, "The search for any biological markers of depression, let alone those that might be predictive of antidepressant responsiveness, has been disappointing" (p. 145).

How do antidepressants work? Various theories from the medical model perspective are proposed to explain antidepressant action. Each tends to build on its predecessors. In this sense these theories actually demonstrate one of the ideals of scientific method—new theories are supposed to build on older ones. However, although these theories do build on one another, scientists still do not understand why antidepressants alter mood. Perhaps Healy (2002) captured the ultimate usefulness of theories when he stated, "[H]aving a theory is scientifically useful primarily because having a theory leads to action" (p. 118). In this case the action depends on the theory. From an Integral perspective we will see that even the more rigorous theories of how antidepressants work only correlate the drug mechanisms of action with symptom relief. It must be noted, however, that this correlation is not causation. In the case of depression, many times the theories about medications lead to diagnoses rather than the other way around. This has been emphasized both by psychopharmacologists (such as Healy) and by laypeople such as Elizabeth Wurtzel. In her memoir of suffering from depression, Wurtzel (1994) commented that once she was prescribed Prozac, she had a diagnosis. She wrote,

> Rather than defining my disease as a way to lead us to fluoxetine, the invention of this drug has brought us to my disease. Which seems backward, but . . . this is a typical course of events in psychiatry, that the discovery of a drug to treat, say, schizophrenia, will tend to result in many more patients being diagnosed as schizophrenics. This is strictly Marxian psychopharmacology, where the material—or rather, pharmaceutical—means determine the way an individual's case history is interpreted. (p. 265)

Note that Wurtzel's reflections resonate with the notion of selling depression that we discussed in the introduction to Part Two.

## Amine Theory

The amine theory of depression began with research related to the amount of norepinephrine in the synaptic cleft. Amines are classes of compounds derived from ammonia by replacing one or more hydrogen atoms with organic groups. As noted in Chapter Two, the neurotransmitters serotonin (5-HT), dopamine (DA), norepinephrine (NE), epinephrine (Epi), and acetylcholine (Ach) are all amines. The amine hypothesis began with researchers observing the effects of antidepressants on norepinephrine. Simply put, the amine hypothesis

proposed that people who suffered from depression did not have enough amines, particularly norepinephrine (NE), in their synapses, and if you could increase the NE then they would not be depressed. It was a parsimonious theory but, as with most parsimonious theories, it did not address the complexity of the situation.

The first step in the amine hypothesis is credited to Albert Zeller, a biochemist at Northwestern University in the 1950s. Zeller had discovered that one function of the enzyme monoamine oxidase (MAO) was to disable neurotransmitters after they had been fired from the terminal button. This made sense, because scientists knew neurotransmitters did not just float in the synapse forever and that the body must have a way to disable them (as discussed in Chapter Two). While screening chemicals for this disabling ability, Zeller found that iproniazid (the drug Nathan Kline used as an antidepressant) was a powerful inhibitor of MAO (thus the name *MAO inhibitor*) (Snyder, 1996). Further research confirmed that iproniazid, by disabling MAO, did indeed raise NE levels in the synapse.

Scientists also knew at this time that a drug called *reserpine* depleted the brain of amines. When monkeys were given reserpine alone, they became almost immobile and presented an animal model of depression. Researchers gave both reserpine and iproniazid to monkeys, and the monkeys became highly animated, leading to the notion that perhaps iproniazid was a psychic energizer (Snyder, 1996). Researchers later discovered that reserpine causes both norepinephrine and serotonin to leak out of the synaptic vesicles into the synaptic cleft, where MAO disables it. Thus, disabling MAO greatly increases the newly leaked norepinephrine and serotonin in the synaptic cleft, allowing more binding to area receptors than does an undrugged state. These discoveries were the primary support for the amine theory. Again, to clarify, the amine theory of depression is that people who are depressed do not have enough amines (such as norepinephrine) in the synapses between important neurons. Drugs that increase the lacking amines thus alleviate depression.

As noted, the amine theory proved too parsimonious. For one thing, the idea of depressed clients being deficient in a neurotransmitter should correlate with lower levels of the metabolite for the neurotransmitter they are supposed to be lacking. Although some subjects in studies show this correlation, others do not. Stahl (2000) noted that when the metabolite for 5-HT is low, it is more likely correlated with impulsive behavior than with depression proper.

In the introduction to Part Two, we noted how tricyclic antidepressants evolved in Europe about the same time MAO inhibitors were developing in the United States. Given the MAO research, investigators thought tricyclics worked in the same way, by disabling MAO or some related enzyme and increasing NE in the synaptic cleft. The clinical actions of both drugs, after all, are quite similar. This assumption soon ran into problems, however, when researchers discovered that much of the MAO in the nervous system exists inside the cells rather than in the synaptic cleft. Also, all antidepressants seemed to have a time lag of at least two weeks before they took effect. This didn't make sense, because MAO began to inhibit iproniazid within hours after the patient took the first dose. Research continued.

### The Discovery of Reuptake Inhibition

The next researcher to make important discoveries in this area was Julius Axelrod. In the 1950s, working at the National Institutes of Health in Bethesda, Maryland, Axelrod discovered that norepinephrine was inactivated not by being broken down by enzymes but by a reuptake mechanism. We discussed this in Chapter Two, but a brief review may be helpful. The mechanism works like this: When norepinephrine (NE) is released into the synaptic cleft, it has a period of time to bind to receptors. After this period, a transporter molecule attaches to the NE neurotransmitter and takes it back inside the cell that released it in the first place, where enzymes store it in synaptic vesicles so it can be released again. In this way the transporter molecule provides something like a recycling service. Other researchers have identified a similar mechanism for most other neurotransmitters, with the exception of acetylcholine, which is deactivated by the enzyme acetylcholinesterase (just as norepinephrine can be

deactivated by monoamine oxidase). This discovery only served to reinforce the amine theory of depression, because researchers eventually discovered that drugs such as tricyclic antidepressants work by inhibiting this reuptake mechanism and thus allowing released neurotransmitters to stay longer in the synaptic cleft. For his work in this area, Axelrod shared the 1970 Nobel Prize in Medicine with Ulf von Euler and Sir Bernard Katz.

Nevertheless, the same time lag noted for MAO inhibitors existed with drugs such as tricyclic antidepressants that inhibited reuptake. For example, about an hour after the person takes a tricyclic antidepressant the reuptake inhibition begins and the amount of neurotransmitter in the synaptic cleft increases, but symptoms do not abate for between two to four weeks (maybe even as long as six weeks). So, despite making important contributions to the understanding of reuptake inhibition, Axelrod had not solved the riddle of how tricyclic antidepressants work.

### Downregulation Theory

Although enzyme deactivation and reuptake inhibition are important elements in most antidepressants' mechanism of action, they still don't account for the two- to six-week lag of the antidepressant effect. The reuptake properties of tricyclic antidepressants and selective serotonin reuptake inhibitors begin increasing levels of neurotransmitters within an hour of someone's taking the medicine. Another problem is that other drugs that dramatically boost the levels of similar neurotransmitters (cocaine) do not act as antidepressants. Although they may induce euphoria, they also cause an emotional "crash" when the drug wears off. This knowledge contributed to the development of postsynaptic receptor desensitization (downregulation) theory as a complement to the amine theory. This theory proposes that initially the receptors in the depressed person are hypersensitive to neurotransmitter because depressed people have less neurotransmitter. Because there is supposedly less neurotransmitter, the researchers hypothesized that receptors act as if they are "starved" for it, so they upregulate (increase in number). (Remember, this is a theory using metaphors—not concrete truths. In the metaphor used to explain this theory, receptors are not really "starved" for a neurotransmitter but if they had human qualities one might say they would act as if they were.) With antidepressant treatment, as more neurotransmitter becomes available the receptors get more than is needed because they previously increased in number (upregulated) to make use of the available neurotransmitter in the synaptic cleft. At this point the cell gets bombarded with neurotransmitter, because the increased levels of neurotransmitter are now binding with the increased numbers of receptors. The cells then adjust by decreasing the number and sensitivity of receptors, because more neurotransmitter is available. Theoretically, this normalizes transmission or provides the "chemical balance" that is correlated with decrease of symptoms. So according to downregulation theory, the antidepressant effect is the result of two mechanisms. The first is the increase to normal of neurotransmitter released into the synapse (accomplished through reuptake inhibition), and the second is the downregulation of receptors to a normal level of responsiveness (to adapt to the increased levels of neurotransmitter). The timeframe required for neurons to decrease the number of receptors correlates closely with the lag time between taking a drug and experiencing the antidepressant effect (two to six weeks depending on the client and dosage of medication).

The downregulation theory led researchers to consider the role of receptor sensitivity in mental/emotional disorders. This combination of the amine theory and downregulation theory was used to account for the action of antidepressants until very recently. Remember, these were and still are just theories. Researchers never had conclusive evidence that the theories fully explained the function of antidepressants nor that there was any "chemical imbalance" that caused depression. Variations on these theories were proposed, such as the permissive theory, which restated the amine hypothesis but included serotonin rather than exclusively focusing on norepinephrine. The permissive theory also tried to explain the role of serotonin in regulating levels of norepinephrine and dopamine. Although all these theories expanded available data on antidepressant action, none fully accounted for

antidepressant effects or the strong placebo responses in many studies of antidepressants (we return to these later). The latest hypothesis to explain antidepressant effects takes the discussion deeper into the mysteries of the cells called *neurons*, as we describe next.

### Neurotransmitter Receptor Hypothesis

The neurotransmitter receptor hypothesis asserts that in depression, something is wrong with particular receptors for monoamine neurotransmitters. Researchers think this "something wrong" leads to depression. It is also related to the upregulation of receptors discussed earlier. Because this hypothesis focuses on the receptors and because receptors are a function of gene expression, this hypothesis also considers that depression may relate to some function (or malfunction) of gene expression. Certainly this is a possibility; however, where genetics is concerned it is important to state hypotheses tentatively and concisely to avoid lapsing into word magic. Although admitting that direct evidence to support the genetic hypothesis is lacking, Stahl (2000) discusses postmortem studies of the brains of suicide victims where test results show that the tissue in parts of these brains have increased numbers of 5-HT2 receptors. He concludes that further research may support a genetic variation of the neurotransmitter receptor hypothesis.

## The Cellular/Molecular Theory of Antidepressant Action

The latest theory of how antidepressants work—the cellular/molecular theory of antidepressant action—required advances in medical technology that allowed scientists to peer inside neurons. The result is a theory that transcends the other theories outlined so far. At the outset we want to stress that this is unlikely to be the final word on the biological theories of depression, because it also leaves many questions unanswered.

The cellular/molecular theory of depression was first outlined by Duman, Heninger, and Nestler (1997). In a sense it is a metatheory, in that it encompasses and transcends its predecessor theories. The authors begin by summarizing the complementarity of amine theory and downregulation theory, noting that these theories accurately outline certain actions of antidepressants but fail to explain why such drugs would improve mood. They then assert that increases in the levels of available neurotransmitters and the resulting downregulation are merely the beginning of antidepressant action. Next they document intracellular changes in response to someone taking antidepressant medications. Note that these authors maintain that once a person takes an antidepressant medication, these intracellular changes occur *after* the drug increases the neurotransmitter levels and persist after downregulation. These authors explain that within the cell, antidepressants cause an increase in cyclic adenosine monophosphate (cyclic AMP or cAMP). Cyclic AMP is a molecule with many functions. Some of these functions are activating enzymes in the neuron, amplifying the effects of hormones and neurotransmitters, and providing other vital functions in the cell. The cAMP levels raised by taking antidepressants apparently do not return to lower levels as the person adjusts to the presence of the drug. Interestingly, cAMP governs the production and processing of cell nutrients called *brain-derived neurotrophic factors (BDNFs)*, and as cAMP increases in response to the antidepressant medication, these cell nutrients also increase.

Without unpacking all the molecular biology involved, let's say the basic idea is that the cell goes through many changes after an antidepressant is introduced into the system and that the increase in cell nutrients may be one of the most important. The developers of the cellular/molecular theory of depression are proposing that stress and disease processes cause neurological atrophy ranging from reversible to irreversible. One manifestation of this hypothesized atrophy is depression. Such damage may be reversed by an increase in cell nutrients that is one of the many results of taking an antidepressant medication. Brain-derived neurotrophic factor holds promise for treating degenerative brain disorders such as Parkinson's disease. In a recent study in the United Kingdom, researchers injected neurotrophic factor directly into the brain of patients suffering from Parkinson's disease. These patients experienced dramatic decreases in their symptoms (Schorr, 2004). Such work may hold promise for mental and emotional disorders that have clear biological correlates, but those correlates must be conclusively determined.

The following flow chart summarizes these theories of depression and how each one builds on previous ones.

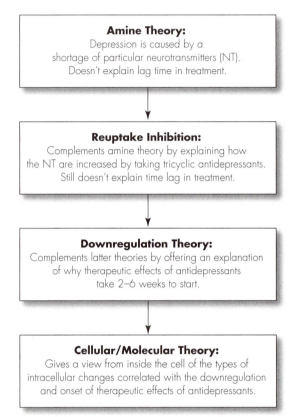

**Amine Theory:**
Depression is caused by a shortage of particular neurotransmitters (NT). Doesn't explain lag time in treatment.

**Reuptake Inhibition:**
Complements amine theory by explaining how the NT are increased by taking tricyclic antidepressants. Still doesn't explain time lag in treatment.

**Downregulation Theory:**
Complements latter theories by offering an explanation of why therapeutic effects of antidepressants take 2–6 weeks to start.

**Cellular/Molecular Theory:**
Gives a view from inside the cell of the types of intracellular changes correlated with the downregulation and onset of therapeutic effects of antidepressants.

If introducing antidepressants boosts cell nutrients, alleviating depression, this theory also needs to posit what happens to cause cell nutrients to fall in the first place. Although we noted earlier that the theorists suggest stress and vulnerability, Stahl (2000) wrote that this stress affects the gene that governs BDNF and represses its expression, resulting in decreased BDNF. He says that it may be that antidepressants act to reverse the decrease in BDNF by causing the genes for BDNF to be activated. Only time and further research will tell whether this speculation is accurate.

Not only does the cellular/molecular theory of depression hold promise for providing a fuller understanding of how antidepressants work, it also promises a fuller understanding of nonpharmacologic approaches to treating depression. Scientists have known for some time that physical exercise is effective in reducing depressive symptoms (Salmon, 2001). Researchers have already documented that general physical exercise rapidly increases the cell nutrients called brain-derived neurotrophic factors (Russo-Neustadt, Beard, & Cotman, 1999). In studies using brain scan technology, depressed participants taking an antidepressant medication and depressed participants engaging in interpersonal therapy showed similar changes in their brain scans as their depression improved. Although the therapy group took longer to manifest these changes, they were as significant as the changes in the group taking the antidepressant (Brody et al., 2001). Apparently exercise and counseling/psychotherapy may induce the same types of intracellular changes as antidepressants. If future research supports this hypothesis, it is important for counselors and other mental health professionals to understand, because this radically expands a client's treatment options. This is also why we emphasize an Integral openness regarding the mind–brain issue in this book: Mind—intention, attention, and awareness—may well be as effective or more effective than pharmacologic interventions.

Finally, it is important to hearken back to the Integral Model at this point. Reviewing physiological theories of how antidepressants work can be dizzying as well as impressive. The key is to not forget that although these theories encompass truths about antidepressants and depression, they are only partial truths. These theories give us important truths from the medical model perspective. However, they are only partial truths; resist the temptation to simplify the complexity of something such as recovering from depression with word magic claiming that antidepressants corrected a "chemical imbalance." Recovery from depression for clients taking antidepressants is hardly remarkable. Although 70% of clients in most studies respond to antidepressants, that response is only partial in some cases. As Ross (1995) pointed out, even in those studies up to 30%

of the clients may respond to placebo, but this finding is never systematically followed up. Finally, Stahl (2000) noted that in terms of recovery, follow-up studies of depressed clients after one year of treatment indicate that approximately 40% still meet the criteria for the same diagnosis and 20% never recover fully or meet the criteria for dysthymia (low-grade depression). Further, Stahl notes that in 18-month follow-ups, many clients who respond to antidepressants report that the antidepressants stop working. This is given the highly technical name "pooping out." The percentage of clients whose antidepressants "poop out" after 18 months is as high as 20 to 30% in some studies.

Research by Antonuccio, Danton, and DeNelsky (1995) supported the hypothesis that cognitive therapy alone may be a better or at least as effective treatment for depression than are cognitive therapy and antidepressants together. Future research on the intracellular theory of depression should investigate whether the intracellular changes correlated with antidepressants are also correlated with engaging in cognitive or other psychological therapies for depression in the absence of antidepressant medication. Here again, the power and politics of culture will determine whether such research gets funded or is allowed to take place.

## A Medical Model Overview of Antidepressant Medications

In this section of the chapter we convey a more standard presentation of the antidepressants. It is difficult to make global statements about the efficacy of antidepressants in general; however, the literature does seem to agree that all the different classes of antidepressants are about equally effective. Stahl (2000) summarized this agreement, noting it is a "good news / bad news" scenario. The good news is that one half to two thirds of depressed clients on any antidepressant respond positively to it, and 90% or more are likely to respond if tried on several different compounds. Half of these responders may progress into full remission within six months of treatment. In addition, antidepressants seem to significantly reduce relapses as well. The bad news is that many responders never reach full remission and that in 20 to 30% of the people who respond at all to antidepressants the effects tend to "poop out" or wear off after about 18 months.

Although Stahl emphasizes the medical model perspective of depression, equating it with diabetes or hypertension, the "bad news" merely means that in some cases biological interventions are time limited. This is only truly "bad news" if in fact there are no other treatments for depression, which is not the case. Given that many people don't maintain their response to antidepressants, it makes sense to view a response as a time-limited window of opportunity within which to employ an Integral approach to treatment. An Integral approach uses all the perspectives we have been discussing in this book. In Integral treatment, medication is one useful component of a whole.

### The Role of Vegetative Symptoms

In the treatment of Major Depressive Disorder (MDD), note that the more **vegetative symptoms** a client suffers from, the better candidate the person is for antidepressant medication, because these symptoms are most affected by the medication. Maybe because depression is overdetermined (meaning it may be caused by biological, psychological, cultural, social and perhaps even spiritual factors), a preponderance of vegetative symptoms point toward a stronger biological component in etiology. Table 5.1 contains a list of common vegetative symptoms for MDD.

### Monoamine Oxidase (MAO) Inhibitors

We noted that the first MAO inhibitor was iproniazid, but this compound fell into disfavor because some physicians reported heptotoxicity (liver toxicity). The drug seemed to cause a type of cell death in the liver. Less toxic MAOIs such as Marplan (isocarboxazid) and Nardil have been introduced. To review the mechanism of action, MAOIs inhibit the enzyme (MAO) that breaks down neurotransmitters thought to be related to depression (specifically norepinephrine). When the drugs inhibit this enzyme, more NE is in the synaptic cleft to bind to receptors. This binding then causes downregulation of receptors and the cellular/molecular changes described earlier. When this chain of events occurs, the person's depressive symptoms tend to improve.

**TABLE 5.1**   Common Vegetative Symptoms in Major Depressive Disorder

Sleep disturbance (early morning waking, frequent awakening, occasional hypersomnia)

Appetite disturbance (decreased or increased appetite with accompanying weight fluctuations)

General fatigue

Decreased sex drive

Restlessness, agitation, or psychomotor retardation

Diurnal variations in mood (usually feeling worse in the morning)

Impaired concentration and forgetfulness

Pronounced anhedonia (loss of pleasure in most or all things)

MAO inhibitors are not specific to any type of MAO, so they inhibit all types of MAO throughout the body and not just in specified areas thought related to depressive symptoms. In addition, the effects of older MAOIs, as noted by Julien, are irreversible; such irreversible effects are rare in psychopharmacology. Thus the chemical bond of the MAO inhibitor with the MAO cannot be broken and enzyme function returns to normal only when the body's DNA creates new enzymes. This attribute has earned MAO inhibitors the nickname "suicide inhibitors," because their binding to MAO is irreversible meaning that the MAO molecule "suicidally" binds and "goes down with the ship." Further, there are two types of MAO in the body, labeled MAO A and MAO B. Both forms are inhibited by the older, original MAO inhibitors, which are nonselective. The MAO A form metabolizes the neurotransmitters most closely linked to depression (serotonin and norepinephrine). The MAO B form is thought to convert some ligands (called *prototoxins*) into toxins that cause cell damage. Researchers have linked MAO B inhibition to prevention of neurodegenerative processes such as those in Parkinson's disease. Table 5.2 lists some available MAO inhibitors by brand and generic names and dosage range. Please note that the dosage ranges are those common in the United States and that dosage range, as well as minimum effective dose, changes from nation to nation.

**TABLE 5.2**   Examples of MAO Inhibitor Antidepressants and Common Daily Dosage Ranges

| Generic Name | Brand Name | Common Daily Dosage Range |
|---|---|---|
| Selegiline | L-Deprenyl | 10 mg |
| Isocarboxazid | Marplan | 20–50 mg |
| Moclobemide | Manerix | 150–500 mg (available in Canada) |
| Phenelzine | Nardil | 30–75 mg |
| Tranylcypromine | Parnate | 20–40 mg |

## Common Side Effects of MAOIs

The side effects of MAOIs are more severe and more frequent than those of other antidepressants. Most are related to the increased activity of norepinephrine, but some are related to the enzyme inhibition that causes the NE increases. Table 5.3 lists common side effects of MAOIs.

**TABLE 5.3**   Common Side Effects of MAO Inhibitors

Orthostatic hypotension (a drop in blood pressure that results in dizziness on standing)

Nighttime insomnia, daytime sedation

Headache

Muscle cramps

Weight gain

Difficulty urinating

Tyramine intolerance

### *Inhibition of MAO A and Tyramine Intolerance*

One of the most dangerous side effects of traditional MAO inhibitors is tyramine intolerance. We noted that MAO A metabolizes neurotransmitters that are linked to depression. By slowing down this metabolism, the neurotransmitters remain active longer and this sets in motion the events correlated with symptom improvement. MAO A also metabolizes tyramine, a dietary amine. If the MAO A is not there to break it down, this amine can build up and cause the release of norepinephrine and other sym-

pathomimetic amines, raising blood pressure. In severe reactions, the blood pressure elevation can cause hemorrhage and death. The side effect is easily controlled with a diet low in tyramine-containing foods. Table 5.4 lists examples of foods to avoid when taking MAO inhibitors. A physician should give a complete list to the clients for whom they prescribe these medications.

**TABLE 5.4**   Examples of Foods High in Tyramine Content to Avoid When Taking MAOIs

Cheeses (cream cheese, such as the common Philadelphia brand, and cottage cheese are safe)

Chicken liver and beef liver

Yeast preparations (avoid brewer's yeast, and powdered and caked yeast as sold in health food stores)

Broad beans and fava beans

Herring

Beer, sherry, ale, red wine, liqueurs

Canned figs

Protein extracts (such as soup cubes and commercial gravies)

Obviously, because most MAOIs bind irreversibly, there is no specific antagonist that people can take if they accidentally ingest a food high in tyramine while taking their MAOIs. In such a situation, clients are usually advised not to lie down as this will exacerbate the increase in blood pressure. Clients are directed to go to an emergency room for treatment. Treatment may include taking a calcium-channel blocker such as nifedipine that can lower blood pressure to avert a hypertensive crisis. A note on discontinuation: If MAOIs are stopped, the client should maintain dietary restrictions for about two weeks. That's how long it takes to build up an adequate level of monoamine oxidase. The same holds for making a transition from an MAO inhibitor to another antidepressant medication.

In general, MAOIs are used to treat depression that has been resistant to treatment with other types of antidepressants. This is more due to the side effect profile than to questions of efficacy, because this MAOI class of antidepressants is just as effective as the other classes. In addition to being used against depression, MAO inhibitors have been used with mixed results in treating Bulimia Nervosa, Social Phobia, migraine headaches, neurodermatitis, Borderline Personality Disorder, and Panic Disorder with Agoraphobia.

### Contraindications for MAOI Therapy

Clients with a history of liver disease, congestive heart failure, recreational drug use/abuse/dependence, hypertension, or uncontrollable tyramine consumption are not good candidates for MAOI therapy. In addition, clients who, for whatever reason, are unlikely to abide by the dietary restrictions are also poor candidates for this type of therapy.

### Newer MAO Inhibitors

We briefly want to note two developments in MAO inhibitors. The latest efforts of pharmaceutical companies have resulted in MAO inhibitors that form *reversible* bonds with MAO. These are called *RIMAs* (*reversible inhibitors of MAO*). Also, certain MAO inhibitors are selective for A and B. One new drug that offers both developments is selegiline (Eldepryl and L-Deprenyl). This drug is metabolized to an amphetamine molecule, which slows dopamine reuptake. It is reversible, and in low doses (5 to 10 mg a day) it affects only MAO B. At low doses, no dietary restrictions seem necessary. It does not act as an antidepressant at low doses, however. The prescribing professional must raise the dosage to get an antidepressant effect, and at this level the drug affects both MAO A and MAO B. At this level, although still reversible, dietary restrictions are necessary. Selegiline is very expensive (about $5 a pill) and should not be abruptly stopped, because doing so can cause a discontinuation syndrome (nausea, dizziness, hallucinations).

Although MAO inhibitors are rarely the medication of first choice, they may be used after other medications have failed to provide results. The following case illustrates that dynamic while also illustrating the inadequacy of strictly viewing a client's symptoms through the medical model perspective.

## The Case of Allan

Allan, a 54-year-old lower-middle-class Caucasian male of Baptist faith, was referred for treatment as part of coordinated services at a mental health agency. Ten years prior to referral he was diagnosed as severely depressed and prescribed a tricyclic antidepressant (TCA) (imiprimine/Tofranil) that he took for about 10 weeks. During this period he was hospitalized twice, more for his complaints about his reactions to the medication than his depression. After the second hospitalization he was prescribed an SSRI (fluoxetine/Prozac) for his ongoing depression and buspirone (BuSpar) for his bouts of anxiety. At no time in the record of his assessment was there any mention of personality impairment or disorder.

Within two weeks of beginning Prozac, Allan became very agitated, anxious, and paranoid, and had to be hospitalized a third time. The treatment team felt Allan might be suffering from an Atypical Depression, and he was taken off the Prozac and put on an MAOI (tranylcypromine/Parnate). Allan was advised about the important dietary restrictions he had to follow while on Parnate. Soon after, his condition did improve and some of the depressive symptoms lifted. A month later Allan was transferred to a different case manager because his current one left the agency. Within two weeks he was hospitalized a fourth time for a severe allergy reaction. It was soon determined that Allan had deliberately eaten some cheese because he was in a rage about losing his case manager. By the time Allan was discharged and assigned to a counselor, he was threatening suicide almost daily and refusing to come to counseling. Eventually, however, he began to attend counseling.

The treatment was very challenging, and because of Allan's feelings and suspicions about his care he basically did all he could to undermine his counselor's efforts. Gradually the counselor learned three very important facts about Allan and his life. The first was his enormous fear and then absolute rage about being abandoned and then turned over to someone else for care. The second was his great skill and talent as an electrician and his very fragile self-appraisal of his skills. The third was his gradual discovery of his homosexuality and deep attraction to his male therapist.

The therapist developed a treatment plan to address all three themes. He and Allan planned better for therapeutic interruptions by improving backup support, he referred Allan to a vocational rehabilitation office for additional training in electronics, and he helped Allan talk more concerning his feelings of homosexuality. Gradually Allan stopped taking all medications and worked on his issues in therapy. Here is an example of a case where the client masked severe issues in both intrapsychic and cultural realms and presented a picture of a complex clinical depression. It took time, a great deal of disruption, medication changes, hospitalizations, and careful listening to get a more accurate therapeutic focus on Allan. Being alert only to a client's depressive symptoms with the sole intent of administering psychotropic medications would inevitably have missed the important Integral aspects of Alan's dilemmas. Overall, Allan's MAOI treatment stabilized him for several years. He continued with the medication in conjunction with bimonthly psychotherapy until he was 62. Then he was titrated off the MAOI and saw his therapist only on an as-needed basis. He continues to work as an apartment superintendent 40 hours a week in his neighborhood.

## Tricyclic Antidepressants

As noted, the word *tricyclic* in "tricyclic antidepressants" refers to the three-ring molecular core of the drugs in this class of compounds. According to Stahl (2000), the term "tricyclic antidepressant" is outdated by the standards of current psychopharmacology. Newer and similar agents can have more than three rings to their structure, and these agents are used on-label for a variety of disorders other than depression. Nevertheless, for instructional purposes we use the term *tricyclic antidepressants*, or *TCAs*. As noted in the history section in the introduction to Part Two, the TCAs were unexpectedly born from chlorpromazine, the first antipsychotic, also known as a *neuroleptic*. TCAs were created because drug companies were seeking compounds with fewer side effects and with application to other disorders. Table 5.5 lists commonly prescribed TCAs by their brand and generic names and the typical dosage range for each compound.

**TABLE 5.5**   Examples of Tricyclic Antidepressants and Common Daily Dosage Ranges

| Generic Name | Brand Name | Common Daily Dosage Range |
|---|---|---|
| Amitriptyline | Elavil | 75–250 mg |
| Amoxapine | Asendin | 200–300 mg |
| Clomipramine | Anafranil | 50–200 mg |
| Doxepin | Sinequan, Adapin | 75–250 mg |
| Imipramine | Tofranil | 75–250 mg |
| Nortriptyline | Pamelor | 50–100 mg |
| Maprotiline | Ludiomil | 50–200 mg |

The primary mechanism of action in all TCAs is inhibition of the reuptake norepinephrine and serotonin (and to a slight extent dopamine). As the cellular theory of depression described earlier suggests, researchers assume that other changes in the affected neurons are related to the reuptake inhibition. In addition, all tricyclic compounds block receptors on acetylcholine, histamine, and epinephrine neurons. These additional mechanisms of action have no therapeutic effects for depression and cause most of the side effects of taking TCAs.

### Side Effects of TCAs

We have listed the side effects of TCAs in Table 5.6 by class. As noted, the side effects come from the drug molecules binding to certain receptors and blocking them. In Chapter Two we described this "blocking" as an antagonist effect, meaning the molecule binds, does not initiate an effect on the neuron, and prevents other ligands from binding and exerting their effect. Because this is an antagonistic action, we use the prefix "anti-" when describing the side effect. For example, a TCA molecule blocking an acetylcholine neuron exerts an "anticholinergic" effect. A TCA molecule blocking a histamine neuron exerts an "antihistaminic" effect. Conversely, if a drug molecule has an agonist action we do not use the "anti-" prefix and we simply say the drug had a cholinergic or histaminic effect. Table 5.6 is just a general introduction to possible side effects, not an exhaustive list. Please note that not every TCA drug produces every side effect and that effects also vary depending on the specific responses of the individual taking the drug.

**TABLE 5.6**  Common TCA Side Effects Listed by Class

| Class | Description of Side Effect |
|---|---|
| Anticholinergic | Dry mouth, dizziness, constipation, difficulty urinating, blurred vision |
| Adrenergic | Sexual dysfunction, sweating, orthostatic hypotension |
| Antihistaminic | Sedation and weight gain |

TCAs also have potent effects on the peripheral nervous system. Especially in combination with other medications, they can cause cardiac depression and increased electrical activity that results in arrhythmia. Both can lead to heart failure.

For a prescribing professional, choosing the right TCA seems to be a matter of preference based on matching the TCA to the client's symptoms. Some TCAs are more sedating (Elavil), others are more stimulating (Norpramin). Pointing out the contrast to some of the other classes of antidepressants, Schatzberg and Nemeroff (1998) have argued that if a client does not respond to one TCA, it is unlikely that he or she will respond to any other TCA and the prescribing professional is best advised to try another class of antidepressants. Note that some other medications can significantly raise or lower a client's TCA plasma level. For example, SSRI antidepressants or stimulants such as methylphenidate (Ritalin) can increase TCA plasma levels as much as eight-fold, whereas substances such as carbamazepine (Tegretol) and nicotine can significantly lower TCA plasma levels. This simply indicates that clients need quality care from the professional prescribing the medications. Medical professionals are trained to be alert to drug–drug interactions, which is becoming a crucial aspect of psychopharmacology as more and more compounds come to market. TCAs are indicated for depression and are approved by the FDA for anxiety, childhood enuresis, and Obsessive-Compulsive Disorder (OCD). Off-label uses include insomnia, Panic Disorder with agoraphobia, PTSD, Generalized Anxiety Disorder (GAD), chronic pain (all classes of antidepressants have been tested as analgesics for chronic pain and frequently are more effective than placebo), and Bulimia Nervosa.

### Tricyclic Derivatives

There is a subclass of antidepressants derived from TCAs that is referred to by several labels, including "secondary amines," "second-generation antidepressants," or "atypical" antidepressants. The numerous labels are unfortunate because they make it hard to tell what is being referred to, because some of the labels (such as "second-generation antidepressants") are also used to refer to totally different classes of drugs. To avoid confusion, we call these compounds *tricyclic derivatives*. Most have a two-ring molecular structure and have been discovered from metabolites of the tricyclic antidepressants. As we noted in Chapter Two, one strategy for creating marketable compounds is to examine the metabolites of a parent compound. The metabolites can be found in the urine of people taking the parent compound. If the metabolites are active, they can be synthesized into a similar agent that acts like the parent compound but is probably weaker in therapeutic and side effects. As such, these compounds may still produce the desired therapeutic effect with lower levels of side effects. Table 5.7 lists some examples of TCA derivatives. Note how the generic name is similar to the parent compound.

**TABLE 5.7**  Examples of TCA Derivatives and Their Parent Compounds

| TCA Derivative Generic Name | Parent Compound Generic Name | Dosage Range |
|---|---|---|
| Nortriptyline | Amitriptyline | 50–100 mg |
| Desipramine | Imipramine | 75–250 mg |

### Benefits and Drawbacks to TCAs and TCA Derivatives: A Summary

As you have read this chapter, you probably have already guessed what the benefits and drawbacks of TCAs and TCA derivatives are. The benefits center around two things. First, these drugs are among the most extensively studied psychotropic medications on the market. This is largely because they have been on the market about 50 years. When TCAs were put on the market, their only competition was MAO inhibitors. Because MAOIs had the potentially dangerous "cheese effect" related to tyramine intolerance, they were quickly displaced by the TCAs, which did not require a focused dietary regimen (other than avoiding alcohol and other drugs that may interact). Thus TCAs became the drug of first choice for depression and remained so well into the 1980s, when Prozac was introduced. Once established as a drug of first choice, they then provided the baseline against which all other newer antidepressants were measured. The result is a wealth of information on the TCAs, a situation that makes even conservative medical practitioners comfortable prescribing them to patients. Although the SSRIs (which we discuss next) are currently thought of as the drug of first choice for people with depression, no one disputes that far more data are available on the TCAs. The other advantage to TCAs is their lower cost. After a pharmaceutical company is approved to sell a drug for a given purpose, the company usually gets patent rights to the compound for only 17 years. After this time, other companies can produce the drug generically and sell it for a lower price. The result is that clients with no insurance and little income will likely be able to afford a tricyclic antidepressant as opposed to an SSRI that has not yet "gone generic." For example, in 2000 a common wholesale price for a nongeneric SSRI was approximately $150 for a 30-day supply. By contrast, the same supply of generic Elavil (amitriptyline) was approximately $5 . Note that the first SSRI, fluoxetine (Prozac), is currently available in generic form. Although its manufacturer (Eli Lilly) is trying to recapture the patent, if fluoxetine remains generic this will likely become the drug of first choice for the populations referred to. It is logical to imagine that after several newer antidepressant compounds become available in less expensive generic formulations, the use of TCAs will continue to decrease.

The several key drawbacks to TCA include slow onset of action (a drawback for all antidepressants), unreliable effectiveness from client to client, diffi-cult side effects, and (perhaps most disturbing) a high overdose potential. Suicidal patients are therefore frequently never given more than a week's worth of pills at a time. Moreover, investigations have probed deaths in several children being treated with TCAs. As noted, the drugs have strong effects on the peripheral nervous system and can cause heart rate variability (Walsh, 1998). As you will see in Chapter Nine, TCAs are now thought to be no better than placebo in children and, as such, should be prescribed only under particular conditions. The following case demonstrates how TCA medication played an important role in the treatment of one client.

## The Case of Rita

Rita, 31, sought counseling for several years in the late 1970s for generalized sadness, some hopelessness, lack of energy, great worry, a loss of a genuine sense of pleasure, and a recurrent sense of loneliness. Although she went to several mental health professionals during this period, not one suggested assessment for depression. Rita experienced almost no relief, as evidenced by her therapist shopping. She complained to her few friends, "They are all good listeners, but I don't feel I'm getting any help. Maybe that's just my lot in life." About this time she stopped all therapy and began a very aggressive program of exercise and vitamin therapy. Also, she began to see a massage therapist for body massage. twice a month and she began to meditate every morning. She felt some relief and improvement, but those feelings were short-lived. In November of the same year she became despondent with great personal anguish, had plaguing suicidal thoughts, and isolated herself from friends and family. Living single, she told one friend, "I might as well not live, no one will ever love me and I'm not lovable." After a terrible period of two weeks, one of her friends took her to a local emergency room. There the attending physician diagnosed Major Depressive Disorder; prescribed imipramine (Tofranil), which is a TCA as well as one of the most commonly used antidepressants at that time; and referred her to a female psychiatrist for follow-up. Gradually Rita improved. She followed up three times with the psychiatrist and continued on imipramine as pre-scribed for six months.

In the middle of this six-month period, Rita met a man whom she began to date. Rita quickly became attached, which seemed to frighten her companion and he abruptly ended the brief rela-tionship. This termination triggered a severe sui-cidal depression in Rita, and she slit her wrists. Her landlord found her, and she was rushed to a local hospital and admitted to the psychiatric ward. After two weeks in the hospital, the treating team noted almost no improvement in Rita. She remained on suicidal precaution (being monitored closely for suicidal ideation), and she was sleeping poorly. The team decided to titrate her off the imi-pramine and began a course of nortriptyline (Pamelor), a different type of TCA, as soon as pos-sible. The team also introduced a low dosage of diazepam (Valium), an anxiolytic, to address her sleep and anxiety problems.

Rita was hospitalized for nine weeks, and the medication change and the milieu of in-patient therapies assisted her recovery. After discharge Rita remained on diazepam for an additional two months and on nortriptyline for an additional 15 months. She also began treatment with a skilled li-censed counselor who was very knowledgeable about psychopharmacology. Rita remained in therapy until two months after titrating off nortrip-tyline. Five years later she remained stable, with no recurrence of her major depressive episode with an attempted suicide.

Most of Rita's treatment was in the medical model realm through the introduction of TCAs. It was not uncommon during the 1970s, when Rita received treatment, for psychiatrists to try different TCAs with a patient who demonstrated little re-sponse with one type. Also, it was not uncommon to add an anxiolytic in conjunction with a TCA to address symptoms of anxiety and sleeplessness. It is clear from the case material that Rita's earlier at-tempts with psychotherapy, in the intrapsychic realm, were very unsuccessful and the therapists seemed naive to the importance of medication as-sessment because of Rita's chronic symptoms. We believe Rita's recovery after discharge resulted from careful interventions in both the medical model and intrapsychic perspectives.

# Selective Serotonin Reuptake Inhibitors: The Real Second-Generation Antidepressants

Although we noted that TCA derivatives were sometimes referred to as "second-generation" anti-depressants, the label more accurately belongs with the selective serotonin reuptake inhibitors (SSRIs) (Olver, Burrows, & Norman, 2001). We begin the story returning to some historical high points.

## A Bit More History

We noted in the beginning of this chapter that the amine theory was expanded to include the effects of serotonin on mood. This opened up a line of re-search looking at the effects on depression of drugs that made more serotonin available in the central nervous system. The first such agent (trazodone) had been released in 1981, but because of a rare but problematic side effect (priapism—prolonged and painful erection in males), it failed to gain widespread use. In the early 1970s, a research team at Eli Lilly (Byron Malloy, David Wong, & Ray Fuller) had synthesized an agent labeled LY86032. Healy (1997) notes that the team created the com-pound in a series of "moonlighting experiments" and finally decided it was an inhibitor of serotonin reuptake. Following their discovery, they conducted several meetings to explore uses for the new com-pound. Ironically, when someone first suggested that the drug be tested as an antidepressant, the re-sponse was that it would not likely be useful in treating depression and that there was not much of a market for antidepressants anyway (Coppen & Healy, 1996).

Because serotonin is widely distributed in the body, any agent that affects its action is likely to have numerous effects. Research teams initially de-cided that fluoxetine might be an antihypertensive agent, partially because in the 1970s the antihyper-tensive market was larger than the antidepressant market. In 1976, Marie Asburg and Lil Traskmann demonstrated that serotonin metabolites were sig-nificantly decreased in the cerebrospinal fluid of suicidally depressed people. This led to speculation about the role of serotonin in depression. Accord-ing to Healy (1997), this development and the ever expanding antidepressant market of the early 1980s led to clinical trials of fluoxetine as an antidepressant, and the first evidence to support this hypothesis became available in 1985. Fluoxetine (Prozac) was licensed in the United States in 1987. Several other compounds were made available at this time, including SmithKline and Beecham's paroxetine (Paxil). Paxil hit the U.S. market in 1993, delayed by SmithKline and Beecham's skepticism about the market. In an effort to distinguish its compound, SmithKline and Beecham created the category *selective serotonin reuptake inhibitor (SSRI)*, and the label "stuck" as the category in which all similar agents were grouped.

The SSRIs seemed to have treatment effects similar to those of TCAs without as many side effects. Interestingly, whereas TCAs are molecularly similar across compounds, SSRIs are remarkably different in chemical structure. SSRI effects across the range of 5-HT receptor systems also vary. Thus, whereas Schatzberg and Nemeroff (1998) noted that if patients don't respond to one TCA it is unlikely they will respond to another, the situation is quite different with SSRIs and physicians may try patients on several agents before finding one that provides optimal symptom relief.

As Kramer (1993) has noted, no drug in the history of psychiatry has received more positive and negative attention than Prozac. At the height of its popularity, sales of the drug topped $1.2 billion annually in the United States alone. This success, as has been the pattern, led to a plethora of SSRI agents being released in a short period of time. Stahl (2000) has concluded that there are five prominent compounds in the SSRI category. These compounds, and their general dosage range, are listed in Table 5.8 in addition to a sixth, newer compound (released after Stahl's conclusions were published).

### Mechanism of Action

As already noted, although SSRIs are classed together many clients may have very different reactions to the drugs. This is one reason we provide no charts on when certain clients should get particular drugs: There is no database of knowledge from which to create such a chart. Whereas fluoxetine (Prozac) may work for one client, another may respond only to citalopram (Celexa). A strictly medical model perspective offers no explanation for this,

**TABLE 5.8**  Examples of SSRI Antidepressants and Common Daily Dosage Ranges

| Generic Name | Brand Name | Common Daily Dosage Range |
|---|---|---|
| Citalopram | Celexa | 20–40 mg |
| Escitalopram oxalate | Lexapro | 10–20 mg |
| Fluoxetine | Prozac | 10–60 mg |
| Fluvoxamine | Luvox | 50–250 mg |
| Paroxetine | Paxil | 10–40 mg |
| Sertraline | Zoloft | 50–200 mg |

and although biological differences in client nervous systems may someday be found to underlie the phenomenon, we believe an Integral research approach to the problem may also yield useful hypotheses (Stahl, 2000). A great deal of research has been done on SSRIs, and many authors now note that although more data on the TCAs are available, the SSRIs are really the drugs of first choice for depression. This is due in large part to a less severe profile of side effects and the difficulty of overdosing on the drugs. As Stahl explained, taking a two-week supply of a TCA would be lethal to many clients, whereas SSRIs rarely cause death in overdose unless combined with other agents.

As the name *selective serotonin reuptake inhibitor* suggests, the primary mechanism of action is the inhibition of reuptake of serotonin back into the neuron. However, researchers have learned over the past decade that a great deal more is going on than this. Once taken, the drug inhibits the reuptake, so more serotonin molecules are near the cell body area. Whereas researchers used to think that the increase was immediate, in the synapses it appears that the increase is first felt near the dendrites on the cell body, and scientists currently believe this increase produces many of the side effects. Over time, the increase of serotonin in this area causes the autoreceptors to decrease in number (to downregulate) as well as to become desensitized. Researchers believe this information is communicated to the cell's nucleus, where the **genome** sends out instructions to cause these same receptors to become less sensitive over time. Note that this hypothesis regarding genetic expression still requires more research. In addition, from an Integral perspective, if medications do affect gene expression in a particular fashion researchers then need to investigate whether nonpharmalogic elements may also affect gene expression in the same manner. According to recent theories of gene expression, it appears experience plays as much of a role in gene expression as gene expression does in experience (Ridley, 2003)

Recall from Chapter Two that autoreceptors act as regulators and the more they are triggered, the more frequently they send an impulse into the neuron to decrease the release of whatever neurotransmitters that neuron produces and releases. By downregulating and becoming less sensitive, the cells less frequently send a signal into the cell to slow down release, and this results in increased release of serotonin from the cell. Scientists now believe that as well as downregulating, the postsynaptic neurons also desensitize over time in the same way as autoreceptors on the presynaptic neuron do. This is a *ripple effect*, or what Stahl calls a *cascade effect*, wherein SSRIs affect the brain.

### Common Side Effects

Another advantage to SSRI antidepressants is that, unlike TCAs, they have far fewer anticholinergic or antihistaminic side effects. The side effects listed in Table 5.9 are due almost exclusively to the selective serotonin reuptake inhibition. There are many serotonin receptor systems throughout the central and peripheral nervous systems, and SSRIs can significantly affect them. Also, as noted in Chapter Two, there are multiple serotonin receptor systems and different SSRI compounds have different effects across these families.

**TABLE 5.9**   Common SSRI Side Effects

| |
|---|
| Headache |
| Nausea |
| Nervousness |
| Diarrhea |
| Insomnia |
| Weight gain |
| Sexual dysfunction |

These side effects often decrease or cease after therapeutic effects take hold, with the exception of sexual dysfunction. As we stated earlier in the chapter, SSRIs have a variety of on-label and off-label uses. Currently, different SSRIs have on-label uses approved for Major Depressive Disorder, Dysthymia, Social Phobia, Post-Traumatic Stress Disorder, and Obsessive-Compulsive Disorder. Off-label uses have included Panic Disorder, Generalized Anxiety Disorder, chronic pain syndromes, Personality Disorders, Bulimia Nervosa, and insomnia.

### Antidepressant-Induced Sexual Dysfunction

A particularly troubling side effect for many people is antidepressant-induced sexual dysfunction (AISD). This has been a problem for many clients taking a wide range of antidepressants, and the earliest documentation of it dates back to the early 1960s (Healy, 1997). Initially researchers found it hard to determine how much of the problem was due to the drugs and how much to the depression, because decreased libido is one of the vegetative signs of depression. George Beaumont (1973), who published one of the first papers on the topic, noticed that clients treated with clomipramine (brand name Anafranil), a TCA with stronger effects on serotonin, had delayed orgasm. Beaumont learned that varying the client's dosage could somewhat control the problem. Also in the case of clomipramine, an orgasm rebound apparently could result when the drug was discontinued. Healy (1997) recounts the story of a nun who experienced three days of spontaneous orgasms when withdrawing from clomipramine.

With serotonin-related AISD, apparently the drug's stimulation of serotonin receptors in the spinal cord can inhibit the spinal reflexes, orgasm, and ejaculation (Stahl, 2000). Although early market research with SSRIs reported that approximately 4% of patients taking them would experience this side effect, Healy (1997) states that the number is now confirmed to be well over 50% and may be closer to 90%. There are multiple approaches to treating this side effect, and it is worth discussing, because this problem is often why clients stop taking the medication. From the intrapsychic perspective, it is important that counselors tune into clients' comfort in discussing sexual issues. Many clients are uncomfortable with the topic, and this seems to have contributed to under-reporting of the side effect when SSRIs were first released. It is above all important to communicate to clients that prescribing professionals can do many things to decrease or ameliorate this side effect, including switching the client to another medication, supplementing the SSRI with a second medication, or altering the dosage.

### Do Antidepressants Induce Dependence?

The simple answer to the politically delicate question "Do antidepressants induce dependence?" is yes. We are deliberately using the word "dependence" rather than "addiction," because colloquial overuse of the latter has attached a great deal of emotional baggage to it. This baggage has rendered it almost meaningless except when one wants to elicit strong emotional reactions from a reader. We prefer the construct of dependence, defined as a physical tolerance produced by repeated administration of a drug and a concomitant withdrawal syndrome (Stahl, 2000). Given this definition of dependence, we can state that SSRI antidepressants can induce dependence. As Julien (2001) stated, "If drug dependence is defined as a change in physiology or behavior following drug discontinuation, a person can become dependent on SSRIs" (pp. 435–436). Julien described a serotonin withdrawal syndrome that he estimated may occur in 60% of SSRI-treated patients after stopping the drug. The onset is usually within a few days and may last up to a month. Table 5.10 summarizes the symptoms of serotonin withdrawal.

**TABLE 5.10**  Symptoms of Serotonin Withdrawal

Lethargy

Fatigue

Gastrointestinal disturbance (nausea, vomiting, diarrhea)

Paresthesias (numbness or tingling in extremities)

Insomnia

Agitation/anxiety

Schatzberg, Cole, and DeBattista (1997) offered the first definition of what they called "serotonin reuptake inhibitor discontinuation syndrome." They noted that the syndrome typically consisted of physical and psychological symptoms. The physical symptoms include disequilibrium; gastrointestinal symptoms such as nausea, vomiting, and diarrhea; flulike symptoms including lethargy, fatigue, and chills; sensory disturbances such as paresthesia; and sleep disturbances such as insomnia. The psychological symptoms may include anxiety, agitation, and crying spells. One important distinction between dependence on SSRI antidepressants and dependence on a drug that, for example, induces a "high" or euphoria (such as heroin) is that it appears a person who has developed physiological dependence on an SSRI antidepressant does not experience a "craving" for the drug as does someone dependent on heroin (or other opioids). This is why there is little abuse potential for antidepressants and no real "street value" for the drugs.

Another type of dependence is psychological dependence. In this syndrome a person comes to believe he or she cannot function without a particular drug. In such cases we would say the person in question is psychologically dependent on the drug. Although there may not be physiological tolerance and withdrawal, psychological dependence can be every bit as difficult to deal with as physical dependence. Certainly a client could develop psychological dependence on SSRI antidepressants (or any medication, for that matter). Prescribing professionals and mental health professionals must help clients understand their relationship to the medication. It is important for clients to understand what the medication can do for them, and what they must do for themselves. In our opinion, the people least likely to develop psychological dependence on antidepressants are those who undergo counseling while they are taking the medication. In the counseling relationship, clients learn to differentiate their role from the role played by medications.

### SSRI Notes from the Intrapsychic Perspective

In the late 1980s and early 1990s a backlash arose against SSRIs in general and Prozac in particular. We briefly review this episode here, because questions about it still come up in dialogue with clients and because, at the time of this writing, there are some serious concerns about using SSRIs with children and adolescents. The concern at the center of the backlash was whether SSRIs and other antidepressants could in fact instill violent, suicidal behaviors in people. The Church of Scientology launched the attack against Prozac in 1989. Its main ammunition appeared to be a 1990 (February) *American Journal of Psychiatry* article (Teicher, Glod, & Cole, 1990) reporting that after two to seven weeks on Prozac, 6 patients became preoccupied with obsessive, violent suicidal thoughts. These patients had not been responsive to other drugs, but 4 of the 6 were also on other medications. Although this was a small sample of cases, the authors were concerned because, as they wrote, "None of these patients had ever experienced a similar state during treatment with any other psychotropic drug" (p. 207).

Because some links appear between serotonin and aggression, there was concern that Prozac might cultivate sociopathy. Scientologists cited the case of Joseph Wesbecker, who in 1989 attacked his coworkers with an assault rifle, killing 8, wounding 12, then killing himself. Scientologists blamed Prozac; however, the case history and witnesses indicate that he had a history of violent preoccupation before taking Prozac. In 1991 the FDA announced that Prozac and other antidepressants do not cause suicide or violent behavior and actually tend to reduce them. Researchers now estimate that less than 5% of clients on Prozac develop violent suicidal preoccupations, and these patients might have developed it even if not taking the drug. Although Scientology's claims about antidepressants (and psychotropic medications in general) are not all substantiated, it is interesting that in 2004 the FDA issued a public warning about possible connections between adolescent suicides and SSRI medication. Hearkening back to Ken Wilber's Integral maxim that "everyone is right about something but not everyone is equally right," Scientologists must be given credit for questioning some of the word magic from extreme proponents of the medical model perspective. The FDA has required that SSRI antidepressants come with a warning on the label (called a "black box warning," because the warning is situated in a black box on the label) that SSRIs can sometimes spur suicidal behavior in children and adolescents (Neergaard, 2004).

The concern about SSRI medication remains, and we discuss it further in Chapter Nine. More recently, one of the shooters at Columbine High School was noted to have been taking an SSRI at the time he participated in that attack. From the medical model perspective, the links between SSRI medication and aggression appear minimal but the relationship is still questioned in many areas of society and exists as a concern in the worldview of many clients. Counselors should be alert to these concerns and should place a priority on exploring them with clients when they come up. Currently the FDA is reclassifying and recategorizing the research to determine whether SSRI use is a causal factor for suicidal ideation in adolescents and children (Brown University Psychopharmacology Update, 2004). In addition, the attorney general of New York State is currently charging one SSRI manufacturer (SmithKline and Beecham) with fraud. According to the charges, the company withheld negative outcomes of studies on paroxetine (Paxil) in children and misrepresented data on prescribing the drug to children (Agovino, 2004).

## Cases Involving SSRI Medication

In the following two cases SSRI medication proved helpful, but not a panacea. We recommend an exercise with these cases. In both cases, assign elements of the case to the four perspectives of the Integral Model. This can increase your awareness of how medication can be a helpful, if only partial, component of treatment.

### The Case of Linda

Linda, a 39-year-old Latina, came to therapy after a painful and difficult divorce. She had three children, ages 6, 8, and 11. Her concerns were focused on family survival; she had great worries about the children and feelings of worthlessness. The process of divorce was very difficult, and there were many terrible moments with her ex-husband, some of which the children witnessed. Linda quickly established a therapeutic relationship and began to put her life back together. Around the time of what would have been her 14th wedding anniversary, Linda showed signs of slipping into a clinical depression. After discussing these symptoms and changes with her therapist, she agreed to consult a psychiatrist, who recommended a course of treatment using sertraline (Zoloft).

Linda reluctantly agreed and began taking the medication. Her therapist was aware of the necessity of Zoloft at this time for her and spoke to her in every session about its impact in her life. Linda experienced relatively few side effects, with some general nervousness at the beginning of treatment and a mild loss of sexual excitement, about which she talked in therapy. Linda's clinical symptoms lifted after four months and she was titrated off the Zoloft.

Linda worked with her therapist for 17 months and made several changes to improve her life and inner attitude. The combining of talk therapy with psychiatric medication was crucial to the success of the overall treatment. Her therapist recognized Linda's serious depressive signs, referred her to a psychiatrist, and continued to see her during this period. Without the medication Linda's condition would likely have deteriorated, with little hope for progress in therapy. The success of this treatment depended on a well-trained therapist who, recognizing the severity of Linda's depression, referred her for medical evaluation in a timely and appropriate manner.

## The Case of Jack

Jack, a 29-year-old single bisexual man, came to therapy ostensibly to sort out issues of great career ambivalence. Raised in a strict religious family, Jack lost his mother at age 20 and his father at 12. During his teenage years he was isolated, rebellious, and naive. He completed high school but never quite settled on college. After high school he had sustained heterosexual and homosexual relationships. He was brilliant, with an IQ over 155 and a great capacity to synthesize complex material. Recently he had ended a five-year homosexual relationship, had made peace with an older sister who supported him, and had applied and been accepted to a prestigious East Coast college to study philosophy.

As the treatment unfolded, very complex material and conflicts entered into the work with Jack. He suffered greatly from the losses of both parents and seemed unable to grieve for them and move on. He expressed a great deal of excitement for female companionship, yet remained constantly disappointed in these relationships. In the transference he was meek and dependent, challenging and demanding, and rebellious and attacking. He sought to find from therapy quick-fix solutions to his historical problems and current dilemmas. He loved to philosophize and gossip. During moments of his greatest anguish and chaos, he identified with the antigovernment types of Montana who felt totally trapped by the rules of living in a democracy. About a year into the treatment he became seriously depressed and was referred to a psychiatrist who, after an evaluation, prescribed paroxetine (Paxil). Jack took the medication as ordered for about six months, and he reported relief from many of his depressive symptoms.

Gradually he then became disenchanted with the Paxil. He said he had all but lost his sexual drive and desire and wondered if the medication was a method to modify or control his radical thinking about some of the absurdities of American culture. At first it seemed he was expressing symptoms of paranoia, but when therapy explored the meanings, it appeared his feelings and meanings were rooted in a genuine disagreement with much of the fabric of American life. He identified with groups and cultures that deeply questioned the rules and values of Western culture. Jack's experiences were particularly poignant because of the many hateful reactions he encountered from society when he lived openly with his partner. Some of his agony was rooted in life experiences that were discriminatory and threatening. Although the medication was temporarily helpful, it could not address issues and conflicts he experienced as a result of internal group identifications. Understanding these dilemmas in his life allowed exploration of many alternative options for his present and future life choices. He gradually came off the Paxil in consultation with his psychiatrist.

In this case we can see how a psychopharmacological intervention was helpful temporarily and that its limited effectiveness led to a deepened understanding of the client's struggles and therapeutic interventions. In this case we see the Paxil as a bridge to more critical unfolding of Jack's psychic and political life.

## Third-Generation Antidepressants

SSRIs constituted the second generation of antidepressants; there is now a third generation of antidepressants that includes drugs with diverse properties and that were chemically inspired by the development of the SSRIs (Olver, Burrows, & Norman, 2001). This category of drugs has a variety of actions that may include but are not confined to serotonin reuptake inhibition. Like the second-generation SSRIs, these drugs have better side effect profiles and more safety than MAO Inhibitors and TCAs. However, despite much initial speculation that they might be more effective than SSRIs, they seem, at most, to be only equally effective and subject to the same "pooping out" problems as SSRIs. The third-generation antidepressants include such drugs as bupropion (Wellbutrin), mirtazapine (Remeron), venlafaxine (Effexor), duloxetine, and reboxetine (Edronax). At the time of this writing, another third-generation antidepressant (nefazodone/Serzone) was taken off the market by manufacturer Bristol Myers Squibb because of rare but lethal side effects related to liver failure. Table 5.11 summarizes the current third-generation antidepressants.

**TABLE 5.11**   Current Third-Generation Antidepressants

| Generic Name | Brand Name | Common Daily Dosage Range |
| --- | --- | --- |
| Bupropion | Wellbutrin | 200–450 mg daily |
| Remeron | Mirtazapine | 15–45 mg daily |
| Venlafaxine | Effexor | 75–375 mg daily |
| Reboxetine | Edronax, Vestra | 4–8 mg daily |
| Duloxetine | Cymbalta | 40–60 mg daily |

### Bupropion: A Norepinephrine-Dopamine Reuptake Inhibitor

The mechanism of action for bupropion was unclear for some time. Although it at first seemed to have potent reuptake inhibition properties for NE and DA, the drug itself was actually a weak inhibitor of these reuptake processes. Researchers recently discovered that when taken into the body, the drug goes through an anabolic metabolism, which means that as the drug is metabolized, initially it becomes more potent. This is why psychopharmacologists sometimes call it a "prodrug," meaning a drug that acts like a precursor and then becomes activated through the body's metabolic processes. From the intrapsychic perspective, clients report that bupropion is somewhat stimulating and (from the medical model perspective) is not associated with AISD, which makes it an alternative for clients who are troubled by AISD. Interestingly, bupropion is marketed with two different brand names for two different purposes: Wellbutrin as an antidepressant and Zyban as a smoking cessation aid. Bupropion seems to decrease the craving sensations associated with nicotine withdrawal.

Bupropion is available in an extended-release (XR) formulation that requires two doses per day. The dosage range for bupropion is from 150 to 350 mg. daily. Side effects can include insomnia, gastrointestinal distress, and treatment-emergent hypertension. Bupropion has been shown to reduce the seizure threshold and is contraindicated for people who suffer from a seizure disorder, a head injury, or an eating disorder. Alcohol use is also contraindicated while taking bupropion, because it also lowers the seizure threshold.

### Mirtazapine: A Serotonin-Norepinephrine Antagonist

Mirtazapine (Remeron) is a drug that increases both serotonin and norepinephrine release by blocking the appropriate autoreceptors (in this case the alpha-2 autoreceptors on both the NE and 5-HT neurons). Recall from Chapter Two that autoreceptors help neurons regulate their output of whatever neurotransmitter the neurons happen to produce. Artificially blocking these with the mirtazapine molecule so they cannot be naturally stimulated to give the slow-down signal the neuron is "fooled" into increasing its release of neurotransmitter. This increase then theoretically causes the same ripple effect in the central nervous system that we summarized in discussing the molecular/cellular theory of depression. Stahl (2000) offers the analogy that this mechanism of action is like "cutting the brake cable" (p. 251) and thus increasing neurotransmitter release. Like all drugs, mirtazapine has side effects. It also blocks various serotonin and histamine receptors, resulting in sedation and weight gain. The typical dosage range for mirtazapine is 15 to 45 mg daily. It is also available in an orally dissolving "Soltab" formulation (Organon, 2003).

## Venlafaxine:
### A Serotonin-Norepinephrine Reuptake Inhibitor

Venlafaxine has earned the label "dual reuptake inhibitor," because it combines the SSRI mechanism of action with potent reuptake inhibition of norepinephrine. It is currently available in an extended-release formulation (XR) and can be taken once daily. Researchers consider this once-daily administration significantly reduces side effects. Stahl (2000) asks, "Are two antidepressant mechanisms better than one?" Because reality is complex, the answer is "It depends." For some clients who have not responded to more specific, single-action agents (such as SSRIs), additional mechanisms of action can result in enhanced efficacy. From an Integral perspective we must note that the question presupposes a clear medical model etiology to depression, and this hypothesis has not been confirmed. Common side effects associated with venlafaxine include gastrointestinal distress and insomnia. The common dosage range for venlafaxine is 75 to 300 mg per day.

## Reboxetine:
### A Selective Noradrenergic Reuptake Inhibitor

First recall from Chapter Two, that *noradrenaline* is synonymous with *norepinephrine* (the difference being that the latter term is derived from the Latin and the former from Greek). Thus reboxetine is a selective inhibitor of norepinephrine reuptake. You may think this sounds like a tricyclic antidepressant,

and that is correct. The difference is that reboxetine does not have the "dirty" quality of binding to histamine and acetylcholine receptors (which cause many of the side effects associated with the TCAs). As such, reboxetine may be useful for patients who respond better to NE reuptake inhibition or as a complement to SSRI therapy where response has been partial. The efficacy of reboxetine is equal to the TCAs and the SSRIs. Side effects may include tremor, agitation, and changes in heart rate and blood pressure. Stahl (2000) also describes a milder set of side effects, similar to TCA anticholinergic side effects (dry mouth, constipation, and urine retention). He noted that these effects are milder and shorter in duration, because they do not result from direct blockage of acetylcholine receptors. These effects are more a result of reboxetine's effects on the sympathetic and parasympathetic nervous systems, both of which are highly populated with norepinephrine receptors.

## Duloxetine: A Newer
### Serotonin-Norepinephrine Reuptake Inhibitor

At the time of this writing, duloxetine is an investigational serotonin-norepinephrine reuptake inhibitor (SNRI). Although it seems to have the same side effect profile as do SSRI medications, researchers hope it will have more rapid onset and be correlated with higher symptom remission rates than currently available antidepressants ("Duloxetine," 2001). Duloxetine is also being looked at for use in chronic pain syndromes. Although the initial results are promising, remember that initial results usually are. As Olver, Burrows, and Norman (2001) noted, pharmaceutical companies had similar hopes for the third-generation antidepressants. As mentioned earlier, these hopes were not actualized in long-term, systematic trials.

We end this section of the chapter with a few key points to communicate to clients about antidepressants. These are paraphrased from Julien (2001):

- Onset of clinical action may take from two to six weeks.
- Symptomatic improvement is usually most seen in physiological symptoms. Many other symptoms may respond only partially to the drugs.

- Although these medications may improve mood, they do not erase all sadness or one's ability to experience the full range of emotions.
- The best indication of medical response includes improved sleep, less daytime fatigue, and some improvement in emotional control, and mental clarity.
- There may be side effects, but these can often be managed by dosage adjustment, augmentation, or switching to another antidepressant.
- Length of treatment varies with the client. It takes four to eight weeks for symptoms to subside, and if you quit at this point the relapse rate can be as high as 80%. A general guideline is to continue for six months and then gradually decrease.
- SSRI antidepressants (and possibly other types) do induce a type of dependence. Although not dependence inducing, as is cocaine, they do induce a tolerance effect that can result in a withdrawal syndrome, which can be pronounced if clients do not appropriately go off the medication under their doctor's supervision.

## Case of Joshua

Joshua is 36-year-old African-American businessman who recently came to counseling because of many changes in his life, including sleeplessness, loss of energy, feelings of hopelessness, lack of concentration, and difficulties with his relationships at home and at work. After a three-session assessment, which included an evaluation of Joshua's thoughts and feelings, he reluctantly agreed to see a psychiatrist for an evaluation to determine his need for an antidepressant medication. The psychiatrist recommended that Joshua begin a course of treatment with Prozac (fluoxetine). A week later he began taking the Prozac while continuing weekly therapy with his counselor. Almost immediately Joshua complained of sleeplessness, irritability, and nervousness. His therapist encouraged him to give the Prozac time, at least three weeks, which he did. However, the side effects did not subside. In fact, Joshua reported that they worsened.

Throughout this period, Joshua continued to attend his weekly sessions to talk both about his depression and his reaction to the medication. Both the counselor and Joshua felt that their work together deepened. After four weeks on the Prozac, Joshua decided to talk over his problem with the psychiatrist. The counselor and Joshua prepared for this meeting, which went well, and as a result, Joshua was titrated off the Prozac. The psychiatrist prescribed a course of Effexor (venlafaxine), an SNRI for Joshua.

Joshua took the Effexor as prescribed, and after about 25 days on the medication reported to his counselor that he was feeling better. It is clear from the medical model perspective that the Prozac was not helping Joshua, and it was equally clear that Effexor began to alleviate some of his symptoms. What is more difficult to ascertain is the impact of the emerging counseling relationship and how Joshua's growing trust in his counselor also contributed to his psychological relief. Joshua continued the Effexor and the counseling for nine months and made almost a complete recovery. Although the technical aspects of this case are clear, it is most difficult to tease out the impact of the authentic counseling relationship on Joshua's movement back to health.

## Antidepressants in Older Clients

Depression in elderly people is thought to be under-reported (Satlin & Wasserman, 1997). Elderly people compose 12% of the population and account for approximately 20% of all suicides. Men account for 81% of suicides in those 65 and older. Risk factors for later life depression include female gender, unmarried status, stressful life events, lack of social support, and concurrent medical illness.

Satlin and Wasserman (1997) have noted that the literature is an imperfect guide to pharmacologic treatment of the elderly for several reasons.

- Published antidepressant trials use clients 55 to 65, whereas antidepressants are being prescribed for people considerably older.
- Participants in studies are atypical in that they are often free from medical illness. Although this makes it easier to see the relationship of the drug under study to the symptoms, it does not mirror

the reality that many older clients with depression have complicating medical conditions.

- Most studies include only those clients with moderate depression.
- Therapeutic response is measured only by the decline on depression scales, thus many people who showed "therapeutic response" have significant residual symptoms that continue to interfere with quality of life.
- With elderly clients it is important to screen for substance abuse, current nonpsychotropic medications, and general medical conditions. SSRIs are primary drugs of choice, starting at half-dose. Julien (2001) advises prescribers to start with a lower dose and titrate slowly. In addition, apparently bupropion and venlafaxine are promising treatments. Low doses of stimulant medication have also been used to improve mild dysphoric states (Satlin & Wasserman, 1997).

## Focus on Intrapsychic, Cultural, and Social Perspectives

In this section we return to exploring antidepressants through intrapsychic, cultural, and social perspectives—several issues concerning antidepressants that are rarely (if ever) mentioned in standard psychopharmacology texts. As we noted in the cases for this chapter, the various quadrants offer us important perspective on these issues.

### Intrapsychic Perspectives

What does it mean to someone to take an antidepressant? As with many things in life, the meaning varies from person to person. Researchers working from the medical model perspective have tried to determine whether a given depressive episode was biological or psychological in etiology (Stahl, 2000). From an Integral perspective, this does not go far enough, because in the intrapsychic realm alone many variations of psychological responses to stress or trauma can be delineated. John Teasdale (Teasdale, Segal, & Williams 1999; Teasdale et al., 2000) hypothesized that even if biological mechanisms in some people allowed sadness to slide into depression, these same people could learn to stop that series of events through intrapsychic, nonphar-macologic means. Using a variation of awareness meditation (described in Chapter Three) Teasdale was able to help clients disidentify from their thoughts to the point where they could preclude depressive episodes that likely would otherwise have followed periods of normal stress or sadness.

Another perspective regarding the variety of intrapsychic experiences of depression views the subjective experience of depression in relation to a client's level of development. Human development can progress far beyond the stage of having a healthy ego. Most people have the capacity for growth beyond the levels of healthy ego development (Alexander & Langer, 1990). This further development is referred to as "transpersonal," meaning "going beyond" or "including and transcending" the personal (Walsh & Vaughan, 1980). On the personal level of development, the subjective experience of depression is qualitatively different from that on the transpersonal level. Moving from personal to transpersonal frequently includes an existential component wherein the person feels a sense of meaninglessness and horror when confronted with the existential givens of the world (aging, illness, death, human cruelty). After passing such a developmental milestone, people who have stabilized ego functioning may experience the world without benefit of the filters the ego puts in place. This experience calls on such people to develop a deeper and broader philosophy or "big picture" in order to continue living and growing. Sometimes the spiritual personages considered saints in both Eastern and Western traditions report an experience called "dark night of the senses," which qualitatively resembles anhedonia (a loss of joy or pleasure in all things). The dark night of the senses is a period of desolation where one no longer finds joy in life. Rather, one confronts the stark pain inherent in human existence and seeks a way to deal with that pain. Far from being a chemical imbalance of the brain, such a state is frequently a prelude to a more expanded state of spiritual understanding. We realize that in a society that values materialistic explanations, it is hard enough to accept various psychological theories for things such as depression, let alone to consider a worldview that, for lack of a better term, is spiritual in nature. Yet an Integral exploration of any topic must be broad enough to include a place for such worldviews. With these worldviews come technologies such as meditation that have rich potential for treating symptoms such as those seen in depressed clients.

## Different Perspectives on the Placebo Problem

We discussed the placebo problem in the introduction to Part Two and return to it again in Chapter Nine when discussing the use of antidepressants for children. Placebo responses are common, according to researchers such as Fisher and Greenberg (1997) and practitioners such as Colbert (2002). These professionals begin by claiming that the evidence of efficacy of counseling and psychotherapy (from the intrapsychic perspective) is not given equal weight with the evidence supporting pharmacologic interventions (medical model perspective). They then note that although medical research on psychotropic medication is lavishly funded by the pharmaceutical companies, research on counseling and psychotherapy struggles, because it has far fewer resources. Finally, many have claimed that many research results from the medical model perspective that do not distinguish between placebo and drug never get published and are not as accessible to the public as the published studies that support the efficacy of the drugs over placebo.

For example, Khan and colleagues (2002) demonstrated that in over 50% of the trials on antidepressants in the FDA database, researchers found no significant difference between active placebo and the drug being tested. Many of these studies are never published in peer-reviewed journals, because they are less likely to be published than studies that showed significant differences between placebo and drug. Another scenario is that when pharmaceutical companies sponsor studies, they may include clauses that allow them to "hold" results for a period of time before releasing them back to the researchers, who may then try to publish them. Bodenheimer (2000) has documented cases where companies prevented important research findings from being published because the results were not favorable regarding the compound being tested.

From the cultural perspective, one question is how far the culture of the pharmaceutical industry may go in protecting its interests. Although more research needs to be done regarding client responses to placebos, it is unlikely the companies themselves would carry out such research. Government is more likely to fund it with tax dollars targeted for such research, but again, how will politicians who receive financial support from pharmaceutical companies view such research?

Pomerantz (2003) offers another perspective on antidepressants and placebo effects. Summarizing prescription trends, he notes that spending for antidepressants increased 600% during the 1990s and that in 2000 alone over $7 billion was spent on SSRI medications. He then cites studies from the United States and Italy suggesting that a significant percentage of clients stop taking the SSRIs after one or two months. He reminds us that off-label uses for SSRI antidepressants keep growing despite little evidence to support such uses. This practice includes using SSRIs for mild depression, for which SSRIs are no more effective than placebo in many studies. Pomerantz contends that in cases where SSRIs are being used off label, this use is akin to using them as active placebos. Because most clients feel *something* on beginning the medication, they assume something is working to help them, without realizing they are just feeling drug effects that may be unrelated to their problem. Because Streater and Moss (1997) have demonstrated that large numbers of patients are taking SSRIs for off-label uses, Pomerantz concludes this is simply very expensive (wastefully so) placebo therapy.

## Other Treatments for Depression

You can see that the systematic use of RCTs and the standardization of categorical psychiatry rely predominantly on the medical model perspective. Despite the dominance of the medical model perspective, many people seek out alternative and/or complementary treatments (herbs, and so forth), which we discuss more thoroughly in Chapter Ten. One battle in mental health treatment is between the proponents of the intrapsychic perspective, who point to successful psychosocial treatments for mood and anxiety disorders, and proponents of strictly adhering to the medical model perspective, which reduces mental disorders to biochemical entities ignoring their social, cultural, and personal meaning. More studies are now showing the efficacy of the psychosocial methods. Two studies have even documented through brain scans that the neurological changes attributed to antidepressants also occur with psychotherapy (Brody et al., 2001; Martin, Martin, Rai, Richardson, & Royall, 2001).

Nevertheless, U.S. trends show an increased number of people given medication for depression, a decreased number receiving counseling or psychotherapy, and a lowered percentage of treatment costs covered by insurance (Olfson, Marcus, Druss, Elinson, Tanielian, & Pincus, 2002). In addition to the standard psychosocial interventions, an increasing number of studies show that exercise is effective in alleviating symptoms of depression (Babyak et al., 2000; Leppamaki, Partonen, Hurme, Haukka, & Lonnqvist, 2002; Salmon, 2001), as are yoga postures and breathing exercises (Jorm, Christensen, Griffiths, & Rodgers, 2002; Ray et al., 2001). Continued research on these nonpharmacologic treatment options is important.

### When to Recommend Medication

For mental health therapists, all these considerations raise the question "When should I recommend a medication?" As the cases in this chapter illustrate, antidepressant medication ideally provides a chemical window of opportunity for clients to gather the energy for making changes through counseling and psychotherapy. When to recommend this "window of opportunity" depends primarily on client factors: in particular, the severity of the depression and the associated risks to the client (or others) such as suicidal thinking or failing to meet caregiving responsibilities. Ideally, the counselor can develop some alliance with the client and work through the question with him or her. Clients who resist the idea of medication can use this resistance to apply themselves to counseling. Clients at risk for harming themselves or others by omission or commission require a more aggressive intervention to stabilize them.

### The Culture of Pharmaceutical Companies: Are Newer Antidepressants Medical Innovations or "One-Trick Ponies"?

The issue of whether the newer antidepressants are just "one-trick ponies" relates directly to the culture of pharmaceutical companies and the legal-economic aspects of drug development in the United States. When pharmaceutical companies find a mechanism of action that seems effective, they focus research on finding as many permutations of that mechanism as possible. There are likely several reasons for doing so. Certainly one is that by fully exploiting the mechanism they may break through to advances that will help clients. The other reason may be less noble and more related to the amount of time and money it takes to really develop new compounds. Consider the FDA regulations we discussed in Chapter Four. There we noted that the FDA requires companies to show through randomized, double-blind, placebo-controlled studies that their medication treats the symptoms of some disorder. These regulations are objectively built into this society through the authority of the FDA and related laws passed by state and federal legislators. Given these structures, it costs millions of dollars just to begin the long journey toward FDA approval. This increases the probability that once a single company has cleared part of the path to FDA approval, other companies will follow in that wake.

Recall that the first company to break SSRIs into the market was Eli Lilly, with fluoxetine (Prozac), and that after this, numerous other companies spent a great deal of money putting similar and equally effective SSRI compounds on the market (fluvoxamine [Luvox], sertraline [Zoloft], paroxetine [Paxil], citalopram [Celexa], and so on). These compounds were similar but different enough to garner FDA approval and be able to compete in the marketplace. The National Institute for Health Care Management (NIHCM) (2002) reported that approximately two thirds of the medications the FDA approved in the 1990s were merely modified versions of existing drugs. Only 15% were for drugs containing new active ingredients.

Companies often seek to extend their patent rights over an existing compound either by bringing out a slightly different version of the compound or by seeking FDA approval for a new use for the existing compound. About a year before its patent ran out for fluoxetine (Prozac), Eli Lilly brought out fluoxetine under a new name (Sarafem) and received FDA approval for its use for Pre-Menstrual Dysphoric Disorder (PDD). This is curious, because the latter was technically not a *DSM* category at the time and only a condition for which further research was needed. It was also deemed by the writers of *DSM* one of the "not otherwise specified (NOS) conditions under Mood Disorders.

At the same time, rival companies are constantly seeking ways to bring out generic versions of compounds other companies have patented. For example, in 1998, Apotex Corporation filed for approval of a generic form of paroxetine (Paxil). Paroxetine was worth $2.1 billion in 2001, and the company with the patent rights (GlaxoSmithKline) sued Apotex for patent infringement. The suit was not yet settled at the time of this writing. Critics thus question whether enough energy is going into the study of new compounds or whether pharmaceutical companies are relying on "one-trick ponies" for guaranteed profits, and such ponies tend to pay off a great deal. So what begins as serendipity, the possibility that a drug may have other uses with varied disorders, becomes a corporate strategy to fully support a new diagnostic category without the necessary research.

These issues have been summarized as the Matthew effect (Merton, 1968) and the Luke effect (Healy, 1997). Both paraphrase quotations from the biblical texts bearing these proper names. Merton summarized the Matthew effect as "To him who has, more shall be given, and from him who has not, even more shall be taken away." He noted that the survival of ideas depends on how effective they are. In addition, Healy (1997) added that whose interests the ideas coincide with and the degree to which they have commercial application for brand name recognition also influence how much effort and energy is put into them. Thus SSRIs in general and the outdated theories about why they work (for example, the "chemical imbalance" theory) garner a great deal of support and name recognition, and any company with a similar compound can "jump on the bandwagon" for an increased probability of

success. Conversely, Healy noted that this effect may reduce the chance that different (and thus financially riskier) ideas will not get funded by pharmaceutical companies.

Based on this logic, Healy proposed the Luke effect, which followed the biblical parable that when a sower sows seed, some will fall on thorny ground and wither, some will fall on fertile ground and be choked by weeds, and some will fall on fertile ground and flourish. Thus the now outdated metaphor of "chemical imbalance" provides fertile ground on which to sow the seeds of compounds that work like others that correct this hypothetical "imbalance." Healy concludes, "This parable ends with an exhortation to those who have ears to listen, which I will argue is what drug companies do very successfully, as part of the business of bringing the development of their compounds to fruition" (p. 180).

We want to emphasize that we are not raising these issues to condemn pharmaceutical companies for seeking to make profits. Again from the social perspective, the principles of the free market and how those principles are implemented through laws are an integral part of our society. This does not mean, however, that they should evade inspection, commentary, and a system of checks and balances.

## Summary

Antidepressants have a huge presence in our culture, not all of which is well deserved. Although there are several theories of how antidepressants work from the medical model perspective, depressive symptoms are highly overdetermined and biological variables are only one group of many related to the development and resolution of depression. We noted in Chapter One that the Integral Model requires consideration of lines and levels of development. The current concern over the extent to which antidepressant medications may induce or exacerbate suicidal thinking in children and adolescents points to the importance of developmental studies on the effects of all psychotropic medications. Although antidepressants have efficacy in treating depression, research indicates that depressed clients also respond well to counseling or psychotherapy, exercise, and perhaps even activities such as yoga and meditation. Whereas antidepressants are an important component of treatment for some clients, mental health professionals will benefit from an Integral overview of depression and how the intrapsychic, cultural, and social perspectives can complement what antidepressants can offer.

## Study Questions and Exercises

1. Describe your understanding of the placebo effect and your sense of the current state of effectiveness of antidepressants (TCAs, MAOIs, and SSRIs).

2. Discuss vegetative symptoms and your understanding of how antidepressants work in general to relieve these symptoms. Demonstrate how the medical model theories in psychopharmacology build on one another.

3. Discuss the impact of Prozac (fluoxetine) on the antidepressant model, and in your response focus on its significance from the intrapsychic, cultural, and social perspectives.

4. After reading this chapter, summarize your thoughts about how you could talk to your clients about beginning a course of antidepressant treatment and about the potential side effects of the medication.

5. Some might say the era of antidepressants was an "incidental" outcome of scientific research that fueled a range of diagnostic categories (*DSM IV-TR*). Discuss.

6. Detail the strengths and limitations of TCAs, MAOIs, and SSRIs.

7. From the chapter, what is your understanding of a serotonin-norepinephrine reuptake inhibitor? Identify one, give an example of a type of client for whom it could be prescribed, and explain why.

8. Discuss some potential multicultural problems with using antidepressants as the only mode of treatment with certain populations.

9. Identify several problems encountered with prescribing antidepressants to children.

10. What is your understanding of an SSRI and SNRI? Identify an SNRI, and give an example of a type of client for whom it could be prescribed.

11. Discuss some cultural problems with using antidepressants as the only mode of treatment.

12. Describe some ways that an informed counselor can speak to a client about the effectiveness and uses of antidepressants when the client is uncertain about the course of action he or she wants to take.

13. Based on your knowledge after reading this chapter, would you take an antidepressant that was recommended to you? Why or why not?

CHAPTER SIX

# The Age of Anxiety

The multiple perspectives we have been using in this book are particularly useful in understanding the impact anxiety has on U.S. society. Anxiety disorders are believed to be the most common mental health problem in the United States (Danton & Antonuccio, 1997). Preston, O'Neal, and Talaga (2002) estimated that about 25% of all people in the United States will experience an anxiety disorder in their lifetime. Although psychotropic medications (medical model) are available for anxiety disorders, many psychological treatments (intrapsychic) also have excellent track records. Remember, from an Integral perspective it is not enough to describe anxiety symptoms, posit a biological explanation, then describe how certain drugs act biologically to (at least temporarily) decrease or eliminate these symptoms. Believing that biology is the only approach to anxiety is just more word magic.

We recall a client (Elijah) who lived in what could be described as a **"toxic environment."** Elijah's urban residence was the regular scene of violence, and he himself had witnessed two shootings in his 23 years. He was court-ordered to receive treatment for an alcohol-related charge (drunk and disorderly conduct). Even after abstaining from all drugs for 60 days, Elijah was what could only be described as "a nervous wreck." He showed symptoms of both Panic Disorder and Post-Traumatic Stress Disorder (the latter related to stimuli associated with the shootings he had witnessed). In consultation with a psychiatrist,

who prescribed SSRI medication, Elijah asked why he had his symptoms, and the doctor replied, "Some people have a genetic predisposition to such things." As Charlie Brown would say, "Good grief!" In this client's case, genetic predisposition not withstanding, there were clearly social and cultural contributors to his anxiety. His alcohol use was a classic example of self-medication. Although the SSRI medication provided a window of opportunity for Elijah, it was going to take far more than new and improved brain chemistry to alleviate his anxiety. Tragically, Elijah was stabbed in a fight at his residence, and although he recovered from that, he never re-entered treatment. As we have urged in previous chapters, mental health professionals must not lose sight of clients like Elijah nor surrender them to the partial truths of medical model explanations.

Although society has effective psychological interventions for anxiety, researchers estimate that only 30% of people suffering from an anxiety disorder seek treatment, although treatment is effective for 70 to 90% of those clients who seek it (Preston, O'Neal, & Talaga, 2002). Why is there so much anxiety in this population? It is not enough for mental health professionals to treat clients and refer them for psychiatric consultations. From an Integral perspective, we must wrestle with the question of why there are so many anxious people. Although moderate alcohol use can be perfectly appropriate, mental health professionals need to ask why there is so much abuse of alcohol in Western societies When reflecting on cases like Elijah's, the counselor must also remember that anxiety symptoms are just as prominent in people living in nontoxic environments. What are people so anxious about, and is medication really the best solution? Although mental health clinicians must know about medications that can provide relief for clients, they must also address these broader questions.

## Changes in Antianxiety Medication

Twenty years ago we would probably have titled this chapter "Central Nervous System (CNS) Depressants," because those were the primary compounds available for treating anxiety. Currently, psychotropic medications from numerous classes are used to treat anxiety symptoms, including CNS depressants, SSRI antidepressants, and unique compounds such as buspirone (BuSpar). In general, anxiolytics are the most commonly used psychotropic medications and nonpsychiatrists prescribe the vast majority (less than 20% are prescribed by psychiatrists). This situation required us to structure this chapter differently from the others in this book. Although we could structure Chapter Five around theories of antidepressant action, some history of antidepressants, and the compounds dedicated to treating depression, the great variety of medications for anxiety requires a different structure. For this chapter, we begin with a general discussion of anxiety, then describe anxiety from the medical model perspective, and then describe the different classes of drugs for anxiety. In discussing each class of drugs, we outline some of the drug's history; mechanisms of action; side effects; and potential for tolerance, dependence, and overdose. Finally we outline recommended pharmacologic approaches as well as other treatments for particular anxiety disorders. In Chapter Nine we discuss the treatment of anxiety in children and adolescents.

## The Construct of Anxiety

Anxiety, in and of itself, is natural and adaptive. A moderate amount of anxiety enhances physical and intellectual performance. This is reflected in what is called the Yerkes-Dodson law (Yerkes & Dodson, 1908). Simply stated, it means people all perform a little better when they are slightly anxious, but too much anxiety tends to impair performance and too little leaves them unmotivated to do their best (Barlow & Durand, 2002). You may have been initially anxious picking up this book. If you were moderately anxious, the anxiety likely helped you motivate yourself to get to this chapter. Readers who felt crippled with anxiety reading Chapter One probably didn't get this far.

Anxiety was instrumental in the birth of psychoanalysis and psychodynamic models of the mind. In *Inhibitions, Symptoms, and Anxiety* (1925), Freud unfolded his thinking about anxiety and its relationship to the structural model of the mind: id, ego, and superego. In this seminal work, he developed the notion of anxiety neurosis and identified two forms. The first was a sense of worry or dread that originated in a repressed wish or thought that generated conscious and unconscious conflict and was curable through the intrapsychic treatment he developed into psychoanalysis. The second was an overwhelming sense of *panic*, accompanied by autonomic nervous system arousal (sweating, increased heart rate, and diarrhea). This, he thought, resulted from a buildup of libido and required a sexual outlet. Freud viewed anxiety as a result of conflict between unconscious sexual or aggressive wishes in the id and the corresponding punishment (or threat of punishment) from the superego. Anxiety is thus seen as a signal of danger in the unconscious, which could then result in a dangerous behavior or in inhibition. In response to the signal, the ego mobilizes defense mechanisms to prevent unacceptable feelings from emerging into consciousness. If the signal fails, the anxiety just keeps getting more intense and becomes immobilizing.

As you can see from this summary, Freud actually differentiated panic from anxiety and would not be the last to do so. Anxiety is often differentiated from panic and fear. Anxiety is defined as a future-oriented, negative mood state characterized by bodily symptoms of physical tension and by apprehension about the future. A key feature of the apprehension is related to the sense that the person cannot control upcoming events (Barlow & Durand,

2002). Anxiety itself can be seen in the eleven Anxiety Disorders listed in the *DSM*, in several of the Personality Disorders (Histrionic, Dependent, and Obsessive-Compulsive), Delirium, Delusional Disorder, Major Depressive Disorder, Schizophrenia, and Substance Abuse Disorders. (This overlap highlights the importance of investigating comorbidity and doing adequate differential diagnosis.) Fear is an immediate alarm reaction to danger and is characterized by autonomic nervous system stimulation (for example, increased heart rate and respiration). The autonomic nervous system stimulation is thought to help the person escape the feared stimulus. Panic, in contrast, is an abrupt onset of intense fear, usually accompanied by physical symptoms such as heart palpitations, shortness of breath, and dizziness. Barlow and Durand (2002) described panic as a fear response when there is nothing (apparently) to be afraid of (in other words, a false alarm).

### The Case of Marcia

Marcia a 36-year-old female teacher, married with two adolescent teenagers, has struggled with mental and emotional issues for the past 11 years. She has been diagnosed with (not at the same time) Major Depressive Disorder, Dysthymic Disorder, Seasonal Affective Disorder, Avoidant Personality Disorder, and Personality Disorder Not Otherwise Specified (NOS). During the course of her treatment, Marcia was a very compliant patient. She always took her medications, mostly TCAs, and seldom missed therapy sessions. During the 11 years of her treatment, she had cognitive-behavioral therapy with a feminist female therapist, gestalt therapy with a male therapist, and holistic therapy with another female, and she tried various workshops and techniques such as art therapy. Almost always the intervention or theoretical approach was combined with a psychotropic medication. Marcia improved slightly, only to return to what appeared to be a depressed and irritable state.

In the 10th year, after much frustration, Marcia was referred to a psychoanalytically oriented psychotherapist who spent several sessions with her conducting an assessment. After this thorough and extensive evaluation period, he made the diagnosis of Generalized Anxiety Disorder (GAD) and began

to speak with her about the ways anxiety and panic manifested in her life. She seemed to talk about being incurably worried, exhausted, and never able to relax. Marcia existed in a state of agitation. They also discovered together that the closer Marcia got to a performance, a test in graduate school, giving a party, or being at a party, the more she panicked and fretted. The therapist referred her to a psychiatrist for assessment for medications and she prescribed Tranxene (clorazepate) for her anxious conditions. The combination of insight therapy and Tranxene was very beneficial. Marcia gradually decreased her irritability, learned more about the triggers and pressures on her life from inside herself, and appeared less depressed.

In the first session Marcia said three things that helped the therapist clarify his diagnosis: (1) "As I get closer to an obligation or performance, I begin to worry, ruminate, fret, and feel totally overwhelmed"; (2) "I fight these terrible battles within myself, should I do this or should I do that? How can I ever find a peace of mind?"; and (3) "Most of the time I disagree with my other doctors and therapists that I have depression, it always felt like something else, not depression." Thus from her own words and her various therapeutic journeys, it is evident that Marcia had a strong personal hunch that her previous diagnoses and treatments were not quite accurate. (We might say her intrapsychic intuition was working fine.) Marcia was most helped by a dynamic psychotherapy and a benzodiazepine, Tranxene. Although we have not delved into the social and cultural influences in Marcia's case, it illustrates a very common error in current diagnostic thinking, namely that many anxiety symptoms often get subsumed in a diagnosis of depression (as mentioned in Chapter Three). It is true that Marcia did get depressed and exhibited depressive symptoms, but her primary problem was anxiety, showing the importance of thorough diagnosis before any referral for medication.

## Theories of Anxiolytic Action From the Medical Model Perspective

As with depression, theories of anxiety rooted in the medical model hypothesize that some physiological process is deficient or impaired and that this deficiency or impairment results in a person having anxiety. Although some research supports this hypothesis, it is far from conclusive. As noted at the beginning of this chapter, there are more successful psychosocial (intrapsychic) interventions for anxiety than any other category of disorders. If anxiety were due solely to a physiological problem, why would psychological interventions be so successful? At the very least, the success of psychological interventions points to the mysterious mind–brain problem outlined in Chapter One. Even the most rigorous medical model theory of anxiety cannot dismiss the importance of the mind and of the type of knowledge available from the intrapsychic perspective.

## Anxiety, Brain Circuits, Brain Structures, and Neurotransmitters

In Chapter Two we described several brain structures and some of the neurotransmitters in the brain associated with the types of symptoms psychotropic medications are designed to treat. In this section we return to this topic to summarize the more popular medical model explanations of anxiety. A primary brain circuit associated with anxiety is called the *behavioral inhibition system (BIS)* (McNaughton & Gray, 2000). This circuit leads from the limbic system to the frontal cortex and is triggered from the brain stem. Recall from Chapter Two that in the limbic system meaning attaches to incoming stimuli and the frontal cortex processes executive functions. The circuit is triggered by things such as unexpected events that act as signals for danger; for example, abrupt changes in bodily functioning or visual stimuli. In abrupt changes in body functioning, the signals arise from the brain stem, and in changes in visual stimuli they descend from the cortex. Either way, BIS activation leads the person to freeze, experience anxiety, and evaluate the situation for danger (Barlow & Durand, 2002).

This brain circuit is hypothesized to underlie the type of anxiety seen in Generalized Anxiety Disorder and creates effects that differ from the "fight or flight" circuit. The fight-or-flight circuit originates in the brain stem (associated with vital body processes such as heart rate and respiration) and proceeds through several limbic system structures. Stimulating this circuit produces an "alarm and escape response" that researchers believe manifests as panic such as that seen in Panic Disorder. In the panic response, the limbic system, hypothalamus, and pituitary gland release a cascade of neurotransmitters and hormones that prepare the body for action.

## A Hypothesized Braking System

Preston, O'Neal, and Talaga (2002) note that the brain does have a "brake system" of sorts. This brake system consists of the ion channels on most neurotransmitters that allow negative ions (particularly chloride) to flow into the neuron to decrease its excitability (see Chapter Two). Researchers hypothesize that an as-yet-undiscovered endogenous benzodiazepine molecule binds with receptors to allow this influx of chloride ions. The hypothesis basically states that a deficiency of this yet-to-be-discovered substance causes anxiety disorders. Like the amine theory of antidepressant action, this hypothesis is a convenient extrapolation from the minimal data available on these brain circuits but is hardly convincing when you consider all the environmental and intrapsychic factors that can also trigger anxiety.

Much research on anxiety and brain structures points to action in the amygdala. Recall from Chapter Two that the amygdala is the almond-shaped structure in the limbic system that helps attach emotional meaning to incoming stimuli. Julien (2001) has summarized research showing that electrical lesions of the amygdala result in an anxiolytic effect as well as research documenting amygdala abnormalities in patients with Panic Disorder. The latter two examples have a "chicken-and-egg" problem. Saunders, Morzorati, and Shekhar (1995) showed that chronically blocking GABA receptors in rat amygdalas produced anxiety responses. Recall from Chapter Two that GABA is a neurotransmitter that tends to function in the brain to calm the organism. As noted, although this research certainly supports the hypothesis that the amygdala plays a role in anxiety symptoms, it does not confirm that defects in the amygdala cause anxiety symptoms.

## Neurotransmitters Involved in Anxiety

GABA has clearly been indicated as playing a role in relief from anxiety in that facilitation of GABA binding is one mechanism that decreases anxiety.

Less well understood are the roles of serotonin and norepinephrine. Currently some medications prescribed for anxiety target either serotonin (for example, SSRI antidepressants) and/or norepinephrine. Perhaps it is easier to understand how norepinephrine is involved in anxiety, because the fight-or-flight circuit includes large releases of norepinephrine via the locus coeruleus. Recall from Chapter Two that the locus coeruleus ("blue disk") is a small brain structure whose neurons project to most other norepinephrine neurons in the brain. This structure can trigger the release of norepinephrine, stimulating the sympathetic nervous system, resulting in tachycardia, tremor, sweating, and anxiety. One medication (Catapres/clonidine) paradoxically treats such stimulation by releasing norepinephrine in a way that triggers surrounding autoreceptors. Recall from the discussion of mechanisms of action in Chapter Two that triggering autoreceptors decreases production of whatever neurotransmitter is produced in the triggered neuron. In this case, the clonidine-induced release of norepinephrine actually decreases **noradrenergic** activity. Although this medication successfully reduces physiological symptoms associated with noradrenergic overactivity, it does not relieve the intrapsychic aspects of anxiety.

Another neurotransmitter implicated in anxiety is serotonin. Although its role is still unclear, apparently several serotonin agonists are helpful with anxiety. For the nonmedical therapist, a perplexing aspect of pharmacologic interventions is the use of antidepressants to treat anxiety disorders. As with antidepressant agents, researchers still do not have clear evidence as to whether anxiolytic agents are targeting specific brain sites to exert symptom relief or (as Breggin, 1997, puts it) whether anxiolytics are just one of any number of agents that temporarily disable the brain.

In the last 10 years researchers have made numerous advances in conceptualizing and treating anxiety disorders. Some may argue that the anxiety disorders are so heterogeneous that it is not accurate to include them all under one category, and there is much to support this assertion. Nevertheless, we treat all the known anxiolytics in this chapter. We start by reviewing the medical model perspective of central nervous system depressants. At the end of the chapter, to help organize the material on anxiolytics, we review pharmacologic treatment strategies by diagnosis.

## Central Nervous System Depressants: The Medical Model Perspective

Central nervous system (CNS) depressants are a group of medications with diverse chemical structures that all induce behavioral depression. They produce many effects ranging from relief from anxiety and inhibitions, to inducing relaxation and sleep, to inducing unconsciousness, general anesthesia, and (in overdose) coma and death. The predominant tendency of all these drugs is to inhibit the excitability of neurons.

Unfortunately, several terms are used to refer to CNS depressants, including *sedatives, tranquilizers, hypnotics,* and *anxiolytics.* In the first half of the 20th century, anxiety was not a common construct and most patients were medicated with sedatives for their "nerves." These sedatives were usually **bromides** or barbiturates combined with everything from cannabis to digitalis. With refined diagnostic criteria, counselors would now say that many of these cases of "nerves" were actually depression and would be more likely to treat them with compounds described in Chapter Five (Healy, 2002).

The inducement of sleep is referred to as a "hypnotic effect." This is inaccurate, because sleep induction is actually very different from what happens in hypnosis, but the term was coined at a time when people believed hypnosis induced a sleeplike trance. **Anxiolytics** are drugs used for treating anxiety. We prefer the term *anxiolytic* throughout this book. The inaccurate phrase "minor tranquilizers" is often used for anxiolytics but indicates only that these drugs treat milder symptoms than those treated by drugs labeled "major tranquilizers." As you will see in Chapter Seven, the phrase "major tranquilizer" is also sometimes misapplied to certain types of antipsychotic medication. So many poorly chosen words! At this point the reader may conclude that the field of psychopharmacology could benefit from the services of a grammarian. Although we want readers to be familiar with all these terms, we encourage the use of the more accurate terms "anxiolytics" and "hypnotics." Next we discuss the CNS depressants that are currently (or historically have been) used to treat anxiety.

## Barbiturates

The first barbiturates were created in the late 19th century and introduced to the United States in 1912, the first being phenobarbital. According to Julien (2001) between 1912 and 1950, hundreds of barbiturates were tested and at least 50 were marketed. Although these medications are rarely used for anxiety now, they dominated the antianxiety market until about 1960, when their dangers and drawbacks became widely known. We discuss barbiturates in this book not so much because they are often used but because their undesirable qualities set the baseline for desirable qualities researchers wanted in the anxiolytic drugs they were trying to develop and that currently dominate the market. As Stahl (2000) points out, barbiturates do not really have a specific anxiolytic effect but merely reduce anxiety as a side effect of their overall sedating effects, much like drinking too much whisky might.

The name "barbiturate" is said to have been chosen *either* because the urine of a girl named Barbara was used to derive the compound *or* because it was synthesized on St. Barbara's Day (Snyder, 1996). For the curious minded, Saint Barbara's Day is December 4 and she is the patroness of miners (and perhaps barbiturate users, for all we know). She was martyred in C.E. 235 or 238. As far as using urine to synthesize compounds, the curious minded might also wonder what that is about. The answer is, as mentioned earlier, that drug companies examine the urine of subjects taking medications, to check for active metabolites of the drug. These active metabolites then provide the blueprint for synthesizing the compound or similar compounds.

Barbiturates have rapidly become the dinosaurs of drugs. As anxiolytics, they have been displaced by benzodiazapines. The effects of barbiturates are quite similar to those of alcohol, and their main advantage is that they are cheap because their patents have expired. Barbiturates differ from each other primarily in terms of how quickly they act and in

the intensity and duration of their action. The differences in these properties are the main consideration in deciding which barbiturate to use. Current clinical uses include treatment of epileptic seizures, alleviation of migraine headaches, and use as a component of anesthesia. They once were used more for insomnia but can dangerously induce sedation to the point where a drugged person may not hear a smoke alarm or similar sounds. They also disrupt REM sleep, and discontinuing the barbiturate results in **REM rebound**, a period of fitful sleep characterized by a rapid, dense sequence of dream images.

### Mechanisms of Action

The mechanisms of action of barbiturates have never been clearly understood, and, as Julien (2001) notes, they are complex and controversial. Their dangers had already resulted in decreased use by the time the technology was available to more fully understand how they acted on the nervous system. Researchers once believed barbiturates caused a general decrease in neuron excitability throughout the nervous system. They believed the dominant action was to hyperpolarize many types of neurons (recall from Chapter Two that "to hyperpolarize" means to increase the probability that a neuron will *not* fire). As with reality, the truth appears more complex than that. In Chapter Two we wrote that glutamate tends to be a generally excitatory neurotransmitter and that GABA is generally an inhibitory neurotransmitter. Some evidence indicates that barbiturates may act as glutamate antagonists (Zhu, Cottrell, & Kass, 1997), although other research indicates they also act as GABA agonists (Tomlin et al., 1999). Barbiturates seem to bind to GABA receptors, facilitating their binding of GABA.

Also recall from Chapter Two that when a drug allows an influx of negatively charged ions into the neurons, it hyperpolarizes the neurons, decreasing the probability that they will fire. In addition to facilitating the binding of GABA, barbiturates also allow the influx of chloride, a negatively charged ion, into the neurons. This effect accounts for the increased toxicity of barbiturates compared to benzodiazepines (Julien, 2001). Table 6.1 summarizes

**TABLE 6.1**   Hypothesized Mechanisms of Action in Barbiturate Medications

| Action | Result |
| --- | --- |
| First-messenger binding | Facilitates the actions of to GABA receptors GABA (acts as a GABA agonist) at those receptor sites, decreasing neuronal activity |
| Antagonism of glutamate | Decreases neuronal activity |
| Facilitation of chloride conductance into neurons | Further hyperpolarizes neurons |

**TABLE 6.2**   Examples of Barbiturate Drugs, Their Duration of Effect, and Common Uses

| Name | Duration of Effect | Common Uses |
| --- | --- | --- |
| Thiopental | 15 minutes | Anesthetic |
| Secobarbital | 30 minutes | Hypnotic |
| Pentobarbital | 4 hours | Hypnotic |
| Phenobarbital | 6 hours | Anticonvulsant |

these hypothesized mechanisms of action in barbiturates. You can imagine that combining all these mechanisms of action would have a potent inhibiting effect on the nervous system.

The neurons in the reticular activating system are particularly sensitive to barbiturate drugs. The reticular activating system is involved in sleep, and this is one reason why barbiturates have a hypnotic effect. In addition, sites of action include the cerebellar **pyramidal cells** (involved in fine movement), the substantia nigra (motor skills), and the thalamus (processing sensory information). Barbiturate action on these brain structures results in loss of coordination (ataxia), which increases with dosage. In terms of pharmacokinetics, barbiturates are rapidly absorbed and distributed to most body tissues. The ultra–short-acting barbiturates are lipid soluble, cross the blood–brain barrier quickly, and can induce sleep in seconds. As noted, barbiturates differ in their length of action. Table 6.2 lists commonly used barbiturates, duration of effect, and common uses.

### Common Side Effects

Common side effects for barbiturates include behavioral depression, sleepiness and particularly disruption of REM sleep, motor and cognitive inhibition similar to those seen with alcohol, ataxia (loss of muscle coordination), and respiratory depression. Barbiturates are contraindicated in people with severe respiratory disease or liver impairment,

or who are concomitantly using other CNS depressants. They are clearly contraindicated for people who may be experiencing suicidal ideation, because the drugs are so easy to overdose on.

### Tolerance and Dependence

Barbiturates can induce both physical and psychological tolerance and dependence. Physical tolerance occurs via metabolic and cellular mechanisms (discussed in Chapter Two). Metabolic tolerance is caused by an increase in the enzymes that metabolize barbiturates, resulting in a need for higher and higher doses. Cellular tolerance is the condition of the neurons adapting to the presence of the drug. Physical dependence is usually manifested by sleep difficulties when withdrawing from barbiturates, but withdrawal from high doses may also be accompanied by hallucinations and lethal convulsions (Julien, 2001). The psychological dependence results from the anxiolytic action. Depending on the individual and on the set and setting of barbiturate administration, some people may experience a euphoric response that is also linked to psychological dependence. The phrase "set and setting" refers to the mind set of the person taking the drug and the physical place and context (setting) where the person is taking a drug.

### Barbiturates and Overdose

Researchers estimate that barbiturates have been involved in nearly one third of drug-related deaths, including the deaths of several celebrities (Boston University Medical Center, 2002). Actresses Rachel Roberts and Carol Landis both committed suicide with barbiturates, and actresses Judy Garland and Marilyn Monroe are said to have died of barbiturate overdoses (although signs of overdose were conspicuously lacking in Monroe's case). Although many of these deaths appear to be intentional suicides, others are accidental or possibly murders. The effects of barbiturates can be so disorienting that a person may take one dose and then a second or third, having forgotten the previous doses. The toxicity of barbiturates is also apparent in their approval as euthanasia agents for lab animals. Partly in response to the toxicity of barbiturates and to their multiple uses, pharmaceutical companies in the early to mid 20th century began to seek out nonbarbiturate alternatives with all the efficacy of barbiturates but without their toxicity and dangers.

### The Case of Francis

In the late 1990s, Francis, a 42-year-old unmarried stock broker working in a high-powered investment firm, found himself increasingly tense, edgy, and agitated, which he expressed in an aggressive temper with coworkers and friends. He remembered that his father in his 40s had taken some sort of "-barbital" to help him calm down. He called his father, who even in his late 70s was very sharp. His father remembered that he had taken pentobarbital and it was very helpful in low doses. He even remembered the physician who had prescribed the medication and encouraged Francis to give him a call, because he was a friend and still in practice. Francis did, and the doctor, simply basing his decision on how helpful pentobarbital had been for his father, prescribed it for Francis. Francis did not seek assistance from therapy or a psychiatrist.

Francis began to use the sedative medication and found it very helpful. In fact, as time went on, he felt he needed more and more to get into the same calm and soothing state. He slept longer and deeper, but found waking up very difficult. Even though his physician warned him, Francis continued to need an ever greater supply of pentobarbital. Colleagues and friends began to worry about Francis's unpredictable behavior, his barbiturate-induced stupors, and his impaired decision-making skills. Francis continued to deteriorate until one day he didn't come to work, nor did he call. One of his worried colleagues went to his home and found him in a deep sleep. He noticed the bottle of pen-

tobarbital and immediately called for help from an EMT (emergency medical technician). Francis was taken to a nearby emergency clinic, revived and treated, and released with a referral to a psychiatrist who specialized in anxiety disorders. He never followed up.

We have not yet addressed an intrapsychic factor crucial to this case: Sometimes adult children who have overidentified with their parents seek out treatments that were helpful to their parents, even if those treatments are outdated. Francis kept himself outside the appropriate treatment nucleus and found treatment for his anxiety in exactly the same manner that his father had 20 years earlier—and it was not effective.

### Nonbarbiturate Alternatives: Mother's Little Helpers

The subtitle of this section, "Mother's Little Helpers," refers to the Rolling Stones song of the same name that is said to have referred to some of the drugs described next. Nonbarbiturate alternatives are extremely similar to barbiturates in everything except molecular structure. Although each one was initially marketed with great fanfare as a safe alternative to barbiturates, most were equally dangerous and many were subsequently withdrawn from the market. The important result of research on nonbarbiturate alternatives is that it led to discovering the benzodiazepines, which we discuss shortly.

### *Meprobamate*

In 1945 Czechoslovakian pharmacologist Frank Berger was attempting to develop antibacterial agents. In his research he stumbled onto a sedating compound that seemed to act like a barbiturate but did not induce sleep as readily. He noted it seemed to induce "tranquilization" without necessarily inducing sleep, and that term was used in marketing the new compound, to present it as different from barbiturates. The compound was marketed as *meprobamate* in 1955 (Berger, 1970). Its primary success was that while reducing anxiety, it allowed people to remain awake. Like barbiturates, meprobamate produced daytime sedation, relief from anxiety, and sometimes euphoria. Although not as toxic in overdose as barbiturates, meprobamate seemed to induce tolerance and dependence to the same degree and appeared more teratogenic than barbiturates (Julien, 2001). Meprobamate is still prescribed under the trade names Equanil and Miltown.

### The Quaalude Years

Glutethimide (Doriden) was introduced in 1954, and methaqualone (Quaalude) in 1965. Both were hailed as nonbarbiturate alternatives but experience showed otherwise. In the 1970s and 1980s Quaalude rivaled marijuana and alcohol in level of abuse in the United States. By 1972 the practice of mixing Quaalude with wine ("luding out") was widespread across college campuses. Far from being nonbarbiturate alternatives, Doriden and Quaalude induced tolerance and dependence syndromes, and Quaalude overdose proved even harder to treat than barbiturate overdose. Quaalude was linked to numerous deaths, so it was banned from the U.S. market in 1984. When taken off the market, Quaalude was placed on federal drug Schedule I. Doriden was placed on Schedule II because of overdose deaths. As noted in Chapter Four, the federal drug schedules are really a listing on five levels of drugs considered least to most dangerous. Schedule I is for drugs that are illicit and supposedly have no medical uses although, as you will see in Chapter Ten, this classification is debatable. As with barbiturates, euphoria associated with Quaalude seemed dependent on the set and setting of the drug user.

### The Case of John

John, a 36-year-old waiter, ex-con, and entrepreneur, was a product of the late 1960s and early 1970s. He believed one should be mellow at all times and should not become stressed under any circumstances. He was in a methadone treatment program to overcome his long-standing addiction to heroin. With the pressures of new marriage and a child, John felt he was becoming tense, agitated, and anxious. He visited his primary care doctor and told him about everything except the methadone treatment. After a brief assessment, the doctor prescribed Quaalude (methaqualone) for John. The year was 1979, and given this drug's street reputation John was pleased. He called it his "cool-down script." Soon it seemed to others that the "ludes" became John's substitute for his heroin addiction. He became a quasi-dealer for Quaalude and eventually became dependent on it. He deteriorated gradually but eventually lost his job and family as a result of his Quaalude abuse/dependence. Fortunately, John had the inner resilience to request in-patient treatment and follow-up therapy to address his serious dependence.

Although scenarios such as John's are not common today, clinicians recognize that in the history of developing pharmaceuticals for mental and emotional disorders some drugs, if abused, are very dangerous.

## Benzodiazepines

Benzodiazepines are the prototypic anxiolytic medications. Over the past 40 years barbiturates were replaced by benzodiazepines, which are less dependence inducing and have less abuse potential. Benzodiazapines are still the leading treatment for anxiety (Stahl, 2002) and currently account for 90% of the anxiolytic market.

### Some Anxiolytic History

Ever since Frank Berger had synthesized meprobamate, researchers had tried numerous combinations of muscle relaxers and sedatives to come up with an anxiolytic drug that would not totally sedate a person but would decrease anxiety significantly. Following up on research begun by Berger, Leo Sternbach, a Polish chemist working for Roche Drug Company in New Jersey, first synthesized chlordiazepoxide (Librium) and diazepam (Valium). In trying to learn how meprobamate acted at a molecular level, Sternbach and his colleague Earl Reeder were synthesizing chemicals called *quinazolines* and screening them for anti-anxiety properties. He screened 19 out of 20 compounds with no success, and moved on.

As the story goes (Snyder, 1996), a year and a half later, while cleaning his lab, he found the 20th compound and decided to have it screened. It turned out quite active. The final steps of its synthesis completely altered its chemical properties from a quinazoline to what we now call a *benzodi-*

*azepine*. The first benzodiazepine (chlordiazepoxide) was patented in 1959 and marketed as Librium in 1960. Research continued, and diazepam (Valium) was released in 1963. Currently over 40 benzodiazepines are on the market, and research for nonbenzodiazepine alternatives continues (Ballenger, 1995).

In time researchers concluded that benzodiazepines were effective in reducing anxiety-related symptoms in 70 to 80% of people. This result must be considered in light of the fact that the symptoms vary considerably across time and go into remission with a placebo in 25 to 30% of clients. Benzodiazepines also serve as sedatives, muscle relaxants, intravenous anesthetics, and anticonvulsants.

### Varieties of Benzodiazepine Compounds

The three families or subclasses of benzodiazepines vary in potency, duration of action, and amount of time they take to clear out of the body. The older compounds rely more heavily on the liver for metabolism. The more drug metabolism relies on the liver, the more the drug induces moderate metabolic tolerance. The names of the three families of benzodiazepines are related to their chemical properties. Table 6.3 summarizes the benzodiazepines and their mean elimination half-lives.

#### 2-Keto Compounds

Of the three types, 2-keto benzodiazepines are the oldest and most lipophilicitous. These compounds are oxidized primarily in the liver, a relatively slow process. As a result, these benzodiazepine compounds have the longest elimination half-lives (up to 60 hours). Many have multiple active metabolites, so it takes the body longer to clear them out of the system. An example of a 2-keto compound is diazepam (Valium). Diazepam (like many 2-keto compounds) is a prodrug, meaning (as noted earlier) it actually enters the body relatively inactive and becomes active as the body begins to metabolize it. The initial compound (diazepam) acts as a precursor for methyldiazepam, which is further metabolized to oxazepam. The 2-keto compounds are more likely to induce tolerance and dependence because of their potency. Because people taking these compounds still have active metabo-

**TABLE 6.3** Examples of Benzodiazepines

| Brand Name | Type | Generic Name | Mean Half-Life (in hours) |
|---|---|---|---|
| Dalmane | 2-keto | Flurazepam | 80 |
| Centrax | 2-keto | Prazepam | 60 |
| Tranxene | 2-keto | Clorazepate | 60 |
| Librium | 2-keto | Chlordiazepoxide | 60 |
| Paxipam | 2-keto | Halazepam | 60 |
| Valium | 2-keto | Diazepam | 24 |
| Klonopin | 2-keto | Clonazepam | 30 |
| ProSom | 3-hydroxy | Estazolam | 18 |
| Ativan | 3-hydroxy | Lorazepam | 15 |
| Restoril | 3-hydroxy | Temazepam | 12 |
| Xanax | Triazolo | Alprazolam | 12 |
| Serax | 3-hydroxy | Oxazepam | 8 |

lites in their urine, pharmaceutical companies found they could synthesize less potent compounds that would clear more quickly and still produce the desired anxiolytic effects.

#### 3-Hydroxy Compounds

The 3-hydroxy compounds are also metabolized through the liver, as well as through direct joining with endogenous compounds, which brings about more rapid oxidation (negative charging and water solubility) and thus a shorter half-life (10 to 15 hours). Examples of 3-hydroxy compound benzodiazepines include oxazepam (Serax), lorazepam (Ativan), and temazepam (Restoril). Although less likely to induce tolerance and dependence than the 2-keto compounds, these medications still possess these drawbacks and should not be used for long-term treatment of symptoms.

#### Triazolo Compounds

The triazolo benzodiazepine compounds are very similar to the 3-hydroxy compounds. They are more quickly oxidized, rely less on the liver to metabolize, and leave fewer active metabolites in the system than do the hydroxy compounds. They also have short half-lives (15 hours). An example of a triazolo compound is alprazolam (Xanax). The triazolo compounds are the most frequently prescribed for anxiety (Ballenger, 1995).

### Pharmacokinetics

All classes of benzodiazepines are well absorbed. The majority of shorter-acting benzodiazepines have no active metabolites and thus are excreted more quickly. The rest are metabolized first into active metabolites and then are further metabolized, taking longer to excrete from the body.

### Mechanisms of Action

Research continues to shed new light on mechanisms of action (summarized in Table 6.4) in the benzodiazapines. First and foremost, benzodiazepines (like barbiturates) facilitate the binding of GABA. Also like barbiturates, benzodiazepines facilitate conductance increases in chloride (a negative ion), which inhibits synaptic action. Like barbiturates, the benzodiazepine molecules actually bind on GABA receptors and facilitate the binding of GABA. Since the 1970s, research has been building to support the hypothesis that the brain actually has a naturally occurring benzodiazepine receptor, which has led to speculation that the brain produces its own natural benzodiazepine-like substance, although this has yet to be confirmed. Currently some researchers speculate that benzodiazepines may also block stress-induced increases in norepinephrine, serotonin, and dopamine as well as other neurotransmitters that have GABA receptors.

**TABLE 6.4**   Mechanisms of Action of Benzodiazepines

---

Facilitate the binding of GABA through binding at a benzodiazepine receptor

Facilitate the flow of chloride into the neuron to decrease its excitability

Block stress-induced increases in NE, 5-HT, and DA

---

### Side Effects

The side effects of benzodiazepines are dose related and are extensions of their therapeutic effects. The side effects include sedation, lethargy, ataxia, motor and cognitive impairments, slurred speech, and amnesia (depending on the benzodiazepine used). Side effects may also include respiratory suppression, depression, and in some cases a paradoxical excitation/agitation (Pies, 1998). Note that unlike barbiturates, benzodiazepines do not appear to significantly disrupt REM sleep. Although they may disrupt deeper, delta-wave sleep, these effects are experienced as less troublesome than disruption of REM sleep.

### Tolerance and Dependence

Benzodiazepines can induce physical tolerance and both psychological and physical dependence. Although the benzodiazepines do not induce as much metabolic tolerance as barbiturates, they do increase production of hepatic drug-metabolizing enzymes. They also cause cellular tolerance in the form of downregulation or decreased sensitivity of the receptors. Patterns of dependence can develop even at therapeutic dosages if continued over a long-enough period of time. If benzodiazepines are taken short term or infrequently (for example, p.r.n., for Latin *pro re nata*, "as circumstances require"), clients generally do not develop tolerance to the therapeutic effects of the medications. As we mentioned, although a great deal of hysteria surrounds the abuse of drugs with reinforcing properties, only a minority of clients on benzodiazepines abuse them (Julien, 2001). When tolerance and dependence do occur, early withdrawal signs include insomnia, restlessness, and irritability, and the return of the anxiety for which the medication was being taken in the first place. The compounds with the highest affinity for receptors and the longest half-lives are more likely to induce tolerance and dependence. Most people taking benzodiazepines as prescribed do not develop tolerance but still experience the anxiolytic effects. Also note that any dependence that occurs is not associated with the types of craving experienced by people withdrawing from drugs such as cocaine or heroin. If rebound anxiety is experienced during a benzodiazepine withdrawal, it is transient and usually lasts 48 to 72 hours (Perry, Alexander, & Liskow, 1997).

## Overdose Potential

Although the overdose potential of benzodiazepines is less than that of barbiturates, they are still toxic in overdose. Perry, Alexander, and Liskow (1997) report that doses of diazepam as high as 1355 milligrams have been reported without significant toxicity. Apparently when oral benzodiazepines are involved in overdoses, they are only one of several substances ingested. Intravenous benzodiazepines, in contrast, have a high potential for toxic overdose, but of course the availability of these compounds is restricted. One of the more positive advances in this area is the development of a benzodiazepine antagonist (flumazenil). This compound binds to the same receptors as benzodiazepines but exerts no activity. It also competitively blocks these receptors, so it displaces benzodiazepines that have bound there. This drug can be used to treat a benzodiazepine overdose, although it may have to be injected multiple times, because its half-life is much shorter than the benzodiazepines it is intended to displace.

## The Case of Jennifer

Jennifer, a 26-year-old ballet dancer, began to experience mild panic attacks prior to both rehearsal and performances. She developed powerful resistance to dancing, accompanied by tightness in her chest, rapid breathing, and sweaty palms. Until the recent attacks, Jennifer had been recognized as one of the premier young dancers in the ballet company. Now she could barely perform. The director of the company referred her to a panic/phobia specialist at a local teaching hospital. Jennifer went for an assessment and complete psychological and physical workup. As a result of the evaluation, he recommended group therapy and a regimen of prazepam (Centrax) for Jennifer.

Jennifer expressed some reluctance to him about both treatments. She said her Eastern European culture frowned on sharing your deep personal problems in a group of people, and she was worried about the impact of the medication on her

functioning and dancing. The psychiatrist addressed both issues (cultural and intrapsychic) with Jennifer and paid very close attention to her feelings about the panic and the treatment. Eventually Jennifer agreed to both treatments.

This treatment protocol was very successful for Jennifer. The prazepam gave her relief from her panic and agitation almost immediately and continued for her 12-week course of treatment. The 10-week group helped Jennifer talk about some of her fears and anxieties about professional dance, provided hope and support, and facilitated her catharsis with some rage issues that had been building in her. She was a willing and positive contributor to the group process, and she benefited from both treatment interventions.

We believe it is important to provide realistic cases about panic and anxiety with some that demonstrate improvement by the client. This well-designed treatment easily could have soured if Jennifer had become dependent on her prazepam and was not able to titrate off of it or if she had become overly dependent on her group.

## The Case of Sherry

Sherry is a 46-year-old sexual abuse survivor with three children. She is divorced and works as an administrative assistant for a local accounting firm. Sherry has been in treatment on and off for over 20 years with several therapists and group approaches. Sherry has tried many medications during this time: TCAs, SSRIs, antipsychotics, antimanics, and more recently, a short–half-life benzodiazepine, alprazolam (Xanax).

Sherry reported that most medications helped her only for brief periods during the course of her treatment. Eventually all were either ineffective or caused her some discomfort because of side effects. Most recently Sherry felt her therapy was going well. She reported less agitation, fewer intrusive memories of her abuse, almost no nightmares, and far less panic. She also reported improved relationship with her children, as well as comfort and success at work, and she began to date again. Sherry attributed her improvement to her twice-a-week therapy with an eclectic female therapist and her ability to take alprazolam p.r.n. when she felt mounting agitation or anxiety in herself. She has learned to self-monitor these feelings, often derived from her chronic sexual abuse by her father between age 5 and 9. Sherry has learned in therapy that at certain times in her daily life she needs the help of alprazolam. This occurs about once or twice a week, and Sherry believes the alprazolam is very helpful at these times. Sherry has been using alprazolam in this way for three and a half years. She is not dependent on it and uses it very appropriately. Both Sherry and her therapist have begun to talk about what her life would be like without the alprazolam.

We believe there are many varied uses for the benzodiazapines and that clients, therapists, and physicians can discover their uses by a careful understanding of the client and/or by applying the Integral Model. Here is a case analysis using the Integral Model.

### The Case of William

William, a 27-year-old, African-American firefighter, developed panic attacks after a very serious fire. Almost immediately the department physician prescribed diazepam (Valium) for him, which he began taking. William did not like the drowsy, stuporous feeling from taking diazepam. In fact, after a week he became more agitated by the medication. His panic attacks worsened, and they got so intense that his supervisors recommended him for a disability leave because he could not function at work. William was distraught. He did not feel he had had an opportunity to talk with anyone about his panic and fears, and he detested the impact of the diazepam on him. Finally, William's minister recommended to him an African-American therapist at a neighborhood mental health center.

Certainly many factors influence this case. From the medical model perspective, William was speedily administered diazepam for his panic, with no evaluation or other considerations. From the intrapsychic perspective, William certainly had a reaction to the medication, and it is possible to hypothesize from the information presented that he also may have been very reluctant to take it. From a cultural perspective, William is an African American, and he seems to trust the counsel of his minister about his mental health concerns first.

In considering the social perspective, a few issues loom. One could assume that Valium was the benzodiazepine of choice by the fire department physician. Certainly many social forces are at work in recommending William for leave, including the potential stigma against firefighters with mental health problems. None of William's spheres of experience or vantage points were explored in detail except by his minister.

William had several complex psychological issues that he discussed with his therapist. The first was his personal fear of medication, accompanied by a need to know more about the impact of the diazepam and its side effects. William was a Gulf War veteran, and elements of the fire that triggered his panic seemed reminiscent of some of the horrors he had witnessed in that war. Over a three-month therapy, William and his therapist worked on these issues, consulted with the staff psychiatrist, and developed a plan for him to return to work. Through some selective cognitive-behavioral therapy, William learned about his repressed fears by experiencing an all-engulfing fire that kills humans, and he gained some control over his panic. After a consult with the staff psychiatrist at the mental health center and a careful evaluation, they agreed to a course of oxazepam (Serax) p.r.n. for times when William could not manage his growing panic. Oxazepam is from a different chemical family and is less potent than diazepam. The psychiatrist carefully explained all aspects of oxazepam to William and empowered him to take it only as needed. Together William and his therapist developed a strategy whereby he returned to work at full salary on "light" duty as a dispatcher, with the goal that he could request a return to regular duty. The minister initiated a treatment regimen that addressed William's issues from an integral perspective, and assisted in his recovery. The diazepam was not helpful, but the combination of oxazepam and therapy was.

### Nonbenzodiazepine Alternatives

Researchers have made numerous efforts in recent years to synthesize some nonbenzodiazepine compounds that have the therapeutic effects of benzodiazepines without the possibility of tolerance and dependence. Let's briefly discuss two of these compounds.

Zolpidem (brand name Ambien) was marketed in 1993 as a short-term hypnotic. Chemically it is structurally different from a benzodiazepine but it acts in much the same manner. It binds at the benzodiazepine receptor but tends to induce sleep far more than providing a wakeful anxiolytic effect. It has the same side effects as benzodiazepines and likely has the same pattern of tolerance and dependence, although that has not yet been determined. Part of the reason for this is because zolpidem is prescribed only short term for insomnia.

Zaleplon (brand name Sonata), like zolpidem, is structurally dissimilar to benzodiazepines but functions in much the same manner. Released in 1999 as a hypnotic agent, this compound has a very short half-life (about one hour) and induces sleep fairly effectively. Because of the short half-life, Julien (2001) notes, a pattern of tolerance and dependence is unlikely.

## Buspirone: A Unique Anxiolytic

Davis Temple and Michael Eison of Bristol-Myers Company (now Bristol-Myers-Squibb) developed buspirone (BuSpar) in 1968. Like so many other psychotropic medications, its development as an anxiolytic was serendipitous. The initial research goal for Temple and Eison was to develop an improved antipsychotic medication. Chemically, BuSpar resembles butyrophenone antipsychotics (about which we say more in Chapter Seven) more than anxiolytics. Although ineffective in alleviating symptoms of psychosis, buspirone did seem to have antianxiety properties in humans and antiaggression properties in other primates (Schatzberg, Cole, & DeBattista, 1997). In 1986 the FDA approved it for the market, to treat anxiety. Buspirone is classed as an azaspirodecanedione. Buspirone was the first serotonergic drug that showed efficacy for treating anxiety.

Although more will be said about buspirone later, we want to address a small detail that students invariably raise in our seminars. We are frequently asked, "Why is BuSpar (the brand name for bu-

spirone) spelled with an upper case "S"? This is a good question for which we had no answer. Finally one of our students (personal communication, Barry Zabielinski, June 1999) tracked down an answer through numerous phone calls to the manufacturer. The manufacturer said there was no esoteric meaning underlying the odd spelling, but the marketing team wanted the brand name to stand out and so capitalized the first and third letters. Another insight into the culture of the pharmaceutical industry!

### Mechanisms of Action

As noted, buspirone is unlike the anxiolytic compounds discussed thus far. Although the vast majority exert CNS depression by acting as GABA agonists, buspirone is actually a serotonin agonist and antagonist. Because serotonin is related to certain types of disinhibition of behavior and such disinhibition is also related to relief from anxiety, researchers have hypothesized since the 1980s that serotonin agonists may alleviate anxiety (Feldman, Meyer, & Quenzer, 1997). Buspirone is believed to act as a serotonin antagonist at the 5-HT1a receptors. These receptors are found in parts of the brain associated with fear and anxiety responses including the amygdala, septum, and hippocampus. Readers may be pondering the phrase "serotonin agonist" and wondering if buspirone would be helpful for depression, given that most of the newer antidepressants discussed in Chapter Five are serotonin agonists. Buspirone also acts on the noradrenergic system to increase the firing of neurons in the locus coeruleus. Recall from Chapter Two that such neuronal firing would seem to increase anxiety, not decrease it. How do we account for the fact that in this case the stimulation of these neurons by buspirone is associated with an anxiolytic action? Perry, Alexander, and Liskow (1997) explain that buspirone's effects on the hippocampus and raphe nucleus seem to override this stimulation of the locus coeruleus.

Although not as powerful an agonist of serotonin as a drug such as fluoxetine (Prozac), buspirone has shown some efficacy for treating depression (Julien, 2001) but is more often used as a supplement to more conventional antidepressants (Stahl, 2000). Researchers have noted that buspirone may interact with dopamine as a weak agonist in some areas of the brain and as a weak antagonist in others. These effects are not considered clinically significant (Perry, Alexander, & Liskow, 1997). Note that buspirone does not interact with GABA or benzodiazepine receptors, so it does not have significant sedative, muscle relaxant, or anticonvulsive properties.

### Side Effects and Dosing

The side effects of buspirone primarily include headache, dizziness, GI upset, and sometimes anxiety and tension. Some patients taking buspirone have reported restlessness or fidgeting. Patients suffering from Parkinson's disease may show a worsening of their Parkinsonian symptoms on buspirone. Buspirone is not recommended during pregnancy or while breastfeeding, mainly because researchers have no data about its effects on fetuses or neonates. Buspirone is not associated with tolerance, dependence, or overdose. Because the drug is not associated with any euphoric or other reinforcing effects, it is not likely to be abused.

Interestingly, buspirone has a more desirable side effect profile than the benzodiazepines, because it does not impair motor performance to any great degree and does not show any negative interactions with alcohol. Buspirone may exacerbate psychotic symptoms in patients suffering from Schizoaffective Disorder because of its weak dopamine agonism. Given this favorable side effect profile, many clinicians have wondered why it is not more routinely prescribed, because it has FDA approval for Generalized Anxiety Disorder. Schatzberg, Cole, and DeBattista (1997) have recommended buspirone as the drug of choice for treating Generalized Anxiety Disorder, Social Phobia, Mixed Anxiety and other combinations of depression, and anxiety in patients with a history of substance abuse.

Schatzberg, Cole, and DeBattista point out that many psychiatrists and physicians assume buspirone is weaker and slower to work than benzodiazepines, particularly in patients who have a history of being treated with benzodiazepines. These authors note that if patients like the more immediate effects of sedation that follow the first dose of benzodiazepines, they may think buspirone is not working,

because it lacks this effect. Both benzodiazepines and buspirone take two to four weeks before reaching maximum therapeutic effects, although the patient feels the impact of benzodiazepines within an hour of the first dose. Schatzberg and colleagues did not note that until going generic, buspirone was one of the most expensive anxiolytics on the market (Modell, 1995), which may have accounted for its less frequent use by prescribing professionals. Benzodiazepines can be problematic in that their withdrawal effects that may be similar to (or worse than) the anxiety symptoms clients initially began taking them to dispel. Buspirone has no tolerance or withdrawal effects and therefore is a more flexible drug to use with such clients.

Because buspirone does not interact with GABA receptors at all, it has some advantages over benzodiazepines. These are summarized in Table 6.5.

**TABLE 6.5** Advantages of Buspirone Over Benzodiazepines

| |
| --- |
| Lacks hypnotic, anticonvulsant, and muscle relaxant properties |
| Much less likely to induce drowsiness and fatigue |
| Does not impair psychomotor or cognitive function |
| Shows little potential for abuse and dependence |
| Does not induce tolerance |
| Has no synergistic effect with alcohol |
| Lacks affinity for GABA and benzodiazepine receptors |
| Is not cross-tolerant with benzodiazepines |

As Schatzberg, Cole, and DeBattista (1997) noted, though, buspirone does not give the immediate effect of drowsiness that is typically anxiolytic. Many people with anxiety who have taken benzodiazepines may mistake the lack of this effect for evidence that the buspirone is not working. Clients need to be informed that buspirone does work differently from benzodiazepines and should be told not to expect the same sensations when taking buspirone.

Although dosing is done by the prescribing professional, mental health clinicians should be aware some psychiatrists think that many clients go off buspirone because they do not believe it is working and that this in turn is related to not having a high-enough initial dose. Perry, Alexander, and Liskow (1997) advise that the usual dosage for anxiety is between 15 and 45 mg per day, given b.i.d or t.i.d.(from the Latin *bis in die*, "twice a day"; *ter in die*, "three times a day"), but this can be increased to as high as 60 mg. per day.

## Tolerance, Dependence, and Overdose

As noted in Table 6.5, some of the strongest arguments in favor of using buspirone are that it does not induce tolerance and dependence. In addition, it is highly unlikely that clients could overdose on buspirone. These effects seem minimal to nonexistent with buspirone, primarily because of its mechanisms of action, which are wholly different from those of benzodiazepines. A note of caution should be added, though. Recall from Chapter Five that serotonergic antidepressants were once believed to not induce tolerance and dependence and that this has since been disproved (Schatzberg, 1997). Therefore, prescribers may do well to watch for a discontinuation syndrome in longer-term users of buspirone at higher doses.

Before discussing a case, let's summarize when buspirone may be better for a client than a benzodiazepine. Benzodiazepines are effective when used over short periods or infrequently (p.r.n.). Clients with fairly severe anxiety on a chronic basis are good candidates for trying buspirone. A review of studies indicated that buspirone may be helpful in clients with GAD. There are mixed results for buspirone's effectiveness in other disorders (Perry, Alexander, & Liskow, 1997). Thus clients would likely be taking something every day to treat their anxiety, so buspirone is attractive in that it has not been shown to induce tolerance or dependence. Generally speaking, many clinicians believe buspirone is worth trying with anxious patients who have a history of abusing alcohol or benzodiazepines. Because alcohol is something adults have access to, these clients may drink but the alcohol does not interact negatively with the buspirone. Finally, Stahl (2000) wrote that buspirone may help older clients with anxiety because it is well tolerated and does not seem to have significant pharmacokinetic drug interactions.

## The Case of Meredith

Meredith, a 38-year-old married defense attorney, has suffered from extreme anxiety for most of her life. She has a very strong aversion to psychotherapy and believes there should be a pill to cure her worries. Over the years she has expressed a dislike for the benzodiazepines (she tried several) because they often induced drowsiness and fatigue. She also tried an SSRI, which made her more agitated after two weeks.

At her next appointment, her primary care physician suggested buspirone (BuSpar), a drug that for some reason Meredith had not known about. She began a course of buspirone 15 mg b.i.d. for her anxiety. After about six weeks Meredith noted a decrease in her daily levels of anxiety and reactions to stress. She also felt herself gain some perspective on the professional and personal issues that she often avoided. She recognized that the buspirone did not impair her level of functioning at work, and in fact she found she was more effective now that her anxiety had diminished. She also appreciated that the side effect profile of buspirone was better than that of the benzodiazepines.

Meredith took the buspirone for over 18 months and then recognized a need for psychotherapy to address conflicts and issues not resolved by the medication, exercise, or stress reduction techniques that she incorporated into her life. In the treatment, Meredith focused on her sense of isolation and unhappiness in her marriage, her surfacing sexual feelings toward women, and the pain from her childhood because her family moved 10 times to different cities. Once in therapy, after seven months Meredith stopped taking the buspirone. Meredith is one of many who discovered buspirone as an effective anxiolytic.

## Other Similar Agents

By the time this book has been published, some newer anxiolytic agents, similar to buspirone, may be on the market. Gepirone is also a serotonin agonist that has been in clinical trials for GAD. This compound seems to have a delayed onset similar to that of SSRI antidepressants (up to six weeks). As with buspirone, taking Gepirone correlated with decreased aggression in mice (Julien,

2001). Unfortunately, Gepirone, at last reports, was not as well tolerated by humans as buspirone and was not as effective as benzodiazepines in treating GAD (Rickels, Schweitzer, DeMartinis, Mandos, & Mercer, 1997). A second compound, Alnespirone, is also a serotonin agonist, shows anxiolytic and antiaggression properties, and is currently under investigation (Munoz & Papp, 1999).

## Noradrenergic Agents as Anxiolytics

Two noradrenergic agents have been thought helpful for anxiety, although neither one has FDA approval for that use. Still, it appears that until research more conclusively rules on the use of these agents, clinicians will meet clients who are taking these medications for anxiety symptoms. Recall from Chapter Two that the word *noradrenergic* refers to compounds that impact noradrenaline, which is synonymous with *norepinephrine* (remember your Greek!). The two agents in question are propranolol (Inderal) and clonidine (Catapres). Both drugs affect the sympathetic nervous system. The hypothesis that they may decrease anxiety stems from the observation that many people experience anxiety as sympathetic nervous system stimulation (sweating, increased heart rate, palpitations).

### Propranolol

Propranolol is called a "beta-blocker," because it blocks a receptor referred to as the *beta-adrenergic receptor*. Although the mechanism of action in anxiety is not well known, researchers hypothesize that perhaps in anxious people these receptors are "sensitive" and the drug decreases this hypothesized "sensitivity" (Perry, Alexander, & Liskow, 1997). The FDA approved beta-blockers for hypertension and as prophylactics against migraine headaches and angina. Because they decrease sympathetic nervous system stimulation, these drugs have a strong effect on the physical symptoms of anxiety but are not effective for the subjective symptoms of anxiety. Propranolol has been around for more than 40 years (it was introduced in 1964) and has yet to earn a reputation for efficacy or effectiveness in treating anxiety. Some studies report that beta blockers are helpful for treating acute, situational anxiety (Lader, 1988). Although some researchers thought they held promise for generalized anxiety, beta blockers are clearly ineffective for more severe types of anxiety such as panic attacks (Schatzberg, Cole, & DeBattista, 1997).

### Side Effects

The small number of studies researching propranolol's effects on anxiety turned up numerous side effects. The most severe involved decreased cardiac functioning or even cardiac failure in older clients. These severe side effects involved approximately 9% of subjects (Perry, Alexander, & Liskow, 1997). In addition, some clients reported GI distress, typically involving nausea and/or diarrhea. Perhaps the most frequently reported side effect is fatigue and lethargy.

### Conclusions

Propranolol is of limited use as a second-line treatment for anxiety. It may reduce situational or performance-related anxiety but is unlikely to be helpful in Social Phobia and Panic Disorder.

### Clonidine

Another compound that seems to affect norepinephrine is clonidine (Catapres). Many hoped that clonidine would have wide application for treating anxiety, but this has yet to transpire. Clonidine is one of the few drugs whose mechanism of action involves stimulation of autoreceptors. Recall from Chapter Two that when stimulated, autoreceptors signal the cell to which they are attached to decrease the amount of neurotransmitter synthesized and released. Thus stimulating an autoreceptor has an antagonist effect. Stahl (2000) likens it to stimulating the brake system in your car.

The FDA has approved clonidine, like propranolol, for treating hypertension. Because it decreases the release of norepinephrine, it has been explored in treating anxiety, mania, and Attention-Deficit-Hyperactivity Disorder (ADHD). Its usefulness in any of these applications still remains to be seen. Stahl (2000) noted that interest in clonidine as an anxiolytic stemmed from research showing that artificial stimulation of the locus coeruleus (remember the "blue disk" from Chapter Two?) induced anxiety-like symptoms in animal models. Because clonidine decreased the activity of cells in the locus coeruleus, researchers assumed it might help alleviate anxiety. Again, like propranolol, clonidine helps reduce sympathetic (physical) symptoms of anxiety but is not as useful in blocking subjective symptoms of anxiety. Although clonidine has shown some efficacy in anxiety and panic disorder, researchers now believe tolerance develops to the anxiolytic effects. Interestingly, clonidine has shown efficacy in decreasing symptoms of opioid withdrawal. The primary side effects reported are hypotension and sedation. Perry, Alexander, and Liskow (1997) recommend that the patient's blood pressure be monitored regularly when taking clonidine.

### The Case of Starr

Starr, a local 18-year-old high school track and field star, began to get very nervous before each meet and this worsened before each approaching event. Her symptoms were increased heart rate, sweaty palms and feet, and palpitations. As a result of these symptoms, she experienced a loss of concentration and confidence. She discussed this mounting problem with her coach, who suggested she talk to her family physician. The physician prescribed a low dose of clonidine (Catapres) to take before her track meets. Starr reported that the medication helped her and relieved most of her pre-event physical symptoms. As a result, Starr performed up to expectations during her senior year and was awarded a scholarship to the college of her choice.

We recognize the efficiency of this medical model treatment with Starr, but we caution that a family physician prescribed the clonidine, and there seemed to be no consideration of any therapy for her concerns. It should be noted that researchers recommend that blood pressure should be monitored regularly while taking Catapres, yet Starr's was not. Furthermore, no one discussed with Starr, her family, or coaches the potential risk to her heart by taking the clonidine before intense physical exertion. Fortunately, Starr did not experience any cardiac problems from the clonidine. Starr did not compete athletically in college and never needed the clonidine again.

## SSRI Treatment of Anxiety

Clinicians have long known that antidepressants also reduce anxiety in clients taking them. Recall from Chapter Five that anxiety and depression are often comorbid; in fact, several opponents of categorical psychiatry feel anxiety and depression may form two ends of a symptom continuum. Researchers as early as Klein (1967) have noted the impact of antidepressants on symptoms of anxiety. Although most antidepressants seem to have some value in treating anxiety (Rickels & Rynn, 2002), some of the more chemically atypical agents such as bupropion do not, and actually may exacerbate anxiety. Clinicians must also allow for the possibility of an unpredicted, idiosyncratic response. Because, as we have pointed out, depression and anxiety are probably overdetermined disorders, it is not possible to state with certainty what the impact of taking any particular medication will be. Indeed, we have known clients to take SSRI medications that have actually induced full-blown panic attacks.

### The Case of Katrina

Katrina, a 57-year-old widow who worked as a secretary for a local grocery distributor, developed immobilizing anxiety symptoms about four years after her husband's death. In fact, over time she was diagnosed with Generalized Anxiety Disorder, Panic Disorder with Agoraphobia, and Dysthymia. Katrina staunchly opposed taking any form of medication, even aspirin or vitamins, but she did believe in talk therapy. She said, "I have heard many people on television and radio speak to the benefits that they received from psychotherapy." In fact, after her husband's death Katrina was helped a great deal by a female therapist at the local mental health center. The therapy was supportive and insight-oriented and the therapy lasted six months on a weekly basis, with two follow-up sessions.

Katrina had sought help from a cognitive-behavioral male therapist, a feminist therapist, a support group for people suffering with anxiety and phobias, a hypnotherapist, and now a psychoanalytically oriented psychotherapist. None of the approaches appeared helpful in reducing Katrina's symptoms. Four of the five therapists recommended she have a psychiatric evaluation. Katrina refused all recommendations.

In her work with the dynamic therapist, Katrina gradually discovered aspects of her resistance to any changes and great distrust in both modern medicine and medications. Her therapist diligently explored these issues with her and began to teach her about more recent psychopharmacologic developments related to anxiety disorders. Katrina became slightly more open to discuss the possibility of a psychiatric assessment, and she expressed interest in the SSRIs. Eventually Katrina saw a psychiatrist who prescribed paroxetine (Paxil), and she reluctantly agreed to it. After eight weeks Katrina noticed a lessening of her fears and anxiety. Her panic all but disappeared. She did have several life issues that she continued to address with her therapist, but the SSRI treatment greatly reduced her symptoms of anxiety.

In Katrina's case, by addressing her intrapsychic issues her therapist was able to maximize therapeutic impact by combining a medical model intervention with an intrapsychic intervention. Katrina improved, and 16 months later titrated off the paroxetine. We summarize the efficacy of antidepressants later, while discussing pharmacologic interventions by disorder.

### The Case of Nicole

Nicole, a 35-year-old single woman, sought, from her psychiatrist, relief for a long-standing depression with features of anxiety. At the time of referral, Nicole was experiencing great difficulty sleeping, constant worry, mild panic, and a constant depressive affect (mood). Her physician prescribed paroxetine (Paxil) at 10 mg and told her to increase to 20 mg at the end of the first week. Nicole noticed during the first week that she was more agitated and slept even less. Because her doctor had not warned her about these possible side effects, she increased the dosage at the end of the week to 20 mg. By the second day after the increase, Nicole was experiencing total panic and terror. At times she could not breathe, and in her hypervigilant state she could barely speak to her neighbor, who wisely called the EMT service. Nicole was taken to the emergency room at the local hospital, where she was prescribed

a mild tranquilizer. The attending physician called her psychiatrist, and they agreed that Nicole was experiencing an SSRI-induced panic attack and she was taken off the paroxetine. When Nicole recovered from her panic attack, her psychiatrist prescribed alprazolam (Xanax) p.r.n. and encouraged her to seek therapy. He also indicated that if she still felt depressed in about two weeks, he would try a different class of antidepressant.

### The Case of Rhonda

Rhonda was a 38-year-old divorced mother who had been in weekly therapy about a year. Near the end of the first year of her work, Rhonda became very depressed and requested a psychiatric consult. The psychiatrist recommended sertraline (Zoloft), a new SSRI that had just received FDA approval. Rhonda began the Zoloft at 100 mg and soon was taking 200 mg per day. She reported feeling better but noticed she was losing large amounts of her beautiful hair daily, which she linked directly to the sertraline. Her therapist recommended she talk to the psychiatrist, who checked the side effects and found nothing about hair loss. However, she decreased the sertraline for Rhonda to 100 mg daily and the hair loss ceased.

I (Rak) also noticed this hair loss in two other female clients who took sertraline at 200 mg. I reported this to a middle manager at Pfizer, who indicated he would look into the situation, but I never received a further response. Sertraline now is seldom prescribed at 200 mg per day.

## Anxiolytic Therapy by Diagnosis

As stated earlier, in this section we summarize recommended therapies for anxiety symptoms by diagnosis. We summarize the pharmacologic interventions and also touch on the intrapsychic or psychological interventions. As we have stated from the beginning, an Integral view of the topic demands that these interventions be held in mind so that the reader does not unwittingly become mesmerized by the word magic of pharmacologic interventions. We cover Generalized Anxiety Disorder, Panic Disorder, Social and Specific Phobias, Obsessive-Compulsive Disorder, and Post-Traumatic Stress Disorder.

## Generalized Anxiety Disorder

Generalized Anxiety Disorder (GAD) is considered the basic anxiety disorder, because it is characterized by intense, unfocused anxiety. *DSM* criteria for this classification require excessive anxiety and apprehensive expectation more often than not for at least 6 months before the diagnosis is made. Adults must manifest three of the symptoms in the symptom list; children, only one. In children this used to be called Overanxious Disorder of Childhood and has a high comorbidity with ADHD and Major Depressive Disorder as well as other anxiety disorders. The focus of the intense anxiety varies developmentally. Adults tend to worry about minor daily life events, whereas children tend to worry about athletic, academic, or social competence. It is crucial that clinicians explore the worry of children and adults for other emotions such as sadness, loss, rage, and other symptoms that reflect the aspects of "worry." People with GAD are vigilant regarding potential threats in the environment but do not have particular images of threats. These people actually show less physiological responsiveness (heart rate, blood pressure, respiration) to anxiety-provoking stimuli than do people with other anxiety disorders. For this reason people with this disorder have been called "autonomic restrictors." This may be explained as follows.

Recall that the autonomic nervous system regulates involuntary sympathetic and parasympathetic functions. Autonomic restriction has been linked to intense thought processes or worry that never develops to specific, consistent images of potential problems. The images would elicit more negative emotions. Their style keeps such autonomic restrictors from feeling these potentially negative emotions but also from working through their anxiety in therapy (Barlow & Durand, 2002).

### *Medical Model Treatments for GAD*

GAD is considered a challenging disorder to treat. Although benzodiazepines have been a staple of treatment until recently, they do not alleviate all symptoms and are rarely studied over periods longer than two months (Barlow & Durand, 2002). Schweizer and Rickels (1996) concluded from their study that the therapeutic effects begin to decline after six months. Although most benzodiazepine users do not abuse their medication, tolerance and dependence are still a risk, which is problematic for long-term use of benzodiazepines to treat GAD. Many researchers (such as Schatzberg, Cole, & DeBattista, 1996) thus believe buspirone is the ideal medication of first choice for GAD. According to Perry, Alexander, and Liskow (1996), seven controlled studies have found that buspirone compared favorably with the benzodiazepines. Unlike benzodiazepines, buspirone cannot be used on a p.r.n. basis. Like the serotonergic antidepressants, it seems to require daily dosing to exert its effects. Buspirone may also take two to four weeks for the full therapeutic benefit to be achieved (although as Schatzberg, Cole, and DeBattista argued, the same may hold true for benzodiazepines).

Antidepressants are also being used more frequently for GAD (Schatzberg, 2000) and venlafaxine (Effexor) and paroxetine (Paxil) have FDA approval for on-label use to treat this disorder. Although the newer antidepressants may all have tolerance- and dependence-inducing properties, these may be easier to manage than the same properties in benzodiazepines.

### *Psychological (Intrapsychic) Treatments for GAD*

Regardless of the pharmacotherapy used when treating GAD, it is important to combine medication with some form of counseling or psychotherapy. The long-term nature of the condition and the lack of long-term efficacy studies both support supplementing medication with a psychosocial intervention. In reviewing the treatment literature, Hoehn-Saric, Borkovec, and Nemiah (1994) found that behavior therapy and cognitive-behavioral therapy (CBT) consistently show superiority over no treatment at all. These authors also note that the dropout rates in psychosocial treatment trials have been low and that the combination of CBT with progressive relaxation and/or exposure seems to have the best possibility of long-lasting change.

This recommendation is not intended to rule out other types of therapy such as psychodynamic therapy but, as is often the case, there are more studies of CBT and behavior therapy, partly because they are easier to study with operationalized variables. Psychodynamic therapy for GAD aims to help clients gain awareness of unconscious conflicts and underlying anxiety-provoking drives, recognize the environmental cues that activate anxiety, and understand the origins of anxiety in early life experience. Three questions typically underlie this treatment:

1. What inner drive is the client afraid of?
2. What consequences of overt behavioral expression of the drive does the client fear?
3. What psychological and behavioral measures does the client take to control the drive?

In seeking to answer these three questions, the clinician also confronts various perplexing symptoms expressed by the client, and defense mechanisms that initially hinder the therapy. Clients considered good candidates for insight-oriented therapy are those willing to engage in (and capable of) introspection and to reflect on that introspection, those who can tolerate the expression of painful intrapsychic material, and those who can form meaningful relationships. It is important that these clients be motivated to aim for psychological change and growth as opposed to just symptom relief.

## Panic Disorder

Panic Disorder is typically treated in two phases. The first is aimed at reducing the frequency and/or intensity of the panic attacks. This phase is frequently accomplished pharmacologically. The second phase involves administering the psychosocial treatment in the hope of decreasing the dysfunctional responses that become panic attacks (American Psychiatric Association, 2000a). Interestingly, numerous drugs that affect different parts of the central nervous system all seem effective in reducing panic attacks (Speigel, Wiegel, Baker, & Greene, 2000). For the first phase of treatment, high-potency benzodiazepines are very effective, work quickly, and reduce anticipatory anxiety. Over 60 trials on benzodiazepines have been made on subjects with Panic Disorder, and the data suggest that these clients continue to improve up to six months, at which point gains stabilize. These medications can be prescribed p.r.n., so clients need only take the dose when they feel in imminent dan-

ger of a panic attack. Obviously, the more frequently clients use any benzodiazepine, the more likely the problem of tolerance and dependence. Thus the benzodiazepines from the 3-hydroxy or triazolo families are preferable, because of their shorter half-life.

Numerous trials have been conducted to assess the efficacy of antidepressants for the treatment of Panic Disorder. Summarizing literature across 15 years, Perry, Alexander, and Liskow (1996) noted that approximately 67% of subjects could be said to respond to treatment with tricyclic antidepressants and MAO inhibitors. "Response" was defined as anywhere from an 80% reduction in panic attacks to complete remission. SSRI medications generally showed a 60% response rate, where response was defined as a decrease in panic severity. Several SSRI compounds have on-label FDA approval for treatment of Panic Disorder, including sertraline (Zoloft) and paroxetine (Paxil).

Several psychosocial interventions are highly successful for the second phase of Panic Disorder treatment, and from an Integral perspective we would be remiss if we omitted mention of these. Traditionally, treatment centered on gradual exposure to feared situations (in cases where agoraphobia was a component) and anxiety-coping mechanisms such as relaxation. Barlow and Durand (2002) describe a treatment they developed called Panic Control Treatment, which concentrates on exposing clients to sensations that remind them of their panic attack sensations. These researchers found that by inducing these quasi-panic attacks they could bring to the client's awareness previously unconscious cognitive processes and responses that increased the probability of full-blown panic attacks. They note that follow-up studies as long as two years after treatment support the efficacy of these tactics.

## Social and Specific Phobias

Although social and specific phobias may vary in the focus of the fear, they share several similarities that allow us to group them together in this section. They both seem to be an outgrowth of an evolutionary mechanism that prepared humans to flee dangerous situations, and they are both problematic in that the flight response is out of proportion to the actual danger posed by the situation. Again, these are disorders for which several effective psychological interventions are available. Specific phobias seem to respond well to structured exposure-based treatments that may use models as part of the treatment. These are paired with relaxation exercises to decrease the strength of a physiological anxiety response.

### Social Phobia

Having a Social Phobia is being extremely and painfully shy. It manifests as a marked or persistent fear of one or more social or performance situations in which the person is exposed to unfamiliar people or possible scrutiny. The main fear is that the person fears acting in a way that will be humiliating or embarrassing to him- or herself. Although social phobia treatments are newer, group therapy involving role-play and rehearsal of the feared situation both seem effective (Turk, Heimberg, & Hope, 2001). As with specific phobias, exposure to the anxiety-provoking situation is an important part of the treatment.

Given that psychological treatments are so effective, what is the rationale for prescribing medications? The answer is that often the medications can give clients a window of opportunity (of relief from symptoms) that then allows them to confront their issues in counseling and make the necessary changes. This is particularly important for clients who are so limited by their symptoms that they cannot fulfill important obligations. Social Phobia in particular has received a great deal of attention over the past five years from the makers of SSRI medications. Recall the opening lines in Chapter Five describing a commercial for paroxetine (Paxil), focusing on a young man with Social Phobia. Several SSRI medications have received FDA approval for treating Social Phobia, including paroxetine (Paxil) and sertraline (Zoloft). Interestingly, about two thirds of study participants with Social Phobia respond to these agents. Two thirds also respond to MAO inhibitors and the tricyclic clomipramine (Anafranil) but, as noted in Chapter Five, the SSRI side effects are less difficult to manage than those from MAO inhibitors or TCAs.

### Obsessive-Compulsive Disorder

In some ways Obsessive-Compulsive Disorder (OCD) combines elements from most of the other disorders, making it quite complex. People with OCD may also have panic attacks, depression, and generalized anxiety. OCD is characterized by obsessions, which are recurrent mental processes that the person experiences as inappropriate and intrusive and as causing marked anxiety or distress. Compulsions may be actions or thoughts that the person uses to suppress the obsessions. The compulsions provide relief because the client imbues them with a magical quality to prevent a dreaded event from occurring, such as the man who repeatedly washes his hands before touching anything, to ward off infectious illness or death. Although compulsive acts or thoughts may provide some relief in the short term, the client's obsessions almost always return.

Although most people experience intrusive thoughts at one time or another and may even engage in compulsive behavior to block the thoughts, few develop OCD. Although many theories from the medical model and intrapsychic perspectives seek to explain how OCD develops, there are no firm conclusions and the disorder is probably overdetermined, like most other mental/emotional disorders. From the medical model perspective, the neurotransmitter serotonin is definitely related to OCD, although how it is related remains a mystery (Stahl, 2000). The SSRI medications all seem to show efficacy for treating the symptoms of OCD. This efficacy was discovered by accident when physicians prescribed fluoxetine (Prozac) for depressed clients whose tendencies to obsess exacerbated their symptoms; the clients reported that they spent less time obsessing. Controlled studies supported this result, and the first SSRI to receive FDA approval for treating OCD was fluvoxamine (Luvox). Note that the medication provides only modest gains. Generally, 40 to 60% of subjects with OCD respond partially to SSRI medication. Here, "partial response" is defined as a 20 to 35% reduction in their obsessions and compulsions (Goodman et al., 1993).

Stahl (2000) has summarized how dopamine may play a role in the development of OCD. Researchers have long noted that amphetamines can cause people to engage in purposeless, repetitive motor behaviors that appear similar to compulsions. There has also been a long-standing relationship between obsessive-compulsive behavior and Tourette's Disorder. Up to 90% of study participants suffering from Tourette's Disorder also suffer from obsessions and compulsions. Participants who receive medications that decrease dopamine activity also report relief from obsessions and compulsions. Given these data, Stahl (2000) noted that clients may be prescribed more than one agent in the hopes of more effectively decreasing OCD symptoms by affecting both serotonin and dopamine transmission. Table 6.6 summarizes combined treatments outlined by Stahl, after which we explain them.

**TABLE 6.6**  Psychotropic Medications That Combine With SSRs to Treat OCD

SSRI and Buspirone

SSRI and Trazodone

SSRI and Lithium

SSRI and Benzodiazepine

SSRI and Zolpidem

SSRI and typical antipsychotic

SSRI and atypical antipsychotic

The strategy in the first two combinations is to boost the serotonergic activity (because SSRIs, buspirone, and trazodone all are serotonergic agents). The strategy of combining an SSRI with lithium, a benzodiazepine, or zolpidem (a hypnotic that acts in a manner similar to a benzodiazepine) is to boost the SSRI by altering transmission at the norepinephrine or GABA receptors. Combining an SSRI and a typical antipsychotic enhances 5-HT transmission while decreasing DA transmission (a good strategy for people with Tourette's). Finally, pairing an SSRI with an atypical antipsychotic is still in the experimental stages and thus far seems to worsen symptoms for as many participants as gain relief from the combination.

Although medications may help clients with OCD, counseling is also recommended. The evidence for this approach is primarily anecdotal, but

behavior therapy and an SSRI medication appear more effective in reducing symptoms than either one alone. The behavior therapy best documented is exposure and ritual prevention. In this process the client is exposed to feared thoughts or stimuli and then prevented from engaging in the compulsions (rituals) typically engaged in to bring about relief (Foa & Franklin, 2001).

### The Case of Roger

Roger, a 48-year-old married father of three, is a plant manager at a local automobile assembly plant. For at least 20 years he has suffered from obsessive-compulsive disorder (OCD). For years he took a TCA, clomipramine (Anafranil), to relieve his obsessions and compulsions, with only marginal success. At times his compulsions were so severe that he was unable to work or attend family functions. He reluctantly tried various psychotherapists, hypnotherapists, healers, and herbal therapies. He even tried a course of acupuncture treatment. About 10 years ago he was recommended for psychoanalysis, which he declined. Roger was very reluctant to try any other psychotropic medications after the clomipramine, but his psychiatrist persisted and spoke to him about a newer SSRI, fluvoxamine (Luvox), which had FDA approval for the treatment of OCD.

About that time Roger learned about brief solution-focused therapy and decided to give it a try for 10 sessions. During treatment, Roger's therapist suggested he might want to consider his psychiatrist's recommendation of the fluvoxamine, because his rigid thinking made their work together difficult. Roger was both angered and curious, so they talked more about the "potential" impact of an SSRI on his condition. After careful reflection, Roger decided to try the fluvoxamine and, after a period of adjustment, found some relief from his compulsions and less relief from his obsessive thought patterns. He returned to the brief therapist and began to focus on strategies to improve his condition even more. Roger eventually reported a 40 to 50% reduction in his compulsive behaviors and 25% reduction in his obsessive thoughts. To him, this was relief.

OCD is a very complex disorder, and Roger's case reflects the long-term and frustrating nature many clients have in seeking assistance with their suffering. For people with OCD, we believe treatment from the intrapsychic perspective is essential in conjunction with medications.

### Post-Traumatic Stress Disorder

Post-Traumatic Stress Disorder (PTSD) is perhaps easiest to conceptualize from multiple perspectives. PTSD symptoms include "reliving" the trauma through nightmares or memories in which the person re-experiences the emotions of horror, helplessness, and fear that accompanied the trauma. Such people also seek to avoid anything that reminds them of the trauma. These people often appear chronically vigilant, quick to anger, and easy to startle. Although the cause of the disorder from the perspective of the trauma is easy enough to identify, why some people who suffer traumas develop PTSD and others do not is not as easy to fathom. Barlow and Durand (2002) summarize contributions from each perspective discussed in this book. Some people may be more vulnerable to PTSD through some as-yet-undiscovered biological mechanism, intrapsychic dispositions, cultural attitudes, or sociological circumstance.

Although medication may serve as an adjunct to treatment, most clinicians agree that a psychosocial treatment that helps the client reapproach the original trauma, work through responses, and develop effective coping mechanisms is the staple of effective PTSD treatment (Keane & Barlow, 2002). Although most antidepressants have proven helpful in treating PTSD, sertraline (Zoloft) currently has FDA approval for treating this disorder. Again, as in most anxiety disorders, the medication can provide a window of opportunity for the client to engage in therapy and make the changes necessary to reduce or eliminate symptoms. Note that although benzodiazepines can help in the short term, clients who use or abuse alcohol regularly are best prescribed a different medication.

## Focus on Perspectives

In this section we explore some of the confounding issues surrounding anxiety disorders that are frequently not covered in psychopharmacology books. We address issues from the intrapsychic, cul-

tural, and social perspectives outlined in Chapters Three and Four. It is important to remember that the discussion of issues from these other perspectives is meant to complement medical model perspectives of anxiety and treatment with anxiolytic medication.

### Intrapsychic Issues
#### *Anxiety Disorders: Myth or Reality*

The debate about the nature and source of anxiety continues. Is anxiety a product of an overwhelming state of tension (Barlow & Durand, 2002), a sign of intrapsychic conflict (Freud, 1925), or both (Gabbard, 1994)? If we examine anxiety from the intrapsychic perspective covered in Chapter Three, it is possible to arrive at one point of agreement: Clinicians who treat clients suffering from anxiety disorders understand that these clients have cognitive, affective, and interpersonal struggles that are entwined in their anxiety symptoms. No medication is going to address all of these struggles which is where counseling and psychotherapy enter the picture. We sometimes wonder whether our thinking so far in this chapter has been overly optimistic in relationship to the prospects for clients finding relief from anxiolytics. In every case we reviewed and shared here, counseling played a crucial role in the client's recovery. When talking with clients, we find that intrapsychic issues range from anxiety resulting from situational stress to severe PTSD. Each disorder potentially encompasses underlying issues and conflicts that cannot be ameliorated by medication alone.

I (Rak, the second author of this book) have trained to become a psychoanalyst. This training involved four to five days a week treatment focused on intrapsychic conflicts and is designed to prepare one to be a psychodynamic therapist. (A psychoanalyst provides four- to five-day-a-week treatment focused on the intrapsychic conflicts of the patient who usually lies on a couch. Intensive psychotherapy is one- or two-day-a-week counseling that is eclectic in nature, and psychodynamic psychotherapy is counseling or therapy that is guided by psychoanalytic principles, but is not an analysis.) My view of profound anxiety resonates with that of some clinicians in the field. I believe serious anxiety can be understood only in the context of the transference in intensive psychotherapy where counselor and client search beyond the symptoms for underlying beliefs, feelings, and attitudes, conscious or unconscious. These conflicts and wishes repeatedly trigger the client's anxiety and must be integrated into the client's concept of self before any long-lasting relief can be accomplished.. Taking a broader perspective, Barber and Luborsky (1991) have argued that specific anxiety disorders required varied treatments with different clients. Psychodynamic psychotherapy may be the treatment of choice for those clients who are psychology minded and willing to invest the time to explore their anxiety. Clients who want more direction from their mental health clinician may do better with a cognitive behavioral approach. Other clients whose anxiety is directly tied to a felt need to make difficult but necessary choices (such as whether to keep a safe but boring job or risk an exciting but less secure job) will likely benefit from an existential approach to therapy. As we have discussed throughout the chapter, anxiolytics have a range of effectiveness with symptoms of anxiety disorders, but they may or may not be the total solution for the client's problem. Understanding the intrapsychic elements of each client's anxiety guides us in selecting an appropriate counseling intervention to complement whatever medication regimen they may be on.

Gabbard (1994) concluded that the treatment of anxiety disorders must begin with careful and thorough psychodynamic evaluation. In making this evaluation the therapist should be aware that the symptoms may only be the proverbial "tip of the iceberg" for the client. The mental health professional needs to assess the nature of the client's underlying fears, capacity to tolerate treatment that explores those fears, worry that the anxiety is destroying the self, and the client's relationship with important others or lack thereof. After an assessment and evaluation, the professional considers the range of treatments for anxiety, including brief therapies, cognitive-behavioral therapy, existential and humanistic therapies, psychodynamic theory, psychoanalysis, and long-term expressive-supportive psychotherapy. In cases such as those presented in this chapter, the professional must consider which

approach may be most helpful to each client.

We believe the complex intrapsychic issues that arise in clients contribute to the complexity and mystery of anxiety disorders. Some clients maintain their high levels of anxiety in order to live out their lives in a compromised fashion. In one example provided earlier, I (Ingersoll) worked with a client who chose not to pursue the exciting job opportunities and stay in the safe but boring job. Although his anxiety decreased significantly after making his choice, he was then beset by bouts of depression. From an existential perspective the client had traded freedom for comfort and this was signaled by the depression. He re-entered treatment five years later when another opportunity to take a more exciting but less secure job presented itself and his anxiety reappeared. Some clients can find relief only from supportive counseling, whereas others require compulsive behaviors to distract them from their suffering. This strategy of seeking relief through distraction is one of the prominent motivations driving the consumer culture in the United States. From an existential perspective, the consumer culture provides distractions from the anxiety that comes when one is aware of the freedom one has and the consequences of trading it for security. For the client with the job dilemma, his current (but boring) job paid well and he was able to afford expensive pleasures (like vacations), but the relief these pleasures provided was temporary. It is most beneficial to clients not to oversell medications as a definitive treatment, but to help them understand that anxiety is an important sign of issues to explore in counseling or psychotherapy.

### Cultural Issues

The pressures of American culture in general are enormous external contributors to anxiety. The continued struggle for civil rights for all Americans, psychological responses to war, the horror of the terrorist attacks on the World Trade Center, the uncertainty of the stock market, an increasing mistrust of government, the increased turmoil and violence of our youth, and the dismantling and or transformation of traditional values all trigger anxiety reactions. Our culture is infused with paradigms of violence, revenge, conquest, and dominance. The influence of culture is a powerful variable in understanding the rise of anxiety disorders. The impact of these external stressors varies with the psychological makeup of each client.

The American tendency, particularly in the consumer culture and mass media, to glorify violence continues to make major contributions to stress and anxiety in Americans, although evolutionary dynamics related to reproduction can always account for a certain percentage of violence (fighting for the best mate to reproduce with) (Wright, 1994). Violence is also reinforced by unrealistic portrayals in almost all mass media (Bushman & Anderson, 2001). The question remaining is the extent to which this contributes to anxiety, but it is certainly a useful working hypothesis in that being the target of or viewing aggression increases anxiety.

Perform this simple experiment. Using a blood pressure cuff (available at most retail pharmacies), chart your blood pressure two to three times a day for a week, to establish a baseline. Take the range of average readings per day as your baseline. Then watch a national or local news program on television and take your blood pressure again. Is it higher or lower? Our guess is that for many people, watching the news tends to correlated with higher blood pressure, thus identifying the activity with a stress response. By becoming aware of your body's responses to stress, try to monitor them when you are viewing movies or television programming. To what extent does viewing these entertainments seem correlated with stress responses? Although we are not advocating "media blackouts," we are advocating conscious media engagement. Conscious media engagement simply means being aware of your responses to various media and deciding consciously if you want to expose yourself to those media.

Tseng (2001) further elaborated on the external cultural pressures of anxiety by exploring its cross-cultural dimensions. He addressed the issues of how different cultures reveal their emotions. Some do so with gestures and facial expressions, others with words, still others through the body. Some cultures have highly elaborate cultural ways of expressing emotions through "somato organ language," incorporating into the language words or terms that represent somatic pain without a complete awareness of its psychological origins for affective expressions. For instance, *fa pi qi* ("lost spleen spirit,"

meaning losing one's temper) and *gan fuo da* ("elevated liver fire," meaning emotionally irritated) in Chinese are equivalent to organ language expressions used in English, such as "butterflies in stomach" or "a pain in the neck" (p. 292).

Tseng further elaborated that it is difficult for patients to present a clear picture of their distress if they are from a culture where the condition is viewed as a holistic experience rather than as a series of specific symptoms from the descriptive psychiatry perspective. Tseng further discussed specific culture-related syndromes such as Dhat syndrome in India (fear that excessive semen loss will result in illness) and Malignant Anxiety syndrome in Africa (intense feelings of fear and anger from extreme cultural disruption that lead to homicidal feelings). From the cultural perspective, it is clear that anxiety disorders are subject to a variety of cultural influences and the cultural "language of expression" of the client. Therapists need to be alert to these both subtle and overt manifestations of anxiety from clients. Most therapists in practice today, especially in urban settings, encounter increased numbers of clients from diverse cultural backgrounds.

### Social Issues

From the perspective of third-party payers (managed care), the most appropriate treatment for a client (counseling) is not always the most cost-effective (Gabbard, 1994). This further deepens the dilemma we have noted so often throughout the book: that psychotropic drugs alleviate many symptoms of anxiety disorders, even though we do not fully understand the pharmacokinetics and the pharmacodynamics of the drugs, yet they do not necessarily lead to deep and maintained gains for all clients. The pressures from managed care to treat most, if not all, anxiety disorders with psychotropics and brief models of counseling are enormous. It is crucial that we become and remain alert to clients whom these strategies do not help.

In an effort to counter the forces and impact of managed care, Hubble, Duncan, and Miller (2001) attempted to address the dilemmas and controversies among the various theoretical models and paradigms of therapy to provide research-based knowledge on what is most effective in the therapeutic process. This seminal work identified the **pantheoretical** or common therapeutic factors shared by all effective orientations. Later in the book, Brown, Deis, and Nace (2001) discussed the poignant intersection between effective counseling and the mandates of managed care in the context of current market pressures. They identified how market forces on managed behavioral health care organizations (MBHCOs) have now focused their reimbursement power on client outcomes. Nowhere are the issues of client outcomes more complex than in the anxiety disorders. In this chapter we have endeavored to demonstrate this fact not only by discussing the limited and successful impact of psychotropics on anxiety disorders but also by identifying the complex layers of "partial truths" that underlie these disorders. The findings of Brown, Deis, and Nace underscored the critical importance of recognizing the client's response to treatment and outcomes. Even with the best therapeutic protocols, a client's early failure to respond to treatment decreases the chances of a positive outcome.

As detailed in other chapters, the role and influence of the pharmaceutical companies cannot be overlooked in treating anxiety disorders. The surge in the uses of SSRIs for anxiety conditions indicates the drive of these companies to influence the psychiatric treatment market with an arsenal of psychotropics. This occurs in the context of growing confusion, as discussed in earlier chapters, about distinctions between anxiety and depressive disorders and about their comorbidity.

## Summary

In this chapter we have provided an overview of both the psychotropics and the therapeutic interventions used with anxiety disorders. In one sense you, the reader, may feel optimistic about both interventions. We caution that many therapists are surprised to discover, after what they feel were successful courses of psychotherapy, that their clients have developed new or altered symptoms and that their suffering has increased.

Medications to treat anxiety are among the most prescribed psychotropic medications in Western societies. Anxiolytic medications have evolved a great deal from the barbiturates and similar central nervous system depressants to the point where an array of medications may be used to treat client anxiety depending on the diagnosis. Although researchers have made strides in the pharmacologic treatment of anxiety, we believe that therapists must approach this work with wisdom and humility. For all we know about the psychotropic medications that can be used for anxiety disorders, we still encounter the powerful and insidious nature of human anxiety that has intrapsychic, cultural, and social dynamics. We are learning that beneath the anxiety lie some of the fundamental struggles of human existence, struggles that cannot be altered easily, if at all.

## Study Questions and Exercises

1. Describe your understanding of the complex construct of anxiety. Relate this working knowledge to one or two clients whom you have counseled.
2. Describe with detail the mechanism(s) of action of barbiturates, benzodiazepines, early nonbarbiturates, and noradrenergic agents.
3. Let's assume your client is taking one medication of those listed in the preceding question; indicate how you would speak to him or her about the side effects of the medication chosen. Also, discuss how you would stay alert for the more dangerous side effects of drug overdose or dependence.
4. Select one of the cases from the benzodiazepine section of the chapter, and discuss different vantage points (based on the four perspectives in the Integral framework) from which to analyze the case.
5. Reread the first paragraph of this chapter, and discuss what we mean by "from an Integral perspective it is not enough to describe anxiety symptoms, posit a biological explanation, then describe how certain drugs act biologically to (at least temporarily) decrease or eliminate these symptoms."
6. From the chapter on depression, you learned about the impact of the SSRIs on the symptoms of depression; in this chapter you have discovered they can be helpful with anxiety.

What does this overlap say about the medication? About the mind–brain problem as it relates to anxiety? Depression? Comorbidity issues of depression and anxiety?

7. Are you as optimistic about the treatment of anxiety disorders as the authors seem to be? Why or why not?

8. Develop your own question about the material from this chapter, and give a comprehensive response.

9. Using the chapter and your own experience, express your understanding of the similarities and differences of fear, panic, and anxiety.

10. Discuss how you understand the complexity of obsessive-compulsive disorder (OCD), and then discuss the effectiveness (as described in Stahl, 2000) of the psychotropic medication combinations used to treat OCD. Highlight the strengths and limitations of three of these combinations.

11. What cautions are raised in this chapter about the long-term use and effectiveness of psychotropic medications with Post-Traumatic Stress Disorder (PTSD)? Explain.

# CHAPTER SEVEN

# Antipsychotic Medications

## *The Evolution of Treatment*

Many readers may begin this chapter with some familiarity with antipsychotic medications. Others may think antipsychotic medications or the research related to them has not affected their lives. These latter readers may be wrong. Have you ever taken a prescription antihistamine such as Seldane or Allegra? Perhaps during the flu season you have had a cough syrup that included promethazine. If so, your life has been affected by research into antipsychotics. As with so many other areas of research in psychotropic medication, antipsychotics and theories about their use have been developed through combined scientific effort, clinical research, market-driven agendas, and serendipity. Let's look at some history to introduce this topic. The primary source for the following is Healy's compelling narrative (2002). We know of no better history of the field.

## The Current Impact of Antipsychotics

In a video designed for psychiatrists (Novartis Pharmaceuticals, 1998) a young man suffering from treatment-resistant Schizophrenia is shown in an inpatient setting. Although his psychotic symptoms are temporarily under control, he is so incapacitated by medication side effects that he can barely walk across a small room. His movements are jerky contractions of muscle groups that he can hardly control. Anyone who has treated clients taking conventional antipsychotic medications knows that this

young man is living a worst-case scenario in which the treatment is worse than the disorder being treated. The video progresses, showing the young man at monthly intervals as he is slowly weaned off the medications causing the side effects, and gradually titrated onto a new medication (clozapine). With each passing month we see that the young man's psychotic symptoms remain under control but that he is gradually regaining control of his body. In the final video frame we see the same young man enjoying a game of basketball and apparently having no problems with movement or symptoms of psychosis.

This was one of the first videos promoting what we describe later as an atypical antipsychotic, and we can fairly say that clozapine and drugs modeled after its molecular structure have launched yet another revolution in psychopharmacology. Like the SSRI revolution in antidepressants, the new antipsychotics are changing the way psychotic disorders are treated as well as the quality of life that patients can expect during treatment. The current impact of antipsychotics is a high point in a story that goes back at least 50 years. Before we turn to that story, however, let's briefly review Schizophrenia.

## Schizophrenia

Schizophrenia is best thought of as constituting a heterogeneous spectrum of symptoms occurring variably in stages or phases and affecting a person's emotion, volition, perception, thinking, and social behavior. Although theories of etiology focus on the medical model (Schizophrenia as a brain disease), investigators currently think it may also be induced genetically or environmentally (Thaker & Tamminga, 2001), although research has yet to consistently support this hypothesis. Prevalence among adults is thought to be between 1 and 1.5% of the adult population (Ingersoll & Burns, 2001). Although this chapter focuses on treatments for Schizophrenia, the spectrum of schizophrenic disorders includes Brief Psychotic Disorder and Schizophreniform Disorder. The latter two differ from Schizophrenia only in the time frame of symptoms.

### The Spectrum of Symptoms in Schizophrenia

The spectrum of symptoms in Schizophrenia includes both positive and negative symptoms. This concept derives from the work of the 19th-century neurologist John Hughlings Jackson. **Positive symptoms** of Schizophrenia are things the client experiences but likely should *not* be experiencing, such as **hallucinations, illusions, delusions**, and **paranoia**. Clients with positive symptoms usually lack insight into the sense outsiders have that these experiences are not real or normal and frequently cannot distinguish between them and the consensual reality shared by others.

**Negative symptoms** of Schizophrenia are deficits in the client's functioning expressed as things like **anhedonia** (lack of pleasure in life), isolation, withdrawal, flat or restricted affect, and reduced motivation. These negative symptoms severely affect quality of life for afflicted clients and can be exacerbated by certain antipsychotic medications clients are given to control the positive symptoms. In addition to the positive and negative symptoms, clients suffering from Schizophrenia experience conceptual disorganization, which used to be called "**thought disorder**." This disorganization can range from concrete thinking to severe **loose associations** and **word salad**. These symptoms may also severely reduce clients' quality of life (Thaker & Tamminga, 2001). From an Integral perspective, all these symptoms need to be addressed. Although pharmacological interventions are the first line of treatment

for Schizophrenia, it is important also to include psychosocial and educational components (American Psychiatric Association, 2000a).

Gelman (1999) divides the history of medicating psychotic disorders into four periods. The first period encompasses the 1950s and 1960s and began with the appearance of chlorpromazine (Thorazine). In this period, the mechanisms of action for chlorpromazine were not known, and although many people believed this drug would usher in an age of deinstitutionalization, others felt it would likely just make hospital wards more manageable.

The second period begins in the early 1960s with the emphasis (begun in the Kennedy administration) of community care versus hospital care. At this time the National Institute of Mental Health was labeling antipsychotics "**antischizophrenic.**" At this time intrapsychic explanations for mental disorders were dropped in favor of medical model theories. Some writers at the time (Swazey, 1974) even posited that chlorpromazine was a "**magic bullet**" for Schizophrenia. This second period ends in the 1980s with the disappearance of such overly optimistic views. By the 1970s clinicians accepted that neuroleptics could produce "alarming side effects, non-profound benefits in most cases, and no benefit at all in many" (Gelman, 1999, p. 7).

The third period, encompassing the 1980s and early 1990s, found many clinicians still clinging to the vague medical model notion of a chemical imbalance as causing Schizophrenia despite the theory's decline. Although researchers and clinicians began to understand Schizophrenia as a complex, overdetermined disorder, many psychiatrists continued to follow the chemical imbalance theory. Research in this period birthed the atypical antipsychotics, and for many psychiatrists these drugs seemed to continue to support the chemical imbalance theory, although they operate very differently from the neuroleptics that actually spawned the theory.

The fourth and current period began in the mid-1990s and continues to the present. This period is marked by new imaging technology that allows neurologists and psychopharmacologists to more closely examine the brain and the effects of medications on the brain. During this period researchers will likely continue to construct newer theories to account for the action of antipsychotic medications.

## Theories of Neuroleptic Action From the Medical Model Perspective

In this section we outline the mechanism of action in typical antipsychotics (neuroleptics), detail their common side effects, and discuss how to deal with side effects. It is interesting that neuroleptics, and chlorpromazine in particular, were widely used before their mechanisms of action were isolated. As you are now aware, this is not unusual in the history of psychopharmacology, but the neuroleptics were being used on a global scale before the mechanisms of action were identified.

### The Dopamine Hypothesis of Schizophrenia

The **dopamine hypothesis of Schizophrenia** (the first "chemical imbalance" theory for the disorder) actually was formulated in the 1960s but had no impact on the field of psychiatry until the 1970s. The hypothesis proposes that Schizophrenia is caused by an undefined problem in dopamine transmission. The hypothesis grew out of the realization that chlorpromazine and haloperidol both seemed to interrupt dopamine transmission and both seemed to decrease the symptoms of Schizophrenia. As you may recall from Chapter Five, this is similar to the **amine hypothesis of depression.** It posits a simple (too simple) cause-and-effect relationship from observations of medical trials. As in other cases, though, the reality is far more complex, and emotional defense of the simple dopamine hypothesis today carries the same authority as emotional arguments espoused by the Flat Earth Society.

So how was the dopamine hypothesis developed, and what relevance has it for mental health clinicians? Since the early administration of chlorpromazine, researchers had noted that the drug caused symptoms similar to those in Parkinson's disease (so named for James Parkinson, who outlined the symptoms in 1812). Carlsson and Lindqvist (1963) proposed the first variation on the dopamine hypothesis, but remember that at the time people knew little about neurotransmitters and nothing

at all about neurotransmitter receptors. Arvid Carlsson discovered dopamine in the central nervous system, where, researchers learned, dopamine was also a precursor to norepinephrine. Studies with reserpine demonstrated that it depleted norepinephrine and serotonin from the brain, but when these neurotransmitters were replaced they did not counter the effects of the reserpine. Carlsson and his colleagues, hot off their discovery that dopamine was also present in the brain, assumed that dopamine too was depleted by reserpine and discovered that giving research animals a precursor for dopamine (levodopa) did in fact reverse the effects of reserpine. Thus was born the first variation of the dopamine hypothesis—that psychoses were somehow related to deficiencies in dopamine.

The first response to this theory was that it did not make sense, because chlorpromazine did not empty the presynaptic neuron of dopamine (recall that researchers had not yet learned about receptors). Carlsson and Lindqvist (1963) demonstrated that chlorpromazine and haloperidol acted on the postsynaptic neurons. Only after Solomon Snyder and Candace Pert confirmed the presence of receptors could researchers make the conceptual leap linking the effects of chlorpromazine to dopamine receptors. Snyder, Banerjee, Yamanura, and Greenberg (1974) also demonstrated that there were many dopamine receptors, and subsequent research showed that antipsychotic drugs had a particular affinity for binding at the dopamine-2 (D2) receptor. This paved the way for the inordinate focus on receptors in today's pharmacologic research. Researchers concluded that neuroleptic drugs such as chlorpromazine and haloperidol blocked the D2 receptors, preventing dopamine from binding at those receptors and exerting an effect. Thus decreasing dopamine activity in this manner lessened symptoms of Schizophrenia in many patients. When researchers assumed that people suffering from Parkinson's disease were suffering from decreased dopamine activity, this hypothesis further explained why people taking neuroleptics might suffer Parkinsonian side effects. Although the drug they were taking, not Parkinson's disease, had disrupted their dopamine transmission, the result was the same.

This variation of the dopamine hypothesis was supported by observations of amphetamine users as well. Researchers had long known that heavy amphetamine users could develop symptoms similar to those seen in Schizophrenia. Because amphetamines were later shown to increase dopamine in the synaptic cleft, it made sense that if problems in dopamine transmission could cause Schizophrenia, drugs that artificially increased dopamine levels might cause symptoms similar to those of Schizophrenia, just as decreased levels of dopamine would cause symptoms similar to those of Parkinson's disease.

As noted, the dopamine hypothesis was a starting point but too simplistic. Despite warnings from researchers such as Solomon Snyder and Arvid Carlsson that the hypothesis was merely a correlation and should not be mistaken for a cause-and-effect relationship, by the 1970s the dopamine hypothesis of Schizophrenia was quite popular. It is still espoused by some clinicians with great certainty today.

To summarize: It is now clear that neuroleptics (also called *typical antipsychotics*) bind to a subfamily of dopamine receptors called the D2 receptors. Here the drugs act as **antagonists,** meaning they block the receptor but exert no effect. They merely block dopamine molecules from binding. The dopamine molecules would exert an effect if they *could* bind, but they are prevented from doing so as long as the person is taking a neuroleptic medication. The dopamine hypothesis was a mainstay for understanding drug treatment for Schizophrenia until the 1990s.

The following two cases illustrate both (1) the use of neuroleptics to treat disorders in the spectrum of Schizophrenia and (2) the reliance on the dopamine hypothesis as the cornerstone for treating Schizophrenia until the early 1990s. This approach met with both success and failure, showing that the dopamine hypothesis was too simplistic.

## The Case of Colin

Colin, a 27-year-old father of four, began to notice that he experienced strange thoughts, maybe voices, during his workday. His wife noticed that he was

more agitated and tense at home, even impatient with the children. In his work as a media specialist at a major university, Colin had a range of responsibilities linked to a very tight schedule. His immediate supervisor noticed his growing disorganization at work and a gradual deterioration of his performance. Colin insisted he was receiving messages that preoccupied his mind and distracted him from his daily routine. He became frightened and paranoid, and said people were out to destroy him. He stopped sleeping and eating, and believed his food was poisoned. Finally his wife called the emergency room and was advised to bring Colin in as soon as possible. He resisted her efforts, but finally agreed to go when his best friend insisted he should to demonstrate to the world that he was not insane.

Colin was hospitalized for 18 days and prescribed 24 mg of a typical antipsychotic called *thiothixene* (Navane). Colin also participated in group and art therapy during his hospitalization. On release Colin continued the thiothixene (reduced to 12 mg a day) and began individual and couples therapy at a mental health center. Colin continued both therapies for several years, stopping the thiothixene after nine months. Ten years after his hospitalization, Colin remains relatively stable both at work and at home, leading an active and productive life. Colin was never hospitalized again, nor did he decompensate to such a state that he needed to go back on thiothixene or into the hospital. This episode occurred in the early 1980s, and the diagnosis at the time was Brief Reactive Psychosis.

Colin's case also illustrates several of the perspectives we have discussed in this book. He suffered from a brief but serious cognitive impairment that included hearing voices, losing some contact with reality, and becoming paranoid. From the medical model perspective, Colin had psychotic symptoms and was hospitalized for them. The neuroleptic, thiothixene, was very helpful, and Colin never developed any serious side effects. As usual though, the medical model perspective provides only part of the story. From the intrapsychic perspective, Colin experienced enormous pressure to earn more money for his growing family at the same time he learned of his parents' divorce. He also learned there was little promotion potential for him at work, and he began to sense a growing stress with his wife. Culturally, Colin, as a second-generation Irishman to the United States, was ashamed of the dramatic nature of his psychological disorder and his need to take a psychotropic medication. The influence of his family's rigid interpretation of Catholic dogma made Colin ashamed to share this experience with others. In addition, Colin felt a covert stigmatization at work from his immediate supervisor, who was Japanese and who failed to grasp the seriousness of Colin's illness and to be empathic toward him during his recovery.

Therapy was invaluable to Colin as he focused on some personal issues that bothered him and also worked on many of the difficulties in his marriage. Throughout the therapy Colin became alert to the signs that indicated that he could become ill again and, as of this writing, he has had no further serious problems.

## The Case of Ethel

For many years Ethel suffered from Undifferentiated Schizophrenia accompanied with many negative symptoms. Ethel's psychiatrist had prescribed 600 mg of chlorpromazine (Thorazine) daily. Because Ethel was single and lived alone, it was very difficult for her case manager to assess how compliant she was with her medication, including her Cogentin (taken to treat side effects from her chlorpromazine). Over a period of two years Ethel had to be hospitalized six times, for periods ranging from eight days to four weeks, because she was unable to function or care for herself. Eventually the pattern became clear: Ethel would stop taking her chlorpromazine and gradually retreat into a nonfunctioning catatonic state. During her last hospitalization the treatment team recommended haloperidol (Haldol) by injection on a monthly basis to assist her with compliance. This strategy altered Ethel's response to her illness. Although it remained essential for her to take her Cogentin orally, getting an injection once a month at the mental health center ended her cycle of hospitalizations, seemed to ease her negative symptoms, and allowed her to participate in group activities sponsored by the center.

Neuroleptic therapy by injection was a strategy implemented for noncompliant patients before the advent of the atypical antipsychotics. This intervention was only partially successful, because many clients remained resistant to treatment with all neuroleptics and/or suffered such serious side effects that neuroleptic treatment became a burden.

### Side Effects of Neuroleptic Medication

Perhaps one of the greatest influences for the development of newer antipsychotic medications was the side effects of the neuroleptic medications. Table 7.1 lists the most common neuroleptic drugs still in use today. Note that all these drugs are associated in different degrees with the difficult side effects we describe next.

To fully understand the side effects of neuroleptic antipsychotic medications, we must look at four primary dopamine pathways in the brain that are affected by these medications. Table 7.2 summarizes these pathways, and then we discuss each.

### The Four Primary Dopamine Pathways in the Brain

#### The Mesolimbic Pathway

Without dispute, the mesolimbic pathway is most clearly associated with the positive symptoms of Schizophrenia. Stahl (2000) has noted that the auditory hallucinations, delusions, and even thought disorder symptoms of Schizophrenia have been correlated with this pathway. Stahl has suggested that perhaps the dopamine hypothesis of Schizophrenia should be renamed the "mesolimbic dopamine hypothesis of positive psychotic symptoms" (p. 374), because that more accurately describes the correlation between neuroleptic medications acting at this brain site and decreased symptoms. Obviously one problem in medicating clients with Schizophrenia is that the effects of the medications (at least to date) cannot be isolated to this one dopamine pathway.

#### The Mesocortical Pathway

The mesocortical pathway is related to cognition, but its role (if any) in the symptoms of Schizophrenia is undetermined. It does appear that the blockade of the dopamine-2 receptors in this pathway by

**TABLE 7.1**   Examples of Neuroleptic (Typical) Antipsychotics

| Generic Name | Class or Subclass | Brand Name | Daily Oral Dose |
|---|---|---|---|
| Chlorpromazine | Phenothiazine (aliphatic) | Thorazine | 150–1000 mg[a] |
| Promazine | Phenothiazine (aliphatic) | Sparine | 25–1000 mg |
| Triflupromazine | Phenothiazine (aliphatic) | Vesprin | 20–50 mg |
| Fluphenazine | Phenothiazine (piperazine) | Prolixin | 2–20 mg |
| Perphenazine | Phenothiazine (piperazine) | Trilafon | 8–40 mg |
| Trifluoperazine | Phenothiazine (piperazine) | Stelazine | 5–30 mg |
| Mesoridazine | Phenothiazine (piperidine) | Serentil | 75–300 mg |
| Thioridazine | Phenothiazine (piperidine) | Mellaril | 100–800 mg |
| Chlorprothixene | Thioxanthene | Taractan | 30–600 mg |
| Thiothixene | Thioxanthene | Navane | 6–50 mg |
| Haloperidol | Butyrophenone | Haldol | 2–40 mg |
| Molindone | Dihydroindolone | Moban | 20–225 mg |
| Loxapine | Dibenzoxazepine | Loxitane | 30–150 mg |
| Pimozide | Diphenylbutylpiperidine | Orap | 2–12 mg |

[a]Schatzberg, Cole, and DeBattista (1997) have summarized research suggesting that little benefit is gained from chlorpromazine by exceeding a dose 400 mg a day.

**TABLE 7.2**   Four Primary Dopamine Pathways in the Brain

| Name | Location |
|---|---|
| Mesolimbic pathway | Projects from the ventral tegmental area of the brain to the limbic system. Plays a role in emotional behavior |
| Mesocortical pathway | Projects from the ventral tegmental area of the brain all the way to the cerebral cortex. Plays a role in cognition. |
| Nigrostriatal pathway | Projects from the substantia nigra of the brain stem to the basal ganglia and is part of the extrapyramidal nervous system. |
| Tuberoinfundibular pathway | Projects from the hypothalamus to the pituitary and governs prolactin release. |

neuroleptic medications causes an emotional blunting (sometimes referred to as **flat affect)** and cognitive problems that look like thought disorder. This has sometimes been called **neuroleptic-induced deficit syndrome** (Stahl, 2000, p. 405). Neuroleptic-induced deficit syndrome is particularly problematic, because it mirrors the negative symptoms of Schizophrenia that we discussed at the beginning of this chapter. Part of the ongoing debate is whether neuroleptic medications acting on this pathway actually exacerbate the negative symptoms of Schizophrenia and in turn degrade the client's quality of life. Further, if clients have pronounced negative symptoms before receiving neuroleptic medication, such medications may make the symptoms worse.

## The Nigrostriatal Dopamine Pathway

The nigrostriatal dopamine pathway as part of the extrapyramidal nervous system governs motor movements. Any deficiency of dopamine in this pathway causes a movement disorder. Parkinson's disease is caused by a deficiency of dopamine in this pathway, in turn caused by degeneration of dopamine neurons in the pathway. What we describe later as extrapyramidal symptoms are the **Parkinsonian side effects** that result when neuroleptic medications block dopamine receptors in this pathway and cause movement disorders. One of the more serious disorders is **tardive dyskinesia**, or late-appearing abnormal movement. Although the effects of neuroleptics on this pathway and thus movement confirmed initial hypotheses about the role played by dopamine in their mechanism of action, such effects have also confirmed fears that for some clients the treatment may be as difficult to live with as the symptoms.

## The Tuberoinfundibular Pathway

The tuberoinfundibular pathway is much shorter than the previous three and, as noted in Table 7.2, controls the prolactin levels that normally rise in breast-feeding women. The firing of dopamine neurons in this pathway inhibits the release of prolactin, precluding lactation. When a woman is pregnant, part of the hormonal changes she experiences include inhibition of these neurons. This inhibition increases prolactin release so the woman can lactate to feed her child after birth. Herein lie more problematic side effects from neuroleptic medications. When the medications artificially inhibit the dopamine neurons in this pathway by blocking DA receptors, the result is an unintended increase of prolactin and symptoms such as galactorrhea (breast secretion) and amenorrhea (cessation of menses) in females as well as development of female secondary sex characteristics in males. Clients of both genders may also experience sexual dysfunction.

Given this overview of important pathways affected by neuroleptic medications, you can surmise the basic problem. As we noted, the only antipsychotic actions from these medications result from their blockage of D2 receptors in the mesolimbic pathway. The blocking of D2 receptors in the remaining three pathways all result in undesirable side effects. In addition, neuroleptics are "dirty" drugs, meaning that they not only block dopamine receptors but also may block histamine, acetylcholine, and adrenergic receptors. These properties also result in undesirable side effects. Having introduced the different ways in which side effects can occur from neuroleptic medication, let's now look more closely at the primary side effects of these medications. Please note that this discussion of the topic is not exhaustive and does not include rare side effects. These descriptions should give clinicians a sense of what clients may expect and what to listen for as clients describe effects they are experiencing.

### Allergic Reactions to Neuroleptics

Allergic reactions to neuroleptics occur in approximately 7% of patients and usually manifest between two weeks and two months of treatment. The primary symptom is a rash on the face, neck, upper chest, or extremities. The rash (local or general) results in red pimples accompanied by a burning or stinging sensation. These are usually treated with antihistamines or, in more severe cases, steroids (Malhotra, Litman, & Pickar, 1993).

### Anticholinergic Effects of Neuroleptics

As the name implies, anticholinergic effects of neuroleptics result from the neuroleptic medication blocking acetylcholine receptors in both the peripheral and the central nervous systems. The secondary results are called **autonomic side effects** because of their impact on the autonomic nervous system. The primary CNS side effect related to anticholinergic action is **delirium**. The peripheral effects of anticholinergic action are described later. Note that all these side effects may be exacerbated if the client is also taking an anticholinergic agent with the neuroleptic. We explain the rationale for using these agents later, when we address extrapyramidal symptoms.

## Blurred Vision

The anticholinergic action of neuroleptics can paralyze the ciliary muscle in the pupil of the eye, causing difficulty in focusing on objects within a close field of vision. Sometimes prescribers lower the dosage temporarily or recommend reading glasses to provide relief (Perry, Alexander, & Liskow, 1997). We have found that although not all clients experience this (or any other side effect), those who do often prefer to have the doctor change their medication.

### Dry Mouth

Dry mouth can be particularly bothersome for clients, depending on the strength of the effect. Both the antihistaminic and anticholinergic effects of neuroleptics cause dry mouth. Many clients can obtain relief with sugarless gum or candy, but many clients find it necessary to carry a drinking bottle with them at all times. Our clients often preferred sweetened, caffeinated soft drinks, which, combined with other poor dietary habits, exacerbated the weight gain associated with the antihistaminic effects of neuroleptics.

### Constipation

Constipation can be seriously aggravated by neuroleptic medication, although it may resolve as the client adjusts to the medication. Routine use of laxatives is to be discouraged (Perry, Alexander, & Liskow, 1997). Malhotra and colleagues (1993) noted that in severe cases, constipation can progress into fatal intestinal dilation or paralytic ileus. Paralytic ileus can result in death through intestinal obstruction. Although this is rare, clients need regular checkups with regard to intestinal functioning.

### Urinary Retention

Urinary retention may be noticed two to four weeks from beginning the neuroleptic regimen. According to Perry and colleagues (1997), blocking the acetylcholine neurons affects the detrusor muscle that governs the flow of urine. Although the effect is dose related, acute urinary retention is a sign for the prescribing professional to consider another medication as it can lead to kidney problems and bladder or urinary tract infections.

### Withdrawal Reactions

Although neuroleptic medications are not drugs of abuse per se, regular and long-term use can induce tolerance, which can lead to withdrawal reactions if medications are discontinued abruptly. The symptoms usually begin two or three days after discontinuation and include headache, nausea, vomiting, diarrhea, and insomnia. Any client who has taken a neuroleptic for at least one month should have the medication tapered off if it is to be discontinued. Perry, Alexander, and Liskow (1997) recommend at least a one-week period (inpatient) or a two-week period (outpatient) where the dosage is titrated down before the drug is discontinued.

## Cardiovascular Side Effects From Neuroleptics

As with some of the antidepressants we discussed in Chapter Five, neuroleptics can cause orthostatic hypotension, which is due to the antiadrenergic effects of these drugs. This effect inhibits the normal constriction of blood vessels associated with postural change, resulting in the lightheadedness and dizziness characteristic of orthostatic hypotension (Malhotra, Litman, & Pickar, 1993). This side effect usually begins within the first few hours or days of treatment and is more pronounced when the neuroleptic has been administered **parenterally** (by injection). In most cases clients can easily manage this by standing up slowly and by elevating their feet when lying down. In cases where clients have complained about this effect, lowering the medication dose has also been effective as long as the therapeutic effects are not diminished to the point that symptoms begin to interfere with the client's life again. Clients on neuroleptics may also experience electrocardiogram changes, which are of debatable clinical significance. Although case reports exist of lethal cardiovascular events in people taking neuroleptics, they have not been linked to the neuroleptic medication per se.

## Dermatological Side Effects From Neuroleptics

Perhaps the most common dermatologic side effect is photosensitivity. This sensitivity to sunlight occurs in approximately 3% of clients taking neuroleptic medications. Most cases are related to chlorpromazine, but all clients on neuroleptics should limit their exposure to the sun and should use sunscreen and protective clothing. Approximately 1%

of clients on neuroleptics develop a bluish pigmentation in their skin. This rare effect depends on the neuroleptic used, dosage, and extent of exposure to sunlight. These disorders are thought to be much less frequent today because use of neuroleptics has decreased and lower doses are used (Perry, Alexander, & Liskow, 1997).

### Endocrinological Side Effects of Neuroleptic Medications

Neuroleptics can cause hormonal side effects partly because of their impact on dopamine transmission in the tuberoinfundibular pathway, described earlier. As mentioned, galactorrhea and amenorrhea can occur in females. It is important to note that breast enlargement and engorgement can occur in both males and females (Sullivan & Lukoff, 1990). Elevated prolactin levels may subside within two to three days of discontinuing treatment of oral antipsychotics, but in some cases this may take weeks or months (Perry, Alexander, & Liskow, 1997). In addition, clients may experience polydipsia (excessive thirst and water drinking) or a deficiency of sodium in the blood (hyponatremia).

### Weight Gain

Studies done in the 1970s correlated weight gain with neuroleptic medications. The average gain was approximately 13 pounds. Weight gain is tied to the antihistaminic properties of the neuroleptics, as is drowsiness and sedation (Julien, 2001). Perry, Alexander, and Liskow (1997) caution that although weight gain may be a property of neuroleptic medications, it may also be due to a combination of factors such as the medication, a sedentary lifestyle, and poor diet habits. Although these authors encourage clinicians to monitor patients' weight, they remind us that under no circumstances should clients use amphetamine-based appetite suppressants, because of the connection between dopamine stimulation and exacerbated symptoms.

### Extrapyramidal Symptoms Caused by Neuroleptic Medication

As you may recall from our discussion of the nigrostriatal dopamine pathway in the brain, neuroleptic medications block the dopamine-2 receptors in this pathway and cause movement disorders. These extrapyramidal symptoms (EPSs), can range from mild to severe, and may have early or late onset. For most clients, these symptoms are problematic and are one reason that many psychiatrists believe newer, atypical antipsychotics should be the first line of treatment.

### Early-Onset Extrapyramidal Symptoms

Estimates of early-onset EPSs fluctuate wildly, ranging between 2 and 95% of clients taking neuroleptics (Lavin & Rifkin, 1992). **Dystonias** or **dystonic reactions** occur in 2 to 10% of clients on neuroleptic medications. The onset is sudden (1 to 3 days after neuroleptic medication is taken) and consists of involuntary contractions of possibly any striated muscle group. The most common dystonic reactions are in the muscles of the head and face, producing tics, facial grimacing, or spasms. The reactions are possible with all neuroleptics but are less likely with the piperazine phenothiazines (see Table 7.1). Although these side effects often cease without treatment, they can be easily treated with Benadryl or benztropine (Cogentin), an anticholinergic agent. The etiology of dystonic reactions is not known.

The term *akathisia* refers to a subjective experience of motor restlessness, a condition that is much more difficult to treat than dystonic reactions. In our clinical work with clients, the intrapsychic experience of this particular side effect can be profound. Clients report feeling that they cannot sit still, and they tap their foot/feet, pace back and forth, shake their hands, or rock back and forth when standing. Observed behaviorally, they are always in constant motion. The incidence of akathisia in studies ranges from 21 to 75% (Perry, Alexander, & Liskow, 1997). The majority of clients who develop akathisia experience symptoms within about two months. Schatzberg, Cole, and DeBattista (1997) note that sometimes akathisia has been misdiagnosed as psychotic agitation. Obviously, this misdiagnosis may lead doctors to increase the dosage of the very compound causing the problem.

One sign from which to discern the difference between psychotic agitation and akathisia is the degree of psychological contact the client can make. It is important that someone who has a therapeutic alliance with the client talk to him or her about the symptoms. Most clients suffering from akathisia can, to some extent, describe the symptoms and differentiate them from psychotic symptoms they have experienced in the past. Schatzberg and colleagues note that asking the client whether the restlessness is "a muscle feeling or a head feeling" (p. 145) often helps differentiate akathisia (the muscle feeling) from anxiety that may accompany agitation (the head feeling). These authors consider that to assume akathisia over agitation is to err on the side of caution. Doctors may treat akathisia with a benzodiazepine, an anti-Parkinsonian agent such as Cogentin, or even a beta-blocker such as propranolol. Although some clients may not even be aware of their akathisia, the symptoms greatly distress others. Furthermore, sometimes agents used to treat akathisia exacerbate the sedation the client experiences, making such treatment problematic.

Parkinsonianism is a set of side effects that manifest as muscular rigidity, slowed movement, tremors (usually in the hands), or **bradykinesia** (fatigue when performing repetitive motion). The tremors may occur at rest or while in motion and may include the mouth, chin, and lips. Clients with Parkinsonianism appear depressed, but it is important to differentiate this from actual depression. The incidence ranges in studies from 2 to 56% of clients taking neuroleptics. Again it depends on the neuroleptic used, the dosage, and the individual's response to it. Parkinsonianism is typically treated with anticholinergic agents (such as Cogentin). There is debate as to whether or not all neuroleptics should be given with an anti-Parkinsonian agent (Stanilla & Simpson, 1995). Advocates claim that doing so precludes the appearance of many extrapyramidal symptoms, and opponents claim the neuroleptics are toxic enough without adding a second agent if not needed. It is hoped that with continued success in atypical antipsychotics, the debate will soon be nothing but a historical artifact.

### Late-Onset Extrapyramidal Symptoms

Two identified late-onset EPSs are similar to the early-onset symptoms and differ only in the time it takes them to manifest. Frequently these are called tardive syndromes, meaning delayed-onset, abnormal, involuntary movement disorders (Fernandez & Friedman, 2003). Bear in mind that the word *tardive* means "late appearing"; thus tardive dystonia and tardive akathisia are the same as dystonic reactions and akathisia as described earlier, but with a much later onset (sometimes after a patient has taken the neuroleptic for years). Although there is no developed literature regarding these two late-onset EPSs, there is a great deal of literature on tardive dyskinesia.

Tardive dyskinesia is a late-appearing abnormal movement of the mouth, lips, and tongue that may be accompanied by involuntary twitching and jerking of muscles (choreic movement). The primary differential diagnoses include Huntington's chorea and other disorders that affect the basal ganglia (Casey, 1993). The most common symptoms are sucking and smacking lip movements, lateral movements of the jaw, and puffing of cheeks with tongue-thrusting motions (Perry, Alexander, & Liskow, 1993). Tardive dyskinesia affects on average 15 to 20% of clients on neuroleptics, although gender (7:1 male-to-female ratio), age, diagnosis, dosage, and duration of neuroleptic regimen all seem to play a role. Perry and colleagues (1993) noted, "Tardive dyskinesia is present in 5%–10% of patients over 40 years of age but may occur in 50%–80% of the elderly" (p. 51).

There are several theories of etiology for tardive dyskinesia, including hypersensitivity to dopamine, imbalances between the dopamine and acetylcholine systems, GABA dysfunction, and excitotoxicity. Most recently a theory has been proposed that oxidative stress and resulting structural abnormalities are the key factors in people who develop tardive dyskinesia (Kulkarni & Naidu, 2003). At present there is no one accepted theory.

Tardive dyskinesia is unpredictable. Although a six-month regimen of neuroleptics is generally considered safe, some patients develop tardive dyskinesia after only a few weeks of taking neuroleptics. When clients show signs of tardive dyskinesia and the neuroleptic is discontinued, often the symptoms vanish within weeks to months. Tardive dyskinesia appears irreversible in some cases, whereas in others it may only remit years after the neuroleptic is discontinued. Schatzberg, Cole, and DeBattista (1997) noted that about 25% of their clients developed dyskinesia when the neuroleptic was tapered off or stopped. These authors also note that dyskinesia develops in some individuals who have never been exposed to neuroleptics. Schatzberg and colleagues (1997) state there is no single effective or standard treatment for tardive dyskinesia and clinicians should consider the risks and benefits of extended treatment with neuroleptics in patients likely to be kept on the medication more than a few months.

Schatzberg and colleagues (1997) conclude that "this issue must be discussed with the patient and his or her family unless there are defensible clinical reasons for not doing so" (p.151). From our clinical experience, the only reasons for not discussing this with clients and/or family members is if a client's symptoms preclude making psychological contact and the family members are clearly judged to be incapable of acting, or unwilling to act, in the client's best interest. As you will see, researchers hope that the newer, atypical antipsychotics are not associated with tardive dyskinesia. Although the jury is still out, the outlook is optimistic. It appears the incidence of tardive dyskinesia in the newer antipsychotics is substantially lower than in the neuroleptics (Dolder & Jeste, 2003; Friedman, 2003; Lykouras, Agelopoulos, & Tzavellas, 2002), although the newer compounds are still associated with some tardive dyskinesia (Bella & Piccoli, 2003).

### Neuroleptic Malignant Syndrome

Although rare, neuroleptic malignant syndrome (NMS) is a potentially life-threatening complication of neuroleptic medications. Although rates of occurrence are low, they should be noted. Approximately 1% of all psychiatric admissions may have this response to standard neuroleptic medications. Hyperthermia, severe extrapyramidal symptoms, and autonomic disturbances characterize NMS. Caroff and Mann (1993) have noted that the onset may occur within an hour to two months after the first dose of the neuroleptic. In most cases, the clients show signs within a week. Once NMS begins, it progresses rapidly over a one- to three-day period. If the medication is discontinued in time, most cases resolve within a month. Fatalities from NMS are rare, because use of neuroleptics has decreased and the syndrome is detected early.

### Agents to Treat Extrapyramidal Side Effects

Antiparkinsonianism agents are used for treating early-onset extrapyramidal symptoms. Recall that these side effects result from neuroleptic-induced blockade of dopamine receptors in the nigrostriatal pathway that cause decreased dopamine transmission. Table 7.3 lists drugs commonly used to treat EPSs.

Looking at Table 7.3, readers may sense the paradox of all the agents listed. As for the dopaminergic agent (amantadine), you may ask, "If neuroleptics are decreasing dopamine transmission, won't the addition of a dopamine agonist worsen symptoms?" Similarly, you may look at all the anticholinergic agents and wonder, "If neuroleptics cause anticholinergic symptoms, won't adding an anticholinergic

**TABLE 7.3**   Drugs Commonly Used to Treat Extrapyramidal Side Effects

| Generic Name | Brand Name | Type of Drug | Daily Dosage Range |
| --- | --- | --- | --- |
| Amantadine | Symmetrel | Dopaminergic | 100–300 mg |
| Benztropine | Cogentin | Anticholinergic | 2–6 mg |
| Biperiden | Akineton | Anticholinergic | 2–8 mg |
| Diphenhydramine | Benadryl | Anticholinergic | 50–300 mg |
| Ethopropazine | Parsidol | Anticholinergic | 100–400 mg |
| Procyclidine | Kemadrin | Anticholinergic | 10–20 mg |
| Trihexyphenidyl | Elixir | Anticholinergic | 4–15 mg |

agent worsen these side effects?" Both are good questions. To understand why any of these agents may be given to a client taking neuroleptic medication for psychotic symptoms, it is first important to understand something we discussed in Chapter Two, the delicate balance of neurotransmission and the ripple effect of how impact on one neurotransmitter system eventually influences others.

Recall that although most neurons produce only one type of neurotransmitter, most neurons have receptors for multiple neurotransmitters. When we clinicians interfere with neurotransmission by introducing an agent such as a neuroleptic, we set in motion a ripple effect that can upset the function and balance of many other systems. One of these is the cholinergic system. It seems the neurons that make acetylcholine depend on dopamine transmission. If we interfere with dopamine transmission, we disrupt acetylcholine transmission as well. Thus one theory about extrapyramidal symptoms is that they result from disruption in balance between dopamine neurons and acetylcholine neurons. Therefore two ways to restore balance logically present themselves. The first is to decrease the acetylcholine transmission so it "evenly matches" the dopamine transmission. That is done with anticholinergic agents. The second solution is to boost dopamine transmission so it more evenly matches acetylcholine transmission. The obvious challenge here is not to increase it in an area or in a way that exacerbates the psychotic symptoms that were the problem in the first place.

Both solutions to addressing EPSs have their problems. Although amantadine does in fact diminish dystonia, akathisia, and Parkinsonianism more effectively than placebo, it also causes orthostatic hypotension, skin rashes, and GI disturbance and can exacerbate psychotic symptoms or induce agitation. Similarly, anticholinergic agents effectively treat dystonia, akathisia, and Parkinsonianism, but can cause allergic reactions (rash or dermatitis), increase heart rate, exacerbate all anticholinergic side effects listed earlier for neuroleptics, cause urinary retention, impair memory, and may induce confusion and/or delirium. Although helpful with EPSs, clearly neither type of agent is a panacea, and prescribing professionals must carefully balance the

**TABLE 7.4**   Rational Prescribing Practice for Treating Extrapyramidal Symptoms

First, try lowering the dose of the neuroleptic or switch the client to an atypical antipsychotic.

Generally speaking, anticholinergics should not be routinely added as prophylactics when a client is prescribed neuroleptic medication.

Every three months reassess a client who is prescribed medication for EPSs, because not all clients need long-term treatment with these agents.

If a client does not respond to one agent, try another, because responses differ person to person.

There is no support for combining anticholinergic agents.

intended therapeutic effects with the emergence or exacerbation of side effects.

Table 7.4 describes the rational prescribing practice recommended by Perry, Alexander, and Liskow (1997).

The following two cases address some of the complex side effect issues linked to neuroleptics and potential dependency issues related to some anticholinergics.

## The Case of Teana

Teana, a 37-year-old divorced biracial mother of three, suffered from Schizoaffective Disorder and polysubstance dependence. Most recently her presenting symptoms seemed more like the positive symptoms of Schizophrenia than those of a manic profile. The psychiatrist was acutely aware of Teana's polysubstance dependence. Both Teana and her case manager vouched for the fact that Teana was attending Narcotics Anonymous (NA) and was not currently using. The psychiatrist reluctantly prescribed fluphenazine (Prolixin) 20 mg daily, accompanied by the anticholinergic benztropine (Cogentin) 2 mg daily.

About a month later Teana scheduled an appointment with the psychiatrist, indicating that it was an emergency. Both the psychiatrist and case manager were puzzled, because she had enough medication for 90 days. In the waiting room another case manager overheard Teana talking about what a "sweet" high she got from that "cognitive stuff" and that she was totally out and needed more. The case manager alerted the psychiatrist, who took Teana off the Cogentin and substituted a dopaminergic, amantadine (Symmetrel). Teana was upset and acted out both in the physician's office and in the waiting room, and she went back to using for a time. Eventually she returned to her drug treatment and accepted the Symmetrel in place of the Cogentin.

## The Case of Maurice

Maurice, a 39-year-old, single, auto assembly-line worker, became acutely psychotic at work. He spoke in a "language" that could not be understood, and he appeared delusional and paranoid. He was hospitalized for seven weeks and released on 30 mg of trifluoperazine (Stelazine) daily. Maurice could not return to work, and three months after being released from the hospital he was evicted from his apartment. He had been homeless and on the streets for over four months when he was accepted by a Christian house of hospitality, which offered to house him and monitor his medication. Over time Maurice changed from the positive symptoms of Schizophrenia to an array of negative symptoms. He became withdrawn, isolated, and detached, with slurred speech and impaired movement. The monk who was in charge of the house noticed that he seemed fatigued, that his hands trembled constantly, and that his movements were rigid and very slow. He called the mental health center to alert them to these changes in Maurice, and the psychiatrist saw him the following week. The case manager also had reported that Maurice had seemed more withdrawn lately. The psychiatrist evaluated Maurice, found he was suffering from Parkinsonianism, and treated him with Cogentin, an anticholinergic.

Maurice's symptoms improved gradually, but he never returned to any previous level of functioning. He remained in a state of isolation with minimal Parkinsonian symptoms, but with little hope of improving the quality of his life. We lost track of Maurice when he was recommended for clozapine in 1990. He had already been on neuroleptics for 13 years.

## Uses and Efficacy of Neuroleptic Medications

Thus far you are likely aware that the neuroleptics we have described have several drawbacks. Despite persistent and troublesome side effects, how well do these traditional agents really work? As we noted while summarizing the history of neuroleptics, compared to no medication at all they were a breakthrough. The questions remain, though, What is the efficacy today for neuroleptics? and For what disorders are clinicians likely to see them employed? Pies (1998) has emphasized that the main indication for any antipsychotic is, of course, for psychosis. He noted that although it is not necessarily inappropriate to use an antipsychotic for a nonpsychotic disorder, antipsychotics are often misused for other conditions, such as agitation. Certainly this is where the "practice" of medicine comes in and doctors must make clinically informed judgments to the best of their ability. At the same time, mental health clinicians should be aware of the difference between common and uncommon uses for neuroleptics. Table 7.5 lists common uses of antipsychotics outlined by Pies (1998) and Stahl (2000).

**TABLE 7.5**    Common Uses for Neuroleptic Medications

| |
| --- |
| All forms of Schizophrenia |
| Schizophreniform Disorder |
| Brief Psychotic Disorder |
| Schizoaffective Disorder |
| Major Depression with Psychotic Features |
| Psychosis secondary to cocaine intoxication |
| Manic states |
| Dementia related to various causes/disorders |
| Noncompliant client in an acute setting where fast onset of action is desired |
| Noncompliant client needing intramuscular formulations |
| Tics associated with Tourette's syndrome |
| Severe cases of Obsessive-Compulsive Disorder |
| Agitated State of PTSD |

And what about efficacy? As you learned in Chapter Five, many antidepressants fare no better than placebo in controlled trials, making the question of efficacy an important one to explore in great depth. All the available neuroleptic (typical) antipsychotics have conclusively been shown to be more effective than placebo in reducing the positive symptoms of Schizophrenia. The positive symptoms are typically the target symptoms, because they are the most disruptive to the client and others in the client's life. However, negative symptoms do not respond well (if at all) to neuroleptics (Kane & Marder, 1993).

Schatzberg, Cole, and DeBattista (1997) concluded that even where positive symptoms are concerned, neuroleptics do better than placebo but "in many respects, the nature and timing of clinical response to antipsychotics are unsatisfactory" (p. 122). They add that at most, only 75% will respond (some studies cite lower response rates), and many of these responders never achieve full remission. These drugs are not satisfactory regarding maintenance therapy, with approximately 50% of clients relapsing within two years, compared to 85% in placebo groups (Schatzberg, Cole, & DeBattista, 1997). Again, neuroleptics are clearly better than placebo—but are they good enough?

Although some clients may respond within hours to days of receiving a neuroleptic, an adequate trial should be at least four weeks, and maximum improvement in symptoms is expected to occur within the first six months of therapy. Although evidence suggests that early antipsychotic treatment in recently diagnosed clients improves long-term outcomes, over two to three years the relapse rates of even those with a diagnosis of first-time psychosis are in the 60 to 90% range (Szymanksi, Cannon, Gallagher, Erwin, & Gur, 1996). Table 7.6 summarizes strategies outlined by Perry, Alexander, and Liskow (1997) for clients who do not respond to neuroleptics or who respond only partially.

Clearly, although they offer some relief from the symptoms of psychosis, neuroleptics are of limited utility and carry side effects so severe that many clients are not motivated to comply with medication regimens. By the 1980s, these issues seemed so daunting that two rather hostile camps arose regarding neuroleptics. One camp believed these treat-

**TABLE 7.6** Strategies for Clients Taking Neuroleptics Who Partially Respond or Do Not Respond

Continue the same neuroleptic at the same dose.

Increase the dose of the current neuroleptic.

Switch to a different class of neuroleptic.

Add another medication to the neuroleptic.

Switch to an atypical (second-generation) antipsychotic.

ments were the best that could be done at the time, whereas the other questioned the ethics of placing clients on medications with such harsh side effect profiles. Although there appeared no common ground between these perspectives, all that was about to change with the introduction of the first atypical antipsychotic: clozapine.

### The Atypical Antipsychotics

There were two early attempts to develop antipsychotics that were structurally different from the neuroleptics. Molindone (Moban) was a structurally unique molecule in that it resembled the neurotransmitter serotonin. Despite this similarity, its binding properties resemble neuroleptics in the affinity for dopamine receptors. Although its use is less frequently associated with tardive dyskinesia, it seems to induce many of the same early-onset EPSs of the neuroleptics. Its efficacy is similar to that of haloperidol, and these similarities lead researchers to group it with the neuroleptics. Loxapine (Loxitane) is structurally more related to serotonergic antipsychotics (such as clozapine) than a neuroleptic, but it too functions more like a neuroleptic than like anything else. Loxapine binds to both dopamine and serotonin receptors but has many of the same side effect problems as the neuroleptics.

## The Case of Bonnie

Bonnie experienced her first psychotic episode when she was 17 years old. Bonnie's mother had been institutionalized off and on for 18 years, diagnosed with Schizophrenia. Her father left Bonnie and her mother when Bonnie was only 2 years old, and she had no siblings. Bonnie had been diagnosed with Schizophrenia, Disorganized subtype. She suffered from delusions, magical thinking, and bizarre behavior such as storing feces in mason jars under her bed, believing they would turn to gold if stored long enough. Bonnie would masturbate openly with little concern for where she was and would only say, "The voices are fucking me."

Bonnie showed marked negative symptoms and conceptual disorganization. These became substantially worse when she was treated with neuroleptic medication. When Bonnie was referred to the partial hospitalization program (PHP), she was 28 years old. She had three children of her own with three different men but had lost custody because of her inability to care for them. She was not allowed visits with them in their foster home because her bizarre behavior upset them. On first coming to the PHP from an inpatient unit, Bonnie was taking 500 mg of chlorpromazine daily as well as 6 mg of benztropine. This medication produced pronounced EPSs and worsened her anhedonia and social withdrawal. Over the course of two years, the psychiatrist at the PHP switched Bonnie's medication four times (constantly adjusting dosages), trying to maximize the therapeutic benefits and minimize the side effects. The best combination seemed to be haloperidol (20 mg daily) and benztropine (2 mg daily). This "best" combination, the doctor reluctantly agreed, allowed Bonnie to reside in a maximum-supervision group home and attend (but rarely participate in) PHP programming. Apparently Bonnie was in for a life living on the fringes of the community.

In 1990, we became aware of a new drug called *clozapine* and a patient management program sponsored by Novartis Pharmaceuticals. As a person suffering from treatment-resistant Schizophrenia with pronounced negative symptoms, Bonnie was an ideal candidate for the program. Further, her Social Security disability benefits would cover the costs of the medication. The program was rigorous, including weekly blood draws to check Bonnie for potentially lethal side effects (described later). After several months Bonnie was titrated off her haloperidol and benztropine and titrated onto clozapine. Although she experienced many of clozapine's side effects (weight gain, excessive salivation, GI upset), these seemed acceptable compared to what she had experienced on the neuroleptic.

Further, several months into treatment the PHP staff noticed a pronounced change in Bonnie. One day as she was coming to the PHP to have her blood drawn, a staff member greeted her, joking that she looked as if she had just gotten up. Bonnie, who had rarely responded with more than one- or two-syllable answers, turned to the staff member and said, "Yes, as you can see I am quite tired." This marked a dramatic decrease in Bonnie's negative symptoms. She began to participate in groups and to engage in conversations with other clients about day-to-day activities. Further, she became more independent in the group home and moved to a moderate-supervision setting. Perhaps the most rewarding aspect of her case was that she improved to the point that she was allowed to have biannual visits with her children, who lived about an hour away. Certainly Bonnie did not fully recover from Schizophrenia, but the clozapine brought about a diminishment of symptoms that greatly improved her quality of life. At last check, Bonnie was still stable and tolerating the clozapine therapy.

## A New Era

As we have noted, the discovery of antipsychotic drugs in 1950 was a breakthrough in treating mental illness. Lieberman (1997) noted that the magnitude of this advance in psychiatry has been compared to the discovery of insulin for diabetes, antibiotics for infectious disease, and anticonvulsants for epilepsy. At the same time, almost a half-century's experience with these compounds has made clinicians and consumers painfully aware of their limitations. According to Lieberman, almost 50% of patients respond only partially to treatment, and 20 to 30% may be wholly refractory to treatment. And, as you have seen, the therapeutic effects of the neuroleptics predominantly reduce the positive symptoms; neuroleptics are less beneficial for the negative symptoms and conceptual disorganization. Finally, the therapeutic effects of neuroleptics come with a great number of side effects (Brown & Levin, 1998).

Lieberman draws the metaphor that after 40 years of wandering in the proverbial pharmacological wilderness (1950 to 1990), many researchers and clients thought the introduction of clozapine was the gateway to a "promised land." Although clozapine was actually synthesized in 1959, it took 30 years before it was released for use in the United States.

What makes clozapine atypical? First, it alleviates psychotic symptoms while causing significantly fewer extrapyramidal side effects. Second, it is a more effective antipsychotic agent than conventional neuroleptics. Finally, clozapine has an impact on both the negative and the positive symptoms of Schizophrenia. Melzer (1993) noted that clozapine is very effective in treating a set of symptoms we have been referring to as *conceptual disorganization* (Lencz, Smith, Auther, Correll, & Cornblatt, 2003). Haloperidol has typically been the neuroleptic baseline against which all other antipsychotic drugs are tested. In numerous studies clozapine is more effective than haloperidol. A useful meta-analysis of these is done by Wahlbeck, Cheine, Essali, and Adams (1999).

### Placebo Versus Active Control Trials

Before exploring the atypical antipsychotic medications, we want to briefly note an important difference in the way newer antipsychotic medications are tested. In the introduction to Part Two and in Chapter Five, we covered the problem of placebo response, particularly with regard to antidepressant medications. In tests of newer medications designed to help people suffering from psychotic symptoms, an ethical problem arises with placebo-controlled trials. First, placebo responses from people suffering psychotic disorders have historically been very small in number, which raises the ethical concern of testing new medications against placebo. If a person is suffering from psychotic symptoms, it simply is not ethical to withhold treatment from the person for the purposes of having the person in a placebo control group. Therefore, new antipsychotics are frequently tested against the older neuroleptic medications. Such *active control trials* (Fleischhacker, Czobor, Hummer, Kemmler, Kohnen, & Volavka, 2003) are more designed to test the medication's side effect profile than to test efficacy against placebo. For the most part, the newer antipsychotics (with the exception of clozapine) work just as well as haloperidol but have a more favorable side effect profile.

### Mechanisms of Action

How does clozapine work? Whereas we noted the mechanism of action in neuroleptics focused on the blocking of dopamine receptors, clozapine is one of the most complicated drugs on the market. Researchers have found it has noteworthy interactions with at least nine neurotransmitter receptors. Six of the nine receptors are dopamine or serotonin receptors. Researchers currently do not know which of these receptors (or which combination of receptors) accounts or account for the antipsychotic effects. Table 7.7 details the mechanisms of action of clozapine.

**TABLE 7.7**  Mechanisms of Action of Clozapine

| Receptor | Action | Strength of Action |
|---|---|---|
| Dopamine 4 | Antagonist (blocks receptor, most DA antagonism here) | Weak |
| Dopamine 1 | Antagonist (blocks receptor) | Weak |
| Dopamine 2 | Antagonist (blocks receptor) | Weak |
| Dopamine 3 | Antagonist (blocks receptor) | Weak |
| 5-HT2 | Antagonist (blocks receptor) | Strong |
| 5-HT2C | Antagonist (blocks receptor) | Strong |
| 5-HT3 | Antagonist (blocks receptor) | Strong |
| Histamine | Antagonist (blocks receptor) | Unknown |
| Ach | Antagonist (blocks receptor) | Unknown |
| Adrenergic | Antagonist (blocks receptor) | Unknown |

Reviewing Table 7.7, perhaps the most striking thing you note is that the primary mechanism of action is strong serotonin antagonism and weak dopamine antagonism. Recall that all the neuroleptics worked by powerful dopamine antagonism, particularly at the D2 receptor. As far as clozapine goes, although the overall effects on dopamine are weak, those effects are more pronounced on the D1 receptor than the D2 receptor. Without having to understand the biochemistry involved, you can draw the significant conclusions: (1) This compound is more effective in treating Schizophrenia than neuroleptics that rely on D2 antagonism, and (2) this result certainly weakens any interpretation of the dopamine hypothesis of Schizophrenia that ties symptoms to dopamine transmission. The most that can be said is that by significantly interfering with dopamine transmission, neuroleptics can attenuate the positive symptoms of Schizophrenia. Schatzberg, Cole, and DeBattista (1997) remind us that clozapine, although an exciting development, is not a panacea. They warn, "The drug does have problems and dangers, it does not work for everyone, and patients who are helped substantially may still be far from well" (p. 157). With those cautions in mind, we turn now to the side effects of clozapine.

### Clozapine Side Effects

We cover the more common side effects of clozapine here. Those seeking a more elaborate discussion, including rare side effects, should see Perry, Alexander, and Liskow (1997) or Pies (1998).

### Agranulocytosis

The most potentially dangerous side effect of clozapine is agranulocytosis. This hematologic (related to blood-performing organs) side effect causes white blood cell count to drop dramatically in about 1.2% of treated patients. In a sense, this problem is related to the normal functioning of the immune system. In such cases the clozapine molecule attaches to the white blood cells, which the body then mistakenly interprets as foreign substances and discards. Mounting evidence suggests that people who develop agranulocytosis have a genetic predisposition to it. After clozapine has been around for more than one generation of clients to

receive it, researchers will likely know more about this disposition.

The first reports of agranulocytosis came from Finland in 1975, where 13 trial subjects had the reaction and 8 died from resulting secondary infection. Of the 73 agranulocytosis cases reported in the United States, 84% occurred in the first 3 months of treatment, 12% between 3 and 6 months, and the remaining 4% after 6 months. So the longer clients tolerate the drug, the less likely they are to develop agranulocytosis (Pisciotta, 1992). Clients must be monitored closely, though, and the manufacturer (Novartis Pharmaceuticals) mandates a weekly white blood cell count. This mandate is based on the hope that the white blood cell decrease is gradual and that therefore advance warning is possible. All patients must be cleared through a national registry (the Clozaril Patient Management System, CPMS), and the doctor and pharmacy are responsible for making blood counts as long as the patient is on the medication. New medication supplies are delivered at the time blood is drawn. Most patients stay on between 200 and 350 mg per day. Despite these precautions, 12 fatalities had occurred by 1994, with 5 of these people dying despite drug discontinuation. A baseline white blood cell count (WBC) must be obtained before the first dose is given, and the cell count must be 3500/mm or higher. If the WBC falls below 3000, Clozaril should be discontinued and never given again. The client should also be admitted to a hospital for observation. Table 7.8 lists the side effects of clozapine, drawn from Perry, Alexander, and Liskow (1997) and Schatzberg, Cole, and DeBattista (1997).

### Autonomic Side Effects of Clozapine

Autonomic side effects result from the antiadrenergic and anticholinergic actions of clozapine. These include constipation, hypersalivation, nausea/vomiting, and syncope. For some clients the constipation may be severe. Dosage reduction, increased exercise, and increased fluid intake may alleviate the problem. Hypersalivation is a still unexplained side effect that 6 to 31% of clients experience (Perry, Alexander, & Liskow, 1997). This typically manifests as excessive drooling at night but may include gagging. Although this decreases over the first two to three months, it will likely persist at

**TABLE 7.8**   Common Side Effects of Clozapine

| Type | Side Effect | Proposed Cause |
| --- | --- | --- |
| Hematologic | Agranulocytosis | Potentially lethal drop in white blood cell count related to drug binding to white blood cells and immune system response |
| Autonomic | Constipation Hypersalivation Nausea/vomiting Syncope | Likely caused by anticholinergic and antiadrenergic properties |
| Cardiovascular | Hypertension Hypotension ECG changes | Possibly caused by antiadrenergic properties |
| Metabolic | Weight gain | Possibly caused by antihistaminic and antiserotonergic properties |
| Neurologic | Delirium Seizures | Rarer effect caused by anticholinergic properties Mechanism not known |
| Psychiatric | OC symptoms | Possibly caused by antiserotonergic properties |
| Sexual dysfunction | Anorgasmia Impotence Priapism Decreased libido | Possibly caused by antiadrenergic or anticholinergic properties |
| Other CNS effects | Problems with temperature regulation | Mechanism not known |

some level. Some clinicians have prescribed other medications such as amitriptyline to help clients deal with salivation (Copp, Lament, & Tennent, 1991); other clinicians try to help clients adjust by sleeping with a towel on their pillow. This latter solution was in fact preferred in the case of Bonnie, given earlier. Although Bonnie was bothered by the salivation, she did not want to take any additional medications—and who could blame her?

Nausea and vomiting may occur after weeks or months of treatment, because there are large numbers of serotonin receptors in the gut that the drug affects, but the exact etiology is still unclear. Taking the medicine with food may help some clients. Syncope is a sudden loss of muscle tone (but not consciousness) that may be localized or more general. It appears dosage related, and reducing dosage may solve the problem.

## Cardiovascular Side Effects

Cardiovascular side effects may range from hypertension to hypotension and tachycardia. Hypotension is more often reported (11 to 13% of clients) than hypertension (4% of clients). Although dosage reduction may alleviate both symptoms, tolerance to the hypotensive side effects usually develops within a month (Perry, Alexander, & Liskow, 1997). As for tachycardia, the client may experience an increase of heart rate of 20 to 25 beats per minute. Onset is usually within a week of starting clozapine, and although the symptom may decrease, it rarely abates completely.

## Metabolic

The most problematic metabolic side effect is weight gain, with clients gaining between 9 and 25 pounds on average. The side effect is thought to be due to antihistaminic and antiserotonergic mechanisms of action in clozapine. In one study, which covered 7½ years, Umbricht, Pollack, and Kane (1994) noted that half the clients in the study gained over 20% of their pretreatment weight. In a retrospective analysis of weight gain across several different atypical antipsychotics, Wirshing et al. (1999) concluded that weight gain associated with clozapine tended to be most persistent. In the case described earlier, Bonnie gained a total of 30 pounds over two years of clozapine treatment. She was close to her ideal weight at the start of treatment, and this side effect troubled her. She did not want to discontinue the medication, although. Perry and colleagues (1997) noted that at the time of their writing, there were no effective approaches to counter this side effect.

### Neurological Side Effects

Of the neurological side effects in Table 7.8, the one of greatest concern is seizures. Grand mal seizures can occur in patients on high dosages. The maximum dosage is 900 mg a day. Approximately 5% of clients receiving between 600 and 900 mg suffer from seizures, about 3% of those receiving dosages between 300 and 600 mg develop seizures, and some 1% of those receiving up to 300 mg develop seizures (Perry, Alexander, & Liskow, 1997). If seizures occur, discontinue clozapine until the patient has a normal neurological exam. If the neurological exam is normal, clozapine can be reintroduced at 50% the original dose. Sometimes anticonvulsant medication can be used with clozapine to preclude further seizures.

### Extrapyramidal Side Effects

As noted, clozapine is associated with a low incidence of severe EPSs. Approximately 3% of clients experience muscular rigidity or tremor, and approximately 6% develop akathisia. There have been no reports of dystonias or late-onset EPSs.

## The Serotonin/Dopamine Antagonists

Despite its side effects, clozapine shifted the momentum of antipsychotic research. With the dopamine hypothesis of Schizophrenia, there was little research on how to treat clients who did not respond to neuroleptic medication and there was little research developing new neuroleptics. The creation and introduction of clozapine ushered in a new research direction in antipsychotics. Whereas researchers up to this point had focused on antihistamines and dopamine antagonists, clozapine raised a new possibility, which was that some combination of serotonin balanced against dopamine antagonism would have an antipsychotic effect. Further, this approach held much more promise for impacting both positive and negative symptoms. Serotonin dopamine antagonists (SDAs) have been developed in the hopes of maximizing therapeutic benefits. Since clozapine's U.S. release in 1989, several drugs have been developed that to differing degrees are intended to balance serotonin against dopamine antagonism. SDAs are atypical antipsychotics patterned after clozapine.

Another way to view this mechanism is by looking at relative percentages of antagonism of various receptors (Stahl, 2000). With therapeutic doses of neuroleptic agents, 70 to 90% of D2 receptors are blocked with little (if any) blockage of serotonin receptors. With therapeutic doses of clozapine, only 30 to 60% of D2 receptors are blocked, whereas 85 to 90% of serotonin receptors are blocked. SDAs fall midway on the range, with 30 to 50% of D2 receptors blocked and 60% of 5-HT receptors blocked.

The primary goal for side effects has been to eradicate the risk of agranulocytosis. Many new atypical medications have been developed that are "clozapine-like" without causing agranulocytosis. Note that although these agents appear generally just as effective as neuroleptics, they are not as effective as clozapine. Nevertheless, they are superior to clozapine in that none have yet been associated with agranulocytosis. They are superior to neuroleptics in that they have a milder side effect profile and may ameliorate the negative symptoms of Schizophrenia. Table 7.9 lists the SDA antipsychotics.

### The Specter of Side Effects

Before exploring the individual SDA compounds, we want to emphasize that the primary problems driving this research were the lack of EPSs in clozapine and the presence of agranulocytosis in

**TABLE 7.9**   Serotonin-Dopamine Antipsychotics

| Generic Name | Brand Name | Date Released |
|---|---|---|
| Risperidone | Risperdal | 1994 |
| Risperidone Intramuscular | Risperdal | 2003 |
| Risperidone M-Tab | Risperdal M-Tab | 2003 |
| Olanzapine | Zyprexa | 1996 |
| Sertindole | Serlect | 1997 |
| Quetiapine | Seroquel | 1998 |
| Ziprasidone | Geodon | 2001 |
| Ziprasidone Intra Muscular | Geodon | 2002 |
| Amisulpride | Solian (in Europe) | 1997 |

clozapine. The underlying theme of these forces was legal liability. With this liability in mind, apparently the most problematic side effect with the SDAs is related to a cardiac process called the *QTc interval.* The QTc interval is the length of time the heart ventricles need to electrically discharge and repolarize. Prolonging this interval can cause cardiac arrhythmia, including a potentially serious condition called *torsades de pointes (TdP)* and sudden death. Seldane had a similar effect and was therefore taken off the market. This effect also caused drug regulation authorities in the United Kingdom to pull the SDA sertindole (Serlect) off the market between 1999 and 2001.

Healy (2002) notes that many other antipsychotics, including neuroleptics, have this side effect, which came to light when Paul Leber of the FDA had experts testify on both sides of the argument. The results were that sertindole was pulled from the market in Europe and the release was significantly delayed in the United States. Presently the drugs with the most profound effects on QTc interval are contraindicated in patients with cardiac conditions, but as with all newer drugs, only time will tell how significant this potential side effect is. It is also important to understand that other drugs may contribute to QTc prolongation and that these medications are contraindicated with sertindole.

These medications include tricyclic antidepressants and their derivatives, and neuroleptics (particularly thioridazine). Mental health clinicians should check with prescribing professionals for more information about drug–drug interactions related to QTc prolongation. An overview of QTc can be found at http://www.sads.org/, a web site devoted to sudden arrhythmia death syndromes.

In addition to the problems with QTc prolongation, some atypical antipsychotics are now being linked to an increased risk for diabetes and other metabolic problems (Lebovitz, 2003). Liberty, Todder, Umansky, and Harman-Boehm (2004); Lindenmayer and Patel (1999); and Goldstein et al. (1999) noted that the use of atypical agents is associated with increased risk of diabetes and diabetic **ketoacidosis** in adults. Koller, Cross, and Schneider (2004) have reported the same problem in pediatric populations. Liberty et al. (2004) and Lebovitz (2003) recommend screening patients for risks associated with the disorder prior to putting them on an atypical antipsychotic regimen, and then monitoring them closely. In September 2003, the FDA requested that manufacturers of atypical antipsychotics update their product information labeling to contain additional information about diabetes and hypoglycemia.

Currently researchers are trying to sort out how much increased risk users of atypical antipsychotics may have for developing diabetes or hyperglycemia and what the mechanisms of this risk may be. It is also important to sort out this risk from the increased incidence of diabetes and hyperglycemia in the general population (Brown University Psychopharmacology Update, 2003). One study comparing the risk in olanzapine versus risperidone found that cases of patients on olanzapine seem associated with significantly higher risk of medication-related diabetes (Fuller, Shermock, Secic, & Grogg, 2003). Alas, whereas researchers once believed that moving from neuroleptic antipsychotic medications to atypical antipsychotic medications resulted in fewer medical complications and higher quality of client life, that conclusion requires more consideration, based on the client's health risks as well as on the prescriber's carefully weighing symptom relief against morbidity and mortality (Abidi & Bhaskara, 2003).

**TABLE 7.10**   Common Side Effects Associated With Risperidone

| Type | Description | Percentage of Patients |
|------|-------------|------------------------|
| Autonomic | None noted | |
| Cardiovascular | Prolonged QTc interval<br>Hypotension, dizziness | Unknown<br>10% |
| Hematologic | None noted, no agranulocytosis | |
| Hepatic | None noted, no monitoring necessary | |
| Metabolic | Weight gain of 7% body weight<br>Increased risk of diabetes | 18% |
| Endocrinologic | Increased prolactin levels | Unknown |
| Gastrointestinal | Nausea | 18% |
| Neurological | Agitation/anxiety | 58% |
| Early-onset EPS | Dose related | |
| Tardive dyskinesia | Dose related | |
| Neuroleptic malignant syndrome | 2 cases noted by 1997 | |
| Respiratory | Rhinitis (nasal congestion) | Approx. 9% |
| Other | Headache<br>Insomnia<br>Sedation | 16%<br>54–58%<br>Approx. 9% |

## Risperidone

Risperidone has been called a "novel" antipsychotic (Perry, Alexander, & Liskow, 1997) because at low doses it does not cause EPSs but does at higher doses. This reversal arises because its dopamine antagonism is far greater than that of clozapine. On the positive side, it does not appear associated with agranulocytosis. In the studies comparing risperidone to haloperidol, the results are split, with about half the studies concluding it is just as effective as haloperidol and half concluding it is more effective. Compared to clozapine, risperidone seems slightly less effective, although these studies also show mixed results (Perry, Alexander, & Liskow, 1997). Stahl (2000) notes that risperidone has a far simpler pharmacologic profile than clozapine but still seems to decrease positive and negative symptoms. There are some EPSs with risperidone, particularly at higher doses. Although risperidone does not block histamine or acetylcholine receptors, some weight gain is still associated with it. Because the SDAs are so similar and, in many cases marketed solely on the basis of differences (sometimes minor) in side effects, we include tables of the side effects for each SDA. Risperidone is now available in parenteral and oral dissolving-tab formulations. The injectable, long-acting form of risperidone appears efficacious and well tolerated (Kane, Eerdekens, Lindenmayer, Keith, Lesem, & Karcher, 2003). Table 7.10 summarizes the side effects associated with risperidone.

## Olanzapine

Olanzapine (Zyprexa) is of interest to us not just because it has on-label approval to treat Schizophrenia but also because it has on-label approval to treat the acute mania seen in Bipolar I Disorder (more about that in Chapter Eight). As we mentioned in Chapter Four, once a compound is licensed for one use by the FDA, a common marketing tool is to then struggle to expand the potential market by getting approval for more and more con-

**TABLE 7.11**   Common Side Effects Associated With Olanzapine

| Type | Description | Percentage of Patients |
|---|---|---|
| Autonomic | Constipation, dry mouth | Approx. 8% |
| Cardiovascular | Minor changes in blood pressure | Unknown |
| Hematologic | None noted, no agranulocytosis | |
| Hepatic | Minor changes in enzyme levels | Unknown |
| Metabolic | Weight gain<br>Increased risk of diabetes | Unknown |
| Endocrinologic | Increased prolactin levels | Unknown |
| Neurologic | Early-onset EPS | Dose related |
| Tardive dyskinesia | Unknown | |
| Neuroleptic malignant syndrome | No cases known | |
| Other | Sedation | 26% |

ditions. This can have profound payoffs, because the companies do not have to develop a new agent but simply test the existing agent on different disorders. Although this testing costs a great deal, it is millions of dollars less than ushering a new compound through the entire process of approval.

When compared in clinical trials, olanzapine performs just as well as haloperidol. We do not yet have much data comparing olanzapine with clozapine. Olanzapine has a chemical structure similar to clozapine but is different from both clozapine and risperidone. This unique structure differs enough from both the latter compounds as to have neither agranulocytosis nor short-term EPSs associated with it. There is a very low incidence of tardive dyskinesia with long-term use. Olanzapine is not as sedating as clozapine but is associated with weight gain. Table 7.11 outlines the common side effects for olanzapine.

## Sertindole

Sertindole (Serlect) is the fourth atypical antipsychotic introduced to the United States in 1997. Although sharing the serotonin and dopamine antagonist properties that mark the atypical antipsychotics, it does not bind to histamine receptors (unlike clozapine and risperidone) and so is less sedating. In addition, the half-life is considerably

longer than risperidone and clozapine, allowing dosing once a day or, in some cases, once every other day (Julien, 2001). Initial studies confirmed that sertindole was significantly more effective than placebo in decreasing negative and positive symptoms of Schizophrenia. It is also equally effective to haloperidol in treating the positive symptoms of Schizophrenia with far fewer side effects and better than haloperidol at decreasing negative symptoms (Kane, 1998).

The biggest problem with sertindole, as noted earlier, is its potential for QTc interval prolongation and cardiac failure. According to Perry, Alexander, and Liskow (1997), sertindole was thought to prolong the QTc interval by an average of 21 milliseconds, which is significant in the context of cardiac functioning. Although this prolongation was thought to affect 4% of patients in clinical trials, note that 40% of patients in clinical trials had abnormal EKGs at baseline. This baseline makes it difficult to control for effects. In the initial concern over some fatalities, the drug was pulled from the market in Europe between 1999 and 2001 and its release was delayed in the United States. Currently, cardiac monitoring is recommended while clients are taking sertindole. The longer the client is on the medication, the less frequently EKGs need to be performed. We further discuss the implications

**TABLE 7.12**   Common Side Effects Associated With Sertindole

| Type | Description | Percentage of Patients |
|---|---|---|
| Autonomic | Dry mouth, decreased ejaculatory volume | Unknown |
| Cardiovascular | Prolonged QTc interval | Unknown |
| | Hypotension, dizziness | Unknown |
| Hematologic | None noted at this point | |
| Hepatic | None noted at this point | |
| Metabolic | Weight gain of 5% body weight | Unknown |
| | May be associated with increased risk of diabetes | |
| Endocrinologic | Minor, short-term prolactin increase | Unknown |
| Gastrointestinal | None noted at this point | |
| Neurologic | None noted at this point | |
| Respiratory | Rhinitis (nasal congestion) | Unknown |

of this issue later in the chapter. Table 7.12 summarizes the information we have been able to gather on the side effects of sertindole. Please note that the more recently a drug has been released, the less information is available on its effects.

### Quetiapine

Quetiapine (Seroquel) has a chemical structure similar to clozapine but is also different enough from clozapine, olanzapine, and risperidone to have some atypical advantages. First, it appears to be associated with no prolactin increases nor EPSs. It appears useful in Schizophrenia and Bipolar Disorders (Stahl, 2000). As with other SDAs, the goal with quetiapine was to have the therapeutic effects of clozapine without the agranulocytosis. At this point quetiapine is not associated with agranulocytosis. It has a half-life of about 7 hours, which may necessitate dosing two to three times a day. Table 7.13 details the side effect profiles from Phase 2 and 3 studies. This material is drawn from Casey (1996), Ereshefsky (1996), Green (1999), and Hirsch, Link, Goldstein, and Arvanitis (1996).

### Ziprasidone

Ziprasidone is the sixth atypical antipsychotic to be released. It was initially slated for release with the brand name of Zeldox but the FDA felt there were too many new drugs with brand names that began with "z," so it was released as Geodon. Julien (2001) points out that ziprasidone has some unique receptor actions. Like all other SDAs, ziprasidone blocks a combination of dopamine and serotonin receptors. Unlike the other SDAs, ziprasidone is an agonist of a particular serotonin receptor (the 5-HT1a receptor), giving it a buspirone-like action. Julien feels this may make the drug useful for depressive symptoms as well. Although at the time of this writing there is not enough research to produce a table of side effects, we can summarize what has been found. As with the other SDAs, the most common side effects of ziprasidone are sedation, nausea, constipation and/or diarrhea, dizziness, restlessness, respiratory congestion, and some uncontrollable movements such as tremor and shuffling. As with several other drugs in this category, clients need to be monitored for prolongation of QTc interval (Rivas-Vasquez, 2001). Time will tell if ziprasidone really offers anything unique compared to the other SDAs. Ziprasidone is also available in parenteral formulations. The following case demonstrates the effective use of Geodon after a long and complex history with neuroleptics and their side effects.

**TABLE 7.13**   Common Side Effects Associated With Quetiapine

| Type | Description | Percentage of Patients |
|------|-------------|------------------------|
| Autonomic | Constipation, dry mouth | Approx. 6% |
| Cardiovascular | Prolonged QTc interval | None noted |
|  | Dizziness | Approx. 7% |
|  | Orthostatic hypotension | Approx. 6% |
|  | Tachycardia | Approx. 4% |
| Hematologic | None noted at this point |  |
| Hepatic | None noted at this point |  |
| Metabolic | Weight gain | None noted |
| Endocrinologic | Prolactin increase | Rare |
| Gastrointestinal | Dyspepsia | Approx. 4% |
| Neurologic | None noted at this point |  |
| Respiratory | Rhinitis (nasal congestion) | Unknown |
| Other | Sedation | 18% |
|  | Priapism | Rare |

## The Case of Melanie

Melanie, a 16-year-old high school sophomore, was referred to a psychiatrist because she developed a schizophrenic break. She was very disorganized and suffered from visual, olfactory, and auditory hallucinations. She was first put on 25 mg of Thorazine, and she experienced an array of side effects, including severe postural hypotension. Melanie was taken off the Thorazine, and Mellaril at 25 mg was attempted, with the same result. Even with Cogentin, Melanie developed severe postural hypotension. This prevented her from working and going to school, because she was very lightheaded and fainted frequently. Therefore her psychiatrist switched her to first Stelazine and then Haldol, and with both Melanie developed akathisia with restlessness and pacing. She felt as if she was "crawling out of her skin." These side effects persisted even with Artane (trihexiphenidyl) to combat this movement disorder.

After many trials she and her psychiatrist found she could tolerate Trilafon (perphenazine) at 4 to 8 mg and up to her eventual stabilizing dose of 16 mg. Melanie stayed on the Trilafon for many years, with very good results. Her psychiatrist noted that during this time her organization improved to a paranoid Schizophrenia. Although her course fluctuated, she was able to graduate from college, marry, and have a child while on the Trilafon; the child was born healthy. She became an effective K–6 teacher and mothered her child well. Later she developed a severe tardive dystonia that affected her neck and back muscles, and she suffered incapacitating back spasms that hot baths or massages could not assuage. Gradually she was taken off the only neuroleptic that helped her, Trilafon, which she had taken for 17 years.

After careful consideration and evaluation, her psychiatrist now put Melanie on Seroquel (quetiapine) 400 mg, but she experienced a very serious relapse. This was her first psychotic break in over a decade, so for the time Melanie was put back on Trilafon and the dystonia (which never fully went away) worsened. Her psychiatrist also tried the SDAs Risperdal (risperidone) and Zyprexa (olanzapine), but both were too sedating. Then in June

2001 Melanie began a course of treatment with Geodon (ziprasidone), with great success. Her tardive dystonia is improving and although she cannot risk going off the medication to have another baby, Melanie is learning to cope with this limited sense of choice. Melanie had no drowsiness on Geodon. Finally she told her psychiatrist that her feelings were back and she was learning how to love.

This case reflects the efforts of a diligent and determined psychiatrist and a courageous patient. They addressed each medication and side effect dilemma as it arose and sought to provide options from among both the neuroleptic and the serotonin-dopamine antipsychotics. Issues from several perspectives were certainly addressed during the course of treatment. The most significant factor was that the quality of Melanie's life improved.

### Conclusions About the SDAs

At this point, what general conclusions can we draw? The new atypical medications work at least as well as the old drugs and possibly better. In some ways they are safer (as with the risk for tardive dyskinesia), but they hold their own dangers (agranulocytosis, QTc interval prolongation, and now diabetes and hyperglycemia). So does the evidence support their use as first-line treatments for Schizophrenia? Although many clinicians believe it does, there is the issue of cost, which we address later when addressing issues from different perspectives.

From the medical model perspective, if you compare the side effect profiles of the atypical antipsychotics with neuroleptics, the atypicals still seem to have more favorable side effect profiles, although the risk of diabetes may temper this conclusion. Even drugs such as risperidone, although associated with some EPSs, are not as severe in their side effects as are the neuroleptics (DeQuardo & Tandon, 1998). Again, reviewing the side effect profiles given earlier, newer agents such as quetiapine appear promising, having even fewer side effects than risperidone. It is interesting that the more chemically complex agents (such as clozapine and olanzapine) may have a broader array of side effects, whereas the chemically simpler agents such as neuroleptics and risperidone have more focused but disruptive side effects. This points to the possibility that the more chemically complex agents spread all their effects across several sites in the CNS and may, in some ways, be more tolerable.

Another factor that must be considered is that the initial evidence seemed to indicate the atypical antipsychotics were associated with significantly decreased relapse rates in patients taking them (Weiden, Aquila, & Standard, 1996). These relapse rates have a profound impact on the overall cost of caring for people suffering from Schizophrenia as well as on their overall quality of life, as discussed later. More recent research (Rosenheck et al., 1999) concluded that substantial cost savings because of decreased relapse was only apparent in clients with histories of heavy hospital use before beginning treatment.

Although the initial research on atypical antipsychotics seemed to promise a revolution in recovery, these expectations have become far more modest over the past seven years. Perhaps the most important point to be gleaned from this history is stated by Lewis (2002): Overall, the atypical antipsychotics' modest treatment gains and new, different side effects underscore the need for researching more effective treatments. On that note, let's look at two newer agents.

## Newer Agents: The Dopamine Hypothesis Revisited

Although newer agents do not act at all like neuroleptics, two appear primarily dopaminergic and do not block serotonin at all. One wonders, will these agents bring about a formal revision of the dopamine hypothesis?

### Amisulpride

At the time of this writing, amisulpride has been released in Europe (brand name Solian) and is pending release in the United States. At between 400 and 800 mg a day, amisulpride appears effective in treating Schizophrenia and may have efficacy for dysthymia. Amisulpride is unique in that it has high specificity for blocking D2 and D3 receptors in the limbic system but not in other areas such as the basal ganglia. It is twice as selective for D3 as D2 receptors. At low doses it blocks autoreceptors, but at high doses it shows postsynaptic antagonism. This increases DA action in the limbic system at low doses and decreases DA action at high doses. The combination seems to result in low EPSs. In low doses it also seems to alleviate depression and dysthymia but would not be subject to the same types of abuse as other dopaminergic compounds (such as amphetamines). In higher doses it seems effective in treating psychosis (Danion, Rein, Fleurot, & the Amisulpride Study Group, 1999). In controlled studies, amisulpride has been associated with the following side effects: insomnia, anxiety, and agitation (5 to 10% of clients); sedation, constipation, nausea, vomiting, and dry mouth (2% of patients); and weight gain, acute dystonia, tardive dyskinesia, hypotension, and QTc prolongation. Amisulpride has also been associated with increased prolactin release. Researchers have recently concluded that amisulpride is equal in efficacy to risperidone and may surpass it in subsequent studies (Sechter, Peuskens, Fleurot, Rein, Lecrubier, & the Amisulpride Study Group, 2002). As with any new drug, only time will tell if these optimistic reports are warranted and whether this drug is really contributing anything new or improved.

### Aripiprazole

Aripiprazole (Abilify) is a new antipsychotic that may open up yet another approach to treating the symptoms of Schizophrenia. The initial studies on the drug were presented at the 2002 annual American Psychiatric Association meeting in Philadelphia. Aripiprazole presents us with yet another set of mechanisms of action. It appears to be a potent partial agonist of D2 receptors, a partial agonist of serotonin 1a receptors, and an antagonist of serotonin 2a receptors. These studies indicate that it is better than haloperidol at treating positive and negative symptoms as well as having fewer side effects. Bristol-Myers Squibb filed a regulatory application with the FDA, and the drug was approved in November 2002 (Barclay, 2002).

Stahl (quoted in Manisses Corporation, 2002) stated that aripiprazole belongs to a class of drugs called *dopamine system stabilizers.* He calls them "Goldilocks drugs" because they balance the dopamine so that there is not too much or too little.

Aripiprazole seems to have a decent side effect profile, but initial reports state there is risk of QTc prolongation, weight gain, headache, agitation, insomnia, and nervousness. As with amisulpride, only time and further research will tell the worth of aripiprazole and dopamine system stabilizers in general.

## Focus on Other Perspectives

### Intrapsychic Considerations

What is it like to experience psychotic symptoms? One of our clients told us that to suffer from Schizophrenia was to suffer from interminable boredom. This client knew what it felt like to be intellectually and interpersonally engaged and knew what her symptoms were robbing her of. Her treatment with olanzapine was an important part of her recovery, and her psychotherapy was another crucial component. Another client spoke of his experience in terms of stark terror. He was plagued by voices he felt sure were demonic in origin, and he was convinced his very soul would not survive his ordeal. For this client, a series of seven antipsychotic medications were tried, with only minimal success. Counseling with an ego-strengthening focus helped this client retain some quality of life. We note these narratives because we have encountered clinicians who thought people with psychotic disorders could not benefit from counseling or psychotherapy. Quite to the contrary, such clients are unlikely to improve much if only treated with medication.

In Chapter Three we discussed a study by Sayre (2000) that examined clients' perceptions of their symptoms. Their perceptions fell into five distinct themes, summarized in Table 7.14.

Regardless of the extent to which one agrees with the ultimate truth of each conclusion, each theme obviously opens a gateway for counseling and psychotherapy. When a client with psychotic symptoms can make psychological contact, it is crucial that a trained therapist begin establishing a relationship with the person so that when able to use it, that person has access to therapy that will help him or her through the intrapsychic realm. The type of therapy employed will vary with the developmental level of the client. Many clients

**TABLE 7.14**   How Clients Understand Their Symptoms, by Theme

| Theme | My symptoms are . . . |
|---|---|
| Disease | . . . the result of a brain disease |
| Psychology | . . . related to my personality and behaviors |
| Crisis | . . . the result of a trauma or crisis |
| Ordination | . . . a sign of significance or special power |
| Punishment | . . . a punishment for past behavior |

with psychotic disorders are struggling with establishing adequate ego functioning, and counseling them focuses on ego-strengthening techniques. Some clients who have adequate ego functioning may be struggling with transpersonal development. These clients are likely a minority, but they do exist, and several clinicians have offered guidelines for working with them (Grof, 1998, 2000; Lukoff, Lu, & Turner, 1996).

Lauriello, Lenroot, and Bustillo (2003) provided an overview of some of the counseling approaches that have shown success with clients suffering from Schizophrenia. Although the studies reviewed did not favor psychodynamic approaches, they found that personal therapy, cognitive behavioral therapy, social skills training, and family therapy all had some support in the literature. In addition to vocational and job coaching, these treatments are an important part of an overall treatment plan and have been shown to decrease the number of hospitalizations that clients experience (Bichsell, 2001; Fenton & McGlashon, 1997).

In the spirit of an Integral approach, it is also important to note that clients who have significant improvements on atypical antipsychotics may also suffer psychological sequelae. Weiden, Aquila, and Standard (1996) point to clients experiencing "awakenings" phenomena, in which their improvement allows them to be more in touch with their losses and intrapsychic pain. Weiden, Aquila, and Standard (1998) concluded that the long-term psychological issues many clients must deal with include changes in self-image, sexuality, and intimacy concerns. That such researchers are addressing these issues alongside medication management is encouraging and leads us to our discussion of counseling and psychotherapy with clients who are suffering from Schizophrenia.

### *Dealing With Ambivalence About Taking Medication*

Clinicians encounter many clients who are ambivalent about taking medication that is going to cause them severe side effects. Even though the newer medications hold promise for allowing clients to regain a great deal of functioning, there is no getting around the side effects of weight gain, potentially fatal blood disorders, the risk of diabetes, and annoying side effects such as hypersalivation. The most important thing (as in any form of counseling or psychotherapy) is the quality of the therapeutic alliance. Counselors who have a good relationship with the client and client's family (or caregivers) know the client's personality, the client's values, and the client's degree of insight and the extent to which symptoms are impairing ability to function.

Although not a unitary concept, insight assessment is possible and to a large extent depends on the qualities of the therapeutic alliance just listed. David and Kemp (1997) have summarized five intrapsychic barriers to insight. The first two are psychopathology and cognitive deficits. Both interfere with the abstract reasoning processes that are necessary to have a sense of how others are experiencing you. If these deficits are a result of symptoms and medication reduces the symptoms, then after the deficits have been addressed clinicians can work with the client. The third and fourth barriers to insight are ego defense mechanisms and aspects of personality. Assuming the client can make psychological contact, these can be handled within the context of the therapeutic relationship. The last barrier to insight is culturally and socially determined attitudes, which may be intricately woven together with ego defenses and aspects of personality. Ideally, an Integral assessment will take these social and cultural attitudes into account. When consciously acknowledged by the clinician, they can be worked with in the counseling relationship.

## Issues From the Cultural Perspective

### *The Culture of Stigma*

Perhaps the most prominent issue from the cultural perspective is stigma. The idea of suffering from a mental/emotional disorder still carries the belief, shared by many, that the afflicted person is somehow "defective," not equal to others in the eyes of society, and, in some cases, even being justly punished by whatever god there may be. Although the United States and other countries have made strides in addressing this through education, advocacy, and community action, stigma still persists (Corrigan et al., 2000; Penn & Corrigan, 2002; Schreiber & Hartrick, 2002). In our brief historical outline of the antipsychotics, you saw how when the first neuroleptics were leading to deinstitutionalization of recovering clients, towns lobbied hospitals with petitions to keep the recovering people behind hospital walls (Healy, 2002).

In some societies a stigma is equally associated with the use of psychotropic medications. Jorm (2000) detailed a study in which many people expressed negative beliefs about medication for mental health disorders, although they favored medication for physical disorders. As we have argued in this book, a healthy skepticism about what medications can and cannot provide is important; however, negative beliefs about medication can also develop into negative beliefs about people who choose to take such medications. This is where mental health clinicians can intervene with advocacy and education. It should be noted that a recent study also commented on stigmatization of individuals receiving psychotherapy. The perspectives of mental health consumers reflected in the study is that they are portrayed particularly negatively in the media. The researcher in this case felt that this stigma may prevent people from seeking help in the first place (Ben-Porath, 2002).

The issue of stigma is particularly pronounced in severe disorders such as Schizophrenia. Positive and negative symptoms of Schizophrenia severely decrease clients' quality of life by decreasing their social interactions or the receptivity of others to interacting with them. Add the severe extrapyramidal side effects associated with neuroleptic medications, and the problem is unnecessarily compounded. We say "unnecessarily" because more and more clinicians are advocating the atypical antipsychotics as a first line of treatment. It is important for mental health clinicians to participate in this advocacy. Assuming a client is willing to take a medication to deal with the life-disrupting symptoms of Schizophrenia, that client deserves every opportunity to be given the most effective agent with the fewest side effects. At this point, clozapine is still reserved for treatment-refractory clients, because of the risk of agranulocytosis. However, the SDAs (olanzapine in particular) may be excellent first-line medical treatments for Schizophrenia (Psychlink, 1998). As most clinicians are aware, the lives of many people with Schizophrenia have been so disrupted by their symptoms that they frequently lack financial resources such as health insurance. Many of these clients receive Medicaid or Social Security disability. Therefore, those responsible for paying for treatment may balk at the cost. Advocacy must be directed to these payers, which takes us next to the social issues.

## Social Issues

### *Pharmacoeconomics*

Perhaps the most important obstacle to the widespread adoption of atypical antipsychotics is cost. Pharmacoeconomics is an area of which mental health clinicians need to be aware. In a recent study, Ernst et al. (2000) found that even physicians frequently don't know the cost of generic and brand name medications. Bearing in mind that over a 12-year period a new drug may cost $400 million to $500 million to bring to market, the costs of newer agents are going to be substantially more than older ones. Atypical antipsychotics cost approximately 10 times what neuroleptics cost. In the United States, a 30-day supply of olanzapine costs approximately $325 and a 30-day supply of clozapine is approximately $320. Even in countries such as Canada with more government subsidy of health care, clozapine costs $16 a day, in contrast to a neuroleptic that would cost approximately 30 cents a day.

In the United States, the decisions about what drugs to use for Medicaid patients are often made by state formulary boards, pharmacy committees, or state medical directors and pharmacy directors. In a 1998 video symposium (Psychlink, 1998), pharmacologist Larry Ereshefsky and psychiatrists Bill Glazer and Jay Fawver reviewed a protocol for lobbying state officials, which can be useful to mental health professionals. Depending on the regulatory agency and personnel involved, clinicians cannot assume that audiences for advocacy know about the symptoms of Schizophrenia and so are advised to consider the following steps when advocating for atypical antipsychotics to be routinely available to indigent clients. This protocol can also be helpful in educating the public about the long-term benefits of allowing clients access to the atypical antipsychotics.

### First Steps

First, make sure the parties involved (whether a formulary board or the lay public) understand the positive and negative symptoms of Schizophrenia. Next, explain the mechanism of D2 blockade and the severe side effects associated with it. A discussion of compliance is important, because many clients go off neuroleptic medications to avoid the severe side effects. Clinicians should then discuss how the newer atypical antipsychotics are more complex drugs than the neuroleptics, with multiple mechanisms of action. These more complex molecules are associated with better outcomes. It is also important to emphasize that each atypical is structurally different from the others, to preclude the assumption that one atypical is just as good as any other. Much like antibiotics, some clients respond to one atypical and not to another, so it is important that prescribing professionals have access to all of them.

### Efficacy and Compliance

As we have documented here, the atypical antipsychotics appear to have greater efficacy on the overall symptoms and are better tolerated than neuroleptics. Although the initial excitement over the atypicals was somewhat euphoric, more recent studies note that it may be time to tone down that excitement (Volavka, 2002). Still, clozapine and the SDAs seem to have better side effect profiles than do the neuroleptics and are at least as good as the neuroleptics at addressing the symptoms of Schizophrenia. Although clinicians hoped as recently as

1998 that the atypicals would clearly improve quality of life and decrease suicidality, these hopes have yet to be consistently confirmed (Sernyak, Desai, Stolar, & Rosenheck, 2002). As far as compliance goes, clients do seem more likely to continue taking clozapine as opposed to haloperidol, because clozapine offers greater symptom relief and reduced side effects (Rosenheck et al., 2000).

### Cost

Although five years ago, researchers believed that the long-term savings from decreased relapse rates would more than pay for the drugs, today the reviews are mixed. Sernyak et al. (2001) noted that in actual practice clozapine treatment may cost substantially more than treatment with neuroleptics. Although the 1998 Psychlink symposium put a lot of emphasis on long-term savings projected from using atypical antipsychotics as a first line of treatment, current data do not seem to support the argument. Another argument also overlaps with the cultural perspective: What cost is too high to ease human suffering? This question was eloquently raised by Rosenheck (2000), who documented that services for mentally ill homeless people were in fact effective. He noted, though, that these services will likely increase costs in many areas and their value ultimately depends on the value society places on caring for its less well-off members.

Just as many pharmaceutical companies set up medication access programs for indigent clients, many state and county systems have set up what are called "central pharmacies" where indigent clients can get certain medications at lower costs. For example, in Ohio each county puts money in a central pool in Columbus (Ohio's capital) and that money is then used to set up the central pharmacy in Ohio. Counties then direct client prescriptions to the central pharmacy for discounted medications. Doctors frequently prefer these programs to pharmaceutical company programs, because the latter require the prescribing doctor to store and dispense the medication as well as do all the paperwork involved.

### Whom Do We Trust?

A final note is called for as we end this long journey through the world of antipsychotic medications. Readers are likely aware that many issues remain unresolved about just how good the newer, atypical antipsychotics are. One variable that continues to play a role from an Integral perspective is the economic power of pharmaceutical companies. It is interesting that many of the initial studies that were optimistic about the revolution atypicals could bring about were funded by pharmaceutical companies and were short-term studies. One of the latest studies that suggests the initial response to the atypicals was too enthusiastic was sponsored by the National Institute of Mental Health, with only moderate funding from the pharmaceutical industry. We hope that through such independent, large-scale, long-term studies, the truth will be easier to pursue.

Healy (2002) documented how Eli Lilly Pharmaceuticals recruited well-known figures from psychiatry beginning in the 1970s to conduct research and write papers. He connected this effort to meta-analyses on drug efficacy that have been written entirely by people on the pharmaceutical company payroll. One example is the meta-analysis on fluoxetine that appeared in the *British Medical Journal* (Beasley et al., 1991), supposedly refuting the connection between Prozac (a Lilly product) and suicide. It stated, "Until then, papers written solely by company personnel would never have been published in a leading journal like the *British Medical Journal*. This article cracked the dam that had separated the academic and commercial universities" (p. 263). We ask, where is that flood leading us?

## Summary

Antipsychotics play a vital role in the treatment of severe mental and emotional disorders such as Schizophrenia. Although there are many theories of how antipsychotics work, the jury is still out on what these medications tell us about the nature of Schizophrenia and its etiology. Until recently, antipsychotic medications were basically all neuroleptic and worked through dopamine antagonism. The creation of clozapine and now the serotonin dopamine-antagonists (SDAs) has opened a new avenue of treatment for Schizophrenia and provided more options to clients with the disease. No drug can be taken without a cost and the newer antipsychotics are still associated with side effects. For the newer medications such as clozapine and the SDAs, there is a new concern about these medications inducing diabetes and other metabolic problems. Newer compounds such as aripiprazole will likely help us continue developing theories about the nature of Schizophrenia. Although medication is a first line of treatment for Schizophrenia, mental health clinicians must remain advocates of psychosocial interventions to improve the quality of life for people with Schizophrenia. In addition, mental health professionals must remain mindful of the pharmacoeconomics of the newer, more expensive antipsychotics and advocate for indigent clients to have access to these drugs.

## Study Questions and Exercises

1. From your clinical experience, discuss two clients who have been diagnosed in the spectrum of Schizophrenia and who have been on a neuroleptic. Describe the effectiveness of the neuroleptic and the side effects experienced by the clients.

2. What is deinstitutionalization? Why did chlorpromazine have such an impact on this phenomenon?

3. In your own words, how do neuroleptics work in the brain? How effective are they with the positive symptoms of Schizophrenia? With the negative symptoms?

4. Summarize some major side effects of the neuroleptics. How might you speak to a schizophrenic client or his or her family about these effects?

5. What are the extrapyramidal symptoms (EPSs) of the neuroleptics? Discuss Parkinsonianism.

6. What is your reaction to the case of Bonnie? Discuss how and why even with the successes of the neuroleptics, it was necessary to develop atypical antipsychotics.

7. What are some characteristics of drugs from the "new era" of antipsychotics?

8. What is agranulocytosis? How is it related to clozapine?

9. Select a atypical antipsychotic other than clozapine, and discuss its treatment features and side effect profile.

10. What is the "culture of stigma"? How does it affect people diagnosed with Schizophrenia?

# CHAPTER EIGHT

# Mood Misnomers

## *Mood-Stabilizing Agents*

The very phrase "mood stabilization" is curious. Webster's Unabridged Dictionary (1989) notes that a stabilizer makes or holds things stable. That is simple enough, but the very nature of mood in us human beings is rarely stable. In fact, our range of affect and the manner in which we express it may be one of the hallmarks of being (or becoming) human. Clinically speaking, "normal" mood is referred to as a state of "**euthymia.**" This word, however, has two slightly different meanings. The more clinical meaning of euthymia is a state that is neither manic nor depressed. Simple enough—perhaps too simple where human beings are concerned. A more important meaning of "euthymia" is rooted in the etymology of the word (almost never referred to by mental health clinicians). The original Greek meaning of *euthymia* is being "tranquil or joyous." *Eu-* is a Greek prefix meaning "good or well," and *thymus* refers to "mind." Unfortunately clinicians typically restrict the word *euthymic* to the shallower, clinical meaning, when perhaps we would better serve clients if we aimed for the deeper, original meaning. Imagine what mental health delivery would be like if joy and tranquility were viewed as desirable goals for clients! As philosopher Alan Watts (1973) noted, mental health clinicians seem to be suspicious of things such as joy and prefer that consensual reality be defined as the frame of mind one has going to work on Monday morning. Be that as it may, mood stabilization is the practice of introducing

pharmacologic agents that keep clients' moods within parameters clinically described as "normal" or "euthymic." The psychotropic agents used to do this are called **mood stabilizers.**

Regrettably, as you will see, the agents administered rarely bring clients the deeper experience of euthymia, described by the ancient Greeks as tranquil or joyous. In this society, suspicion of joy is perhaps reflected in the severe restriction of access to those drugs that actually seem to induce joy. More often, clients taking mood stabilizers report feeling constricted mood, something even less than the normal fluctuations of mood. Clinically, such clients are described as being neither manic nor depressed, but many tell us this is not a pleasant state. What does it mean to feel *neither* manic nor depressed? Describing a state by what it is *not* (called the *via negativa* in the spiritual logic of St. Thomas of Aquinas) usually fails to give a clear picture of what the state really *is*. We suspect that the clinical meaning of euthymia is perhaps more word magic retreated to by exhausted clinicians who simply want to say, "The client is neither manic nor depressed." So we are somewhat back where we started.

Why *did* we begin this chapter by calling "mood stabilization" a curious phrase? For one thing, the phrase is caught up in semantic problems. We have already discussed depressed mood and antidepressants at length in Chapter Five. In Chapter Six we discussed anxiety, which is also referred to as a

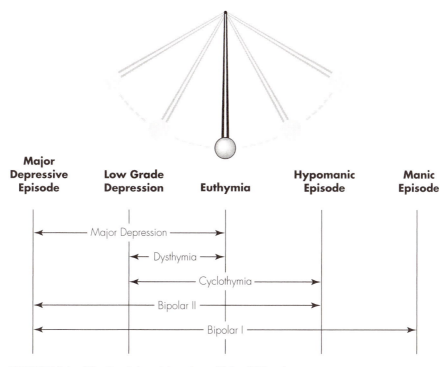

**FIGURE 8.1** The Pendulum Metaphor of Mood Disorders

mood state (Barlow & Durand, 2002). The literature on anxiety and depression makes no consistent use of the phrase "mood stabilization." It is as if mood needs to be stabilized only if it becomes severely elevated and/or severely depressed.

In an effort to operationalize for readers the mysterious phrase "mood stabilizer," we use the parameters set by clinical logic and draw on the work of Schou (1997) and Keck (Interactive Medical, 2001). Schou noted that a mood stabilizer should have far-reaching effects. Ideally, it should show efficacy for relieving manic episodes and depressive episodes, and as a prophylactic treatment, for preventing any further severe mood symptoms. Keck agreed, noting that mood stabilizers should (1) show efficacy in an acute manic phase, (2) show such efficacy in one stage of Bipolar illness without exacerbating another stage, and (3) show some efficacy for mood, psychotic, and cognitive symptoms. Keck also added that mood stabilizers should show some efficacy as a prophylactic (Interactive Medical, 2001). The key to these definitions is that an ideal

mood stabilizer does more than simply calm a person suffering from mania. That calming could easily be accomplished with one of the benzodiazepines described in Chapter Six or one of the neuroleptics described in Chapter Seven; however, the neuroleptic would have little impact on the depressive symptoms or as a prophylactic.

Clinically, the words used to describe mood disorders are important for understanding mood stabilizers. We all need to understand the terms bequeathed to us from *DSM* to describe mood symptoms that may require mood stabilization. Figure 8.1 offers the metaphor of a pendulum to illustrate these concepts.

As you can see in Figure 8.1, euthymia is at the pendulum's center, implying a "centered" state, meaning normal. In the figure, elevated mood is shown as movement to the right of euthymia and depressed mood is shown as movement toward the left of euthymia. Mood elevated above normal is not described as pathology in *DSM* until it reaches hypomanic. Hypomanic episodes are new in *DSM-IV*

(American Psychiatric Association, 1994) and can be difficult to diagnose. The primary difficulties lie in confirming the symptoms and in the fact that hypomanic symptoms eventually shade into manic symptoms. No "hard and fast" line separates them. Hypomanic episodes are described in terms exactly similar to manic episodes, except they are of shorter duration and less severe. As the pendulum of mood moves further to right toward elevated mood, the next descriptor is "manic episode." This is mood so elevated that it is "sufficiently severe to cause marked impairment in occupational functioning or in usual social activities or relationships with others, or to necessitate hospitalization to prevent harm to self or others" (American Psychiatric Association, 1994, p. 332). In the direction of depressed mood, there is a low-grade depression spectrum referred to in *DSM* first as Dysthymia and finally Major Depression, described in Chapter Five. Figure 8.1 includes arrows, spanning the range of a client's mood, that correspond to *DSM* criteria for particular disorders. Mood stabilization comes into play in Cyclothymia (fluctuations between hypomania and dysthymia), Bipolar II Disorder (fluctuations between major depression and hypomania), and Bipolar I Disorder (fluctuations between major depression and mania).

We are primarily concerned in this chapter with medications used to treat Bipolar I Disorder, colloquially known as "manic-depressive illness." Although so-called mood stabilizers are used to treat Schizoaffective Disorder, Bipolar II Disorder, Borderline Personality Disorder, and Cyclothymia, these uses are not yet systematic, the literature is inconsistent, and mood stabilization focuses on manic symptoms (Delgado & Gelenberg, 2001). We cover lithium and several anticonvulsant medications, some of which have demonstrated efficacy for treating Bipolar I Disorder and others of which are still under study. We also discuss atypical antipsychotic medications, as well as a new, hybrid medication combining olanzapine (Zyprexa) with fluoxetine (Prozac).

Note that the literature on medications for Bipolar I Disorder often use "mood stabilizer" as synonymous with "antimanic." We use the phrase "mood stabilizer." It is also important to note that

the so-called mood-stabilizing medications described in this chapter are increasingly being used in an attempt to control aggressive behavior, particularly in children and adolescents (Viesselman, 1999). We discuss this use in the next chapter, as well as the fact that little research supports this practice.

## Bipolar I Disorder

As noted, Bipolar I Disorder is predominantly characterized by symptoms that meet the criteria for major depression and symptoms that meet the criteria for mania. The estimated lifetime prevalence fluctuates between 0.4 and 1.6% of the adult population (Kessler et al., 1994). Estimates are thought to include the other bipolar-type disorders (Bipolar II and Cyclothymia); however, this may not be the case, particularly because Bipolar II did not exist as a category prior to 1994. The mean age of onset for Bipolar I Disorder is 18 (Weissman, Bruce, Leaf, Florio, & Holzer, 1991), although there is currently debate about how many cases actually begin in childhood and go undiagnosed until adolescence (see Chapter Nine). The American Psychiatric Association (2000a) describes Bipolar I Disorder as a long-term illness with a variable course. The association estimates that 90% of clients who suffer a single manic episode repeat the experience. The majority of manic episodes (60 to 70%) occur immediately before or after an episode of major depression (American Psychiatric Association, 1994).

Prevalence estimates are very difficult to come by, and some practices used to justify them are questionable. In Ohio in 2003, a psychiatrist on a cable-access news program stated that the incidence of Bipolar I Disorder is significantly higher than currently believed. To support this assertion, he cited some survey research (Hirschfeld et al., 2003). He did not say that the survey in question was extrapolating diagnoses from a 10-item questionnaire (which is not clinically ethical), that the 10-item questionnaire had only fair validity, and that 10 of the 11 authors received substantial financial support from pharmaceutical companies. From an Integral perspective, this was hardly a good citation of a supposedly objective, scientific study. Our point is that most viewers may not have even bothered to look up the study to which the speaker was referring and might believe him simply because he was a psychiatrist.

Scientists do not know what causes Bipolar I Disorder. This is surely dismaying to the clients who suffer its symptoms, but the truth is, the well-intentioned theorists who share a strong medical model perspective tend to theorize exclusively from this perspective. Although a great deal of attention has been placed on heritability, this focus has not provided clues as to the etiology of Bipolar I Disorder other than giving people the luxury of speculating that it *may* be genetic. From an Integral perspective, this hypothesis is not terribly useful. It might be just as useful to say that the disorder "appears karmic." Some promising developments are occurring in molecular psychiatry, but more work needs to be done before a coherent theory can be articulated (Manji, Moore, Rajkowska, & Chen (2000). Despite the ignorance about etiology, as with Schizophrenia, the spectrum of symptom presentation in Bipolar I Disorder requires comment.

### The Spectrum of Symptoms in Bipolar I Disorder

Bipolar I Disorder is unique in that symptoms manifest heterogeneously, which influences treatment (Bowden, 1998). The manic and depressive symptoms may fluctuate slowly (one or two mood episodes per year) or more quickly in a subtype of the disorder called "rapid cycling" (meaning four or more mood episodes in a 12-month period). The symptoms may also present (appear) as mixed where over a one-week period the person has met the criteria for mania and depression nearly every day (American Psychiatric Association, 1994).

In addition, about half of all clients suffering from Bipolar I Disorder have psychotic symptoms and these clients respond less well to some treatments, lithium in particular (Bowden, 1998). Clinicians must also be aware that researchers estimate over half of clients suffering from Bipolar I Disorder have a history of substance abuse (Sonne & Brady, 1999), so this factor requires careful screening and treatment of the substance abuse as well as

of the mood disorder. Most clients suffering from Bipolar I Disorder return to adequate functioning between episodes (approximately 80%); however, many require continued pharmacologic interventions to avoid future episodes. As with Schizophrenia, clients with Bipolar I Disorder are at a greater risk for suicide: An average of 19% complete the act (Goodwin & Jamison, 1990).

Researchers estimate that 35 to 50% of clients who do stay on medication are likely to suffer relapse despite medication compliance (Julien, 2001). Many clinicians assume that patients stabilized on lithium will continue on the medication indefinitely. There is some evidence in favor of slowly titrated withdrawal in patients who have made therapeutically based life changes and seem able to manage their illness. We say more about this later when we explore the disorder from various perspectives.

## Some History on Mood Stabilizers

In the 19th century a popular theory called *uric acid diathesis* was a dominant concept in medicine used to explain the etiology of disorders as diverse as manic-depressive illness and cardiac problems (Healy, 2002). As Barlow and Durand (2002) have noted, "diathesis" means vulnerability (as in the diathesis–stress model of psychopathology), in this case, vulnerability to the effects of uric acid on one's system. Uric acid is a breakdown product of urea, which is a compound, found in urine, that is the result of protein metabolism.

In the 19th century, as today, theories followed the technologies available to test them. The ability to peer inside neurons is followed by theories of mental disorders that hypothesize intraneuronal (and interneuronal) causes, as you saw in our Chapter Five discussion of depression (remember the molecular/cellular theory of depression?). In the 19th century, chemical analysis was the newest technology of that time, so researchers used it to investigate substances eliminated from the body and then proposed theories about disorders, based on the analysis. Although the uric acid diathesis theories are now recognized as no more accurate than the chemical imbalance theories of depression, they did provide a starting point for research that led to lithium being used for Bipolar I Disorder.

Uric acid was also found to be a major constituent in kidney stones and gout. Gout is a painful inflammation of the joints, caused by uric acid in salt form settling in joints. In the 19th century gout was also linked to disturbances in mood (although these surely could have been side effects of the unpleasant experience). In 1817 a new element called *lithium* had been discovered. Lithium is a light, positively charged metal ion that has been used therapeutically in a number of ways for almost 200 years. Researchers realized that lithium dissolved kidney stones, so perhaps it would be useful for other disorders related to uric acid. From a period spanning 1840 to 1870, Alexander Ure and Alfred Garrod began experimenting with lithium as a treatment for disorders believed related to uric acid (Lenox & Manji, 1998).

As Healy (2002) documents, the effects of lithium on **urates** gave rise to an industry in lithium-laced products. Although many readers may know that Coca-Cola at one time had coca leaf extract as one of its ingredients, you may be surprised to know that 7-Up came on the market as a lithium-containing beverage. Spring waters containing lithium were carried by spas and were supposed to induce a sense of well-being, and lithium was even used as a salt substitute for patients with heart problems (Julien, 2001). As early as 1870, the Danish neurologist Carl Lange (co-creator of the James-Lange theory of emotions) found that lithium had therapeutic effects in clients with manic-depressive illness. In the United States, William Hammond gave lithium to patients with mood disorders and also reported positive results (Healy, 2002). One problem with lithium, however, is that in large enough doses it can be toxic, and there were some fatalities from these enthusiastic additive uses of the substance. This, coupled with the decline of the uric acid diathesis hypothesis of illness, contributed to the FDA removing lithium from the market in 1949. Ironically, this same year a little-known psychiatrist from Australia was about to put lithium "back on the map."

## Developments Down Under

John Cade was a psychiatrist and state hospital superintendent in Australia in the mid 20th century.

Under the influence of the uric acid diathesis theory, Cade hypothesized that a toxin that entered the brain caused mania. He further asserted that this toxin could be detected in urine. He proposed injecting uric acid from manic patients into guinea pigs, thinking that if the hypothetical toxin were active, it would induce manic activity in the guinea pigs. Alas, uric acid is highly toxic and the first guinea pigs died. He then decided to dissolve the acid by mixing it with a metal to form a soluble salt. After failing with a number of metals, he found lithium ideal for his mixture. He then injected the dissolved mixture of uric acid and lithium into the guinea pigs, and they responded not with mania but lethargy. Cade thought the lethargy was a calming effect and eventually tried injecting just lithium into the guinea pigs. It had the same effect (in actuality, the lithium did not calm the guinea pigs, it just made them sick). At any rate, although this was not at all what he had expected to find, Cade (1949) concluded that lithium might have some effects on mood (calming what he called "psychotic excitement"), and he proposed to test it in humans, including himself (Snyder, 1996). Although Cade had some success using lithium in manic patients, several of his patients died from its toxicity (Healy, 2002).

Although some give Cade all the credit for discovering lithium (Snyder, 1996), others (Healy, 2002) cite the important contributions of Morgens Schou, a Danish researcher. Schou (1978) did the first randomized, controlled trials that demonstrated the efficacy of lithium. Although Cade had some success, it was anecdotal and not based on standard trials. Schou's research confirmed the usefulness of the compound and led to standards for safe dosage levels. Note that there is still no theoretical basis for lithium's use. As Snyder (1996) concludes, "One of the fascinations of the discovery process is that we often find the right answer by looking in the wrong place" (p. 119).

As noted, lithium was taken off the market in 1949 (the same year it appeared to have efficacy for manic-depressive illness) and was not reapproved by the FDA for psychiatric use until 1970. Some think part of the reason for this time lag was that because lithium is a naturally occurring element, no pharmaceutical company could get a patent on it, thus limiting its profitability. The toxicity of lithium was surely another reason for the caution in approval. The early deaths related to lithium were all caused by lithium-induced cardiac problems. Researchers now think these cases were all cases of lithium toxicity, but when monitored and given in appropriate doses, the cardiac side effects of lithium are typically minor (Tilkian, Schroeder, Kao, & Hultgren, 1976). As we outline later, lithium therapy must be closely monitored, because the therapeutic dose is very close to the toxic dose. The only FDA-approved use of lithium is for mood stabilization.

## Lithium: The Prototypical Mood Stabilizer

As noted, lithium is a naturally occurring, positively charged alkali metal ion. Johan August Arfvedson in Stockholm, Sweden, discovered it in 1817. Its name derives from the Greek *lithos*, meaning "stone" because Arfvedson discovered it in a mineral source. It can be mixed with magnesium and aluminum to form metal alloys, is used in some glasses and batteries, and of course has use in psychopharmacology. Lithium has good efficacy in treating acute mania as well as being a prophylactic for both manic and depressive episodes (American Psychiatric Association, 2000a). Newer evidence correlates long-term lithium therapy with decreased suicide rates in clients suffering from Bipolar I Disorder (Goodwin & Ghaemie, 1999). Lithium may also have neuroprotective properties, which would mean that Bipolar I Disorder is progressive and/or degenerative and lithium protects neurons from the progression of the disorder. As with most hypotheses, more work needs to be done to confirm this one (Manji et al., 2000). Lithium is least effective in clients suffering from mixed episodes or rapid cycling of mood symptoms (Bowden, 1995).

Lithium is typically available in capsules, tablets, slow-release tablets, and as lithium citrate syrup (Keck & McElroy, 2002). Common lithium formulations are listed in Table 8.1.

Clients show an initial response within one week to one month of beginning lithium therapy. Because of this time lag and because clients suffering from manic symptoms may endanger themselves or others, additional medications may be

**TABLE 8.1** Examples of Lithium Formulations

| Generic | Brand Names | Formulation |
|---|---|---|
| Lithium citrate | Cibalith-S | Syrup |
| Lithium carbonate | Eskalith | Capsule |
| | Eskalith-CR | Scored tablet |
| | Lithobid | Tablet |
| | Lithotabs | Tablet |
| | Lithane | Gelatin capsule |

used, including typical antipsychotics and benzodiazepines (Price & Heninger, 1994). Once a client starts to show a response to lithium, symptoms usually diminish quickly. If lithium is discontinued abruptly during the manic phase of the illness, relapse may occur rapidly (Perry, Alexander, & Liskow, 1997).

In placebo-controlled studies, approximately 60 to 80% of clients suffering from mania respond to lithium over placebo. Some researchers (Grof, Alda, Grof, Fox, & Cameron, 1993; Grof & Alda, 2001) challenge this estimate and believe the response rate closer to 50%. Stahl (2000) concluded that lithium is effective in only 40 to 50% of clients. Regardless, with the placebo, response is clearly less substantial than that seen in trials with antidepressants. Julien (2001) writes that only 23% of clients taking lithium appear to be total responders, with 28 to 50% of clients who take lithium discontinuing the medication against medical advice, and 38% relapsing despite remaining on the medication. For those who respond to lithium, the drug does offer protection against relapse, although the protection decreases the longer the person is on lithium and protection increases when other drugs are used in addition to lithium (Peselow, Fieve, DiFiglio, & Sanfilipo, 1994). Of clients on maintenance therapy with lithium alone, approximately 50% may relapse despite staying on the lithium (Dunner, Fleiss, & Fieve, 1976). Lithium treatment cannot occur until clients have several lab tests done, including checking sodium, calcium, and phosphorous levels, and an electrocardiogram, urinalysis, thyroid battery, and complete blood cell count.

Because the average duration of a manic episode is three months, plasma levels of lithium effective for the client should be maintained for three to six months afterward. If lithium is to be discontinued, Perry, Alexander, and Liskow (1997) recommend that the daily dosage be tapered by 25% each day over a period of four weeks. About half of patients stabilized successfully on lithium and then switched to placebo relapse within six months. There are stories of patients relapsing in a few days, but these are not from controlled studies and are rare.

Unlike antidepressants, there are more often significant statistical differences between lithium and placebo groups in participants with Bipolar I Disorder. Clearly something is happening, but what? To address that question, we begin by discussing the mechanisms of action of lithium.

### Mechanisms of Action

The pharmacology of lithium is incredibly complex and a matter of ongoing speculation (Ikonomov & Manji, 1999; Lenox & Manji, 1998). Lithium affects different parts of the brain differently at different times. Lithium's effects extend to multiple neurotransmitters and second-messenger systems.

As Schatzberg, Cole, and DeBattista (1997) point out, we are still uncertain of the key factors in lithium's effectiveness. Table 8.2 outlines the mechanisms of action we know lithium exerts. Note that part of the complexity of lithium is due to the fact that it can affect the brain differently in different regions (for example, increasing neurotransmitter release in some areas and decreasing release of the same neurotransmitter in other areas). These mechanisms are summarized from Lenox and Manji (1998); Perry, Alexander, and Liskow (1997); and Schatzberg, Cole, and DeBattista (1997).

The best-studied effects of lithium are on serotonin, and these effects also demonstrate the complexity of lithium's pharmacodynamics. After short-term use (one to two weeks), lithium appears to increase serotonin synthesis by increasing tryptophan reuptake in synapses. After two to three weeks, it appears to enhance release of 5-HT from neurons in the parietal cortex and the hippocampus. Long-term taking of lithium seems to cause downregulation in 5-HT1 and 5-HT2 receptors. Again, how these effects may relate to mood is currently unknown.

Lithium's effects on norepinephrine are equally curious. Lithium appears to increase the rate of

**TABLE 8.2**   Mechanisms of Action of Lithium

| *Neurotransmitter System* | *Effects* |
|---|---|
| Serotonin | Increase in tryptophan (precursor) uptake after short- and long-term treatment. General increases in serotonin levels. Increased release of serotonin in the hippocampus, hypothalamus, and parietal cortex. Serotonin receptor decreases in hippocampus. Long-term administration causes downregulation of 5-HT1 and 5-HT2 receptors. |
| Dopamine | Long-term administration diminishes neostriatal dopamine activity. May block the effects of highly sensitive DA receptors, thus decreasing the behaviors associated with DA stimulation. |
| Norepinephrine | Increases rate of synthesis of NE in some parts of the brain but decreases the synthesis in other parts. Decreases the excretion of NE metabolites in manic patients and increases the excretion of NE metabolites in depressed patients. |
| Second-messenger systems | Lithium appears to reduce the activity of second-messenger systems in undetermined ways. |
| Ionic effects | Lithium, being a positively charged metal ion, may have stabilizing effects on neurons in the CNS. |

norepinephrine synthesis in some parts of the brain. It decreases excretion of norepinephrine metabolites in manic patients but increases excretion of norepinephrine metabolites in depressed patients. Lithium appears to block postsynaptic DA receptors, which seems to partly explain the controlling effects on mania and psychosis. There appears to be evidence that lithium affects the **G-proteins** in second-messenger systems. Apparently it inhibits some enzymes, in particular second-messenger systems, which in turn is believed to bring about some of the therapeutic effects.

If even after reviewing our brief description of lithium's mechanisms of action you are confused, you are not alone. Scientists do have molecular clues as to lithium's pharmacodynamics, but these clues do not help explain how it alters mood. From an Integral perspective, this is likely because mood cannot be explained in terms of brain chemistry alone. In fairness though, researchers have likely only seen the proverbial "tip of the iceberg" in terms of lithium's mechanisms of action, and continued research will likely yield a deeper understanding of its effects on brain chemistry. Newer theories about additional mechanisms of action are currently under study (Manji, Bowden, & Belmaker, 2000). Currently researchers simply do not know enough about the etiology of Bipolar I Disorder or the effects of lithium to speculate further.

### Theories of Lithium Action From the Biomedical Perspective

The short answer to the question "How does lithium work?" is "We don't know." Because researchers do not really know what causes Bipolar I Disorder, it is hard to draw definitive conclusions as to how lithium corrects the disorder in people who respond to it as a treatment. Next we briefly outline some medical model theories that have implications for psychosocial interventions as well.

### Lithium and Neurotransmission

#### *The Amine Theory Revisited*

In Chapter Five we discussed the amine theory of depression, which in essence proposed that people whose nervous systems did not produce enough amines (specifically norepinephrine) become depressed. From here it was a simple leap to propose that some people's nervous systems produce amines erratically, sometimes producing too many, and at other times producing too few. When the nervous system of such afflicted people produces too many amines, the result is manic mood. When the person's nervous system produces too few amines, the result is depression. This appeared to have limited support in that (as noted in Table 8.2) lithium is correlated with decreased norepinephrine (NE) metabolites in manic patients and increased NE metabolites in depressed patients. These data led researchers to conclude that lithium helped the body achieve some innate homeostasis that had been lacking. Obviously, in light of how complex lithium's effects are, this chemical imbalance theory turns out to be as oversimplistic and inadequate as is the chemical imbalance theory of depression.

#### *Lithium's Ionic Impact on Neurotransmission*

That lithium is a positively charged metal ion may account for lithium's effects on the nervous system. As Preston, O'Neal, and Talaga (2002) note, "Since neurotransmitter production, release, and reuptake rely on various ions (sodium, calcium, potassium, and magnesium), lithium's ionic properties may affect neurotransmission-mediated depression and mania" (p. 187). This hypothesis is certainly plausible. As you saw in Chapter Two, all neurons have ion channels that allow the passage of positively or negatively charged particles into the cell. We noted that an influx of positively charged ions (such as sodium) tends to excite cells and an influx of negatively charged ions (such as chloride) tends to inhibit or hyperpolarize cells.

#### *Lithium's Effect on Second-Messenger Systems*

In the late 1980s and early 1990s, researchers proposed that intraneuronal effects caused lithium's therapeutic effects. They specified second-messenger systems as a primary site where lithium exerted a powerful influence. In this theory, the lithium acts to slow down second-messenger systems (Avissar & Schreiber, 1989; Weber, Saklad, & Kastenholz, 1992). Recall from Chapter Two that second-messenger systems may play a role in neuronal excitation and subsequent firing. In this theory, the slowing of the second-messenger systems may decrease cell firing and (theoretically) decrease manic symptoms. It now appears these effects may be only one of many effects that ultimately translate into therapeutic gains.

### Lithium and Gene Expression

Research continues into the extent to which lithium may affect gene expression in the central nervous system. Ikonomov and Manji (1999) explored the possibility that lithium administration may alter the expression of specific genes related to the central nervous system. The idea is that in regulating gene expression, neurons are stabilized through some sort of as-yet-undefined neuroprotective mechanisms related to lithium's effects. Stahl (2000) ties the idea of modification in genetic expression to second-messenger systems, positing that lithium may regulate gene expression by modulating **protein kinase** C. In Chapter Two, we gave an overview of second-messenger systems and how they impact enzyme action. Another possibility of how lithium affects gene expression is that it somehow alters the enzymes that interact with second-messenger systems. As with most questions about how lithium works, these are good hypotheses but likely partial.

### Lithium and Circadian Rhythms

As early as 1990, researchers have sought to explore the connection between Bipolar I Disorder and sleep–wake cycles (Goodwin & Jamison, 1990) that are part of our circadian rhythms (biologic cycles within the course of a day). This theory reflects the psychosocial intervention of optimizing sleep and setting regular patterns of sleep and wakefulness with clients suffering from Bipolar I Disorder. The circadian rhythm hypothesis of lithium's action derives from the fact that lithium slows the circadian rhythm in species ranging from plants to human beings (Lenox & Manji, 1998). Although studies with humans are hampered by several ethical limits that do not constrain animal models, it appears that lithium significantly slows and lengthens the circadian cycle.

### Side Effects of Lithium

Approximately three fourths of clients on lithium experience side effects (American Psychiatric Association, 2000), which constitutes a primary reason that clients stop taking the drug (Atack, 2000; Julien, 2001). One problem is that the therapeutic dosage is often close to the toxic dosage, so the drug requires regular blood monitoring in clients. The side effects of lithium are summarized in Table 8.3 and then described more fully in the text. The types and degrees of side effects clients will suffer are difficult to estimate. Even recent analyses of the literature give broad ranges of the percentage of patients complaining of adverse effects (35 to 93% according to Lenox and Manji, 1998). Price and Heninger (1994) noted that the side effects increase as the serum levels of the drug increase. It is important to note that clients will have different numbers and degrees of side effects, as well as that lithium's difficult side effect profile is a main reason that continued research on different mood stabilizers is important. When the percentage is generally known, we have also listed in parentheses the proportion of clients thought to suffer from a given side effect. Data for Table 8.3 are drawn from Lenox and Manji (1998); Perry, Alexander, and Liskow. (1997); and Schatzberg, Cole, and DeBattista (1997).

### CNS Side Effects of Lithium

The cognitive side effects of lithium may be the most troubling for clients but remain the least studied (Jamison & Akiskal, 1983; Lenox & Manji, 1998; Shaw, 1986). From the intrapsychic perspective, clients say lithium decreases creativity and concentration and increases forgetfulness. Schatzberg, Cole, and DeBattista (1997) have noted that forgetfulness is one of the most common reasons given by clients who stop taking lithium. The few existing studies have produced conflicting data. Judd, Squire, and Butters (1987) reported slowed rate of central information processing with short-term use of lithium. Some of these effects seem to diminish with long-term use, suggesting there is some accommodation to the effects. More research on this problem is warranted, and clinicians should monitor cognitive functioning in clients receiving lithium. Cognitive impairment can also be a sign of lithium toxicity.

TABLE 8.3   Side Effects of Lithium

| Type of Effect | Description |
|---|---|
| CNS effects | Contradictory evidence of deleterious cognitive effects on concentration, memory, and creativity<br>Seizures can occur as a result of lithium toxicity |
| Neuromuscular | Tremors at rest or although moving (4%–65%)<br>Muscle weakness (40% in short-term treatment) |
| Gastrointestinal | Chronic nausea, diarrhea, occasional blood in stool |
| Endocrine | Weight gain (11%–64%)<br>Hypothyroidism (approx. 4%)<br>Goiter (approx. 6%)<br>Elevated thyroid-stimulating hormone (30%) |
| Renal | Polyuria/polydipsia (20%) |
| Dermatologic | Acne and rashes<br>Aggravation of psoriasis<br>Alopecia |
| Hematologic | Increase in white blood cells (75%–100%) |
| Teratogenic | Increased risk of Epstein's anomaly a congenital heart defect characterized by displacement of the tricuspid valve |
| Sexual | Decreased libido in males and females, erectile dysfunction in males |

## Neuromuscular Side Effects of Lithium

The most reported neuromuscular side effect of lithium is tremor. The tremor can occur while the client is at rest or moving. The incidence of tremor is quite broad (4 to 65%) and seems positively correlated with the client's lithium level. Emotional stress and stimulants such as caffeine can worsen the tremor. Although the tremor is reversible with discontinuation of the medication, it may also be controlled by lowering the lithium dosage or by administering a beta-blocking agent (such as described in

Chapter Six). Although the source of lithium-induced tremor is uncertain, it is not related to the extrapyramidal side effects described in Chapter Seven. Several studies have shown that medications used for EPS are ineffective with lithium-induced tremor. General muscle weakness is also a common neuromuscular side effect of lithium and is reported in about 70% of clients within the first two weeks of taking lithium. Again, this side effect is dose related and appears to resolve on its own after the first two or three weeks of lithium use.

## Gastrointestinal Side Effects of Lithium

Gastrointestinal side effects can range from mild to severe, with milder effects that include bloating and slight abdominal pain and severe effects that include nausea and vomiting. It is important for clinicians to monitor these side effects closely, because they are also signs of lithium toxicity. Perry, Alexander, and Liskow (1997) noted that GI side effects frequently subside on their own and can be diminished if the medication is taken with food. Sometimes the daily required dosage can be divided into more numerous, smaller portions. Although there are currently sustained-release formulations of lithium, studies indicate no real benefits in terms of side effect profile.

## Endocrine Side Effects of Lithium

The most problematic endocrine-related side effect of lithium is weight gain. It has been clearly tied to lithium use and is another of the more common reasons that people stop taking lithium (Peselow, Dunner, Fieve, & Lautin, 1980). Weight gain is variable, ranging from about 7 to 60 pounds. Clients who are overweight to begin with seem to gain more weight while taking lithium. Also, the better the therapeutic response to lithium, the more weight the person typically gains (Perry, Alexander, & Liskow, 1997). Although the reasons for the weight gain are not entirely clear, lithium does exert an insulin-like effect in lowering blood glucose levels and inducing hypoglycemia. This hypoglycemia then promotes eating and weight gain. Dietary regulation and exercise require close monitoring by a physician, because both can disrupt levels of lithium in the client's system. Lithium treatment may also disrupt thyroid functioning, most commonly as an increase in thyroid-stimulating hormone

### Renal Side Effects of Lithium

The most common renal side effects of lithium administration are **polydipsia** (chronic, excessive thirst) and **polyuria** (excessive urination). These effects occur in about 20% of clients on lithium. The polyuria is caused by lithium reducing the kidneys' ability to concentrate urine. Although these effects may wear off on their own, lowering the dosage or discontinuing the drug can relieve them. A more problematic (albeit rarer) side effect from lithium is inflammation of the renal tubules, blood vessels, and surrounding tissue (called *interstitial nephritis*). Although rare, it can cause renal scarring and destruction. Patients exposed to multiple periods of lithium toxicity are at greater risk for this disorder. These side effects have led to the recommendation that clients on lithium have kidney function checked every 6 to 12 months (Schatzberg, Cole, & DeBattista, 1997).

### Dermatologic Side Effects of Lithium

The dermatologic side effects from lithium include various rashes and outbreaks on the skin, aggravation of existing dermatologic conditions, and hair loss (alopecia). Cases of rashes, acne, or other outbreaks on the skin may resolve by themselves. Lowering the dosage frequently relieves them. Few studies have been done on hair loss and lithium treatment. Although more rare than other dermatologic problems, it seems associated with disrupted thyroid function. On discontinuation of the drug, hair loss stops and hair typically regrows. The mechanisms of action of these dermatologic side effects are at present unknown.

### Sexual Side Effects of Lithium

Only a few studies have looked at incidence of sexual dysfunction related to lithium use. These and anecdotal clinical evidence suggest lithium does interfere with sexual functioning. Note that hypersexuality is sometimes associated with mania, and for such clients, returning to baseline levels of sexuality may seem like impairment but that is only

relative to the hypersexual state they experienced in manic episodes (Rojansky, Wang, & Halbreich, 1992). Under double-blind conditions, lithium has been reported to cause decreased libido as well as erectile failure (Vinarova, Uhlir, Stika, & Vinar, 1972).

### Lithium Toxicity

As noted, the therapeutic dosage of lithium is frequently close to the toxic dosage. Prescribing professionals cannot know the correct dose in advance, because each person eliminates lithium at different rates. In addition, lithium is one of the few psychotropic medications that is not highly fat soluble. As a result, it has a more difficult time crossing the blood–brain barrier and requires higher concentrations in the blood to reach adequate concentrations in the central nervous system (Lickey & Gordon, 1991). Clients must have regular blood tests to ensure that their levels are within safe parameters.

The balance of lithium in a person's bloodstream is delicate. Many things can affect it, including physical and emotional stressors that alter sodium levels. For example, changes in diet and exercise can easily lower sodium levels, which in turn alter the plasma levels of lithium to the point where the person could suffer lithium toxicity. In some documented cases, medical illnesses seemed to tip the balance and bring about toxicity (Decina, Schlegel, & Fieve, 1987). Because the kidneys excrete lithium almost intact, any impairment of kidney functioning (such as mild dehydration, reduced salt intake, or dieting) can result in lithium toxicity.

The toxicity is of a type described as "excitotoxicity" (West, 1996). This means the brain's excitatory neurotransmitter systems become overstimulated and produce excess calcium (a positively charged ion) and free radicals and break down cell defenses. West and Melzer (1979) studied clients under severe psychological stress and found these clients were at higher risk for developing lithium toxicity. These authors were concerned that the ego disintegration typical of severe mental and emotional disorders actually functioned as a risk factor for lithium toxicity; ironically, it was ego disintegration that partially made people candidates for lithium. Also note that clients with a history of

**TABLE 8.4**  Signs of Lithium Toxicity

Nausea

Drowsiness

Confusion

Dizziness

Mental dullness

Slurred speech

Muscle twitches

Irregular heartbeat

Blurred vision

brain injury may have increased vulnerability to lithium toxicity (Moskowitz & Altshuler, 1991).

Lithium toxicity primarily affects the brain. The symptoms include confusion, slurred speech, loss of balance, tremor, GI upset, and possibly coma and death. Although some of these symptoms are side effects that are most likely to occur at the beginning of therapy, if they emerge in a client who has been on lithium for some time, the drug should be discontinued and immediate medical attention should be sought (Lickey & Gordon, 1991). There is no antidote to lithium poisoning, and the condition is usually treated by halting the drug administration and giving the client sodium-containing fluids. If the toxicity is serious enough, other medical interventions may be necessary (Paragas, 1984). Julien (2001) notes that complete recovery from lithium toxicity can take weeks to months, depending on the severity of the case. Table 8.4 summarizes the signs of lithium toxicity.

Some authors (Sheean, 1991; West, 1996) feel that the dangers of lithium toxicity are minimized in the literature. Sheean (1991) estimated that 10% of lithium toxicity survivors suffer some permanent neurologic damage. Aronson and Reynolds (1992) recommend that clients have their blood checked as close as possible to 12 hours after the last dose. At this time the drug absorption is complete and allows for the most consistent reading. Mental health clinicians often have to help clients organize schedules to make sure these tests are done consistently at the appropriate time. Although lithium toxicity is a problematic side effect, the chances of developing

it can be greatly reduced through conservative dosing strategies, care in combining lithium with other medications, regular blood monitoring, and educating clients and significant others about the core symptoms (Delva & Hawken, 2001).

### Lithium and Aggression

An important footnote to lithium in the history of psychopharmacology is the work of Michael Sheard. He has conducted several studies exploring the effects of lithium on aggressive behavior (Sheard, 1971; Sheard, 1975; Sheard, Marini, Bridges, & Wagner, 1976; Sheard & Marini, 1978).

Sheard began his work on rodents, assuming that because serotonin was implicated in aggression and because lithium affected serotonin transmission, it might affect levels of aggression in rodents. These initial studies seemed to indicate the lithium did decrease aggression, so he then treated prison inmates with lithium in a placebo-controlled study. Although lithium had no impact on nonviolent behaviors such as lying and stealing, it appeared to fully suppress serious assault in the inmates, as guards observed and documented. Sheard's conclusion was that only impulsive aggression was affected. More importantly, on discontinuation of the lithium the aggression returned. Sheard's work laid the basis for many different populations being treated with lithium for aggression. As we discuss in Chapter Nine, children and adolescents are among those regularly being given lithium and other mood stabilizers for aggressive behavior and for the condition diagnosed as Conduct Disorder (Malone, Luebbert, Pena-Ariet, Biesecker, & Delaney, 1994)

Although lithium therapy is still an effective treatment for the symptoms of Bipolar Disorder (Baldessarini, Tondo, Hennen, & Viguera, 2002), that alone does not mean clients comply with lithium treatment. In addition, not all clients have a therapeutic response to lithium and need alternatives. After presenting some cases of clients taking lithium, we discuss those alternative treatments.

### Lithium Cases

The following cases illustrate several different ways in which lithium has been used in mental health treatment.

## The Case of William

Near the end of summer William, a 27-year-old, single construction worker, began to act very oddly and irrationally. He missed work or was often late. Coworkers noticed that he seemed "hyper" and silly, because he would toss tools, speak rapidly, and lose his train of thought. Friends recognized that William, an avid sports fan, was becoming obsessed with the owner of the local professional football team. William would talk at great lengths about his long conversations with this man and the inside advice he gave William just before each season. At present he said the two of them were in intense discussions about strategies for the preseason games. One evening William's girlfriend, Sharon, called two of his best friends, a psychologist and attorney, to alert them of William's increasing bizarre behavior. She said he had invested most of his savings in what she believed was a scam to save dying children in Africa, was not sleeping, and had extreme mood swings she had never seen before. This evening she was afraid, because when he stormed out of her house, he told her he was going to walk on the center rail of the major highway at sunrise and he believed only the traffic driving west would be able to see him. He also believed this was the only way he could communicate with the sports owner about a disagreement they had had about a rookie on the team. She indicated she had never seen him like this, and she said she felt that William had slept little in recent weeks.

Eventually his two friends found William at the local YMCA, where he was being escorted out by police for creating a scene and using profanity with the manager. His friends spoke to the police, who released William to them. Over the next several hours William talked with his friends about many grandiose plans, his paranoid fears, his worries that there wasn't enough time in a day, and his growing, spiteful hatred of the football team owner. Gradually, after long and circuitous arguments, William's two friends convinced him he needed medical help and took him to the emergency room of a local hospital. William was admitted and put on lithium carbonate 450 mg, three times a day, until he stabilized and was discharged. At three- and six-month follow-up William remained stable and his blood

levels remained in the therapeutic range. Now, 10 years later, William has had only one, minor manic episode, which did not demand hospitalization. He no longer takes the lithium and leads a relatively normal life. He is now married, with three children, and continues to work in construction.

## The Case of Lincoln

Lincoln is a 38-year-old trade laborer who has suffered from Bipolar I Disorder for 19 years. He has had to be restrained or arrested for 31 of his 32 hospitalizations. Lithium, supportive counseling, and case management have failed to manage his disorder. It is important to mention that the lithium worked well enough to stabilize Lincoln so that he could be discharged from the hospital, but even when taken as prescribed it could not keep him from decompensating into a psychotic and manic state. In these states Lincoln becomes menacing and violent. During his manic episodes no one can talk to or reason with Lincoln, and he seems to become more agitated and grandiose when safety personnel or mental health staff attempt to reason with him, resulting in hospitalization and restraint.

On discharge Lincoln could return to work for short periods of time, but eventually he would again begin to decompensate into a manic state. His psychiatrist recommended both case management and a counselor. Lincoln began a 10-year counseling regimen with the same counselor. The work was problematic and very difficult. It emerged that Lincoln was the oldest of seven children and that his domineering father was an alcoholic. As a child Lincoln had sustained several beatings from his father, and yet as an adult he intermittently worked for him. The counselor could not predict when Lincoln would become manic and often found out about the episodes only after Lincoln was hospitalized. It appeared there was no way to break the cycle of Lincoln's hospitalizations, and he refused any other medications beside lithium and diazepam for his agitation. His severe Bipolar I Disorder with psychotic features and extreme manic states seemed impossible to control or manage.

During the 10th year of treatment, Lincoln recognized for the first time that he could self-admit to the hospital without the struggle of being either forcibly taken in or probated. This was a major breakthrough, and he externalized this decision by blaming the episode on his counselor when he spoke with the hospital staff. His counselor accepted this twist of events and worked with Lincoln to help him understand how this hospitalization was different from all the rest. Lincoln was never hospitalized again, except for the time he volunteered to participate in the Depakote (divalproex sodium) studies at a local research hospital. During the study Lincoln unfortunately got the placebo, and his mania went off the charts. He had to be put in isolation and administered both lithium and Depakote. This was also quite a learning experience for him.

When he returned to therapy, still on lithium and Depakote, Lincoln began to explore his family-of-origin issues, his current depressive feelings and enormous fear of them, and his desire to have a relationship with a woman. The combination of drugs seemed to stabilize Lincoln, and the counseling deepened his understanding of himself and his illness. He eventually married and managed to establish his own business, but he remains on his medication, is alert for side effects, and tries to cope with the anxiety and hyper states in his life.

Lincoln suffered tremendously from his Bipolar I illness, yet he managed to find the resilience to survive the numerous hospitalizations and connect with a counselor who maintained a tolerant, empathic, and focused relationship with him until he could begin to manage his illness in a more proactive way. In therapy he explored intrapsychic issues and cultural examination of the impact of his Eastern European heritage. It is a miracle that Lincoln survived his illness and chaotic life. Both the combined drug therapy and the counseling facilitated Lincoln's improvement.

### The Case of Kelly

Kelly is a 39-year-old, married, African-American art teacher with no children. Over the holiday break her husband noticed increased signs of agitation in Kelly, along with insomnia and heightened irritability. He also noticed that her daily activity increased dramatically and he could not keep up with everything she was trying to accomplish.

Kelly's state became so exaggerated that other family members became quite worried. Kelly would call members of her family at all hours of the night and try to enlist them in her ongoing activities. Finally her husband had the good judgment to take Kelly to her family physician. She assessed Kelly briefly and referred her to a psychiatrist, whom she called immediately to alert her about Kelly's manic state. The psychiatrist evaluated Kelly the next day and recommended that she begin a course of lithium. She began on 450 mg daily and gradually increased to 1350 mg. The psychiatrist spoke with Kelly and her husband about lithium toxicity. Kelly returned to work and took the lithium as prescribed. She also had her blood levels checked regularly over the next several months. She never had a case manager or therapist.

In the seventh month Kelly's husband began to notice a change in her skin, indicated by acne and rashes, one of the known side effects of lithium. Both he and Kelly noticed her continued drowsiness, frequent nausea, and mild dizziness. Kelly also complained of forgetfulness and mental dullness as she tried to remember her lessons for class. Most recently she complained of blurred vision. She contacted her family physician, who immediately consulted with the psychiatrist who recognized the signs of lithium toxicity. He saw Kelly immediately, diagnosed toxicity from the signs, discontinued the lithium, and began sodium fluids. Even after this intervention it took Kelly eight weeks to recover from the symptoms of lithium toxicity. She did not try another mood-stabilizing agent and tried to manage her rather moderate mood symptoms with diet, exercise, and meditation.

## Anticonvulsants as Mood Stabilizers

Anticonvulsant medications are used in treating Bipolar Disorder and appear to have some efficacy as antimanic agents. Researchers have hypothesized that manic episodes resemble seizures in the sense that they "kindle," or catch fire, just as fires "kindle" and then grow if enough is kindling present. For clients with seizure disorders, each episode seems to increase the probability of later episodes or to act as "kindling" for these later episodes. This has been reported with manic episodes, in that many clients who suffer from a manic episode are more likely to suffer from subsequent episodes. Thus earlier episodes are said to somehow "kindle" the brain for other episodes. Deserved or not, this theoretical similarity has been used as a justification for treating mania with anticonvulsants (Stahl, 2000). This has birthed a line of research in which drugs that are approved as anticonvulsants seem to find their way into trials for treating Bipolar I Disorder. Further research is needed to clarify the role these medications play in treating mania and whether, or the extent to which, each one represents any improvement over lithium (Macdonald & Young, 2002). The following anticonvulsant medications are used in treating Bipolar Disorder and mania.

### Carbamazepine

Researchers developed carbamazepine (brand name Tegretol) in the late 1950s as an anticonvulsant medication with efficacy in treating epilepsy. Pharmaceutical companies introduced it to the European market in 1960. In the early 1960s physicians believed carbamazepine had beneficial psychotropic effects in people taking it for epilepsy, and in the 1970s Japanese researchers documented its effectiveness in manic-depressive illness (Keck & McElroy, 1998). This latter research was confirmed in a double-blind, crossover trial (Ballenger & Post, 1980). The FDA approved carbamazepine in 1974 as an antiepileptic drug for adults, in 1978 as an antiepileptic for children over 6 years of age, and finally in 1987 as an antiepileptic without age restriction. Carbamazepine comes in several liquid formulations (solutions, syrups) as well as slow-release and chewable formulations.

As we pointed out in the introduction to Part Two of this book, the categorical approach to diagnosis has always been challenged by the dimensional approach. Most mental and emotional disorders, far from appearing as discrete entities, usually share characteristics with other disorders. Bipolar Disorder is no different in this respect, and for years researchers have speculated on the relationships among Bipolar Disorder, epilepsy, and explosive behavior disorders (Julien, 2001). Is it possible these are really different variations on a continuum of similar disorders? This is a question only continued

research and effective political lobbying for flexibility in diagnostic categories can answer. That many antimanic drugs are effective in treating epilepsy continues to fuel this speculation.

### Mechanisms of Action in Carbamazepine

Table 8.5 summarizes the mechanisms of action for carbamazepine.

**TABLE 8.5**   Proposed Mechanisms of Action for Carbamazepine

| |
|---|
| Reduce neuronal firing through inhibition of sodium channels |
| Increased potassium conductance |
| Decreased glutamate release |
| Increase in adenosine receptors |
| Also alters neurotransmission mediated by NE, 5-HT, DA, GABA, Substance P, and aspartate |

As you can see from Table 8.5, carbamazepine has many proposed mechanisms of action; however, researchers do not know which ones, or which combinations, account for carbamazepine's efficacy in clients suffering from Bipolar I Disorder (Keck & McElroy, 2002). Keck and McElroy (1998) and Mitchell and Malhi (2002) have proposed two basic mechanisms in carbamazepine that may influence the symptoms of Bipolar Disorder. The first is effects on ion channels to reduce the firing of neurons, and the second is effects on presynaptic and postsynaptic neurotransmission.

### Ion Channel Effects of Carbamazepine

Recall from Chapter Two, that each neuron has ion channels that allow the influx of either positively charged or negatively charged ions. The influx of positively charged ions increases the likelihood of a cell firing, and the influx of negatively charged ions decreases the likelihood of the cell firing. Carbamazepine seems to reduce neuronal firing by binding to and deactivating sodium ion channels. Sodium is a positively charged ion, and when its ion channel is deactivated it cannot enter the neuron and exert its excitatory effects. Some studies also support the notion that carbamazepine increases potassium conductance (Post, Weiss, & Chuang, 1992).

These mechanisms occur shortly after a person takes the drug and account for carbamazepine's anticonvulsant properties. These mechanisms do not explain why it is an effective mood stabilizer, however, because the mood-stabilizing effects usually do not appear for 10 to 14 days (Perry, Alexander, & Liskow, 1997).

### Carbamazepine's Effects on Neurotransmission

Carbamazepine has numerous effects on neurotransmission. It decreases glutamate release (recall from Chapter Two that glutamate is an excitatory neurotransmitter) and affects norepinephrine, dopamine, and adenosine. Adenosine was not covered in Chapter Two but is what is called a *neuromodulator*, which is similar to a neurotransmitter except that its actions are not limited to the synaptic cleft. Carbamazepine causes an increase in adenosine receptors, which overall, would have an inhibitory effect on the nervous system. As noted, knowledge of these mechanisms has not helped explain why carbamazepine has efficacy for manic-depressive symptoms.

### Efficacy of Carbamazepine in Bipolar Disorder

Although the scant literature supports the efficacy of carbamazepine for manic-depressive symptoms, the drug does not appear as effective as once thought (Dardennes, Even, Bange, & Heim, 1995; Kleindienst & Greil, 2002). Although other researchers challenge this view, carbamazepine is listed as a second-line treatment for mania (Julien, 2001). Like lithium, response to carbamazepine is correlated to the dosage and many nonresponders have been on inadequate doses of the drug. Studies have also supported carbamazepine as a maintenance therapy for manic-depressive illness (Kishimoto, Ogura, Hazama, & Inoue, 1983). Many researchers believe that trials with appropriate methodologies and adequate samples would find carbamazepine equal to lithium in efficacy (Mitchell & Malhi, 2002).

### Side Effects of Carbamazepine

Table 8.6 summarizes the more common side effects associated with carbamazepine, according to Perry, Alexander, and Liskow. (1997) and Schatzberg, Cole, and DeBattista (1997).

**TABLE 8.6** Common Side Effects Associated With Carbamazepine

| Type | Description |
|---|---|
| Dermatologic | Rash that may foreshadow WBC problems |
| Endocrine | Hyponatremia (dangerous drop in sodium levels)<br>Water intoxication |
| Gastrointestinal | Nausea, vomiting |
| Hematological | Leukopenia (elevated WBC count)<br>Agranulocytosis (rare)<br>Aplastic anemia (rare) |
| Hepatic | Elevated liver enzymes (20%) |
| Neurologic | Sedation/ataxia, dizziness<br>Dystonic reactions |
| Psychiatric | Delirium, hallucinations<br>Minimal cognitive impairment |
| Teratogenic | Associated with craniofacial defects and spina bifida |

### Dermatologic Side Effects of Carbamazepine

Within 2 weeks to 5 months of beginning carbamazepine, approximately 7% of users show general dermatologic problems such as rash or acne. Some data connect these dermatologic side effects to a more serious side effect of bone marrow suppression, particularly in children (Silverstein, Boxer, & Johnson, 1983). Another possible side effect is Stevens-Johnson syndrome, a rash involving the skin and mucous membranes. The lesions can include conjunctivitis as well as oral and genital lesions. Severe forms of the syndrome can include hepatitis and pneumonia and can be fatal. Once detected, this syndrome resolves when medication is discontinued.

### Endocrine Side Effects of Carbamazepine

Carbamazepine can cause sodium depletion (hyponatremia) as well as water intoxication (defined as too much water in the body). Although this occurs in only 5% of clients, hyponatremia can be fatal if not corrected. The symptoms of sodium depletion include headache, nausea, puffiness about the face, muscle weakness, and disorientation. Frequently lithium is combined with carbamazepine, and sodium depletion (as noted earlier) can in turn cause lithium toxicity.

### Gastrointestinal Side Effects of Carbamazepine

The most commonly experienced GI side effects of carbamazepine are vomiting and nausea. If people experience these side effects, their dosage can be reduced to resolve the side effect. Frequently clients experience this while the prescribing professional is titrating the dose upward. In that case, the prescribing professional usually slows the titration.

### Hematologic Side Effects of Carbamazepine

Elevated white blood cell counts (leukopenia) are experienced in approximately 12% of adults and 7% of children taking carbamazepine. Symptoms include fever, sore throat, and ulcers in the mouth. Although the blood count should be monitored for problems, most blood counts return to baseline without intervention. Patients with low counts should be monitored every two weeks for the first 3 months of medication treatment. If the count falls below a certain point (3000 per millimeter), the drug should be discontinued. More problematic are agranulocytosis (drop in white blood cell counts) and aplastic anemia (failure of the bone marrow to produce white and red blood cells).

### Hepatic Side Effects of Carbamazepine

The most common side effect related to the liver is an elevated level of liver enzymes that govern metabolism. This side effect occurs in about 20% of clients on carbamazepine and is generally thought benign. There are rare occurrences of liver toxicity, the majority of which occurred in the first four weeks of treatment. Symptoms include fever, jaundice, rash, anorexia, and/or nausea. If liver toxicity occurs, the medication should be discontinued.

### Neurologic Side Effects of Carbamazepine

Two of the most common side effects of taking carbamazepine in general are sedation and dizziness. These typically occur within the first few weeks of therapy. Some children on carbamazepine experience dystonic reactions in the first two to three weeks of treatment. This response is possibly due to dopamine antagonism. If carbamazepine is combined with lithium, about 12% of clients taking the combination risk neurotoxicity. Symptoms include confusion, disorientation, slurred speech, and problems with coordination.

### Psychiatric Side Effects of Carbamazepine

No estimates exist on how many people experience psychiatric complications from carbamazepine, but the typical symptoms include delirium and hallucinations, insomnia, irritability, and mood lability. If these occur, the medication should be discontinued. There are also reports of some minimal cognitive impairment from carbamazepine; however, this impairment is not as great as is reported with lithium.

### Teratogenic Side Effects of Carbamazepine

The use of carbamazepine in pregnant women has been associated with craniofacial defects, spina bifida (underdeveloped neural tube), underdeveloped fingernails, and developmental delays. Although some studies dispute these figures, there is not enough evidence to support safe use during pregnancy.

## The Case of Molly

Molly is a 24-year-old single woman who has suffered from Bipolar I Disorder for over a year. She has had a great deal of difficulty on lithium, and her attending physician recognized that Tegretol (carbamazepine) had just received FDA approval for use with Bipolar I Disorder in adults. He titrated Molly off the lithium and began a course of treatment on the carbamazepine. Over time, Molly noticed that her intermittent manic symptoms lessened while she was taking Tegretol, and she agreed to begin therapy to focus on issues surrounding her sexual orientation and great issues of anxiety and concern about "coming out" as a lesbian.

In this case the carbamazepine served as an important alternative to lithium, and it stabilized Molly enough that she was able to explore other psychological issues in counseling. Another outcome of the counseling was that Molly was able to tolerate her depressive symptoms and link them to the losses she experienced in her life and to deep personal sadness. Molly remained on carbamazepine for six years and then successfully titrated off the psychotropic with minimal adverse effects. Molly's case is a good illustration of how psychotropic medication provides a window of opportunity for clients to explore intrapsychic issues.

## The Case of Roger

Roger, a 32-year-old single male has suffered from a variety of mood and psychotic disorders over the past decade. Sometimes his chronic manic symptoms would intensify and Roger would become psychotic and have to be hospitalized. During these hospitalizations Roger was given various diagnoses: He has been variously diagnosed with Schizophrenia, Schizoaffective Disorder, Cyclothymia, and Bipolar I Disorder. He was treated with several medications, including lithium, perphenazine(Trilafon), loxapine (Loxitane), haloperidol (Haldol), and thiothixene (Navane). None of these medications seemed very helpful to Roger, and his case remained a mystery to his psychiatrist.

Recently Roger was prescribed carbamazepine (Tegretol) for his symptoms, and after three months he began to report some relief from his chronic manic symptoms. After six months on the drug, however, Roger began to experience continuous auditory and tactile hallucinations. He had never experienced either of these symptoms before, although the variety of his symptoms was extensive. After a careful assessment, his attending psychiatrist recognized that there was a very strong possibility that Roger was experiencing psychiatric side effects of the carbamazepine. The psychiatrist discontinued the medication, and after about five days the hallucinations disappeared.

Given the complexity and range of Roger's symptoms and diagnoses, it is remarkable that his psychiatrist was able to link his hallucinations to an adverse reaction to the carbamazepine rather than to new psychotic symptoms. This case is a good illustration of the importance of good medical care, particularly where multiple medications are involved.

## Valproic Acid

Valproic acid is another anticonvulsant that is used as a mood stabilizer. There are several formulations of valproic acid with different names, including divalproex, Depakene, and Depakote. We use *valproate* because that is the most general term in use. Valproate was first synthesized in the United States in 1882. Its initial use was as a solvent, and its anticonvulsant properties were not discovered until 1963. This discovery (like many in psychopharmacology) was made by accident: In France, researchers were mixing valproate (as a solvent) with other compounds thought to have anticonvulsant properties. The researchers soon discovered that the other compounds worked only when mixed with valproate and that only the valproate had anticonvulsant properties. It was tested and introduced as an anticonvulsant in Europe in 1967, becoming available in the United States in 1978. In the 1990s the FDA approved it for treating acute manic episodes.

### Mechanism of Action

Table 8.7 summarizes proposed mechanisms of action for valproate.

Valproic acid differs chemically from all other anticonvulsants and psychotropic compounds. Like carbamazepine and lithium, it has many mechanisms of action. Scientists do not know why it acts effectively as an anticonvulsant or as a mood stabilizer. One theory, summarized by Keck and McElroy (1998), is that valproate slows down metabolism of GABA, increases its release, and increases GABA receptor density. Recall from Chapter Two that GABA serves an inhibitory function in the nervous system, so any agent that increases its presence would increase inhibition of the nervous system. Although valproate acts on the body in many ways, this inhibition seems to be a key to its therapeutic applications, However, more evidence is needed.

**TABLE 8.7**   Proposed Mechanisms of Action for Valproate

| |
|---|
| Inhibits sodium and calcium channels |
| Slows metabolism of GABA |
| Increases release of GABA |
| Increases GABA receptor density |
| Reduces glutamate action |

## Efficacy of Valproate in Bipolar I Disorder and Aggression

Current data suggest that valproate is as effective as lithium in treating acute mania and may be more effective than lithium in mixed-state or rapid-cycling subtypes of Bipolar I Disorder (Freeman, Clothier, Pazzaglia, Lessem, & Swann., 1992; Bowden et al., 1994; Mitchell & Malhi, 2002). Schatzberg, Cole, and DeBattista (1997) have noted that open trials indicate that valproate is also effective as a prophylactic. The antimanic effects of valproate begin within 7 to 14 days of a patient beginning the medication. It is currently being used in both children and adults (Wagner et al., 2002).

Some support exists for the notion that valproate is better tolerated than lithium. French researchers Lambert and Venaud (1992) noted in their study that valproate decreased aggression in animal models, may increase cognitive functions in humans (as opposed to the impairment of cognitive function associated with lithium), and may provide "awakening" effects on personality. An example would be a client whose emotional flattening and avolition improve after being put on valproate. Perry, Alexander, and Liskow (1997) make the point that in comparing valproate to lithium, it is important to separate the participants in various studies into those who have taken lithium and responded, those who have taken it and not responded, and those who have never taken it. This would give us more accurate information on how valproate compares to lithium, but many researchers do not give the participants' lithium history. It appears valproate is also useful in reducing aggression and irritability in people suffering from personality disorders. Like lithium, it is also useful in treating impulsive aggression (Davis, Ryan, Adinoff, & Petty, 2000).

### Side Effects of Valproate

Table 8.8 outlines the most common side effects of valproate. Note that the percentage of clients who suffer from a given side effect varies, as does the reported percentage of side effects, depending on which source you consult.

#### *Cardiovascular Side Effects of Valproate*

Edema is a condition characterized by swelling of body parts, particularly the limbs. Pitting edema is

**TABLE 8.8**   Common Side Effects Associated With Valproate

| Type | Description |
| --- | --- |
| Cardiovascular | Pitting edema |
| Dermatologic | Transient alopecia |
| Endocrinologic | Weight gain |
| Gastrointestinal | Anorexia<br>Nausea, indigestion<br>Vomiting<br>Transient diarrhea |
| Hematologic | Neutropenia (low count of a particular white blood cell)<br>Thrombocytopenia (low platelet count) |
| Hepatic | Increase in hepatic enzymes<br>Hepatotoxicity |
| Neurologic | Sedation<br>Fatigue<br>Confusion<br>Headache |
| Teratogenic | Neural tube defects<br>Craniofacial defects |

when pressure applied to the swelled area leaves a pit for some time after the pressure is released. This is caused by excess fluid under the skin and in the tissue outside the blood vessels. The condition is caused by excess salt in the system, and the valproate in some manner seems to disrupt the balance of salt in the system. Although this side effect is relatively rare, clients should know how to recognize it and report it to the doctor if it occurs.

#### *Dermatologic Side Effects of Valproate*

The transient alopecia (hair loss) that is a side effect of valproate is similar to that seen with lithium. The hair tends to regrow when the drug is discontinued and may regrow even if the drug is continued. Obviously, most clients find this distressing enough to discontinue medication.

#### *Endocrinologic Side Effects of Valproate*

Weight gain and increased appetite are common side effects of valproate. Perry, Alexander, and Liskow (1997) note that although dietary counseling may be recommended, caloric restriction may not solve the problem. Although it is hard to determine which clients suffer from this side effect and how much they gain, all clients should have baseline weight measured before beginning valproate therapy.

### Gastrointestinal Side Effects of Valproate

This category of side effects of valproate has the broadest range. It is the second most common set of side effects attributed to valproate. Although many clients suffer from gastrointestinal side effects, researchers really do not understand the mechanisms of action. Both Perry, Alexander, and Liskow (1997) and Schatzberg, Cole, and DeBattista (1997) have emphasized that often these side effects can be alleviated by changing the formulation of valproate used. In addition, an over-the-counter histamine blocker such as Pepcid can also provide relief.

### Hematologic Side Effects of Valproate

Platelet dysfunction (thrombocytopenia) can be a problem for clients on valproate. The symptoms include easy bruising or bleeding. Platelet levels can be checked, and if the counts are low the prescribing professional can lower the dose or try a different medication. Another problem in this category is neutropenia, which is a low count of a particular type of white blood cell. Again, if this occurs the drug dosage can be decreased or the medication discontinued.

### Hepatic Side Effects of Valproate

The most common hepatic side effect from valproate is elevated levels of liver enzymes. This side effect, which seems benign, occurs in almost half the participants taking valproate in some studies. A more serious although rare problem is hepatotoxicity. This may be fatal and can be detected through tests of liver functioning. Symptoms of hepatotoxicity include lethargy, vomiting, anorexia, and weakness.

### Neurologic Side Effects of Valproate

Sedation is the most common neurologic side effect of valproate. Less commonly, clients may experience headache, fatigue, and confusion. Small studies have also reported onset of hand tremor within one month of beginning treatment.

### Teratogenic Side Effects of Valproate

Like carbamazepine, valproate is associated with increased risk of neural tube defects and craniofacial defects in infants of mothers taking valproate.

As can be seen from the side effect descriptions of lithium, carbamazepine, and valproate, there are some very unpleasant side effects associated with all these drugs. Although they all show efficacy to some extent in treating the symptoms of Bipolar I Disorder, many clients will not take them because of the side effect profiles. In addition, the truth is that scientists still do not understand why any of these medications are effective against the symptoms of Bipolar I Disorder and aggression. For these and many other reasons, the search continues for better mood stabilizers.

# The Case of José

José is a 15-year-old Latino student who was placed in a Severe Emotionally Disturbed (SED) classroom for his aggressive and acting-out behavior. José had beaten up several boys and one girl over the past three years, and one of the boys had to be hospitalized for head injuries. After a recent fight, one of José's teachers noticed that José became very tired, even though he was the violent and uncontrolled aggressor. He slept in the dispensary for over an hour, and when he woke up he seemed very dazed and disoriented. The teacher consulted with the school psychologist, who was aware of many studies and efforts to administer mood stabilizers to aggressive youth. The psychologist also wondered if José might be experiencing some sort of atypical seizure disorder. As a result, the intervention teams met with the mother (his parents were divorced) and recommended a psychiatric consult for José.

José was referred to a psychiatrist who had an excellent reputation for treating children and adolescents. After a careful evaluation of José that included a complete neurological evaluation, he recommended that José begin a combined psychotropic medication treatment of lithium and Tegretol (carbamazepine) for his atypical seizure disorder and his extremely aggressive behavior.

The intervention team included an explanation of this pharmacologic treatment in their staff meetings, and they monitored the administration of both drugs while José was at school. This therapy, along with milieu support, greatly reduced José's outbursts and his aggressive behavior. In fact, over the next 18 months he only threatened, but did not assault, one student.

## The Case of Beverly

Beverly, age 67, is a widow of 17 years who has suffered from Schizoaffective Disorder for over 17 years. Her psychiatrist had tried to manage her extreme manic episodes with both lithium and carbamazepine, with only marginal effectiveness. Over time Beverly had several side effect problems with lithium, including tremors, weight gain, goiter problems, severe rashes, and muscle weakness. Carbamazepine was ineffective in managing her manic episodes, which often necessitated that Beverly be hospitalized for long periods.

Beverly was not responsive to counseling, because she lacked insight and seemed to blame all her problems on either her husband's death or bad luck. She did connect with a female case manager, who helped her with daily living and survival skills, medication management, and support with her loneliness. The case manager was very knowledgeable about psychotropic medications, and she wondered if Depakote might be helpful to Beverly. She not only brought her idea to the attention of the staff psychiatrist but also spoke with Beverly about the medication. Beverly began a course of treatment on Depakote, and her manic episodes and symptoms diminished significantly. She was hospitalized once for a brief period over the next four years, and she had minimal side effects on the Depakote.

In this case the knowledge, experience, and diligence of the mental health professional helped the client and alerted the psychiatrist to an alternative medication. This decision addressed Beverly's extreme suffering from her manic symptoms and the side effects. When counselors are well educated about psychopharmacology, they can competently assist both the client and the attending physician.

**TABLE 8.9**   Newer Anticonvulsants Being Investigated for Efficacy in Treating Bipolar I Disorder

| Generic Name | Brand Name |
| --- | --- |
| Oxcarbazepine | Trileptal |
| Lamotrigine | Lamictal |
| Topiramate | Topamax |
| Gabapentin | Neurontin |

## Newer Anticonvulsants as Mood Stabilizers

Ever since valproate first showed promise as a treatment for Bipolar I Disorder, the search has continued for new mood stabilizers. Most drugs approved as anticonvulsants were considered for efficacy as mood stabilizers. Newer anticonvulsants may hold promise as mood stabilizing agents, but they must be thoroughly researched, because their structures, effects, and side effects are heterogeneous (Calabrese, Shelton, Rapport, & Kimmel, 2002). Although research has just begun on these agents, the following sections summarize what we know about them so far. Table 8.9 lists newer anticonvulsant agents being research for efficacy in treating Bipolar I Disorder.

### Oxcarbazepine

Oxcarbazepine (Trileptal) is an antiepileptic drug that the FDA approved in 2000. It is a chemical variation of carbamazepine and differs primarily in having more oxygen molecules than carbamazepine and in its metabolic properties (Hellewell, 2002; Hummel et al., 2002). Although current studies show promise (Evins, 2003; Ghaemi, Berv, Klugman, Resenquist, & Hsu, 2003; Hummel et al., 2002), more work needs to be done before firm conclusions can be reached. It is noteworthy that because it is metabolized differently from carbamazepine, oxcarbazepine appears better tolerated than other anticonvulsants used to treat Bipolar Disorder (Aldencamp, DeDrom, & Reijs, 2003; Harranz & Argumosa, 2002). A complete list of side effects from oxcarbazepine has yet to be produced, but more severe side effects include cognitive slowness, fatigue, coordination problems, sodium deficiency (hyponatremia), and rare cases of liver malfunction or failure.

## Lamotrigine

The FDA approved lamotrigine (Lamictal) as an anticonvulsant in 1994. Since that time researchers have been studying its efficacy in treating Bipolar I Disorder, making it the most studied of the newer anticonvulsants (Yatham, Kusumakar, Calabrese, Rao, Scarrow, & Krocker, 2002). Macdonald and Young (2002) have noted that in terms of its efficacy lamotrigine is one of the more promising of the newer anticonvulsants . Lamotrigine has shown some initial efficacy in treating Borderline Personality Disorder, Post-Traumatic Stress Disorder, and Schizoaffective Disorder (Bowden et al., 1999; Calabrese, Bowden, Sachs, Asher, Monaghan, & Rudd, 1999). In terms of Bipolar I Disorder, lamotrigine seems to have more efficacy in acute bipolar depression, longer-term bipolar depression, and Bipolar Disorder, rapid cycling type. Double-blind trials have failed to show efficacy for lamotrigine in treating acute mania, however (Yatham et al., 2002).

### *Mechanism of Action of Lamotrigine*

Although lamotrigine is still under study, research to date has identified several mechanisms of action. The drug seems to stabilize neuronal membranes by blocking sodium, calcium, and potassium ion channels. Lamotrigine also inhibits release of glutamate in the hippocampus. Recall from Chapter Two that glutamate is an excitatory neurotransmitter, thus inhibiting glutamate would generally tend to inhibit the neurons in those areas of the brain.

### *Side Effects of Lamotrigine*

Table 8.10 summarizes the side effects so far known from taking lamotrigine. Unlike the other side effect tables in this chapter, these are not listed by category, on which more research is needed.

Probably the most serious side effect in Table 8.10 is the rash, which could be related to Stevens-Johnson syndrome (an immune-complex–mediated hypersensitivity disorder that may be caused by

**TABLE 8.10**   Side Effects of Lamotrigine

| Side Effect | Percentage Reporting |
| --- | --- |
| Dizziness | 38% |
| Headache | 29 |
| Double vision | 28 |
| Unsteadiness | 22 |
| Nausea | 19 |
| Blurred vision | 16 |
| Sleepiness | 14 |
| Rash | 10 |
| Vomiting | 10 |

many drugs and can be fatal). Clients taking lamotrigine who notice a rash should contact their doctor immediately. In addition to these, some psychiatric side effects have been reported, including depression, confusion, irritability, and mania (Asghar, 2002; Ferrier, 1998).

### *Preliminary Conclusions About Lamotrigine for Bipolar I Disorder*

Although there have been some positive reports on lamotrigine, its use in treating Bipolar Disorders may lie in using it as an adjunct to complement other agents such as lithium. Lamotrigine seems to have the most impact on depression, typically being significantly more effective than placebo. It is also useful for preventing future depressive episodes. Although it has not yet shown efficacy in treating acute mania, it may be a useful complement for the depressive end of the cycle (Calabrese et al., 1999). As Hurley (2002) noted, lamotrigine costs two to four times as much as lithium and when this is considered along with lamotrigine's adverse effects and efficacy, lamotrigine appears slated as a second line of treatment.

## Topiramate

Topiramate (brand name Topamax) is a new anticonvulsant that has shown some promise in open trials for treating Bipolar I Disorder. Although initial studies seemed to indicate weight loss was a side effect (Marcotte, 1998), recent analyses indicate that any lost weight is regained after 12 to 18 months of therapy (Gordon & Price, 1999). At this point it appears topiramate may serve as a useful adjunct to more traditional mood stabilizers in treatment-resistant cases (Chengappa, Gershon, & Levine, 2001; Letmaier, Schreinzer, Wolf, & Kasper, 2001).

### Gabapentin

Gabapentin (brand name Neurontin) was introduced to the United States in 1993 as an anticonvulsant. In addition, it has been used off label for a variety of disorders, including Bipolar I Disorder, impulsive behaviors, anxiety disorders, substance use disorders, and chronic pain. Some of these uses have proven quite problematic, and we return to this issue later. Gabapentin is designed to mimic the effects of GABA in the central nervous system (and is hence referred to as a GABA analog). Although initial trials proved promising (Stanton, Keck, & McElroy, 1997), later controlled studies and meta-analyses have found gabapentin no more effective than placebo (Frye et al., 2000; Maidment, 2001; Pande, Crockatt, Janney, Worth, & Tsaroucha, 2000). Gabapentin may yet show efficacy for agitation in psychiatric patients (Megna, Devitt, Sauro, & Mantosh, 2002), but thus far it has not sufficiently demonstrated antimanic properties. At the time of this writing, a great deal of controversy surrounds gabapentin and criminal fraud in its off-label uses that we explain shortly.

One of the more promising groups of agents are the newer antipsychotics covered in Chapter Seven. We now review the use of these in treating Bipolar I Disorder and finish the section by giving overviews of newer agents that may yet rise to prominence as useful compounds.

## Atypical Antipsychotics as Mood Stabilizers

Throughout the book we have written about the lack of accuracy in the *DSM* categories and in the psychotropic drug categories. For example, we noted that drugs categorized as antidepressants seem to have efficacy for a variety of disorders. So are they really "antidepressants" proper? The same problem crops up when we consider the use of atypical antipsychotics for Bipolar I Disorder. Olanzapine (Zyprexa) was approved in 2000 for treating Bipolar I Disorder. Although the dosing is somewhat higher for Bipolar I Disorder than for Schizophrenia, current evidence suggests that olanzapine may also be useful in the long-term treatment of Bipolar I Disorder and is at least as effective as lithium (Berk, Ichim, & Brook, 1999). In a large, randomized, clinical trial, Tohen et al. (2002) concluded that olanzapine was more effective than valproate in treating acute mania over a three-week period.

Current research is also looking at risperidone's role in treating mania. Because these medications must be used at higher doses than used for treating Schizophrenia, there is an increased risk of tardive dyskinesia. It also seems that atypical antipsychotics, although showing promise for treating mania, may induce depression in some clients with Bipolar I Disorder (Yatham, 2002). The most attractive feature of the atypical antipsychotics is the possibility that they would be better tolerated in terms of side effects than any of the mood stabilizers discussed so far. Although not associated with side effects such as hair loss, they are associated with weight gain, sedation, and the increased risk of diabetes (in some cases) that may be equally problematic for some clients (McIntyre, 2002).

One of the newer uses of atypical antipsychotics is as complements for another mood stabilizer (Kafantaris, Coletti, Dicker, Padula, & Kane, 2001). Delbello, Schwiers, Rosenberg, and Strakowski (2002) outlined a course of treatment for adolescents diagnosed with Bipolar I Disorder, complementing valproate with quetiapine (Seroquel). The study found that the combination therapy was more effective than valproate alone. Likewise, Weizman and Weizman (2001) concluded that the atypicals had promise both alone and used in addition to other mood stabilizers, although these authors point readers to the debate on whether or not the atypical antipsychotics have significant advantages in terms of side effects.

## General Conclusions on Mood Stabilizers

Although we have yet to explore mood stabilizers through the other perspectives of the Integral Model, we can draw some conclusions from the medical model summary of these drugs covered thus far. First, as we noted at the beginning of the chapter, the very notion of mood stabilization is as illusive as the etiology of Bipolar I Disorder. All the medications discussed in this chapter were originally developed to treat other conditions, and their effects on mood states were accidentally discovered. Researchers really need to understand the etiology of Bipolar I Disorder and the action mechanisms of the effective drugs before they can move forward to designing drugs and other treatments specifically to treat Bipolar I. The inclusion of the phrase "and other treatments" implies that causes of Bipolar I Disorder may in fact not be limited to biological ones. From an Integral perspective, looking at psychological and even spiritual aspects of the disorder may help therapists radically redirect treatment efforts. Finally, it is becoming clear that the most difficult aspect of mood stabilization is the prophylactic one. Mitchell and Malhi (2002) noted that one large problem with researching this area is that clients eligible for the trials usually suffer from less severe forms of the disorder. This makes the clinical trial easier to carry out but decreases the generalizability in the field.

## Issues From Other Perspectives

In this section we explore some of the many issues surrounding mood stabilizers that frequently are not covered in psychopharmacology books. From an Integral perspective there are numerous non-pharmacologic issues that, if engaged, could have profound implications for treatment.

### Intrapsychic Issues

#### Bipolar Illness and Creativity

Several of our students have asked whether there is a significant connection between Bipolar I Disorder and creativity. Jamison (1989) conducted a study with an admittedly small number of participants that supported the notion that clients who identified themselves as artists seemed to have a higher incidence of manic-depressive illness. Jamison (1993a, 1993b) revisits this study with several other case studies that seem to support the hypothesis. She notes that medical model theorists resist this connection. One possible source of the resistance is the difficult question of how treatments may stifle creativity, raising the question as to whether the treatment is worse than the disorder. The case of Robert illustrates this situation.

### The Case of Robert

Robert worked as a visual artist, suffered severe mood swings, and met the criteria for Bipolar I Disorder. When he was depressed, he described himself as being in a liminal state between life and death. In this liminal state he claimed to "peer across the narrow vale" that separated the living and the dead. In peering across that valley, Robert felt overwhelmed by the immensity of both the horrors and beauty of being alive; he became acutely aware of the needless cruelty that human beings inflict on one another. His conclusion was that most people were suicidal and expressed their suicidality outwardly in cruel actions. In such periods he frequently contemplated suicide, and the only thing that stopped him was a profound conviction that suicide did not bring about the cessation of consciousness that, in these states, Robert so desperately desired. As a practicing Wiccan, Robert believed souls would continue to deal with the same problems in the afterlife that they faced in this life, so suicide would not be "an easy out." Robert's practice of Wicca also led him to see his own alienation from mainstream society as an illness of the society more than his illness. To cope, Robert drank and abused opioids until he could create a buffer of numbness between himself and the terrors and pain of the world.

When Robert was in a manic mood, his creative output was indeed amazing. He was able to capture on canvas the rapture he could feel in contemplating the beauty of life as well as the desolation that so frequently overtook him. He could often work for days and even weeks on little or no sleep. Robert's manic episodes usually ended in a more restrictive setting as he would take his paintings out to museums and offer them to personnel there for display. His insistence and manner usually resulted in law enforcement officers being called and transporting Robert to an inpatient facility. Although certainly disruptive, Robert never threatened or hurt anyone.

After his third manic episode, Robert was stabilized and agreed to try lithium therapy. He suffered from forgetfulness, weight gain, sexual dysfunction, and hand tremors. Although the forgetfulness and hand tremor interfered with his painting, he said it was his total *lack* of mood that he found unacceptable. He said in essence that the medication took away all feeling and passion from his mind. He said it reminded him of the "zombie powder" used in voodoo ceremonies in the B-grade horror movies he watched. In addition, Robert found the regular blood testing uncomfortable and disruptive to his life. He discontinued lithium under his doctor's care after 3 months. The doctor then tried treating Robert with divalproex, with similar results.

Robert eventually stopped all medical treatments for his condition and chose instead to return to his previous lifestyle. Family members twice tried to have him involuntarily committed but were unsuccessful. Robert stated that if his condition were going to kill him at least he would be able to function as an artist until death. While on medication he was not an inconvenience to society, he said, but neither was he fully alive. In his last therapy session, Robert said he did not expect his therapist or most people to understand, because most people hated life and hated to see anyone truly living the mystery of it. When told by family that his lifestyle was a risk to his well-being, he was fond of quoting the saying, "The candle that burns twice as bright burns half as long."

Again, from an Integral perspective there is much to reflect on in Robert's story. Do people have a right to live as they wish even if that lifestyle may cause them impairment and distress and possibly shorten their life? Is Robert really any different from other people who engage in unhealthy behaviors (such as smoking, fighting, creating unnecessary anger and stress for themselves and others)?

Certainly it would be ideal if a medication existed that his doctor could have used to treat Robert without the severe side effects on his creativity, but this has never been an ideal world.

Robert's story also brings in the spiritual aspects of life. Although many adherents to positivism and the medical model perspective abhor the mere mention of the word, if spirituality reflects a person's ultimate concerns in life then Robert's spirituality was an important component of his story. From an Integral perspective, clients' spirituality is as important as the medications they are taking and the cultural/social context in which they find themselves.

### Compliance With Mood Stabilization Therapy

Cases such as Robert's raise the issue of compliance with mood stabilizer therapy. One of our clients said to us, "I don't like taking lithium, but I seem to always get in trouble when I don't take it." This client—let's call him Jack, for convenience—was suffering some fairly severe side effects from lithium in the early 1990s but had failed to respond to carbamazepine. Weight gain and forgetfulness particularly bothered Jack. In addition, Jack, like Robert, deeply disliked having blood drawn and found the regular blood testing very difficult to comply with. On one occasion he went on a drinking binge, almost winding up in the emergency room. He recovered from that but became deeply depressed over his situation. Twice the doctor had titrated Jack off lithium, and twice he relapsed within 18 months. The relapses were crushing blows to his sense of self-efficacy, and he began to refer to himself as a "chemical cripple."

Compliance can be a difficult challenge for clients who are taking lithium. Studies on compliance show that about half the clients who begin lithium therapy stop taking the drug against medical advice. This also holds true for other mood stabilizers such as carbamazepine and valproate. Predictors regarding who is likely to be noncompliant include clients with histories of noncompliance, clients with denial regarding the severity of their illness, and the length of time the client has been on the mood stabilizer (the longer, the less compliant) (Scott & Pope, 2002). Most clients stop taking the medication because of the side effects, and it is not hard to understand why (Silverstone & Romans, 1996). As we see later, numerous medications may be as effective as lithium in treating Bipolar I Disorder, and mental health clinicians need to be prepared to advocate for their clients should lithium be unacceptable to the client. Although some clients can manage their symptoms without medication, many may require long-term or even life-long pharmacologic intervention. For these people the dangers of going off medication include not only relapse but also a significantly increased risk for suicide (Baldessarini, Tondo, & Hennen, 1999).

We have also found from the intrapsychic perspective that clients tend to miss the "high" associated with manic states. There is no simple solution to this other than to establish a good therapeutic alliance with the client and, early in the relationship, to construct a history of the client's symptoms, making sure you discuss the symptoms that were most troubling for the client. When the client misses the manic states, it is important to balance what may be an idealization of these past states with the reality of the problems they caused the client. This dialogue must take place within a trusting relationship. Family therapy and support can also help clients face difficult existential issues. The bottom line, though, is that it is not the mental health clinician's job to "talk the client into" staying on medications. If the client cannot come to this decision autonomously, then clinicians need to explore alternatives to lithium therapy.

## Issues From the Cultural and Social Perspectives

### Living in a Violent Culture

It is not rocket science to notice some oddities about aggression in U.S. society in general. The author Kurt Vonnegut (1991) has pondered aggression in the United States and what it means that we live in a time when killing is a leading entertainment form. Although many scholarly works support this description (Shifrin, 1998), we recommend instead that readers check their local cable listings and the "new release" shelf at the video store. Other estimates indicate that many categories of violent crime have increased between the 1980s and 1990s, and this may continue into this 21st century

(Goldstein & Conoley, 1998). The linguist and activist Noam Chomsky (2002) has noted that U.S. society has a history of violent imperialist policies requiring that citizens be distracted to other things (such as forms of violent entertainment). When you pair this aspect of U.S. society with the rates of psychotropic medication use, you may begin to wonder if perhaps everyone needs something to "take the edge off."

In Chapter Nine we discuss the controversy that surrounds diagnosing younger and younger children with Bipolar I Disorder. At this point, though, we want to examine from an Integral perspective the connection between the violent nature of U.S. society and the use of "mood-stabilizing" medications. We have already noted that more and more mood stabilizers are being prescribed off label to treat children who engage in aggressive/violent behaviors, but we question if this is really treating the cause of the behaviors. The American Academy of Pediatrics (Shifrin, 1998) has summarized the literature that has concluded that viewing violence on television does influence the aggressive behaviors of children. Nevertheless, few studies look at how much violence children are exposed to who are also being treated with mood stabilizers for violent medication.

From an Integral perspective, we would do well to examine any correlation between viewing such violence on television or in video games and being on mood-stabilizing medication. Further, as we document in Chapter Nine, resources are decreasingly available for psychosocial interventions with children who have suffered or witnessed violence. Psychosocial interventions help children make meaning out of these horrible experiences, and the meaning they make has everything to do with how well they function after the event (Garbarino, 1998).

Although in U.S. society we discourage and punish some forms of aggression, others are blatantly rewarded. A good example is marketing strategies. Marketers frequently use martial vocabulary speaking of "conquering" a market, "exploiting" a competitor's weakness, or "destroying" the competition. The culture of marketing takes on special meaning in the pharmaceutical industry and, as we noted earlier, requires special monitoring.

The lawsuit discussed below, regarding the anti-convulsant gabapentin (Neurontin), illustrates some of the problems of aggressive marketing.

### The Gabapentin Controversy: Corruption in Corporate Culture

As we noted earlier, studies from the medical model have not supported gabapentin as having efficacy in treating Bipolar I Disorder. Yet the drug continues to be prescribed off label. One such prescription became the center of this mess. This story was reported on National Public Radio on January 16, 2003 (Prakash, 2003). Although drug companies must follow rules in promoting medications to physicians, there are also ways around these rules. The case in question deals with a 16-year-old who committed suicide while under the care of his doctor, ostensibly for Bipolar I Disorder. The doctor was treating the teenager with gabapentin, although the young man said it was not helping. The patient's statements make sense in light of a review of the literature that does not support gabapentin as having efficacy for Bipolar I Disorder.

What has come to light and became the center of a criminal fraud lawsuit is that the drug's manufacturer (Warner-Lambert, a subdivision of Parke-Davis) was accused of illegally marketing the drug for unapproved uses. The basic strategy was that the company encouraged the off-label use of gabapentin by directing money at influential doctors, who then wrote favorable reports for medical journals about gabapentin's efficacy in Bipolar I Disorder. By also talking about such findings at meetings of professional organizations, drug companies create "buzz" about the possible uses and increase the probability of increased off-label experimentation by others in the field. The "loophole" is that a company cannot market a drug for off-label uses but can "educate" doctors about those uses.

Parke-Davis contracted with a company called Medical Education Systems in Philadelphia, paying MES $160,000 to develop 12 scientific papers to "support epilepsy education." In actuality, 3 of these papers were on gabapentin and Bipolar Disorder. The documents indicate that Parke-Davis made sure the articles printed what it wanted included, preapproved the authors and topics, and even chose the journals to which they would be submitted. According the NPR story, some of the papers may have been entirely written by MES ghost-writers. The NPR reporter interviewed a former editor-in-chief of the *New England Journal of Medicine*, who stated that this arrangement is not unusual and that pharmaceutical companies often hire medical education companies to write such papers and then pay prominent physicians to basically sign the paper.

In another story (Prakash, 2002) documented that Warner-Lambert / Parke-Davis planned the strategy to promote gabapentin for unapproved uses and that a company committee formulated the strategy. This strategy was enacted after the company determined in 1995 that clinical trials would be too expensive and take too long. The fear was that by the time the clinical trials were completed, the patent on gabapentin would have expired, and competitors would flood the market with generic formulations of the compound. The lawsuit involving Parke-Davis's Warner-Lambert division (recently acquired by Pfizer) maintained that this strategy was illegal. In addition, Warner-Lambert withheld one study from publication that concluded gabapentin was less effective than placebo for treating Bipolar I Disorder. The question arises, To what extent did the illegal strategy contribute to the physician prescribing gabapentin for the young man who committed suicide?

We are aware that we are writing this at a time when corporate scandal has been prominent in the headlines, first with the Enron scandal and then the WorldCom story. We feel the gabapentin story describes an extension of the immoral practices that seem to be such a large part of the U.S. corporate culture. Any Integral view of psychopharmacology must take this corporate culture into account when considering the impact of pharmaceuticals on the person. Any mental health clinician operating in the United States must consider these perspectives when treating clients taking psychotropic medication. Ideally, clinicians can get the client's agreement to monitor prescriptions for off-label uses of medications and when necessary, advocate for the client. As noted, the pharmaceutical company Pfizer acquired the Warner-Lambert division of Parke-Davis and was held responsible for the subdivision's activities between 1996 and 2000.

Pfizer pleaded guilty to criminal fraud and agreed to pay $240 million dollars in criminal fines (the second-largest ever in health care fraud) and an additional $152 million in civil fines to be shared among state and federal Medicare agencies (JournalNews.com, 2004). Perhaps the most difficult thing to comprehend is that this fine was a fraction of the money made through the off-label uses of gabapentin. *Time* magazine (2004) estimated that gabapentin made Pfizer $2.7 billion in 2003 and that 90% of that figure was from off-label uses. This would mean that almost $2.25 billion was made in off-label uses, making the $430 million in fines a proverbial "drop in the bucket."

Ingersoll, Bauer, and Burns (2004) have explored the role of advocacy in light of possible corruption in the corporate culture of the pharmaceutical industry. These authors recommend the following steps. First, mental health clinicians must know how to read and evaluate research. In an ideal world this would be enough, but in the real world clinicians must also work to understand how papers come to be published and whether the trial was conducted by a neutral party or a vested interest (including the pharmaceutical company itself). Clinicians need to know how well psychological treatments work and advocate with their professional organizations to focus on this material in professional journals and conferences. In addition, clinicians need to know the limits of diagnostic categories and that they are not descriptions of diseases capable of a single allopathic treatment but rather clusters of symptoms occurring together that can help guide treatment. Finally, mental health clinicians should consider advocating for regulatory oversight of pharmaceutical marketing to preclude dishonest or misdirected marketing efforts.

## Issues From the Social Perspective

### The Role of the Law in Pharmaceutical Company Regulation

Certainly the gabapentin suicide described in the last section has components that should be addressed from the social perspective. First and foremost are the laws that allow companies to use loopholes such as the ones described. All too often there is an assumption that if something is not against the law, there is no problem. This of course ignores the rich history of unjust laws in our, as well as other, societies as well as discriminant enactment and adjudication. What protection does the individual citizen have when competing with vested power interests such as pharmaceutical companies that have the power to speak directly to elected representatives who supposedly represent us all? Here oversight—supervision—becomes an issue. Although many say that government oversight of corporations is already too great in this country, this is hard to believe when you look at scandals such as those involving Enron, WorldCom, and now Pfizer. If anything, these scandals point to the need for further oversight and for internal checks and balances on the government regulatory agencies and courts, as well as legislation, and on media and advertising.

### The Social Costs of Bipolar Disorder

Another social issue that needs to be considered concerns the social costs of Bipolar Disorder as well as the costs of treatment. An interesting study by Wyatt, Henter, and Jamison (2001) looked at the social costs of the disorder and then tried to estimate the amount society saved by using lithium. Reporting that the estimated social cost of manic-depressive illness in 1991 was roughly $45 billion, these authors noted that by comparing the actual social costs and the projected costs had lithium never been introduced, they could estimate how much money was saved. Recall that the FDA did not approve lithium for manic-depressive illness until 1970, so estimated social costs from that year in 1991 dollars may be considered an estimate of typical social costs prior to lithium's approval.

These authors concluded that in terms of direct social costs, lithium appeared to save approximately $8 billion a year, or a total of over $170 billion. These direct costs included inpatient and outpatient care and research dollars. In addition, the authors sought indexes of indirect costs and estimated that introducing lithium saved society approximately $155 billion. Indirect social costs included factors such as lost productivity of wage earners, homemakers, and caregivers as well as the unhappiness and waste of those people who languished in institutions or of those who, without lithium, may have committed suicide. Although many complex variables cannot be represented adequately in such studies, it is safe to assume that although not a perfect treatment, lithium has worked well enough for enough individuals to effect substantial savings in the social costs of treating manic-depressive disorders. The unaddressed issues in large-scale "guesstimates" about "costs to society" include general questions about the relative health of the society and the pointed question, If the society were healthier, would the need for intrusive interventions such as lithium treatment remain the same?

## Conclusion

We hope this chapter on mood stabilizers has at least increased the complexity with which readers think about the issue. In many ways the topic is like the mythic Hydra, with each problem representing a head. Once one head is cut off, several more arise in its place. Probably, until scientists can more clearly outline the etiology of manic-depressive illness, clinicians will continue to approach treatment in a "hit-or-miss" fashion. Although newer research on the human genome may accelerate the quest for the "perfect" medication, research must also continue examining the most effective psychosocial treatments for clients who take medications as well as for those who choose not to.

## Summary

Bipolar I Disorder is a serious and in many ways mysterious mental/emotional disorder. Although there are medications that help people suffering from the disorder, researchers are still unclear as to how the disorder develops and how to discern which medications will work best for individual clients. Although the drugs to treat Bipolar I Disorder are referred to as *mood stabilizers*, this is an inexact term. The oldest mood stabilizer is lithium, although researchers are not clear exactly how it exerts its therapeutic effects. Although lithium is still in use, not all clients respond well to it and many must try other medications. Alternatives to lithium include carbamazepine and valproic acid. Both of these compounds have proven efficacy for treating Bipolar I Disorder. There are several new drugs that the jury is still out on including oxcarbazepine,

lamotrigine, and topiramate. As with antidepressants, pharmaceutical companies must be closely monitored in the claims they make for mood stabilizers, as the gabapentin controversy illustrates. Because so little is known about the etiology of Bipolar I Disorder, it is important to take an Integral view of efficacy claims made by pharmaceutical companies.

## Study Questions and Exercises

1. Discuss your understanding of the pendulum metaphor of mood disorders. From your experience, describe one client whose disorder "swung" on this pendulum.

2. What is a mood stabilizer? Discuss how this term is applied in this chapter to help explain Bipolar I Disorder.

3. Discuss the discovery of the effectiveness of lithium against mania. Why did the FDA delay approval of its use for mania in the United States?

4. Why is Bipolar I considered such an insidious mental and emotional disorder? Discuss some conundrums and problems of Bipolar I.

5. What is lithium toxicity? What are some manifestations of it? How should it be addressed once detected?

6. Discuss the work of Sheard in exploring the effects of lithium on aggression. Have you had any aggressive clients who were treated with lithium? How did they respond?

7. What is an anticonvulsant? Discuss why carbamazepine is one, and describe its mechanisms of action. List some of its side effects.

8. In this chapter we discuss psychotropic medications that combat the symptoms of Bipolar I Disorder. From your perspective, have psychopharmacologists been more successful treating the psychotic disorders or mood disorders? Explain.

9. What does it mean to you that valproate is better tolerated than lithium?

10. Discuss how some atypical antipsychotics may be effective as mood stabilizers.

11. Describe your reflections and reactions to the issues surrounding the gabapentin lawsuit discussed in this chapter.

# PART THREE

# Newer Issues

This part of the book explores new ground in psychopharmacology on two important topics: the use of psychotropic medications with children and herbaceuticals. There is nothing new about prescribing psychotropic medications to children; however, in the last decade there has been an exponential increase in this practice. One of the biggest problems with this practice is that very few psychotropic medications are FDA approved for use in children, and the younger the child is developmentally, the more that child's nervous system differs from an adult's. In addition, we are seeing annual decreases in the amount of funding set up to support mental health services for children. From an Integral perspective this is a disaster, because many mental and emotional problems children experience respond very well to psychosocial interventions. If no resources are provided for these interventions, then more and more children are referred for medication therapy alone despite an absence of evidence to support such referrals. Finally, an Integral view of this issue requires people to examine this culture's view of children. If work and achievement are given higher priority than family, where does that leave children?

Much has been written on herbaceuticals, but the topic is really just becoming accessible to English-speaking audiences, because the majority of the research has been conducted in European countries and published in journals written in European languages. Herbaceuticals are somewhat controversial in general in the United States, because technically they can be sold as "supplements" and do not require FDA oversight. As such, there is no guarantee on dosage, potency, or quality of formulation. Without FDA oversight, it is unlikely that herbaceuticals will be prescribed for mental or emotional disorders. We also cover the controversial marijuana plant in the herbaceuticals chapter. Although this book does not cover the pharmacology of drugs of abuse, a substantial case has been made for marijuana having medicinal uses, and we review that literature.

One thing that the material in these two chapters on newer issues have in common is that the importance of these issues can be underemphasized. We are now learning that antidepressants, prescribed off label for decades to children, may in fact exacerbate suicidal thinking in that population. In addition, we have also learned there are some herbaceuticals, such as the recently banned ephedrine, that can be lethal. We are certain that the topics in these two chapters will be making headlines for years to come.

# CHAPTER NINE

# Medicating Children

## *Perspectives, Dilemmas, and Future Paradigms*

Thus far we have explored the medical model and intrapsychic, cultural, and social perspectives as they relate to psychopharmacology. In this chapter we show that using psychotropic medications with children and adolescents raises particular problems and concerns from several perspectives. Many category errors are being committed by some medical and mental health practitioners, but particularly by the pharmaceutical industry, to justify the use of all types of psychotropic medications with children. As discussed in Chapter Three, we frequently see explanations and justifications from the medical model perspective used to reduce childhood disorders to chemical and genetic problems, excluding crucial consideration of environmental traumas, developmental foreclosures, or life stressors.

We explore child and adolescent psychopharmacology primarily from the medical model perspective but complement this approach with information from the other perspectives (intrapsychic, cultural, and social). We set the stage by exploring the current status of the treatment of children and adolescents with mental and emotional disorders. This chapter is structured differently from the others in this book. We begin by discussing the context from the social and cultural perspectives and the problems with prescribing psychotropic medications to children. Then we cover an introduction to stimulants used to treat symptoms of Attention-Deficit/Hyperactivity Disorder (ADHD). Finally we cover the medications discussed in previous chapters and outline the status of their current use with children and adolescents.

## The Complex State of Therapy

Dr. Frank O'Dell, Professor Emeritus of Counseling in the College of Education and Human Services at Cleveland State University, has argued in all his lectures on counseling children and adolescents that we are an "anti-kid" society (personal communication, 2001). By that he means fewer and fewer therapists and psychiatrists choose to treat or continue to work with children in counseling. To support his argument O'Dell points out that resources for children, including the number of hospital beds in mental health wards for children, have been shrinking. He believes the rules of managed care companies, dwindling personnel resources, and increasing difficulty working with parents or guardians and their struggling children all contribute to the current trend. This has been a problem for at least 35 years. It was the subject of an editorial in the *American Journal of Psychiatry* in 1968 (Tarjan, 1968). The American Academy of Child & Adolescent Psychiatry (2001) summarized the following facts, which support O'Dell's assertion, indicating little has changed since 1968:

- There is a dearth of child psychiatrists. The U.S. Surgeon General's Report (2001) stated further that many barriers remain that prevent children, teenagers, and their parents from seeking help from the small number of specially trained professionals who are available and that places a burden on pediatricians, family physicians, and other gatekeepers to identify children for referral and treatment decisions (U.S. Department of Health and Human Services, 2001).

- The academy's report projected that between 1995 and 2020 the need for child and adolescent psychiatrists will increase by 100%, whereas need for general psychiatry is projected to increase at 19% for the adult population.

- In November 2000, the Coalition for Juvenile Justice estimated that 50 to 75% of teenagers in the juvenile justice system nationwide have a diagnosable mental disorder, and these numbers appear to be growing.

- One in 10 children suffers from mental illnesses severe enough to impair development. Fewer than 1 in 5 children get treatment for mental illness.

The U.S. Department of Health and Human Services (2001) concluded that burgeoning numbers of children are suffering needlessly because their emotional, behavioral, and developmental needs are not being met by the institutions and systems created to care for them .As the number of children and adolescents needing psychological treatment rises and the number of service providers falls, the primary treatment modality becomes psychotropic medications rather than therapy.

Debner (2001a) reported that in a one-year period, 350 children needing hospitalization were turned away from hospitals in the Boston area. This phenomenon is occurring in most major U.S. cities and is exacerbated by hospitals holding onto children who are ready to be discharged, because there is no suitable placement for them. In another article Debner (2001b) noted that the chief pediatricians from the five major academic health centers in Massachusetts indicated there is a serious crisis in psychiatric services for youth in the state. The

doctors said they and their staffs could not find appropriate therapy and other mental health services for mentally ill children. As a result many such children deteriorate to the point of crisis.

Recently, the *Washington Post* (2002) published an article about a woman who desperately needed a psychiatric evaluation for her teenage daughter and who left 36 phone messages for various psychiatrists. She received only 4 replies. All the replies were from practitioners who refused to take the case because they did not treat adolescents. The article further detailed how, more and more, in-network providers (clinicians) prefer not to take patients covered by managed care plans, because reimbursements are so low and restrictions so numerous. The article also highlighted the disparity and arguments between the treating professionals and spokespeople from managed care companies. It is more than fair to say that desperate parents and anguished children are caught in the political policy dilemma over the cost and reimbursement of mental health treatment for children and adolescents.

## The Explosion of Psychotropic Medication Prescriptions for Children and Adolescents

With diminishing psychological supports for children and adolescents, using psychotropic medications with them has become the treatment of choice, even though the majority of medications used with them lack FDA "on-label" approval for them (Werry, 1999). Researchers currently estimate that between 7.5 and 14 million children in the United States experience significant mental health problems (Wozniak, Biederman, Spencer, & Wilens, 1997; Riddle, Kastelic, & Frosch, 2001). These statistics vary a little from the U.S. Surgeon General's Report (2001), cited earlier; clearly millions of children in this country require mental health services. Children are increasingly prescribed psychotropic medications as part of their treatment; in many cases the medications replace the therapy (Jensen, Bhatara, Vitiello, Hoagwood, Feil, & Burke, 1999; Phelps, Brown, & Power, 2002). Authors such as Andreasen (2001) indirectly fuel this negative trend when they (using word magic and category errors) assert that in the future scientists will create medications to correct the abnormal expression of disease-producing genes for all conditions. Given the explosion in the use of psychotropic medication with children, it is important also to note that this population has been *excluded* from clinical trials of these drugs. Hence decisions about juvenile medication obviously rest more on extrapolation of adult data to children and adolescents than on direct research and evaluation of the safety and efficacy of psychotropic medication with children (Riddle, Kastelic, & Frosch, 2001; Vitiello & Jensen, 1999).

Coyle (2000) indicated that 80% of all medications prescribed to children and adolescents in the United States have not been studied for the safety and benefit of these populations. The trend in treating children and adolescents with off-label psychotropic medications, mostly in lieu of counseling and psychotherapy, has triggered concern both in the general public and the mental health community. Coyle (2000), Furman (1993), and Zito (Zito, Safer, dosReis, & Riddle, 2000; Zito et al., 2003) argue there is little or no evidence to support psychotropic drug use with very young children and conclude such treatment could have harmful psychological, developmental, and physical effects.

With the proper research, mental health professionals may be able to head off disasters such as aspirin precipitating Reye's syndrome or valproate leading to sudden death in infants (Riddle, Kastelic, & Frosch, 2001). Given the lack of knowledge about the long-term and adverse effects of psychotropic medication on children, it is crucial that mental health clinicians be alert to the impact of these drugs on children and advocate for youth when the evidence that such drugs would be helpful is questionable (Ingersoll, Bauer, & Burns, 2004). At this point we would like to introduce a case that highlights many of the treatment and medication dilemmas children and adolescents encounter.

## The Case of Phillip

Phillip is a 7-year-old first-grader from a single-parent home. His mother is on public assistance, and he is the oldest of four boys. Although some of the details of his developmental history are sparse, Phillip began to exhibit impulse control problems at the age of 2 years and four months, shortly after his father moved out of the house. He was hypervigilant, easily distractible, aggressive with his younger sibling, and frequently irritable. Initially his mother believed he was going through a stage of rebelliousness, but after several months she became concerned about his behavior and mentioned this to the pediatrician. After a brief examination, the pediatrician indicated that Phillip was likely suffering from ADHD and recommended against medication unless his behavior got too out of control at home. However, she felt he would need a course of methylphenidate (Ritalin), a prescription stimulant, once he began preschool. Phillip's mother accepted this recommendation and planned to have him evaluated when he began preschool. Phillip's behavior improved slightly over the next several months, without therapy or psychotropic medication.

When he began preschool, it took only a few days before all his active symptoms returned. After observing him for several weeks, the teacher recommended to Phillip's mother that he see a physician to be assessed for a stimulant medication. After the evaluation, the physician prescribed 10 mg of methylphenidate daily for Phillip. Methylphenidate is one of the most common stimulants used for symptoms of ADHD in children. It is intended to reduce inattentiveness, distractibility, impulsivity, and motor hyperactivity, with a goal of improved academic productivity. Phillip's symptoms slightly improved over the next eight weeks, but his aggressive behavior toward other children increased. Phillip's mother noticed more unpredictable behavior at home, as well as sleeplessness and restlessness followed by long periods of lethargy. She took him back to his physician, who referred them to a psychiatrist. The psychiatrist, after a three-session assessment, diagnosed Bipolar I Disorder, took him off the Ritalin, and prescribed 50 mg of carbamazepine (Tegretol) daily and 0.01 mg of clonazepam (Klonopin). The carbamazepine was used to reduce his manic symptoms. This antiseizure medication has over time been found very effective with Bipolar Disorder (Phelps, Brown, & Power, 2002).

The clonazepam was used to address Phillip's anxious and agitated symptoms. This antianxiety medication often relaxes children and reduces anxiety without inducing sleep.

Many of Phillip's symptoms diminished, but his mother noticed both a sluggishness and apathy in him that were new. Over the course of the next year, Phillip's teacher addressed several of his learning and cognitive processing problems. Up to this point the focus of Phillip's treatment had been psychopharmacologic. No psychosocial interventions were given to Phillip, as is often the case (Phelps, Brown, & Power, 2002). No one seemed to have any awareness or discussion about the optimal level of medication (methylphenidate) for Phillip, and there was no referral for a psychosocial assessment. As his symptoms worsened, he was evaluated by a psychiatrist schooled in prescribing adult psychotropic medications off label to children. Finally Phillip's mother took him to see a therapist, who focused on Phillip's attachment issues, his phobic anxiety triggered by sudden loss or the anticipation of sudden loss, and his physiologic symptoms, which the therapist considered powerful side effects of the pharmacologic therapy.

### Analysis of Phillip's Case

Analyzing the case from the four perspectives of the Integral Model, we see that the initial approach to Phillip was clearly rooted in the medical model, where the scientific method and rational thinking dominate and center on pharmacology. The combination of methylphenidate and carbamazepine on Phillip's system was supposed to reduce some of his externalizing symptoms in the constellation of ADHD or Bipolar I disorders, but the intrapsychic aspects of his personality were ignored. Not until much later in the course of his illness did Phillip get some assistance in those domains. Culturally, Phillip's mother had little power in society and was torn between accepting the opinion of the medical experts, and watching the negative impact the medications were having on her son. As mental health professionals, we need to understand the medical psychiatry's rapid efforts to address most disorders of childhood and adolescents with psychotropic medication. Far too often medicating

professionals view talk therapy and other psychosocial interventions as ineffective and second rate. Because medical professionals hold more power in our society than mental health professionals, their medical opinions are frequently given more weight even when those same opinions are about mental health issues. We must integrate care into a larger model of treatment that addresses each of the four perspectives equally and where mental health professionals' opinions on mental health treatment are given more weight. In addition, the power of pharmaceutical companies must be monitored. Bodenheimer (2000) has documented numerous cases where companies prevented important research findings from being published because they were not favorable regarding the compounds being tested. To what extent may such situations affect clients like Phillip?

Remember, Phillip was in the 4 to 7 age range when he began treatment. Coyle (2000) comments that there is "no empirical evidence to support psychotropic drug treatment in very young children and that such treatment could have deleterious effects on the developing brain" (p. 1060). Furman (1993) posited that psychiatrists in the United States are recklessly "out of control" in prescribing Ritalin and other stimulants for children, in contrast to the extreme caution that physicians in almost all European countries use in recommending this treatment approach. With the increasing trend to medicate a younger and younger population (Zito et al., 2000), mental health professionals not only need to understand the impact and therapeutic effectiveness of these medications, but also their limitations and potential for harming children.

## The Medication of Children and the Federal Laws

As we have noted in previous chapters, the laws of the land hold great influence over cultural and social paradigms. To a large extent laws are the result of a dynamic interaction of forces that influence other areas such as socioeconomic status and the fiscal systems of a society. Socioeconomic status and fiscal systems shape laws in very powerful ways, and people with financial resources are able to buy

**TABLE 9.1**   Major Emphases of Recent Legislation on Pediatric Pharmacology

| Law/Rule | Summary |
|---|---|
| FDA Modernization Act (Public Law Number 105-115, 1997) | Recognizes rights of children as patients<br>Set specific standards for research of pediatric drugs<br>Encouraged pediatric labeling |
| Best Pharmaceuticals for Children Act (Public Law Number 107-109, 2002) | Voluntary pediatric studies of currently marketed drugs<br>Created list of all pediatric drugs needing documentation<br>Requires timely labeling of pediatric drugs<br>Establishes a mandate to include children of all cultures in studies<br>Voluntary studies of new drugs |
| Pediatric Rule Bill of 2002[a] | Required timely pediatric studies and adequate labeling |

[a]US District Court, District of Columbia ruled that the FDA did not have authority to assert the Pediatric Rule, 2002.

influence with lawmakers. This is nothing new, but bears stating in this chapter. Although recent legislation has been introduced to address the many problems of prescribing psychotropic medications for children, most such laws require only voluntary testing of psychotropic drugs, diminishing any real impact. In this section we summarize recent laws and comment on them, beginning with a summary in Table 9.1

### FDA Modernization Act

Buck (2000) traced the unfolding need for greater specific labeling of drugs used with patients less than 18 years of age. The burgeoning use of almost all drugs approved for children by the Food and Drug Administration (FDA) compelled pediatric health care providers to use these drugs off label without a clear knowledge of dosing, administration, or adverse effect information. In 1992 the FDA took steps to improve both pediatric labeling and research, which resulted in support for building a network of pharmacologic research by the National Institutes of Health (NIH). These efforts began to address the problem, and passage of the FDA Modernization Act (1997) for the first time set specific requirements to tighten regulations relating to pediatric pharmacology. This law encouraged pediatric labeling on drugs used widely with children and adolescents where the lack of labeling might lead to serious misuse.

This law goes a long way toward recognizing the rights of children as patients, protecting their health, and assisting pediatric providers with essential information. Unfortunately the law did not go far enough. Many practitioners and lawmakers felt the need for a comprehensive law to mandate pharmacologic research, monitor it, and further protect children. Hence Senator Christopher Dodd led the effort to introduce new legislation to address these issues.

### The Best Pharmaceuticals for Children Act

On January 4, 2002, President George W. Bush signed Public Law Number 107-109, the Best Pharmaceuticals for Children Act (Dodd, 2001), with the anticipation that it would address many of the dilemmas and controversies surrounding the eruption in use of pharmaceuticals for children. This law aims to initiate critical studies with pharmaceuticals already prescribed to a population for whom there exists little research, and it tightens the monitoring and development of new drugs released for children and adolescents. The law seeks to integrate viewpoints on medicating children with the medical, cultural, and social perspectives. Unfortunately, its most powerful provisions regarding the conduct of pharmaceutical companies are voluntary.

The Best Pharmaceuticals for Children Act (BPCA, Public Law Number 107-109, 2002) has 19 sections. This law encourages voluntary pediatric studies of already marketed drugs, the so-called off-label psychotropic drugs in widespread use with children, and it creates a research fund for studying these drugs. Both efforts are critical to understanding the effectiveness and efficacy of psychotropic medications for children and adolescents. Further, the law establishes an ongoing program for the pediatric study of drugs, including a list of all drugs for which documentation is needed. This aspect of the law is monitored by the commissioner of the FDA and the director of the National Institutes of Health, who have the power to make written requests of pharmaceutical companies for pediatric studies. The law requires timely labeling changes for pediatric drugs under study.

We contacted Senator Dodd's office to determine if drug trials would be mandatory or voluntary. Benjamin Berwick (personal communication, December 2, 2002) of Senator Dodd's office confirmed that drug companies are not trying to change the law and that it was never intended for mandatory testing—only voluntary testing. He further stated that Senator Dodd's current efforts are aimed at preserving the Pediatric Rule Bill of 2002 (not yet passed and currently in litigation initiated by the pharmaceutical companies). This legislation would track the pharmacodynamics and pharmacokinetics of new drugs, already marketed drugs, drugs being studied, and drugs that were granted a time deferral before study.

The one exception is that the Pediatric Rule would not jeopardize the availability of new drugs for other populations. Thus the Pediatric Rule would augment and provide funds and security in areas the BPCA cannot support or fund. Maryann Carey (personal communication, December 10, 2002), legislative liaison in Congressman Dennis Kucinich's office, confirmed and supported the voluntary nature of BPCA as it relates to testing psychotropic medication with children and adolescents.

As of this writing the BPCA is being implemented gradually in several key areas. However, the pharmaceutical companies challenged the Pediatric Rule in court on October 17, 2002, and the U.S. District Court for the District of Columbia ruled that the FDA did not have the authority to issue the Pediatric Rule and has barred the FDA from enforcing it. The Pediatric Rule would have required timely pediatric studies and adequate labeling of all human drugs.

# A Word on Cross-Cultural Perspectives

Tseng (2003) proposed many variables and differences in prescribing psychotropic medications to children and adolescents from various cultures. He stressed that one must consider not only the physician's attitudes about treating people from different cultures, but also the patients' perspectives on how they feel about psychotropic medications. Thus the giving and receiving of medications has many implications. This factor is greatly enhanced for children and adolescents, because the physician must not only communicate with the parents about the diagnosis and the psychotropic medications (neither of which may make sense in the parents' worldview) but also must weigh carefully the cultural issues that the family brings to treatment.

Tseng (2003) also addresses the enculturation issues of children. His research has described how not every culture emphasizes the fast-paced and often accelerated approach to growing up that characterizes the United States. **Enculturation** is defined as a process through which an individual, starting in early childhood, acquires a cultural system through the environment, particularly from parents, school, and so on. Some cultures, such as many Asian cultures, have a laid-back attitude toward babies and toddlers that is more indulgent. Yet later they show a dramatic shift for these children, who, when they arrive at latency, the developmental period between the ages of 6 and 11 or 12, experience enormous pressure to be diligent and to achieve. Thus as clinicians treat children and adolescents from all cultures, they need to reconsider cross-cultural adjustment and revise the psychosocial stages of Erikson (1969), which depended on developmental understandings in a particular culture.

With the upsurge in the use of psychotropic medications, it is impossible to monitor the expected and unexpected adverse effects. Given the expanding knowledge of the varying developmental trajectories of children from other cultures, mental health practitioners and psychiatrists need to exercise further caution when prescribing psychotropic medications for these children. Lin and Poland (1995) described in detail the remarkably large interindividual variability in drug responses and side effect profiles. This can be partially accounted for in differences of ethnicity and/or culture apart from physiological pace. Some cultures are very suspicious of medication and may delay the decision for more than a year.

Lin and Poland (1995) have made significant contributions to the understanding of cultural psychiatry and of the fact that genetic factors associated with individual and ethnic backgrounds contribute greatly to responses to medication in children, adolescents, and adults. They point to variations within the same ethnic group and variations among ethnic groups. This further complicates the Integral dilemma, which is how to view psychopharmacology and cases from the four perspectives outlined in Chapter One as well as consider important developmental lines and levels. Mental health professionals recognize that researchers have much to learn about psychopharmacology with children and adolescents, as shown by the research cited in this chapter. We need to integrate our growing understanding of cultural psychiatry with our limited understandings of how psychotropic medications work in children. The Best Pharmaceutical Act for Children (2002) provided for including in studies children from various racial and ethnic backgrounds. The law calls for studying the impact of medications on children of different cultures.

## Intrapsychic Perspectives of Children and Adolescents

Medicating children and adolescents for all types of psychological disorders is a solution that only reflects partial truth. The overt behaviors and symptom profile for which they receive medication may only mask the deeper psychological wounds of loss, trauma, abuse, sibling rivalry, neglect, sexual abuse, or gender conflict. Thus diagnosing and treating children is complex.

Furman (2000) has indicated that if mental health professionals carefully examined the overuse of stimulants with children, they would discover a variety of conflicts and problems fueling the hyperactive behavior. These issues could include cruelty in the home, harsh toilet training, neglect, sexual abuse, delay in language development, and more.

Young children cannot address their inner conflicts without the help of a caring therapist and the modality of play therapy, yet far too often they are diagnosed with Bipolar I or ADHD and medicated in an attempt to quickly suppress their active symptoms. There should be far more effort to get the child to a therapist to uncover the underlying cause(s) of the child's anguish, but this requires resources that, at the time of this writing, lawmakers are not giving a high priority.

The American Academy of Pediatrics (2001) for ADHD makes clear that parent and teacher assessments at home and school, respectively, along with clinical review and examination by pediatrician or psychiatrist, often omit psychological assessment of the child by a mental health professional to rule out abuse, neglect, loss, sleeplessness, or other potential causes of hyperactivity or mania. In this protocol (the AAP guidance), the psychology and clinical history of the child are treated as unimportant. Many authors unfortunately support rapid assessment of ADHD children to speed up treatment with stimulant medication.

## Opposition to the Current Trend of Medicating

Opponents to exclusively medication treatment for ADHD, Bipolar I, and other conditions have pointed out significant regional variations in the amount of psychotropic medications prescribed to children and wide variations in regional diagnostic criteria for ADHD and other conditions (Safer, Zito, & Fine, 1996; Wolraich, Hannah, Pinnock, Baumgaertel, & Brown, 1996). These variances have legislators and mental health advocates from various regions of the country clamoring for more judicious use of psychotropic medications with children, with more careful attention to the range of adverse effects from them, and a more formalized protocol for diagnosing ADHD, Bipolar I, and other conditions. This protocol should go well beyond the traditional oral report from teacher to parent about a child's externalizing behavior. Opponents of psychotropic medication use in children call for a more specific and guided differential diagnosis of these disorders because the symptoms commonly overlap with Oppositional

Defiant Disorder, Conduct Disorder, Major Depressive Disorder, various anxiety disorders, and many developmental disorders (August, Realmuto, MacDonald, Nugent, & Crosby, 1996). Many researchers and practitioners believe that ADHD in particular is a myth and that the explosion in use of the diagnosis renders differential diagnosis impotent (Armstrong, 1997; Furman, 2002).

Furman (2002) concluded,

I have tried to trace the thinking that followed the discovery of the vastly different approaches in the United States and Europe to the management of the active or overactive child. . . . This thinking led to the conclusion that ADHD is not a specific disorder or pathological entity but rather a collection of symptoms that could be manifested by a child in distress, a child in conflict within himself and/or with his environment. It has no more specificity than that, and likewise methylphenidate has no specificity in producing its effects. . . . Suppressing these symptoms by "subduing" the child with medication hides from all the source of the child's troubles, precludes his being able to obtain mastery of his troubles through understanding, and subjects him to a false label of brain pathology. (p. 141)

Furman indicated that his conclusions are not new but have simply been ignored.

## An Overview of Pediatric and Adolescent Psychopharmacology

By the time this text has been published, only a handful of psychotropic medications will have been approved as on label for the preschool age group. Examples include methylphenidate (Ritalin), amphetamine (Adderall), haloperidol (Haldol), and chlorpromazine (Thorazine) (Zito et al., 2003). For preschool-age children, it is aggressive behavior that generally triggers a referral for treatment (Bassarath, 2003). A few more psychotropic medications have been approved for use in older children and adolescents (Kluger, 2003), but those (such as the antidepressant fluoxetine) are hotly debated.

We have mentioned the national dilemma that more children and adolescents demand psychological services each year, yet there are fewer service providers. Concurrent with this expanding problem is the dramatic increase in the use of psychotropic medications off label for a variety of mental and emotional conditions and disorders. Although this is problematic in and of itself, the focus on intrapsychic and interpersonal factors in treating children and adolescents has dangerously diminished. Whereas it used to be common practice for child psychiatrists to choose in each case from among drug therapy, primary drug therapy and secondary counseling, or primary counseling and secondary drug therapy (Kraft, 1968), today these choices are rarely discussed routinely.

Also note that *DSM* criteria are primarily normed on adults and are more difficult to apply with children. House (1999) has indicated that over half of the time, children who meet the criteria for one mental or emotional disorder meet criteria for other disorders as well. This multiple nature of children's problems frequently results in a polypharmacy approach and requires careful decisions by the physician and/or treating team (Brown & Sammons, 2002). How carefully those decisions are made varies from setting to setting and clinician to clinician.

Researchers do know the preschool years are one of the key developmental periods for maturation of the brain dopamine system, which is targeted by stimulants (Coyle, 2000). The FDA-approved package insert on methylphenidate (MPH) warns against its use with children under age 6. Given all the unknowns, many scholars and physicians are concerned about the quality and care and the current explosion of prescribing practices with preschoolers. Mental health professionals do not have enough clear evidence about how preschoolers respond to psychotropic medications, and researchers are very uncertain about the impact of such medications on the development of preschoolers. Let's examine some of the major developmental issues.

### Developmental Issues

For many of you, this section on human growth and development in children and adolescents is a review. Most texts on development emphasize cognitive, language, moral, and psychosocial developmental paths. We briefly consider these lines of development and include others that are potentially affected by the ingestion of psychotropic medication. Understanding development is further complicated by the construct of **developmental lines**—the simultaneous occurrence of several aspects of human growth and development.

## Developmental Lines

Although there are dozens of lines of human development, this multiplicity is still not a focus for mental health professionals outside of developmental studies. What should be common knowledge for mental health professionals is still peripheral to their training. For example, the Council for the Accreditation of Counseling and Related Educational Programs (CACREP) requires only one human development course for a master's degree in school or agency counseling. Wilber (2000) has estimated that there are about 24 lines of human development. These include physical development, cognitive development, emotional development, sexual development, moral development, spiritual development, kinesthetic development, socioemotional development, gender identity, and role-taking ability. As Wilber notes, these are just a few of the lines of development to which every person has access, and, for the most part, everyone proceeds through them unevenly.

The sheer number of developmental lines and the fact that most people proceed unevenly through them raise enormous, unaddressed issues for psychopharmacology. We noted earlier that scientists know very little about how brains develop and that many researchers are concerned that psychotropic medications could profoundly damage the brains of children and adolescents when taken long term. Glen Elliott, director of the Langley Porter Psychiatric Institute Children's Center of the University of California at San Francisco, noted that the current use of psychotropic medications on children "has outstripped our knowledge base . . . we are experimenting on these kids without tracking the results" (Kluger, 2003, p. 51). For example, even when an adolescent truly appears to suffer from Bipolar I Disorder, the sequelae of mood stabilizer side ef-

fects such as weight gain and perhaps hair loss are likely to be more devastating for a person of that age than for an adult—but there is no research on such intrapsychic issues.

Perhaps the greatest problem of studying child and adolescent psychopharmacology from the four Integral perspectives is that whenever the issue of medicating children comes up, the only perspective represented is that of the medical model. A good example is a *Time* magazine cover story, by Kluger (2003), that basically explores only the medical model perspective, with only minor attention to intrapsychic, cultural, and social issues. The same article presents a diagram showing what parts of the brain are believed to be correlated with different mental or emotional disorders. At no point in the article does the author state that these areas are hypothesized to be *correlated with* symptoms and there is no evidence that they *cause* symptoms.

As we have noted throughout the book, many symptoms that are psychogenic in origin register in the brain, but this does not mean the symptoms were *caused* by the brain. This bias toward the medical model perspective leads laypeople to assume that mental/emotional disorders, whether in children or adults, are strictly medical disorders. This assumption is not currently supported by the evidence we have been covering in this book. A full-scale Integral approach to mental and emotional disorders in children and adolescents considers medication and possible brain pathology as only one part of the story in a very complex interactions of tentative causes and interventions.

## Developmental Pharmacology

Developmental psychopharmacology is the study of brain development focused on brain plasticity (the brain's ability to shape itself to environmental or chemical input) and sensitive periods (during which experience can alter neural representation before hardwiring occurs) (Carrey, Mendella, MacMaster, & Kutcher, 2002). Although this discipline is examining development strictly from the medical model perspective, its overarching question is, What happens in the complex process of neural development when an infusion of psychotropic medications is introduced to address particular environmental stressors during periods of accelerated brain development? The research of Nieoullon (2002) concluded that because dopamine is a key neurotransmitter in the brain, altering the dopaminergic transmission through pharmacology may contribute to cognitive impairment. This certainly raises questions about using dopamine agonists such as methylphenidate in children and adolescents, even if approved by the FDA.

Epstein (2001) posited that active brain growth spurts occur stagewise in correlation with Piagetian types of development. Thus a child who is making the transition from the sensory motor stage to Piaget's preoperational stage is in a very active brain growth stage (from age 2 to 4 years). Epstein cites Boothroyd (1997), who noted that lexical knowledge and syntactic knowledge grow rapidly until age 4. At about 6 (from age 6 to 8), the next rapid brain growth period parallels Piaget's concrete reasoning stage, where a child begins to think logically about experienced inputs, the concrete operational stage. Epstein discussed the next brain growth period as slow (from age 12 to 14 years), a time of practicing and consolidating new networks in preparation for the next rapid brain growth stage (between ages 14 and 16 years). Psychotropics often are administered to preschoolers in the rapid growth period of between ages 2 and 4 years, and to early-latency children between the ages of 6 and 8 years. Mental health professionals do not know enough about the impact of both on-label and off-label psychotropics in these rapid brain growth periods to be administering them to children and adolescents. Bramble (2003) concluded that given the changing nature of pediatric pharmacology and developmental pharmacology, this society needs a rapid expansion of pediatric research and academic inquiry into the impact of psychotropics on children's development.

Another problem with pediatric psychopharmacology is **polypharmacy**: the use of more than one psychotropic simultaneously, a usage that interacts with children's metabolism in a variety of unpredictable ways (Brown & Sammon, 2002). Clinicians who observe children and adolescents under the influence of polypharmacy are often startled not only by the dramatic change in the clients' af-

fective and behavioral state but also by the array of side effects they experience. Tonya, a very aggressive 12-year-old, was placed on olanzapine (an atypical antipsychotic), sertraline (an SSRI antidepressant), lorazepam (an anxiolytic), and valproate (a mood stabilizer). This combination of medications was ostensibly for what appeared to the attending psychiatrist as Bipolar I with severe agitation and aggression in the manic phase. Tonya's symptoms diminished, but her teacher noticed new ones: slurred speech, mild tics, and a constant staring off without responding when addressed. Now, rather than disrupting the class, she slept through it. Although from the perspective of the teacher and other students this was an improvement, was Tonya being helped, or was she merely medicated into submission when she might have been more fundamentally helped with assessment and therapy from a wider interpersonal perspective?

Other developmental considerations include adverse cardiovascular effects. We have many reports of sudden deaths of children and adolescents treated with psychotropic medications, including methylphenidate (Ritalin), TCAs, SSRIs, bupropion (Wellbutrin), lithium, and most neuroleptic medications. Gutgesell et al. (1999) detailed the cardiovascular and electrophysiologic effects of commonly used psychotropic medication, which can be deadly. Although the precise causes of the deaths have not been documented, severe heart spasms (cardiac arrhythmias) and delayed repolarization of the heart rhythm make the heart muscle vulnerable to possibly lethal changes (such as ventricular tachycardia). These tragedies call on mental health professionals to be vigilant and cautious when prescribing psychotropic medication. With many high-risk medications, cardiovascular monitoring is particularly important. In fact, Wagner and Fershtman (1993) recommended ECG monitoring at baseline and during drug therapy for children and adolescents who are on the medications associated with cardiovascular side effects. Brown and Sammons (2002) argued that the use of most psychotropic medication exceeds data available for efficacy, effectiveness, and safety.

Many concerns also remain related to the physiological impact on children who take psychotropic medication. One is the controversy about the impact of stimulant treatment on brain growth in children (Bell, Alexander, Schwartzman, & Yu, 1982). Researchers have recently learned that methylphenidate and other stimulants decrease blood flow to selected parts of the brain, specifically the cortex area that controls conscious movement (Zeiner, 1995). In a recent study (Castellanos et al., 2002), the research team concluded that developmental trajectories for all brain structures, except caudal, remain parallel for children and adolescents in ADHD patients and controls. This suggested that genetic and early environmental influences on brain development in ADHD are fixed, nonprogressive, and unrelated to stimulant treatment.

However, initial brain scans of patients with ADHD showed significantly smaller brain volumes in all regions than appeared in the brain scans of the controls. In general, because of brain plasticity (the brain's ability to shape itself), it is possible for children to be highly susceptible to a negative impact on their brain development during one period of development and less so in another period of development (Carrey, Mendalla, MacMaster, & Kutcher, 2002). Does treatment with psychotropic medications constitute a negative impact? These authors further concluded that researchers are only beginning to understand the long-term effect of psychotropic medication on neuron cell factors and their overall impact on brain development. All these developmental concerns or issues involve potential adverse effects for children and adolescents taking psychotropic medication.

At this point we cover the different categories of medications used on children and adolescents. We begin the next section with a more thorough treatment of stimulant medications.

## Stimulant Medication

Even though stimulants are currently the best-studied psychotropic medication used on children, many issues regarding their use are still unresolved. Because stimulants are prescribed almost exclusively for children, we have included information on them in this chapter. Before discussing some of

the controversial issues, let's examine some background and general information on these widely prescribed medications.

### Some History

The first known stimulant in the West was cocaine. It was isolated in the mid-18th century and in 1884 was given to Bavarian soldiers to decrease fatigue. Many people in South American societies still regularly chew coca leaves with little ill effect, because unprocessed leaves are far less dependence inducing than is refined cocaine powder (Siegel, 1989). Efforts to synthesize amphetamine began in 1887, when physicians believed it useful for treating asthma. This belief emerged from the use of an herbaceutical called *ma huang* in Chinese medicine. Ma huang is discussed more thoroughly in Chapter Ten on herbaceuticals, but for now understand that it is the ingredient ephedra that is central to the story of amphetamines. This ingredient produces the bronchial dilation that relieves the wheezing of asthma.

In the 1920s a Chinese pharmacologist working for Eli Lilly (K. K. Chen) was working to isolate and synthesize ephedra. He succeeded in synthesizing a compound so structurally similar to ephedra that it was named *ephedrine*. Although this could be taken orally, the goal for asthma treatment was a compound that could be inhaled. Gordon Alles succeeded in developing another variation of the molecule that could be delivered in an inhaler. Called Benzedrine, this variation was successful in treating asthma. Aside from treating asthma, it also seemed to induce euphoria. People soon realized they could open the inhaler and ingest the contents for what became known as "the amphetamine rush." This also became a popular pastime on college campuses during exams. Amphetamines were experimented with to manage a number of disorders, and one of their early uses was treating children for what was described as "overactivity."

Werry has asserted that research in psychopharmacology for children began with publication of Bradley's (1937) paper on how amphetamine seems to calm overactive children and help children with learning disabilities. The only other noteworthy investigations of the same period were studies on the effects of antihistamines on children (Connors, 1972). These works are thought to be the only primary contributions to child psychopharmacology until very recently (Werry, 1999).

Bradley's work re-emerged in the 1960s after psychiatry began moving away from a psychodynamic model toward the biological model dominant today. Psychiatrists at that time were not well trained in the statistical methods that were becoming the norm in evaluating medications. They turned to psychologists for assistance. The psychologists emphasized the need to look at medication effects on learning and academic performance (Werry, 1999). Such research has, until very recently, remained focused primarily on stimulant medication.

Research in child psychopharmacology received an unintentional boost in the 1960s with the diagnosis of Minimal Brain Dysfunction (MBD). MBD was one of the several precursors to the current ADHD diagnosis. MBD was treated with stimulant medications such as methylphenidate. Although later discarded because it was too vague, the MBD diagnosis did much to lead to the development of a norm for a methodology with which to evaluate the effects of drugs, and particularly stimulants, on children.

In World War II, German, British, American, and Japanese soldiers all used amphetamines, a practice still common in the U.S. Air Force to help pilots keep alert on bombing missions (Knickerbocker, 2002). After World War II the Japanese had such huge surpluses of amphetamines that they marketed them to civilians. These drugs were advertised for the elimination of drowsiness and repletion of spirit. Researchers estimate that by 1948 5% of the Japanese population between the ages of 15 and 25 was dependent on amphetamines.

After World War II it became evident that amphetamines have appetite suppressant qualities, and chemists tried to tease these out from the reinforcing properties that were connected to abuse. However, most of these initial efforts (such as Ritalin) failed, and then the drug was simply marketed as amphetamines.

The amphetamine molecule is a simple and highly malleable molecule that acts as the chemical template for over 50 pharmacologically active substances (Grilly, 1994). Amphetamine is basically made of two compounds (isomers) labeled "L" and "D" amphetamine. D-amphetamine is more potent and was marketed as Dexedrine. A minor modification in this molecule yields methamphetamine marketed as Methedrine. Other variations of the amphetamine molecule can produce MAO inhibitors. Modifying amphetamine to dimethoxymethylamphetamine (DOM) produces a psychedelic compound similar to mescaline, and further modification produces the empathogen methylenedioxymethamphetamine (MDMA, street name "ecstasy"). The latter was a promising psychotherapeutic compound until criminalized (Eisner, 1994). The therapeutic effects revolved around chemically induced states of empathy that facilitated insights that were then to be integrated into clients' normal awareness (Greer, 1985; Greer & Tolbert, 1986).

Table 9.2 outlines stimulant medications used to treat ADHD in children

**TABLE 9.2**   Stimulant Drugs Used to Treat ADHD in Children

| Generic Name | Brand Name | Type of Drug | Daily Dose |
|---|---|---|---|
| Amphetamine and D-amphetamine compound | Adderall | Stimulant | 5–20 mg |
| D-amphetamine | Dexedrine | Stimulant | 5–15 mg |
| Methylphenidate | Ritalin | Stimulant | 5–20 mg |
| Atomoxetine[a] | Strattera | NE reuptake inhibitor | 0.5–1.2 mg |

[a]Atomoxetine is not a stimulant but an SNRI (see Chapter Five).

## Mechanisms of Action in Amphetamines

Amphetamines exert almost all their effects by causing the release of norepinephrine and dopamine from the synaptic vesicles into the synaptic cleft. Julien (2001) noted that the peripheral nervous system effects of amphetamines likely result from the released norepinephrine. Also, studies have suggested that amphetamine reverses the normal action of transporter molecules so that instead of taking neurotransmitter into the cell, they actually bring it out of the cell into the synaptic cleft (Fawcett & Busch, 1998). The excess dopamine stimulates activity in the limbic system and the brain's pleasure centers. This makes the drug very likely to be abused and to induce tolerance and dependence. In a study comparing methylphenidate to cocaine, Volkow et al. (1995) noted that although the mechanisms of action and effects are similar, methylphenidate clears more slowly from the brain, which, they hypothesize, makes it less dependence inducing. Readers are encouraged to think critically about this result, because when a similar mechanism of slow clearance is invoked to defend cannabis (marijuana) as low in dependence-inducing qualities, it is often rejected (DeFonseca, Carrera, Navarro, Koob, & Weiss, 1997). Either the mechanisms discussed decrease the probability of dependence, or they do not. Pharmaceutical and political agendas should be separated from this debate so that people can objectively examine the issues. In previous chapters we have listed the adverse effects of psychotropics being discussed. With ADHD, these effects are interwoven into the complex presentation of the stimulants. We ask you to consider why in the continent of Europe (an area of the world that has about the same population as the United States), stimulant medications are used with children for only about 5 to 8% of the treatment population so treated in the United States. Now let us examine the *DSM IV-TR*.

## ADHD Diagnosis and Assessment

According to the *DSM IV-TR*, the diagnostic criteria for Attention- Deficit/Hyperactivity Disorder are

A. Either (1) or (2):
  (1)  six or more of the following symptoms of inattention have persisted for at least 6

months to a degree that is maladaptive and inconsistent with developmental level:

*Inattention*
(a) often fails to give close attention to details or makes careless mistakes  in schoolwork, work, or other activities
(b) often has difficulty sustaining attention in tasks or play activities
(c) often does not seem to listen when spoken to directly
(d) often does not follow through on instructions and fails to finish schoolwork, chores, or duties in the workplace (not due to oppositional behavior or failure to understand instructions)
(e) often has difficulty organizing tasks and activities
(f)  often avoids, dislikes, or is reluctant to engage in tasks that require sustained mental effort (such as schoolwork or homework)
(g) often loses things necessary for tasks or activities (e.g., toys, school assignments, pencils, books, or tools)
(h) is often easily distracted by extraneous stimuli
(i)  is often forgetful in daily activities
  (2)  six (or more) of the following symptoms of hyperactivity impulsivity persisted for at least 6 months to a degree that is maladaptive and inconsistent with developmental level:

*Hyperactivity*
(a) often fidgets with hands or feet or squirms in seat
(b) often leaves seat in classroom or in other situations in which remaining seated is expected
(c) often runs about or climbs excessively in situations in which it is inappropriate (in adolescents or adults, may be limited to subjective feelings of restlessness)
(d) often has difficulty playing or engaging in leisure activities quietly
(e) is often "on the go" or often acts as if "driven by a motor"
(f)  often talks excessively

*Impulsivity*

    (g) often blurts out answers before questions have been completed

    (h) often has difficulty awaiting turn

    (i) often interrupts or intrudes on others (e.g., butts into conversations or games)

B. Some hyperactive-impulsive or inattentive symptoms that caused impairment are present before age 7 years.

C. Some impairment from the symptoms is present in two or more settings (e.g., at school [or work] and at home).

D. There must be clear evidence of clinically significant impairment in social, or occupational functioning.

E. The symptoms do not occur exclusively during the course of a Pervasive Developmental Disorder, Schizophrenia, or other Psychotic Disorder and are not better accounted for by another mental disorder (e.g., Mood Disorder, Anxiety Disorder, Dissociative Disorder, or a Personality Disorder).

*Source: Diagnostic and Statistical Manual of Mental Disorders*, 4th ed., Text Revision (Washington, DC: American Psychiatric Association, 2000), pp. 91–92. Reprinted by permission.

Both the "Consensus Statement" of the National Institutes of Health (1998) and the "Clinical Practice Guidelines" of the American Academy of Pediatrics (AAP) (2001) recommend careful diagnosis of ADHD and then an appropriate and judicious use of stimulants in combination with other psychosocial treatments to address the symptoms. Most protocols recommend a neurologic exam, a consultation with a psychiatrist or psychologist who specializes in ADHD, behavioral observation reports from parents, grandparents, teachers, and other school personnel. Olfson, Gameroff, Marcus, and Jensen (2003), analyzing national data, reported the increased rates of treatment from 0.9 per 100 children in 1987 to 3.4 per 100 children in 1997. They posited that this increase along with fewer treatments (counseling) per child was attributed to a broader awareness of the diagnosis by special educators, growth of managed behavioral health care, and increased public acceptance of psychotropic medications. But we ask, Has the mushrooming of the ADHD diagnosis in children led to improved assessment and treatment?

The answer is mixed. Although some teachers, school administrators, and pediatricians rapidly diagnose ADHD in children, the National Institutes of Health (NIH) (1998), the National Institute of Mental Health (NIMH) (1996, 2000), and the American Academy of Pediatrics (AAP) (2001) all have developed diagnostic guidelines for ADHD. In all cases these expert societies recommend a careful evaluation by a trained psychiatrist or psychologist in conjunction with teachers, mental health professionals, and family members. They recommend an evaluation period that is not rushed, so the team can rule out other conditions that might be confused with ADHD, and which includes observation and rating scales.

In a 10-year review of rating scales assessing ADHD, Collett, Ohan, and Myers (2003) concluded that *DSM IV*-based rating scales can reliably, validly, and efficiently measure ADHD symptoms in youth. In this comprehensive review, the authors evaluated the validity and sensitivity of subscales on several rating scales to assess the symptoms of ADHD. The greater use of narrowband rating scales in the assessment of ADHD can supplement and complement clinical interviews and behavioral observations in the evaluation of ADHD in children and adolescents. It is now evident that reliable and valid ADHD rating scales can augment the accuracy and specificity of diagnosis.

In a comprehensive response to the Multimodal Treatment Study (Owens et al., 2003), the authors sought to answer the layered question, What do we treat in ADHD? and, Who treats it? based on the needs of the child and her or his circumstances (Paul, 1967, p. 111). Their findings were remarkable. The children least likely to respond well to a combined treatment of stimulants and milieu therapy were those with depressed parents or caregivers and severe ADHD. Owens et al. (2003) examined several outcome predictors, using nine baseline child and family characteristics. None were predictive, but the two issues discussed earlier along with a lower IQ of the identified child correlated with an outcome less than favorable with the combined treatment.

## ADHD Efficacy, Effectiveness, and Conundrum

ADHD has been classified as one of the externalization disorders, along with Conduct Disorder and Oppositional Defiant Disorder. As opposed to the other two, stimulant medication has been the treatment of choice for ADHD for about 25 years in the United States (Phelps, Brown, & Power, 2002). In fact, stimulants for ADHD are the most widely researched and used medications in child psychiatry. The commonly prescribed stimulants are amphetamine (Adderall), D-amphetamine (Dexedrine), and methylphenidate (Ritalin) (Barrickman, Perry, Allen, & Kuperman, 1995; Connors, 1996; Manos, Short, & Findling, 1999). Evidence indicates significant increase in the use of stimulants for both preschoolers and children (Brown & Sammon, 2002; Riddle, Kastelic, & Frosch, 2001; Zito et al., 2000, 2003). The data include empirical evidence on safety, efficacy, and adverse effects.

Research demonstrates the beneficial effects of stimulants on symptoms linked with ADHD. These effects include diminished inattention, impulsivity, overactivity (Bennett, Brown, Carver, & Anderson, 1999), improved classroom attention and academic efficiency (DuPaul & Rappaport, 1993), and improved mother–child relationships (Barkley, Karlsson, Strzelecki, & Murphy, 1984). However, with all the benefits cited for the use of stimulants with ADHD, available literature to date has not supported or demonstrated that stimulants enhance school achievement (Phelps, Brown, & Power, 2002). Short-term efficacy studies supported the impact of stimulants on the target symptoms. From this literature clinicians can conclude that using stimulants with children appropriately diagnosed with ADHD diminish the child's inattention, impulsivity, and hyperactivity, but do not necessarily improve his or her academic achievement. It is very possible that the child will adapt better to the demands of the classroom environment and become less externally driven. However, it would also be interesting to research whether or not stimulants improve performance in children who are not diagnosed with ADHD.

Proponents of stimulant treatment for ADHD are more convinced than ever that the disorder is passed on through heredity via the *DRD4* receptor gene and that, as twin studies have suggested, up to 80% of the variance in the trait of hyperactivity/impulsivity is now considered to be based on genetics (Barkley, 1998). Peter Jaska (1998), president of the Attention Deficit Disorder Association (ADDA), is a staunch advocate of stimulant treatment for ADHD and argues that "we cannot and will not turn back decades of scientific research on the biological basis of ADHD, medical research, educational progress, and federal disability legislation, because some people selling books claim that ADHD is a 'myth'" (p. 1). Both Jaska and Barkley are experts on the biological bases for ADHD derived from the medical model perspective and the resulting medication for treatment, but they seldom address intrapsychic, cultural, or social perspectives of ADHD.

## ADHD and Combined Interventions

Interventions with ADHD usually begin with assessing the child or adolescent for oral stimulant medication, because most studies have indicated short-term behavioral improvement related to the symptoms of the disorder when stimulants are used (American Academy of Pediatrics, 2001; Barkley, DuPaul, & Connor, 1999; Phelps, Brown, & Power, 2002). Until very recently Ritalin (methylphenidate) was the most widely prescribed stimulant. Now studies have demonstrated that Adderall (amphetamine/dextroamphetamine) is equally efficacious and leads to more improvements in teacher and clinician ratings of behaviors (Faraone, Phiszka, Olvera, Skolnik, & Biederman, 2001; Swanson et al., 1998). Pemoline (Cylert) is infrequently prescribed, because studies indicate it can cause hepatotoxicity. Although pemoline has not been removed from the U.S. market (Abbott informs physicians that Cylert should be used as a third-line stimulant with regular monitoring of liver enzymes), Great Britain and other countries no longer permit its use (Riddle, Kastelic, & Frosch, 2001).

Almost all consensus statements on ADHD treatment recommend psychosocial interventions that assist the family as well as the person diagnosed with ADHD. These approaches include psychotherapy, cognitive-behavioral therapy, behavioral therapy, social skills training, impulse control therapy, parenting skills training, support groups and family therapy. Each of these approaches alone or in conjunction with stimulant medication can help ameliorate some of the symptoms of ADHD and/or address some of the underlying factors affecting the person with the disorder. The American Academy of Pediatrics (2001) specifically recommended behavioral therapy as the best adjunct intervention with stimulants to establish targeted outcomes and manage the child's behavior both in the classroom and at home. They also stated that if one stimulant does not work at the highest feasible dose, the physician should recommend another. Clinicians learning about pharmacology may find it helpful to remember that stimulants generally provide only relief of symptoms, thus requiring other treatment modalities and follow-up.

Results of the Multimodal Treatment Study for Children with ADHD (MTA Cooperative Group, 1999) demonstrated that stimulant treatment was slightly more effective than behavioral therapy alone, but the study found parents preferred the behavioral therapy conditions to the stimulants-alone treatment. As with all treatment approaches for ADHD, the MTA study is not without its critics, who argue for a better match of patient with a treatment strategy tailored and selected for the individual's needs (Green & Albon, 2001). When the selected management (interventions) for a child with ADHD has not met targeted outcomes, clinicians must evaluate the original diagnosis, adjust treatments and medications, and evaluate for coexisting conditions.

Another critic of the MTA study (Leo, 2002) noted that the fanfare surrounding publication of the study "was nothing short of extraordinary" (p. 53). Leo pointed out that *ABC News* reported that results indicated drug therapy was much better than counseling for ADHD. Leo contends the MTA study was heavily biased toward medication treatment. He claims the study's authors all had a history of strongly favoring medication, bringing their objectivity into question. He also points out that the MTA study had four groups: one received medication, one received behavior therapy, one received both, and a fourth group received no treatments from the MTA researchers but instead received standard treatment in the community. The most

"robust" changes were reported in ratings by teachers and parents of children in the study. The problem with this, according to Leo, is that the investigators preselected a group of parents who believe it is acceptable to medicate children; in fact, in all cases the parents contacted the investigators to enroll children in the study. This fact, according to Leo, points to a bias in the sample.

Edwards (2002) addressed the important follow-up outcomes of studies and interventions in the wake of the report from the MTA Cooperative Group study (1999). He recommended that a specific family-based intervention be used in a mental health setting in conjunction with pharmacologic treatment. He specifically cited Parent Management Training (PMT) as an approach that through cognitive-behavioral coaching helps parents manage their child's difficulties. Whatever the method, more physicians, researchers, and clinicians are recommending family interventions with children and adolescents diagnosed with ADHD. The research in treatment outcomes of ADHD is complicated, and we encourage you to evaluate many strategies and interventions for your clinical work, especially those that include family/parent strategies.

We spoke with one interventionist who provides a learning/coaching service to children with ADHD (Joyce Kubik, personal communication, April 2003). Kubik not only conducts specific skill-building training/coaching for ADHD children but also conducts support groups for parents. She also gives workshops for teacher in-service programs. Her overall message is that children with ADHD are capable of developing specific learning strategies that will lead to improved academic learning and success. She outlines these specific skills in her book *S.C.O.P.E.: Student Centered Outcome Plan and Evaluation* (Kubik, 2002). The central theme of her work is to help parents and teachers find ways to help students with attention difficulties. The American Academy of Child & Adolescent Psychiatry (2001) stated,

> Research also should include the role of school and community-based professionals, as well as primary care clinicians, in delivering treatment services. Little is known about how short or long-term effectiveness varies as a function of

the school and community-based professional involvement. . . . They should consider child and family outcomes and cost-effectiveness of care. Linking outcomes to service parameters is an important step in encouraging practice in system change. (p. 10)

In this summary statement you can recognize aspects of the Integral model that forms the basis of this book in analyzing and evaluating interventions with children and adolescents diagnosed with ADHD. It calls for more comprehensive research on the multiple factors that contribute to ADHD in children and adolescents and initiates the process to improve research on outcomes with this disorder.

## ADHD and Comorbidity

The American Academy of Pediatrics (2001) has stressed that evaluation for ADHD should include an assessment for coexisting or comorbid conditions. The literature on ADHD identifies several psychological and developmental disorders that coexist in children with ADHD (American Academy of Pediatrics, 2000; Biederman, Mick, Faraone, & Burback, 2001; Phelps, Brown, & Power, 2002; Spencer, Biederman, & Wilens, 2002). These disorders included conduct and oppositional defiant disorders, mood disorders, anxiety and depressive disorders, mental retardation, learning disabilities, tics, substance abuse, and medical conditions. Researchers have estimated that among children with ADHD, the prevalence rate of Oppositional Defiant Disorder is up to 35%, Conduct Disorder up to 26%, anxiety disorders up to almost 26%, and depression up to 18% (American Academy of Pediatrics, 2001). It is more difficult to estimate comorbidity rates of Bipolar Disorder, substance abuse, and tics. Most authors who discuss comorbidity and ADHD tend to discuss the issue from a pharmacologic perspective rather than a counseling perspective (Levy & Hay, 2001; Solanto, Arnsten, & Castellanos, 2001). This is a burgeoning and complex conundrum in the treatment of ADHD. We encourage you to be alert to the great variability in children and adolescents diagnosed with ADHD and to assess for other conditions or factors.

Mental health clinicians should be able to recognize the evidence recommending cautious use of stimulants with children and adolescents diagnosed with ADHD, and should remain alert to the potential for overdiagnosis or misdiagnosis of the disorder and the extensive range of comorbid/coexisting conditions. Phelps, Brown, and Power (2002) summarized issues surrounding comorbidity of ADHD, ODD, and CD related to the evidence that when two or more of these disorders occur together, the prognosis is more guarded. They also addressed the hypothesis that ADHD occurs first in the child and the symptoms of impulsivity and inattention interact with the psychosocial issues of family turmoil, parental problems, and abuse factors to trigger ODD and/or CD. Clinicians need to be alert to the range of symptoms of several disorders when assessing and evaluating symptoms of impulsiveness and hyperactivity. These conditions could emanate from intrapsychic family and environmental factors. Although the debate continues about the effectiveness of stimulant medication with ADHD, Greenhill (1998) and National Institutes of Health (1998) concluded that stimulants used for ADHD children and adolescents

1. Produce moderate to marked short-term improvement in motor restlessness, on-task behavior, compliance, and academic performance.
2. In studies of 6 months or longer, children fail to maintain academic improvement or improve social problem-solving skills (Greenhill, 1998, p. 53).

## Atomoxetine, a Nonstimulant

Recently, atomoxetine (Strattera), a nonstimulant and an inhibitor of the presynaptic norepinephrine transporter, has demonstrated some promising results in reducing ADHD symptoms (Brown University, 2002). It was approved for use in children ages 6 and older in 2002. In the three major studies to date, efficacy outcomes provide clinical hope that this nonstimulant will avoid some of the insomnia and hypervigilance side effects of the stimulants.

Atomoxetine (Strattera) is metabolized primarily through the CYP2D6 enzymatic pathways. It demonstrates an adverse event percentage of between 3.5 and 7% (poor metabolizers) in clinical trials. These adverse events include gastrointestinal problems, irritability, insomnia, aggression, and dizziness. As a nonpsychostimulant, atomoxetine has potential as an alternative to the stimulants now used with ADHD. As with any new medication, only time and continued research will tell if atomoxetine will improve on the side effect profile of stimulant medications.

# Mood Stabilizers and Bipolar I Disorder in Children

The Diagnostic and Statistical Manual of Mental and Emotional Disorders (*DSM IV-TR*) (American Psychiatric Association, 2000b) provides the following diagnostic criteria for Bipolar Disorder, Single Manic Episode:

A. Presence of only one Manic Episode and no past Major Depressive Episodes.
   *Note:* Recurrence is defined as either a change in polarity from depression or an interval of at least 2 months without manic symptoms.
B. The Manic Episode is not better accounted for by Schizoaffective Disorder and is not superimposed on Schizophrenia, Schizophreniform Disorder, Delusional Disorder, or Psychotic Disorder Not Otherwise Specified.

*Criteria for Manic Episode*

A. A distinct period of abnormality and persistently elevated, expansive, or irritable mood, lasting at least 1 week (or any duration if hospitalization is necessary).
B. During the period of mood disturbance, three (or more) of the following symptoms:
   Have persisted (four if the mood is only irritable) and have been present to a significant degree:
   (1) inflated self-esteem or grandiosity
   (2) decreased need for sleep (e.g., feels rested after only 3 hours of sleep)
   (3) more talkative than usual or pressure to keep talking
   (4) flight of ideas or subjective experience that thoughts are racing

   (5) distractibility (i.e., attention too easily drawn to unimportant or irrelevant external stimuli)
   (6) increase in goal-directed activity (either socially, at work, or school, or sexually) or psychomotor agitation
   (7) excessive involvement in pleasurable activities that have a high potential for painful consequences (e.g., engaging in unrestrained buying sprees, sexual indiscretions, or foolish business investments).
C. The symptoms do not meet criteria for a Mixed Episode.
D. The mood disturbance is sufficiently severe to cause marked impairment in occupational functioning or in usual social activities or relationships with others, or to necessitate hospitalization to prevent harm to self or others, or there are psychotic features.
E. The symptoms are not due to the direct physiological effects of a substance (e.g., a drug of abuse, a medication, or other treatment) or a general medical condition (e.g., hyperthyroidism).

*Source: Diagnostic and Statistical Manual of Mental Disorders*, 4th ed., Text Revision (Washington, DC: American Psychiatric Association, 2000), pp. 388–389. Reprinted by permission.

We have seen in the past decade an increasing interest and shift in focus from Conduct Disorder (CD) and Oppositional Defiant Disorder (ODD) to Bipolar Mood Disorder (BMD) in children and adolescents (Kusumaker, Lazier, MacMaster, & Santor, 2002). We illustrated this in the case of Phillip at the beginning of this chapter. Although in our Chapter Eight discussion of mood stabilizers we focused on Bipolar I Disorder, in this chapter we use the more general BMD (Bipolar Mood Disorders), because that is the construct common to the literature on children and adolescents. Many diagnostic scholars tell us the prevalence of BMD is growing, especially in preadolescent children, with almost no gender differences (Bland, 1997; Hirschfield et al., 2003; Zarate & Tohen, 1996). The case for increased incidence is still undecided. Currently the *DSM IV-TR* diagnostic criteria for Bipolar Disorder are used for children and adolescents without any major modifications and the features providing the best distinction between ODD, CD, ADHD, and BMD are the presence of a flight of ideas, grandiosity, and the episodic nature of the grandiosity (Carlson, 1996; Kusumaker et al., 2002). As we summarize the literature on BMD in children and adolescents, we learn that it is difficult to diagnose, more clinicians are recognizing its prevalence at an earlier age of onset, three tentative developmental theories are linked to it (McMahon & DePaulo, 1996), and more clinicians are using antimanic medications to treat BMD in both children and adolescents.

There is a paucity of information on Bipolar I disorder in children and adolescents. King (1997) found that although Bipolar I disorders in children were considered historically rare, they are now being reported more often. Frequency remains an area of some controversy. King also indicated that further research is needed to establish the specificity of symptoms, to distinguish childhood mania from behavior disorders. They stated the existing research examining early-onset Bipolar Disorder is limited. "Methodological problems include small sample sizes, lack of comparison groups, retrospective designs, and lack of standardized measures . . . given these limitations, some of the information presented in this review had to be drawn from the adult literature" (p. 158). King (1997) emphasized that the incidence and validity of the BMD diagnosis in children remains controversial, as many children meet the criteria for mania because of their problems with irritability, emotional lability, increased energy, and reckless/dangerous behavior.

Viesselman (1999) addressed the general symptoms of BMD as expansive mood, inflated self-esteem, decreased need to sleep, talkativeness, flight of ideas, distractibility, psychomotor agitation, and excessive involvement with pleasurable activities. Phelps, Brown, and Power (2002) addressed the fact that BMD youth often are incorrectly diagnosed as having Schizophrenia; thus BMDs are difficult to discern in children and adolescents because many present with an agitated depressed mood rather than mania (Weller, Weller, & Fristad, 1995). Lewinsohn, Klein, and Seeley (1995) stated that pediatric clients with BMD present with more

psychomotor agitation, elevated mood, increased verbalizations, inflated self-esteem, distractibility, and a decreased need for sleep.

The treatment of choice for BMD in children and adolescents is the mood stabilizers covered in Chapter Eight. These drugs include lithium (Eskalith, Lithobid), valproate (Depakote/Depakene, Divalproex), carbamazepine (Tegretol), oxcarbazepine (Trileptal), and olanzapine (Zyprexa). Many scholars already cited in this chapter argue against indiscriminate use of these medications with pediatric populations without further study and argue for more complete awareness of the dynamics affecting the child. Campbell and Cueva (1995) argued that although lithium has been used with children, the data gathered so far have been conflicting. Lithium continues to be used with younger children, although it is approved only for patients 12 and older.

Riddle, Kastelic, and Frosch (2001) discussed the finding that the older antiepileptic drugs had been well researched as mood stabilizers in adults but not in pediatric populations. Campbell, Kafantaris, and Cueva (1995) have studied lithium, carbamazepine, and valproate used for children with nonspecific aggression and found lithium was superior to placebo and to the other antiepileptic drugs in reducing aggression. One very important note: Eberle (1998) found that one type of adverse event of using valproate with girls is that of polycystic ovarian disease, which can have profound consequences for females.

In a nine-child case study of BMD and juvenile mania (in which six subjects began in the study as preschoolers), Mota-Castillo, Torruella, Engels, Perez, Dedrick, and Gluckman (2001) provided clinical evidence of the successful use of valproate (Divalproex) with this population. The key indices that the study evaluated were clinical descriptor, family history of Bipolar Disorder, getting worse on stimulants, and eventual mood stabilization with valproate. This important study offers the partial truth that it is possible, under careful clinical assessment, to diagnose mania or BMD in very young children, to distinguish the diagnostic criteria from ADHD and other similar categories, and to treat the symptoms with the antiepileptic drug valproate.

Ryan, Bhatara, and Perel (1999) agreed with this perspective that mood stabilizers may be effective with children seemingly out of control, but their study offered several cautions for using these drugs without further research and careful attention to the potential adverse effects. They also raised the issues of how to achieve objective assessment of children deemed out of control and how prevalent compliance is with the medications. Finally, as with many adults with BPD, Biederman, Wilens, Mick, Faraone, and Spencer (1998) found relationships among BMD, substance use disorders, and the onset of adolescent mania. The complex interaction of BMD and substance use disorders makes this one of the most severe combinations of psychopathology in children and adolescents.

In our clinical work of over 25 years, we have found that the substance use disorders were a major missing piece in several cases with children and adolescents. These clients were diagnosed with ODD, CD, or BMD and seemingly did not improve with psychotherapy or psychotropic interventions. The missing link and confounding variable was their hidden polysubstance abuse or dependence, which exacerbated some symptoms and masked others. The links in the literature show how the onsets of BPD, ADHD, CD, or ODD become significant risk factors in diagnosing substance use disorders.

The following case may provide additional understanding of these complex variables.

## The Case of Nicole

Nicole, a 14-year-old Caucasian girl currently living in a foster home, had just been referred to a Severe Emotional Disturbance (SED) unit in her school system. Nicole has a history of acting out, impulsivity, distractibility, conduct, and learning problems from a very early age. Initially, Nicole was referred to a specialist for her impulsivity and distractibility both at home and in preschool at the age of 4.

During the assessment the clinician suspected a mood disorder but seemed to have more evidence for ADHD. He recommended a daily course of Adderall with behavior management therapy at home and school, focused on specific age-appropri-

ate behaviors. At the time of the evaluation, he did not notice Nicole's intermittent scratching of her genital area. Over the next six months Nicole showed little improvement in her symptoms and behaviors as a result of the Adderall and the milieu behavioral therapy. In fact, some of her behaviors worsened: She attacked other children, was cruel to animals, and was overtly curious about male and female genitals. After nine months the psychologist consultant at the school recommended another neuropsychiatric evaluation and an outside therapist who would address some of Nicole's apparent intrapsychic conflicts along with her behavior.

The second psychiatric evaluation yielded a change in diagnostic perspective. This time the psychiatrist diagnosed BMD and prescribed divalproex (Depakote) and a low dose of lorazepam (Ativan), an anxiolytic. The new therapist, a female, stopped the behavior therapy and began to treat Nicole with a combination of play therapy and insight-oriented therapy. The play produced associations to remote possibilities of earlier sexual abuse and abandonment, and the insight therapy captured her already highly critical superego (obsessive thought patterns and preoccupation with sexual act) and her deep affection for the rituals of the Catholic Church. Nicole remained on this treatment regimen for about two and a half years. During treatment she never really settled down in class or at home, but her behavior and attention were slightly more manageable. (We have all had cases where there is just enough improvement from the medication to raise expectations even if the client seems not to be making progress in many important areas of her life.) Later Nicole developed a passion for reading 7 to 10 books a week that she got from the local library. On her trips back and forth to the library, she befriended some older boys (ages 10 to 13) who offered her street stimulants at a very low cost. Nicole welcomed the friendship and experimented with the drugs (stimulants, soapers, cocaine), but was gang-raped by the boys one Saturday afternoon. Overwhelmed by this horrific sexual trauma, Nicole did not speak of it to anyone. She also immediately stopped associating with the boys. Her response to this event was alternately to withdraw into a cocoon-like isolation and to become aggressive with people.

She verbally assaulted teachers and foster parents and attacked her friends and other students. She was unreachable and totally out of control. She stopped attending her therapy sessions with the counselor, but she continued to seek street drugs.

Puzzled and frustrated, the school crisis team recommended an additional psychiatric evaluation and assessment for Nicole and possible hospitalization. This triggered a series of episodes in which she ran away, had several foster and specialized school placements, a brief stay at a juvenile detention facility, one abortion, and two attempts at drug rehabilitation for her dependence on stimulants, cocaine, and now alcohol. Somehow Nicole survived and is now in an SED classroom with a specialized social worker as an aide. She is on olanzapine (Zyprexa) for psychotic mania, sertraline (Zoloft) for depression and anxiety, low doses of divalproex (Depakote) for violent and aggressive outbursts, and zolpidem (Ambien) every other night for sleep. In essence, at 14, Nicole was loaded with psychotropic medications (polypharmacy). She was referred to a new female therapist, with whom she rarely spoke; when she did, she mentioned missing her former, caring play therapist, one of the most stable objects (people) in her life. Although Nicole did attend her class regularly and her behavior was quite manageable, her teachers reported very little learning progress and a total inability to interact with her classmates. Her therapist echoed much of the same descriptions, but voiced marginal hope when she and Nicole engaged in drawing or other forms of play therapy or discussed issues related to an all-loving versus all-punishing God. The concluding remarks in her individual educational plan (IEP) at school read, "No change, few academic gains, impulsive/aggressive behavior stabilized, little socialization, continues in counseling."

Examining this case from our four perspectives yields some important insights and omissions. Nicole did receive a more extensive assessment early on and participated in behavioral therapy first, which is recommended by the literature (American Academy of Pediatrics, 2001; Kusumaker et al, 2002; Phelps, Brown, & Power, 2002) followed by art therapy and insight therapy when the behavioral

therapy failed. It is critical to note that the second therapist helped Nicole discuss intrapsychic and cultural issues and learned about the pressure from her complicated feelings about her upbringing in the Catholic Church and her deep awareness of her self-critical feelings and thoughts.

As is so often the situation with a foster child, other social and cultural pressures intervened, such as drug abuse, negative and exploitive peer relationships, and sexual trauma. It is not clear whether Nicole ever experienced sexual or physical abuse earlier in her life. The most recent team is faced with an early adolescent girl with a long history of psychotropic and psychotherapeutic treatments whose life is further complicated and traumatized by rape and drug dependence. Given the assumption that the significant others in her life—case managers, foster parents, teachers—feel she is out of control, the attending psychiatrist then addressed her range of symptoms and conflicts with a polypharmaceutical strategy. This approach numbs and tranquilizes Nicole so she is more appropriate in her various living environments but fails to address the boiling issues, anguish, and conflicts from the other aspects of her life. Treatment for Nicole should begin by recognizing the extreme complexity of her life space and developing a treatment plan and approach to gradually help her titrate off some of her medications while addressing in counseling the complex issues of abuse, drug dependence, abandonment, and loss of self that so plague her. She will need a very extended and interpersonal treatment approach if she is to recapture hope and resiliency in her life. We also would speculate about the accuracy of her diagnosis, because of the interplay of her conflicts and varying presenting problems.

## Children and Antipsychotic Medication

Schizophrenia with childhood or adolescent onset has been noted since the earliest descriptions of the disorder. Readers will recall Emil Kraepelin's initial diagnosis of a patient as having *dementia praecox*, which means "youthful insanity." As Russell (2001) notes, given that the disorder has been linked with children and adolescents through the evolution of its diagnostic forms, one might think there would be an ample treatment literature regarding these populations, but there is not. In a review of controlled studies of antipsychotic agents to treat Schizophrenia, Campbell, Rapoport, and Simpson (1999) found only one controlled study of the use of these agents with adolescents and one report on their use with children younger than age 12. Therefore, Russell (2001) notes, until more research is conducted clinicians must extrapolate from adult studies to children and adolescents. Although he comments this is not cause to adopt a nihilistic attitude, it does call for clinical skepticism. Russell maintains it may be true that people with early-onset Schizophrenia have more severe forms of the disorder, but this has yet to be determined conclusively and it does not mean pharmacologic treatment will not be effective. Further, early-onset Schizophrenia seems to have more severe negative symptoms, making the atypical antipsychotics a better choice (Botteron & Geller, 1999).

Although few data are available regarding the use of antipsychotics with childhood psychoses certain medications have been a mainstay in managing these disorders, such as Haldol (haloperidol), because it tends to be less sedating (Andreasen, 2000). Because of the potential for Parkinsonian-like symptoms, this medication should be prescribed with an anti-Parkinsonian agent such as benztropine (Cogentin). Ernst, Malone, Rowan, George, Gonzalez, and Silva (1999); Phelps, Brown, and Power (2002); and Riddle, Kastelic, and Frosch (2001) also addressed the use of the "atypical" newer neuroleptics for children diagnosed with tics, behavioral problems in autism, psychotic illness, and nonspecific aggression.

Some researchers have made the case that children and adolescents with psychotic disorders should receive atypical agents as the first line of treatment (Jensen et al., 1999) particularly given evidence that children and adolescents may be more susceptible to the side effects of neuroleptics (Lewis, 1998). Although the atypicals have far fewer side effects, Kottler and Devlin (2001) have noted that the associated weight gain can be a problem for many adolescents. Researchers have begun to publish weight gain management protocols, and clini-

cians should be familiar with these (Aquila, 2002). The few trials that exist indicate that the schizophrenic symptoms of children and adolescents respond favorably to both neuroleptics and atypical antipsychotics and that the clinician must balance the therapeutic and side effects for each individual case. As we noted in Chapter Seven, evidence is mounting that atypical antipsychotics are also correlated with increased risk for diabetes and hyperglycemia and that this risk includes children and adolescents (Koller, Cross, & Schneider, 2004). Whatever medication a clinician chooses, Russell (2001) emphasizes the need for multimodal treatment that includes psychosocial interventions such as individual and family therapy, psychoeducational counseling, and social skills training.

A more common problem is raised by Pappadopulos et al. (2002) in a study that examines the range of off-label prescribing of atypical antipsychotics for aggression. These authors state that although in theory doctors seem to agree about optimal prescribing practices, in the "real world" there is wild disparity in the prescriptions written. Apparently even the agreement between researchers and front-line doctors can be influenced by staff pressure, limited staff resources, managed care limits on inpatient stays, and the movement away from physical restraint. It appears use of the atypical antipsychotics for the treatment of aggression will increase. Studies such as Findling's (Findling, McNamara, Branicky, Schluchter, Lemon, & Blumer, 2000) support using the atypical antipsychotics over neuroleptics primarily for their improved side effect profiles. As you saw in Chapter Eight clinicians show increasing interest in using atypical antipsychotics as mood stabilizers (Schaller & Behar, 1999; Heimann, 1999).

Another problem that requires further debate and research concerns the notion that Schizophrenia is a wide spectrum of early-onset disorders manifesting in a variety of the disorder called "schizotaxia," which refers to a genetic predisposition to Schizophrenia (Meehl, 1962). Tsuang, Stone, and Faraone (2001) advocate treating Schizophrenia prophylactically. These authors maintain that the theoretically genetic predisposition toward Schizophrenia may be associated with reversible problems and may improve the child's quality of life. Despite this strong medical model perspective, they admit that psychosocial interventions may also work. They conducted a six-week trial of risperidone (prescribed at low levels) in six subjects identified as schizotaxic. They reported that five of the six reported increased cognitive abilities during the trial as well as greater enjoyment of social activities. Obviously, there is no way to determine the amount of placebo effect until a double-blind, placebo-controlled trial is done.

Great caution needs to be exercised here, as the implications are that asymptomatic children might be given antipsychotics in the hope their diagnosis as schizotaxic is correct. The antipsychotic market currently amasses $5 billion a year, and many fear that the theory of schizotaxia is just another way of bending the parameters of diagnosis to help pharmaceutical companies profit from a new market. Currently no diagnostic system in the world identifies adolescents in the phase *before* onset as ill, so this approach would have ramifications for the diagnosis. Ideally, the issues surrounding the politics of research and publishing described in Chapter Two, need to be more adequately addressed before any further medicating of asymptomatic populations

Recently Bryden, Carrey, and Kutcher (2001) summarized several studies that used Clozaril (clozapine) with 95 children, mostly adolescents, diagnosed with Schizophrenia. Over 80% improved on both the positive and negative symptoms of the disorder. In some of these studies the adverse effects were controlled for, in others they were not and included seizures, drooling, somnolence, hypotension, and neutropenia. These studies did not discuss agranulocytosis (an adverse effect that reduces the body's ability to produce white cells).

In Chapter Seven, we discussed neuroleptics and their affinities for different CNS receptors, their pharmacokinetics, and pharmacodynamics. Marriage (2002) spoke to our inability to predict the response of an individual patient (child or adolescent) to a typical or atypical neuroleptic. He addressed the enormous response variation, especially with adolescent males, Asians, Native Americans, and people suffering from various forms of organicity. For children or adolescents exhibiting symptoms of psychosis, the long-term prognosis is poor

(Phelps, Brown, & Power, 2002), and we need to learn a great deal more about the adverse side effects of both the typical and atypical medications (Riddle, Kastelic, & Frosch, 2001).

## Antianxiety Medications and Children and Adolescents

Despite the high prevalence of anxiety disorders in children (10 to 20%), very few controlled medication trials have been conducted. Brown and Sawyer (1998) concluded that regarding anxiolytic medication with children, "few published empirical studies support their long term efficacy for children and adolescents" (p. 83). Bernstein and Shaw (1997) noted that psychotropic medications should not be the sole intervention but should be used as an adjunct to counseling. Interventions that facilitate active mastery are important, to prevent symptoms returning after discontinuation of medication.

Garland (2002) noted that anxiety disorder categories for children and adolescence are in flux because of the many *DSM-IV* alterations and the elimination of some anxiety disorders from *DSM III-R*. Bernstein, Borschardt, and Perwien (1996) viewed these changes as placing at risk a decade of research on childhood anxiety disorders, although Phelps, Brown, and Power (2002) supported elimination of some categories of childhood anxiety disorders from *DSM III-R* as a research-based simplification of the categories. Although prevalence rates vary for current anxiety disorders with children and adolescents (Botteron & Geller, 1999; Garland, 2002), incidences of Generalized Anxiety Disorders (GAD), Panic Disorder (PD), Post-Traumatic Stress Disorder (PTSD), and Separation Anxiety Disorder (SAD) are frequently thought to require both psychopharmacologic and psychotherapeutic interventions. Currently, although almost all the drugs are used off label, SSRIs such as paroxetine (Paxil), fluvoxamine (Luvox), fluoxetine (Prozac), citalopram (Celexa), and sertraline (Zoloft) are prescribed for children and adolescents with anxiety disorders. The current concern over safety of these medications for children and adolescents applies to their use in anxiety disorders as well as in depression. One of chronic side effect of SSRIs recognized in children is a behavioral activation (Riddle et al., 1991), like an increased agitation different from a mania. At the time of this writing, the Food and Drug Administration (2003) has issued a Public Health Advisory stating that use of SSRIs and similar types of antidepressants with depressed children and adolescents may be linked to increased suicide rates. How this will affect use of these antidepressants for anxiety disorders remains unclear

In a review of the literature on anxiolytic medications used in pediatric populations, Livingston (1995) noted mixed results with benzodiazepines and said that in cases where studies show initial results, the results fail to be significant in replications of the studies. Livingston notes that if children are going to be placed on these medications, prescribers need to "start low and go slow" (p. 248). Recall from Chapter Six, benzodiazepines such as alprazolam (Xanax) and diazepam (Valium) have an inhibitory impact on the CNS at the GABA receptor complex. Originally great hope was held out for the benzodiazepines in treating adult, adolescent, and childhood anxiety disorders (Coffey, 1990), but more recent studies have tended to demonstrate that improvement in anxiety symptoms has a high likelihood with placebo as well as medication (Garland, 2002). Side effects of benzodiazepines include drowsiness, dependency problems, and some withdrawal symptoms. Often studies of anxious children do not report these adverse effects.

## School Issues, Anxiety, and Children

A relevant law when addressing anxiety in children is the Individuals with Disabilities Education Act (IDEA). Services to children are provided under a number of provisions in this act, and often many *DSM* anxiety disorders can be used to qualify a child for services. The diagnostic categories of *DSM* do not automatically correspond to the eligibility categories in IDEA. The interested reader can go to http://www.ed.gov/offices/OSERS/IDEA/the_law.html for a listing of the relevant diagnoses. IDEA services focus on disability conditions that interfere with a child achieving academically or vocationally.

Anxiety disorders have been used to qualify a child for special services. A key symptom is fears associated with personal or school problems that persist over a period of time and adversely affect educational performance. Anxiety disorders are one of the most common childhood disorders and may impair a child's life even if symptoms are below the threshold for a *DSM* diagnosis. For example, some studies show "subclinical" anxiety to be highly correlated with reading difficulty (Bernstein & Shaw, 1997).

Developmental differences exist in the presentation of the anxiety disorders. For example, younger children with Separation Anxiety Disorder have far more symptoms than older children. In adolescents, somatic complaints and school refusal are more common than in younger children. Conversely, older children with Generalized Anxiety Disorder (GAD) show more symptoms than younger ones. This is probably caused by cognitive differences, because older children have more mental tools with which to craft their worries.

Interestingly, in several studies with benzodiazepines, the medicated groups did no better than placebo controls. Two studies did yield significant differences among school refusers and children with selective mutism and social phobia. In one study, the school refusers did better than controls when given Tofranil/imipramine, a tricyclic antidepressant. The other study, on selective mutism and social phobia, showed that the experimental subjects did better than controls when given Prozac.

A related childhood disorder is Separation Anxiety Disorder. Here the anxiety is aroused by separation from familiar people (usually parents) or leaving home. The reaction is excessive and may include fears that something will happen to the parents or to prevent reunification. Somatic complaints are also common. The distinction must be made between developmentally normal separation anxiety and this disorder. If refusal to go to school is thought to be due to Separation Anxiety Disorder, the child will go if accompanied by the parent. Although benzodiazepines and antihistamines have been used to treat this (Wozniak et al., 1997), exposure-based interventions and relaxation are likely to be more effective.

Another subthreshold condition is shyness. It is consistently correlated with adult and childhood anxiety disorders. Although common (90% of people report feeling it at some time in their lives), it can be debilitating as the person gets older. Shy men marry later and become parents later than their counterparts who are not shy. Although shy women marry and become parents at ages comparable to their counterparts who are not shy, they are less likely to attend college or work outside the home. Social phobia is a severe manifestation of shyness that afflicts about 5% of children. It delays social and emotional development. The overwhelming fear of doing or saying something embarrassing or humiliating keeps such people from eating, drinking, or writing in public or engaging in everyday conversations.

Although children generally outgrow shyness, they do not outgrow Social Phobia. Children with social phobias are usually depressed and lonely and almost always solitary. They may show extreme anxiety in situations where they feel they are being evaluated by others. The onset of Social Phobia is usually in adolescence and without treatment, the course is often chronic. There is high comorbidity with depression, other anxiety disorders, and substance abuse to self-medicate. As with other childhood anxiety disorders, the recommended treatments include rehearsal, imagery, and drug treatment with antidepressant compounds. Behavior therapy has a 70% success rate for both children and adults, with systematic desensitization and exposure being the common treatments. Although more children and adolescents are being prescribed antidepressant compounds for shyness and Social Phobia, there is little literature supporting the practice.

## Obsessive-Compulsive Disorder

The symptoms of Obsessive-Compulsive Disorder (OCD) usually emerge in childhood, are underdiagnosed until they become severe, and have an approximate prevalence rate of 1 to 2% in the pediatric population (Phelps, Brown, & Power, 2002; Riddle, 1998; Riddle, Kastelic, & Frosch, 2001). A brief review of the characteristics of OCD from *DSM-IV-TR* (American Psychiatric Association,

2000b) includes intrusive thoughts, impulses, or images (that is, obsessions) that often lead to repetitive behaviors or mental acts. For children, common obsessive thoughts deal with dirt, contamination, and fear of harm. Compulsions include hand washing, counting, and rearranging things (March & Mulle, 1996; Phelps, Brown, & Power, 2002).

Several efficacy studies tested SSRIs with children diagnosed with OCD ages 8 to 15. The outcomes (March et al., 1998; Scahill et al., 1997) demonstrated that more children on SSRI have shown marked improvement of their symptoms than those on placebo. The degree of improvement in both studies with different SSRIs (sertraline and fluvoxamine) was virtually the same. The outcomes of these studies permit cautious optimism that carefully administered SSRIs with children suffering from OCD can be beneficial for symptom relief over time. As with SSRIs in general, though, their ultimate safety for children and adolescents has yet to be determined.

Anxiety disorders in children and adolescents demand careful evaluation and treatment. Many theorists recommend a course of psychotherapy before medication (Furman, 2002; Garland, 2002; Phelps, Brown, & Power, 2002). It is difficult to treat and resolve many of the anxiety disorders in children without careful attention to family, developmental, and trauma variables as well as a complete medical history (an assessment from all four perspectives).

## Antidepressants and Children and Adolescents

Many reports have appeared on an increased incidence of Major Depressive Disorder (MDD) in children and adolescents. Although more studies on this have begun, there is always error in the epidemiologic methods used to gather such data, so such reports are far from conclusive (Ingersoll & Burns, 2001). As McClure, Kubiszyn, and Kaslow (2002b) noted, although many approaches are used for diagnosing and treating mood disorders in children, only a few have any empirical support. It does seem that when identified, childhood or adolescent depression is characterized by high rates of comorbidity with conduct, anxiety and attention deficit disorders, impaired social and vocational functioning, increased rates of substance abuse, eating disorders, and higher risk for completed suicide (West, 1997). Given that, it is important to consider all treatments that may be helpful when a child or adolescent does manifest symptoms of depression.

Depression (unipolar) can be very difficult to discover, discern, and diagnose in children and adolescents. In children the symptoms manifest themselves as hyperactivity, impulsivity, and aggressiveness. Grief and loss may trigger enuresis, sleeplessness, nightmares, and extreme stubbornness, depending on the age of the child (Brown & Sammons, 2002; Riddle, Kastelic, & Frosch, 2001; Ryan, 2002; Viesselman, 1999). In fact, Ryan (2002) noted that depressive illnesses in children and adolescents can be protracted, recurrent, and continue into adulthood.

Newer research into the complexities of antidepressant action can help neurologists and clinicians better understand developmentally important age differences in the nervous system. Researchers are beginning to see that developing animals differ from older ones in serotonin-mediated responses. Very-early-onset stress may compromise later adaptive capacity of some of these systems (Goldman-Rakic & Brown, 1982). Juvenile depression may also differ substantially from adult depression regarding the role of noradrenergic mechanisms and thus in the responsiveness to compounds that target norepinephrine. Practitioners need to be alert to warnings such as those by Coyle (2000), who noted there is "no empirical evidence to support psychotropic drug treatment in very young children and that such treatment could have deleterious effects on the developing brain" (p. 1060).

### Tricyclic Antidepressants in Children

Overall the results have not supported data found in adult studies regarding the efficacy of these tricyclic antidepressants in treating juvenile depression (Cohen, Gerardin, Mazet, Purper-Ouakil, & Flament, 2004; Rosenberg, Holttum, & Gershon, 1994). The weight of currently available evidence suggests that TCAs as a group are indistinguishable from placebo, except in side effects (Kutcher et al., 1994; Puig-Antich et al., 1987). The highest response rate in a study is about 44%. In addition, a sig-

nificant risk arises of serious cardiac problems in developing bodies. The same conclusions hold true for the TCA derivatives such as desipramine and nortriptyline. Both have been fairly well studied, and researchers have failed to show significant therapeutic differences from placebo but did show a high number of adverse side effects. In addition, both still carry the risk of cardiovascular complications.

Research has demonstrated that TCAs (and MAOIs) have not revealed greater efficacy than that for placebo, and their adverse side effect profile is extensive, including reports of sudden cardiac death (Birmaher, 1998; Kye et al., 1996; Brown & Sammons, 2002; Riddle, Geller, & Ryan, 1993; Werry, 1999). There is little support if any for the routine use of TCAs as a first line of treatment in children and adolescents. Therefore it is disturbing that millions of prescriptions for desipramine and related compounds have been written for young people under age 18 (Goleman, 1993). Sommers-Flanagan and Sommers-Flanagan (1996) recommended that such prescriptions be reserved for special cases where other treatments have proven ineffective or intolerable and that a thorough physical (including cardiovascular exam) should be conducted before beginning the medication. TCAs should be used in children only under the following conditions:

- Full informed consent of patient and parent
- A history of lack of response to more appropriate treatments
- Full disclosure of side effect profile
- Disclosure of cardiotoxicity of these compounds
- When trials of more effective, available pharmacotherapies (SSRIs) have failed

Also, TCAs should be used with extreme caution, because the noradrenergic system (on which TCAs operate) does not fully develop until early adulthood (Goldman-Rakic & Brown, 1982).

### SSRIs in Children

As noted, the FDA (2003) has currently issued a Public Health Advisory cautioning about a possible link to the use of certain SSRI antidepressants in pediatric populations and increased suicide rates. The antidepressants in the advisory are listed in Table 9.3.

**TABLE 9.3**   Antidepressants Listed in 2003 FDA Public Health Advisory

| Generic Name | Brand Name |
| --- | --- |
| Fluoxetine | Prozac |
| Fluvoxamine | Luvox |
| Citalopram | Celexa |
| Escitalopram | Lexapro |
| Mirtazapine | Remeron |
| Nefazodone | Serzone |
| Paroxetine | Paxil |
| Sertraline | Zoloft |
| Venlafaxine | Effexor |
| Bupropion | Wellbutrin |

As noted, the SSRIs currently are used with children and adolescents for anxiety and depression. Fluoxetine (Prozac) has received FDA approval for use in pediatric populations, and fluvoxamine (Luvox) is approved for treating OCD in children (Brown & Sammons, 2002). All other SSRIs are prescribed as off label to children with depression as of this writing. Children and adolescents encounter the same adverse effects as when the SSRIs are employed with anxiety disorders. These compounds are more effective in children but not as effective as in adult samples.

It is important to note that adolescent girls are particularly vulnerable to depression when entering puberty (Phelps, Brown, & Power, 2002; Silberg et al., 1999). Clinicians should be sensitive to gender, family history of depression, impacting life events, loss, or death when assessing children for depression. Current trends and preliminary understandings of the research suggest that in addressing childhood depression, the clinician must consider both psychotherapy and medication (Badal, 1988, 2003). Ryan (2002) indicated that 30 to 40% of children do not have a sufficient response to the first SSRI treatment.

There is almost no literature on the effects of SSRIs on infants and preschoolers (McClure, Kubiszyn, & Kaslow, 2002a); however, evidence shows SSRI prescriptions are on the increase for

this age group (Zito et al., 2000). The majority of researchers looked at the effects of fluoxetine (Prozac) on older children and adolescents, which has shown mixed results (Emslie et al., 1997). Some studies looking at the effects of paroxetine on children and adolescents are also promising (Findling, McNamara, Branicky, Schluchter, Lemon, & Blumer, 2000; Keller et al., 2001), but more double-blind, placebo-controlled studies need to be done. Juveniles with a family history for manic or hypomanic symptoms are at higher risk for SSRI-induced manic or hypomanic episodes. If children or adolescents are treated with SSRI medications, treatment should be cautious and should observe the following conditions:

- SSRIs are used in addition to supportive psychotherapy or counseling to deal with psychological issues.
- SSRIs should be supported by education regarding the symptoms, the medication, and what relief the medication is to provide.
- Effective treatment involves parents or caregivers as much as possible.
- Effective treatment includes use of a depression scale (HAM-D or BDI-II) if the child is old enough to take one, to monitor symptoms.
- The acute phase of treatment should take place over 8 to 12 weeks followed by maintenance of 4 to 6 months.

McClure, Kubiszyn, and Kaslow (2002a) conclude that when medication is warranted, the SSRIs are the medication of first choice. Jureidini et al. (2004) disagree, however. They recently reviewed and critiqued seven published randomized, controlled trials of newer antidepressants for depressed children. These researchers found that pharmaceutical companies paid for the trials, the benefits of the drugs were small, and the adverse effects were downplayed, and they concluded antidepressant drugs could not be confidently recommended as a first-line treatment option. This is only one meta-analysis, but it points to the need for validity in published data and full disclosure of biases resulting from funding sources or researchers.

From an Integral perspective, it is important to review all literature as it comes in, as well as review the researchers and the funding sources to check for possible bias. At the time of this writing a new government-funded study of SSRIs and children was completed but not officially released in a peer-reviewed journal. The study was the Treatment for Adolescent with Depression Study (TADS), sponsored by the National Institute of Mental Health (NIMH). When we called NIMH to get a copy of the study, we were told the study needed to be peer-reviewed and the results would not be released until that process was complete. Nevertheless, *Time* magazine (Lemonick, 2004) and the *New York Times* (Harris, 2004) reported (without benefit of peer review) that the study supported the use of the medications with children. When we asked the NIMH representative how the popular press would have gotten the results to report *before* the peer review, she said she didn't know. Until a peer review of the study is concluded, the writers have no basis for these conclusions other than their own opinions of the study. Without including the results of peer review, readers are likely to come away with a "sound byte" interpretation of the results that may not be accurate. Readers can access the latest results of drug trials on the NIMH web site http://www.nimh.nih.gov/studies/2mooddisordersdep.cfm.

## The Placebo Problem

As we noted in Chapter Five, the placebo effects of compounds and the place and type of placebo in studies has yet to be explicated. According to Fisher and Fisher (1997), "A probe of the available scientific reservoir of pertinent studies does not reveal any serious evidence that antidepressants do more for childhood depression than do placebos" (p. 308). An earlier overview of studies by Thurber, Ensign, Punnett, and Welter (1995) concluded that the more adequate the experimental methods in each study, the less likely to be found superior to placebo were the drugs tested. Although Fisher and Fisher (1997) noted that thevidence is still limited for the effectiveness of many counseling/psychotherapy approaches to depressed children and adolescents, this does not excuse the prescribing of compounds for which very little evidence of efficacy exists.

In concluding this section, we remind the reader that clinicians are using off-label psychotropic medication for several other disorders. In each case the clinician must weigh the benefit versus the potential adverse effects of the drug on the child. We must also speak to the child about his or her reaction and feelings about the medication and request feedback from the parents or guardians about the child's progress or struggles with the psychotropic medications. We believe it is an enormous responsibility to counsel children and adolescents who are on psychotropic medication where little research has been conducted on the efficacy, effectiveness, and safety of the drugs.

In April 2003 the recommendations were published of the Research Forum approved by the American Academy of Child and Adolescent Psychiatry (AACAP) on strategies for psychopharmacological studies on preschool children (Greenhill et al., 2003). The six workgroups of the Research Forum were (1) diagnosis/assessment, (2) research design, (3) ethics/institutional review board (IRB), (4) preschool protocol modifications, (5) FDA/regulatory industry, and (6) training/public issues. The workgroups began their efforts before the passage of the Best Pharmaceutical for Children Act (BPCA), and their recommendations are very compatible with the mandates of this act.

## Conclusion

We have sought to highlight the complexity, controversy, and conundrums of child and adolescent psychopharmacology. By now, you are alert to factors from all four perspectives that impinge on this issue, generate "word magic," provide partial truths, or stimulate category errors. In the colossal debate over ADHD, we discover not only category errors but an inflexibility that may harm children rather than treat them. We recognize the power and influence of the pharmaceutical companies to market so many "off-label" psychotropic medications to children and adolescents with such confidence or, more accurately, grandiosity. Central to this dilemma are the shortages of mental health professionals who exclusively treat children and adolescents. This shortage, coupled with the growing confidence of the effectiveness of psychopharmacology with some diagnoses, permitted pharmaceutical companies to market "off-label" drugs for children and adolescents on a grand scale while clinicians observe the phenomenon, almost powerless. Even the passage of the Best Pharmaceuticals Act for Children recently is not enough to slow this trend.

## Summary

The use of psychotropic medications with children and adolescents is very complex. Clearly there is no simple answer to this dilemma. Because most of the medications are prescribed off label, it is important that mental health professionals learn all that they can in order to protect the health and well-being of their clients who are children and adolescents. The information provided here spans the four perspectives to challenge the reader to consider medical, psychological, cultural, and social paradigms. The discussion of stimulant medications serves as a template for practitioners as they consider psychotropic applications with other disorders. When children or adolescents are placed on a psychotropic it is always recommended that they receive counseling or other supportive services. The federal government through recent legislation is emphasizing how important and critical this issue is. Finally, the question is asked, "Do we as a society use psychotropic medication as the ultimate modality of behavior management?"

## Study Questions and Exercises

1. Using the four perspectives of the Integral Model, describe one problem from each perspective with off-label use of psychotropic medications in young children.

2. How would you respond to a parent whose child was taking multiple medications for impulsive behavior and asks you, "What are the medications supposed to do for my child, and why does he have to take so many?"

3. Of the four positions on prescribing stimulant medications for children diagnosed with ADHD, which one do you support most and why?

4. What connections do you see between the material at the beginning of this chapter and the "family values" politicians talk about so much?

5. From the perspective of subjective experience, what do you think some main issues would be for children taking psychotropic medication?

6. From the social perspective, do you feel that pediatric studies of psychotropic medication should be mandatory? Why or why not?

7. How can mental health clinicians best advocate for children around issues related to psychotropic medications?

8. Spend some time reviewing psychosocial treatments for ADHD, anxiety disorders, and mood disorders. What are the most promising nonpharmacologic treatments available, and how well do they work?

9. Summarize the most important components of the Best Pharmaceuticals Act for Children. If you were going to write to your representatives in the Senate or House of Representatives, what points do you think they should be aware of?

10. Interview a mental health clinician who has worked with children and adolescent clients for at least 10 years. What percentage of his or her clients take psychotropic medications? How is this different from 10 years ago?

# CHAPTER TEN

# An Integral View of Herbaceuticals

## *Weeds, Seeds and New Age Needs*

The topic of herbaceuticals strikes at the heart of many issues already raised in this text. In the case of herbaceuticals, questions of efficacy, availability, potency, and responsibility are for the most part unanswered. We use the term *herbaceuticals* for herbal compounds used for medicinal purposes related to mental or physical well-being. It seems the most appropriate term, because to call these compounds "herbal drugs" implies some connection with synthesized drugs sold as pharmaceuticals or street drugs used recreationally, neither of which is true. To call these compounds "medications" also misrepresents them, because they are treated differently from medications, as we will describe. We also briefly discuss the role of herbaceuticals as entheogens (from the Greek, meaning a way to realize the divine within oneself) (Ott, 1993). Ironically, the licit herbaceuticals we discuss here cannot, by law, advertise themselves as anything other than "dietary supplements." We address why later, in discussing social issues and perspectives. The use of herbaceuticals (called **phytotherapy**, from the Greek, meaning "plant therapy") is ancient, and many of these plants have been used for thousands of years, for a range of purposes, including mental, physical, and spiritual healing.

We have structured this chapter a bit differently from other chapters in the book. We begin by introducing general herbaceutical issues from the four perspectives of the Integral model. Next we review what is known (and speculated) about a variety of herbal supplements, and then revisit the perspectives of the Integral model to examine specific issues. Finally, we use the perspectives of the Integral Model to review cannabis. There are no cases in this chapter, because the scope of our practices does not include consultation on herbaceuticals. For reasons we discuss, mental health clinicians who recommend herbal remedies do so at great risk for committing malpractice. Please note that we cite as much literature as possible in this chapter, because our knowledge regarding herbaceuticals is incomplete and the best we can do is keep up with and report to readers the literature that exists.

## The Behavior of Herbaceutical Use

What do we know about people's behavior regarding the use of herbaceuticals? Worldwide, it is estimated that up to 80% of all people use complementary and alternative medicine, including herbaceuticals (LaFrance et al., 2000). From an Integral perspective, it is important to note that the widespread use of herbaceuticals worldwide is likely in part because many people do not have access to other medications for cost or distribution reasons. Herbaceutical approaches are firmly integrated into the medical systems in China, North and South Korea, as well as Vietnam (Northridge & Mack, 2002). Also, in many cultures people use herbaceuticals specifically to enhance well-being (Cocks & Moller, 2002; Perry, 2002). In Germany, herb use is more common than in the United States, and depression is treated with St. John's wort (*Hypericum perforatum*) four times as often as with fluoxetine (Gray, 1999). Herbaceutical use is also said to be increasing in England (Redvers, Laugharne, Kanagaratnam, & Srinivasan, 2001).

Researchers indicate herbaceutical use is increasing worldwide (Boniel & Dannon, 2001). What are the estimates in the United States? Researchers estimate that 40% of Americans have tried "alternative therapies," with herbal therapies being the most common (Gray, 1999). The most rapidly growing herbal market in the United States is for products with supposed efficacy in treating symptoms of mental and emotional disorders (Beaubrun & Gray, 2000). An ongoing problem with herbaceutical use is that, as researchers estimate, 40 to 60% of those using herbal remedies do so without telling their physician (Gutherie, 1999). As you can see in examining various herbal preparations, all have potential for interactions with other drugs as well as for their own adverse effects. Most users in the United States are middle/upper-middle-class Caucasian women paying out-of-pocket (Klesper et al., 2000). In addition, older Mexican Americans suffering from poor health and depressive symptoms are more likely to use herbal supplements than is the general population (Loera, Black, Markides, Espino, & Goodwin, 2001). Increased use among Americans can be directly linked to a 1994 law that allowed herbal preparations to be sold unregulated as dietary supplements.

Do psychiatrists prescribe or recommend herbaceuticals to their patients? Interestingly, there are few data on this question, but a review of the literature seems to indicate significant differences depending on where the psychiatrists reside and practice. American medical practitioners are really not in a position to prescribe or recommend herbaceuticals, because the FDA does not regulate them, so in most cases the prescriber and the consumer have no idea what is actually in the product. Not many more data are available on physicians' atti-

tudes toward herbaceuticals. One study, done with the faculty and students at the State University of New York Science Center, indicated that although most physicians do ask their patients about the use of herbaceuticals, most never research the herbaceuticals that patients report taking. These researchers did note that the younger the doctor, the more likely the doctor was to be aware of herbaceuticals (Silverstein & Spiegel, 2001).

It is interesting that American researchers raise questions about studies examining herbaceuticals that researchers rarely raise (but could raise) in regard to studies of drugs. Some researchers have noted that the medical community seems particularly critical of trials of herbaceuticals and applies to them more conservative standards than to drug compounds (Even, Friedman, & Dardennes, 2001). One problem that has arisen in the United States with regard to herbaceuticals is the "Don't ask, don't tell" syndrome (Boniel & Dannon, 2001). Basically, patients are reluctant to report their use of herbaceuticals with their doctor because they think the doctor would not approve. Similarly, most doctors don't ask patients if they are using herbaceuticals. This "silence" regarding herbaceuticals can be problematic, because they can interact badly with regular pharmaceuticals (Cupp, 1999; Gold, Laxer, Dergal, Lanctot, & Rochon, 2001).

A study of psychiatrists in Australia and New Zealand found that psychiatrists there were far more positive toward herbaceuticals, with 80% of respondents having used St. John's wort (Walter, Rey, & Harding, 2000). In European countries, where herbs such as St. John's wort are regularly prescribed (for example, Germany), psychiatrists have more positive attitudes about herbaceuticals. A crucial difference to consider is that the German government regulates the dosage and potency of herbaceuticals as well as promotes research and public education on them, so psychiatrists know exactly how much of the compound patients are being prescribed (Preston, O'Neal, & Talaga, 2002). Several studies from Germany indicate efficacy for St. John's wort (Kasper & Dienel, 2002).

## Intrapsychic Issues

### Why Do People Take Herbaceuticals?

From the intrapsychic perspective, people report many reasons for turning to herbaceuticals. Table 10.1 summarizes some of the more common reasons given.

#### *Mistrust of Traditional Western Medicine*

Gutherie (1999) noted mistrust of traditional Western medicine as one reason that patients seek alternative and complementary therapies. Many clients and members of the general public are becoming more aware of the adverse effects of medications as well as of questionable practices by pharmaceutical companies. This mistrust may be more pronounced regarding the medical subspecialty of psychiatry—particularly its diagnostic categories. Critics such as Colbert (2002), Breggin (1997), and Healy (2002) all raise substantial questions regarding the accuracy of the *DSM* diagnoses, the degree to which the disorders have biological etiologies, and the extent to which they should be treated with traditional Western medicine.

The state of managed health care in the United States has also decreased consumer confidence in traditional Western medicine. Clients frequently report to us that their health maintenance organization (HMO) will not fill a prescription their doctor has given them, and offers them a different medication. They are usually aware that HMOs routinely make deals with pharmaceutical companies to carry particular drugs and not competing drugs that may have more efficacy in treating the same disorder.

In a nationwide survey, Astin (1998) also explored whether mistrust of traditional medicine was the reason people used herbaceuticals but found in his sample that the primary reasons people sought out alternative therapies were because such approaches were more congruent with their own beliefs, values, and philosophic orientations toward health and life. Rather than framing his participants' preference for herbaceuticals as a reaction to mistrust of traditional Western approaches, Astin sees it as proactive choice based on consciously chosen values. This is certainly the case for many

**TABLE 10.1** Reasons People Report for Taking Herbaceuticals

|  |
| --- |
| Mistrusting traditional Western medicine |
| Believing that "natural" products are safer, less toxic than drugs |
| Sensing that herbaceuticals are more consistent with patient values or philosophy of health |
| Accepting anecdotal testimony about efficacy |
| Not needing a prescription |

whose spiritual or religious paths have a history of using herbaceuticals both medicinally and ritually. Religions like Wicca and Santeria are examples of spiritual paths with rich heritages of herbaceutical use (Hutton, 1999).

#### *Belief That Natural Products Are Safer Than Drugs*

Although people taking herbaceuticals often say they believe that natural products are safer than drugs (Gutherie, 1999; Walter & Rey, 1999), many hazards are actually associated with taking herbaceuticals. You do not have to look very far to find toxic compounds in nature. For example, belladonna, sassafras, licorice, and ephedra are all toxic in large enough amounts. In addition, because herbaceuticals are not regulated in most countries (including the United States), consumers really have no way of knowing exactly what they are taking in terms of contents, dosage, and potency of contents. Later in the chapter we review the growing body of literature that reports on the interactions herbaceuticals can have with medications. Given that a significant percentage of clients taking herbaceuticals do not tell their doctors, these risks for problematic interactions increase (Izzo & Ernst, 2001).

#### *Acceptance of Anecdotal Testimony About Efficacy*

Both of us have treated clients who asked us about herbal supplements to treat symptoms of anxiety and depression. When we ask clients how they heard about these, they frequently say they know people who claim to have had success using herbal supplements to treat one or another symptom. It is possible that belief in anecdotal testimony facilitates some placebo effect. We caution readers that although anecdotal evidence may be a good starting point for research questions, it is not a good source for drawing conclusions. Case histories and individual clients' responses to different treatments help us refine how to research and evaluate those treatments. However, conclusions should not be overgeneralized based on one or two cases.

### Issues of Culture

Issues of culture related to herbaceuticals can be placed in two categories. The first is herbaceutical practices that derive from indigenous cultures and have been handed down to the present day. Examples include older Mexican-Americans' reliance on herbaceuticals (Loera et al., 2001) and those cultures where herbaceuticals are an integral part of medicine and wellness. Here, herbaceuticals could logically be extended to include **entheogens,** meaning "God-manifesting" agents. Despite the **current** prohibition in the United States, entheogens have been used (and continue to be used) here and in traditional societies as ways to facilitate the mystical vision (Smith, 2000). Despite the overgeneralizing rhetoric in the United States about the evils of mind-altering substances, ample evidence shows that in many cultures the moderate use of mind-altering plants is part of human evolutionary legacy as well as a strategy that can enhance well-being (Siegel, 1989; Sullivan & Hagen, 2002).

The second category concerns the subcultures fighting over whether herbaceuticals can be a standard part of medical practice in the United States. This power issue interests not just medical practitioners but also pharmaceutical companies. Imagine what might happen if a plant such as St. John's wort caught on as an effective treatment for depression. Would the FDA seek to regulate its production and distribution? Would it become illegal to grow, as marijuana currently is? If not, would consumers with any gardening savvy pay $80 a month for an antidepressant, or would they grow St. John's wort

in a back yard at a fraction of the cost? In addition, would the medical lobby seek to restrict St. John's wort to prescription-only access? Although many believe there should be an over-the-counter antidepressant (Volz & Laux, 2000), many others contest that possibility. From an Integral perspective, all these are important questions.

Another question implied in the power issue is, How much protection can and should the government give its citizens? People have come to expect regulation in how drugs are accessed as well as what is allowed in terms of advertising. The United States in particular has not defined the extent to which drugs should be regulated by prescription. Some researchers have suggested that compounds such as antidepressants could all be sold over-the-counter, because they are no more dangerous than many other over-the-counter substances (Healy, 1997). The prescription issue has particular relevance when considering such issues as marijuana used for medical purposes. Should citizens have the right to grow plants with psychotropic properties for their own use? Is government's role to protect people from themselves even when they don't want such protection?

## Issues From the Social Perspective

### Legal Issues

In pondering some of the questions ending the last section, you are likely aware that herbaceutical use has legal aspects. Many people wonder why herbaceuticals sales picked up so much in the last 10 years. One answer is a 1994 law called the Dietary Supplement Health Education Act. The law, for which the supplements industry lobbied heavily, restricted the FDA's ability to control herbal products. Passage of that law allowed any product to be labeled a supplement as long as no claims were made that the product affected a disease. As Julien (2001) points out, whereas a manufacturer cannot claim something such as St. John's wort "alleviates depression," it can legally claim that a substance "helps facilitate emotional balance." As the Consumer's Union (1999) points out, the current law allows such products to be marketed with absolutely no demonstrations of safety or efficacy. On the one hand, critics such as Pies (2000) believe that because herbal products can create adverse reactions in users, consumers need stricter FDA regulation of these products. On the other hand, advocates of access to herbaceuticals fear that regulation will turn into unnecessarily harsh, even draconian, restrictions, as happened with marijuana prohibition.

Another important legal issue concerns the types of liability U.S. physicians and mental health care providers may incur if they discuss unregulated compounds with clients. The cost of malpractice insurance in the United States has skyrocketed out of control (Vasankathumar, 2001), and attorneys and a public that seem eager to resort to litigation routinely scrutinize physicians. In such a climate, is it any wonder physicians are unlikely to recommend untested and unregulated herbaceuticals? Again, from an Integral perspective, it is unfair to blame physicians for what actually is an effort to achieve a "best practices" standard.

The legal and ethical issues become more complex for nonmedical mental health clinicians. We have already said clinicians are likely to be practicing ethically when discussing basic information about medication, helping the client work through issues related to medication, or acting as an information broker in helping the client get quality information about a medication (see also Ingersoll, 2000, 2001). Although clinicians should try to answer clients' questions about herbaceuticals, clinicians should restrict themselves to the conclusions in peer-reviewed literature and should recommend that clients check with the doctor before starting any herbaceuticals compound. This conservative approach is important until more data on herbaceuticals are amassed and more standardization is achieved. As Rivas-Vasquez (2001) has pointed out, this is a high-risk area, and clinicians should tread carefully.

## Problems in Studying Medicinal Plants

An important social issue we must also comment on is research practice related to herbaceuticals. Although approximately 5000 medicinal plants are

**TABLE 10.2** Problems in Studying Medicinal Plants

Isolating compounds

Identifying species

Variations in composition

Variations in preparation

Adulteration and substitution

Chemical complexity

Problematic study designs

Language barriers

known, there are only current studies and published papers on about 100 (Northridge & Mack, 2002). Why the dearth of information? Clearly some of this lack is related to difficulties in studying plants that may have hundreds of active compounds and trying to decide which compounds produce the therapeutic effects. Table 10.2 lists some challenges, in studying medicinal plants, that may contribute to the dearth of literature. A brief discussion follows.

Isolating naturally occurring compounds is currently not a front-line research strategy in pharmaceuticals. The most popular research now focuses on drug–receptor interactions as well as on intracell changes. Further, isolating active compounds that produce a supposed therapeutic effect is very difficult and time consuming. In Chapter Seven, writing about the new antipsychotics, we noted an important question: How much dopamine antagonism versus serotonin antagonism is necessary for optimal antipsychotic effects? This is a difficult problem to solve even when there are only two primary variables. In plants with hundreds of active compounds, the variables multiply exponentially, and it is hard to know where to begin. Here, the chemical complexity of medicinal plants continues to be a problem. Plants contain thousands of chemicals. This complexity means each herbal preparation may have a variety of pharmacologic effects. For example, at least 40 chemical compounds contribute to producing the aroma of coffee. That is 40 chemical compounds just for aroma alone, without even considering the pharmacologically active chemicals.

Medicinal plant species also vary, as do individual plants within a species, with each variation having its own combination and concentration of active elements. Inaccurate identification of species thus poses a potential problem for systematic study of medicinal plants. For example, the 250 varieties of the herb valerian vary in concentration of active compounds. Researchers would first have to determine which varieties had the most therapeutic effect and then isolate the active compounds to determine those that produce the effect.

Even if a researcher identifies the correct plants and can isolate the active elements, variations in composition result from genetic factors, climate, growing season, soil quality, rainfall, and post-harvest storage conditions. Any of these can affect the composition of the plant. So researchers would also have to find ways to exercise control over as many of these variables as possible.

Once an herb is harvested, it can be prepared in many different formulations. For example, herbs can be dried and made into tea or concentrated and used as extract. In addition, extracts may be created with various solvents, including alcohol, oils, or water. Amount of active ingredients varies with preparation method.

Even for herbs harvested and prepared in a uniform manner, lack of standardization can affect the end product. Standardization depends on the integrity of the company selling and distributing the herb. Suppliers often adulterate and substitute other plant materials when the target plant is expensive. Tyler (1994) found that many preparations of ginseng have no ginseng but are filled with numerous other substances.

For the hardy researcher ready to tackle these challenges, there are more, including study design and access to current data. As with lithium, no one can patent a naturally occurring element, and this precludes making a lot of money on herbaceuticals. Thus most herbaceuticals have few adequate studies to test their efficacy. Another problem is likely more pronounced for U.S. researchers, who are more likely than researchers in other countries to speak only one language. There are data on many herbaceuticals, but the data are in languages other than English. Although many noteworthy works on phytotherapy are now beginning to be translated into English (Blumenthal, 1998), the process is slow.

## Differences Between Herbs and Drugs

All the latter research problems point to some of the essential differences between herbal preparations and drugs. Although some may seem to be commonsense distinctions, they bear emphasizing, particularly in a society where people are so confused over what constitutes a "drug." Many critics of the current U.S. practice of labeling herbs such as St. John's wort as "dietary supplements" note that if such herbs may negatively interact with medicines, public safety is best served by regulating them as drugs (Stein, 2002). Table 10.3 summarizes important differences between herbs and drugs. This table is also followed by commentary.

As noted earlier, dosage of an herbal product is very difficult to determine, because there are few efficacy studies on varying dosages to determine the optimal dosage range. In addition, lack of standardization in preparing many herbal supplements makes it next to impossible to know the potency of the compound making up each dosage. Drugs are required to have efficacy studies as well as uniformity in dosage and potency. Under U.S. law, herbaceuticals do not. In addition, as noted, drugs must be regulated by the FDA, whereas herbaceuticals do not. Drugs are usually monosubstances, whereas herbaceuticals may have many active elements. Fi-

**TABLE 10.3**   Important Differences Between Herbs and Drugs

Dosage

Efficacy

Complexity of the compound

FDA role

Role of patents

Role of potency standards

nally, when a pharmaceutical company synthesizes a drug, it can get a patent on the compound, which lets the company monopolize the substance for a period of time (usually 17 years) in which to earn back the money it took to research the compound (plus, one assumes, profits).

These differences contribute to many problems with herbaceuticals, including lack of purity. Slifman, Obermeyer, Musser, Correll, Chichowicz, and Love (1998) did a study of chemical analyses for many popular herbal compounds to see what was actually in them, and logged some disturbing results. The herbs studied had many contaminants. In some of the Chinese patent medicines studied, the researchers found mercury, arsenic, aspirin, and phenobarbital. In some of the medicines from India, the researchers found carbamazepine and Valium (diazepam)!

Another related problem concerns unethical marketing. Bear in mind that under the 1994 Dietary Supplement Health Education Act, advertising can be legal without being ethical. One product marketed as an antitension supplement claimed to contain St. John's wort, 10 complementary herbs, and calcium. The product claimed these ingredients worked together for a synergistic effect. The product listed the following ingredients in each tablet:

    300 mg St. John's wort
    90 mg passion flower
    70 mg hops
    30 mg skullcap
    40 mg black cohosh
    30 mg wood betony
    30 mg chamomile
    15 mg lady's slipper
    10 mg cayenne
    5 mg chlorophyll
    40 mg elemental calcium
    10 mg elemental magnesium

Clearly, there is no way the company could have "known" the combination would have a calming effect, because most of the herbs listed had not been studied for any "calming" effect. Further, there would be no way of knowing what the effects of all these ingredients would be on the person taking the

supplement. Should laws prohibit such advertising? It stands to reason that because the claims cannot be backed up by research, such claims should not be made to consumers.

## Examining Better Known Herbaceuticals With Application for Psychiatric Problems

In this section of the chapter we share what we know about some of the more popular herbaceuticals thought to have uses for mental/emotional symptoms. Note that although some herbs have a good deal of research behind them at this point (such as St. John's wort), others have very little, and in some cases the jury is still out regarding efficacy. For each herb, we note the side effects we are aware of. Table 10.4 summarizes the herbs we cover in this section.

**TABLE 10.4**   Herbaceuticals Thought to Have Use in Mental/Emotional Disorders

| Herb | Supposed Therapeutic Property |
| --- | --- |
| St. John's wort | Antidepressant |
| Kava | Anxiolytic |
| Valerian root | Anxiolytic |
| Passion flower | Anxiolytic/hypnotic |
| Hops | Anxiolytic/hypnotic |
| Melatonin | Hypnotic |
| Ginkgo | Cognitive enhancer |
| Ephedra | Stimulant |

### St. John's Wort

St. John's wort (*Hypericum perforatum*) is an aromatic perennial that is native to Europe and grows wild in Asia, North America, and South America. It has bright yellow flowers with red spots and is abundant in June. The red spots are supposed to symbolize the blood of John the Baptist, a Christian figure who was beheaded at the time of year the spots appear (early summer). *Perforatum* refers to the tiny perforation in each leaf of that subspecies; the leaves seen from directly overhead are positioned like a cross, in four directions on the stem; German ethnobotanist Bernhard Becker of Beendorf told the tale that St. John looked down and the devil was hiding beneath the plant; the plant opened up tiny holes to reveal the devil; a version from a less Druidic past says God's all-seeing eye bored the tiny holes. Other legends hold that June (when the plant flowers) is also the birthday of John the Baptist (the word "wort" is derived from the Old English *wyrt* and means "plant" or "vegetable"). St. John's wort has been used medicinally for over 2000 years. Paracelsus called it "arnica of the nerves" ("arnica" referring to perennial herbs) because of its soothing effects on nervous disorders (Bilia, Gallori, & Vincieri, 2002). Its use in treating mood disorders was pioneered by a German physician in 1939. Although traditionally prepared as tea, currently it is also prepared in ethanol and methanol extracts. The methanol extract is the extract used in the most systematic research on the herb and is prepared by a firm in Germany. Any research on St. John's wort in Germany uses this compound (labeled LI 160), as reflected in the literature. St. John's wort is hypothesized to have efficacy in treating depression. We review the studies supporting this hypothesis later; for now it's enough to say that a great deal of research supports the efficacy of St. John's wort in mild to moderate depression.

## Mechanism of Action

St. John's wort has many elements that are biologically active, including naphthodianthrones, flavonoids, and xanthones. The two active ingredients, presumed to be naphthodianthrones, are hypericin and hyperforin. The word *hypericin* is a Greek word meaning "overcoming an apparition," and medical historians think the ancients believed the plant had the ability to ward off evil spirits (Julien, 2001). Modern researchers initially thought hypericin disabled MAO (like an MAO inhibitor), but now they think hypericin is more of a reuptake inhibitor of serotonin, dopamine, and norepinephrine (Wong, Smith, & Boon, 1998). In addition, hypericin seems to bind to GABA receptors, benzodiazepines receptors, and glutaminergic receptors. Hyperforin is also hypothesized to play a key role in

the antidepressant activity of St. John's wort (Cervo, Rozio, Ekalle-Soppo, Guiso, Morazzoni, & Caccia, 2002); however, it is not known what its primary mechanism of action is at the time of this writing.

## Efficacy of St. John's Wort

The consensus of opinion currently seems to be that St. John's wort has efficacy over placebo in treating mild to moderate depression. Several meta-analyses support this conclusion, including Gaster and Holroyd (2000); Kasper and Dienel (2002); Kim, Streltzer, and Goebert (1999); Laakmann, Jahn, and Schuele (2002); Linde, Ramirez, Mulrow, Pauls, Weidenhammer, and Melchart (1996); Linde and Mulrow (2000); and Whiskey, Werneke, and Taylor (2001). In addition, clinical trials have also supported the use of St. John's wort in mild to moderate depression (see Benner, Bjerkenstedt, & Edman, 2002; Ernst, 2002; Friede, Henneicke von Zepelin, & Freudenstein, 2001; Holsboer-Trachsler & Vanoni, 1999; Kelly, 2001; Lecrubier, Clerc, Didi, & Keiser, 2002; Volz, Murck, Kasper, & Moeller, 2002). The extract of St. John's wort used in most studies is labeled LI 160 and is the commonly prescribed compound for depression in Germany. LI 160 is distributed and regulated in Germany with regard to the potency and dosage of the compound. The recommended dosage is at least 900 mg per day.

Of the trials that did not support efficacy, one of the more controversial was that by the Hypericum Depression Trial Study Group (2002), which found no differences among sertraline, St. John's wort, and placebo. This study was followed by no fewer than six commentaries (Cott & Wisner, 2002; Klaus, Mechart, Mulrow, & Berner, 2002; Kupfer & Frank, 2002; Spielmans, 2002; Volp, 2002; Wheatley, 2002), indicating a number of questions regarding the findings. Another trial (large-scale, multisite, placebo-controlled) also did not find St. John's wort significantly different from placebo (Shelton et al., 2001). All the studies showing significance for St. John's wort did so *only* with mild to moderate depression. These studies used participants whose depression was in the moderate to severe range, as measured by the Hamilton Depression Rating Scale. This discrepancy alone could account for the differences in findings.

With regard to studies comparing St. John's wort with standard antidepressants, four studies have compared St. John's wort to Ludiomil (a tricyclic derivative), Tofranil (imipramine) , and Elavil (amitriptyline). No significant differences were found in responses to the St. John's wort and these agents. One severe limitation in these studies was that the antidepressant doses were lower than would be normal in clinical practice (Wheatley, 1997). Another study (Friede, Henneicke von Zepelin, & Freudenstein, 2001) found St. John's wort at 500 mg per day as effective as fluoxetine at 20 mg per day (the minimum therapeutic dosage in the United States) in treating mild to moderate depression. It is hoped that researchers will replicate this latter study.

In addition to treating mild to moderate depression, studies have suggested efficacy for St. John's wort in treating menopausal symptoms (Grube, Walper, & Wheatley, 1999) and Seasonal Affective Disorder (Wheatley, 1999).

### Side and Interaction Effects of St. John's Wort

Although there is no systematic study of the side effects of St. John's wort, some reported side effects in studies can be shared here. Many researchers report that side effects are minimal (Gaster & Holroyd, 2000) and others that St. John's wort is well tolerated (Volz et al., 2002). Parker, Wong, Boon, and Seeman (2001) and Dannawi (2002) found that in sensitive patients, St. John's wort is associated with serotonin syndrome. This is a potentially life-threatening syndrome caused by increased accumulation of serotonin in the central nervous system. The symptoms of serotonin syndrome include disorientation, confusion, agitation, restlessness, fever, chills, diarrhea, hypertension, and sweating.

Far more likely than developing serotonin syndrome just from St. John's wort is that clients could develop the syndrome from combining St. John's wort with another serotonergic drug, as was the case in the Dannawi (2002) study. Parker and colleagues (2001) identified cases where the syndrome was associated only with St. John's wort. These researchers also found a case where St. John's wort was associated with hair loss. This is reminiscent of the case we shared in Chapter Five where the hair loss seemed caused by sertraline. In another study (Holsboer-Trachsler & Vanoni, 1999), gastrointestinal upset was one of the most frequently reported side effects, but in most cases it was rated as mild to moderate. Finally, one researcher noted that sexual dysfunction was a side effect of St. John's wort and could be treated with sildenafil (Viagra) (Asslian, 2000).

Although side effects are always a concern with a substance, they are eclipsed in importance by adverse interactions with other substances. All herbaceuticals exerting a psychotropic effect can have adverse interactions with other herbaceuticals or with other drugs the client may be taking. In one study, 19% of the people who reported taking herbaceuticals also reported an adverse reaction to them (Hailemaskel, Dutta, & Wutoh, 2001). Concern over adverse interactions between herbaceuticals and drugs have been voiced by researchers in Europe (Izzo & Ernst, 2001; Kistorp & Laursen, 2002), the United States (Keller & Lemberg, 2001; Pies, 2000), Canada (Assalian, 2000; Gold, Tullis, & Frost-Pineda, 2001), Israel (Boniel & Dannon, 2001), and Lebanon (Dannawi, 2002). Note that the presence of interaction effects implies pharmacodynamic activity in St. John's wort.

Drug interactions peculiar to St. John's wort include lowering blood concentrations of other drugs (particularly anticoagulants and anti-inflammatory drugs for arthritis). St. John's wort combined with certain oral contraceptives (ethinylestradiol/desogestrel) has been correlated with intermenstrual bleeding (Izzo & Ernst, 2001). These interactions seem related to the effects St. John's wort has on the cytochrome P-450 enzyme system, the liver enzyme system responsible for metabolizing most drugs. St. John's wort, like many FDA-approved pharmaceuticals, appears to elevate these enzymes, making them more efficient at metabolizing other drugs (Bilia, Gallori, & Vincieri, 2002).

### Kava

The kava, or kava kava, shrub (*Piper methysticum*) is native to Polynesia and the Pacific Islands. It has been used there for millennia, primarily in liquid form made by grinding the dried rhizome (underground stem) and mixing with water and coconut milk. Captain James Cook and other European explorers in the 18th century described kava as having a calming effect. The crude drug can be derived from the rhizome, but now most formulations are made as ethanol-water or acetone extracts. Traditionally, kava is used socially similar to the way we use alcohol. At high doses kava, like alcohol, can cause intoxication.

### Mechanism of Action

Kava is one of the few herbal treatments where the active ingredient is known. Meyer (1967) proved that the effects of kava were due to kavapyrones. These act as muscle relaxants and anticonvulsants, and they reduce excitability in the limbic system. They do so by inhibiting voltage-dependent sodium channels, increasing the number of GABA-A receptors, blocking NE reuptake, and suppressing release of glutamate (which metabolizes into glutamic acid, which, recall from Chapter Two, serves an excitatory function).

### Efficacy of Kava as an Anxiolytic

Three double-blind, placebo-controlled studies support the use of kava as an anxiolytic (Warnecke, 1991; Kinzler et al., 1991; Volz, 1997). The only problem with these studies is that the patient population was not clearly defined by diagnosis. Two studies exist researching the effects of kava on symptoms of Generalized Anxiety Disorder (GAD). The first study (Wheatley, 2001) compared two doses of kava in patients suffering from GAD. Both dose schedules (120 mg once daily and 45 mg three times daily) were found effective. In the second, although overall differences from placebo were not significant, the authors felt the improvement warranted further investigation (Connor & Davidson, 2002). More recently, Rex, Morgenstern, and Fink (2002) compared kava with diazepam (Valium) used on rats using a maze test. These authors concluded that the kava exerted an anxiolytic response in the rats similar to that induced by diazepam. They felt the study supported the use of kava as an anxiolytic.

### Side Effects and Adverse Reactions

Although the few studies that exist note minimal side effects, there are some reports of rash, tiredness

(Leak, 1999), and a rare occurrence of nausea (Wheatley, 1997). Although initial studies (few in number) seem to indicate kava is well tolerated, more research is needed to draw conclusions. The risk of adverse reactions for kava includes the possibility that it induces tolerance and dependence (Mischoulon, 2002), and there has been at least one report of acute liver failure tied to kava use (Brauer, Stangl, Siewert, Pfab, & Becker, 2003). Clearly, kava should not be mixed with other CNS depressants (Julien, 2001).

## Ginkgo Biloba

The *Ginkgo biloba* tree is native to East Asia. Gingkos were first imported to Europe from Japan during the 18th century and now are common ornamental trees throughout Europe and North America. According to Wong, Smith, and Boon (1998), they are among the oldest species of deciduous trees on the planet. Ginkgo fruit and seeds have been used in China for medicinal purposes for millennia. Ginkgo has been used to treat people with asthma, and leaves are used to dress wounds. Currently most ginkgo products are derived from the dried leaves (the therapeutic extracts are labeled Egb 761 and LI 1370).

### Mechanisms of Action

Gingko, like other herbs, contains a large number of substances that have been demonstrated to have a wide variety of pharmacologic properties. As with most herbs discussed so far, ginkgo has a wide variety of active ingredients we are only just learning about. A primary active ingredient seems to be flavonoids. Flavonoids are compounds found in numerous plants, and ingesting them is associated with decreased risk of several chronic diseases (Knekt et al., 2002). Flavonoids are effective antioxidants that decrease free radicals in the body. Free radicals are reactive chemicals that attack molecules by capturing electrons from the molecules and then modifying their chemical structure. Free radicals are believed to be one cause of Alzheimer's-type dementia. This connection provides a rationale for testing ginkgo on people suffering from Alzheimer's disease. If ginkgo has flavonoids that decrease the free radicals causing the damage to neurons, researchers hope their administration may slow the disease. Ginkgo leaves are harvested in May when the flavonoid content is highest.

Compounds called *ginkgolides* are another active ingredient in ginkgo. Researchers think ginkgolides inhibit platelet-activating factor. This effect may play a role in patients with vascular dementias, using the same mechanism as aspirin in forestalling additional strokes. It is also related to some of the adverse effects of ginkgo such as prolonged bleeding after chronic administration.

### Efficacy of Ginkgo

So how well does ginkgo work with people suffering from Alzheimer's-type dementia? After several false starts and years of studies, it appears ginkgo does not have efficacy for treating this disorder, as once believed. More than 40 controlled studies were initially conducted in Europe testing ginkgo efficacy for treating dementia. Although these studies seemed to show positive effects, the patient populations were poorly defined, the numbers were small, the randomization poorly done, and the outcome measures were not standard (Kleijnen & Knipschild, 1992).

The LeBars study in 1997 corrected many of these shortcomings. This 52-week, randomized, double-blind, placebo-controlled study was done with 202 patients, who were diagnosed with either Alzheimer's disease (236) or vascular dementia (73). The patients were 45 to 90 years of age. Outcome measures included the Alzheimer's Disease Assessment Scale, Cognitive subscale (ADAS-Cog); the Geriatric Evaluation by Relatives Rating Instrument (GERRI); and the Clinical Global Impression of Change (CGIC).

On average the ADAS-Cog and the GERRI showed significantly less decline in the ginkgo extract group than in the placebo. This difference was equivalent to a 6-month delay in progression of the disease. The results were comparable to the effects of 80 to 120 mg of Cognex (tacrine), a drug used to delay progression of Alzheimer's Disease. Although statistically significant, the results of the LeBars study were actually modest. In a later paper, LeBars and Kastelan (2000) noted that ginkgo is more likely to appear efficacious on broad dependent measures as opposed to more narrow cognitive assessments. Other studies using such narrow assessments do not find any significant differences between patients on

ginkgo and those on placebo (Soloman, Adams, Silver, Zimmer, & DeVeaux, 2002). The evidence to date seems to show that the effects of ginkgo on cognition are minimal (Sommer & Schatzberg, 2002).

### Valerian Root

Valerian root is another herb commonly prescribed in Europe. Valerian is a flowering perennial plant that grows in temperate climates worldwide. The root is believed to be a mild sedative/anxiolytic, although results of research have been conflicting. Valerian is on Germany's list of approved herbs, and supplements can be purchased in various formulations. For thousands of years the Greeks, Chinese, and the people of India used valerian as a mild sedative, and it is still used to flavor foods and beverages such as root beer. The rhizome and roots are harvested, dried, and served as tea or used to make an extract.

### Mechanisms of Action

Valerian extract contains over 100 different constituents. Researchers do not know which of these is or are responsible for its effects, although some believe valerian may have an effect on GABA receptors and act like a mild benzodiazepine (Julien, 2001). Others have hypothesized that valerian inhibits the enzymatic breakdown of GABA, thus producing its tranquilizing effects (Houghton, 1999).

### Efficacy of Valerian

In studies, 400 to 900 mg of valerian extract decreased sleep latency and nocturnal awakenings and improved subjective sleep quality. In some cases the beneficial effects were seen only after two to four weeks of therapy (Balderer & Bobely, 1985; Leathwood & Chauffard, 1982; Leathwood, Chauffard, Heck, & Munoz-Box, 1982). It appears valerian can produce an anxiolytic effect, although the degree of that effect relative to the dose is still debated (Leak, 1999).

### Side and Adverse Effects

The side effects of valerian have been reported to be headache, agitation, uneasiness, and possible liver toxicity (Yager, Siegfried, DiMatteo, 1999). Julien (2001) noted the possibility that valerian could interact with SSRI antidepressants and cause serotonin syndrome. Studies on reaction time, alertness, and concentration indicate that the effects of valerian do not impair these functions on the morning after taking a dose (Kuhlmann, Berger, Podzuweit, & Schmidt, 1999). More research is obviously needed, but at this point valerian may prove promising as a mild anxiolytic.

## Ephedrine

Ephedrine is a sympathomimetic alkaloid derived from any of several species of ephedra. The Asian species *E. sinica* typically has the highest concentration of ephedrine. Perhaps more than any other herbaceutical, ephedrine illustrates the dangers inherent in unregulated products that have powerful mechanisms of action. On February 17, 2003, major-league baseball player Steve Bechler, 23, collapsed and died from heatstroke during spring training. The coroner in Broward County, Florida, believed that Bechler's use of an ephedrine-containing weight loss product contributed to his death. This tragedy reignited the debate over whether products containing ephedrine should be sold as over-the-counter supplements (Fox, 2003). In 2004, the FDA banned the sale in the United States of products containing ephedrine (Parry, 2004).

You may recall from Chapter Nine that ephedrine is an alkaloid (organic, nitrogen-containing compounds) found in the ma huang plant (*Ephedra sinica*), which has been used in Chinese medicine for thousands of years. The primary active constituent of ephedra is ephedrine, which served as the organic model for the first synthesized amphetamine. Ephedrine gained widespread medical use in the United States in the 1920s as a nasal decongestant, CNS stimulant, and asthma treatment, but its use decreased because of safety concerns. Ephedrine reappeared as a dietary supplement to weight loss products sold as herbal supplements. Although ephedrine-containing products account for less than 1% of herbaceuticals purchased, they are responsible for 64% of the adverse effects reported (Bent, Tiedt, Odden, & Shlipak, 2003).

### Mechanisms of Action

Ephedrine is a psychostimulant that exerts its effects by releasing epinephrine, norepinephrine, and dopamine. It resembles amphetamine, although it has a much shorter half-life. Ephedrine has been shown to have pharmacodynamics similar to those of amphetamine (Angrist, Rotrosen, Kleinberg, Merriam, & Gershon, 1977; Ercil & France, 2003; Glennon & Young, 2000). Ephedrine is categorized as a sympathicomimetic agent, because it mimics the sympathetic nervous system. Recall from Chapter Two that the sympathetic nervous system prepares the body's fight–flight-freeze response. Ephedrine stimulates the cardiovascular system and dilates the bronchial tubes (hence its use in treating asthma attacks) (van der Hooft & Stricher, 2002; Wooltorton & Sibbald, 2002). These effects also seem to be responsible for its appetite-suppressing qualities.

### Adverse Effects

The primary adverse effects include stroke, heart attacks, cardiac arrhythmias, and seizures—all potential adverse effects seen in amphetamines as well (Geiger, 2002; Kaberi-Otarod, Conetta, Kundo, & Farkash, 2002; van der Hooft & Stricher, 2002; Wooltorton & Sibbald, 2002). In addition to these adverse effects, there have also been reports of ephedrine-induced mania (Capwell, 1995), psychosis (Jacobs & Hirsch, 2000), and dependence (Gruber & Pope, 1998).

In the wake of the deaths from adverse effects, the FDA heeded Julien's (2001) call to treat ephedrine as a potent psychostimulant to be regulated. Although the Dietary Supplements Health and Education Act of 1994 prohibits regulation of dietary supplements, the FDA may regulate if a supplement poses a significant or unreasonable risk of injury or illness. Given this authority, the FDA called for stricter regulations in 1997 (Maradino, 1997) and then banned ephedrine in 2003. A federal court upheld this decision in 2004 (Parry, 2004).

From an Integral perspective, regulation promises only a partial solution. Far less socially and individually dangerous drugs (such as cannabis) are completely prohibited in the United States, but people who want them find a way to get them. Thus regulation may not solve the problem and may in fact increase the problem, adding immeasurably to the social damage surrounding its use. Many users of ephedrine-containing products seem to be athletes, and many are adolescents. From the intrapsychic perspective of the Integral Model these users report feeling that using the supplement gives them a "competitive edge" or brings them closer to an internalized ideal of thinness. Further, from the cultural perspective, subcultures can easily develop in groups of adolescent athletes where taking supplements becomes a norm, and this norm in turn increases use of supplements and the attendant risks. In one large-scale study, researchers found that trainers had a significant influence on the attitudes and subjective norms of adolescent athletes and the researchers proposed ways to encourage attitudes that discouraged supplement use (Dunn, Eddy, Wang, Nagy, Perko, & Bartee, 2001).

## Other Herbaceuticals

### *Passion Flower and Hops*

Both passion flower and hops are purported to have sedative/anxiolytic properties, but there are little scientific data on either. Passion flower is a climbing vine native to North America. It has fallen into disuse in this country but is still one of the most common herbal hypnotics in Great Britain. Components of its extract appear to bind to GABA receptors.

Hops are the fruit of the hop plant, a vine native to Europe. Although used primarily for making beer, hops have been used as a tonic for over 1000 years. Their use as a sleeping aid resulted from the observation that hop pickers tired easily, possibly due to the transfer of hop resin from hands to mouth. Studies have not confirmed that hop resin, hop extract, or lipophilic hop concentrates have a sedative effect. There do not appear to be sufficient data to support its use as a sleep aid.

### *Melatonin*

Melatonin is a hormone produced by the pineal gland. It binds to the suprachiasmic nucleus (SCN), which is the body's circadian pace maker or internal clock. The SCN normally produces an alerting signal that researchers think is blunted by melatonin. Melatonin is useful in initiating sleep but not really helpful in maintaining sleep, because there may be a rebound in the SCN, causing wakefulness three to four hours after taking the melatonin. Various doses are used (1 to 100 mg), and anything over 5 mg raises the melatonin in the blood to levels higher than normal. The melatonin in health food stores is labeled to range between 1 to 5 mg, but the actual range is much more variable.

## An Integral View of Marijuana: Out of the Frying Pan

Although marijuana is not a licit herbaceutical in the United States, many people around the world still use it for everything from medical purposes, to enhancing sexual experience and well-being, to "finding God"—that is, as an entheogen. We have included this section for two reasons. First, I (Ingersoll) have taught dozens of courses and seminars on psychopharmacology, and in most of them students have questions about marijuana, its efficacy for medical use, and its actual dangers. Although it is not popular to say, many of these students are skeptical about the government media campaign against marijuana use and want to know where to find reliable information. The second reason we have included this section is because it illustrates the Integral Model's capacity to capture the complexity of a topic, revealing the partial truths while also providing a critical view of the issues.

### A Brief History of Marijuana Use

There is something profoundly frightening to the orthodoxies of higher civilization about the shamanistically originated vision quest with drugs. (Wilson, 1993, p. 164)

Marijuana is an ancient drug that apparently has been used since prehistoric times. It is a product of the hemp plant (*Cannabis sativa*, Latin for "planted hemp"), a species that provides a useful fiber, an edible seed, oil, and a medicine (Weil & Rosen, 1993). Until recent times it has been an important cultivated crop. As recently as 1943, farmers were paid to grow hemp; "Hemp for victory" was one of the industrial catch-phrases of World War II. This was industrial hemp, not cultivated for its psychoactive properties, but marijuana was being used recreationally in society at the time.

Marijuana is derived from the flowers and the tops of the leaves from male and female plants.

Cannabis will grow almost anywhere, given adequate water and drainage. *Cannabis sativa* produces a sticky, yellowish resin, which seems to have evolved as a defense mechanism to protect itself from harmful predators. This resin contains the primary psychoactive ingredients of marijuana.

Cannabis is one of the few plants that legend says was not discovered by animals. Typically humans seem to have learned which plants were safe for ingestion by watching animals eat them (and not fall over dead!). According to an Arab legend, in 1155 C. E. Haydar, an ascetic monk who founded an order of Sufis, discovered the plant dancing in the heat of a summer day (Siegel, 1989). Haydar mixed the plant with wine and found the drink made him laugh—little wonder. Medieval Muslim society disapproved of Haydar's discovery, but alas, the proverbial "cat" was out of the bag. The Sufis became heretics in Arab society, but the world was introduced to one of the most versatile and hotly debated plants; after all, how many plants have "wars" declared on them? As Julien (2001) points out, a great deal of emotionalism surrounds marijuana today. Most of the debate does not even ask the most important questions, which we explore through the different perspectives of the Integral Model.

Although we will never know if humans discovered the *Cannabis sativa* plant first, we do know many birds love marijuana seeds, which are rich in protein. For hundreds of years bird breeders have referred to marijuana seeds as "pigeon candy" and noted that birds fed on these seeds border on erotomanic behavior. This is not entirely surprising, because the seeds, and other parts of the plant, have been considered aphrodisiac at least since ancient Roman and Greek times (Grinspoon & Bakalar, 1997; Siegel, 1989). B. F. Skinner's famous pigeons, which played such a pivotal role in putting operant conditioning on the map, were fed a mixture that contained 10% hemp seeds. As Siegel (1989) wrote, people may never know "to what extent the foundations of Skinnerian psychology were made under the influence" (p. 155).

## A Medical Model Perspective on Marijuana

From the medical model perspective, what do scientists know about marijuana? We begin by reviewing the active ingredients and their mechanisms of action. Obviously, like other herbaceuticals discussed in this chapter, cannabis varies a great deal in potency depending on the conditions under which it is grown and on the sex of the plant (Schwartz, 1987).

### Delta-9-Tetrahydrocannabinol

The *Cannabis sativa* plant contains over 400 chemical agents, including over 60 cannabinoids. In 1964 researchers determined delta-9-tetrahydrocannabinol (THC) to be the primary psychoactive ingredient in marijuana. It took another 20 years to determine that THC acted on a specific set of receptors in the brain called *cannabinoid receptors.* Two of these receptors have been discovered and are localized in the brain as well as throughout the body, particularly in the immune system (Herkenham, Little, Johnson, Melvin, deCosta, & Rice, 1990; Matsuda, Lolait, Brownstein, Young, & Bonner, 1990). Cannabinoid receptors are located in the cortex, motor system, limbic system, and hippocampus. This appears to explain some of THC's effects on cognition, motor coordination, memory, and mood. Researchers have further determined that humans produce the equivalent of endogenous cannabinoids, which act on these receptors and appear to play a natural role in pain regulation, control of movement, cognition, memory (Watson, Benson, & Joy, 2000) and possibly as anti-inflammatory agents (Zurier, 2004).

Cannabinoid receptors exist primarily on presynaptic neurons and seem to inhibit the flow of calcium ions and facilitate the influx of potassium ions (Felder & Glass, 1998). Julien (2001) concludes that with these mechanisms, cannabinoid receptors inhibit the release of other neurotransmitters from presynaptic neurons, and this inhibition likely causes THC's psychoactive effects. Some researchers hypothesize that cannabis is also related to dopamine release in the brain's pleasure centers (Voruganti, Slomka, Zabel, Mattar, & Awad, 2001). Watson, Benson, and Joy (2000) point out that scientists are just beginning to understand cannabinoid receptors and the different endogenous and exogenous cannabinoid compounds that may affect them. These authors point out that research on these compounds should not be restricted to THC proper, because a number of cannabinoids may have utility for a variety of uses.

## *Physiological Effects of THC*

Being highly fat soluble, THC quickly enters the central nervous system. Heart rate and blood pressure both increase, and skin temperature falls. The drug calms aggressive behavior in animals, and further research is needed to determine whether this effect is also consistent in humans. Although the subjective high (which we later discuss from the intrapsychic perspective) lasts up to 12 hours, THC is metabolized slowly and can persist in the body for up to two weeks. Although this slow metabolism can lead to a reverse tolerance syndrome when the user becomes more sensitive to the drug, it also minimizes physical tolerance and dependence on THC. The only studies suggesting that marijuana is highly "addictive" (De Fonseca, Carrera, Navarro, Koob, & Weiss, 1997; Gianluigi, Pontieri, & Chiara, 1997) had three serious flaws. First, they used animal models, and results from such studies do not necessarily generalize across species. Second, the researchers disabled this natural process for the slow metabolism of the THC, creating an artificial reaction in the bodies of the lab animals. And third, the researchers did not even use THC but a synthetic compound (HU-210) believed similar to THC. Even these researchers, who seemed biased toward equating marijuana with heroin, admitted that probably only 9% of marijuana users would meet the criteria for dependence. These data were first summarized by Warner, Kessler, Hughes, Anthony, and Nelson (1995), who noted that 9% of the people who ever tried marijuana would develop dependence on it. This question of the dependence-inducing potential of cannabis requires further comment.

## The Issue of Cannabis Dependence and Withdrawal

Although it is fashionable to use the word *addiction*, we find the word emotionally loaded and poorly operationalized, and used more to generate emotionalism than to explore a phenomenon rationally. Generally it is thought bad to be "addicted" to

something. Although *Webster's Unabridged Dictionary* (1989) defines addiction as having yielded to something that is habit forming, such as narcotics, the colloquial understanding seems to be any compulsive need to take a substance or engage in a behavior. However, as pointed out in Chapter Five, if addiction is defined as (1) tolerance to repeated administrations of a drug and (2) withdrawal on discontinuation, then we must conclude that SSRI antidepressants as well as benzodiazepines cause "addiction." These examples illustrate why we prefer to use words such as *tolerance* and *dependence*. Tolerance and dependence are more easily operationalized and explored using the scientific method. As in Chapter Five, dependence here is defined as a physical tolerance produced by repeated administration of a drug and a concomitant withdrawal syndrome (Stahl, 2000) or as a change in physiology or behavior after stopping a drug (Julien, 2001).

In surveys of which drugs are the most and least dependence inducing, marijuana is consistently found to be one of the least dependence inducing (Franklin, 1990). Although some marijuana users develop dependence, most do not (Anthony, Warner, & Kessler, 1994; Watson, Benson, & Joy, 2000). As noted earlier, the pharmacokinetics of cannabis cause it to be stored in the fat cells of the body and then slowly released over a relatively long period (long for a drug, that is). It is interesting that although advocates of marijuana prohibition downplay this mechanism, a similar mechanism in methylphenidate is described with enthusiasm as making it less likely that children on methylphenidate will become dependent on it (Volkow et al, 1995). Mechanisms that allow for slow metabolism seem to decrease the probability of physical dependence for compounds they operate in. Those rules apply regardless of whether the substance in question curries political favor. Heavy use of marijuana, like the heavy use of many substances, can, on stopping, result in mild withdrawal in symptoms such as sleeplessness and restlessness. One such study gave participants oral dosages of 180 to 210 mg of THC (the equivalent of THC that would be smoked in approximately four to eight marijuana cigarettes when less than one cigarette would be closer to what is generally used). Mild withdrawals followed discontinuation of these heavy doses (Jones, Benowitz, & Bachman, 1976). In a minority of chronic users (for example, those who smoked marijuana every day for years), withdrawal can include mental cloudiness, irritability, cramping, nausea, and aggression (Gold, Tullis, & Frost-Pineda, 2001; Watson, Benson, & Joy, 2000). When these effects occur, they are said to be short-lived (Hancy, Ward, Comer, Foltin, & Fischman, 1999).

Researchers have not been able to determine how much of this dependence is physiological and how much is psychological, although both types are likely involved. Psychological dependence is a state in which a person believes he or she cannot get through the day without a particular substance or activity. Researchers do know that, as with antidepressants, chronic cannabis exposure causes downregulation of cannabinoid receptors (Abood & Martin, 1992), which can be thought of as a type of physical tolerance. Recent studies on dependence and withdrawal seem consistent with what we have reported here. In a recent review of the literature, Smith (2002) concluded that studies to date do not provide strong evidence for the existence of a cannabis withdrawal syndrome similar to that with other drugs of abuse such as opioids. Research should continue in this area, and researchers should take care to preclude contaminating studies with political agendas.

Note that other characteristics are found in chronic and/or heavy users of marijuana, characteristics not likely to be found in moderate users. This group of heavy users includes people with Anti-Social Personality Disorder and Conduct Disorder (Watson, Benson, & Joy, 2000). Some studies indicate that these characteristics, and the sequence of drug use, are better predictors of who will become dependent on any given substance than is the use of the substance alone (Eldredge, 1998; Morral, McCaffrey, & Paddock, 2002).

## Is Cannabis a "Gateway" Drug?

Another interesting debate regarding cannabis is whether or not it is a gateway drug similar to alcohol and cigarettes. This gateway theory (also called the *stepping-stone theory*) has yet to be soundly supported (Watson, Benson, & Joy, 2000). The theory basically is that using drugs such as alcohol, tobacco, and marijuana lead to the use of "harder" drugs such as cocaine and heroin. This notion mistakes correlation for causation. It is like noting that most people with pilot's licenses had driver's licenses first and then concluding that getting a driver's license somehow caused such people to get a pilot's license. In the same way, we could make the argument that diapers are "gateway pants."

Proponents of the gateway theory resort to unconvincing logical maneuvers to make their case. While defending the gateway theory from this criticism, Clayton and Leukefeld (1992) wrote, "We often act or react in our professional and personal lives according to observed correlations without solid and irrefutable evidence that two phenomena are causally related . . . shouldn't we do the same with this information on smoking and other drug use?" Our short answer is no. If correlation is enough to pass as causation, then proponents of the gateway theory must account for other correlations. For example, why is it that where cannabis use carries no criminal penalties and is more available (such as in the Netherlands), there is a decreased tendency for people to use harder drugs (Korf, 2002; Model, 1993)? Further, proponents of the gateway theory would have to explain why Dutch studies note that the availability of cannabis has no relationship with heroin use or even with whether people continue to use cannabis (Sifaneck, 1995). The most recent report on the gateway theory, by the think tank Rand Drug Policy Research Center (Morral, McCaffrey, & Paddock, 2002), concludes there are other plausible explanations for hard drug use beside the gateway theory. For these researchers, it is not marijuana but individual propensities to use drugs that determine a person's risk of initiating hard drug use. Further, the researchers propose that the current prohibition policies that rely so heavily on the gateway theory are unnecessarily burdensome to society particularly in filling the courts and prisons with perpetrators of the victimless crime of marijuana possession.

It may be more helpful to examine patterns of drug use in heavy users, who are more at risk to develop dependence on marijuana or other drugs. One study that examined the sequence of drug use among serious users (Mackesy-Amiti, Fendrich, & Goldstein, 1997) found that progression of use in these users did not follow the standard gateway theory progression (alcohol, then marijuana, then harder illicit drugs). Rather, they found that many were more likely to use marijuana before alcohol and even harder drugs before marijuana. Their findings suggest that youths who are most at risk for serious drug use may be less likely to follow the sequence predicted by the gateway theory.

## Proposed Medical Uses for Cannabis

Excellent reviews of the medicinal potential of cannabis are provided by Clark (2000); Gurley, Aranow, and Katz (1998); Mathre (1997); and Watson, Benson, and Joy (2000). Unless elsewhere noted, the following material is drawn from these sources. We noted earlier that cannabinoid receptors seem involved in analgesia (pain relief), and much evidence supports the use of cannabis for pain relief (Williamson & Evans, 2000). Evidence from studies on animals and humans indicates that cannabis can provide significant pain relief. On a related note, cannabinoids seem to treat migraine headaches as well, because they maintain vasoconstriction (constriction of blood vessels). Patients with chronic pain are much less likely to develop dependence on cannabis than on a regimen of opioids. Cannabis also has efficacy as an antiemetic (antinausea) drug for patients undergoing chemotherapy and for patients suffering from wasting syndrome associated with AIDS. Researchers have also found that oncologists' attitudes toward medical marijuana are far more favorable than regulatory authorities have believed (Doblin & Kleinman, 1991). Although research in this area is relatively new, taking cannabis to reduce nausea and encourage appetite as well as to reduce pain are well-established uses. We discuss the subjective "high" produced by THC in discussing the intrapsychic perspective.

In addition to treating pain and nausea, medical marijuana may show efficacy in treating spasticity and movement disorders associated with spinal cord injuries, basal ganglia dysfunction, and multiple sclerosis. More data are needed to assess these claims however. Although many people have heard of medical marijuana in association with the treatment of glaucoma, it is not as efficacious as other therapies. Although cannabis does decrease intraocular pressure, the effects are short-lived and require high doses.

Finally, a line of research examines whether cannabinoids may act in the brain as neuroprotective agents. These agents would preclude or slow down a neurodegenerative disease such as Parkinson's disease or Alzheimer's disease. Hampson, Grimaldi, Lolic, Wink, Rosenthal, and Axelrod (2000) examined this property of cannabinoids in rats and found that cannabidiol (a type of cannabinoid) was superior to other agents tested in preventing glutamate toxicity. In addition, both marijuana and synthesized cannabinoids have efficacy to protect the brain from neurotoxic responses after head injury or stroke (Nagayama et al., 1999). Again, regardless of what happens with marijuana as an herbaceutical, such lines of research hold promise for the development of neuroprotective pharmaceuticals.

## Adverse Effects

What are the adverse effects of marijuana? First, it is not a drug that can be taken in lethal quantities, and no fatalities from marijuana are recorded. This is likely because there are no cannabinoid receptors in the brain stem or other parts of the brain controlling vital functions. There are adverse effects that should be considered; however, they are no more severe than any adverse effects for many of the prescription psychotropic medications we have discussed thus far if the drug is not taken by smoking. Table 10.5 summarizes categories of adverse effects of marijuana that we have evidence to support.

**TABLE 10.5** Adverse Effects of Marijuana

Respiratory problems related to smoking the drug

Cardiovascular side effects

Psychiatric side effects

Drug interactions

Infection from contaminated crop

Impairment of motor skills

Problems in pregnancy

## Respiratory Problems

If marijuana is smoked, the user has an increased probability of respiratory problems associated with smoking. As noted earlier, the tar content of marijuana cigarettes is significantly higher than that of tobacco cigarettes. In addition to tar, smoke from the cigarette is likely to cause airway irritation and inflammation in users. The degree of the problem stems from the combination of the user's susceptibility, amount used, and frequency of use (Roth, Arora, Barsky, Kleerup, Simmons, & Tashkin, 1998; Tashkin, 1999). These effects can be totally avoided by ingesting marijuana baked in foods, unless the person taking it is so nauseous that he or she cannot keep any food down at all. In that case, some of the substance can be smoked and then once nausea subsides, more can be ingested.

## Cardiovascular Side Effects

Marijuana is associated with a number of cardiovascular effects that can be significant (El-Mallakh, 1987). Users can suffer from pronounced tachycardia, with an increase in heart rate of up to 50%. Users may also have transient hypertension. Although this hypertension is usually tolerated well in young users, it should be closely monitored in older users. One implication of this side effect is its propensity to lead the user to suffer panic and anxiety (Gurley, Aranow, & Katz, 1998). This is further discussed under psychiatric effects.

## Psychiatric Effects

One of the most important factors in using psychoactive substances is referred to as "set and setting." *Set* refers to the psychological makeup and mind set of the user, and *setting* to the environment in which the psychoactive substance is to be used (Smith, 2000). Set and the human response to setting are two things that make it difficult to generalize from animal to human models. Some individuals' mind set and psychological makeup make them poor candidates for using particular psychoactive substances. These individuals are more prone to anxiety and panic under the influence of marijuana. Anxiety and panic can be a function of the setting as well.

Although cognitive effects are experienced during the high after smoking marijuana, studies thus far have found no long-term effects on intelligence (Fried et al., 2002). There have been reports of marijuana triggering or exacerbating psychotic symptoms in people predisposed to such symptoms (Johns, 2001; Shufman & Witztum, 2000), but not in those who are at not at risk for developing psychotic symptoms.

## Drug Interactions

Users of cannabis need to know it can have interactions with other drugs related to decreased intestinal motility (movement) and decreased stomach acid. Prescription use would need to take each of these effects into consideration. As with other herbaceuticals, to preclude any problematic interactions standard dosage and potency would have to be set.

## Infection From Contaminated Crop

The adverse effect of infection from a contaminated crop is largely encouraged by the prohibition of marijuana and could be practically eliminated were the drug grown and processed under regulation. Marijuana can be contaminated with organisms, including fungal species found in the fecal matter of animals. Outbreaks of both hepatitis B and salmonella have been linked to contaminated marijuana (Gurley, Aranow, & Katz, 1998). Contaminated crop effects also include chemical contamination such as that from the U.S. government supporting the spraying of marijuana crops with dipyridylium (Paraquat), which is designed to sicken consumers (Duke & Gross, 1993; Miron, 2004).

## Impairment of Motor Skills

Marijuana clearly impairs motor skills and reaction time (Ashton, 2001). The drug causes temporary impairment in perception, coordination, reaction time, and time perception (Sugrue et al., 1995). Users under the influence should not drive cars or operate other similarly dangerous machinery. Irresponsible behavior is a risk factor for automobile accidents and injuries.

## Problems in Pregnancy

Marijuana use in pregnancy has been correlated with impaired fetal growth and shortened gestation (Zuckerman et al., 1989). Researchers believe that pregnant women underreport marijuana use but that these same women are likely to be polysubstance users.

The notion of medical marijuana raises the same problems inherent in the use of any herb. Problems of dosage, potency, plant gender, type, and so forth all need to be subjected to regulatory scrutiny. As with many other compounds, perhaps the simplest solution is to synthesize the cannabinoid, as has been done with dronabinol (Marinol). The biggest problem with dronabinol for people with severe nausea has been its oral formulation. This problem is being addressed in the United Kingdom, where GW Pharmaceuticals has developed and is currently testing a cannabis spray that is showing efficacy for chronic pain (Hoge, 2002).

## Marijuana From the Intrapsychic Perspective

Examining the evidence from the medical model perspective does not really begin to capture the complexity of the experience of marijuana use. Clearly, people do not smoke marijuana to cause respiratory distress, increased heart rate, and temporarily impaired motor skills. Why do so many people around the world, some legally and others illegally, use marijuana? There is not as much research on this question as on the medical uses of marijuana, and the answer is usually a form of word magic referring to "addiction," when in fact, as noted, only a minority of marijuana users develop dependence on it. Many people smoke or ingest marijuana because they enjoy its euphorant effect. Some who use it for medical purposes also report this. Does this effect make marijuana an attractive drug of abuse? Yes, but several abusable, recreational drugs in our society are licit. Although prohibitionists argue that legalizing even medical marijuana will lead to more abuse of the drug, these fears have not been confirmed in societies more tolerant of cannabis use, and prohibitionist arguments in general have no support if their goal is to decrease drug consumption.

Many government officials would support medical use if the "high" could be taken out of it. This is a curious statement, given the drug's low potential for dependence—clearly much lower than legal drugs such as nicotine, caffeine, and alcohol. What is wrong with responsible enjoyment of the high

that comes from smoking or ingesting marijuana? For that matter, anyone who has ever been on an oncology ward and listened to the suffering and retching of patients receiving chemotherapy would agree that if these people could enjoy a temporary drug-induced euphoria, why not let them? Certainly recreational use differs from medical marijuana use, although many see medical marijuana as the first step toward legalization (Crites-Leoni, 1998). However, the subjective reports of recreational users are an important component of an Integral analysis.

Perhaps the most thorough research on this topic was done by psychologist Charles Tart (1971/2000). His psychological study of marijuana intoxication is perhaps the best available. Current legal restrictions on research have precluded psychological studies on the drug, and researchers today rarely ask the question of what people enjoy so much about marijuana. From an Integral perspective this is an important question, though. First, note that not everybody enjoys the experience of being under the influence of marijuana. This section merely raises the question, For those who do enjoy it, should the drug continue to be prohibited? Tart has noted that the effects of the drug are variable and can be divided into three types: pure, potential, and placebo. Pure effects are almost always manifested regardless of set and setting (for example, alertness produced by amphetamine). Potential effects do not manifest unless numerous nondrug variables are in place related to set and setting. Placebo effects are brought on almost entirely by nondrug effects. The interesting thing about an Integral view of marijuana is that the medical model perspective describes pure effects, whereas potential effects relate more to the intrapsychic perspective.

Although medical users of marijuana experience relief from troubling symptoms, they also experience many of the things reported by Tart's participants. Following are just some of the reinforcing experiences these users associated with marijuana.

### Changes in the Senses

Visually, users reported increased perceptual organization described as meaningful in terms of patterns, designs, and forms not perceived when not under the influence of marijuana. Users reported perceiving more subtle shades of colors and an enhanced visual depth. Commonly users report a sensual quality to vision while under the influence of marijuana. Although visual illusions or hallucinations are infrequent, they did occur occasionally.

In terms of auditory effects, several of Tart's participants reported subtle changes in sound as well as more acuity with regard to sounds. Other users report what would be akin to a three-dimensional sound space that for them took on a beautiful, indescribable quality. Other users reported synesthesias, "the experience of another sensory modality than the one actually stimulating the person" (Tart, 1971/2000, p. 74). An example of a synesthesia is "seeing sound" or "feeling a smell."

Enhancement of the sense of touch seems to be related to marijuana's purported sexual enhancement effects (Lewis, 1973; McGlothlin & West, 1968; Wilson, 1993). As the author Norman Mailer is reputed to have said, "sex with pot is better than sex without pot" (in Wilson, 1993). Although many users felt less sexual drive under the influence of marijuana, others reported more attunement to their own body and to the body of their partner. They also noted that orgasm had new pleasurable qualities. Many participants in Tart's study felt they were better lovers under the influence of marijuana because they were less inhibited and more arousable, gentler and more giving, experienced prolonged duration of lovemaking, (for males) had longer-lasting erections, and were more in the present moment with the other. This ability to be in the present moment was interpreted as a deepening of intimacy.

Finally, subjective entheogenic experiences are associated with marijuana. Recall that an entheogen is a substance that supposedly accelerates or in some cases initiates experiences described as mystical or divine. As Smith (2000) noted, true mystical experiences must be incorporated into daily living, including mundane, sober daily consciousness. Altered states must transform into altered traits. Although entheogens are not a substitute for a spiritual practice, they may enhance a spiritual practice. Although marijuana is not as powerful an entheogen as a substance such as psilocybin, some users report spiritual experiences while under the influ-

ence. In Tart's study, users reported feeling in touch with the divine or more in touch with a spiritual perspective. Several users felt they meditated more effectively under the influence, and 33% of participants felt they had powerful religious experiences under the influence of marijuana, experiences that had long-term effects on them.

## Marijuana From the Cultural Perspective

Marijuana has enjoyed popularity with different groups at different times in different societies. Herer (1992) noted that from approximately the 27th to the 7th century B.C.E. cannabis was incorporated into most cultures of the Middle East, Asia Minor, India, China, Japan, and Europe for uses ranging from the utilitarian to the recreational. We have already mentioned its rejection in 12th-century Muslim society, with the exception of Sufis. It was popular in 19th-century Europe, where in Paris intellectuals would gather with French doctor Jacques Moreau, who was studying the subjective effects of THC. Siegel (1989) has noted that human beings seem to manifest a fourth drive (in addition to hunger, thirst, and sex), seeking mind-altering or intoxicating states. Culture plays a large role in how this drive is going to be channeled. In U.S. society, many people are moderate users of alcohol. Most alcohol users do not drive under the influence, and they do not drink more than is good for them or enough to interfere with their obligations. Although this majority is not studied extensively, what is so different about someone who uses marijuana moderately in the same manner? In tolerating cannabis use, Dutch society has had none of the problems feared by prohibitionists in the United States. Given the lack of evidence for the effectiveness of prohibition, both the United Kingdom and Canada are considering minimizing criminal penalties for possession and use of marijuana (Senate Special Committee on Illegal Drugs, 2002; Reuters Medical News, 2001).

Wilson (1993) and Eldredege (1998) have pointed out that in the United States the "war on drugs" has racist overtones. Marijuana smoking was strongly associated with Mexican immigrants during World War I. It is from this group that the slang "Mary Jane" is derived, because this is the

Mexican-Spanish translation of *marijuana*. Drug laws in many cases are far harsher on users in lower socioeconomic income brackets, and the case could certainly be made that they become a useful measure of class control. For example, the penalties for possessing crack cocaine (derived from powder cocaine) are harsher than those for possessing powder cocaine (the parent compound of crack cocaine). Advocates of drug law reform note that users of powder cocaine are far more likely to be Caucasian and users of crack, to be African-American. In addition, marijuana has been linked in the minds of many with countercultural movements that challenged authority during the Vietnam War era. The phrase "war on drugs" was coined by then-President Richard Nixon. The Carter administration was apparently considering legalization, but this was stopped by the Reagan administration, although prohibition has consistently been shown to be ineffective for both alcohol and marijuana. Some of the largest funders of the "war on drugs" are pharmaceutical companies. As commentator Ariana Huffington (2000) speculated, "It's not that they do not want us on drugs—they just want us on theirs" (p. 167). Pharmaceutical lobbies' influence on laws related to access to medical marijuana needs to be monitored.

Clearly U.S. culture has many issues to consider in relation to medical marijuana, and this review is a rough outline of just a few. Again, for medical purposes many problems could be overcome by allowing the prescription of synthetic cannabinoid inhalers, which would be treated like any other pharmaceutical with abuse potential (such as morphine).

From the cultural perspective, also consider that many groups use drugs (including marijuana) as an escape from a life that, in their opinion, is not worth living. This is one of the secrets (and fears) of American society: that its citizens may not find life worth living. If a majority of a society comes to this conclusion, they may decide they want to change the way the society is structured and this is a constant threat to those in power. Like it or not, we all must acknowledge that currently not all U.S. citizens have equal access to resources and many have little hope of attaining a decent standard of living.

Others, despite having material abundance, feel their lives have a meaningless quality. The promises of consumer culture leave them feeling empty. The question remains: If a government criminalizes the things its citizens use to relieve the pain of their daily existence, does it thus incur any responsibility to helping its citizens pursue other avenues toward happiness to decrease that pain?

### Social/Legal Perspectives on Marijuana

Perhaps the biggest social/legal issue is the current drug laws, which have been described as "draconian" in publications as diverse as libertarian treatises (McWilliams, 1993) to commentaries in medical journals (Kassirer, 1997). Table 10.6 lists the groups who have recommended decriminalization of marijuana for medicinal purposes.

The laws that exist to prosecute people involved in marijuana possession, cultivation, or trafficking include people who, under their own state laws, may be growing or distributing medical marijuana through state-approved medical marijuana clubs. The laws of 15 U.S. states require life sentences for certain nonviolent marijuana offenses. Under federal law the death penalty can be sought for growing or selling a large amount of marijuana, even for a first offense. The 1986 Drug Abuse Act increased

**TABLE 10.6**  Groups Supporting Medical Marijuana

American Bar Association

American Civil Liberties Union

American Public Health Association

National Nurses Society on Addiction

Conference of Episcopal Bishops

The People of the State of Arizona

The People of the State of California

The People of the State of Nevada

The People of the State of Oregon

The People of the State of Alaska

The People of the State of Washington

The People of the State of Canada

penalties for federal drug offenses and established mandatory minimum sentences, a move opposed by the American Bar Association and federal judges. The federal government can seize the property of "suspected drug traffickers" without even filing charges against them. For example, an entire farm can be seized if one marijuana plant is found on its grounds. Perhaps even more disturbing is a little known clause in the laws that allow informers to receive up to 25% of the assets seized in return for their testimony (Schlosser, 1997). The average time served in prison for a nonviolent drug offense is 5 years. Compare these penalties to the average penalty for kidnapping (4.5 years), assault (2 years), and sexual abuse (2.5 years) (McWilliams, 1993). Reviewing these averages, it is hard to avoid feeling as if we all were living in a surrealist novel. The laws passed to prohibit marijuana use appear far more dangerous than the drug itself.

## Conclusions

What does an Integral investigation of marijuana as an herbaceutical tell us? How do the partial truths revealed help us draw conclusions? First, the Integral model does illustrate the complexity of the situation far more effectively than parochial debates in disciplines that rarely converse with each other. It is imperative to discuss marijuana from the medical model, intrapsychic, cultural, and social perspectives. An Integral approach to an issue such as medical marijuana could inform politicians of problems with the federal laws as they are written, particularly if medical marijuana is to receive federal approval. The Integral approach to medical marijuana also demythologizes the subjective high experienced with marijuana use. The intrapsychic perspective requires us to hear the testimony of not just those in the minority whose use has led to personal or legal troubles, but from those who have had positive experiences using marijuana. This is an important complement to the information from the medical model perspective that, although useful, is incomplete. Perhaps the best way to end this section and this chapter is to cite Julien (2001), who noted that rational approaches can solve the dilemma of medical marijuana. He encourages the

federal government to adopt the recommendations of the 1999 report from the Institute of Medicine:

- Continue research into the effects of synthetic and plant-derived cannabinoids.
- Design and conduct clinical trials of cannabinoids for symptom management.
- Evaluate the psychological effects of cannabinoids and their therapeutic potential.
- Continue studying the health risks of smoked marijuana.
- Conduct clinical trials in short-term designs for patients with conditions thought to respond well to medical marijuana.
- Approve short-term use of smoked marijuana (less than six months) for patients with debilitating symptoms, who have not received relief from standard medications, who are treated under medical supervision, and in settings that use an institutional treatment review board.

Julien notes, "It is hoped that the federal government will move forward with support for research along these guidelines. . . . At a minimum, it is hoped that the institute's report will encourage the federal government to become involved in the well-designed experimentation of cannabinoid pharmacology and therapeutics" (pp. 324–325).

## Summary

Herbaceuticals are not FDA-regulated substances in the United States so are not considered medicines proper. They are, however, increasingly used as an alternative and complementary approach to healing, even though federal laws prohibit their being advertised as a cure for any disorder. Mistrust of traditional medicine, cultural beliefs, increasing numbers of proactive consumers, and a belief in the safety of "natural" products all seem to be contributing to the increased use of these substances. Currently research supports the efficacy of some compounds but not of others. It is important for mental health professionals to understand that just as they cannot make recommendations about psychotropic medications to clients, they should not recommend herbaceuticals either. They should, however, keep abreast of the literature on these substances, given their increasing use by consumers.

The herbaceutical with the best support for efficacy is St. John's wort, which is used to treat depression in Europe. Kava seems to be an effective anxiolytic as well. The literature on other substances such as ginkgo, valerian root, passion flower, hops, and melatonin is mixed but at this point does not seem to support their use as psychotropic agents. The most controversial substance in this chapter is marijuana. Although there appear to be some medical uses for it federal law still prohibits its use even if recommended by a physician. It is likely that the cultural and social issues (and the accompanying propaganda) will slow intelligent debate and discussion of both the proposed medical uses as well as the failure of prohibition.

## Study Questions and Exercises

1. What is the "don't ask, don't tell" syndrome related to herbaceuticals in the United States?
2. Discuss at least three reasons why people report preferring herbaceuticals to prescription medications. How would you counsel a client with this perspective who wanted to use St. John's wort rather than a prescription antidepressant?
3. What are some legal issues affecting the use of herbaceuticals in U.S. culture?
4. List and discuss some of the important differences between herbs and drugs.
5. What is the consensus of opinion on the efficacy of St. John's wort? Discuss one study that does *not* support its efficacy.
6. Discuss some of the dangers associated with ephedrine. How would you counsel a client who told you he or she wanted to use ephedrine-containing products? What legal and ethical issues are involved your responses to the client?
7. What is your reaction to the Integral exploration of medical marijuana? What position do you take on the topic, and why?
8. Compare the dependence-inducing qualities of methylphenidate and marijuana. What conclusions do you reach in this exercise?
9. Debate whether or not the gateway theory of drug use is accurate.
10. Compare the side effect profile of marijuana with side effects of lithium and of an SSRI antidepressant. What conclusions do you reach about their relative usefulness, based on this exercise?

# Glossary

**acetate**  A salt or ester of acetic acid, which is the essential component in vinegar.

**adherence**  The degree to which a client adheres to a medication regimen particularly with regard to dosage and time of day taken.

**allopathic treatment model**  A type of treatment that works by introducing agents (usually medications) that act in a manner opposite to the symptoms. In this book the allopathic model represents what we are calling the *medical model perspective*.

**amine hypothesis of depression**  The hypothesis that depression is caused by a lack of amine-based neurotransmitters such as norepinephrine and that antidepressant medication somehow corrects this "chemical imbalance." This has been found to be too simplistic to explain the dynamics of antidepressant medication.

**anhedonia**  One of the so-called vegetative signs of depression, meaning a loss of pleasure or joy in all things.

**antagonists**  Drugs whose main mechanism of action is to block a receptor site without exerting any particular action.

**antihistamines**  A class of drugs that block histamine receptors in the body and decrease the influence of histamine.

**antihypertensive**  A class of drugs whose effects decrease blood pressure.

**antischizophrenic**  An early word used to describe medications that decreased the symptoms of Schizophrenia. Later replaced by the word *antipsychotic*.

**anxiolytic**  "Anxiety reducing"; medications used to treat anxiety.

**arborization**  The process of dendritic growth in which dendrites grow to make connections with other neurons.

**atypical antipsychotics**  A class of antipsychotic medications that work very differently from the older or "typical" antipsychotics. The atypical antipsychotics include clozapine and the serotonin-dopamine antagonists.

**autonomic nervous system**  The system of nerves that innervates the blood vessels, heart, viscera, smooth muscles, and glands. This system controls involuntary functions and is divided into the sympathetic and parasympathetic nervous systems (see glosses).

**autonomic side effects**  Side effects that are affecting the autonomic nervous system.

**autoreceptors**  These receptors, when stimulated, send a message back inside the neuron to decrease the output of whatever neurotransmitter the neuron produces.

**bradykinesia**  Fatigue when performing repetitive movements

**brain stem**  A component of the central nervous system also called the "reptilian brain," because it is evolutionarily the oldest section of the brain. The brain stem controls many vital functions such as respiration and heart rate.

**Broca's area**  A cerebral area in the inferior frontal gyrus associated with the movement necessary for speech. Named after Paul Broca, the nineteenth century neurologist who concluded that the left frontal lobe was implicated in articulation of speech.

**bromide**  A salt of hydrobromic acid consisting of two elements, one of which is bromine.

**category error**  Using the wrong knowledge tool to pursue an issue or answer a question. An example is using a blood test to find out who a person's favorite actress is. In a category error the tool or questions are not illegitimate, but the wrong tool is selected. Category errors are common when disciples of one approach to reality (such as scientists) believe their tools are the right tools for all approaches.

**central nervous system**   The brain and spinal cord.

**cognitive triad of depression**   Three elements that according to Aaron Beck's cognitive therapy are present in depression: negative views about self, negative views about the world, and negative views about the future.

**comorbidity**   Term used when a child, adolescent, or adult has more than one diagnosis in Axis I of the section of a five-axis diagnosis.

**compliance**   The overall extent to which a client takes medication as prescribed.

**contraindications**   Conditions that prohibit the use of a medication. For example, lithium is contraindicated in patients with kidney or liver disease because such diseases make it difficult for the body to metabolize and eliminate lithium.

**corpus striatum**   A striped mass of white and gray matter located in the front of the thalamus in each brain hemisphere. This area is related to regulating motor behavior and the brain's reward centers.

**cultural perspective**   One of four perspectives referred to in this book. This one reflects shared worldviews and beliefs that are loosely referred to as *culture*. These could also include what we might refer to as "subcultures"; for example, the subculture of the pharmaceutical industry or the subculture of the helping professions in general.

**cultural psychiatry**   A special field of psychiatry concerned with the cultural aspects of human behavior, mental health, psychopathology, and treatment. It promotes culturally competent treatment and aims to expand human knowledge of human behavior.

**cytochrome P-450 enzyme system**   The enzyme system in the human liver that governs most of the metabolism of psychotropic medications that is done by the liver.

**delirium**   A disturbance in consciousness (usually temporary) characterized by restlessness, excitement, and sometimes hallucinations.

**Delphic motto**   The Delphic injunction "Know thyself" is inscribed over the archway leading into the Temple of Delphi, which was dedicated to the god Apollo and occupied by the Delphic oracle.

**delusions**   False beliefs that persist despite a preponderance of evidence to the contrary

**dendrites**   The branching processes of a neuron with receptors on them that conduct signals toward the cell.

**dendritic growth**   The constant growth of dendrites to form synapses or connections with other neurons. Also sometimes called *arborization*, because its appearance is similar to the branching growth of a tree (from *arbor*, Latin for tree).

**dependence**   In reference to drug dependence, dependence is defined physically and mentally. Physical dependence is the tolerance built up to the effects of a drug so that more and more of the drug become necessary to get the same effect. This type of dependence is also associated with withdrawal symptoms on discontinuation of the drug. Psychological dependence is the conviction that one cannot get through the day without taking some of the drug on which one is psychologically dependent.

**depolarization**   The state of a neuron when it fires. This state is characterized by an influx of positive ions and a pumping out of negative ions.

**developmental lines**   The simultaneous occurrence of several aspects of human growth and development. Cognitive, emotional, linguistic, psychomotor, and gender development (to name a few) occur simultaneously in the toddler.

**developmental pharmacology**   The study of brain development in children and adolescents after the infusion of a psychotropic medication focusing on brain development in two key areas, including the impact on brain plasticity or the brain's ability to shape itself in response to environmental or chemical input and the impact on sensitive periods, which are developmental epochs when neural representation is happening before hard wiring occurs.

**diphtheria**   An infectious disease caused by bacteria that cause the formation of false membranes in the air passageways, especially the throat.

**direct-to-consumer (DTC) advertising**   Advertising for psychotropic medications that is aimed at the consumer of the medication (the client or patient) rather than the prescriber of the medication (the physician). This type of advertising was prohibited by law until the 1980s.

**disinformation**   False information intentionally spread to advance a political agenda.

**dopamine hypothesis of Schizophrenia**   The hypothesis that Schizophrenia was somehow caused by too much dopamine in the brain, the overactivity of dopamine, or the oversensitivity of dopamine receptors. This theory, although useful for understanding some antipsychotic medications, is too simplistic to account for the spectrum of symptoms seen in Schizophrenia.

**double-blind, randomized, placebo-controlled trials** The "gold standard" of design for clinical trials of medication. These trials are conducted in a manner so that the participants and doctors do not know who is getting the medication and who is getting the placebo (double blind), assignment of drug conditions is random (randomized), and a placebo is used. A placebo is a compound that might appear to be a drug but that is thought to exert no influence on the symptoms being examined. A placebo can be active or inert. Studies with active placebos produce smaller effect sizes.

**downregulation** The decrease in the number and sensitivity of receptors on a neuron in response to the presence of a drug.

**dysthymia** A category of mood disorder in the *Diagnostic and Statistical Manual* of the American Psychiatric Association that refers to a low-grade, chronic depression that persists for two years or longer.

**ego-dystonic symptoms** Symptoms that are in contrast to the way a client views himself or herself. These are typically easier to treat than symptoms that the client identifies with (ego-syntonic).

**dystonia** A neurological disorder marked by involuntary muscle spasms that can causing painful twisting of the body.

**dystonic reaction** A reaction to a psychotropic medication that manifests as various dystonias.

**ego-dystonic symptoms** Symptoms that contrast with the way a client views himself or herself. These are typically easier to treat than symptoms with which the client identifies (ego-syntonic).

**encephalon** Generally referring to the brain.

**enculturation** The process through which people, starting in childhood, acquire a cultural system through their environment, particularly from parents and schools. This does not always mean that the individuals acculturate to the major culture.

**endocrine glands** Glands such as the thyroid, adrenal, and pituitary glands that secrete certain substances, particularly hormones, directly into the blood.

**entheogen** Literally, "god-manifester"; a drug that has been highly correlated with mystical insights, such as psilocybin or LSD.

**epiphenomenon** Any secondary phenomenon—in the context of this book, referring to the mind as a secondary phenomenon to the brain.

**equanimity** A state of mental or emotional composure, especially under stressful circumstances. It can be cultivated in various meditative practices and is viewed as one of the tools whereby a person can develop a healthy detachment (not dissociation) from powerful emotions, which allows the person so detached to have more choices in how to respond to such emotions. Equanimity is a disposition introduced by Buddhism as one of the four sublime states. In the Buddhist context it is the practice of approaching an interaction with respect and caring while remaining unattached to how the interaction unfolds and how one is treated.

**ethnopharmacotherapy** A newer subdiscipline of psychopharmacology that explores how objectively different groups of people respond differently to medications. The differences explored include race, ethnicity, sex, and gender.

**etiology** The cause or origin of a disease.

**euphorant** A drug that induces euphoria

**euthymia** A clinical term meaning neither manic nor depressed. Derived from a Greek root meaning joyous and tranquil.

**extrapyramidal motor system** This system is made up of the subthalamus and the basal ganglia and is involved in fine motor movement. This system is seriously disrupted by the older antipsychotic medications called *neuroleptics*.

**extrapyramidal symptoms or side effects** Side effects caused by drugs interfering with dopamine neurons in these nervous system structures. Usually refers to side effects of neuroleptic drugs (also called *typical* or *first-generation antipsychotics*).

**extrapyramidal** Outside the pyramidal system.

**first-generation antipsychotics** Phrase that refers to the first antidopiminergic antipsychotics called neuroleptics or "typical" antipsychotics. Although several classes of drugs fall into this category, they all exert their effects by dopamine antagonism.

**first-messenger effect** The effect of a drug molecule or neurotransmitter binding to a receptor.

**flat affect** The lack of emotional expression that is one of the negative symptoms of Schizophrenia. Flat affect is also a side effect of neuroleptic or typical antipsychotic medication.

**G protein** A family of receptors so named because they bind guanine nucleotides. This family plays an important role in second-messenger systems described in this book.

**genome** A single set (haploid set) of chromosomes.

**glucose** A simple sugar that is the principal source of energy for all living organisms.

**hallucinations**   The experience or perception of physical stimuli when none appears to exist (such as hearing voices when no voices are within hearing range). Hallucinations are one of the positive symptoms of Schizophrenia.

**homeostasis**   A state of balance.

**Huntington's Chorea**   A hereditary chorea (disease of the nervous system characterized by jerky, uncontrolled movements) characterized by gradual deterioration of the brain and loss of movement.

**hyperpolarization**   the state of a neuron characterized by being negatively charged (more negative ions inside the cell and positive ions outside). This negative charge decreases the probability that a cell will fire.

**hypertension**   Medical term for high blood pressure.

**hypnotic**   A classification of drugs used to induce or assist with sleep.

**illusion**   Similar to a hallucination, the misperception of stimuli that actually exist.

**Integral**   In this book, *Integral* refers specifically to Ken Wilber's Integral Model, which requires that the exploration of any topic include the four perspectives represented by his four quadrants: levels of development, lines of development, states of consciousness, and types.

**intrapsychic perspective**   One of four perspectives referred to in this book; the perspective that represents the subjective experience of the client. This includes thoughts, feelings, and worldviews as well as such things as mystical or intuitive experiences. Although this perspective registers changes in brain activity, to date we cannot conclude that the experiences divulged through exploring this perspective are "caused by" the brain.

**ketoacidosis**   A feature of uncontrolled diabetes that combines two sets of symptoms: ketosis and acidosis. Ketosis is an accumulation of substances called *ketone bodies* in the blood. These bodies are made when there is not enough insulin in the blood and the body must break down fat instead of sugar (glucose) for energy. Acidosis is increased acidity of the blood.

**Kluver-Bucy syndrome**   Emotional and behavioral changes associated with damage to the amygdala and inferior temporal cortex. Symptoms include emotional blunting, extreme weight gain, and inappropriate sexual behavior. The syndrome can also result from Pick's disease, a progressive dementia beginning in middle life thought to be caused by an abnormal buildup of the tau protein.

**lability**   The quality of being labile or prone to sudden emotional changes ("swings") from one extreme to the other.

**lifetime prevalence**   An estimate at a given time of all the individuals who have ever suffered from a particular disorder

**lipophilicitous**   The quality of being fat soluble.

**lobe**   Roundish projection or division of an organ, in this case, the brain. The four brain lobes discussed are the frontal, temporal, parietal, and occipital.

**locus coeruleus**   A cluster of neurons that release norepinephrine and appear to have projections to most norepinephrine neurons in the brain.

**loose associations**   A positive symptom of Schizophrenia in which mental associations are not governed by logic but idiosyncratically.

**lysergic acid diethylamide (LSD)**   A hallucinogen characterized as a nonspecific amplifier of intrapsychic contents; discovered in 1943.

**macromolecule**   A very large molecule composed of hundreds or thousands of atoms.

**magic bullet**   Colloquially, an ideal drug that targets only a problematic area or tissue without disturbing surrounding areas or tissues.

**major tranquilizer**   Colloquially—and inaccurately—antipsychotic medications.

**mammalian brain**   The portion of the brain that encompasses the midbrain and limbic system characteristic of brains in mammals (colloquial).

**medical model perspective**   One of four perspectives referred to in this book, this is the perspective of scientific materialism and the dominant perspective in biological psychiatry. This perspective uses scientific method to explore observable, measurable aspects of the individual. Although this perspective has been very successful in allopathic medicine, it has been less successful in treating mental and emotional disorders.

**megalomania**   A highly exaggerated and/or delusional concept of one's self-importance.

**mesencephalon**   Midbrain.

**midbrain**   Referring to mesencephalon.

**minimal brain dysfunction (MBD)**   This diagnosis from the 1960s vaguely attempted to categorize some symptoms of both ADHD and ODD. This diagnosis prompted the development of a norm for methodology to evaluate the effects of drugs, particularly stimulants on children.

**minor tranquilizer**   Anxiolytic medications such as the benzodiazepines; colloquial.

**misinformation**   Typically, a misunderstanding that arises from one of several factors. Not to be confused with "disinformation," which is the intentional spread of false information.

**mitochondrion** (plural, **mitochondria**)   An organelle (cell organ) in the cell cytoplasm that has its own DNA inherited from the maternal line and that produces enzymes essential for energy.

**molecular structure**   In psychopharmacology, the arrangement of molecules in a particular drug compound.

**mood stabilizer**   An ill-defined category of psychotropic medication whose main purpose is treating bipolar mood disorders and aggressive, acting-out behaviors.

**Multimodal Treatment Study, The**   A study sponsored by the National Institute on Mental Health (NIMH) to examine children with ADHS who received stimulant medication only, received behavioral therapy only, or received both stimulant and behavioral therapy. In general almost all children improved in their symptoms, but the children with the combined treatment demonstrated greater gains.

**narrow-band rating scale**   A psychometric scale developed to assess or evaluate a more precise range of symptoms in a client, as a specific diagnosis in the *DSM IV-TR*.

**negative feedback loop**   A description, from behavioral theory, of a cycle that is thought to underlie depression. It assumes some stressors have disrupted normal behavior, and the reinforcers that normal behavior used to bring have stopped. This can set up a cycle of self-criticism and further withdrawal or depressive behaviors that then bring new reinforcement to make up for the reinforcers that were lost. This is called a *negative feedback loop (secondary gain)* when the depressive behaviors cause the people in the support network to gather together around the crisis of the person's depression.

**negative symptoms of Schizophrenia**   Symptoms of Schizophrenia that are characterized by the absence of a quality that normally exists, such as a range of emotion, volition, and sociability.

**neocortex**   Literally, "new brain"; the outermost layer of the brain to develop latest in the evolutionary history of the brain.

**neurolepsis**   The action of early antipsychotic medication. Literally, the "clasping" of the neuron; researchers thought these drugs inhibited the neurons in a fashion that could be described as "clasping."

**neuroleptic**   Older or "typical" antipsychotic medications, most of which work through dopamine antagonism. Literally, "neuron clasping."

**neurons**   Specialized impulse-conducting cells that are the functional units of the nervous system.

**nonlocal qualities of consciousness**   Qualities that do not appear to require energy to be transmitted nor a physical body to reside in. In other words, the nonlocal qualities of consciousness seem to transmit faster than the speed of light. Nonlocal qualities of consciousness are currently being explored in group mind phenomena, healing, and consciousness studies.

**noradrenergic**   Activity related to norepinephrine; synonymous with *noradrenalin*.

**nosology**   Any systematic classification of diseases.

**nucleus** (plural, **nuclei**)   Mass of gray matter in the brain or spinal cord.

**object loss**   A psychodynamic concept that refers to a traumatic early loss in a person's life of someone important to that person.

**off-label use**   A drug being used for a purpose not reviewed or approved by the Food and Drug Administration.

**olfaction system**   The sensory system that governs the sense of smell.

**on-label use**   A drug used in a manner that the Food and Drug Administration has approved. Approval means that evidence for efficacy and effectiveness has been presented with regard to the on-label use.

**overdetermined**   In reference to symptoms of many mental or emotional disorders, we say that the disorders and symptoms are "overdetermined," meaning that they likely are caused by multiple variables ranging from biological, to psychological, to cultural, to spiritual.

**pantheoretical**   Transcending and including many different theories, not tied to just one or a few.

**paranoia**   One of the positive symptoms of Schizophrenia; manifests as an unwarranted mistrust of others.

**parapraxes**   Manifest elements that reveal unconscious feelings or thoughts. A common parapraxis is the colloquial "slip of the tongue" when you say something that you did not mean to say but that reflects the way you really feel.

**parasympathetic nervous system**   A subdivision of the autonomic nervous system that is active during conservation of energy.

**parenteral**   Administered by injection.

**Pediatric Rule**   In 1998 the FDA came out with this rule to *require* pharmaceutical companies to assess the safety and effectiveness of new drugs. On October 17, 2002, the U.S. District Court of Columbia ruled that the FDA did not have authority to issue this rule.

**peripheral nervous system**   The nervous system lying outside the brain and spinal cord and containing the somatic and autonomic nervous systems.

**permeable**   Capable of being permeated. In psychopharmacology, usually refers to cell membranes through which drug molecules can pass.

**pharmacodynamics**   The mechanisms of how drugs act on the body.

**pharmacokinetics**   The mechanisms of how the body reacts to and acts on drug molecules introduced into it.

**phenomenological**   The subjective experience of phenomena.

**phenothiazine compounds**   One of many compounds derived from coal tar technology that was developed into a class of antipsychotic medications.

**phytotherapy**   From the Greek, meaning "plant therapy." Used in reference to herbaceuticals.

**placebo response**   Response similar to a response to a drug that occurs when the patient is given a placebo (a substance thought to be inert with regard to the symptoms under study). This is not a well-researched area although in many drug trials, the placebo response is almost as strong as the response to the medication.

**pleasure centers** (of the brain)   Neural pathways in the brain thought to mediate rewards. These pathways are typically dopaminergic in quality.

**point prevalence**   An estimate of the percentage of the population thought to suffer from a particular disorder at a given point in time.

**polarization**   The resting state of a cell in which the cell is in a state of homeostasis between positive and negative ions.

**polypharmacy**   Mixing several medications to alleviate symptoms.

**positive symptoms**   Symptoms of Schizophrenia that are present and are not normal (such as hallucinations, delusions, and paranoia).

**postsynaptic**   In the sequence of events in neural transmission, refers to the part of the sequence enacted after the neurotransmitters pass through the cleft and bind to receptors.

**precursor compounds**   Compounds that are combined to make neurotransmitters (for example, tryptophan is a precursor compound necessary for production of serotonin).

**prepubertal**   Prior to the onset of puberty.

**presynaptic**   In the sequence of events in neural transmission, refers to the part of the sequence enacted before

neurotransmitters pass through the cleft and bind to receptors.

**prophylactic**   Having some preventive quality.

**protein kinase C**   A second-messenger-system–dependent protein kinase (substance that helps create enzymes) that plays a pivotal role in how a cell responds to extracellular stimuli.

**psychic energizers**   A psychodynamic concept prevalent in U.S. psychiatry in the 1950s. If a drug was thought to be a psychic energizer, it was believed to somehow liberate repressed id energy that the ego could then use.

**psychotropic**   From the Greek; "acting on" or "moving toward" the mind.

**pyramidal cells**   Large neurons shaped like pyramids found in the hippocampus and frontal cortex and implicated in motor function.

**radical constructivism**   Where constructivism is a postmodern brand of philosophy that holds "reality" to be in part socially, culturally, or psychologically constructed, radical constructivism is an extreme expression of this philosophy that maintains (without convincing evidence) that all reality is socially, culturally, or psychologically constructed.

**relativism**   A philosophical position that any one position or perspective is just as good as any other position or perspective. As Ken Wilber points out, this is an irrational position in that it is self-contradictory, because it assumes that the proposition that no position is any better than another itself presumes to be better than alternative propositions.

**REM rebound**   The rapid eye movement (REM) stage of sleep associated with theta wave activity in the brain. A person deprived of REM sleep (or sleep in general) will have a REM rebound when able to re-enter the REM state. The state of REM rebound is characterized by multiple dream images exceeding what is normal for the person experiencing it.

**reptilian brain**   Colloquially, the brain stem, the part of the human brain hypothesized to appear earliest in evolution.

**resting state**   The state of a cell when it is polarized (its electrical charge is balanced).

**schizotaxia**   A genetic predisposition to Schizophrenia, which is considered a wide spectrum of disorders with early onset. This notion is complex and controversial.

**second-messenger effects**   Effects that occur through second-messenger systems that include the impact of G-proteins and enzymes after a neurotransmitter binds to a receptor.

**self-efficacy**   A construct pioneered by Albert Bandura that is related to a person's belief that he or she can accomplish things in life and do some things well. People with low self-efficacy believe they cannot do what they need to get what they want in life.

**sense receptors**   Receptors that relay signals relevant to the senses.

**shock**   Severely diminished blood circulation, caused by severe injury or pain.

**side effects**   Effects distinct from main effects. Side effects are just effects unnecessary to the proposed therapeutic action of a drug. They occur to the extent that a drug is "dirty" or affects areas other than the desired area.

**social perspective**   One of four perspectives referred to in this book, the social perspective deals with the measurable aspects of groups, namely, institutions of society related to psychopharmacology. These include institutions such as the Food and Drug Administration.

**somatic nervous system**   The part of the peripheral nervous system that connects with sense receptors and skeletal muscles.

**somatosensory cortex**   The region of the cortex whose primary input is from the somatosensory nuclei.

**sympathetic nervous system**   The part of the autonomic nervous system that is active during arousal, such as in fight, flight, or freeze responses.

**synapse**   The combination (juncture) of the presynaptic neuron, the synaptic cleft, and the postsynaptic neuron.

**tardive dyskinesia**   Late-appearing, abnormal movement. One of four extrapyramidal side effects attributed to some antipsychotic medications.

**telencephalon**   The anterior (front) section of the forebrain, consisting of the cerebrum and olfactory lobes.

**teratogen**   Literally, an agent that may produce monsters or monstrous growths. Medically speaking, agents correlated with the presence of birth defects.

**teratogenesis**   The development of birth defects. The adjective *teratogenic* refers to agents that may produce monsters or monstrous growths. Medically this is understood as referring to agents that are correlated with the presence of birth defects.

**third-party payers**   In reference to insurance, arrangements in which the first party is the client or patient, the second party is the service provider, and the third party is the insurance company that may pay for all or part of the services provided.

**thought disorder**   A positive symptom of Schizophrenia. Can manifest as a disorder in the stream, content, or form of thoughts.

**tolerance**   The clinical state of reduced responsiveness to a drug that can be produced by a variety of mechanisms, all of which result in the person needing increased doses of the drug to achieve effects previously attained by lower doses.

**toxic environment**   A phrase we first came across in workshops with psychologist James Garbarino, who used the word to describe environments typified by high rates of poverty, little access to resources, and high rates of violence.

**tubercle bacillus**   The bacterium that causes tuberculosis.

**typical antipsychotics**   While several classes of drugs fall into this category, they all exert their effects by dopamine antagonism. Also known as neuroleptic or first-generation antipsychotics.

**upregulation**   The increase in number and sensitivity of receptors on a neuron in response to the presence of a drug.

**urate**   Salt of uric acid.

**vegetative symptoms**   Generally, symptoms relating to bodily processes that are performed involuntarily or unconsciously. In psychopharmacology, symptoms that express physically (poor appetite, sleep disturbance) rather than psychologically.

**visual cortex**   The section of the cortex associated with input from the visual system

**Wernicke's area**   A section of the left temporal lobe in the human brain that is involved in comprehending words and producing meaningful speech.

**word magic**   In this book, using words to create an illusion of certainty where only speculation exists.

**word salad**   A positive symptom of Schizophrenia that manifests as linguistic disorganization so pronounced it can impair effective communication.

# References

Abboud, L. (2004, June 18). Drug makers seek to bar "placebo responders" from trials. *Wall Street Journal*, pp. B1, B5.

Abidi, S., & Bhaskara, S. M. (2003). From chlorpromazine to clozapine: Antipsychotic adverse effects and the clinician's dilemma. *Canadian Journal of Psychiatry, 48*, 749–755.

Abood, R., & Martin, B. R. (1992). Neurobiology of marijuana abuse. *Trends in Pharmacological Sciences, 13*, 480–485.

Agovino, T. (2004, June 3). Company faces suit over use of Paxil for children. *Record Courier*, p. B1.

Aldencamp, A. P., DeDrom, M., & Reijs, R. (2003). Newer antiepileptic drugs and cognitive issues. *Epilepsia, 44*, 21–29.

Alexander, C. N., & Langer, E. J. (1990). *Higher stages of human development.* New York: Oxford University Press.

Altschuler, L. L., Burt, V. K., McMullen, M., & Hendrick, V. (1995). Breast feeding and sertraline: A twenty-four hour analysis. *Journal of Clinical Psychiatry, 56*, 243–245.

American Academy of Child & Adolescent Psychiatry. (2001, January 9). *AACAP Work Force Fact Sheet.*

American Academy of Pediatrics. (2001). Clinical practice guidelines: Treatment of the school-aged child with attention deficit/hyperactivity disorder. *Journal of Pediatrics, 108*, 1033–1044.

American Psychiatric Association. (1994). *Diagnostic and statistical manual of mental disorders* (4th ed.) [*DSM-IV*]. Washington, DC: Author.

American Psychiatric Association. (2000a). *Diagnostic and statistical manual of mental disorders* (4th ed., Text Revision) [*DSM-IV TR*]. Washington, DC: Author.

American Psychiatric Association. (2000b). *Practice guidelines for the treatment of psychiatric disorders: Compendium 2000.* Washington, DC: Author.

American Psychological Association [APA]. (1995). *Curriculum for level one training in psychopharmacology.* Washington, DC: Author.

Anderla, G. (1973). *Information in 1985: A forecasting study of information needs and resources.* Paris: Organization for Economic Cooperation and Development.

Anderla, G. (1974). *The growth of scientific and technical information: A challenge.* Washington, DC: National Science Foundation.

Andreasen, N. (2000). Schizophrenia: The fundamental questions. *Brain Research Reviews, 31*, 106–112.

Andreasen, N. (2001). *Brave new brain.* New York: Oxford University Press.

Angrist, B., Rotrosen, J., Kleinberg, D., Merriam, V., & Gershon, S. (1977). Dopaminergic agonist properties of ephedrine: Theoretical implications. *Psychopharmacology, 55*, 115–120.

Anthony, J. C., Warner, L. A., & Kessler, R. C. (1994). Comparative epidemiology of dependence on tobacco, alcohol, controlled substances, and inhalants: Basic findings from the national comorbidity survey. *Experimental and Clinical Psychopharmacology, 2*, 244–268.

Antonuccio, D. O., Danton, W. G., & DeNelsky, G. Y. (1995). Psychotherapy versus medication for depression: Challenging the conventional wisdom with data. *Professional Psychology: Research and Practice, 26*, 574–585.

Aquila, R. (2002). Management of weight gain in patients with schizophrenia. *Journal of Clinical Psychiatry, 63*(Suppl. 4), 33–36.

Armstrong, T. (1997). *The myth of the ADD child: 50 ways to improve your child's behavior and attention span without drugs, labels, or coercion.* New York: Plume.

Aronson, J. K., & Reynolds, D. J. M. (1992). ABC of monitoring drug therapy: Lithium. *British Medical Journal, 305*, 1273–1276.

255

Asghar, S. A. (2002). Case report of 5 bipolar disorder patients (rapid cycling) followed for 3 years, treated with lamotrigine. *European Psychiatry, 5*(Suppl. 1), 109.

Ashton, C. H. (2001). Pharmacology and effects of cannabis: A brief review. *British Journal of Psychiatry, 178,* 101–106.

Asslian, P. (2000). Sildenafil for St. John's wort–induced sexual dysfunction. *Journal of Sex and Marital Therapy, 26,* 357–358.

Astin, J. A. (1998). Why patients use alternative medicine: Results of a national study. *JAMA, 279,* 1548–1553.

Atack, J. R. (2000). Lithium, phosphatidylinositol signaling, and bipolar disorder. In H. K. Manji, C. L. Bowden, & R. H. Belmaker (Eds.), *Bipolar medications: Mechanisms of action* (pp. 1–30). Washington, DC: American Psychiatric Press.

August, G. J., Realmuto, G. M., MacDonald, A. W., Nugent, S. M., & Crosby, R. (1996). Prevalence of ADHD and comorbid disorders among elementary school children screened for disruptive behavior. *Journal of Abnormal Child Psychology, 24,* 571–595.

Avissar, S., & Schreiber, G. (1989). Muscarinic receptor subclassification and G-proteins: Significance for lithium action in affective disorders and for the treatment of extrapyramidal side effects of neuroleptics. *Biological Psychiatry, 26,* 113–130.

Babyak, M., Blumenthal, J. A., Herman, S., Khatri, P., Doraiswamy, M., Moore, K., Craighead, W. E., Baldewicz, T. T., & Krishnan, K. R. (2000). Exercise treatment for major depression: Maintenance of therapeutic benefit at 10 months. *Psychosomatic Medicine, 62,* 633–638.

Badal, D. W. (1988). *Treatment of depression and related moods: A manual for psychotherapists.* Northvale, NJ: Jason Aronson.

Badal, D. W. (2003). *Treating chronic depression: Psychotherapy and medication.* Northvale, NJ: Jason Aronson.

Balderer, G., & Bobely, A. A. (1985). Effect of valerian on human sleep. *Psychopharmacology (Berl[in]), 87,* 406–409.

Baldessarini, R. J., Tondo, L., & Hennen, J. (1999). Effects of lithium treatment and its discontinuation on suicidal behavior in bipolar manic depressive disorders. *Journal of Clinical Psychiatry, 60*(Suppl. 2), 441–448.

Baldessarini, R. J., Tondo, L., Hennen, J., & Viguera, A. C. (2002). Is lithium still worth using? *Harvard Review of Psychiatry, 10,* 59–75.

Ballenger, J. C. (1995). Benzodiazepines. In A. F. Schatzberg & C. B. Nemeroff (Eds.), *The American Psychiatric Press textbook of psychopharmacology* (pp. 231–246). Washington, DC: American Psychiatric Press.

Ballenger, J. C., & Post, R. M. (1980). Carbamazepine (Tegretol) in manic-depressive illness: A new treatment. *American Journal of Psychiatry, 137,* 782–790.

Balon, R. (1999). Positive aspects of collaborative treatment. In R. Balon & M. B. Riba (Eds.), *Psychopharmacology and psychotherapy: A collaborative approach* (pp. 1–32). Washington DC: American Psychiatric Association.

Barber, J. P., & Luborsky, M. L. (1991). A psychodynamic view of simple phobia in prescriptive matching: A commentary. *Psychotherapy, 28,* 469–472.

Barclay, L. (2002). Aripiprazole may change schizophrenia treatment. *Medscape Wire, 1,* 2–4.

Barkley, R. A. (1998). *Attention-deficit hyperactivity disorder: A handbook for diagnosis and treatment* (2nd ed.). New York: Guilford.

Barkley, R. A., DuPaul, G. J., & Conner, D. F. (1999). Stimulants. In J. Werry & M. Aman (Eds.), *Practitioner's guide to psychoactive drugs for children and adolescents* (2nd ed., pp. 213–247). New York: Plenum.

Barkley, R. A., Karlsson, J., Strzelecki, E., & Murphy, J. V. (1984). Effects of age and Ritalin dosage on the mother–child interactions of hyperactive children. *Journal of Consulting and Clinical Psychology, 52,* 750–758.

Barlow, D. H., & Durand, V. M. (2002). *Abnormal psychology: An integrative approach.* Belmont, CA: Wadsworth.

Barrickman, L. L. & Perry, P. J., Allen, A. J., & Kuperman, S. (1995). Bupropion versus methylphenidate in the treatment of ADHD. *Journal of the American Academy of Child and Adolescent Psychiatry, 34,* 649–657.

Bassarath, L. (2003). Medication strategies in childhood aggression: A review. *Canadian Journal of Psychiatry, 48,* 367–373.

Beasley, C. M., Dornseif, B. E., Bosomworth, J. C., Sayler, M. E., Rampey, A. H., Heiligenstein, J. H., Thompson, V. L. Murphy, D. J., & Masica, D. N. (1991). Fluoxetine and suicide: A meta-analysis of controlled trials of treatment for depression. *British Medical Journal (Clinical Research Edition), 303,* 685–692.

Beaubrun, G., & Gray, G. E. (2000). A review of herbal medicines for psychiatric disorders. *Psychiatric Services, 51,* 1130–1134.

Beaumont, G. (1973). Sexual side effects of clomipramine. *Journal of International Medical Research, 1,* 469–472.

Beck, A. T., Rush, A. J., Shaw, B. F., & Emery, G. (1979). *Cognitive therapy of depression.* New York: Guilford Press.

Bell, C. C., & Mehta, H. (1980). The misdiagnosis of black patients with manic-depressive illness. *JAMA, 72,* 141–145.

Bell, C. C., & Mehta, H. (1981). The misdiagnosis of black patients with manic-depressive illness: Second in a series. *JAMA, 73,* 101–107.

Bell, R. D., Alexander, G. M., Schwartzman, R. K., & Yu, J. (1982). The methylphenidate-induced stereotypy in the awake rate: Local cerebral metabolism. *Neurology, 32,* 377–381.

Bella, V. L., & Piccoli, F. (2003). Olanzapine-induced tardive dyskinesia. *British Journal of Psychiatry, 182,* 81–82.

Benner, R., Bjerkenstedt, L., & Edman, G. V. (2002). *Hypericum perforatum* extract (St. John's wort) for depression. *Psychiatric Annals, 32,* 21–26.

Bennett, C. F., Brown, R. T., Carver, J., & Anderson, D. (1999). Stimulant medication for the child with attention deficit/hyperactivity disorder. *Pediatric Clinics of North America, 46,* 924–944.

Bennett, J., & Brown, C. M. (2000). Use of herbal remedies by patients in a health maintenance organization. *Journal of the American Pharmacists Association, 40,* 353–358.

Ben-Porath, D. (2002). Stigmatization of individuals who receive psychotherapy: An interaction between help-seeking behavior and the presence of depression. *Journal of Social and Clinical Psychology, 21,* 400–413.

Bent, S., Tiedt, T. N., Odden, M. C., & Shlipak, M. G. (2003). The relative safety of ephedra compared with other herbal products. *Annals of Internal Medicine, 138,* 468–471.

Berardinelli, C., & Mostade, J. (2003, July 11). *Supervision of psychopharmacology.* Unpublished presentation given at John Carroll University.

Berger, F. M. (1970). The discovery of meprobamate. In F. Ayd & B. Blackwell (Eds.), *Discoveries in biological psychiatry* (pp. 115–129). Philadelphia: Lippincott.

Berk, M., Ichim, L., & Brook, S. (1999). Olanzapine compared to lithium in mania: A double-blind, randomized, controlled trial. *International Clinical Psychopharmacology, 14,* 339–343.

Bernstein, G. A., & Shaw, K. (1997). Practice parameters for the assessment and treatment of children and adolescents with anxiety disorders. *Journal of the American Academy of Child and Adolescent Psychiatry, 36*(Suppl. 1), 69–84.

Bernstein, G., Borschardt, C. M., & Perwien, A. R. (1996). Anxiety disorders in children and adolescents: A review of the past 10 years. *Journal of American Academy of Child and Adolescent Psychiatry, 35,* 1110–1119.

Bhugra, D., & Bhui, K. (2001). *Cross-cultural psychiatry: A practical guide.* New York: Oxford University Press.

Bichsell, S. (2001). Schizophrenia and severe mental illness. In E. R. Welfel & R. E. Ingersoll (Eds.), *The mental health desk reference: A practice-based guide to diagnosis, treatment, and professional ethics* (pp. 142–154). New York: Wiley.

Biederman, J., Mick, E., Faraone, S. V., & Burback, M. (2001). Patterns of remission and symptom decline in conduct disorder: A four-year prospective study of an ADHD sample. *Journal of the American Academy of Child and Adolescent Psychiatry, 40,* 290–298.

Biederman, J., Wilens, T. E., Mick, E., Faraone, S. V., & Spencer, T. (1998). Does attention-deficit hyperactivity disorder impact the developmental course of drug and alcohol abuse and dependence? *Biological Psychiatry, 44,* 269–273.

Bilia, A. R., Gallori, S., & Vincieri, F. F. (2002). St. John's wort and depression: Efficacy, safety, and tolerability—an update. *Life Sciences, 70,* 3077–3096.

Birmaher, B. (1998). Should we use antidepressant medication for children and adolescents with depressive disorders? *Pediatric Clinics of North America, 46,* 926–944.

Bland, R. (1997). Epidemiology of affective disorders: A review. *Canadian Journal of Psychiatry, 42,* 367–377.

Bloom, F., Nelson, C. A., & Lazerson, A. (2001). *Brain, mind, and behavior* (3rd ed.). New York: Worth.

Blumenthal, M. (Ed.). (1998). *The complete German commission E monographs: Therapeutic guide to herbal medicines.* Austin, TX: American Botanical Council.

Bodenheimer, T. (2000). Uneasy Alliance: Clinical investigators and the pharmaceutical industry. *New England Journal of Medicine, 342,* 1539–1544.

Bond, W. S. (1990). Therapy update: Ethnicity and psychotropic drugs. *Clinical Pharmacology, 10,* 467–470.

Boniel, T., & Dannon, P. (2001). The safety of herbal medicines in the psychiatric practice. *Harefuah, 140,* 780–783.

Boothroyd, A. (1997). Auditory development of the hearing child. *Scandinavian Audiology, 26*(Suppl. 46), 9–16.

Bostic, J. Q., Wilens, T., Spencer, T., & Biederman, J. (1997). Juvenile mood disorders and office psychopharmacology. *Pediatric Clinics of North America, 44,* 1487–1503.

Boston University Medical Center. (2002). Barbiturate drugs. Available at http://web.bu.edu/cohis/subsabse/hypnotic/barb.htm. Accessed on November 16, 2002.

Botteron, K. N., & Geller, B. (1995). Pharmacologic treatment of childhood and adolescent mania. *Pediatric Psychopharmacology II, 4,* 283–304.

Botteron, K. [N.], & Geller, B. (1999). Disorders, symptoms, and their pharmacotherapy. In J. S. Werry & M. G. Aman (Eds.), *Practitioner's guide to psychoactive drugs for children and adolescents* (pp. 183–209). New York: Plenum.

Bowden, C. L. (1995). Predictors of response to divalproex and lithium. *Journal of Clinical Psychiatry, 56*(Suppl. 3), 25–30.

Bowden, C. L. (1998). Treatment of bipolar disorder. In A. F. Schatzberg & C. B. Nemeroff (Eds.), *Textbook of psychopharmacology* (2nd ed., pp. 733–743). Washington, DC: American Psychiatric Press.

Bowden, C. L., Brugger, A. M., Swann, A. C., et al. (1994). Efficacy of divalproex vs. lithium and placebo in the treatment of mania (The Depakote Mania Study Group). *JAMA, 271*, 918–924.

Bowden, C. L., Calabrese, J. R., McElroy, S. L., Rhodes, L. J., Keck, P. E., Cookson, J., Anderson, J., Bolden-Watson, C., Ascher, J., Monaghan, E., & Zhou, J. (1999). The efficacy of lamotrigine in rapid cycling and non-rapid cycling patients with bipolar disorder. *Biological Psychiatry, 45*, 953–958.

Boyd, E. A., & Bero, L. A. (2000). Assessing faculty financial relationships with industry: A case study. *JAMA, 284*, 2209–2214.

Bradley, C. (1937). The behavior of children receiving benzedrine. *American Journal of Orthopsychiatry, 9*, 577–585.

Bramble, D. (2003). Annotation: The use of psychotropic medications in children: A British view. *Journal of Child Psychology and Psychiatry, 44*, 169–179.

Brauer, R. B., Stangl, M., Siewert, J. R., Pfab, R., & Becker, K. (2003). Acute liver failure after administration of the herbal tranquilizer kava-kava (*Piper methysticum*). *Journal of Clinical Psychiatry, 64*, 216–218.

Breggin, P. R. (1997). *Brain disabling treatments in psychiatry: Drugs, electroshock, and the role of the FDA.* New York: Springer.

Brenner, R., Bjerkenstedt, L., & Edman, G. V. (2002). *Hypericum perforatum* extract (St. John's wort) for depression. *Psychiatric Annals, 32*, 21–26.

Brent, J. S. (1998). A time-sensitive method for assisting adults in transition. *Journal of Humanistic Psychology, 38*, 7–24.

Britten, N. (1998). Psychiatry, stigma, and resistance. *British Medical Journal, 10*, 963–973.

Brody, A. L., Saxena, S., Stoessel, P., Gillies, P., Fairbanks, L. A., Alborzian, S., Phelps, M. E., Huang, S. C., Wu, H. M., Ho, M. L., Ho, M. K., Au, S. C., Maidment, K., & Baxter, L. R. (2001). Regional brain metabolic changes in patients with major depression treated with either paroxetine or interpersonal therapy: Preliminary findings. *Archives of General Psychiatry, 58*, 631–640.

Brown University Psychopharmacology Update. (2003). Debate continues about atypical antipsychotics and diabetes. *Brown University Psychopharmacology Update, 14*, 1. Providence, RI: Manisses Communications.

Brown University Psychopharmacology Update. (2004). Experts, FDA debate whether SSRIs are safe for children and adolescents. *Brown University Psychopharmacology Update, 15*, 1. Providence, RI: Manisses Communications.

Brown University, Manisses Communications Group. (2002). *Child and Adolescent Psychopharmacology Update, 4*, 3–5. Available on the Web at http://www.medscape.com/viewarticle/423374print. Accessed in September 2002.

Brown, J., Deis, S., & Nace, D. K. (2001). What really makes a difference in psychotherapy outcome? What does managed care want to know. In M. Hubble, B. L. Duncan, & S. A Miller (Eds.), *The heart and soul of change: What works in therapy* (pp. 389–406). Washington, DC: American Psychological Association.

Brown, L. A., & Levin, G. M. (1998). Sertindole: A new atypical antipsychotic for the treatment of schizophrenia. *Pharmacotherapy, 18*, 69–83.

Brown, R. T., & Sammons, M. T. (2002). Pediatric psychopharmacology: A review of new developments and recent research. *Professional Psychology: Research and Practice, 33*, 135–147.

Brown, R. T., & Sawyer, M. G. (1998). *Medications for school-age children: Effects on learning and behavior.* New York: Guilford.

Bryden, K. E., Carrey, N. J., & Kutcher, S. P. (2001). Update and recommendations for the use of antipsychotics in early-onset psychoses. *Journal of Child & Adolescent Psychopharmacology, 11*, 113–130.

Buck, M. (2000). The FDA Modernization Act of 1997: *Impact on pediatric medicine.* Available on the Web at http://www.medscape.com/viewarticle/410910. Accessed on February 14, 2002.

Buelow, G., Herbert, S., & Buelow, S. (2000). *Psychotherapist's resource on psychiatric medications: Issues of treatment and referral.* Belmont, CA: Brooks/Cole.

Bushman, B. J., & Anderson, C. A. Media violence and the American public: Scientific facts versus media misinformation. *American Psychologist, 56*, 477–489.

Buston, K. (2002). Adolescents with mental problems: What do they say about health services? *Journal of Adolescence, 25*, 221–242.

Butterman, K. N., & Geller, B. (1995). Pharmacologic treatment of children and adolescent mania. *Pediatric Pharmacology II, 4*, 283–304.

Cade, J. F. (1949). Lithium salts in the treatment of psychotic excitement. *Medical Journal of Australia, 36*, 349–352.

Calabrese, J. R., Bowden, C. L., McElroy, S. L., Cookson, J., Anderson, J., Keck, P. E., Rhodes, L., Bolden-Watson, C., Zhou, J., & Ascher, J. A. (1999). Spectrum of activity of lamotrigine in treatment-refractory bipolar disorder. *American Journal of Psychiatry, 156*, 1019–1023.

Calabrese, J. R., Bowden, C. L., Sachs, G. S., Asher, J. A., Monaghan, E., & Rudd, G. D. (1999). A double-blind placebo-controlled study of lamotrigine monotherapy in outpatients with bipolar I disorder. *Journal of Clinical Psychiatry, 60*, 79–88.

Calabrese, J. R., Shelton, M. D., Rapport, D. J., & Kimmel, S. E. (2002). Bipolar disorders and the effectiveness of novel anticonvulsants. *Journal of Clinical Psychiatry, 63*(Suppl. 3), 5–9.

Campbell M., & Cueva J. E. (1995). Psychopharmacology in child and adolescent psychiatry: A review of the past seven years. Part I. *Journal of the American Acad-*

*emy of Child and Adolescent Psychiatry, 34,* 1124–1132.

Campbell, M., Kafantaris, V., & Cueva, J. E. (1995). An update on the use of lithium carbonate in aggressive children and adolescents with conduct disorders. *Psychopharmacology Bulletin, 31,* 93–102.

Campbell, M., Rapoport, J., & Simpson, G. (1999). Antipsychotics in children and adolescents. *Journal of the American Academy of Child and Adolescent Psychiatry, 38,* 537–545.

Capwell, R. R. (1995). Ephedrine-induced mania from an herbal diet supplement. *American Journal of Psychiatry, 152,* 647.

Carlson, G. A. (1996). Compared to attention deficit hyperactivity disorder. *American Journal of Psychiatry, 153,* 1128–30.

Carlson, G. A. (2002). Clinical aspects of child and adolescent psychopharmacology. In S. Kutcher (Ed.), *Practical child and adolescent psychopharmacology* (pp. 70–90). Cambridge, UK: Cambridge University Press.

Carlson, N. R. (2001). *Physiology of behavior* (7th ed.). Boston: Allyn and Bacon.

Carlsson, A., & Lindqvist, M. (1963). Effect of chlorpromazine or haloperidol on the formation of 3-methoxytyramine and normetanephrine in mouse brain. *Acta Pharmacologica, 20,* 140–144.

Caroff, S. N., & Mann, S. C. (1993). Neuroleptic malignant syndrome. *Medical Clinics of North America, 77,* 185–202.

Carrey, N., Mendella, P., MacMaster, F. P., & Kutcher, S. (2002). Developmental psychopharmacology. In S. Kutcher (Ed.), *Practical child and adolescent psychopharmacology* (pp. 38–69). Cambridge, UK: Cambridge University Press.

Casey, D. A. (1993). Neuroleptic-induced extrapyramidal syndromes and tardive dyskinesia. *Psychiatric Clinics of North America, 16,* 589–610.

Casey, D. E. (1996). Side effect profiles of new antipsychotic agents. *Journal of Clinical Psychiatry, 57*(Suppl. 11), 40–45.

Castellanos, F. X., Lee, P. P., Sharp, W., Jeffries, N. O., Greenstein, D. K., Blumenthal, J. D., James, R. S., Ebens, C. L., Walter, J. M., Zijdenbos, A., Evans, A. C., Giedd, J. N., & Rappaport, J. L. (2002). Developmental trajectories of brain volume abnormalities in children and adolescents with attention-deficit/hyperactivity disorder. *JAMA, 288,* 1740–1748.

Cervo, L., Rozio, M., Ekalle-Soppo, C. B., Guiso, G., Morazzoni, P., & Caccia, S. (2002). Role of hyperforin in the antidepressant-like activity of *Hypericum perforatum* extracts. *Psychopharmacology, 164,* 423–428.

Chalmers, D. J. (1995). The puzzle of conscious experience. *Scientific American, 273,* 80–86.

Chengappa, K. N., Gershon, S., & Levine, J. (2001). The evolving role of topiramate among other mood stabi-lizers in the management of bipolar disorder. *Bipolar Disorder, 3,* 215–232.

Chomsky, N. (2002). *Distorted morality: America's war on terror?* (Lectures on DVD). New York: Silent Films.

Chopra, D. (1993). *Ageless body, timeless mind.* New York: Harmony Books.

Churchland, P. S. (1995). *Neurophilosophy: Toward a unified science of the mind/brain.* Cambridge, MA: MIT Press.

Churchland, P. S. (1999). Toward a natural science of the mind. In Z. Houshmand, R. B. Livingston, & B. A. Wallace (Eds.), *Consciousness at the crossroads: Conversations with the Dalai Lama on brain science and Buddhism* (pp. 17–32). Ithaca, NY: Snow Lion Press.

Clark, P. (2000). The ethics of medical marijuana: Government restrictions vs. medical necessity. *Journal of Public Health Policy, 21,* 40–60.

Clayton, R. R., & Leukefeld, C. G. (1992). The prevention of drug use among youth: Implications of legalization. *Journal of Primary Prevention, 12,* 289–303.

Cocks, M., & Moller, V. (2002). Use of indigenous and indigenised medicines to enhance personal well being: A South African case study. *Social Science and Medicine, 54,* 387–397.

Coffey, B. (1990). Anxiolytics for children and adolescents: Traditional and new drugs. *Journal of Child and Adolescent Psychopharmacology, 1,* 57–83.

Cohen, D., Gerardin, P., Mazet, P., Purper-Ouakil, D., & Flament, M. F. (2004). Pharmacological treatment of adolescent major depression. *Journal of Child and Adolescent Psychopharmacology, 14,* 19–31.

Colbert, T. C. (2002). Drugs or psychotherapy? What's the answer? Symposium conducted in Beachwood, Ohio, June 14, 2002.

Collett, B. R., Ohan, J. L., & Myers, K. M. (2003). Ten-year review of rating scales. V: Scales assessing attention-deficit/hyperactive disorder. *Journal of the American Academy of Child and Adolescent Psychiatry, 42,* 1015–1037.

Connor, K. M., & Davidson, J. R. (2002). A placebo-controlled study of kava kava in generalized anxiety disorder. *International Clinical Psychopharmacology, 17,* 185–188.

Connors, C. K. (1972). Pharmacotherapy. In H. C. Quay & J. S. Werry (Eds.), *Psychopathological disorders of childhood* (pp. 316–347). New York: Wiley.

Connors, D. (1996). Bupropion hydrochloride in attention deficit disorder with hyperactivity. *Journal of the American Academy of Child and Adolescent Psychiatry, 35,* 1314–1321.

Consumer's Union. (1999). Herbal Rx: The promises and pitfalls. *Consumer Reports, 64,* 44–48.

Copp, P. J., Lament, R., & Tennent, T. G. (1991). Amitriptyline in clozapine-induced sialorrhoea (letter). *British Journal of Psychiatry, 159,* 166.

Coppen, A., & Healy, D. (1996). Biological psychiatry in Britain. In D. Healy (Ed.), *The psychopharmacologists* (pp. 265–286). London: Chapman & Hall.

Corrigan, P., River, P., Lundin, R., Wasowski, K., Campion, J., Methsien, J., Goldstein, H., Bergman, M., & Gagnon, C. (2000). Stigmatizing attributions about mental illness. *Journal of Community Psychology, 28*, 91–102.

Cott, J., & Wisner, K. L. (2002). Effect of *Hypericum perforatum* (St. John's wort) in major depressive disorder: A randomized controlled trial: Comment. *JAMA, 288*, 448.

Coyle, J. T. (2000). Psychotropic drug use in very young children. *JAMA, 283*, 1059–1060.

Crites-Leoni, A. (1998). Medicinal use of marijuana: Is the debate a smoke screen for movement toward legalization? *Journal of Legal Medicine, 19*, 273–304.

Cupp, M. J. (1999). Herbal remedies: Adverse effects and drug interactions. *American Family Physician, 59*, 1661–1662.

Cyranowski, J. M., Frank, E., Young, W. E., & Shear, M. K. (2000). Adolescent onset of the gender difference in lifetime rates of major depression. *Archives of General Psychiatry, 57*, 21–27.

Damasio, A. (1995). *Descartes' error: Emotion, reason and the human brain.* New York: Putnam.

Damasio, A. (2000). *The feeling of what happens: Body and emotion in the making of consciousness.* New York: Harvest.

Danion, J. M., Rein, W., Fleurot, O., & the Amisulpride Study Group. (1999). Improvement of schizophrenic patients with primary negative symptoms treated with amisulpride. *American Journal of Psychiatry, 156*, 610–616.

Dannawi, M. (2002). Possible serotonin syndrome after combination of buspirone and St. John's wort. *Journal of Psychopharmacology, 16*, 401.

Danton, W. G., & Antonuccio, D. O. (1997). A focused empirical analysis of treatments for panic and anxiety. In S. Fisher & R. P. Greenberg (Eds.), *From placebo to panacea: Putting psychiatric drugs to the test* (pp. 229–280). New York: Wiley.

Dardennes, R., Even, C., Bange, F., & Heim, A. (1995). Comparison of carbamazepine and lithium in the prophylaxis of bipolar disorders: A meta-analysis. *British Journal of Psychiatry, 166*, 378–381.

Daumit, G. L, Crum, R. M., Guallar, E., Powe, N. R., Primm, A. B., Steinwachs, D. M., & Ford, D. E. (2003). Outpatient prescriptions for atypical antipsychotics for African Americans, Hispanics, and whites in the United States. *Archives of General Psychiatry, 60*, 121–128.

David, A., & Kemp, R. (1997). Five perspectives on the phenomenon of insight in psychosis. *Psychiatric Annals, 27*, 791–797.

Davis, L. L., Ryan, B., Adinoff, B., & Petty, F. (2000). Comprehensive review of the psychiatric uses of

valproate. *Journal of Clinical Psychopharmacology, 20*(Suppl. 1), 1–7.

De Fonseca, F. R., Carrera, M. R. A., Navarro, M., Koob, G. F., & Weiss, F. (1997). Activation of corticotropin-releasing factor in the limbic system during cannabinoid withdrawal. *Science, 276*, 2050–2054.

Debner, A. (2001a, April 10). Many children can't get mental care. *Boston Globe*, p. B1.

Debner, A. (2001b, May 8). Doctors see crisis in youth psychiatry. *Boston Globe*, p. B2.

Decina, P., Schlegel, A. M., & Fieve, R. R. (1987). Lithium poisoning. *New York State Journal of Medicine, 87*, 230–231.

Delbello, M. P., Schwiers, M. L., Rosenberg, H. L., & Strakowski, S. M. (2002). A double-blind, randomized, placebo-controlled study of quetiapine as adjunctive treatment for adolescent mania. *Journal of the American Academy of Child and Adolescent Psychiatry, 41*, 1216–1223.

Delgado, P. L., & Gelenberg, A. J. (2001). Antidepressant and antimanic medications. In G. O. Gabbard (Ed.), *Treatments of psychiatric disorders* (3rd ed., pp. 1137–1180). Washington, DC: American Psychiatric Publishing.

Delva, N. J., & Hawken, E. R. (2001). Preventing lithium intoxication: Guide for physicians. *Canadian Family Physician, 47*, 1595–1600.

Demyttenaere, K. (2001). Compliance and acceptance in antidepressant treatment. *Journal of Psychiatry in Clinical Practice, 5*, 529–535.

Demyttenaere, K., Mesters, P., Boulanger, B., Dewe, W., Delsemme, M., Gregoire, J., & Van Ganse, E. (2001). Adherence to treatment regimen in depressed patients treated with amitriptyline or fluoxetine. *Journal of Affective Disorders, 65*, 243–252.

Dennett, D. C. (1991). *Consciousness explained.* Boston: Little, Brown.

DeQuardo, J. R., & Tandon, R. (1998). Do atypical antipsychotic medications favorably alter the long-term course of schizophrenia? *Journal of Psychiatric Research, 32*, 229–242.

Dilts, S. L. (2001). *Models of the mind: A framework for biopsychosocial psychiatry.* Philadelphia: Brunner/Rutledge.

Doblin, R. E., & Kleinman, M. A. R. (1991). Marijuana as antiemetic medicine: A survey of oncologists' experiences and attitudes. *Journal of Clinical Oncology, 9*, 1314–1319.

Dodd, C. (2001). *Dodd and Dewine introduce bill to provide better drug safety.* Available on the Web at www.senate.gov/~dodd/press/Release/01/0504.htm. Accessed on September 2002.

Dolder, C. R., & Jeste, D. V. (2003). Incidence of tardive dyskinesia with typical versus atypical antipsychotics in very high-risk patients. *Biological Psychiatry, 53*, 1142–1145.

Dossey, L. (2001). *Healing beyond the body: Medicine and the infinite reach of the mind.* Boston: Shambhala.

Duke, S. B., & Gross, A. C. (1993). *America's longest war: Rethinking our tragic crusade against drugs.* New York: Putnam.

Duloxetine significantly reduces symptoms of depression. (2001). Available on the Web at http://www.medscape.com/viewarticle/411151. Accessed on January 20, 2005.

Duman, R. S., Heninger, G. R., & Nestler, E. J. (1997). A molecular and cellular theory of depression. *Archives of General Psychiatry, 54,* 597–608.

Dunn, M. S., Eddy, J. M., Wang, M. Q., Nagy, S., Perko, M. A., & Bartee, R. T. (2001). The influence of significant others on attitudes, subjective norms and intentions regarding dietary supplement use among adolescent athletes. *Adolescence, 36,* 583–591.

Dunner, D. L., Fleiss, J. L., & Fieve, R. R. (1976). Lithium carbonate prophylaxis failure. *British Journal of Psychiatry, 129,* 40–44.

DuPaul, G. J., & Rappaport, M. D. (1993). Does methylphenidate normalize the classroom performance of children with attention deficit disorder? *Journal of the American Academy of Child and Adolescent Psychiatry, 32,* 190–98.

Eberle, A. J. (1998). Valproate and polycystic ovaries. *Journal of the American Academy of Child and Adolescent Psychiatry, 37,* 1009.

Edwards, J. H. (2002). Evidenced-based treatment for child ADHD: "Real world" practical implications. *Journal of Mental Health Counseling, 24,* 126–129.

Eisenberg, D. M., Davis, R. B., Ettner, S. L., et. al. (1998). Trends in alternative medicine use in the United States, 1990–1997. *JAMA, 280,* 1569–75.

Eisner, B. (1994). *Ecstasy: The MDMA story.* Berkeley, CA: Ronin.

Eldredge, D. C. (1998). *Ending the war on drugs: A solution for America.* Bridgehampton, NY: Bridgeworks.

El-Mallakh, R. (1987). Marijuana and migraine. *Headache, 27,* 442–443.

Emslie, G. J., Rush, A. J., Weinberg, W. A., Kowarch, R. A., Hughes, C. W., Carmody, T., & Rintelmann, J. (1997). A double-blind, randomized, placebo-controlled trial of fluoxetine in children and adolescents with depression. *Archives of General Psychiatry, 54,* 1031–1037.

Engler, J. (1986). Therapeutic aims in psychotherapy and meditation: Developmental stages in the representation of self. In K. Wilber, J. Engler, & D. P. Brown (Eds.), *Transformations of consciousness: Conventional and contemplative perspectives on development* (pp. 17–51). Boston: Shambhala.

Epstein, H. T. (2001). An outline of the role of brain in human cognitive development. *Brain and Cognition, 45,* 44–51.

Ercil, N. E., & France, C. P. (2003). Amphetamine-like discrimination stimulus effects of ephedrine and its stereoisomers in pigeons. *Experimental & Clinical Psychopharmacology, 11,* 3–8.

Ereshefsky, L. (1996). Pharmacokinetics and drug interactions: Update for new antipsychotics. *Journal of Clinical Psychiatry, 57*(Suppl. 11), 12–25.

Erikson, E. (1968). *Identity, youth, and crisis.* New York: Norton.

Ernst, E. (2002). The risk-benefit profile of commonly used herbal therapies: Ginkgo, St. John's wort, ginseng, echinacea, saw palmetto, and kava. *Annals of Internal Medicine, 136,* 42–53.

Ernst, M. E., Kelly, M. W., Hoehns, J. D., Swegle, J. M, Buys, L. M., Logemann, C. D., Ford, J. K., Kautzman, H. A., Sorofman, B. A., & Pretorius, R. W. (2000). Prescription medication costs: A study of physician familiarity. *Archives of Family Medicine, 9,* 1002–1007.

Ernst, M., Malone, R. P., Rowan, A. B., George, R., Gonzalez, N. M., & Silva, R.R. (1999). Antipsychotics (neuroleptics). In J. S. Werry & M. Aman (Eds.), *Practitioner's guide to psychoactive drugs for children and adolescents* (pp. 297– 325). New York: Plenum.

Even, C., Friedman, S., & Dardennes, R. (2001). Antidepressant trials generally have methodological defects. *British Medical Journal, 323,* 574.

Evins, E. A. (2003). Efficacy of newer anticonvulsant medications in bipolar spectrum mood disorders. *The Journal of Clinical Psychiatry, 64,* 9–14.

Express Scripts. (2001). Fact sheet: Express scripts drug trend report. Available on the Web at http://www.express-scripts.com/. Accessed on November 14, 2001.

Faraone, S. V., Phiszka, S. R., Olvera, R. L., Skolnik, R. S., & Biederman, J. (2001). Efficacy of adderall and methylphenidate in attention deficit hyperactivity disorder: A reanalysis using drug–placebo and drug–drug response curve methodology. *Journal of Child and Adolescent Psychopharmacology, 11,* 171–180.

Fawcett, J., & Busch, K. A. (Eds.). (1998). *Textbook of psychopharmacology* (2nd ed). Washington, DC: American Psychiatric Association.

Felder, C. C., & Glass, M. (1998). Cannabinoid receptors and their endogenous agonists. *Annual Review of Pharmacology and Toxicology, 38,* 179–200.

Feldman, R. S., Meyer, J. S., & Quenzer, L. F. (1997). Sedative and hypnotic drugs. In A. L. Sinauer (Ed.), *Principles of neuropsychopharmacology* (pp. 702–703). Sunderland, MA: Sinauer.

Fenton, W. S., & McGlashan, T. H. (1997). We can talk: Individual psychotherapy for schizophrenia. *American Journal of Psychiatry, 154,* 1493–1495.

Fernandez, H. H., & Friedman, J. H. (2003). Classification and treatment of tardive syndromes. *Neurology, 9,* 16–27.

Ferrier, I. N. (1998). Lamotrigine and gabapentin: Alternatives in the treatment of bipolar disorder. *Neuropsychobiology, 38,* 192–197.

Findlay, A. (1938). *A hundred years of chemistry.* New York: Macmillan.

Findling, R. L., McNamara, N. K., Branicky, L. A., Schluchter, M. D., Lemon, E., & Blumer, J. (2000). A double-blind pilot study of risperidone in the treatment of conduct disorder. *Journal of the American Academy of Child and Adolescent Psychiatry, 39*, 509–516.

Findling, R. L., Reed, M. D., Myers, C., O'Riordan, M. A., Fiala, S., Branicky, M. A., Waldoref, B., & Blumer, J. L. (1999). Paroxetine pharmacokinetics in depressed children and adolescents. *Journal of the American Academy of Child and Adolescent Psychiatry, 38*, 952–959.

Fisher, R. L., & Fisher, S. (1997). Are we justified in treating children with psychotropic drugs? In S. Fisher & R. P. Greenberg (Eds.), *From placebo to panacea: Putting psychiatric drugs to the test* (pp. 307–322). New York: Wiley

Fisher, S., & Greenberg, R. P. (Eds.). (1997). *From placebo to panacea: Putting psychiatric drugs to the test.* New York: Wiley.

Flaherty, J. A., & Meagher, R. (1980). Measuring racial bias in inpatient treatment. *American Journal of Psychiatry, 137*, 679–682.

Flam, F. (1994). Hints of language in junk DNA. *Science, 266*, 1320.

Fleischhacker, W. W., Czobor, P., Hummer, M., Kemmler, G., Kohnen, R., & Volavka, J. (2003). Placebo or active control trials of antipsychotic drugs? *Archives of General Psychiatry, 60*, 458–464.

Foa, E. B., & Franklin, M. E. (2001). Obsessive compulsive disorder. In D. H. Barlow (Ed.), *Clinical handbook of psychological disorders: A step-by-step treatment manual* (3rd ed.). New York: Guilford.

Food and Drug Administration [FDA]. (2003). FDA public health advisory: Reports of suicidality in pediatric patients being treated with antidepressant medication for major depressive disorder. Available on the Web at www.fda.gov/cder/drug/advisory/mdd.htm Accessed on November 1st, 2003.

Food and Drug Administration Act and Best Pharmaceuticals Act for Children, Law No. 107–109. S. 1789, 1–17.

Food and Drug Administration Modernization Act of 1997: Impact on pediatric medicine. Available on the Web at http://www.medscape.com/viewarticle/410910. Accessed on February 14, 2002.

Fox, M. (2003). Baseball player's death re-ignites ephedra debate. *Reuters Daily News, 2* C1.

Franklin, D. (1990). Hooked–not hooked: Why isn't everyone an addict? *Health, 1*, 39–52.

Freeman, T. W., Clothier, J. L., Pazzaglia, P., et al. (1992). A double-blind comparison of Valproate and lithium in the treatment of acute mania. *American Journal of Psychiatry, 149*, 108–111.

Freud, S. (1925). Inhibitions, symptoms, and anxiety. In *The standard edition of the complete psychological works of Sigmund Freud* (pp. 77–178). Edited by J. Strachey. London: Hogarth Press.

Freud, S. (1955). *The standard edition of the complete psychological works of Sigmund Freud.* Vol. 2: Studies on hysteria. (J. Strachey, A. Freud, A. Strachey, & A. Tyson, Trans.) London: Hogarth Press. (Original work published in 1895).

Freud, S. (1966). *Introductory lectures on psychoanalysis.* New York: Norton.

Fried, P., Watkinson, B., James, D., & Gray, R. (2002). Current and former marijuana use: Preliminary findings of a longitudinal study of effects on IQ in young adults. *Canadian Medical Association Journal, 166*, 887–891.

Friede, M., Henneicke von Zepelin, H. H., & Freudenstein, J. (2001). Differential therapy of mild to moderate depressive episodes (ICD-10 F 32.0; F 32.1) with St. John's wort. *Pharmacopsychiatry, 34*(Suppl. 1), 38–41.

Friedman, J. H. (2003). Atypical antipsychotics in the EPS-vulnerable patient. *Psychoneuroendocrinology, 28*, 39–51.

Frye, M. A., Ketter, T. A., Kimbrell, T. A., Dunn, R. T., Speer, R. M., Osuch, E. A., Luckenbaugh, D. A., Cora-Ocatelli, G., Leverich, G. S., & Post, R. M. (2000). A placebo-controlled study of lamotrigine and gabapentin monotherapy in refractory mood disorders. *Journal of Clinical Psychopharmacology, 20*, 607–614.

Fuller, M. A., Shermock, K. M., Secic, M., & Grogg, A. L. (2003). Comparative study of the development of diabetes mellitus in patients taking risperidone and olanzapine. *Pharmocotherapy, 23*, 1037–1043.

Furman, R. (1993). Kuhn, chaos and psychoanalysis. *Child Analysis 4*, 133–150.

Furman, R. (1996). Methylphenidate and "ADHD" in Europe and the U.S.A.. *Child Analysis 7*, 132–145.

Furman, R. (2000). Attention deficit/hyperactivity disorder: An alternative viewpoint. *Journal of Infant, Child and Adolescent Psychotherapy 2*, 125–144.

Gabbard, G. O. (1994). *Psychodynamic psychiatry in clinical practice: The DSM-IV edition.* Washington, DC: American Psychiatric Press.

Gabbard, G. O. (2001). Mind and brain in psychiatric treatment. In G. O. Gabbard (Ed.), *Treatment of the DSM-IV psychiatric disorders* (3rd ed., pp. 3–21). Washington, DC: American Psychiatric Press.

Gadow, K. D. (1999). Prevalence of drug therapy. In J. S. Werry & M. Aman (Eds.), *Practitioner's guide to psychoactive drugs for children and adolescents* (pp. 355–385). New York: Plenum.

Garbarino, J. (1998). Children in a violent world: A metaphysical perspective. *Family and Conciliation Courts Review, 36*, 360–367.

Gardiner, H. W., & Kosmitzki, C. (2001). *Lives across cultures: Cross cultural human development* (2nd ed.). Boston: Allyn and Bacon.

Garland, E. J. (2002). Anxiety disorders. In S. Kutcher (Ed.), *Practical child and adolescent psychopharma-*

cology (pp. 187–229). Cambridge, UK: Cambridge. University Press.

Gaster, B., & Holroyd, J. (2000). St. John's wort for depression: A systematic review. *Archives of Internal Medicine, 160,* 152–156.

Geiger, J. D. (2002). Adverse events associated with supplements containing ephedra alkaloids. *Clinical Journal of Sport Medicine, 12,* 263.

Gelman, S. (1999). *Medicating schizophrenia: A history.* New Brunswick, NJ: Rutgers University Press.

Ghaemi, S. N., Berv, D. A., Klugman, J., Resenquist, K. J. & Hsu, D. J. (2003). Oxcarbazepine treatment of bipolar disorder. *Journal of Clinical Psychiatry, 64,* 943–945.

Gianluigi, T., Pontieri, F. E., & Chiara, G. (1997). Cannabinoid and heroin activation of mesolimbic dopamine transmission by a common opioid receptor mechanism. *Science, 276,* 2048–2049.

Gilbert, S. F. (2003). *Developmental biology,* 7th ed. New York: Sinauer.

Glazer, W. M., Morgenstern, H., & Doucette, J. (1994). Race and tardive dyskinesia among outpatients at a CMHC. *Hospital Community Psychiatry, 45,* 38–42.

Glennon, R. A., & Young, R. (2000). Amphetamine-stimulus generalization to an herbal ephedrine product. *Pharmacology, Biochemistry, & Behavior, 65,* 655–688.

Gold, J. L., Laxer, D. A., Dergal, J. M., Lanctot, K. L., & Rochon, P. A. (2001). Herbal–drug interactions: A focus on dementia. *Current Opinion in Clinical Nutrition and Metabolic Care, 4,* 29–34.

Gold, M. S., Tullis, M., & Frost-Pineda, K. (2001). Cannabis use, abuse, and dependence. In G. O. Gabbard (Ed.), *Treatment of psychiatric disorders* (3rd ed., pp. 703–719). Washington, DC: American Psychiatric Association.

Goldman, L., Genel, M. Bezman, R., & Slanetz, P. (1998). Diagnosis and treatment of attention-deficit/hyperactivity disorder in children and adolescents. *JAMA, 279,* 1100.

Goldman-Rakic, P., & Brown, R. M. (1982). Postnatal development of monoamine content and synthesis in the cerebral cortex of rhesus monkeys. *Developmental Brain Research, 4,* 339–349.

Goldstein, A. P., & Conoley, J. C. (1998). Student aggression: Current status. In A. P. Goldstein & J. C. Conoley (Eds.), *School violence intervention: A practical handbook* (pp. 3–19). New York: Guilford Press.

Goldstein, L. E., Spron, J., Brown, S., Kim, H., Finkelstein, J., Gaffey, G. K., Sachs, G., & Stern, T. A. (1999). New-onset diabetes mellitus and diabetic ketoacidosis associated with olanzapine treatment. *Psychosomatics, 40,* 438–443.

Goleman, D. (1993, December 15). Use of antidepressants in children at issue. *New York Times,* p. 7.

Goodman, W. K., McDougle, C. J., Barr, L. C., Aronson, S. C., & Price, L. H (1993). Biological approaches to treatment resistant obsessive compulsive disorder. *Journal of Clinical Psychiatry, 54,* 16–26.

Goodwin, F. K., & Ghaemi, S. N. (1999). The impact of the discovery of lithium on psychiatric thought and practice in the USA and Europe. *Australian New Zealand Journal of Psychiatry, 33*(Suppl. 1), 54–64.

Goodwin, F. K., & Jamison, K. R. (1990). *Manic depressive illness.* New York: Oxford University Press.

Gordis, E. (2000). Why do some people drink too much? The role of genetic and psychosocial influences. *Alcohol Research and Health, 24,* 17–26.

Gordon, A., & Price, L. H. (1999). Mood stabilizers and weight loss with topiramate. *American Journal of Psychiatry, 156,* 968–969.

Gould, E., Beylin, A., Panapat, P., Reeves, A., & Shors, T. J. (1999). Learning enhances adult neurogenesis in the hippocampal formation. *Nature Neuroscience, 2,* 260–265.

Gray, G. E. (1999). A psychiatric perspective on herbal remedies. *Directions in Psychiatry, 19,* 349–359.

Green, B. (1999). Focus on quetiapine. Available on the Web at http://www.priory.com/focus4.htm. Accessed on January 21, 2003.

Green, R. W., & Albon, J. S. (2001). What does the MTA study tell us about effective psychosocial treatment for ADHD? *Journal of Clinical Child Psychology, 30,* 114–121.

Greenberg, R. P., & Fisher, S. (1997). Mood-mending medicines: Probing drug, psychotherapy, and placebo solutions. In S. Fisher & R. P. Greenberg (Eds.), *From placebo to panacea: Putting psychiatric drugs to the test* (pp. 115–172). New York: Wiley.

Greenhill, L. L. (1998). Childhood attention deficit hyperactivity disorder: Pharmacological treatments. In P. Nathan & J. Gorman (Eds.), *A guide to treatments that work* (pp. 42–64). New York: Oxford University Press.

Greenhill, L. L., Jensen, P. S., Abikoff, H., Blumer, J. L., DeVeaugh-Geiss, J., Fisher, C., Hoagwood, K., Kratochvil, C. J., Lahey, B., Laughgren, T., Leckman, J., Petti, T. A., Pope, K., Shaffer, D., Benedetto, V., & Zeanah, C. (2003). Developing strategies for psychopharmacological studies on preschool children. *Journal of the American Academy of Child and Adolescent Psychiatry, 42,* 406–414.

Greer, G. (1985). Using MDMA in psychotherapy. *Advances, 2,* 57–62.

Greer, G., & Tolbert, R. (1986). Subjective reports on the effects of MDMA in a clinical setting. *Journal of Psychoactive Drugs, 18,* 319–327.

Grilly, D. M. (1994). *Drugs and human behavior* (3rd ed.). Boston: Allyn and Bacon.

Grinspoon, L., & Bakalar, J. B. (1997). *Psychedelic drugs reconsidered.* New York: Lindsmith Center.

Grof, P., & Alda, M. (2001). Discrepancies in the efficacy of lithium. *Archives of General Psychiatry, 57,* 191.

Grof, P., Alda, M., Grof, E., Fox, D. & Cameron, P. (1993). The challenge of predicting response to stabilising lithium treatment: The importance of patient selection. *British Journal of Psychiatry*, (Suppl. 21), 16–19.

Grof, S. (1998). *The transpersonal vision: The healing potential of nonordinary states of consciousness*. Boulder, CO: Sounds True.

Grof, S. (2000). *Psychology of the future: Lessons from modern consciousness research*. Albany: SUNY Press.

Grube, B., Walper, A., & Wheatley, D. (1999). St. John's wort extract: Efficacy for menopausal symptoms of psychological origin. *Advances in Therapy*, 16, 177–186.

Gruber, A. J., & Pope, H. G. (1998). Ephedrine abuse among 36 female weightlifters. *American Journal on Addictions*, 7, 256–261.

Gunaratana, B. H. (2002). *Mindfulness in plain English*. Boston: Wisdom Publications.

Gurley, R. J., Aranow, R., & Katz, M. (1998). Medicinal marijuana: A comprehensive review. *Journal of Psychoactive Drugs*, 30, 137–147.

Gutgesell, H., Atkins, D., Barst, R., Buck, M., Franklin, W., Humes, R., Ringel, R., Shaddy, R., & Taubert, K. A. (1999). AHA Scientific statement: Cardiovascular monitoring of children and adolescents receiving psychotropic drugs. *Journal of the American Academy of Child & Adolescent Psychiatry*, 38, 1047–1050.

Gutherie, S. K. (1999). Herbaceuticals in psychiatry. Unpublished lecture given at the Medical College of Ohio, Toledo, September 24.

Hailemaskel, B., Dutta, A., & Wutoh, A. (2001). Adverse reactions and interactions among herbal users. *Issues in Interdisciplinary Care*, 3, 297–300.

Hamilton, J. A. (1986). An overview of the clinical rationale for advancing gender related psychopharmacology and drug abuse research. In B. A. Ray & M. C. Baude (Eds.), *Women and drugs: A new era for research* (pp. 14–20). (NIDA [National Institute on Drug Abuse] manuscript). Washington DC: U.S. Government Printing Office.

Hampson, A. J., Grimaldi, M., Lolic, M., Wink, D., Rosenthal, R., & Axelrod, J. (2000). Neuroprotective antioxidants from marijuana. *Annals of the New York Academy of Sciences*, 899, 274–282.

Handen, B. L., Feldman, H. M., Lurier, A., & Murray, P. J. (1999). Efficacy of methylphenidate among preschool children with developmental disabilities and ADHD. *Journal of American Academy of Child and Adolescent Psychiatry*, 38, 805–812.

Haney, M., Ward, A. S., Comer, S. D., Foltin, R. W., & Fischman, M. W. (1999). Abstinence symptoms following smoked marijuana in humans. *Psychopharmacology*, 141, 395–404.

Harranz, J. L., & Argumosa, A. (2002). Characteristics and indications of oxcarbazepine. *Revista de Neurologia*, 35(Suppl), S101–S109.

Harris, G. (2004). Study shows medication helps teens in depression. *New York Times*, A10.

Healy, D. (1997). *The antidepressant era*. Cambridge, MA: Harvard University Press.

Healy, D. (2002). *The creation of psychopharmacology*. Cambridge, MA: Harvard University Press.

Heimann, S. W. (1999). High-dose olanzapine in an adolescent. *Journal of the American Academy of Child and Adolescent Psychiatry*, 38, 496–498.

Heinrich, M., & Gibbons, S. (2001). Ethnopharmacology in drug discovery: An analysis of its role and potential contribution. *Journal of Pharmacy and Pharmacology*, 53, 425–432.

Hellewell, J. S. E. (2002). Oxcarbazepine (Trileptal) in the treatment of bipolar disorders: A review of efficacy and tolerability. *Journal of Affective Disorders*, 72 (Suppl.), S32–S34.

Herer, J. (1992). *The emperor wears no clothes: Hemp & the marijuana conspiracy* (rev. ed.). Van Nuys, CA: HEMP Publishing.

Herkenham, M. L., Little, M. D., Johnson, M. R., Melvin, L. S., deCosta, B. R., & Rice, K. C. (1990). Cannabinoid receptor localization in the brain. *Proceedings of the National Academy of Science*, 87, 1932–1936.

Hirsch, S. R., Link, C. G., Goldstein, J. M., & Arvanitis, L. A. (1996). ICI 204, 636: A new atypical antipsychotic drug. *British Journal of Psychiatry*, 168(Suppl. 29), 45–46.

Hirschfeld, R. M. A., Calabrese, J. R., Weissman, M. M., Reed, M., Davies, M. A., Frye, M. A., Keck, P. E., Lewis, L., McElroy, S. L., McNulty, J. P., & Wagner, K. D. (2003). Screening for bipolar disorder in the community. *Journal of Clinical Psychiatry*, 64, 53–59.

Hoehn-Saric, R., Borkovec, T. D., & Nemiah, J. C. (1994). Generalized anxiety disorder. In G. O. Gabbard (Ed.), *Treatment of psychiatric disorder* (2nd ed., vol. 2). Washington, DC: American Psychiatric Association.

Hoge, W. (2002). Britain to relax marijuana laws. Available at http://www.hempfarm.org/Papers/Britains_Relax.html. Accessed on October 14, 2004.

Hollon, M. F. (1999). Direct-to-consumer marketing of prescription drugs: Creating consumer demand. *JAMA*, 281, 1227–1228.

Holmer, A. F. (1999). Direct to consumer prescription drug advertising builds bridges between patients and physicians. *JAMA*, 281, 380–382.

Holsboer-Trachsler, F., & Vanoni, C. (1999). Clinical efficacy and tolerance of the hypericum special extract LI 160 in depressive disorders: A drug monitoring study. *Schweizerische Rundschau für Medizin Praxis*, 88, 1475–1480.

Houghton, P. J. (1999). The scientific basis for the reputed activity of valerian. *Journal of Pharmacy and Pharmacology*, 51, 505–512.

House, A. E. (1999). *DSM-IV diagnosis in the schools.* New York: Guilford.

Hubble, M., Duncan, B. L., & Miller, S. A. (2001). *The heart and soul of change: What works in therapy.* Washington, DC: American Psychological Association.

Huffington, A. (2000). *How to overthrow the government.* New York: Regan Books.

Hummel, B., Walden, J., Stampfer, R., Dittmann, S., Amann, S., Benedikt, A., Sterr, A., Schaefer, M., Frye, M. A., & Grunze, H. (2002). Acute antimanic efficacy and safety of oxcarbazepine in an open trial with an on-off-on design. *Bipolar Disorders, 4,* 412–417.

Hurley, S. C. (2002). Lamotrigine update and its use in mood disorders. *Annals of Pharmacotherapy, 36,* 860–873.

Hutton, R. (1999). *The triumph of the moon: A history of modern pagan witchcraft.* Oxford, UK: Oxford University Press.

Hypericum Depression Trial Study Group. (2002). Effect of *Hypericum perforatum* (St. John's Wort) in major depressive disorder: A randomized controlled trial. *JAMA, 287,* 1807–1814.

Ikonomov, O. C., & Manji, H. K. (1999). Molecular mechanisms underlying mood stabilization in manic-depressive illness: The phenotype challenge. *American Journal of Psychiatry, 156,* 1506–1514.

Ingersoll, R. E. (2000). Teaching a course in psychopharmacology to counselors: Justification, structure, and methods. *Counselor Education and Supervision, 40,* 58–69.

Ingersoll, R. E. (2001). The nonmedical therapist's role in pharmacological interventions with adults. In E. R. Welfel & R. E. Ingersoll (Eds.), *The mental health desk reference* (pp. 88–93). New York: Wiley.

Ingersoll, R. E. (2002). An integral approach for teaching and practicing diagnosis. *Journal of Transpersonal Psychology, 34,* 115–127.

Ingersoll, R. E., & Burns, L. (2001). Prevalence of adult disorders. In E. R. Welfel & R. E. Ingersoll (Eds.), *The mental health desk reference* (pp. 3–9). New York: Wiley.

Ingersoll, R. E., Bauer, A. L., & Burns, L. (2004). Children and psychotropic medication: What role should advocacy counseling play? *Journal of Counseling and Development, 82,* 342–348.

Institute of Medicine. (1999). *Marijuana and medicine: Assessing the science base.* Washington, DC: Author.

Interactive Medical Networks (producer). (2001). What makes a drug a mood stabilizer? A video symposium. Carrolton, TX: Interactive Medical Networks.

International Committee of Medical Journal Editors. (2001). *Uniform requirements for manuscripts submitted to biomedical journals.* Available on the Web at www.icmje.org .

Izzo, A. A., & Ernst, E. (2001). Interactions between herbal medicines and prescribed drugs: A systematic review. *Drugs, 61,* 2163–2175.

Jacobs, K. M., & Hirsch, K. A. (2000). Psychiatric complications of ma-huang. *Psychosomatics: Journal of Consultation Liaison Psychiatry, 41,* 58–62.

Jamison, K. R. (1989). Mood disorders and patterns of creativity in British writers and artists. *Psychiatry, 52,* 125–134.

Jamison, K. R. (1993a). Mood disorders, creativity, and the artistic temperament. In J. J. Schildkraut (Ed.), *Depression and the spiritual in modern art: Homage to Miro* (pp. 15–32). New York: Wiley.

Jamison, K. R. (1993b). *Touched with fire: Manic-depressive illness and the artistic temperament.* New York: Macmillan.

Jamison, K. R., & Akiskal, H. S. (1983). Medication compliance in patients with bipolar disorder. *Psychiatric Clinics of North America, 6,* 175–192.

Jaska, P. (1998). Fact sheet on attention deficit hyperactivity disorder (ADHD/ADD). Available on the Web at www.add.org/content/abc/factsheet.htm. Accessed on February 26, 2003.

Jensen, P. S., Bhatara, V. S., Vitiello, B., Hoagwood, K., Feil, M., & Burke, L. (1999). Psychoactive medication practices for U.S. children: Gaps between research and clinical practice. *Journal of the American Academy of Child and Adolescent Psychiatry, 38,* 557–565.

Jensvold, M. F., Halbreich, U., & Hamilton, J. A. (Eds.). (1996). *Psychopharmacology and women: Sex, gender, and hormones.* Washington, DC: American Psychiatric Association.

Johns, A. (2001). Psychiatric effects of cannabis. *British Journal of Psychiatry, 179,* 116–122.

Jones, K. Lacro, R. V., Johnson, K. A., & Adams, J. (1989). Patterns of malformations in the children of women treated with carbamazepine during pregnancy. *New England Journal of Medicine, 320,* 1661–1666.

Jones, R. T., Benowitz, N., & Bachman, J. (1976). Clinical studies of cannabis tolerance and dependence. *Annals of the New York Academy of Sciences, 282,* 221–239.

Jorm, A. F. (2000). Mental health literacy: Public knowledge and beliefs about mental health disorders. *British Journal of Psychiatry, 177,* 396–401.

Jorm, A. F., Christensen, H., Griffiths, K. M., & Rodgers, B. (2002). Effectiveness of complementary and self-help treatments for depression. *Medical Journal of Australia, 176*(Suppl. 1), 84–96.

JournalNews.com. (2004). *The Pfizer settlement.* Available on the Web at www.thejournalnews.com/newsroom/051604/edpfizer.html. Accessed on May 20th, 2004.

Judd, L. L., Squire, L. R., Butters, N., et al. (1987). Effects of psychotropic drugs on cognition and memory in normal humans and animals. In H. Y. Melzer (Ed.), *Psychopharmacology: The third generation of progress* (pp. 1467–1475). New York: Raven.

Julien, R. M. (2001). *A primer of drug action: A concise, nontechnical guide to the actions, uses, and side effects of psychoactive drugs* (9th ed.). New York: Worth.

Jureidini, J. N., Doecke, C. J., Mansfield, P. R., Haby, M. M., Menkes, D. B., & Tonkin, A. L. (2004). Efficacy and safety of antidepressants for children and adolescents. *British Medical Journal, 328,* 879–883.

Kaberi-Otarod, J., Conetta, R., Kundo, K. K., & Farkash, A. (2002). Ischemic stroke in a user of thermadrene: A case study in alternative medicine. *Clinical Pharmacology, and Therapeutics, 72,* 343–346.

Kafantaris, V., Coletti, D. J., Dicker, R., Padula, G., & Kane, J. M. (2001). Adjunctive antipsychotic treatment of adolescents with bipolar psychosis. *Journal of the Academy of Child and Adolescent Psychiatry, 40,* 1448–1456.

Kalat, J. W. (2001). *Introduction to psychology* (6th ed.). Belmont, CA: Wadsworth.

Kane, J. M. (1998). Sertindole: A review of clinical efficacy. *International Clinical Psychopharmacology, 13*(Suppl. 3), 59–63.

Kane, J. M., & Marder, S. R. (1993). Psychopharmacologic treatment of schizophrenia. *Schizophrenia Bulletin, 19,* 287–302.

Kane, J. M., Eerdekens, M., Lindenmayer, J. P., Keith, S. J., Lesem, M., & Karcher, K. (2003). Long-acting injectable risperidone: Efficacy and safety of the first long-acting atypical antipsychotic. *American Journal of Psychiatry, 160,* 1125–1132.

Kasper, S., & Dienel, A. (2002). Cluster analysis of symptoms during antidepressant treatment with hypericum extract in mildly to moderately depressed out-patients: A meta-analysis of data from three randomized, placebo-controlled trials. *Psychopharmacology, 164,* 301–308.

Kassirer, J. P. (1997). Federal foolishness and marijuana. *New England Journal of Medicine, 336,* 366–367.

Keane, T. M., & Barlow, D. H. (2002). Post traumatic stress disorder. In D. H. Barlow (Ed.), *Anxiety and its disorders: The nature and treatment of anxiety and panic* (2nd ed.). New York: Guilford.

Keck, P. E., & McElroy, S. L. (1998). Antiepileptic drugs. In A. F. Schatzberg & C. B. Nemeroff (Eds.), *Textbook of psychopharmacology* (2nd ed., pp. 431–454). Washington, DC: American Psychiatric Press.

Keck, P. E., & McElroy, S. L. (2002). Clinical pharmacodynamics and pharmacokinetics of antimanic and mood stabilizing medications. *Journal of Clinical Psychiatry, 63*(Suppl. 4), 3–11.

Keller, K. B., & Lemberg, L. (2001). Herbal or complementary medicine: Fact or fiction? *American Journal of Critical Care, 10,* 438–443.

Keller, M. B., Ryan, N. D., Strober, M., Klein, R. G., Kutcher, S. P., Birmaher, B., Hagino, O. R., Koplewicz, H., Carlson, G. A., Clarke, G. N., Emslie, G. J., Feinberg, D., Geller, B., Kusumakar, V., Papatheodorou, G., Sack, W. H., Sweeney, M., Wagner, K. D., Weller, E. B., Winters, N. C., Oakes,

R., & McCafferty, J. P. (2001). Efficacy of paroxetine in the treatment of adolescent major depression: A randomized, controlled trial. *Journal of the American Academy of Child and Adolescent Psychiatry, 40,* 762–772.

Kelly, B. D. (2001). St John's wort for depression: What's the evidence? *Hospital Medicine, 62,* 274–276.

Kessler, R. C., McGonagle, K. A., Zhao, S., Nelson, C. B., Hughes, M., Eshleman, S., Wittchen, H. U., & Kendler, K. S. (1994). Lifetime and 12-month prevalence of DSM-II-R psychiatric disorders in the United States. *Archives of General Psychiatry, 51,* 8–19.

Khan, A., Leventhal, R. M., Khan, S. R., & Brown, W. A. (2002). Severity of depression and response to antidepressants and placebo: An analysis of the Food and Drug Administration database. *Journal of Clinical Psychopharmacology, 22,* 40–45.

Kim, H. L., Streltzer, J., & Goebert, D. (1999). St. John's wort for depression. *Journal of Nervous and Mental Diseases, 187,* 532–539.

King, R. A. (1997). Practice parameters for the psychiatric assessment of children and adolescents. *Journal of the American Academy of Child & Adolescent Psychiatry, 36* (Suppl. 10), 1386–1402.

Kinzler, E., Kroner, J., & Helman, E. (1991). Effect of a special kava extract in patients with anxiety, tension, and excitation states of non-psychotic genesis: Double blind study with placebos over 4 weeks. *Arzneimittelforschung, 41,* 584–588.

Kishimoto, A., Ogura, C., Hazama, H., & Inoue, K. (1983). Long-term prophylactic effects of carbamazepine in affective disorder. *British Journal of Psychiatry, 143,* 327–331.

Kistorp, T. K., & Laursen, S. B. (2002). Herbal medicines: Evidence and drug interactions in clinical practice. *Ugeskrift For Laeger, 164,* 4161–4165.

Klaus, L., Mechart, D., Mulrow, C. D., & Berner, M. (2002). Effect of *Hypericum perforatum* (St. John's wort) in major depressive disorder: A randomized controlled trial: Comment. *JAMA, 288,* 447–448.

Kleijnen, J., & Knipschild, P. (1992). *Ginkgo biloba. Lancet, 340,* 1136–1139.

Klein, D. F. (1967). Importance of psychiatric diagnosis in prediction of clinical drug effects. *Archives of General Psychiatry, 16,* 118–126.

Kleindienst, N., & Greil, W. (2002). Inter-episodic morbidity and drop-out under carbamazepine and lithium in the maintenance treatment of bipolar disorder. *Psychological Medicine, 32,* 493–501.

Klesper, T. B., Doucette, W. R., & Horton, M. R., Buys, L. M., Ernst, M. E., Ford, J. K., Hoehns, J. D., Kautzman, H. A., Logemann, C. D., Swegle, J. M., Ritho, M., & Klepser, M. E (2000). Assessment of patients' perceptions and beliefs regarding herbal therapies. *Pharmacotherapy, 20,* 83–87.

Klesper, T. B., & Klesper, M. E. (1999). Unsafe and potentially safe herbal therapies. *American Journal of Health Systems and Pharmaceuticals, 56,* 125–38.

Kluger, J. (2003). Medicating young minds. *Time, 162*, 48–58.

Knekt, P., Kumpulainen, J., Jarvinen, R., Rissanen, H., Heliovaara, M., Reunanen, A., Hakulinen, T., & Timo, A. (2002). Flavonoid intake and risk of chronic disease. *American Journal of Nutrition, 76*, 560–568.

Knickerbocker, B. (2002). Military looks to drugs for battle readiness. *Christian Science Monitor, 8*, 11.

Knudsen, P., Hansen, E. H., Traulsen, J. M., & Eskildsen, K. (2002). Changes in self-concept while using SSRI antidepressants. *Qualitative Health Research, 12*, 932–944.

Koller, E. A., Cross, J. T., & Schneider, B. (2004). Risperidone associated diabetes mellitus in children. *Pediatrics, 113*, 421–422.

Koren, G., & Kennedy, D. (1995). Safe use of valproic acid during pregnancy. *Canadian Family Physician, 45*, 223–228.

Korf, D. J. (2002). Dutch coffee shops and trends in cannabis use. *Addictive Behaviors, 27*, 851–866.

Kottler, L., & Devlin, M. J. (2001). Weight gain with antipsychotic medications in children and adolescents. *Child and Adolescent Psychopharmacology News, 6*, 5–9.

Kraft, I. A. (1968). The use of psychoactive drugs in the outpatient treatment of psychiatric disorders of children. *American Journal of Psychiatry, 124*, 1401–1407.

Kramer, P. D. (1993). *Listening to Prozac: A psychiatrist explores antidepressant drugs and the remaking of the self.* New York: Viking.

Kubik, J. (2002). *S.C.O.P.E.: Student centered outcome plan evaluation.* Avon Lake, OH: Bridge to Success Skill Training.

Kuhlmann, J., Berger, W., Podzuweit, H., & Schmidt, U. (1999). The influence of valerian treatment on reaction time, alertness, and concentration in volunteers. *Pharmacopsychiatry, 32*, 235–241.

Kulkarni, J., & Power, P. (1999). Initial treatment of first-episode psychosis. In P. D. McGorry & H. J. Jackson (Eds.), *The recognition and management of early psychosis: A preventive approach* (pp. 184–205) Cambridge, MA: Cambridge University Press.

Kulkarni, S. K., & Naidu, P. S. (2003). Pathophysiology and drug therapy of tardive dyskinesia: Current concepts and future perspectives. *Drugs of Today, 39*, 19–49.

Kupfer, D. J., & Frank, E. (2002). Effect of *Hypericum perforatum* (St. John's wort) in major depressive disorder: A randomized controlled trial: A reply. *JAMA, 288*, 449.

Kusumaker, V., Lazier, L., MacMaster, F. P., & Santor, D. (2002). Bipolar mood disorder: Diagnosis, etiology, and treatment. In S. Kutcher (Ed.), *Practical child and adolescent psychopharmacology* (pp. 106–133). Cambridge, UK: Cambridge University Press.

Kutcher, S. P. (1998). Affective disorders in children and adolescents: A critical, clinically relevant review. In B. T. Walsh (Ed.), *Child psychopharmacology* (pp. 91–114). Washington, DC: American Psychiatric Association.

Kutcher, S., Boulos, C., Ward, B., Marton, P., Simeon, J., Ferguson, H. B., Szalai, J., Katie, M., Roberts, N., Dubois, C., & Reed, K. (1994). Response to desipramine treatment in adolescent depression: A fixed-dose, placebo-controlled trial. *Journal of the American Academy of Child and Adolescent Psychiatry, 33*, 686–694.

Kye, C. H., Waterman, G. S., Ryan, N. D., Birmaher, B., Williamson, D. E., Iyengar, S., & Dachille, S. (1996). A randomized, controlled trial of amitriptyline in acute treatment of adolescent major depression. *Journal of the American Academy of Child and Adolescent Psychiatry, 35*, 1139–1144.

Laakmann, G., Jahn, G., & Schuele, C. (2002). *Hypericum perforatum* extracts in the treatment of mild to moderate depression: Clinical and pharmacological aspects. *Nervenarzt, 73*, 600–612.

Labruzza, A. L. (1997). *Using DSM-IV: A clinician's guide to psychiatric diagnosis.* Washington, DC: American Psychiatric Association.

Lader, M. (1988). Beta-adrenergic antagonists in neuropsychiatry: An update. *Journal of Clinical Psychiatry, 49*, 213–223.

LaFrance, W. C., Lauterbach, E. C., Coffey, C. E., Salloway, S. P., Kaufer, D. I., Reeve, A. Royal, D. R., Aylward, E., Rummins, T. A., & Lovell, T. R. (2000). The use of herbal alternative medicines in neuropsychiatry. *Journal of Neuropsychiatry and Clinical Neurosciences, 12*, 177–192.

Lambert, P. A., & Venaud, G. (1992). Use of valpromide in psychiatric therapeutics. *Encephale, 13*, 367–373.

Lauriello, J., Lenroot, R., & Bustillo, J. R. (2003). Maximizing the synergy between pharmacotherapy and psychosocial therapies for schizophrenia. *Psychiatric Clinics of North America, 26*, 191–211.

Lavin, M. R., & Rifkin, A. (1992). Neuroleptic-induced Parkinsonism. In J. M. Kane & J. A. Lieberman (Eds.), *Adverse effects of psychotropic medications* (pp. 175–188). New York: Guilford.

Lawson, W. B. (1999). The art and science of ethnopharmacotherapy. In J. M. Herrera, W. B. Lawson, & J. J Sramek (Eds.), *Cross cultural psychiatry* (pp. 67–73). New York: Wiley.

Lawson, W. B., Hepler, N., Holladay, J., & Cuffel, B. (1994). Race as a factor in inpatient and outpatient admissions and diagnosis. *Hospital Community Psychiatry, 45*, 72–74.

Leak, J. A. (1999). Herbal medicine: Is it an alternative or an unknown? A brief review of popular herbals used by patients in a pain and symptom management practice setting. *Current Review of Pain, 3*, 226–236.

Leathwood, P. D., & Chauffard, F. (1982). Quantifying the effects of mild sedatives. *Journal of Psychiatric Research, 17*, 115–122.

Leathwood, P. D., Chauffard, F., Heck, E., & Munoz-Box, R. (1982). Aqueous extract of valerian root (*Valeriana officinalis L.*) improves sleep quality in man. *Pharmacology and Biochemical Behavior, 17*, 65–71.

LeBars, P. L., & Kastelan, J. (2000). Efficacy and safety of *Ginkgo biloba* extract. *Public Health Nutrition, 3*, 495–499.

LeBars, P. L., Katz, M. M., Berman, N., Itil, T. M., Freedman, A. M., & Schatzberg, A. F. (1997). A placebo-controlled , double-blind randomized trial of an extract of *Ginkgo biloba* for dementia. *JAMA, 278*, 1327–1332.

Leber, P. (1996). The role of the regulator. In D. Healy & D. P. Doogan (Eds.), *Psychotropic drug development: Social, economic, and pharmacological aspects* (pp. 69–77). London: Chapman & Hall Medical.

Lebovitz, H. E. (2003). Metabolic consequences of atypical antipsychotic drugs. *Psychiatric Quarterly, 74*, 277–290.

Lecrubier, Y., Clerc, G., Didi, R., & Keiser, M. (2002). Efficacy of St. John's wort extract WS 5570 in major depression: A double-blind, placebo-controlled trial. *American Journal of Psychiatry, 159*, 1361–1366.

Lemonick, M. D. (2004, June 21). Kids and depression. *Time, 163*, 22–29.

Lencz, T., Smith, C. W., Auther, A. M. Correll, C. U., & Cornblatt, B. A. (2003). The assessment of "prodromal schizophrenia": Unresolved issues and future directions. *Schizophrenia Bulletin, 29*, 717–728.

Lenox, R. H., & Manji, H. K. (1998). Lithium. In A. F. Schatzberg & C. B. Nemeroff (Eds.), *Textbook of psychopharmacology* (2nd ed., pp. 379–430). Washington, DC: American Psychiatric Press.

Leo, J. (2002). American preschoolers on Ritalin. *Society, 1*, 52–60.

Leppamaki, S. J., Partonen, T. T., Hurme, J., Haukka, J. K., & Lonnqvist, J. K. (2002). Randomized trial of the efficacy of bright light exposure and aerobic exercise on depressive symptoms and serum lipids. *Journal of Clinical Psychiatry, 63*, 316–321.

Letmaier, M., Schreinzer, D., Wolf, R., & Kasper, S. (2001). Topiramate as a mood stabilizer. *International Clinical Psychopharmacology, 16*, 295–298.

Levy, F., & Hay, D. (2001). *Attention, genes, and ADHD.* Philadelphia: Brunner/ Routledge.

Lewinsohn, P. M., Klein, D. N., & Seeley, J. (1995). Bipolar disorders in a community sample of older adolescents: Prevalence, phenomenology, comorbidity, and course. *Journal of the American Academy of Child and Adolescent Psychiatry, 34*, 454–464

Lewis, B. (1973). *The sexual powers of marijuana.* New York: Wyden.

Lewis, D. A. (2002) Atypical antipsychotic medications and the treatment of schizophrenia. *American Journal of Psychiatry, 159*, 177–179

Lewis, R. (1998). Typical and atypical antipsychotics in adolescent schizophrenia: Efficacy, tolerability, and differential sensitivity to extrapyramidal symptoms. *Canadian Journal of Psychiatry, 43*, 596–604.

Liberty, I. F., Todder, D., Umansky, R., & Harman-Boehm, I. (2004). Atypical antipsychotics and diabetes mellitus: An association. *Israel Medical Association Journal, 6*, 276–279.

Lickey, M. E., & Gordon, B. (1991). *Medicine and mental illness: The use of drugs in psychiatry.* New York: Freeman.

Lieberman, J. (1997). Atypical antipsychotic drugs: The next generation of therapy. *Decade of the Brain, 3*, 3–10.

Lin, K. M. (1996). Psychopharmacology in cross-cultural psychiatry. *Mt. Sinai Journal of Medicine, 63*, 283–284.

Lin, K. M., & Poland, R. E. (1995). Ethnicity, culture, and psychopharmacology. In F. E. Bloom & D. I. Kupfer (Eds.), *Psychopharmacology: The fourth generation of progress.* New York: Raven Press.

Lin, K. M., Poland, R. E., & Anderson, D. (1995). Psychopharmacology, ethnicity, and culture. *Transcultural Psychiatric Residents Review, 32*, 3–40.

Lin, K. M., Poland, R. E., & Nakasaki, G. (Eds.). (1993). *Psychopharmacology and psychobiology of ethnicity.* Washington, DC: American Psychiatric Association.

Linde, K., & Mulrow, C. D. (2000). St. John's wort for depression. *Cochrane Database System Review, 2*, CD000448.

Linde, K., Ramirez, G., Mulrow, C. D., Pauls, A., Weidenhammer, W., & Melchart, D. (1996). St. John's wort for depression. *British Medical Journal, 313*, 253–258.

Lindenmayer, J. P., & Patel, R. (1999). Olanzapine induced ketoacidosis with diabetes mellitus. *American Journal of Psychiatry, 156*, 1471.

Livingston, R. (1995). Anxiety and anxiety disorders. In G. O. Gabbard (Ed.), *Treatment of psychiatric disorders* (2nd ed., pp. 229–253). Washington, DC: American Psychiatric Association.

Loera, J. A., Black, S. A., Markides, K. S., Espino, D. C., & Goodwin, J. S. (2001). The use of herbal medicine by older Mexican Americans. *Journals of Gerontology: Series A: Biological Sciences and Medical Sciences, 56A*, M714–M718.

Logan, L. (2003). A guide to . . . The FDA and the drug development and approval process. Available on the Web at www.namiccns.org/DrugDev.htm. Accessed on May 27, 2003.

Lukoff, D., Lu, F. G., & Turner, R. (1996). Diagnosis: A transpersonal clinical approach to religious and spiritual problems. In B. W. Scotton, A. B. Chinen, & J. R. Battista (Eds.), *Textbook of transpersonal psychiatry and psychology* (pp. 231–249). New York: Basic Books.

Lykouras, L., Agelopoulos, E., & Tzavellas, E. (2002). Improvement of tardive dyskinesia following switch from neuroleptics to olanzapine. *Progress in Neuropsychopharmacology and Biological Psychiatry, 26*, 815–817.

MacCluskie, K. M., & Ingersoll, R. E. (2001). *Becoming a 21st century agency counselor: Personal and professional explorations.* Belmont, CA: Brooks Cole.

MacDonald, J. A. (2001, August 8). Drug ads attract scrutiny of critics. *Akron Beacon Journal,* pp. B1–B4.

Macdonald, K. J., & Young, L. T. (2002). Newer antiepileptic drugs in bipolar disorder: Rationale for use and role in therapy. *Central Nervous System Drugs, 16,* 549–562.

Mackesy-Amiti, M. E., Fendrich, M., & Goldstein, P. J. (1997). Sequence of drug use among serious drug users: Typical vs. atypical progression. *Drug and Alcohol Dependence, 45,* 185–196.

Maidment, I. D. (2001). Gabapentin treatment for bipolar disorders. *Annals of Pharmacotherapy, 35,* 1264–1269.

Malhotra, A. K., Litman, R. E., & Pickar, D. (1993). Adverse effects of antipsychotics. *Drug Safety, 9,* 429–436.

Malone, R. P., Luebbert, J., Pena-Ariet, M., Biesecker, K., & Delaney, M. A. (1994). The Overt Aggression Scale in a study of lithium in aggressive conduct disorder. *Psychopharmacology Bulletin, 30,* 215–218.

Manisses Corporation. (2002). Aripriprazole emerging as next great hope for schizophrenia. *Psychopharmacology Update, 13,* 4–5.

Manji, H. L., Bowden, C. L., & Belmaker, R. H. (Eds.). (2000). *Bipolar medications: Mechanisms of action.* Washington, DC: American Psychiatric Press.

Manji, H. L., Moore, G. H., Rajkowska, G., & Chen, S. (2000). Neuroplasticity and cellular resilience in mood disorders. *Molecular Psychiatry, 5,* 578–593.

Manos, M. J., Short, E. J., & Findling, R. L. (1999). Differential effectiveness of methylphenidate and Adderall in school-age youths with attention-deficit hyperactivity disorder. *Journal of the American Academy of Child and Adolescent Psychiatry, 38,* 813–819.

Maradino, C. (1997). Ephedra falls under FDA jurisdiction. *Vegetarian Times, 241,* 1.

March, J. S., Biederman, J., Wolkow, R., Soffermon, A., Madekian, J., Cook, E. H., Cutler, N. R., Dominquez, R., Ferguson, J., Muller, B., Riesenberg, R., Rosenthal, M., Sallee, F. R., & Wagner, K. D. (1998). Sertraline in children and adolescents with obsessive compulsive disorder: A multicenter randomized control trial. *JAMA, 280,* 1752–1756.

March, J. S., & Mulle, K. (1996). Banishing OCD: Cognitive behavioral psychotherapy for obsessive compulsive disorder. In E. G. Hibbs & P. S. Jensen (Eds.), *Psychosocial treatment for child and adolescent disorders: Empirically based strategies for clinical practice* (pp. 83–102). Washington, DC: American Psychological Association.

Marcotte, D. (1998). Use of topiramate, a new antiepileptic as a mood stabilizer. *Journal of Affective Disorders, 50,* 245–251.

Marriage, K. (2002). Schizophrenia and related psychosis. In S. Kitchner (Ed.), *Practical child and adolescent psychopharmacology* (pp. 134–158). Cambridge, UK: Cambridge University Press.

Martin, S. D., Martin, E., Rai, S. S., Richardson, M. A., & Royall, R. (2001). Brain blood flow changes in depressed patients treated with interpersonal psychotherapy or venlafaxine hydrochloride: Preliminary findings. *Archives of General Psychiatry, 58,* 641–648.

Mathre, M. L. (Ed.). (1997). *Cannabis in medical practice: A legal, historical, and pharmacological overview of the therapeutic uses of marijuana.* Jefferson, NC: McFarland.

Matsuda, L., Lolait, S. J., Brownstein, J. J., Young, A. C., & Bonner, T. I. (1990). Structure of a cannabinoid receptor and functional expression of the cloned cDNA. *Nature, 365,* 61–65.

McClure, E. B., Kubiszyn, T., & Kaslow, N. J. (2002a). Advances in the diagnosis and treatment of childhood mood disorders. *Professional Psychology: Research and Practice, 33,* 125–134.

McClure, E. B., Kubiszyn, R., & Kaslow, N. J. (2002b). Evidence-based assessment of childhood mood disorders: Reply to Lee and Hunsley. *Professional Psychology: Research, Theory, and Practice, 34,* 113–114.

McGlothlin, W. H., & West, L. J. (1968). The marihuana problem: An overview. *American Journal of Psychiatry, 125,* 126–134.

McIntyre, R. S. (2002). Psychotropic drugs and adverse events in the treatment of bipolar disorders revisited. *Journal of Clinical Psychiatry, 63*(Suppl. 3), 15–20.

McMahon, F., & DePaulo, J. (1996). Genetics and age at onset. In K. Schulman, M. Tohen, & S. Kutcher (Eds.), *Mood disorders across the life span* (pp. 35–48). New York: Wiley.

McNaughton, N., & Gray, J. H. (2000). Anxiolytic action on the behavioral inhibition system implies multiple types of arousal contribute to anxiety. *Journal of Affective Disorders, 61,* 161–176.

McWilliams, P. (1993). *Ain't nobody's business if you do: The absurdity of consensual crimes in a free society.* Los Angeles: Prelude Press.

Meehl, P. (1962). Schizotaxia, schizotypy, schizophrenia. *American Psychologist, 17,* 827–838.

Megna, J. L., Devitt, P. J., Sauro, M. D., & Mantosh, J. (2001). Gabapentin's effect on agitation in severely and persistently mentally ill patients. *Annals of Pharmcotherapy, 36,* 12–16.

Melzer, H. Y. (1993). New drugs for the treatment of schizophrenia. *Psychiatric Clinics of North America, 16,* 365–385.

Merton, T. (1968). The Matthew effect in science. *Science, 159,* 59–63.

Meyer, H. J. (1967). Pharmacology of kava. *Psychopharmacology Bulletin, 4,* 10–11.

Meyers, H. F. (1993). Biopsychosocial perspective on depression in African-Americans. In K. M. Lin, R. E. Poland, & G. Nakasaki (Eds.), *Psychopharmacology and psychobiology of ethnicity* (pp. 201–222). Washington, DC: American Psychiatric Association.

Miron, J. A. (2004). *Drug war crimes: The consequences of prohibition*. Oakland, CA: Independent Institute.

Mischoulon, D. (2002). The herbal anxiolytics kava and valerian for anxiety and insomnia. *Psychiatric Annals, 32,* 55–60.

Mitchell, P. B., & Malhi, G. S. (2002). The expanding pharmacopoeia for bipolar disorder. *Annual Review of Medicine, 53,* 173–188.

Model, K. E. (1993). The effect of marijuana decriminalization on hospital emergency room episodes. *Journal of the American Statistical Association, 88,* 11.

Modell, J. G. (1995). The high cost of buspirone. (Letter). *Journal of Clinical Psychiatry, 56,* 375.

Morgenstern, H., & Glazer, W. M. (1993). Identifying risk factors for tardive dyskinesia among chronic outpatients maintained on neuroleptic medications: Results of Yale tardive dyskinesia study. *Archives of General Psychiatry, 50,* 723–733.

Morral, A. R., McCaffrey, D. F., & Paddock, S. M. (2002). Reassessing the marijuana gateway effect. *Addiction, 97,* 1493–1504.

Moskowitz, A. S., & Altshuler, L. (1991). Increased sensitivity to lithium-induced neurotoxicity after stroke: A case report. *Journal of Clinical Psychopharmacology, 11,* 272–273.

Mota-Castillo, M., Torruella, A., Engels, B., Perez, J., Dedrick, C., & Gluckman, M. (2001). Valproate in very young children: An open case serves with a brief follow-up. *Journal of Affective Disorders, 67,* 193–197.

MTA Cooperative Group. (1999). A 14 month randomized clinical trial of treatment strategies for attention-deficit/hyperactivity disorder. *Archives of General Psychiatry, 56,* 1073–1086.

Munoz, C., & Papp, M. (1999). Alnespirone (S 20499), an agonist of 5-HT1A receptors, and imipramine have similar activity in a chronic mild stress model of depression. *Pharmacology, Biochemistry, and Behavior, 63,* 647–653.

Nagayama, T., Sinor, A. D., Simon, R. P., Chen, J., Graham, S. H., Jin, K., & Greenberg, D. A. (1999). Cannabinoids and neuroprotection in global and focal cerebral ischemia and in neuronal cultures. *Journal of Neuroscience, 19,* 2987–2995.

National Institute for Health Care Management. (2002). *Changing patterns of pharmaceutical innovation: A research report by the National Institute for Health Care Management Research and Education Foundation.* Washington, DC: Author.

National Institute of Mental Health. (1996). *Attention deficit hyperactivity disorder.* No. 96-3572. Washington DC: Author.

National Institute of Mental Health. (2000, September). Treatment of children with mental disorders. No. 00-4702. Available on the Web at http://www.nimh.nih.gov.publicat/childqa.cfm. Accessed on April 22, 2002.

National Institutes of Health. (1998). *National Institutes of Health Consensus Development conference statement: Diagnosis and treatment of attention deficit hyperactivity disorder (ADHD). Effectiveness of methylphenidate and Adderall in school-age youths with ADHD.* Washington, DC: Author.

National Institutes of Health. (2002). Diagnosis and treatment of attention deficit hyperactivity disorder. National Institutes of Health Consensus Development statement November 16–18, 1998. Retrieved September 25, 2002, Available on the Web at http://consensus.nih.gov.cons/110/110_statement.htm. Accessed on September 25, 2002.

Neal, D. L., & Calarco, M. M. (1999). Mental health providers: Role definitions and collaborative practice issues. In R. Balon & M. B. Riba (Eds.), *Psychopharmacology and psychotherapy: A collaborative approach* (pp. 65–110). Washington, DC: American Psychiatric Association.

Neergaard, L. (2004, September 15). U.S. urged to red-flag depressed kids' pills. *Cleveland Plain Dealer,* pp. 1, 14.

Nieoullon, A. (2002). Dopamine and the regulation of cognition and attention. *Progress in Neurobiology, 67,* 53–83.

Nietzche, F. (1974). *Twilight of the idols or, how to philosophize with the hammer.* Trans. Anthony Ludovici. New York: Gordon Press.

Northridge, M. E., & Mack, R. (2002). Integrating ethnomedicine into public health. *American Journal of Public Health, 92,* 1561.

Novartis Pharmaceuticals (producer). (1998). *Brian's story.* (Video). Available from Novartis Pharmaceuticals Corporation, East Hanover, NJ 07936.

Olds, J., & Milner, P. (1954). Positive reinforcement produced by electrical stimulation of septal area and other regions of the rat brain. *Journal of Comparative and Physiological Psychology, 47,* 419–427.

Olfson, M., Gameroff, M. J., Marcus, S. C., & Jensen, P. S. (2003). *National trends in the treatment of attention deficit hyperactive disorder, 160,* 1071–1077.

Olfson, M., Marcus, S. C., Druss, B., Elinson, L., Tanielian, T., & Pincus, H. A. (2002). National trends in the treatment of outpatient depression. *JAMA, 287,* 203–209.

Olson, C., Drummond, R., Cook, D., Dickersin, K., Fanagin, A., Hogan, J., Zhu, Q., Reiling, J., & Pace, B. (2002). Publication bias in editorial decision making. *JAMA, 287,* 2825–2828.

Olver, J. S., Burrows, G. D., & Norman, T. R. (2001). Third-generation antidepressants: Do they offer advantages over the SSRIs? *Central Nervous System Drugs, 15,* 941–954.

Organon. (2003). Life without depression. Available at www.remeronsoltab.com. Accessed on October 10, 2004.

Ott, J. (1993). *Pharmacotheon.* Occidental, CA: Natural Products.

Owens, E. B., Hinshaw, S. P., Arnold, L. F., Cantwell, D. P., Elliott, G., Hechtman, L., Jensen, P. S., Newcorn, J. H., Severe, J. B., Vitiello, B., Kraemer,

H. C., Abikoff, H. B., Conners, C. K., Greenhill, L. L., Hoza, G., March, J. S., Pelham, W. E., Swanson, J. M., Wells, K. C., & Wigal, T. (2003). *Which treatment for whom for ADHD?: Moderators of treatment response in the MTA, 71*, 540–550.

Pande, A. C., Crockatt, G. J., Janney, C. A., et al. (2000). Gabapentin in bipolar disorder: A placebo-controlled trial of adjunctive therapy. *Bipolar Disorder, 2*, 249–255.

Pappadopulos, E., Jensen, P. S., Schur, S. B., MacIntryre, J. C., Ketner, S., Van Oreden, K., Sverd, J., Sardana, S., Woodlock, D., Schweitzer, R., & Rube, D. (2002). "Real world" atypical antipsychotic prescribing practices in public child and adolescent inpatient settings. *Schizophrenia Bulletin, 28*, 111–121.

Paragas, M. G. (1984). Lithium adverse reactions in psychiatric patients. *Pharmacology, Biochemistry, and Behavior, 21*(Suppl. 21), 65–69.

Parker, V., Wong, A. H., Boon, H. S., & Seeman, M. V. (2001). Adverse reactions to St. John's wort. *Canadian Journal of Psychiatry/Revue Canadienne de psychiatre, 46*, 77–79.

Parry, W. (2004, April 13). Ban on ephedra upheld; appeals of makers denied. *Cleveland Plain Dealer*, p. A6.

Patterson, L. E. (1996). Strategies for improving medication compliance. *Essential Psychopharmacology, 1*, 70–79.

Paul, G. L. (1967). Strategy of outcome research in psychotherapy. *Journal of Consulting*

Pediatric Pharmacotherapy. (1995). The FDA approval process. Available on the Web at http://www.people.virginia.edu/~smb4v/pedpharm/v1n11.html. Accessed on January 23, 2002.

Penn, D., & Corrigan, P. (2002). The effects of stereotype suppression on stereotype stigma. *Schizophrenia Research, 55*, 269–276.

Perry, E. K. (2002). Plants of the gods: Ethnic routes to altered consciousness. In E. K. Perry & H. Ashton (Eds.), *Neurochemistry of consciousness: Neurotransmitters in mind* (pp. 205–225). Philadelphia: J. Benjamins.

Perry, P. J., Alexander, B., & Liskow, B. I. (1997). *Psychotropic drug handbook* (7th ed.). Washington, DC: American Psychiatric Association.

Peselow, E. D., Dunner, D. L., Fieve, R. R., & Lautin, A. (1980). Lithium carbonate and weight gain. *Journal of Affective Disorders, 2*, 303–310.

Peselow, E. D., Fieve, R. R., DiFiglia, C., & Sanfilipo, M. P. (1994). Lithium prophylaxis of bipolar illness: The value of combination treatment. *British Journal of Psychiatry, 164*, 208–214.

Phelps, L., Brown, R. T., & R. Power, T. J. (2002). *Pediatric psychopharmacology: Combining medical and psychosocial interventions.* Washington, DC: American Psychological Association.

Pi, E. H., Gutierrez, M. A., & Gray, G. E. (1993). Tardive dyskinesia: Cross-cultural perspectives. In K. M.

Lin, R. E. Poland, & R. E. Nakasaki (Eds.), *Psychopharmacology and psychobiology of ethnicity* (pp. 153–167). Washington, DC: American Psychiatric Association.

Pies, R. (2000). Adverse neuropsychiatric reactions to herbal and over-the-counter "antidepressants." *Journal of Clinical Psychiatry, 61*, 815–820.

Pies, R. W. (1998). *Handbook of essential psychopharmacology.* Washington, DC: American Psychiatric Association.

Pisciotta, A. V. (1992). Hematologic reactions associated with psychotropic drugs. In J. M. Kane & J. A. Lieberman (Eds.), *Adverse effects of psychotropic medications* (pp. 376–394). New York: Guilford.

Polanyi, M. (1958). *Personal knowledge: Towards a postcritical philosophy.* Chicago: University of Chicago Press.

Pomerantz, J. M. (2003). Antidepressants used as placebos: Is that good practice? *Drug Benefit Trends, 15*, 32–33.

Post, R. M., Weiss, S. R., & Chuang, D. M. (1992). Mechanisms of action of anticonvulsants in affective disorders: Comparison with lithium. *Journal of Clinical Psychopharmacology, 12*(Suppl. 1) 23–25.

Prakash, S. (2002). Actions by drug company Parke-Davis to promote the drug Neurotin for uses that had not yet been approved by the government. Transcript of story run December 19, 2002, *All Things Considered*, National Public Radio.

Prakash, S. (2003). Drug companies marketing promotion in the name of education. Transcript of story run January 16, 2003, *All Things Considered*, National Public Radio.

Preston, J. D., O'Neal, J. H., & Talaga, M. C. (2002). *Handbook of clinical psychopharmacology for therapists* (3rd ed.). Oakland, CA: New Harbinger.

Price, L. H., & Heninger, G. R. (1994). Lithium in the treatment of mood disorders. *New England Journal of Medicine, 331*, 591–598.

Priest, R., Vize, C., Roberts, M., & Tylee, A. (1996). Lay people's attitudes to treatment of depression: Results of opinion poll for Defeat Depression Campaign just before its launch. *British Medical Journal, 313*, 858–859.

Psychlink. (1998, September 9). *Access to atypical antipsychotics: A public debate.* New York: Interactive Medical Network. [Video]

Puig-Antich, J., Perel, J., Lupatkin, W., Chambers, W. J., Tabrizi, M. A., King, J., Goetz, R., Davies, M., & Stiller, R. L. (1987). Imipramine in prepubertal major depressive disorders. *Archives of General Psychiatry, 44*, 81–89.

Rabiner, D. (1999). Medication treatment for child and adolescent psychiatric disorders: What is the evidence? *ADHD Research Update, 21.*

Rabiner, D. (2002). Medication treatment for child and adolescent psychiatric disorders: What is the evidence? *ADHD Research Update, 21.* Available on the Web at http://user.cyberzn.com/~kenyonk/add/rabiner/med_psych_child.htm. Accessed on September 2002.

Radin, D. (1997). *The conscious universe: The scientific truth of psychic phenomena.* San Francisco: Harper.

Ray, U. S., Mukhopadhyaya, S., Purkayastha, S. S., Asnani, V., Tomer, O. S., Prashad, R., et al. (2001). Effect of yogic exercises on physical and mental health of young fellowship course trainees. *Indian Journal of Physiology and Pharmacology, 45,* 37–53.

Redvers, A., Laugharne, R., Kanagaratnam, G., & Srinivasan, G. (2001). How many patients self-medicate with St. John's wort? *Psychiatric Bulletin, 25,* 254–256.

Reuters Medical News. (2001, September 5). Cannabis spray helps ease chronic pain. Available on the Web at *News in Science,* www.abc.net.au/science/news/pring/print_358716.htm, Accessed on October 14, 2004.

Rex, A., Morgenstern, E., & Fink, H. (2002). Anxiolytic-like effects of Kava-Kava in the elevated plus maze test: A comparison with diazepam. *Progress in Neuro-Psychopharmacology & Biological Psychiatry, 26,* 855–860.

Rickels, K., & Rynn, M. (2002). Pharmacotherapy of generalized anxiety disorder. *Journal of Clinical Psychiatry, 63,* 9–16.

Rickels, K., Schweizer, E., DeMartinis, N., Mandos, L., & Mercer, C. (1997). Gepirone and diazepam in generalized anxiety disorder: A placebo-controlled trial. *Journal of Clinical Psychopharmacology, 17,* 272–277.

Riddle, M. (1998). Obsessive-compulsive disorder in children and adolescents. *British Journal of Psychiatry, 173,* 91–96.

Riddle, M. A., Geller, B., & Ryan, N. (1993). Another sudden death in a child treated with desipramine. *Journal of the American Academy of Child and Adolescent Psychiatry, 32,* 792–797.

Riddle, M. A., Kastelic, E., & Frosch, E. (2001). Pediatric psychopharmacology. *Journal of the Child Psychological Psychiatrist, 42,* 73–90.

Riddle, M. A., King, R. A., Hardin, M. T., et al. (1991). Behavioral side effects of fluoxetine in children and adolescents. *Journal of Child and Adolescent Psychopharmacology, 1,* 193–198.

Ridley, M. (2003). *Nature via nurture: Genes, experience and what makes us human.* New York: Harper Collins.

Rivara, F. P., & Cummings, P. (2002). Publication bias: The problem and some suggestions. *Archives of Pediatric and Adolescent Medicine, 156,* 424–425.

Rivas-Vasquez, R. (2001). Ziprasidone: Pharmacological and clinical profile of the newest atypical antipsychotic. *Professional Psychology: Research and Practice, 32,* 662–665.

Robinson, G. E. (2002). Women and psychopharmacology. *Medscape Women's Health e-Journal, 7,* 1–8. Available on the Web at www.medscape.com/viewarticle/423938. Accessed on October 14, 2004.

Rogers, C. R. (1957). The necessary and sufficient conditions of therapeutic personality change. *Journal of Consulting Psychology, 21,* 95–103.

Rojansky, N., Wang, K. E., & Halbreich, U. (1992). Reproductive and adverse effects of psychotropic drugs. In J. M. Kane & J. A. Lieberman (Eds.), *Adverse effects of psychotropic drugs* (pp. 356–375). New York: Guilford.

Rosa, F. W. (1991). Spina bifida in infants of women treated with carbamazepine during pregnancy. *New England Journal of Medicine, 324,* 674–677.

Rosenberg, D. R., Holttum, J., & Gershon, S. (1994). *Textbook of pharmacotherapy for child and adolescent disorders.* New York: Brunner/Mazel.

Rosenheck, R. (2000). Cost-effectiveness of services for mentally ill homeless people: The application of research to policy and practice. *American Journal of Psychiatry, 157,* 1563–1570.

Rosenheck, R., Chang, S., Choe, Y., Cramer, J., Xu, W., Henderson, W., & Chareny, D. (2000). Medication continuation and compliance: A comparison of patients treated with clozapine and haloperidol. *Journal of Clinical Psychiatry, 61,* 382–386.

Rosenheck, R., Cramer, J., Allan, E., Erdos, J., Frisman, L. K., Xu, W., Thomas, J., Henderson, W., & Charney, D. (1999). Cost-effectiveness of clozapine in patients with high and low levels of hospital use. *Archives of General Psychiatry, 56,* 565–572.

Ross, C. [A.], & Pam, A. (1995). *Pseudoscience in biological psychiatry.* New York: Wiley.

Ross, C. A. (1995). Errors of logic in biological psychiatry. In C. A. Ross & A. Pam (Eds.), *Pseudoscience in biological psychiatry: Blaming the body* (pp. 85–128). New York: Wiley.

Roth, M. D., Arora, A., Barsky, S. H., Kleerup, E. C, Simmons, M. S., & Tashkin, D. P. (1998). Airway inflammation in young marijuana and tobacco smokers. *American Journal of Respiratory and Critical Care Medicine, 157,* 1–9.

Russell, A. T. (2001). Childhood-onset schizophrenia. In G. O. Gabbard (Ed.), *Treatments of psychiatric disorders* (pp. 339–358). Washington, DC: American Psychiatric Association.

Russo-Neustadt, A., Beard, R. C., & Cotman, C. W. (1999). Exercise, antidepressant medications, and enhanced brain derived neurotrophic factor expression. *Neuropsychopharmacology, 21,* 679–682.

Ryan, N. D. (2002). Depression. In S. Kutcher (Ed.), *Practical child and adolescent psychopharmacology.* Cambridge, UK: Cambridge University Press.

Ryan, N. D., Bhatara, V. S., & Perel, J. M. (1999). Mood stabilizers in children and adolescents. *Journal of the American Academy of Child and Adolescent Psychiatry, 38,* 529–536.

Safer, D. S., Zito, J. M., & Fine, E. M. (1996). Increased methylphenidate usage for attention deficit disorders in the 1990s. *Pediatrics, 98,* 1084–1088.

Salmon, P. (2001). Effects of physical exercise on anxiety, depression, and sensitivity to stress: A unifying theory. *Clinical Psychology Review, 21,* 33–61.

Satlin, A., & Wasserman, C. (1997). Overview of geriatric psychopharmacology. In S. L. McElroy (Ed.), *Psychopharmacology across the lifespan* (pp. 143–172). Washington, DC: American Psychiatric Association.

Saunders, S. K., Morzorati, A., & Shekhar, S. (1995). Priming of experimental anxiety by repeated subthreshold GABA blockade in the rat amygdala. *Brain Research, 699,* 250–259.

Sayre, J. (2000). The patient's diagnosis: Explanatory models of mental illness. *Qualitative Health Research, 10,* 71–83.

Scahill, L., Riddle, M. A., King, R. A., Hardin, M. T., Rasmusson, A., Makutch, R. W., & Leckman, J. F. (1997). Fluoxetine has no marked effect on tic symptoms in patients with Tourette's syndrome: A double blind placebo controlled study. *Journal of Child and Adolescent Psychopharmacology, 2,* 75–85.

Schaller, J. L., & Behar, D. (1999). Quetiapine for refractory mania in a child. *Journal of the American Academy of Child and Adolescent Psychiatry, 38,* 498–499.

Schatzberg, A. F. (1997). Serotonin reuptake inhibitor discontinuation syndrome: A hypothetical definition. *Journal of Clinical Psychiatry, 58*(Suppl. 7), 5–10.

Schatzberg, A. F. (2000). New indications for antidepressants. *Journal of Clinical Psychiatry, 61*(Suppl. 11), 9–17.

Schatzberg, A. F., Cole, J. O., & DeBattista, C. (1997). *Manual of clinical psychopharmacology* (3rd ed.). Washington, DC: American Psychiatric Press.

Schatzberg, A. F., & Nemeroff, C. B. (Eds.). (1998). *The American Psychiatric Association textbook of psychopharmacology* (2nd ed.). Washington, DC: American Psychiatric Association.

Schlosser, E. (1997). More reefer madness. *Atlantic Monthly, 279,* 90–102.

Schorr, M. (2004). Neurotrophic factor improves motor function in Parkinson's patients. *MedScape Medical News.* Available on the Web at www.medscape.com/viewarticle/474873_print. Accessed on June 11, 2004.

Schou, M. (1978). The range of clinical uses of lithium. In F. N. Johnson & S. Johnson (Eds.), *Lithium in medical practice* (pp. 34–57). Baltimore, MD: University Park Press.

Schou, M. (1997). Forty years of lithium treatment. *Archives of General Psychiatry, 54,* 9–13.

Schreiber, R., & Hartrick, G. (2002). Keeping it together: How women use the biomedical explanatory model to manage the stigma of depression. *Mental Health Nursing, 23,* 91–105.

Schulman, K. A., Seils, D. M., Timbie, J. W., Sugarman, J., Dame, L. A., Weinfurt, K. P., Mark, D. B., & Califf, R. M. (2002). A national survey of provisions in clinical-trial agreements between medical schools and industry sponsors. *New England Journal of Medicine, 347,* 1335–1341.

Schwartz, J. M., & Begley, S. (2002) *The mind and the brain: Neuroplasticity and the power of mental force.* New York: Regan

Schwartz, R. (1987). Marijuana: An overview. *Pediatric Clinics of North America, 34,* 305–317.

Schweizer, E., & Rickels, K. (1996). Pharmacological treatment for generalized anxiety disorder. In M. R. Mavissakalian & R. F. Prien (Eds.), *Long-term treatments of anxiety disorders.* Washington, DC: American Psychiatric Association.

Scott, J., & Pope, M. (2002). Nonadherence with mood stabilizers: Prevalence and predictors. *Journal of Clinical Psychiatry, 63,* 384–390.

Sechter, D., Peuskens, J., Fleurot, O., Rein, W., Lecrubier, Y., & the Amisulpride Study Group. (2002). Amisulpride vs. risperidone in chronic schizophrenia. *Neuropsychopharmacology, 27,* 1071–1081.

Seligman, M. E. P., & Csikszentmihalyi, M. (2000) Positive psychology: An introduction. *American Psychologist, 55,* 5–14

Senate Special Committee on Illegal Drugs. (2002). *Discussion paper on cannabis.* Canada: Author. Available on the Web at http://www.parl.gc.ca/37/1/parlbus/commbus/senate/com-e/ille-e/library-e/summary-e.pdf. Accessed on October 14, 2004.

Sernyak, M. J., Desai, R., Stolar, M., & Rosenheck, R. (2001). Impact of clozapine on completed suicide. *American Journal of Psychiatry, 158,* 931–937.

Shaw, E. (1986). Lithium noncompliance. *Psychiatric Annals, 16,* 583–587.

Sheard, M. H. (1971). Effect of lithium on human aggression. *Nature, 230,* 113–114.

Sheard, M. H. (1975). Lithium in the treatment of aggression. *Journal of Nervous and Mental Disease, 160,* 108–118.

Sheard, M. H., & Marini, J. L. (1978). Treatment of human aggressive behavior: Four case studies of the effect of lithium. *Comprehensive Psychiatry, 19,* 37–45.

Sheard, M. H., Marini, J. L., Bridges, C. I., & Wagner, E. (1976). The effect of lithium on impulsive aggressive behavior in man. *American Journal of Psychiatry, 133,* 1409–1413.

Sheean, G. L. (1991). Lithium neurotoxicity. *Clinical and experimental neurology, 28,* 112–127.

Shelton, R. C., Keller, M. B., Gelenbert, A., Dunner, D. L., Hirschfeld, R., Thase, M. E., Russell, J., Lydiard, R. B., Crits-Christoph, P., Gallop, R., Todd, L., Hellerstein, D., Goodnick, P., Keitner, G., Stahl, S. M., & Halbreich, U. (2001). Effectiveness of St. John's wort in major depression: A randomized, controlled trial. *JAMA, 285,* 1978–1986.

Shifrin, D. (1998). Three-year study documents nature of television violence. *American Academy of Pediatrics News, 8,* 1.

Shors, T. J., Miesegaes, G., Beylin, A., Zhao, M., Rydel, T., & Gould, E. (2001). Neurogenesis in the adult is involved in the formation of trace memories. *Nature, 410,* 372–376.

Shufman, E., & Witztum, E. (2000). Cannabis—a drug with dangerous implications for mental health. *Harefuah*, 138, 410–413.

Siegel, R. K. (1989). *Intoxication: Life in pursuit of artificial paradise.* New York: Dutton.

Sifaneck, S. J. (1995). Keeping off, stepping on and stepping off: The steppingstone theory reevaluated in the context of the Dutch cannabis experience. *Contemporary Drug Problems*, 22, 483–512.

Silberg, J., Pickles, A., Rutter, M., Hewitt, J., Simonoff, E., Maes, H., Carbonneau, R., Murrelle, L., Foley, D., & Eaves, L. (1999). The influences of genetic factors and life stressors on depression among adolescent girls. *Archives of General Psychiatry*, 56, 225–232.

Silverstein, D. D., & Spiegel, A. D. (2001). Are physicians aware of the risks of alternative medicine? *Journal of Community Health: The Publication for Health Promotion & Disease Prevention*, 26, 159–174.

Silverstein, F. S., Boxer, L., & Johnson, M. F. (1983). Hematological monitoring during therapy with carbamazepine in children. *Annals of Neurology*, 13, 685–686.

Silverstone, T., & Romans, S. (1996). Long-term treatment of bipolar disorder. *Drugs*, 51, 367–382.

Simeon, J. G., Knott, V. J., Thatte, S., Dubois, C. D., Wiggins, D. M., & Geraets, I. (1992). Pharmacotherapy of childhood anxiety disorders. *Clinical Neuropharmacology*, 15, 229–230.

Slifman, N. R., Obermeyer, W. R., Musser, S. M., Correll, W. A., Chichowicz, S. M., & Love, L. A. (1998). Contamination of botanical dietary supplements by *Digitalis lanata*. *New England Journal of Medicine*, 339, 806–811.

Smith, N. T. (2002). A review of published literature into cannabis withdrawal symptoms in human users. *Addiction*, 97, 621–632.

Smith, H. (2000). *Cleansing the doors of perception: The religious significance of entheogenic plants and chemicals.* New York: Tarcher.

Snyder, S. H. (1996). *Drugs and the brain.* New York: Scientific American Library.

Snyder, S., Banerjee, S. P., Yamanura, H. I., & Greenberg, A. (1974). Drugs, neurotoxins, and schizophrenia. *Science*, 188, 1243–1245.

Solanto, M. C., Arnsten, A. T. F., & Castellanos, F. X. (2001). *Stimulant drugs and ADHD: Basic and clinical neuroscience.* New York: Oxford University Press.

Soloman, P. R., Adams, F., Silver, A., Zimmer, J., & DeVeaux, R. (2002). Ginkgo for memory enhancement: A randomized control trial. *JAMA*, 288, 835–840.

Sommer, B. R., & Schatzberg, A. F. (2002). *Ginkgo biloba* and related compounds in Alzheimer's disease. *Psychiatric Annals*, 32, 13–18.

Sommers-Flanagan, J., & Sommers-Flanagan, R. (1996). Efficacy of antidepressant medication with depressed youth: What psychologists should know. *Professional Psychology: Research and Practice*, 27, 145–153.

Sonne, S. C., & Brady, K. T. (1999). Substance abuse and bipolar comorbidity. *Psychiatric Clinics of North America*, 22, 609–627.

Sowell, T. (2002). *Controversial essays.* Stanford, CA: Hoover Institution.

Speigel, D. A., Wiegel, M., Baker, S. L., & Greene, K. A. (2000). Pharmacological management of anxiety disorders. In D. I. Mostofsky & D. H. Barlow (Eds.), *The management of anxiety disorders* (pp. 36–65). Boston: Allyn and Bacon.

Spencer, T., Biederman, J., & Wilens, T. (2002). Attention deficit/hyperactivity disorder. In S. Kutcher (Ed.), *Practical child and adolescent psychopharmacology* (pp. 230–264). Cambridge, UK: Cambridge University Press.

Sperry, R. W. (1988). Psychology's mentalist paradigm and the religion/science tension. *American Psychologist*, 43, 607–614.

Spielmans, G. I. (2002). Effect of *Hypericum perforatum* (St. John's wort) in major depressive disorder: A randomized controlled trial: A reply. *JAMA*, 288, 446–447.

Stahl, S. M. (2000). *Essential psychopharmacology: Neuroscientific basis and practical applications* (2nd ed.). Cambridge, UK: Cambridge University Press.

Stahl, S. M. (2002). Don't ask, don't tell, but benzodiazepines are still the leading treatments for anxiety disorder. *Journal of Clinical Psychiatry*, 63, 756–757.

Stanilla, J. K., & Simpson, G. M. (1995). Drugs to treat extrapyramidal side effects. In A. F. Schatzberg & C. B. Nemeroff (Eds.), *American Psychiatric Association textbook of psychopharmacology* (pp. 289–299). Washington, DC: American Psychiatric Association.

Stanton, S. P., Keck, P. E., & McElroy, S. L. (1997). Treatment of acute mania with gabapentin. *The American Journal of Psychiatry*, 154, 287.

Stein, M. C. (2002). Are herbal products dietary supplements or drugs? An important question for public safety. *Clinical Pharmacology and Therapeutics*, 71, 411–413.

Stivers, R. (2001). *Technology as magic: The triumph of the irrational.* New York: Continuum.

Stratkowski, S. M., McElroy, S. L., Keck, P. E., & West, S. A. (1996). Racial influences on diagnosis in psychotic mania. *Journal of Affective Disorders*, 39, 157–162.

Streator, S. E., & Moss, J. T. (1997). Identification of off-label antidepressant use and costs in a network model HMO. *Drug Benefit Trends*, 9, 48–56.

Strickland, T. L., Lin, K-M., Fu, P., Anderson, D., & Zheng, Y. (1995). Comparison of lithium ratio between African-American and Caucasian bipolar patients. *Biological Psychiatry*, 37, 325–330.

Sugrue, M., Seger, M., Dredge, G., Davies, D. J., Ieraci, S., Bauman, A., Deane, S. A., & Sloane, D (1995). Evaluation of the prevalence of drug and alcohol abuse in motor vehicle trauma in Southwestern Sydney. *Australian and New Zealand Journal of Surgery*, 65, 853–856.

Sullivan, G., & Lukoff, D. (1990). Sexual side effects of antipsychotic medication: Evaluation and interventions. *Hospital and Community Psychiatry, 41,* 1238–1241.

Sullivan, R. J., & Hagen, E. H. (2002). Psychotropic substance-seeking: Evolutionary path or adaptation? *Addiction, 97,* 389–400.

Suurkula, J. (1996). Junk DNA: Over 95 percent of DNA has largely unknown function. Available on the Web at http://www.psrast.org/junkdna.htm. Accessed on May 2, 2004.

Swanson, J., Wigal, S., Greenhill, L., Browne, R., Walik, B., Lerner, M., Williams, L., Flynn, D., Agler, D., Crowley, K., Fineberg, E., Baren, M., & Cantwell, D. (1998). Analog classroom assessment of Adderall in children with ADHD. *Journal of the American Academy of Child and Adolescent Psychiatry, 37,* 519–526.

Swazy, J. P. (1974). *Chlorpromazine in psychiatry.* Cambridge, MA: MIT Press.

Szasz, T. (1992). *Our right to drugs: The case for a free market.* Syracuse, NY: Syracuse University Press.

Szymanksi, S., Cannon, T. D., Gallagher, F., Erwin, R. J., & Gur, R. E. (1996). Course of treatment response to first-episode and chronic schizophrenia. *American Journal of Psychiatry, 153,* 519–525.

Tanner, L. (2004, September 9). Medical journals' policy aims to help enlighten public. *Cleveland Plain Dealer,* p. A16.

Tarjan, G. (1968). Orientation or training? An urgent issue for child psychiatry. *American Journal of Psychiatry, 124,* 1450–1451.

Tart, C. T. (2000). *On being stoned: A psychological study of marijuana intoxication.* Lincoln, NE: Authorsguild. Originally published 1971.

Tart, C. T. (Ed.). (1997). *Body, mind, spirit: Exploring the parapsychology of spirituality.* Charlottesville, VA: Hampton Roads.

Tashkin, E. (1999). Effects of marijuana on the lung and its defenses against infection and cancer. *School Psychology International, 20,* 23–37.

Task Force on Financial Conflicts of Interest in Clinical Research. (2001). Protecting subjects, preserving trust, promoting progress: Policy and guidelines for the oversight of individual financial interests in human subjects research. Washington, DC: Association of American Medical Colleges.

Teasdale, J. D., Segal, Z., & Williams, J. M. G. (1999). How does cognitive therapy prevent depressive relapse and why should attentional control (mindfulness) training help? *Behavior Research and Therapy, 33,* 25–39.

Teasdale, J. D., Segal, Z. V., Williams, D. M. G., Ridgeway, V. A., Soulsby, J. M., Lau, M. A. (2000). Prevention of relapse/recurrence in major depression by mindfulness-based cognitive therapy. *Journal of Consulting and Clinical Psychology, 68,* 615–623.

Teicher, M. H., Glod, C., & Cole, J. O. (1990). Emergence of intense suicidal preoccupation during fluoxetine treatment. *American Journal of Psychiatry, 147,* 207–211.

Temin, P. (1980). Taking your medicine: Drug regulation in the United States. Cambridge, MA: Harvard University Press.

Thaker, G. K., & Tamminga, C. A. (2001). Schizophrenia and other psychotic disorders. In G. O. Gabbard (Ed.), *Treatment of psychiatric disorders* (3rd ed., pp. 1005–1025).Washington, DC: American Psychiatric Press.

Thompson, R. F. (2000). *The brain: A neuroscience primer* (3rd ed.). New York: Worth Publishers.

Thurber, S., Ensign, J., Punnett, A. F., & Welter, K. (1995). A meta-analysis of antidepressant outcome studies that involved children and adolescents. *Journal of Clinical Psychology, 51,* 340–345.

Tilkian, A. G., Schroeder, J. S., Kao, J., & Hultgren, H. (1976). The cardiovascular effects of lithium in man. *American Journal of Medicine, 61,* 665–670.

*Time.* (2004). Notebook numbers. *Time, 163,* 23.

Tohen, M., Baker, R. W., Altshuler, L. L., Zarate, C. A., Suppes, T., Ketter, T. A., Milton, D. R., Risser, R., Gilmore, J. A., Breier, A., & Tollefson, G. A. (2002). Olanzapine versus divalproex in the treatment of acute mania. *American Journal of Psychiatry, 159,* 1011–1017.

Tomlin, S. L., Jenkins, A., Lieb, W. R., & Franks, N. P. (1999). Preparation of barbiturate optical isomers and their effects on GABA(A) receptors. *Anesthesiology, 90,* 1714–1722.

Torrey, E. F. (1997). *Out of the shadows: Confronting America's mental illness crisis.* New York: Wiley.

Tseng, W. (2001). *Handbook of cultural psychiatry.* San Diego: Academic Press.

Tseng, W. S. (2003). *Clinician's guide to cultural psychiatry.* San Diego, CA: Academic Press.

Tsuang, M. T., Stone, W. S., & Faraone, S. V. (2001). Toward prevention of schizophrenia. *Child and Adolescent Psychopharmacology News, 6,* 9–11.

Turk, C. L., Heimberg, R. G., & Hope, D. A. (2001). Social phobia and social anxiety. In D. H. Barlow (Ed.), *Clinical handbook of psychological disorders: A step-by-step treatment manual* (3rd ed., pp. 99–136). New York: Guilford.

Tyler, V. E. (1994). *Herbs of choice: The therapeutic use of phytomedicinals.* New York: Pharmaceutical Products Press.

Umbricht, D. S., Pollach, S., & Kane, J. M. (1994). Clozapine and weight gain. *The Journal of Clinical Psychiatry, 55,* 157–160.

U.S. Department of Health and Human Services. (2001). *Report of the Surgeon General's conference on children's mental health: A national action agenda.* Rockville, MD: U.S. Department of Health and Human Services, Substance Abuse and Mental Health Administration, Center for Mental Health Services, National Institute of Mental Health.

Van Praag, H., Christie, B. R., Sejnowski, T. J., & Gage, F. H. (1999). Running enhances neurogenesis, learning and long-term potentiation in mice. *Proceedings of the National Academy of Sciences of the United States of America, 96,* 13427–13431.

Van der Hooft, C. S., & Stricher, B. H. (2002). Ephedrine and ephedra in weight loss products and other preparations. *Nederlands Tijdschrift Coor Geneeskunde, 146,* 1335–1336.

Vasankathumar, N. B. (2001). *Medical malpractice: A comprehensive analysis.* New York: Auburn House.

Viesselman, J. O. (1999). Antidepressant and antimanic drugs. In J. S. Werry & M. G. Aman (Eds.), *Practitioner's guide to psychoactive drugs for children and adolescents* (2nd ed., pp. 249–296). New York: Plenum.

Vinarova, E., Uhlir, V., Stika, J., & Vinar, O. (1972). Side effects of lithium administration. *Activas Nervosa Superior, 14,* 105–107.

Vitiello, B., & Jensen, P. (1997). Medication development and testing of children and adolescents. *Archives of General Psychiatry, 54,* 871–876.

Volavka, J. et al. (2002). Clozapine, olanzapine, risperidone, and haloperidol in the treatment of patients with chronic schizophrenia and schizoaffective disorder. *American Journal of Psychiatry, 159,* 255–262.

Volkow, N. D., Ding, Y., Fowler, J. S., Wang, G., Logan, J., Gatley, J. S., Dewey, S., Ashby, C., Liebermann, J., Hitzemann, R., & Wolf, A. P. (1995). Is methylphenidate like cocaine? *Archives of General Psychiatry, 52,* 456–463.

Volp, A. (2002). Effect of *Hypericum perforatum* (St. John's Wort) in major depressive disorder: A randomized controlled trial: Comment. *JAMA, 288,* 447.

Volz, H. P. (1997). Controlled clinical trials of hypericum extracts in depressed patients: An overview. *Pharmacopsychiatry, 30*(Suppl. 2), 72–76.

Volz, H. P., & Laux, P. (2000). Potential treatment for subthreshold and mild depression: A comparison of St. John's wort extracts and fluoxetine. *Comprehensive Psychiatry, 41,* 133–137.

Volz, H. P., Murck, H., Kasper, S., & Moeller, H. J. (2002). St. John's wort extract (LI 160) in somatoform disorders: Results of a placebo-controlled trial. *Psychopharmacology, 164,* 294–300.

Vonnegut, K. (1991). *Fates worse than death: An autobiographical collage.* New York: Berkley.

Voruganti, L. N., Slomka, P., Zabel, P., Mattar, A., & Awad, A. G. (2001). Cannabis induced dopamine release: An in-vivo SPECT study. *Psychiatry Research, 107,* 173–177.

Wagner, K. D., & Fershtman, M. (1993). Potential mechanism of desipramine-related sudden death in children. *Psychosomatics, 34,* 80–83.

Wagner, K. D., Weller, E. B., Carlson, G. A., Sachs, G., Biederman, J., Frazier, J. A., Wozniak, P., Tracy, K., Weller, R. A., & Bowden, C. (2002). An open-label trial of divalproex in children and adolescents with bipolar disorder. *Journal of the American Academy of Child and Adolescent Psychiatry, 41,* 1224–1230.

Wahlbeck, K., Cheine, M., Essali, A., & Adams, C. (1999). Evidence of clozapine's effectiveness in schizophrenia: A systematic review and meta-analysis of randomized trials. *American Journal of Psychiatry, 156,* 990–999.

Wallace, B. A. (1999). A Buddhist response. In Z. Houshmand, R. B. Livingston, & B. A. Wallace (Eds.), *Consciousness at the crossroads: Conversations with the Dalai Lama on brain science and Buddhism* (pp. 33–36). Ithaca, NY: Snow Lion, 1999.

Walsh, R. N., & Vaughan, F. (1980). *Beyond ego: Transpersonal dimensions in psychology.* Los Angeles: Tarcher.

Walsh, T. (Ed.). (1998). *Child psychopharmacology.* Washington, DC: American Psychiatric Association.

Walter, G., & Rey, J. M. (1999). Use of St. John's wort by adolescents with a psychiatric disorder. *Journal of Child and Adolescent Psychopharmacology, 9,* 307–311.

Walter, G., Rey, J. M., & Harding, A. (2000). Psychiatrists' experience and views regarding St. John's wort and alternative treatments. *Australian and New Zealand Journal of Psychiatry, 34,* 992–996.

Warnecke, G. (1991). Psychosomatic dysfunctions in the female climacteric: Clinical effectiveness and tolerance of kava extract KS 1490. *Fortschr Med., 109,* 119–122.

Warner, L. A., Kessler, R. C., Hughes, M., Anthony, J. C., & Nelson, C. B. (1995). Prevalence and correlates of drug use and dependence in the United States: Results from the National Comorbidity Survey. *Archives of General Psychiatry, 52,* 219–229.

*Washington Post.* (2002). The System: A weekly check-up on health care costs and coverage, section F3. Available on the Web at http://www.washingtonpost.com. Accessed in July 2002.

Watson, S. J., Benson, J. A., & Joy, J. E. (2000). Marijuana and medicine: Assessing the science base. *Archives of General Psychiatry, 57,* 547–552.

Watts, A. W. (1973). *What is reality?* Sound recording from *Philosophy and Society.* San Anselmo, CA: Electronic University.

Weber, S. S., Saklad, S. R., & Kastenholz, K. V. (1992). Bipolar affective disorders. In M. A. Koda-Kimble, L. Y. Young, W. A. Kradjan, & B. J. Guglielmo (Eds.), *The clinical use of drugs* (pp. 62–90). Vancouver, WA: Applied Therapeutics.

*Webster's new universal unabridged dictionary.* (1989). New York: Barnes & Noble.

Wechsler, H., Grosser, G. H., & Greenblatt, M. (1965). Research evaluating antidepressant medications on hospitalized mental patients: A survey of published reports during a 5-year period. *Journal of Nervous and Mental Disease, 141,* 231–239.

Weiden, P. J., Aquila, R., Emanuel, M., & Zygmunt, A. (1998). Long-term considerations after switching antipsychotics. *Journal of Clinical Psychiatry, 59*(Suppl. 19), 36–49.

Weiden, P., Aquila, R., & Standard, J. (1996). Atypical antipsychotic drugs and long-term outcome of schizophrenia. *Journal of Clinical Psychiatry, 57* (Suppl. 11), 53–60.

Weil, A., & Rosen, W. (1993). *From chocolate to morphine: Everything you need to know about mind altering drugs* (rev. ed.). Boston: Houghton Mifflin.

Weissman, M. M., Bruce, M. L., Leaf, P. J., Florio, L. P., & Holzer, C. (1991). Affective disorders. In L. N. Robins & D. A. Regier (Eds.), *Psychiatric disorders of America: The epidemiologic catchment area study* (pp. 53–80). New York: Free Press.

Weizman, R., & Weizman, A. (2001). Use of atypical antipsychotics in mood disorders. *Current Opinion in Investigational Drugs, 2*, 940–950.

Weller, E. B., Weller, R. A., & Fristad, M. A. (1995). Bipolar disorder in children: Misdiagnosis, underdiagnosis, and future directions. *Journal of the American Academy of Child and Adolescent Psychiatry, 34*, 709–714.

Werry, J. S. (1999). Introduction: A guide for practitioners, professionals, and public. In J. S. Werry & M. G. Aman (Eds.), *Practitioner's guide to psychoactive drugs for children and adolescents* (pp. 3–22). New York: Plenum.

West, A. P. (1996). Excitotoxic aspects of lithium neurotoxicity. *Psycholoquy, 7*, 14–32.

West, A. P., & Melzer, H. Y. (1979). Paradoxical lithium neurotoxicity: Five case reports and an hypothesis about risk for neurotoxicity. *American Journal of Psychiatry, 136*, 963–966.

West, S. A. (1997). Child and adolescent psychopharmacology. In S. L. McElroy (Ed.), *Psychopharmacology across the lifespan* (pp. 129–142). Washington, DC: American Psychiatric Association.

Westermeyer, J. (1989). *Psychiatric care of migrants: A clinical guide.* Washington, DC: American Psychiatric Association.

Wheatley, D. (1997). LI 160, an extract of St. John's wort, versus amitriptyline in mildly to moderately depressed outpatients: A controlled 6-week clinical trial. *Pharmacopsychiatry, 30*(Suppl. 2), 77–80.

Wheatley, D. (1999). Hypericum in seasonal affective disorder (SAD). *Current Medical Research and Opinion, 15*, 33–37.

Wheatley, D. (2001). Kava-kava in the treatment of generalized anxiety disorder. *Primary Care Psychiatry, 7*, 97–100.

Wheatley, D. (2002). Effect of *Hypericum perforatum* (St. John's wort) in major depressive disorder: A randomized controlled trial: Comment. *JAMA, 288*, 446.

Whiskey, E., Werneke, U., & Taylor, D. (2001). A systematic review and meta-analysis of *Hypericum perfora-*

*tum* in depression: A comprehensive review. *International Clinical Psychopharmacology, 16*, 239–252.

Wigal, S., Swanson, J., & Greenhill, L. (1998). Evaluation of individual subjects in the analog classroom. II: Effects of dose of amphetamine (Adderall). *Psychopharmacology Bulletin 34*(4), 833–838.

Wilber, K. (1995). *Sex, ecology, spirituality: The spirit of evolution.* Boston: Shambhala.

Wilber, K. (1997). *The eye of spirit: An integral vision for a world gone slightly mad.* Boston: Shambhala.

Wilber, K. (1999a). *The collected works of Ken Wilber* (vol. 3). Boston: Shambhala.

Wilber, K. (1999b). *One taste: The journals of Ken Wilber.* Boston: Shambhala.

Wilber, K. (2000). *A theory of everything: An integral vision for business, politics, science, and spirituality.* Boston: Shambhala.

Wilber, K. (2003). *Kosmic consciousness.* Audio interview with Tami Simon. Boulder, CO: Sounds True Productions.

Williamson, E. M., & Evans, F. J. (2000). Cannabinoids in clinical practice. *Drugs, 60*, 1303–1314.

Wilson, R. A. (1992). *Right where you are sitting now: Further tales of the Illuminati.* Berkeley, CA: Ronin.

Wilson, R. A. (1993). *Sex and Drugs: A journey beyond limits* (4th ed.). Phoenix, AZ: New Falcon.

Wilson, R. A. (2002). *TSOG: The thing that ate the Constitution and other everyday monsters.* Tempe, AZ: New Falcon Publications.

Wirshing, D. A., Wirshing, W. C., Kysar, L., Berisford, M. A., Goldstein, D., Pashdag, J., Mintz, J., & Marder, S. R. (1999). Novel antipsychotics: Comparison of weight gain liabilities. *Journal of Clinical Psychiatry, 60*, 358–363.

Wolraich, M. L., Hannah, J. N., Pinnock, T. Y., Baumgaertel, A., & Brown, J. (1996). Comparison of diagnostic criteria for attention deficit hyperactivity disorder in a county-wide sample. *Journal of the American Academy of Child and Adolescent Psychiatry, 35*, 319–324.

Wong, A. H., Smith, M., & Boon, H. S. (1998). Herbal remedies in psychiatric practice. *Archives of General Psychiatry, 55*, 1033–1044.

Wooltorton, E., & Sibbald, B. (2002). Ephedra/ephedrine: Cardiovascular and CNS effects. *Canadian Medical Association Journal, 166*, 633.

Wozniak, J., Biederman, J., Spencer, T., & Wilens, T. (1997). Pediatric psychopharmacology. In A. J. Gelenberg & E. L. Bassuk (Eds.), *The practitioner's guide to psychoactive drugs* (4th ed., pp. 385–415). New York: Plenum.

Wright, R. (1994). *The moral animal: Why we are the way we are: The new science of evolutionary psychology.* New York: Vintage.

Wurtzel, E. (1994). *Prozac nation: A memoir.* New York: Houghton Mifflin.

Wyatt, R. J., Henter, I. D., & Jamison, J. C. (2001). Lithium revisited: Savings brought about by the use of lithium, 1970–1991. *Psychiatric Quarterly, 72,* 149–166.

Yager, J., Siegfreid, S. L., & DiMatteo, T. L. (1999). Use of alternative remedies by psychiatric patients: Illustrative vignettes and a discussion of the issues. *American Journal of Psychiatry, 156,* 1432–1438.

Yalom, I. (1995). *The theory and practice of group psychotherapy* (4th ed.). New York: Basic Books.

Yatham, L. N. (2002). The role of novel antipsychotics in bipolar disorders. *Journal of Clinical Psychiatry, 63*(Suppl. 3), 10–40.

Yatham, L. N., Kusumakar, V., Calabrese, J. R., Rao, R., Scarrow, G., & Kroeker, G. (2002). Third generation anticonvulsants in bipolar disorder: A review of efficacy and summary of clinical recommendations. *Journal of Clinical Psychiatry, 63,* 275–283.

Yerkes, R. M., & Dodson, J. D. (1908). The relation of strength of stimulus to rapidity of habit formation. *Journal of Comprehensive Neurologic and Psychology, 18,* 459–482.

Zametkin, A. J., & Yamada, E. M. (1999). Monitoring and measuring drug effects: Vol. 1. Physical effects. In J. Werry & M. Aman (Eds.), *Practitioner's guide to psychoactive drugs for children and adolescents* (2nd ed., pp. 69–97). New York: Plenum.

Zarate, C., & Tohen, M. (1996). Epidemiology of mood disorders throughout the life cycle. In K. Schuman, M. Tohen, & S. Kutcher (Eds.), *Mood disorders across the life span* (pp. 17–34). New York: Wiley.

Zeiner, P. (1995). Body growth and cardiovascular function after extended treatment (1.75 years) with methylphenidate in boys with attention deficit hyperactivity disorder. *Journal of Child and Adolescent Psychopharmacology, 5,* 129–138.

Zhu, H., Cottrell, J. E., & Kass, I. S. (1997). The effect of thiopental and propofol on NMDA- and AMPA-mediated glutamate excitotoxicity. *Anesthesiology, 87,* 944–951.

Zillman, E. A., & Spiers, M. V. (2001). *Principles of neuropsychology.* Belmont, CA: Wadsworth.

Zito, J. M., Safer, D. J., dosReis, S., & Riddle, M. A., (1998). Racial disparity in psychotropic medications prescribed for youths with Medicaid insurance in Maryland. *Journal of the American Academy of Child and Adolescent Psychiatry, 37,* 179–184.

Zito, J. M., Safer, D. J., dosReis, S., Gardner, J. F., Boles, M., & Lynch, F. (2000). Trends in prescribing psychotropic medications to preschoolers. *JAMA, 283,* 1025–1030.

Zito, J. M., Safer, D. J., dosReis, S., Gardner, J. F., Magder, L., Soeken, K., Boles, M., Lynch, F., & Riddle, M. A. (2003). Psychotropic practice patterns for youth: A 10-year perspective. *Archives of Pediatric and Adolescent Medicine, 157,* 17–25.

Zuckerman, B., Frank, D., Hingson, R., Amaro, H., Levenson, S. M., Kayne, H., Parker, S., Vinci, R., Aboagye, K., & Fried, L. E. (1989). Effects of maternal marijuana and cocaine use on fetal growth. *New England Journal of Medicine, 320,* 762–768.

Zurier, R. B. (2004). Prospects for cannabinoids as anti-inflammatory agents. *Journal of Cellular Biochemistry, 88,* 462–466.

# Name Index

# Subject Index

TO THE OWNER OF THIS BOOK:

I hope that you have found *Psychopharmacology for Helping Professionals: An Integral Exploration* useful. So that this book can be improved in a future edition, would you take the time to complete this sheet and return it? Thank you.

School and address:_____

Department:_____

Instructor's name:_____

1. What I like most about this book is:_____

_____

_____

2. What I like least about this book is:

_____

_____

3. My general reaction to this book is:

_____

_____

4. The name of the course in which I used this book is:

_____

5. Were all of the chapters of the book assigned for you to read?_____

   If not, which ones weren't?_____

6. In the space below, or on a separate sheet of paper, please write specific suggestions for improving this book and anything else you'd care to share about your experience in using this book.

_____

_____

_____

**THOMSON**

**BROOKS/COLE** ™

# BUSINESS REPLY MAIL
FIRST-CLASS MAIL          PERMIT NO. 34          BELMONT CA

POSTAGE WILL BE PAID BY ADDRESSEE

Attn:  Marquita Flemming, Counseling

BrooksCole/Thomson Learning
10 Davis Drive
Belmont, CA      94002-9801

OPTIONAL:

Your name:_____    Date: _____

May we quote you, either in promotion for *Psychopharmacology for Helping Professionals: An Integral Exploration* or in future publishing ventures?

Yes: _____          No: _____

Sincerely yours,

*R. Elliott Ingersoll and Carl F. Rak*